WITHDRAWN
FROM
OF PLYMOUTH
SERVICES

D1438905

This book is to be returned on or before
the last date stamped below

20. MAR. 1986

CANCELLED

-3. MAR. 1992

18.

13 JAN 2000

20. DEC. 1989

-2 FEB 2000

CANCELLED 2 8 NOV 2000

2 6 APR 2001

PLYMOUTH POLYTECHNIC
LEARNING RESOURCES CENTRE
Telephone: (0752) 21312 ext.5413
(After 5p.m. (0752) 264661 weekdays only)
This book is subject to recall if required by another reader.
Books may be renewed by phone, please quote Telepen number.
CHARGES WILL BE MADE FOR OVERDUE BOOKS

WITHDRAWN
FROM
UNIVERSITY OF PLYMOUTH
LIBRARY SERVICES

Subviral Pathogens
of Plants and Animals:
Viroids and Prions

Academic Press Rapid Manuscript Reproduction

Subviral Pathogens of Plants and Animals: Viroids and Prions

Edited by

Karl Maramorosch

Waksman Institute of Microbiology
Rutgers—The State University of New Jersey
Piscataway, New Jersey

John J. McKelvey, Jr.

The Rockefeller Foundation
New York, New York

1985

ACADEMIC PRESS, INC.

(Harcourt Brace Jovanovich, Publishers)

Orlando   San Diego   New York   London
Toronto   Montreal   Sydney   Tokyo

PLYMOUTH POLYTECHNIC
LIBRARY

Accn. No.	178384
Class No.	576.64 SuB
Contl. No.	0124702309

COPYRIGHT © 1985, BY ACADEMIC PRESS, INC.
ALL RIGHTS RESERVED.
NO PART OF THIS PUBLICATION MAY BE REPRODUCED OR
TRANSMITTED IN ANY FORM OR BY ANY MEANS, ELECTRONIC
OR MECHANICAL, INCLUDING PHOTOCOPY, RECORDING, OR
ANY INFORMATION STORAGE AND RETRIEVAL SYSTEM, WITHOUT
PERMISSION IN WRITING FROM THE PUBLISHER.

ACADEMIC PRESS, INC.
Orlando, Florida 32887

United Kingdom Edition published by
ACADEMIC PRESS INC. (LONDON) LTD.
24–28 Oval Road, London NW1 7DX

Library of Congress Cataloging in Publication Data

Main entry under title:

Subviral pathogens of plants and animals.

    "Proceedings of a symposium ... sponsored by the
Rockefeller Foundation, held in Bellagio, Italy, June
27-July 2, 1983."--
    Includes index.
    1. Viroids--Congresses.   I. Maramorosch, Karl.
II. McKelvey, John J.   III. Rockefeller Foundation.
IV. Title: Prions.
QR500.S83   1984 ╲ 616'.0194   84-45725
ISBN 0-12-470230-9 (alk. paper)

PRINTED IN THE UNITED STATES OF AMERICA

85 86 87 88   9 8 7 6 5 4 3 2 1

Contents

Part I
Subviral Pathogens

Part II
Viroid Diseases

Part III
Viroid Structure and Replication

Part IV
Subviral Pathogens of Animals

Contributors

Numbers in parentheses indicate the pages on which the authors' contributions begin.

D. H. Adams (393), *Medical Research Council, Department of Virology Annexe, Newcastle upon Tyne, NE 2 4A3, England*

Paul E. Bendheim (337), *Departments of Neurology and Biochemistry and Biophysics, University of California, San Francisco, California 94143*

Guido Boccardo (75), *Laboratorio fi Fitovirologia Applicata, C. N. R., Universita di Torino, 10135 Torino, Italy*

David C. Bolton (337), *Departments of Neurology and Biochemistry and Biophysics, University of California, San Francisco, California 94143*

Karen A. Bowman (337), *Departments of Neurology and Biochemistry and Biophysics, University of California, San Francisco, California 94143*

Andrea D. Branch (201), *Laboratory of Genetics, The Rockefeller University, New York, New York 10021*

George Bruening (235), *Department of Biochemistry and Biophysics, University of California, Davis, California 95616*

Sharon M. Callahan (425), *Institute for Basic Research in Developmental Disabilities, Staten Island, New York 10314*

Richard I. Carp (425), *Institute for Basic Research in Developmental Disabilities, Staten Island, New York 10314*

P. W. G. Chu (265), *Department of Plant Pathology, Waite Agricultural Research Institute, The University of Adelaide, South Australia*

S. Patricia Cochran (337), *Departments of Neurology and Biochemistry and Biophysics, University of California, San Francisco, California 94143*

Dean E. Cress (315), *Tissue Culture and Molecular Genetics Laboratory, Beltsville, Maryland 20705*

George Davatelis (201), *Memorial Sloan–Kettering Cancer Center, New York, New York 10021*

T. O. Diener (3, 299), *Plant Protection Institute, Agricultural Research Service, United States Department of Agriculture, Beltsville, Maryland 20705*

R. I. B. Francki (265), *Department of Plant Pathology, Waite Agricultural Research Institute, The University of Adelaide, South Australia*

ix

D. Carleton Gajdusek (483), *National Institute of Neurological and Communicative Disorders and Stroke, National Institutes of Health, Bethesda, Maryland 20205*

J. Galindo A. (299), *Centro De Fitopatología. Colegio de Postgraduados, Chapingo México, Mexico*

Dalip S. Gill (235), *Roche Institute of Molecular Biology, Nutley, New Jersey 07110*

F. Gonzalez-Scarano (465), *Departments of Neurology and Microbiology, School of Medicine, University of Pennsylvania, Philadelphia, Pennsylvania 19104*

Karl H. J. Gordon (235), *Adelaide University Centre for Gene Technology, Department of Biochemistry, The University of Adelaide, South Australia*

Hans J. Gross (165), *Institut für Biochemie, Universität Würzburg, D-8700 Würzburg, Federal Republic of Germany*

Darlene F. Groth (337), *Departments of Neurology and Biochemistry and Biophysics, University of California, San Francisco, California 94143*

James Haseloff, (235), *M.R.C. Laboratory of Molecular Biology, Cambridge, England*

T. Hatta (265), *Department of Plant Pathology, Waite Agricultural Research Institute, The University of Adelaide, South Australia*

Paul Keese (235), *Adelaide University Centre for Gene Technology, Department of Biochemistry, The University of Adelaide, South Australia*

Michael C. Kiefer (315), *Department of Botany, University of Maryland, College Park, Maryland 20742*

T. Kiss (183), *Institute of Plant Physiology, Biological Research Center, Hungarian Academy of Sciences, Szeged, Hungary*

R. Lizárraga (137), *The International Potato Center, Lima, Peru*

Karl Maramorosch (151), *Waksman Institute of Microbiology, Rutgers—The State University of New Jersey, Piscataway, New Jersey 08854*

Michael P. McKinley (337), *Departments of Neurology and Biochemistry and Biophysics, University of California, San Francisco, California 94143*

Patricia A. Merz (425), *Institute for Basic Research in Developmental Disabilities, Staten Island, New York 10314*

Roger C. Moretz (425), *Institute for Basic Research in Developmental Disabilities, Staten Island, New York 10314*

Peter J. Murphy (235), *Adelaide University Centre for Gene Technology, Department of Biochemistry, The University of Adelaide, South Australia*

N. Nathanson (465), *Departments of Neurology and Microbiology, School of Medicine, University of Pennsylvania, Philadelphia, Pennsylvania 19104*

Robert A. Owens (315), *Plant Virology Laboratory, Beltsville, Maryland 20705*

D. Peters (21), *Department of Virology, Agricultural University, Wageningen, The Netherlands*

Tien Po (123), *Institute of Microbiology, Academia Sinica, Beijing, China*

Stanley B. Prusiner (3, 337), *Departments of Neurology and Biochemistry and Biophysics, University of California, San Francisco, California 94143*

J. W. Randles (39, 265), *Department of Plant Pathology, Waite Agricultural Research Institute, The University of Adelaide, South Australia*

Hugh Robertson (201), *Laboratory of Genetics, The Rockefeller University, New York, New York 10021*

J. Rohozinski (265), *Department of Plant Pathology, Waite Agricultural Research Institute, The University of Adelaide, South Australia*

W. T. Runia (21), *Glasshouse Crops Research and Experiment Station, Naaldwijk, The Netherlands*

L. F. Salazar (137), *The International Potato Center, Lima, Peru*

L. Schilde-Rentschler (137), *The International Potato Center, Lima, Peru*

Eishiro Shikata (101), *Department of Botany, Hokkaido University, Sapporo, Japan*

D. R. Smith (299), *Plant Protection Institute, Agricultural Research Service, Beltsville, Maryland 20705*

F. Solymosy (183), *Institute of Plant Physiology, Biological Research Center, Hungarian Academy of Sciences, Szeged, Hungary*

Robert A. Somerville (425), *Institute for Basic Research in Developmental Disabilities, Staten Island, New York 10314*

Robert H. Symons (235), *Adelaide University Centre for Gene Technology, Department of Biochemistry, The University of Adelaide, South Australia*

Jane E. Visvader (235), *Adelaide University Centre for Gene Technology, Department of Biochemistry, The University of Adelaide, South Australia*

Kerry K. Willis (201), *New York University Medical Center, New York, New York 10016*

Henry M. Wisniewski (425), *Institute for Basic Research in Developmental Disabilities, Staten Island, New York 10314*

Preface

Prior to 1971 all infectious agents of animal and plant diseases were believed to be limited to bacteria, viruses, fungi, and protozoa, but in 1971 the existence of a new group of pathogens, smaller and less complex than viruses, was discovered. These are autonomously replicating RNA molecules named viroids. In the years intervening between 1971 and the present a dozen plant diseases, earlier believed to be caused by viruses, were found to be associated with viroids. So far, viroid diseases have been linked with higher plants only, not with higher animals, arthropods, or bacteria.

The smallest genomes of independently replicating viruses have a molecular weight of one million. So-called satellite viruses and defective viruses have smaller genomes but they are unable to replicate without helper viruses. Viroid genomes are in the range of 50,000 to 100,000 daltons, and the molecular structure of several has been recently established. The replication of viroids by a rolling circle mechanism, using enzymes from RNA templates, has been unraveled. The viroids are not translated into viroid-specified polypeptides.

Viroids have provided a convenient model for the study of subviral pathogens of animals. Several neurological disorders of man and higher animals, so-called spongiform encephalopathies, were found to be infectious diseases, and their causative agents were described as "slow viruses." The enigmatic scrapie disease of sheep and goats, kuru disease in New Guinea, and Creutzfeldt–Jakob senility of man belong to this group. For several years it was suspected that the "slow viruses" might actually be viroids. Recently it has been demonstrated that the scrapie agent is smaller than viroids and that an essential hydrophobic protein is required for its infectivity. The term prion has been coined for these pathogens. So far, no prion diseases have been found in plants or arthropods. The true nature of prions is still a riddle.

Using viroid research as a model, investigators could proceed most proficiently in determining the physical and chemical nature of the scrapie agent. Experimentation has not borne out the speculation that this agent might be akin to plant viroids. On the contrary, it has been demonstrated that the scrapie pathogen is radically different from either viruses or viroids. Even in highly concentrated preparations the involvement of nucleic acid could not be demonstrated, and the hydrophobic protein alone seemed to be essential for an expression of infectivity. It remains to be determined whether a small nucleic acid yet to be detected or destroyed by present-day techniques is present in prions. Should the prion's protein constitute the complete pathogen, prions would contradict all established beliefs of molecular biologists. No wonder that recent findings in prion research are not accepted universally. The revolutionary concept that prions are complete pathogenic entities could have far-reaching implications for virology, for human and veterinary medicine, and indeed for basic molecular biology as well.

We have invited several contributors who support the concept of the nature of prions as well as some who oppose it so that a balanced presentation of views, evidence, and diverse conclusions could be made available to the scientific community to stimulate further work on so far unrecognized plant, human, and animal types of subviral pathogens. We hope this research will advance our knowledge of subviral pathogens and contribute to the eventual control of several important diseases in animals and plants.

Twenty chapters have been devoted to the nature of subviral pathogens of plants and animals. The authors, all recognized authorities in their scientific disciplines, have compared the newly emerging concepts and current research results. Important work on the control of plant viroid diseases is now in progress in several countries which may also be relevant for similar research efforts to control the spongiform encephalopathies. Thus the subject of this treatise should be of considerable scientific interest and importance and one that will appeal to an audience representing human and veterinary medicine, virology, zoology, microbiology, plant pathology, entomology, as well as other branches of biology.

The decision to publish this volume was made following an international workshop at the Rockefeller Foundation's Study and Conference Center in Bellagio, Italy, under the sponsorship of the Rockefeller Foundation, the U.S. Public Health Service, as well as universities and research institutes of Australia, Germany, Hungary, Italy, Japan, Netherlands, People's Republic of China, and Peru. We express our sincere gratitude to these sponsors and particularly to the Rockefeller Foundation, not only for providing ideal conditions for the stimulating discussions which took place but also for the preparation of the final typescript of the book. Thanks are due to the contributors for the effort and care with which they have prepared their chapters and to the staff of Academic Press for their part in the production of this volume.

KARL MARAMOROSCH
JOHN J. MCKELVEY, JR.

PART I
Subviral Pathogens

Chapter 1

THE RECOGNITION OF SUBVIRAL PATHOGENS

T. O. Diener

Plant Virology Laboratory
Plant Protection Institute
Agricultural Research Service
United States Department of Agriculture
Beltsville, Maryland   20705

and

Stanley B. Prusiner

Departments of Neurology and of Biochemistry and Biophysics
University of California
San Francisco, California   94143

I.   INTRODUCTION

Until about 12 years ago, it was generally believed that all infectious diseases of plants and animals are caused either by microorganisms (bacteria, fungi, etc.) or by viruses. Since then, disease-causing agents that are smaller and less complex than viruses have come to light. First, in 1971, the potato spindle tuber disease was shown to be caused by small, unencapsidated molecules of autonomously replicating RNA (Diener, 1971). Today, about a dozen diseases of higher plants are known to be caused by similar subviral agents for which the term *viroid* has been adopted. Second, the agent of a neurological disease of sheep and goats, scrapie, which has long been known to possess a number of properties unlike those of viruses, has recently been shown to contain an essential protein and is therefore fundamen-

Copyright © 1985 by Academic Press, Inc.
All rights of reproduction in any form reserved.
ISBN 0-12-470230-9

tally distinct from viroids. The scrapie agent appears to be even smaller than viroids. For this and similar pathogens, the term *prion* has been proposed (Prusiner, 1982).

The discovery of subviral pathogens has opened new vistas in plant pathology, veterinary medicine, and human medicine, as well as in cell and molecular biology.In the following chapters, various aspects of these pathogens will be described in detail;the book as a whole represents an up-to-date account of our present knowledge in this new scientific area.

Purified viroid preparations have been available to biochemists and molecular biologists for about 10 years, permitting application of conventional biochemical procedures, whereas properties of the scrapie agent must still be deduced indirectly by virtue of its biological activity. It is not surprising, therefore, that our knowledge of viroids (particularly of their structural properties) is far greater than that of the scrapie agent. This imbalance is reflected in the unequal number of chapters dedicated to each of the two known types of subviral pathogen. In this introductory chapter we present an overview of the field as it has developed during the last 12 years.

II. VIROIDS AND VIROID DISEASES

Twelve viroids causing eleven naturally occurring diseases have been discovered over the last decade (Table I). Originally the term viroid was introduced on the basis of newly established properties of the infectious agent responsible for the potato spindle tuber disease. These properties were found to differ fundamentally from those of viruses in 4 important respects as listed in Table II.

Because the smallest known viruses capable of independent replication contain genomes of a size corresponding to a molecular weight (M_r) of about one million, it appeared reasonable to assume twelve years ago that this size represents the minimal amount of genetic information required for a virus to code for virus-specified products and to subjugate the metabolism of the host cell. Indeed, viruses with smaller genomes, although known, are not capable of independent replication but require certain functions provided by a helper virus present in the same cell. In the absence of helper virus, no replication of these "defective" or "satellite" viruses takes place.

Viroids, on the other hand, introduce into their host cells a far smaller amount of genetic information than do viruses, yet their replication does not require the assistance of detectable helper viruses. Because of this, the discovery of viroids came as a surprise and was greeted,

TABLE I
Viroid Diseases

	Disease	Viroid	References
1.	Potato spindle tuber	PSTV	Diener, 1971
2.	Citrus exocortis	CEV	Semancik and Weathers, 1972
3.	Chrysanthemum stunt	CSV	Diener and Lawson, 1973
4.	Chrysanthemum chlorotic mottle	CCMV	Romaine and Horst, 1975
5.	Cucumber pale fruit	CPFV	Van Dorst and Peters, 1974; Sänger. *et al.*, 1976
6.	Coconut cadang-cadang	CCCV	Randles, 1975
7.	Hop stunt	HSV	Sasaki and Shikata, 1977
8.	Columnea latent	CV	Owens *et al.*, 1978
9.	Avocado sunblotch	ASBV	Dale and Allen, 1979; Thomas and Mohamed, 1979
10.	Tomato apical stunt	TASV	Walter, 1981
11.	Tomato planta macho	TPMV	Galindo *et al.*, 1982
12.	Burdock stunt	BSV	Chen *et al.*, 1983

TABLE II
Properties of Viroids Differentiating them from Viruses[*]

1. The pathogen exists *in vivo* as an unencapsidated RNA; that is, no virion-like particles are detectable in infected tissue.
2. The infectious RNA is of low molecular weight.
3. Despite its small size, the infectious RNA is replicated autonomously in susceptible cells; that is, no helper virus is required.
4. The infectious RNA consists of one molecule only.

[*]Diener, 1971, 1972a.

initially, with considerable skepticism. Acceptance of the viroid concept was not facilitated by the fact that, at the time, the viroid could not be recognized as a physical entity, but only by virtue of its biological activity, that is, by its capacity to induce disease in susceptible plants. Molecular biologists, particularly, were not too comfortable with such an indirect approach of determining physical-chem-

ical properties of a biological agent. Fortunately, evidence
for the correctness of the viroid concept soon became indis-
putable and work from a number of laboratories resulted in a
vast increase in our knowledge of viroids.

Once purified viroid preparations had become available,
elucidation of the structure of viroids was rapid. As
highlights, the following events might be mentioned: determination of the thermal denaturation properties of a viroid
(Diener, 1972b); electron microscopic visualization of a
native viroid (Sogo *et al.*, 1973); and of fully denatured
viroids (McClements, 1975; Sänger *et al.*, 1976; McClements
and Kaesberg, 1977), leading to the important discovery that
viroids are single-stranded, covalently closed circular RNA
molecules with extensive regions of intramolecular complementarity. Detailed quantitative thermodynamic and kinetic
studies of their thermal denaturation(Langowski *et al.*, 1978;
Domdey *et al.*, 1978; Henco *et al.*, 1979; Gross and Riesner,
1980) revealed that viroids exist in their native conforma-
tions as extended rodlike structures characterized by a
series of double-helical sections and internal loops. These
structural studies culminated in the determination of the
complete nucleotide sequence and most probable secondary
structure of the potato spindle tuber viroid (PSTV) (Gross *et
al.*, 1978). Thus, in less than 10 years, viroids advanced
from entities whose very existence was doubted by some to RNA
pathogens whose molecular structure is completely known.

In contrast to our extensive knowledge of viroid structure, functional aspects of viroid-host relationships are
still inadequately understood. Consensus exists, however,
that viroids are (1) not translated into viroid-specified
polypeptides (for example, Davies *et al.*, 1974; Semancik *et
al.*, 1977; Conejero and Semancik, 1977; Symons, 1981; Zelcer
et al., 1981); (2) replicated by host enzymes from RNA
templates (Grill and Semancik, 1978; Rackwitz *et al.*, 1981;
Boege *et al.*, 1982); and (3) probably replicated by a rolling
circletype mechanism with the circular viroid (or its complement) serving as a template, resulting in the synthesis of
oligomeric strands of the viroid and its complement (Owens
and Cress, 1980; Branch *et al.*, 1981; Rohde and Sänger,
1981; Owens and Diener, 1982).

Today, with the growing library of viroid nucleotide sequences, we appear to be at the threshold of being able to
correlate particular viroid regions with biological properties and to investigate the effects of specific nucleotide
exchanges, insertions, or deletions on host specificity,
viroid replication efficiency, and pathogenicity. Undoubtedly, availability of infectious, viroid-complementary, recombinant DNA clones, as reported in this volume, will be

invaluable in this endeavor. It is possible that, partly because of the relative simplicity of viroids, partly because of the intensity of research dedicated to the problem, our understanding of viroid-host cell interactions at the molecular level will grow in coming years at a greater rate than our knowledge of analogous processes with other pathogens. Thus, from the vista of molecular biology, viroids may soon become the most thoroughly understood host-pathogen system known. Ironically, at the same time, we still possess only sketchy knowledge of many more traditional aspects of viroids and viroid diseases, such as their natural mode of transmission, disease epidemiology, and possible existence of wild plant reservoirs, for example.

The finding of circular and linear viroid-like RNAs ("virusoids") that are encapsidated, together with linear viral RNAs of usual size (M_r=1.5 x 10^6), in conventional isometric viral capsids (Randles *et al.*, 1981) has added a new dimension to viroid research. In contrast to genuine viroids, viroid-like, encapsidated RNAs are incapable of independent replication, but specifically require the viral RNA of the same virus for their replication (Gould *et al.*, 1981). Surprisingly, in at least two such systems, velvet tobacco mottle virus and *Solanum nodiflorum* mottle virus, the converse also appears to be true: the viral RNA depends on the viroid-like RNA for its own replication (Gould *et al.*, 1981). Other viroid-like, encapsidated RNAs, however, appear to represent satellite RNAs of conventional viruses (see report in chapter 13). Also, thermodynamic investigations have shown that the encapsidated viroid-like RNAs do not possess features typical of viroids (Randles *et al.*, 1982). Evidently more work is needed before the relationships, if any, between viroids and the encapsidated, viroid-like RNAs are fully understood.

III. PRIONS AND PRION DISEASES

For more than four decades, the unusual properties of the scrapie agent have presented an increasingly fascinating puzzle. Numerous hypotheses for the structure of the scrapie agent have been offered to explain its perplexing molecular characteristics (Prusiner, 1982). The hydrophobicity of the scrapie agent and a prolonged, tedious endpoint titration assay hampered efforts to purify and characterize it. Attempts to define its molecular properties in crude extracts have frequently been inconclusive. In 1972, one of us called attention to the fact that a number of properties of the scrapie agent were compatible with the hypothesis that its molecular structure could be akin to that of the then newly discovered plant viroids (Diener, 1972c). However, efforts to verify viroid-like properties of the scrapie agent were fruitless.

No infectious RNA could be isolated from brain homogenates of scrapie-infected animals and procedures used in the isolation of viroids, such as phenol extraction or treatment with sodium dodecyl sulfate, inactivated the scrapie agent (Hunter and Millson, 1967; Prusiner *et al.*, 1980).

The development of a more rapid and economical bioassay for the scrapie agent permitted significant progress to be made in the development of a purification protocol (Prusiner *et al.*, 1980, 1982a, 1982b). Once substantial amounts of contaminating molecules could be removed, convincing evidence that the scrapie agent contains a hydrophobic protein that is essential for the expression of infectivity was obtained (McKinley *et al.*, 1981; Prusiner *et al.*, 1980, 1981), whereas, even in highly enriched preparations, a requirement for nucleic acid could not be demonstrated (Prusiner, 1982).

A scrapie protein, designated PrP, has an apparent M_r of 27,000 to 30,000. Under nondenaturing or native conditions PrP is resistant to protease digestion (Bolton *et al.*, 1982). After denaturation, PrP is readily degraded by digestion with amino acid nonspecific proteases. Many lines of evidence support the hypothesis that PrP is a structural component of the scrapie agent. The results of these recent investigations clearly place the scrapie agent outside the realm of viruses and viroids and have led to the introduction of the term "prion" (Prusiner, 1982). Scrapie prions appear to contain only one major protein; it remains to be established whether or not they contain minor proteins (McKinley *et al.*, 1983). There are between 10^4 and 10^5 PrP molecules per ID_{50} unit, but how many PrP molecules are contained within a single infectious prion is unknown.

Current studies do not permit us to exclude the possibility that a nucleic acid is present in the core of the prion (Prusiner, 1982). Nevertheless, to date it has not been possible to demonstrate the dependence of prion infectivity in purified fractions upon nucleic acid molecules.

Although only the infectious agent causing scrapie of sheep and goats has been purified and characterized sufficiently to classify it as a prion, five other diseases are probably also caused by prions (Table III). The agents causing transmissible mink encephalopathy (TME), chronic wasting disease (CWD), kuru, Creutzfeldt-Jakob disease (CJD) and Gerstmann-Sträussler syndrome (GSS) are tentatively classified as prion diseases (Table IV) because many characteristics of these disorders are similar to those of scrapie (Gajdusek, 1977; Hartsough and Burger, 1965; Masters *et al.*,

TABLE III

Prion Diseases[1]

Disease	Natural Host
Scrapie[2]	Sheep & goats
Transmissible mink encephalopathy (TME)	Mink
Chronic wasting disease (CWD)	Mule deer & elk
Kuru	Humans − Fore
Creutzfeldt−Jakob disease (CJD)	Humans
Gerstmann−Straussler syndrome (GSS)	Humans

[1]Alternative terminologies include subacute transmissible spongiform encephalopathies and unconventional slow virus diseases.
[2]Prions have been shown to cause only scrapie; they are presumed to cause the other diseases listed.

1981; Williams and Young, 1980). All six diseases have pro-longed incubation periods which precede the onset of a progressive neurological disorder. The brain of the host shows extensive astrogliosis with variable amounts of vacuola-tion (Beck *et al.*, 1964; Zlotnik, 1962). No inflammatory response in any of these diseases has been observed. Firm classification of TME, CWD, kuru, CJD and GSS as prion dis-eases must await molecular characterization of their infect-ious agents. Recent studies on the CJD agent indicate that it possesses many features similar to those of the scrapie prion (Prusiner and Kingsbury, in press).

TABLE IV

Characteristics of Prion Diseases

1. Diseases are confined to the nervous system.
2. Prolonged incubation period of months to decades precedes the onset of clinical illness.
3. Progressive clinical course of weeks to years invariably leads to death.
4. All diseases exhibit a reactive astrocytosis and many show vacuolation of neurons.
5. The infectious agents (prions) causing these diseases exhibit properties which distinguish them from both virus-es and viroids.

TABLE V
Comparison of the Stabilities of Viroids and Prions.

Treatment	Concentration	PSTV[1]	Scrapie Agent[1]
Ribonuclease A	0.1–100 µg/ml	+	–
Deoxyribonuclease I	100 µg/ml	–	–
Proteinase K	100 µg/ml	–	+
Trypsin	100 µg/ml	–	+
Diethylpyrocarbonate	10–20 mM	[–]	+
Hydroxylamine	0.1–0.5 M	+	–
Psoralen (AMT)	10–500 µg/ml	+	–
Phenol	Saturated	–	+
Sodium dodecyl sulfate	1–10%	–	+
Zn^{2+}	2 mM	+	–
Urea	3–8 M	–	+
Alkali	pH 10	[–]	+
KSCN	1M	–	+

[1] – = no change, [–] = small change, + = inactivation.

IV. VIRUSES, VIROIDS, AND PRIONS.

Results of a detailed comparison of the stability characteristics of PSTV with those of the scrapie prion (Diener *et al.*, 1982) are summarized in Table V. The properties of viroids and prions are antithetical. Viroids are inactivated by procedures that modify nucleic acids, while prions are resistant. In contrast, prions are inactivated by procedures that modify proteins, while viroids are resistant. These results support the proposition that the molecular properties of prions differ fundamentally from those of viroids and viruses.

They also strengthen the concept (Prusiner, 1982) that the prion represents the prototype of a novel class of subviral pathogens. It is worth noting that of the two classes of subviral pathogens now recognized, viroids have been identified only in plants and prions only in animals. If further work confirms this host specificity, it will be interesting to determine by what molecular mechanisms these novel infectious agents are restricted to either plants or animals. Some distinguishing molecular properties of viroids and prions are listed in Table VI.

Should viroids and prions be included in the kindgom of viruses or should they be given separate taxonomic status? The answer to this question largely depends on the particular definition of virus that one accepts. Various textbooks of virology propose drastically different definitions of the

term - some of which would include viroids (and possibly
prions), whereas others would not (for a discussion, see
Diener, 1982). Because textbooks differ also in their definitions of certain other biological terms (some, for example,
consider viruses to be microorganisms, whereas others do
not), we have attempted to prepare our own glossary of definitions (see below).

TABLE VI
Some Molecular Properties of Viroids and Prions.

Properties	PSTV	Scrapie agent
Nucleic Acid	+	[ ][1]
Protein	−	+
Molecular Weight	127,000	$\leq$ 50,000
Sedimentation Coefficient	6.7	≤ 2[2]
D_{37}[3] at 254 nm J/m^2	5,000	42,000

[1]Denotes no nucleic acid demonstrated to date.
[2]S_{obs} value calculated with the assumption that the particle
     density is >1.05 g/cm^3.
[3]Dose (D_{37})of ultraviolet light that permits 37% (1/e) survi-
     val of the infectious particle.

Evidently, within the context of our definitions,viroids
and prions are not viruses. From a purely taxonomic standpoint, it would appear preferable to make this distinction.
No useful purpose seems to be served by lumping together biological entities as dissimilar as conventional viruses, viroids, and prions. Whether or not such a distinction is
justified in an evolutionary context remains to be determined.

V. DEFINITIONS

Terms in science are constantly being revised and altered as our knowledge is extended. The definition of a scien -
tific term is generally operational and subject to change as
new scientific evidence emerges.
When a term is useful and reasonably descriptive,scien-
tists generally adopt it. When a term is awkward and nonde-
scriptive, it is often dropped in favor of another word or
group of words. Terms are also dropped when they are confusing - too close to related existing ones or erroneous in
their connotation.
As with language, the users decide the meaning and
usefulness of words. A word would seem ideal when its
definition is neither too broad nor too narrow for the
phenomenon being described. If the definition is too broad,
then it can be confusing to the reader as to what the author

means to imply. If the definition is too narrow, then the word is not as useful as it might otherwise be.

The following glossary is an attempt to assign succinct and accurate definitions to a few words frequently used in virology, microbiology and molecular biology. These definitions have no official sanction but as noted above it is the users, in this case scientists, who either provide the sanction or not. We believe it is an important exercise to list these definitions in an attempt to clarify what is to many a confusing array of terms. Perhaps these definitions will also allow us to create a more organized view of small infectious pathogens. The authors welcome comments, criticisms, and suggestions for refinements.

VI. A GLOSSARY

defective virus – a virus that lacks some of the genetic information required for its replication or for the synthesis of a functional coat protein.

episome – a nucleic acid that replicates as an autonomous unit within the host or as an integrated unit attached to a chromosome of the host.

helper virus – a virus that is required for replication of a defective or satellite virus or a satellite RNA.

infection – the presence and multiplication of microorganisms, viruses, viroids, or prions in a host. Most infections eventually produce disease in the host.

latent virus – a virus infecting a host without producing disease.

microorganism – a microscopic organism. Examples are protozoa, bacteria, rickettsiae, and mycoplasmas. Microorganisms are composed of one or several cells and are capable of reproduction by growth and division. Viruses, viroids, and prions are not microorganisms.

organism – a living being composed of one or more cells capable of reproduction by growth and cell division.

plasmid – a small autonomously replicating molecule of covalently closed circular DNA that is devoid of protein and not essential for the survival of its host. Plasmids have been found only in bacteria.

prion   – a small infectious pathogen containing pro-
                 tein and resistant to procedures that
                 modify or hydrolyze nucleic acids. Whether
                 or not prions contain nucleic acid remains
                 to be established. Presumably, prions
                 reproduce within cells; their mechanism of
                 replication is unknown.

provirus   – the DNA form of an RNA virus. The provirus
                 may be integrated into the host chromosomes
                 and transmitted from one generation to ano-
                 ther.The provirus does not contain protein

satellite RNA – a small RNA that becomes packaged in pro-
                 tein shells made from coat proteins of ano-
                 ther, unrelated, helper virus, on which the
                 satellite RNA depends for its own replica-
                 tion.

satellite virus – a virus whose small RNA codes for its own
                 coat protein, but is dependent for its re-
                 plication on another, unrelated, helper vi-
                 us.

slow virus   – an imprecise term applied to the infectious
                 agents of certain animal diseases that
                 become manifest only after prolonged in -
                 cubation periods (months to years). Some
                 of these diseases are caused by viruses,
                 others by prions.

viroid   – a small infectious pathogen composed entire-
                 ly of a low melecular weight RNA molecule.
                 Within susceptible cells, viroids direct
                 their own replication from host metabo-
                 lites, using the biosynthetic machinery of
                 the cell and host enzymes exclusively.

virus   – a small infectious pathogen composed of one
                 or more nucleic acid molecules usually
                 surrounded by a protein coat. Some viral
                 coats also contain lipid and carbohydrate.
                 The genomic nucleic acid of a virus par-
                 ticle is either DNA or RNA, not both.
                 Within susceptible cells, viral nucleic
                 acids direct their own replication and
                 synthesis of one or more virus specific
                 proteins from host metabolites using the
                 biosynthetic machinery of the cell. In the
                 production of progeny viruses, enzymes or
                 enzyme subunits coded by the virus and,in
                 some cases, also by the host are utilized.

virusoid   – viroid-like RNA encapsidated in a virus
                 shell that also contains viral RNA.

REFERENCES

Beck, E., Daniel, P.M., and Parry, H. B. (1964). Degeneration
    of the cerebellar and hypothalamo-neurohypophysical
    systems in sheep with scrapie; and its relationship
    to human system degenerations. *Brain* *87,* 153-176
Boege, F., Rhode, W., and Sänger, H.L. (1982). In vitro
    transcription of viroid RNA into full-length copies
    by RNA-dependent RNA polymerase from healthy
    tomato leaves. *Biosc. Reports 2,* 185-194.
Bolton, D.C., McKinley, M.P., and Prusiner, S. B. (1982).
    Identification of a protein that purifies with
    the scrapie prion. *Science 218,* 1309-1311.
Branch, A. D., Robertson, H. D., and Dickson, E. (1981).
    Longer-than-unit-length viroid minus strands are
    present in RNA from infected plants. *Proc. Natl.
    Acad. Sci. U.S.A. 78,* 6381-6385.
Chen, W., Tien, P., Zhu, Y. X., and Liu, Y. (1983).
    Viroid-like RNAs associated with burdock stunt
    disease. *J. Gen. Virology. 64,* 409-414.
Conejero, V., and Semancik, J.S. (1977). Exocortis Viroid:
    Alteration in the proteins of *Gynura aurantiaca*
    accompanying viroid infection. *Virology 77,* 221-232.
Dale, J. L., and Allen, R.N. (1979). Avocado affected by
    sunblotch disease contains low molecular weight
    ribonucleic acid. *Australasian Plant Pathol. 8,*
    3-4.
Davies, J. W., Kaesberg, P., and Diener, T.O. (1974). Potato
    spindle tuber viroid. XII . An investigation of
    viroid RNA as messenger for protein synthesis.
    Virology 61, 281-286.
Diener, T. O. (1971). Potato spindle tuber "virus". IV. A
    replicating, low molecular weight RNA. *Virology 45,*
    411-428.
Diener, T. O. (1972a). Viroids. *Adv. Virus Research 17,*
    295-313.
Diener, T. O. (1972b). Potato spindle tuber viroid. VIII.
    Correlation of infectivity with a UV-absorbing
    component and thermal denaturation properties
    of the RNA. *Virology 50,* 606-609.
Diener, T. O. (1972c). Is the scrapie agent a viroid?
    Nature New Biology 235, 218-219.
Diener, T. O. (1982). Viroids and their interactions with
    host cells.   *Ann. Rev. Microbiol. 36,* 239-258.
Diener, T. O., and Lawson, R. H. (1973). Chrysanthemum
    stunt: A viroid disease. *Virology 51,* 94-101

Diener, T. O., McKinley, M.P., and Prusiner, S.B. (1982).
    Viroids and prions. *Proc. Natl. Acad. Sci. U.S.A.*
    79, 5220-5224.
Domdey, H., Jank, P., Sänger, H.L., and Gross, H. J. (1978).
    Studies on the primary and secondary structure of
    potato spindle tuber viroid: products of digestion
    with ribonuclease A and ribonuclease T_1, and
    modification with bisulfite. *Nucleic Acids Res. 5,*
    1221-1236.
Gajdusek, D. C. (1977). Unconventional viruses and the origin
    and disappearance of kuru. *Science 197,* 943-960.
Galindo, J.A., Smith, D.R., and Diener, T.O. (1982). Eti-
    ology of Planta Macho, a viroid disease of tomato.
    Phytopathology 72, 49-54.
Gould, A. R., Francki, R.I.B., and Randles, J. W. (1981).
    Studies on encapsidated viroid-like RNA. IV.
    Requirement for infectivity and specificity of
    two RNA components from velvet tobacco mottle
    virus. *Virology 110,* 420-426.
Grill, L.K., and Semancik, J. S. (1978). RNA sequences
    complementary to citrus exocortis viroid in nucleic
    acid preparations from infected *Gynura aurantiaca.*
    Proc. Natl. Acad. Sci. U.S.A. 75, 896-900.
Gross, H. J., and Riesner, D. (1980). Viroids: A class
    of subviral pathogens. *Angew. Chemie Int. Ed. Engl.*
    19, 231-243.
Gross, H. J., Domdey, H., Lossow, C., Jank, P., Raba, M.,
    Alberty, H., and Sänger, H.L. (1978). Nucleotide
    sequence and secondary structure of potato spindle
    tuber viroid. *Nature 273,* 203-208.
Hartsough, G. R., and Burger, D. (1965). Encephalopathy
    of mink. I. Epizootiologic and clinical observa-
    tions. *J. Infect. Dis. 115,* 387-392.
Henco, K., Sänger, H. L., and Riesner, D. (1979). Fine
    structure melting of viroids as studied by kinetic
    methods. *Nucleic Acids Res. 6,* 3041-3059.
Hunter, G. D., and Millson, G. C. (1967). Attempts to
    release the scrapie agent from tissue debris.
    J. Comp. Pathol. 77, 301-307.
Langowski, J., Henco, K., Riesner, D., and Sänger, H.L.
    (1978). Common structural features of different
    viroids: serial arrangement of double helical
    sections and internal loops. *Nucleic Acids Res.5,*
    1589-1610.
Masters, C.L., Gajdusek, D. C., and Gibbs, C.J., Jr.
    (1981). Creutzfeldt-Jakob disease virus isolations
    from the Gerstmann-Sträussler syndrome. *Brain 104,*
    559-588.

McClements, W. (1975). Electron microscopy of RNA: Examina-
    tion of viroids and a method for mapping single-
    stranded RNA. Ph.D. Thesis. University of
    Wisconsin, Madison.
McClements, W.L. and Kaesberg, P. (1977). Size and second-
    ary structure of potato spindle tuber viroid.
    Virology 76, 477–484.
McKinley, M.P., Masiarz, F. R., and Prusiner, S. B. (1981).
    Reversible chemical modification of the scrapie
    agent. *Science 214*, 1259–1261.
McKinley, M. P., Bolton, D.C., and Prusiner, S. B. (1983).
    A protease-resistant protein is a structural component
    of the scrapie prion. *Cell 35*, 57–62.
Owens, R. A., and Cress, D.E. (1980). Molecular cloning and
    characterization of potato spindle tuber viroid
    cDNA sequences. *Proc. Natl. Acad. Sci. U.S.A.77*
    5302–5306.
Owens, R. A., and Diener, T.O. (1982). RNA intermediates
    in potato spindle tuber viroid replication.
    Proc. Natl. Acad. Sci. U.S.A. 79, 113–117.
Owens, R. A., Smith, D.R., and Diener, T.O. (1978). Measure-
    ment of viroid sequence homology by hybridization
    with complementary DNA prepared *in vitro*. *Virology
    89*, 388–394.
Prusiner, S.B. (1982). Novel proteinaceous infectious par-
    ticles cause scrapie. *Science 216*, 136–144.
Prusiner, S. B., Groth, D.F., Bildstein, C., Masiarz, F.R.,
    McKinley, M.P., and Cochran, S.P. (1980). Electro-
    phoretic properties of the scrapie agent in agarose
    gels. *Proc. Natl. Acad.Sci. U.S.A. 77*, 2984–2988.
Prusiner, S. B., Mc Kinley, M.P., Groth, D.F., Bowman,
    K.A., Mock, N.I., Cochran, S.P., and Masiarz, F.R.
    (1981). Scrapie agent contains a hydrophobic
    protein. *Proc. Natl. Acad. Sci. U.S.A. 78*, 6675–
    6679.
Prusiner, S. B., Bolton, D.C., Groth, D.F., Bowman, K.A.,
    Cochran, S.P., and McKinley, M.P. (1982a). Further
    purification and characterization of scrapie prions.
    Biochemistry 21, 6942–6950.
Prusiner, S.B., Cochran, S.P., Groth, D.F., Downey, D.E.,
    Bowman, K.A., and Martinez, H.M. (1982b). Measurement
    of the scrapie agent using an incubation time interval
    assay. *Ann. Neurol. 11*, 353–358.
Prusiner, S. B., and Kingsbury, D. T. (in press). Prions –
    Infectious pathogens causing the spongiform encepha-
    lopathies. CRC Critical Reviews in Clinical
    Neurobiology.
Rackwitz, H.R., Rohde, W., and Sänger, H.L. (1981). DNA–

dependent RNA polymerase II of plant origin transcribes viroid RNA into full-length copies. *Nature
(London) 291,* 297-301.

Randles, J.W. (1975). Association of two ribonucleic acid
species with cadang-cadang disease of coconut palm.
Phytopathology 65, 163-167.

Randles, J. W., Davies, C., Hatta, T., Gould, A.R., and
Francki, R.I.B. (1981). Studies on encapsidated
viroid-like RNA. I. Characterization of velvet
tobacco mottle virus. *Virology 108,* 111-122.

Randles, J. W., Steger, G., and Riesner, D. (1982).
Structural transitions in viroid-like RNAs associated
with cadang-cadang disease, velvet tobacco mottle
virus, and *Solanum nodiflorum* mottle virus.
Nucleic Acids Res. 10, 5569-5586.

Rohde, W., and Sänger, H.L. (1981). Detection of complementary RNA intermediates of viroid replication by
Northern blot hybridization. *Biosci. Reports 1,*
327-336.

Romaine, C. P., and Horst, R.K. (1975). Suggested viroid
etiology for chrysanthemum chlorotic mottle
disease. *Virology 64,* 86-95.

Sänger, H.L., Klotz, G., Riesner, D., Gross, H.J., and
Kleinschmidt, A.K. (1976). Viroids are single-
stranded covalently closed circular RNA molecules
existing as highly base-paired rod-like structures.
Proc. Natl. Acad. Sci. U.S.A. 73, 3852-3856.

Sasaki, M. and Shikata, E. (1977). On some properties of
hop stunt disease agent, a viroid. *Proceed. Japan
Acad. Ser. B 53,* 109-112.

Semancik, J. S., and Weathers, L.G. (1972). Excocortis virus:
An infectious free-nucleic acid plant virus with
unusual properties. *Virology 47,* 456-466.

Semancik, J.S., Conejero, V., and Gerhart, J. (1977).
Citrus exocortis viroid: Survey of protein synthesis in *Xenopus laevis* oocytes following
addition of viroid RNA. *Virology 80,* 218-221.

Sogo, J.M., Koller, T., and Diener, T.O. (1973). Potato
spindle tuber viroid. X. Visualization and size
determination by electron microscopy. *Virology 55,*
70-80.

Symons, R. H. (1981). Avocado sunblotch viroid: primary
sequence and proposed secondary structure. *Nucl.
Acids Res. 9,* 6527-6537.

Thomas, W., and Mohamed, N.A. (1979). Avocado sunblotch - A
viroid disease? *Australasian Plant Pathol. 8,*
1-3.

Van Dorst, H.J.M., and Peters, D. (1974). Some biological

observations on pale fruit, a viroid-incited disease
of cucumber. *Neth. J. Pl. Path. 80,* 85–96.

Walter, B. (1981). Un viroide de la tomate en Afrique de 1'
ouest: identité avec le viroide du "potato spindle
tuber"? *C. R. Acad. Sc. Paris 292* III, 537–542.

Williams, E.S., and Young, S. (1980). Chronic wasting disease
of captive mule deer: a spongiform encephalopathy.
J. Wildl. Dis. 16, 89–98.

Zelcer, A., Van Adelsberg, J., Leonard, D.A., and Zaitlin,M.
(1981). Plant suspension cultures sustain long-
term replication of potato spindle tuber viroid.
Virology 109, 314–322.

Zlotnik, I. (1962). The pathology of scrapie: a comparative
study of lesions in the brain of sheep and goats.
Acta Neuropathol. (Berl.) [Suppl.] 1, 61–70.

PART II

Viroid Diseases

Chapter 2

THE HOST RANGE OF VIROIDS

D. Peters

Department of Virology
Agricultural University
Wageningen, The Netherlands

W. T. Runia
Glasshouse Crops Research
and Experiment Station
Naaldwijk, The Netherlands

INTRODUCTION

Studies initiated to elucidate the nature of the causal agent of potato spindle tuber disease and citrus exocortis disease (Diener, 1971; Sänger, 1972; Semancik and Weathers, 1972) resulted in the discovery of a new class of pathogens. After this discovery chrysanthemum stunt, cucumber pale fruit, chrysanthemum mottle, hop stunt, cadang-cadang, avocado sunblotch, tomato bushy stunt, tomato "planta macho", tomato apical stunt and burdock stunt appeared to be caused by similar pathogens (Sänger, 1982). Furthermore, a viroid has been isolated from apparently healthy *Columnea erytrophae* plants (Owens *et al.*, 1978).

Considerable progress has been made on the chemical and physical characterization of these agents. Studies revealed that they are single stranded covalently closed ciruclar RNA molecules with a molecular weight of about 120,000 dalton

Copyright © 1985 by Academic Press, Inc.
All rights of reproduction in any form reserved.
ISBN 0-12-470230-9

Table I
The viroid diseases presently known and the
abbreviations of the corresponding viroids*

VIROID DISEASE	VIROID	REFERENCE
avocado sunblotch	ASBV	Thomas & Mohamed, 1979
burdock stunt	BSV	Chen et al., 1983
chrysanthemum chlorotic mottle	CCMV	Romaine & Horst, 1975
chrysanthemum stunt	CSV	Hollings & Stone, 1973
citrus exocortis	CEV	Sänger, 1972
columnea viroid	CV	Owens et al., 1978
coconut "cadang-cadang"	CCCV	Randles, 1975
cucumber pale fruit	CPFV	VanDorst & Peters, 1974
hop stunt	HSV	Sasaki & Shikata, 1977
potato spindle tuber	PSTV	Diener, 1971
tomato apical stunt	TAPV	Walter, 1981
tomato bunchy top	TBTV	McClean, 1931
tomato "planta macho"	TPMV	Galindo et.al., 1982

* This table has been modified after Sänger (1982)

(Gross et al., 1978), existing in their native state as double
stranded rod-like structures. The complete primary and secondary structure of CEV, CSV, CCCV, PSTV and ASBV (see Table
1 for abbreviations of viroid names)(Gross et al., 1981;
Haseloff and Symons, 1981; Gross et al., 1982; Visvader et
al., 1982) has been established recently.

     Not withstanding the limited genetic information com-
prised into such a small molecule, viroid infections have
often a great impact on the infected host. Although the
potential of genetic information of a viroid can code for
only one protein with a molecular weight of 12,000, one must
assume that viroid replication is entirely dependent on
nucleic acid synthesizing enzymes pre-existing in the host.

     Less attention has been paid to the biology of viroids,
and for reasons to be discussed, to their host ranges. In
this chapter we will analyze the results of host range studies. Moreover, we will describe the results of serial passage experiments of CPFV through different hosts. In these
passages a stable change in symptom expression and in the
ability to infect a given host was noticed. The mechanisms
possibly responsible for this unusual biological behavior
will be discussed.

I.   THE NATURAL HOST RANGE

     The number of naturally occurring plant diseases that
are known to be viroid incited is small and occurs only in

nine plant species of economic importance, viz. avocado, burdock, chrysanthemum, citrus, cucumber, coconut palms, hop, potato and tomato. The effect of CCCV in coconut palm trees is quite dramatic. It has been estimated that probably more than 20 million trees were killed from 1926 to 1978. This makes the disease as long as no preventive measures against its spread can be taken, a main threat to coconut production in the Philippines (Randles, 1975). Considerable losses have also been reported for PSTV-infected potato plants in some regions (Singh *et al.*, 1971) and CEV-infected citrus species and varieties (Calavan *et al.*, 1968). Less dramatic are the losses caused by CPFV, ASBV, CEV AND CCMV. The economic losses caused by BSV are difficult to assess. The seeds of *Arctium tomentosum* and *A. lappa* are used for medical purposes in China. Infected plants, the number of which can reach values between 20 to 50% in a crop,do not form seeds (Tien Po, personal communication). From the established nucleotide sequence the viroids PSTV, CEV, CSV, ASBV and CCCV may be considered as distinct viroid species, whereas it can not be ruled out that some of the others, especially those causing diseases in burdock, cucumber, hop and tomato, are strains of PSTV or CSV.

II. THE EXPERIMENTAL HOST RANGE OF VIROIDS

The experimental host range of the different viroids differs considerably. PSTV is able to infect, locally but more often systemically, numerous plant species in thirteen families (Sing, 1973; Diener, 1979). The host range of some viroids seems to be restricted to one family (Table 2). CCMV has been transmitted only to chrysanthemum varieties. CCCV has so far only been inoculated successfully to a few other palm species and ABSV seems to infect avocado *(Persea americana)* and cinnamon *(Cinnamomum zeylanicum)* (Da Graca and Van Vuuren, 1980) which are both members of the family Lauraceae. The host range of the viroids CEV and CSV is limited to species of a few specific plant families. The viroids ABSV, CCCV and CCMV which are restricted to a few related host species can be considered to be host specialized, while those infecting unrelated hosts are generalists. It is striking that species of the Compositae and Solanaceae are susceptible to more viroids than the species of other families. Seven viroids have been found to be able to infect species of the Compositae, and six infect species of the Solanaceae. No suscepts were reported for HSV in the Compositae. As this viroid has a host range very similar to CPFV (Sasaki and Shikata, 1978),suscepts for HSV may occur in the Compositae.

Table 2.
The plant families with susceptibility for
viroids and the number of suscepts found

Families	Viroids											
	ASBV	BSV	CCCV	CCMV	CEV	CPFV	CSV	CV	HSV	PSTV	TBTV	TPMV
Amaranthaceae	–	–	–	–	–	–	–	–	–	1	–	–
Boraginaceae	–	–	–	–	–	–	–	–	–	1	–	–
Campanulaceae	–	–	–	–	–	–	–	–	–	1	–	–
Caryophyllaceae	–	–	–	–	–	–	–	–	–	1	–	–
Compositae	–	2	–	+	2	2	43	–	–	1	1	1
Convolvulaceae	–	–	–	–	–	–	–	–	–	1	–	–
Cucurbitaceae	–	–	–	–	4	30	–	–	10	2	–	–
Dipsaceae	–	–	–	–	–	–	–	–	–	1	–	–
Gesneriaceae	–	–	–	–	–	–	–	1	–	–	–	–
Lauraceae	2	–	–	–	–	–	–	–	–	–	–	–
Leguminosae	–	–	–	–	2	–	–	–	–	–	–	–
Moraceae	–	–	–	–	–	–	–	–	2	–	–	–
Palmae	–	–	4	–	–	–	–	–	–	–	–	–
Rutaceae	–	–	–	–	14	–	–	–	–	–	–	–
Sapindaceae	–	–	–	–	–	–	–	–	–	1	–	–
Scrophulariacea	–	–	–	–	–	–	–	–	–	6	–	–
Solanaceae	–	–	–	–	21	11	9	2	1	140	24	3
Umbellifereae	–	–	–	–	2	–	–	–	–	–	–	–
Valerianaceae	–	–	–	–	–	–	–	–	–	1	–	–

The information presented in this table has been compiled
from data extracted from the papers by Da Graca & Van Vuuren
(1980), Diener (1979), Galindo *et al.* (1982), Runia and Peters
(1980), and obtained from personal communications of Diener,
Randles, and Tien Po.

Although most viroids infect species of more than one
family the attention should be drawn to the fact that each
viroid infects preferential species out of one family (Table
2). The occurrence of suscepts only in the Compositae,
Lauraceae and Palmae for CCMV, ABSV and CCCV, respectively,
has already been referred to. From the 158 suscepts of PSTV
140 are found in the Solanaceae (Diener, 1979). The Rutaceae
include 14 out of 45 susceptible species for CEV. CPFV infects
30 cucurbitaceous species (Van Dorst and Peters,1974),where-
as in total 43 suscepts have been found (Runia and Peters,
1980). CSV finds most of its suscepts in the Compositae. It
is attractive to conclude from this distribution of susceptible species that the preference has to be explained in biological and molecular biological terms. But before doing so
it must be realized that the host ranges discovered so far
for the different viroids may reflect more the interest of

the author(s) than that it gives an image of the real host range.

The number of suscepts of PSTV in the family of the Scrophulariaceae is higher than in all the other families in the group of the non-preferred families. It may be worth while to extend the host range studies in this family with other viroids to explore the possibility to discover more suitable hosts for propagation and assay.

In at least 30 families no species were found which were susceptible for viroids. Several authors have included species of Leguminosae and Cruciferae in their study. So far, only two of the tested species of these families of high agricultural importance proved to be susceptible (Runia and Peters,1980). No susceptible species have been found in the Gramineae. The number of susceptible species found in the preferred families may be only a fraction of those which are susceptible. Ten percent of the species in the Solanaceae has been tested with PSTV and the ratio tested/not tested species in the preferred families is much lower for all the other viroids (Table 3).

Table 3

The Ratio of Tested/not Tested Species in Four Families with a High Preference for Viroid Infection

Family	No.of species (estimated)	No.of species tested	Susceptible	Viroid
Compositae	20000	?	43	CSV
Solanaceae	1500	?	152	PSTV,TBTV
Rutaceae	900	?	14	CEV
Cucurbitaceae	750	38	31	CPFV,HSV

One or two percent or even less of the species comprising the Cucurbitaceae, Rutaceae and Compositeae have been tested with CPFV, CEV and CSV, respectively.

The possibility to find new hosts for viroids will be greater in these families than in those families in which no hosts have been found so far.

However, several biological properties of viroids may discourage virologists to execute experiments to detect new susceptible species. Some of these properties will briefly be described. First of all the long incubation period must be mentioned. In herbaceous host plants the first symptoms appear usually 10 to 60 days after inoculation. The length of this period often depends on the temperature at which the plants are kept. Symptom development in woody plants may take months or years.

Often with most species a low number of plants attract infection after inoculation. This is even the case when high viroid concentrations are used as inoculum.

Thirdly, many species or varieties do not produce recognizable symptoms. This means that infections have to be demonstrated in back inoculations to diagnostic hosts.
Factors which influence the sensitivity will be discussed in more detail in the following section.

Finally, the technique used to inoculate plants plays a role in the number of plants that prove to be susceptible. Rubbing of the inoculum onto carborundum dusted leaves resulted in the establishment of CPFV-infection in 17 cucurbitaceous plants. Stem-slashing with razor blades was more efficient. Out of the 38 species inoculated in this way 30 appeared to be susceptible (Van Dorst and Peters, 1974). The latter technique has also been advocated by Weather and Greer (1972) in the transmission of CEV.

The techniques existing in nature to transmit the viroids may be more effective than those in the laboratory. In experimental conditions only 10% of the inoculated burdock plants may attract infection, whereas 20-50% of the plants in a crop can become infected with BSV (Tien Po, personal communication). Young palm trees can only be infected to a limited number through the application of an injection procedure under high pressure, whereas in the field 500,000 coconut palms die each year in the Philippines as a result of cadang-cadang viroid infections. The effectiveness and rate at which burdock and coconut trees are infected by BSV and CCCV point rather to a specific and biological transmission than to a pure mechanical type of transmission by different agents or cultural practices, as can be the case with PSTV.

III. THE SENSITIVITY OF PLANT SPECIES TO VIROID INFECTIONS

As with each pathogen the sensitivity of an infection by viroids is specified by the genetic constitution of the host plant and the viroid. The sensitivity varies considerably from one species to the other, and is more than with plant viruses dependent on the environmental conditions.

At one of the extremes viroids may cause death of cell and plants. CPFV causes the death of plants of seven cucurbitaceous species (Van Dorst and Peters, 1974).
Hypersensitive reactions have been described on leaves of *Scopolia* species 1 to 2 weeks after inoculation (Singh, 1973). The dramatic effects of CCCV on coconut palms have already been mentioned. At the other extreme susceptible species do not show any perceptible reaction. Some viroids are often latent in many hosts, especially in wild plants, and

cause only disease when transmitted to cultivated plant
species and varieties. Singh (1973) listed 140 solanaceous
species which were susceptible for PSTV, but 113 of them
appeared to be tolerant. Out of 14 susceptible rutaceous
species 8 did not produce symptoms upon infection with CEV
(Diener, 1979). The effect of the genetic make-up on the
severity of symptoms is clearly demonstrated with CEV and
PSTV. CEV causes disease symptoms in six solanaceous plants
which are tolerant for PSTV, and only one species out of 21
suscepts found in the Solanaceae did not produce symptoms
upon infection with CEV. As a rule CEV evokes more severe
symptoms in those species, which are susceptible for both CEV
and PSTV.

A difference in pathogenicity by five different PSTV
strains in tomato could be related to differences in the
primary sequence of the viroids. These strains incite a
range of symptoms from very mild to a severe necrotic reaction by which the plant may be killed. Comparison of the
nucleotides sequence between some of these strains showed
that these differences in pathogenicity can be related to
exchanges of a few nucleotides at some fixed positions in the
viroid molecule (Gross *et al.*, 1981).

It is not only the genetic make-up of the viroid and the
host plant by which the expression of symptoms is determined.
The development of symptoms is critically dependent on environmental conditions. High temperatures increase the severity of symptoms and the rapidity of their appearance. This
was clearly demonstrated in studies on the incubation period
of CPFV in cucumber plants. A mean incubation period of 76
days was found when the plants were grown at day and night
temperatures of 20°C. In case these temperatures were 30°C
the incubation period was 21 days (Table 4).

Table 4
The effect of growth temperature on the mean incubation
period and infectivity of CPFV in cucumber plants

GROWTH TEMPERATURE (°C)		MEAN INCUBATION	INFECTIVITY
DAY	NIGHT	PERIOD	
20	20	76	7/10
25	20	49	9/10
30	25	35	10/10
30	30	21	10/10

Leaf symptoms developed clearly at 30°C, but were less pronounced at lower temperatures. The infectivity of plants
grown at low temperatures was lower when compared with those
kept at high temperatures (Table 4). Similar effects have
also been found with PSTV in tomato plants (Raymer and

O'Brien, 1962). It is also evident that PSTV reaches for higher titers and symptoms are expressed earlier when plants are grown at relatively high temperatures such as 30 to 35°C, than at lower temperatures (Singh and O'Brien, 1970). Sänger. and Ramm (1975) found a more than 500 fold increase in viroid yield by rising the growth temperature of Gynura plants infected with CEV from 15 to 35° C. Under their condition of high temperature severe symptoms usually appear 10 to 14 days after inoculation, whereas it may take 2 to 3 months at 18 to 20°C. These results show clearly that the rate of viroid reproduction depends clearly on the temperature and that as a consequence the viroid concentration determines the severity of symptoms. This phenomenon of temperature dependence of viroid replication differs not worthily from the optimum temperatures found for the replication of plant viruses. They often replicate remarkably well at temperatures around 20°C, or express the most severe symptoms around that temperature. The phenomenon that viroids thrive extremely well at high temperatures means that viroids have greater possibilities to manifest themselves better in the tropics than in temperate regions.

Other environmental conditions than temperatures also influence symptom expression. High intensities of light favor expression of symptoms in PSTV-infected tomato, CEV-infected Gynura and CPFV-infected cucumber plants (Raymer et al., 1964; Sänger and Ramm, 1975; Van Dorst and Peters, 1974).

The effect of nutrients on the symptom expression is not well studied. Symptom formation of PSTV in tomato plants is favored by fertilization to insure vigorous growth (O'Brien and Raymer, 1964). However, Wheathers et a (1965) observed that growth of citrus was not related to the development of CEV symptoms. Factors which disfavored the growth of the host, favored symptom expression. Lee and Singh (1972) observed an increase of symptom severity on PSTV infected tomato plants growing in media with increasing amounts of manganese, whereas inconsistency in symptom expression was encountered without manganese fertilization. Development of local lesions on *Scopolia sinensis* appeared to be also dependent on the level of manganese (Singh et al., 1974). The conditions at which S. sinensis has to be grown for opitimal local lesion formation are perhaps so difficult to define that this host did not find its way to the laboratories in the use of bioassays. Recently a more thorough study has been carried out on the effects of some ions on the symptom expression of PSTV in tomato. Manganese, zinc and borium ions strengthened stunting and epinasty symptoms. These ions were supplied by watering the plants with solutions containing 100

μg of $MnSO_4$, $ZnCl_2$ or Na_3BO_3 per ml. Iron, copper and cobalt
ions weakened the development of symptoms in comparison with
the symptoms on infected control plants. Similar reactions
were found when these nutrients were applied to CEV infected
Gynura aurantiaca plants (Tien, 1984).

In general it can be concluded that the conditions in
which plants have to be grown for optimal symptom expression,
have not extensively and systematically been studied, and are
therefore not well-defined. This situation also makes it
unattractive for the virologist to perform extensive host
range studies.

IV. IMMUNITY OR RESISTANCE TO VIROID INFECTIONS

As shown plants respond in different ways to the introduction of viroids. The outcome does not only depend on the
genetic constitution of the viroid and host, but as discussed
also on the environmental conditions in which the plants are
grown. Many plant species are immune to most viruses. Due
to this innate immunity susceptibility of plants for plant
viruses is an exceptional condition. It is not known whether
this is also valid for viroids. Although most authors do not
report on the number of non-susceptible species, there is
sufficient evidence that under natural and the applied experimental conditions most viroids have a very limited host
range. This may suggest that susceptibility to viroid infections is extremely exceptional. However, since a higher
number of susceptible plant species can be found with improved
inoculation techniques and since viroids will be replicated
on nucleic acid synthesizing enzymes pre-existing in the
host, it can be wondered whether real or true immunity to
viroid infections exists in the plant kingdom. Because such
a condition may not exist the use of the term 'highly resistant' to viroid infections has to be preferred rather than
'immune'.

V. VIROID RANGE OF SOME PLANT SPECIES

In our studies we compared the reaction of CPFV on some
plant species with those of CEV, CSV and PSTV. As a result
we were able to compose a restricted viroid range. Viroid
range in analogy to virus range is defined as the range of
viroids to which a particular plant species may be susceptible (Christie and Crawford, 1978), whereas the host range is
that range of plants which are susceptible to one virus. Our
comparison has been restricted to the viroids CEV, CPFV, CSV
and PSTV and those plant species which are often used in
viroid studies.

The viroid range (Table 5) has been compiled from results found in literature and obtained in our studies. The
viroids used in these experiments were maintained in *G.
aurantiaca* (CEV), chrysanthemum (CSV), tomato (PSTV) and
cucumber (CPFV). CEV, CPFV, CSV and PSTV evoke disease
symptoms on potato cv Katahdin or Arka and tomato plants cv
Rutgers, which cannot essentially be distinguished from each
other. An identical response is observed for CPFV on tomato,
when inoculum is used from potato. No symptoms are seen when
inoculum is taken from CPFV infected cucumber plants. HSV,
which is assumed to be quite similar to CPFV does not produce symptoms on tomato (Sasaki and Shikata, 1978).

Table 5

The susceptibility (right column) and sensitivity (left
column) of some plant species for five different viroids

HOST/VIROID	CEV	CSV	CPFV	HSV	PSTV
Chrysanthemum	++	++	++		++
Gynura	++	−+	−+		++
Cucumber	++	−+	++	++	++
Potato	++	++	++	−	++
Tomato	++	++	++	−+	++

In tests on chrysanthemum cv Mistletoe CPFV, CSV and
PSTV incite numerous yellow leaf spots. The diameters of
these spots varied from one spot to the other and were not
characteristically different for the viroids inoculated. CEV
causes a stunting of the top with leaf distortion and mottling (Fig. la). This reaction is quite similar to one that
is described by Welsh (1948) to CSV.

The symptoms caused by PSTV on cucumber cv Sporu plants
were identical to those observed for CPFV (Van Dorst and
Peters, 1974). The symptoms caused by CEV are of the same
character as the CPFV symptoms, but they are much weaker.
Cucumber was found to be a symptomless carrier of CSV.

CPFV, CSV and PSTV failed to produce symptoms on *G.
aurantiaca*, but were recovered from the inoculated plants on
cucumber, chrysanthemum and tomato, respectively. CEV developed on *G. aurantiaca* symptoms as described by Weathers *et
al.*, (1967). Our results with PSTV are not in agreement with
the results of Singh and Clark (1973) who described symptoms
of PSTV in *G. aurantiaca* which were not different from those
of CEV. The difference in PSTV symptom expression of *G.
aurantiaca* found by us and by Singh and Clark may not be so
much a reflection of strain differences as it is a question
of varietal differences of the plants or environmental differences.

Figure 1. (a) CEV-infected chrysanthemum cv Mistletoe plant
showing a distortion and a slight stunting of the top.
        (b) CPFV-infected egg plant (cv Mammouth) showing
disappearance of leaves by necrotisation.

    The viroids CEV, CSV and PSTV may be considered on the
basis of their nucleotide sequence as distinct viroid 'species'. They differ from each other in 30-40% of their nucleotide composition (Gross *et al.*, 1982). The results presented
here do indicate that the agents compared possess a high
degree of similarity in symptom expression. This means that
symptoms are caused by one and the same mechanism in the
plant by a rather well preserved nucleotide sequence in the
evolution of viroids.

VI.   INFECTION OF TOMATO BY CPFV

    In our studies on the viroid range of plants we noticed
that CPFV changes in symptom expression on tomato after passage over different plant species. This host passage effect
could be confirmed in a number of experiments which will be
described in detail. Host passage is defined in these experiments as the introduction of the viroid into a host species
and its subsequent transfer to another host species.
    Infection of tomato plants by CPFV could be demonstrated
in eight different experiments. No symptoms were produced on

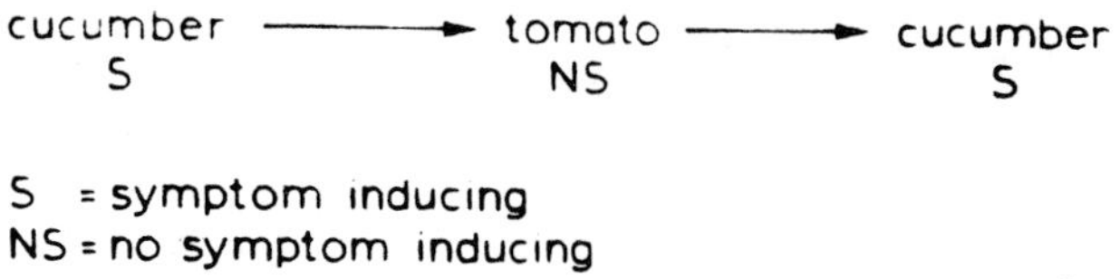

cucumber ——————▶ tomato ——————▶ cucumber
    S   NS   S

S = symptom inducing
NS = no symptom inducing

Figure 2. Scheme and results of host passage of CPFV between cucumber and tomato.

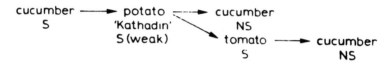

S = symptom inducing
NS = no symptom inducing

Figure 3. Scheme and results of a passage of CPFV from cucumber over potato and tomato to cucumber.

any of the 60 tomato plants inoculated while kept for pro-longed observation for a period of two months, following inoculation. In back inoculations from these tomato to cucumber plants 50% of the cucumber plants became infected and showed the characteristic symptoms of CPFV, indicating that at least half of the tomato plants were infected. In inoculations made simultaneously from cucumber to cucumber an infection rate of 100% was obtained. These experiments, out-lined in Fig. 2, show that (I) CPFV causes a latent infec-tion in tomato plants, (II) no change in symptom expression has occurred on cucumber and (III) an inoculum from tomato is less infectious than from cucumber.

VII. INFECTION OF TOMATO BY CPFV AFTER PASSAGE THROUGH POTATO

When CPFV was transmitted to the potato variety Kathadin and then to tomato plants, symptoms were observed on tomato. The potato plants showed only a slight reduction in growth, whereas a severe stunting occurred on the tomato plants. These symptoms were comparable to those caused by CEV, CSV and PSTV on tomato plants (Semancik and Weathers, 1972 Diener and Lawson 1973; Raymer and O'Brien, 1962) and as observed for CEV, CSV and PSTV on tomato plants in our experiments. These observations were made in four experiments in which 38 potato plants and 60 tomato plants, of which 55 became infected, were used. It seems conclusive that CPFV, of which three different isolates were used, may acquire the capacity to incite symptoms on tomato by passing over potato. The forms of CPFV which are maintained in potato and tomato plants are called CPFVp and CPFVt, respectively.

After inoculating CPFVt to cucumber, no symptoms were produced in 17 experiments, using 207 plants, and no recovery of the viroid could be made by back inoculations to tomato plants. These experiments (Fig. 3) show that CPFV has been converted via potato plants and/or tomato plants into a form which is not anymore able to infect cucumber and which is able to produce or evoke symptoms on tomato plants.

VIII. PASSAGE OF CPFV, CPFVp and CPFVt THROUGH EGGPLANT

CPFV incites severe symptoms on eggplants (*Solanum melongena* cv (Fig. 1b) 'Mammouth'). In a transfer of CPFV from egg plant to tomato plants no symptoms were observed, whereas inoculation of cucumber plants from these tomato plants resulted in a discernible infection (Fig. 4a). These results indicate that after passage over eggplant CPFV behaves in the same way as this viroid does in direct transfers of CPFV from cucumber to tomato and back to cucumber (Fig. 3). This confirmed the observation that the form of CPFV that does not produce symptoms on tomato, evokes them in cucumber.

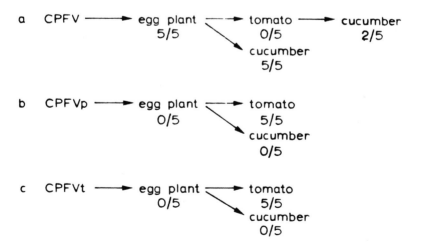

Figure 4. Outline and results of an experiment to study the effects of host adaptation of CPFV in eggplants.

To study the behavior of CPFV$_p$ CPFVt in inciting symptoms on tomato and cucumber similar experiments were carried out (Fig. 4b and c). Inoculation of CPFVp and CPFVt on eggplant resulted in latent infections. In subsequent transfers to tomato plants disease symptoms were observed. An infection could not be demonstrated in cucumber plants after inoculation. Thus, CPFVp and CPFVt exhibit the same biological properties after passage through eggplant as obtained after passage through potato. It is concluded that CPFVp and CPFVt form stable changes of CPFV.

IX. CONCLUDING REMARKS ON HOST PASSAGE EFFECTS

Our results show that after different host passages CPFV may undergo conspicuous changes in its capacity to induce symptoms on tomato and seems to lose its ability to infect cucumber. These changes became stable biological properties of the corresponding viroid progeny. Several possible mechanisms are conceivable to explain the observed alterations. First of all we can assume that the viroid preparations used for inoculation may be a mixed population containing variant molecules. A specific variant might then be able to establish an infection in a given host, in this case potato, so that this molecule is replicated and thus giving rise to a population consisting of only one variant. This variant may then be replicated in tomato and incite symptoms. In subsequent transfers to cucumber no replication and symptom development could be demonstrated. It is a prerequisite that the variant should replicate in cucumber. It is highly unlikely that a variant occurring in an inoculum in cucumber has been selected by replication in potato which cannot be replicated anymore in cucumber.

The presumed existence of mixed populations opens also the possibility that a specific variant is preferentially replicated in a given host. The population of variants formed in cucumber and potato may then differ dramatically in composition. Inoculation of tomato with material from both hosts may cause a differential symptom expression. It might be expected that after inoculation of potato the compostion may be restored during the replication to that formed in tomato plants after a direct transfer of CPFV from cucumber. Then it can be expected that, after back inoculation of tomato, cucumber attracts infection and will develop symptoms. However, since this does not occur after passage over potato it is safe to assume that the observed host passage effect can not be attributed to a preferential replication of variants in the hosts involved.

A mechanisms in which the viroid concentration in the

different hosts differs so much that an adaptation problem occurs, has also be considered. This idea is opposed by the finding that plants with severe symptoms usually contain higher concentration of viroid than plants showing no or weak symptoms. Since after passage over potato tomato reacts with symptoms, whereas no symptoms are observed on tomato, following direct inoculation from cucumber, a concentration effect might also be ruled out.

Since the observed biological changes are stable one may assume that a change in genetic information has occurred during host passage. This can only be demonstrated by the establishment of the primary nucleotide sequence of the corresponding viroid isolates. This will help us in the first place to decide whether the host passage effect is a genetic or biological phenomenon.

The idea of host induced changes is not supported by the work of Dickson *et al.* (1978). Fingerprints made of PSTV and CEV after propagation in tomato and *G. aurantiaca* showed no characteristic changes in the oligonucleotide pattern. Their results showed that gross changes do not occur in the respective hosts. However, their results and conclusions are not necessarily in conflict with ours. In the several passages made in our study, an effect was thus far only encountered after passage of CPFV over potato.

REFERENCES

Calavan, E.C., Weathers, L.G., Christiansen, D.W.(1968). Effect of exocortis on production and growth of Valencia orange trees on trifoliate orange rootstock. In "Proc. 4th Conf. Int. Org. Citrus Virologists" (J.F.L. Childs, ed.), pp.101-104, Univ. Florida Press, Gainesville.

Chen, W., Tien, P., Zhu, Y.X., and Lui Yong (1983). Viroid-like RNAs associated with burdock stunt disease. *J. Gen. Virol. 64,* 409-414.

Christie, S.R., and Crawford, W.E. (1978). Plant virus range of *Nicotiana benthamiana. Plant Dis. Reptr. 62.* 20-22.

Da Graca, J.V., and Van Vuuren, S.P. (1980). Transmission of avocado sunblotch disease to cinnamon. *Plant Dis. 64,* 475.

Dickson, E., Diener, T.O., and Robertson, H.D. (1978). Potato spindle tuber and citrus exocortis viroids undergo no major sequence changes during replication in two different hosts. *Proc. Natl. Acad. Sci. U.S.A. 75,* 951-954.

Diener, T.O. (1971). Potato spindle tuber "virus". IV. A

      replicating, low molecular weight RNA. *Virology 45,* 411-428.

Diener, T.O. (1979). "Viroids and viroid diseases". John Wiley and Son, New York, pp. 252.

Diener, T.O., and Lawson, R.H. (1973). Chrysanthemum stunt: A viroid disease. *Virology 51,* 94-101.

Galindo, J., Smith, D.R., and Diener, T.O. (1982). Etiology of planta macho, a viroid disease of tomato. *Phytopathology 72,* 49-54.

Gross, H.J., Domdey, H., Lossow, C., Jank, P., Raba, M. Alberty, H., and Sänger, H.L. (1978). Nucleotide sequence and secondary structure of potato spindle tuber viroid. *Nature (London) 273,* 203-208.

Gross, H.J., Krupp, G., Domdey, H., Raba, M., Alberty, H., Lossow, C., Ramm, D., and Sänger, H.L. (1982). Nucleotide sequence and secondary structure of citrus exocortis and chrysanthemum stunt virus. *Eur. J. Biochem. 121,* 249-257.

Gross, H.J. Liebl, U., Alberty, H., Krupp, G., Domdey, H., Ramm, K. and Sänger, H.L. (1981). A severe and a mild potato spindle tuber viroid isolate differ in 3 nucleotide exchanges only. *Biosci. Rep. 1,* 235-241.

Haseloff, J., and Symons. R.H. (1981). Chrysanthemum stunt viroid — primary sequence and secondary structure. *Nucl. Acids Res. 9,* 2741-2752.

Hollings, M., and Stone, O.M. (1973). Some properties of chrysanthemum stunt, a virus with the characteristics of an uncoated ribonucleic acid. *Ann. Appl. Biol. 74,* 333-348.

Lee, C.R., and Singh, R.P. (1972). Enhancement of diagnostic symptoms of potato spindle tuber virus by manganese. *Phytopathology 62,* 516-520.

McLean, A.P.D. (1931). Bunchy top disease of tomato. *S. Afr. Dept. Sci. Bull. 100,* pp 36.

O'Brien, M.J., and Raymer, W.B. (1964). Symptomless hosts of the potato spindle tuber virus. *Phytopathology 54,* 1045-1047.

Owens, R.A., Smith, D.R., and Diener, T.O.(1978). Measurement of viroid sequence homology by hybridization with complementary DNA prepared *in vitro. Virology 89,* 388-394.

Randles, J.W. (1975). Association of two ribonucleic acid species with cadang-cadang disease of coconut palm. *Phytopathology 65,* 163-167.

Raymer, W.B., and O'Brien, M.J. (1962). Transmission of potato spindle tuber virus to tomato. *Am. Potato J. 39,* 401-408.

Raymer, W.B., O'Brien, M.J., and Merriam, D. (1964). Tomato

as source of and indicator plant for the potato
spindle tuber virus. *Am. Potato J. 41*, 311-314.

Romaine, C.P., and Horst, R.K. (1975). Suggested viroid
etiology for chrysanthemum chlorotic mottle disease. *Virology 64*, 86-95.

Runia, W.Th., and Peters, D. (1980). The response of plant
species used in agriculture and horticulture to
viroid infections. *Neth. J. Plant Pathol. 86*,
135-146.

Sänger, H.L. (1972). An infectious and replicating RNA of
low molecular weight. The agent of the exocortis
disease of citrus. *Adv. Biosci. 8*. 103-116.

Sänger, H.L. (1982). Biology, structure, functions and possible origin of viroids. *Encycl. Plant Physiol.*
New Series 14B, 368-454.

Sänger, H.L., and Ramm, K. (1975). Radioactive labelling
of viroid-RNA. In "Modification of the Information
Content of Plant Cells", pp 229-252, North-Holland/
American Elsevier Publ. Co., Amsterdam.

Sasaki, M., and Shikata, E. (1978). Studies on hop stunt
disease I. Host range. *Rept. Res. Lab.* Kirin
Brewery Co., Ltd. *21*, 27-39.

Semancik, J.S., and Weathers, L.G. (1972). Exocortis disease:
Evidence for a new species of infectious low molecular weight RNA in plants. *Nature (New Biol.) 273*,
242-244.

Singh, R.P. (1973). Experimental host range of the potato
spindle tuber "virus". *Am. Potato J. 50*, 111-123.

Singh, R.P., and Clark, M.C. (1973). Similarity of host response to both potato spindle tuber and citrus exocortis viruses. *FAO Plant Prot. Bull. 21*, 121-125.

Singh, R.P., Finnie, R.E.,, and Bagnall, R.H. (1971). Losses
due to the potato spindle virus. *Am. Potato J.
48*, 262-267.

Singh, R.P., Lee, C.R., and Clark, M.C. (1974). Manganese
effect on the local lesion symptom of potato spindle tuber virus in *Scopolia sinensis*. *Phytopathology. 64*, 1015-1018.

Singh, R.P., and O'Brien, M.J. (1970). Additional indicator
plants for potato spindle tuber virus. *Am. Potato
J. 47*, 367-371.

Thomas, W., and Mohamed, N.A. (1979). Avocado sunblotch -
a viroid disease? *Austr. Plant Pathol. Soc.* News
Lett. 1-2.

Tien, P. (1984). Viroids and viroid diseases in China. In
"Subviral Pathogens of Plants and Animals - Viroids
and Prions" K. Maramorosch and J.J. McKelvey, Jr.,
eds. Academic Press, New York.

Van Dorst, H.J.M. and Peters, D. (1974). Some biological observations on pale fruit, a viroid-incited disease of cucumber. *Neth. J. Plant Pathol. 80*, 85-96.

Visvader, J.E., Gould, A.R., Bruening, G.E., and Symons, R.H. (1982). Citrus exocortis viroid nucleotide sequence and secondary structure of an Australian isolate. *FEBS Lett. 137*, 288-292.

Walter, B. (1981). Un viroide de la tomate en Afrique de l'Ouest: identite avec le viroide du potato spindle tuber. *C.R. Acad. Sci. Paris 292*, 537-542.

Weathers, L.G., and Greer, F.C. (1972). Gynura as a host for exocortis virus of citrus. In "Proc. 5th Conf. Int. Org. Citrus Virologists" pp 95-98, (W.C.Price, ed.), ed.), Univ. Florida Press, Gainesville.

Weathers, L.G., Greer, F.C., Jr., and Harjung, M.K. (1967). Transmission of exocortis virus of citrus to herbaceous hosts. *Plant Dis. Rep. 51*, 868-871.

Weathers, L.G., Harjung, M.K., and Platt, R.G. (1965). Some effects of host nutrition on symptoms of exocortis. In "Proc. 3rd Conf. Int. Org. Citrus Virologists" (W.C. Price, ed.) pp 102-107, Univ. Florida Press, Gainesville.

Welsh, M.F. (1948). Stunt-mottle virus disease of chrysanthemum. *Sci. Agric. 28*, 422.

Chapter 3

COCONUT CADANG-CADANG VIROID

J. W. Randles

Plant Pathology Department
Waite Agricultural Research Institute
University of Adelaide
South Australia

I. INTRODUCTION

The name 'cadang-cadang' is derived from 'gadan-gadan' which in the Bicol dialect of the Philippines means dead or dying (Rillo and Rillo, 1981). The use of this name emphasizes the mystery which has surrounded this disease since it was first recognized early this century. The name is non-specific, and has led to confusion in the recognition of the disease in the past, but now refers to a premature decline and death of coconut palms in the Philippines which is associated with viroid infection. The synonym 'yellow mottle decline' is not in common use, while 'tinangaja' is the name used for a similar disease with the same etiology in Guam.

This chapter reviews events which led to the recognition of the disease and its cause, describes aspects of disease epidemiology, reports progress in diagnosis, describes properties of the cadang-cadang viroid, and outlines strategies for control.

39

Copyright © 1985 by Academic Press, Inc.
All rights of reproduction in any form reserved.
ISBN 0-12-470230-9

Terms and their abbreviations used in the text are:
RNAs specifically associated with cadang-cadang – ccRNAs;
monomeric form of ccRNA – ccRNA1 or CC1; dimeric form of the
viroid – ccRNA2 or CC2; the agent of the disease without
reference to form is referred to as the coconut cadang-cadang
viroid – CCCV.
     The variants of the viroid with abbreviations are:
fast electrophoretic forms, i.e. the small molecular forms –
CC1S and CC2S; slow electrophoretic forms, i.e. the large
molecular form – CC1L and CC2L. Variants with a single or
double cytosine residue (e.g. at position 198-199 of CC1S)
have the suffix (c) or (cc).

II. HISTORY

The earliest unsubstantiated report of cadang-cadang was
in Camarines Sur province in 1914 (De Leon and Bigornia,
1953; Kent, 1953; Velasco, 1961). A disease with the symptoms
now known to be specific for cadang-cadang was first described
on San Miguel Island in 1931 (Ocfemia, 1937) and its incidence
was reported to be 25% in some areas of the plantation. The
disease subsequently destroyed most of the plantation.
     The early difficulty of distinguishing cadang-cadang
from other diseases is illustrated by a report that the
disease could be controlled by cultural practices (Celino,
1946) and the subsequent suggestion that the disease had a
physiological and an infectious form (Celino, 1947). Therefore, evaluation of the history of cadang-cadang must take
account of the difficulty of recognizing the disease on
symptoms only, and the relatively small number of people
trained to recognize the disease.
     Following the observations on San Miguel Island, a
sequential series of reports of disease occurrence at sites
at increasing distances from the Bicol peninsula was obtained
(Price, 1971), with water or disease-free coconut growing
areas frequently intervening (Fig. 1).
These observations suggested that cadang-cadang had spread
rapidly and extensively from an initial origin in the Bicol
between 1914 and 1963. This hypothesis was supported by
reports that losses increased with time. For example, between 1931 and 1946, disease incidence on San Miguel Island
increased from 25% to 90% in some areas (Kent, 1953) and less
than 100 palms survived to the 1970's. Roadside surveys in
the adjoining Bicol region gave the following estimates for
the number of diseased palms; 1,788,000 in 1951; 4,569,000
in 1952; 5,527,000 in 1953 (Kent, 1953) and 7,927,000 in
1957 when yield losses of $16m were estimated (Price, 1971).
     Disease incidence ranged from 9.1% to 61% in different

provinces and more than 12 x 10^6 palms were estimated to have been killed by cadang-cadang between 1926 and 1971 (Price, 1971). In 1978 and 1980 respectively, 391,000 and 209,000 new cases of disease were estimated to have occured (Zelazny and Pacumbaba, 1982) representing a decline in incidence since 1960. It is estimated that up to 30 x 10^6 palms have been killed by the disease since its recognition (Zelazny *et al.*, 1982).

Speculation on the cause of the disease has been rife (Rillo and Rillo, 1982). International support for research on the disease commenced after 1950 (Reinking, 1950), the importance of the disease became more widely recognized,

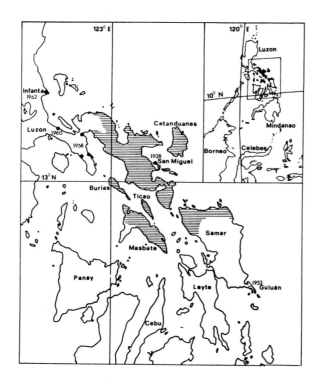

Figure 1. Distribution of cadang-cadang in the Philippines.

and the disease syndrome was described in some detail (Price, 1957;Nagaraj *et al.*, 1965). Despite a failure to define disease etiology up to 1971, the Food and Agriculture Organization of the United Nations continued to support research, but with a change in emphasis to allow an effective collaboration to be established between local laboratories and a foreign laboratory capable of introducing techniques and facilities not available locally (Heinze and Robinson, 1972; see Rillo and Rillo, 1981). This led to an active decade of research (1973-1983) which resolved the etiology of cadang-cadang and allowed the introduction of specific diagnostic tests. Concurrent intensive ecological studies were introduced with the objective of determining the mode of natural spread and developing a model of disease epidemiology.

Continued research on cadang-cadang will run parallel to the coconut improvement program in the Philippines which relies on the introduction of F1 hybrid seedlings to replace local varieties. To minimize the risk of a new epidemic in these lines, an attempt is being made to select plants which are resistant or tolerant to cadang-cadang.

III. EPIDEMIOLOGY

Cadang-cadang provides a useful system for studying the distribution and spread of a plant disease. The appearance of specific symptoms, the longevity of the host plant, and the high frequency of coconut plantations throughout the disease area provided a relatively static base for observing cadang-cadang epidemiology, and information thus gained has been used to study distribution, rates of increase and spread and to infer mode of spread.

Early disease surveys were done in strips along roads with trained observers recording disease incidence, and in plantations where incidence and spread was mapped. It was concluded (Sill *et al.*, 1964; Price and Bigornia, 1971, 1972) that disease incidence was related to the age of the plantation. Incidence was negligible before plantations were 10 years old, but after this, a linear regression of incidence on age was observed, at least until incidence reached 50 to 60%. Evidence supporting the view that cadang-cadang spread from palm to palm was presented by Price and Bigornia (1972), in conflict with a previous hypothesis that other species were the source of cadang-cadang (Holmes, 1961). The reliability of the conclusions drawn from these studies is limited by their restricted scope, a result of inadequate research resources. Nevertheless, the following conclusions were justified. Cadang-cadang is contagious and is not likely to be due to soil,physical, biological or chemical factors as suggested by Velasco (1961; 1982). It has a scattered, apparently random distribution, the rate of spread is slow, and if a vector is responsible for spread it is either rare, inefficient, or sluggish. One immediate benefit of this work was that replanting was shown to be a feasible means of maintaining yields in infected ageing plantations, because young palms had no significantly greater risk of becoming infected when growing adjacent to diseased palms than when grown in new plantations.

More intensive studies since 1975 (Zelazny, 1979, 1980; Zelazny and Niven, 1980; Zelazny and Pacumbaba, 1982a,1982b; Zelazny et al., 1982; Anon.,1982) have confirmed some of the earlier conclusions while giving a more comprehensive picture of rates and type of spread in a number of different situations. Zelazny and his co-workers have concluded from their observations that the area within which cadang-cadang occurs has increased very little in the last 26 years. Surveys at the boundaries of disease distribution showed that outward spread was less than 500 meters p.a. New infections can be found up to several hundred meters ahead of a boundary. Where isolated pockets of infection were known to exist, they appear not to have expanded markedly since 1960. Thus, there is no evidence that cadang-cadang originated at one point.

These conclusions provide an alternative hypothesis to that presented in section II where the sequential identification of cadang-cadang at increasing distances from the site of first recognition implied that the disease had spread rapidly outwards from a single source in the last 70-80 years. This alternative hypothesis states that cadang-cadang is endemic in the Philippines and that some factor is responsible for its present pattern of distribution. A number of factors could be involved, such as, mutation of CCCV to a pathogenic form, protection of some palms because of genotype or 'mild strain protection', distribution of a putative vector, or palm age distribution, but none of these have been implicated so far.

There is no doubt that epidemics of the disease occur, but observations at a number of sites indicate that they have occurred at different times in different places. Thus, an epidemic was observed in the Albay province in 1951-57 (see Section II) but the incidence is now declining. In contrast, parts of the neighboring Camarines Sur province are now experiencing 50-70% incidence of disease whereas in the same area in 1956 the incidence was below 3% (Zelazny et al., 1982).

Within the boundaries of disease distribution (Fig. 1) cadang-cadang incidence is highly variable. In small areas,

diseased palms are not clustered, but over large areas,
centers of high and low incidence are seen. Zelazny (1980)
surveyed an area of 1492 km^2 and attempted to correlate disease incidence with variables such as site, altitude, abun-
dance of different vegetation, palm density and age, rainfall,
and soil conditions. A significant negative correlation was
observed between altitude and incidence and, in agreement with
earlier observations, a positive correlation was observed
between palm age and incidence. Three beetle species *(Oryctes
rhinoceros, Plesispa reichei, and Hemipeplus sp.)* were more
abundant in areas with high disease incidence (Zelazny and
Pacumbaba, 1982a) but so far no insects have been shown to
transmit cadang-cadang.

Patterns of disease increase vary from site to site.
Some fit a 'simple interest' pattern, others a 'compound
interest' pattern (Anon, 1982). The lack of a specific
pattern of disease increase does not allow the source of
infection in plantations to be inferred. The low rates of
spread mean that trials to determine mode of transmission
must be very large. So far, no evidence is available to
implicate either pollen, or mechanical (use of harvesting
scythes) transmission of cadang-cadang.

Figure 2. Early (E), medium (M) and late (L) stages of
cadang-cadang disease.

IV.   SYMPTOMS AND EFFECTS ON YIELD AND GROWTH

Palms infected with CCCV progress through a well defined series of changes culminating in death(Fig. 2). Recognition of these stages is important for field diagnosis, and consequently the more obvious morphological changes have been best described. For convenience, diseased palms in the field are classed as being at early (E) mid or medium (M), or late (L) stage (Randles *et al.*, 1977). The E stage has recently been subdivided because it is involved in major changes in disease and CCCV development (Imperial *et al.*, 1981; Mohamed *et al.*, 1982). The stages are as follows:

E_0 : ccRNA detected in the youngest fronds; symtomless (symptoms appear 1-2 yrs. later).

E_1 : newly developing nuts more rounded with equatorial scarification; no leaf symptoms.

E_2 : more nuts rounded and scarified; chlorotic leaf spots appear; inflorescences stunted.

E_3 : leaf spots enlarged; fewer nuts produced; new inflorescences stunted and sterile.

M   : spathe, inflorescence, and nut production decline then cease; leaf spots more numerous.

L   : fronds decline in size and number; pinnae become brittle; leaf spots coalesce giving a general chlorosis; crown size is reduced, palm dies.

This progression of symptoms is remarkably constant in the Philippines, with some variation in intensity. Tinangaja disease (see the chapter by G. Boccardo) shows different nut symptoms. The E stage lasts an average of about 2 years in 19-30 year old palms (Anon, 1982) but lasts up to 3.75 yr in older palms (Zelazny and Niven, 1980). The M stage lasts for an average of just over 2 yrs (Anon, 1982). The L stage, to death, averages about 5 yrs. Direct estimates give the mean duration of disease to death, as 9 yrs (Anon, 1982), while indirect estimates give a duration of 7.5 yrs for 22 yr old palms, and 15.9 yrs for 44 yr old palms (Zelazny and Niven, 1980). The rare infected palms in the field which show symptoms before they commence bearing do not bear nuts even though they survive well beyond the age of bearing.

Although root deterioration has been reported (Calica and Bigornia, 1962) studies of histological changes have concentrated on the leaf. Rillo *et al.*, (1972) reported that leaflets from infected palms were thinner, and that palisade and mesophyll tissue were disorganized. This hypoplasia suggests that the disease induces changes at the cell differentiation phase of leaf development. The yellow spots on expanded leaves do not develop from a point of necrosis. Light microscopy shows that chloroplasts are distinguishable in the yellow area but are paler than in the

GREEN   YELLOW   2 μ

Figure 3. Electron micrograph of a green-yellow boundary in
a disease associated leaf spot, showing in the yellow area
irregularity of chloroplast outline, vesiculation, starch
accumulation and disorganization of lamellae. Dark structures
resembling tannin bodies accumulate in the vacuole.

adjacent green tissue (Randles, unpublished). Electron microscopy of the green-yellow interface (Fig. 3) showed that
chloroplasts were vesiculate, starch accumulated, lamellae
were disorganized, and that some tannin body accumulation
occurred in vacuoles.

It is noteworthy that the yellow spots (sometimes described as watersoaked spots: Nagaraj *et al.*, 1965) do not
appear until fronds have reached the third or fourth position
in the crown, i.e. 3-4 months after they first expand. Exposure to sunlight is thought to be important in the development of spots as shaded areas show less intense spotting.
Thus, the degeneration of chloroplasts and the production of
yellow zones may be a later phase initiated either by light
or heat, or it may be due to changes in leaf physiology as
the leaf changes from an immature parasitic white state to a
green source of photosynthates. Rasa (1968) reported phloem
necrosis in the apical meristem of diseased palms, but Rillo
et al., (1972)saw neither phloem degeneration nor proliferation.

The availability of inoculated palms for study has confirmed most of these observations in field-infected palms.
Inoculated palms show similar leaf spot development, reduced
frond production and crown size, and slower growth (Fig. 4)
Production of inflorescences, or nuts, in palms inoculated as
seedlings is rare.

V. DETERMINATION OF THE ETIOLOGY OF CADANG-CADANG

As with a number of other diseases subsequently shown to
be caused by pathogens, the history of cadang-cadang is a

catalogue of claims for causes ranging through nutrition,
climate (including catastrophic events such as typhoons),
toxic elements and insect feeding (Bigornia, 1977; Velasco,
1982). The detailed observations up to 1972 on disease
distribution, spread, and the disease syndrome essentially
excluded these hypotheses, in that all the available data
together best fitted the pattern expected for an infectious
disease. Nevertheless, no pathogen was found to be specifically associated with cadang-cadang and the failure to unequivocally transmit the disease by standard microbiological
methods, or by virus inoculation methods left the pathogen

Figure 4. Artificially inoculated seedling (left) showing
stunting, sterility and disordered pinnae compared with a
healthy seedling; 6 yr post inoculation.

hypothesis without direct suport. A significant aspect of
this failure was that the most reliable technique available
to transmit intercellular and vascular pathogens of plants,
grafting, cannot be used with coconut palms.
    The apparent contagious nature of the cadang-cadang
agent, and the absence of either macroscopic or microscopic
evidence for another pathogen, led to the virus hypothesis
for cadang-cadang. The discovery of mycoplasmas as plant
pathogens in 1968 and their involvement in lethal yellowing
of coconut in the West Indies (Plavsic-Banjac *et al.*, 1972;
Beakbane *et al.*, 1972) and the USA (Parthasarathy, 1973) led
to their inclusion in a list of possible agents. Viroids
were also first described in 1969 (Diener, 1979) but little
was known of their properties in 1972.

The events which led to the discovery that cadang-cadang was caused by a viroid commenced with a study to look for mycoplasma, virus, or virus components by both electron microscopy and gel electrophoretic methods. The approach was unconventional in that Koch's postulates were not followed. Instead of attempting to isolate a pathogen, purifying it and reintroducing it to a healthy host plant to induce disease, the approach was to seek any unusual feature of diseased palms, and determine whether it was uniquely associated with the disease. Electron microscopy using the negative staining technique showed the presence of rod-shaped particles(Randles, 1975a) which were shown to be neither virus-like, nor specifically associated with disease. The fraction of palm leaf extracts which was precipitable with polyethylene glycol 6000 was analysed to seek nucleic acids which may have originated from virus particles not detectable by electron microscopy. These assays were done by polyacrylamide gel electrophoresis and showed two sharp low molecular weight RNA bands which were uniquely associated with diseased palms and which had thermal denaturation properties unlike either tRNA or double-stranded RNA, but like a viroid (Randles, 1975b). The discovery of these bands provided, in the first instance, a diagnostic marker for cadang-cadang in coconut. Secondly, they led to a series of experiments designed to determine whether the RNA's were a virus RNA component (perhaps an unnecessarily cautious attitude, but nevertheless an attitude given credence by the discovery of a plant virus with a viroid like RNA component; Randles *et al.*, 1981), or viroids. Aspects such as the presence of two RNA bands, and the absence of an infectivity assay for cadang-cadang precluded the assumption being made that cadang-cadang was viroid induced at this stage. However, the demonstration that the two RNA's (ccRNA-1 and ccRNA-2) appeared in some seedlings following inoculation with crude nucleic acid extracts by a combination of high pressure injection and razor slashing (Randles *et al.*, 1977, and repeated failures to implicate other pathogens such as mycoplasmas (Randles *et al.*, 1977; Imperial, 1980a) supported the view that they were a component of the cadang-cadang agent. Their appearance in inoculated palms preceded the appearance of distinctive leaf symptoms (Randles *et al.*, 1977). Parallel comparative studies were continued with potato spindle tuber viroid (PSTV) and ccRNA-1 was found to have a number of structural properties in common with it (Randles *et al.*, 1976). Electron microscopy showed that preparations of ccRNA-1 and ccRNA-2 contained circular molecules, and that ccRNA-1 was smaller than PSTV while ccRNA-2 was larger (Randles & Hatta, 1979).

The unique nucleotide sequence of ccRNA-1 was demonstrated using a [3]-complementary DNA probe synthesized on a template generated by cleaving ccRNA-1 with S_1 nuclease. The S_1 nuclease products were polyadenylated, primed with oligodeoxythymidylic acid and reverse transcribed with avian myeloblastosis virus reverse transcriptase(Hell *et al.*, 1976: Randles and Palukaitis, 1979). The probe was used in liquid-liquid hybridization assays which allowed analysis of hybridization kinetics, and comparisons of percentage homology. It not only provided a specific and sensitive means of detecting ccRNA-1 particularly when it was in very low concentrations and not detectable by gel electrophoretic assay, but it also showed whether RNA bands associated with cadang-cadang-like diseases in other hosts, or new geographic areas, were homologous with ccRNA.

The cDNA probe was used in hybridization assays to show that:
(i)   ccRNA-1 and ccRNA-2 had sequences in common.
(ii)   ccRNA-1 sequences were not detectable in RNA or DNA from healthy coconut palm, nor were they detectable in the fraction from diseased coconut palm containing RNA higher in MW than ccRNA-2 or in DNA from diseased palms.
(iii)   preparations of ccRNA-1 contained a population of molecules of the same size and sequence, hence the information provided by the molecules was no more than that of any one molecule, i.e. by a sequence of approximately 300 nucleotides.
(iv)   specimens of naturally infected African oil palm *Elaies guineensis* and buri palm *(Corypha elata)* (Randles *et al.*, 1980 and inoculated royal palm *(Oreodoxa regia)* and Manila palm *(Adonidia merrillii)* (Imperial *et al.*, 1980) were shown to be infected with ccRNA.
(v)   diseased coconut palms in India (Kerala wilt and Tatipaka disease) and Vanuatu have no nucleic acids homologous with ccRNA whereas Tinangaja disease in Guam was shown to be synonymous with cadang-cadang (Table 1) (Boccardo *et al.*, 1981).

Although this evidence supported the unique nature of ccRNA, and was consistent with it being a viroid, the final proof of a viroid etiology depended upon a demonstration that the highly purified RNA was infectious. These experiments were complicated by the existence of a number of different forms of ccRNA, but it was considered that the viroid etiology would be proved if the smallest disease specific component, ccRNA-1, was shown to be transmissible and to produce the disease syndrome. Table 2 shows the results of several trials in which ccRNA fractions were inoculated by the com-

TABLE I

Liquid-liquid molecular hybridization of CCCV-cDNA with nucleic acids extracted from coconut palms infected with cadang-cadang, tinangaja, bristle-top, tatipaka, Kerala wilt and Vanuatu diseases.

Disease	RNA extract	%hybridization of cDNA[c]
Cadang -cadang	Low MW fraction[a]	56
Tinangaja	" " "	67
Bristle-top	" " "	7
Tatipaka	LiCl soluble[b]	10
Kerala wilt	" "	0
Vanuatu disease	PEG precipitated[b]	2
	Nil	3

a. Boccardo *et al.*, 1981
b. Randles *et al.*, 1976
c. Values not normalized.

bined high pressure injection – razor slashing technique (Randles *et al.*, 1977). Fractions prepared by sucrose density gradient centrifugation were analysed for their RNA content before inoculation. Maximum infectivity was associated with the fraction containing the highest concentration of ccRNA-1 and 2 (Table 2)and the infectivity cut off in the<4S material indicated that the smallest infectious component of total nucleic acid preparations was the size of the disease specific ccRNA-1 and ccRNA-2. In experiments in which CC1 and CC2 were separated into their small (fast) or large (slow) forms, (CC1S, CC1L, CC2S, CC2L)and also into the circular or linear forms of CC1 (Table 2) all forms except the large linear CC1 were shown to be infectious (J.S. Imperial, N.A. Mohamed and R. Bautista, unpublished results; Anon, 1982; Mohamed and Imperial, 1983). Although CC1S was apparently the most infectious form, the significance of the apparently different estimates of infectivity is not known because no clear relationship between the concentration of inoculum and its infectivity has been established in the transmission trials. The transmission rates may be determined by the number or site of injections rather than the concentration of ccRNA in the inoculum. Nevertheless, these data clearly show the viroid nature of CCCV and demonstrate the infectivity of the smallest molecular form associated with the disease – a molecule of 246 or 247 nucleotides (Haseloff *et al.*, 1982).

TABLE II

Infectivity of nucleic acid components isolated from cadang-cadang infected coconut palm (Anon, 1982).

Experi-ment	Method of fractionation	Fraction	Concentra-tion(μg/ml)	Infectivity Infected/total inoc.)
1. Unfractionated.	Total	48		2/10
	Sucrose density gradient[a]	4–5S		0/10
		5–10S	"	4/10
		ccRNA1+2		
		10–15S	"	1/10
		15–25S	"	1/10
		>25S	"	0/10
		Recombined	"	1/10
2. Unfractionated	Total	–		7/10
	Non-denaturing PAGE[b]	ccRNA1	22	5/10
		ccRNA2	26	1/10
		ccRNA1+2	22 + 26	4/10
3. Denaturing PAGE[c]	CC1S	0.01–100		57/266
		CC2S	"	8/131
		CC1L	"	6/182
4. " "	CC1S circular			2/10
		linear		1/9
		CC1L circular		0/9
		linear		0/10

a. Nucleic acids were fractionated on 10–35% linear sucrose density gradients. Components were collected, assayed by PAGE, adjusted to 48 μg/ml in standard saline citrate buffer and inoculated by combined high pressure injection and razor slashing (Randles *et al.* 1977). Results assayed by PAGE 44 mo post-inoculation.

b. ccRNA1 and 2 separated by elution from 2.5% preparative gels.

c. Small and large forms of ccRNA1 and 2, and their linear and circular forms were prepared by sequential fractionations on a 5% non-denaturing PAGE, a 5% denaturing 8M urea gel, and a preparative 3.3% elution gel (Anon,1982; J.S.Imperial, N.A. Mohamed, R. Bautista, unpublished results; Mohamed and Imperial, 1983).

VI. DIAGNOSTIC METHODS

The development of diagnostic methods for viroid
infection is limited by the low concentration of viroid RNA
in infected host tissue, and their non-immunogenicity.
Infectivity assays for viroids have been the most reliable,
but are not particularly useful for CCCV because they are
inefficient, incubation times are long, and early symptoms
are unreliable.

Routine diagnosis of cadang-cadang became possible with
the discovery that polyethylene glycol(PEG) 6000 and ammonium
sulfate precipitated a fraction from diseased leaf extracts
which was enriched with ccRNA1 and ccRNA2 (Randles, 1975;
Randles *et al.*, 1976). Between 20 and 280µg of ccRNA can be
purified per kg of leaf using PEG precipitation of ccRNA
followed by three cycles of polyacrylamide gel electrophoresis (PAGE) (Anon, 1982). ccRNA concentrations in leaves
determined by R_0t analysis of total leaf nucleic acids with
cDNA in liquid-liquid hybridization assays, were estimated to
be between 82 and 111 µg per kg (Anon, 1982) and the PEG step
therefore recovers and concentrates a major part of the ccRNA
present in the leaf of infected coconut palms. Our observations suggest that it is not an efficient method for concent-
rating ccRNA from other palm species.

For work on coconuts, the PAGE assay for ccRNA has been
favored because of its ease of operation. Currently a maximum
of about 400 samples can be handled per week at the Albay
Research Centre, with 3-4 days required from leaf harvest to
final result. Samples of 10g are harvested, blended in cold
0.1 M Na_2SO_3, and subjected to the steps outlined in the
footnote of Table 3. ccRNA1 and 2 are clearly detected in
extracts from the equivalent of 1-2.5 g leaf, as the toluidine
blue stain routinely used detects around 0.1 µg of ccRNA per
band. An added advantage of PAGE is that variations in the
electrophoretic mobility of different ccRNA isolates are detected at the time the ccRNA is detected.

Improvements to the technique are likely to be achieved
by further simplifying the extraction procedure, modifying
the gel electrophoretic system, and the use of more sensitive
staining procedures. For example, the use of phenol to
extract nucleic acids from the PEG precipitate may be unnecessary as ccRNA can be detected in the ethanol precipitated fraction of the resuspended PEG precipitate by PAGE. A
refinement of the PAGE method has been recently proposed
(Schumacher *et al.*, 1983) which utilized the differing
electrophoretic mobilities of viroid molecules compared with
normal plant RNAs in nondenaturing and partially denaturing
gels. By running extracts first in non-denaturing gels in one
direction, then either in the reverse direction or at 90° to
the first direction under denaturing conditions, viroid bands

can be separated from other nucleic acids. Silver staining allows the detection of viroids in amounts down to 600 pg and tests with purified ccRNA1 clearly detected 0.4 to 1.6 ng.

Molecular hybridization methods are highly sensitive as well as being specific. In the liquid-liquid system, ccRNA hybridization kinetics with homologous cDNA give a R_0t $1/2$ value of 1×10^{-3} mol s 1^{-1} (Randles and Palukaitis, 1979). Thus, in a 96 hr hybridization, ccRNA concentrations down to 1 ng/ml would be detectable. With a reaction volume of, say, 40 μg, amounts down to 40 pg of cc would be detectable. It has been observed that palm nucleic acids should be highly purified to prevent partial denaturation and loss of ^{3}H-cDNA during hybridization. A theoretical limit also applies in that ccRNA concentrations should exceed that of cDNA by at least one order of magnitude to preserve first order kinetics.

Table III.

Relative sensitivity of detection of ccRNA by PAGE and blot hybridization assays. The values given are dilution end points for detection in standard[a] or total[b] nucleic acid extracts.

Sample	PAGE	Hybridization	Sensitivity Ratio
Coconut - healthy[a]	0	0	
- diseased 1	1/5	1/3125	625
2	1/5	1/250	125
3	1/25	1/3125	125
4	1/5	1/3125	625
5	1/5	1/78125	15625
6	1/25	1/390625	3125
Oil palm - inoculated[b]	–	1/3125	–
Royal palm - "	–	1/1	–
Buri palm "	–	1/3125	–

a. Leaf blended in 0.1M Na_2SO_3, polyethylene glycol insoluble fraction extracted in phenol-SDS-chloroform, nucleic acids recovered by ethanol precipitation, fractionated with 2M LiCl. Ethanol precipitated nucleic acids were dissolved, diluted in a 5-fold dilution series, then subjected to either PAGE (4 μl) or blot hybridization (2 μl). (Rodriguez, Haseloff, Symons and Randles, unpublished).

b. Total nucleic acid extracts from these palms were assayed by hybridization only.

Liquid–liquid hybridization methods are relatively laborious but with the successful cloning of DNA complementary to PSTV (Owens and Cress, 1980) it became possible to synthesize large amounts of radioactive DNA complementary to the viroid and to use it in solid–liquid hybridization. A sequence representative of ccRNA1 has been cloned by J. Haseloff (unpublished), labelled with ^{32}P and used in a blot hybridization assay (Owens and Diener, 1981). A comparison of the sensitivity of this assay with PAGE is given in Table 3. Assuming that the limit of detection of ccRNA1 by toluidine blue staining is about 100, the 125 fold to 15,625 fold greater sensitivity of the blot assay would allow amounts of 800 pg down to about 6 pg to be detected in each nucleic acid spot. The advantages of this technique are its sensitivity and its applicability to large numbers of samples. The disadvantage is the difficulty of establishing the assay in laboratories not equipped for biochemical studies.

As mentioned in Section IX, a rapid field test is needed which would detect early stages of infection. Such a method is still being sought.

VII. CCV: FEATURES IN COMMON WITH OTHER VIROIDS

CCCV resembles PSTV, CEV, and CSV in structural properties, in both the static and dynamic sense. Thus, not only are shape, size and structure similar, but also the manner in which these molecules dissociate and reassociate, and perhaps, interact with other molecules in host cells.

A. 'Static' Properties

The original attempts to implicate ccRNA1 as the cadang-cadang pathogen concentrated on a comparison of its molecular properties with those of the other viroids, particularly PSTV (Randles *et al.*, 1976). The critical features, such as nakedness, size, circularity and infectivity were all demonstrated.

Nakedness was demonstrated by showing that both ccRNA1 and 2 were removed from PEG precipitated material by incubation in ribonuclease A at 0.2 μg/ml for 10 h at 0°C (Randles, 1975). ccRNA 1 is the smallest of the viroids being about 80% of the size of PSTV and about the same size as avocado sunblotch viroid (ASBV) (Randles *et al.*, 1976; Randles and Hatta, 1979; Haseloff *et al.*, 1982; Mohamed *et al.*, 1982). Circular forms of both ccRNA1 and 2 were detected by electron microscopy (Randles and Hatta, 1979). The partially basepaired rod-like native structure, was deduced by electron microscopy (Randles and Hatta, 1979), a demonstration of cooperative thermal denaturation round the melting point (Tm) which was also very close to the Tm of

other viroids (Randles 1975;   Randles *et al.*, 1982), and by
partial sensitivity of ccRNAl to the single strand specific
S_1 nuclease (Randles *et al.*, 1976;   Randles and Palukaitis,
1979).   Thermodynamic studies indicate that native molecules
do not adopt significant tertiary folding.   Infectivity has
been discussed in section V.

Linear forms of ccRNA 1 and 2 are isolated with the
circular forms (Mohamed *et al.*, 1982; Randles *et al.*, 1982)
(Fig. 5).   Their lengths are estimated to be the same as the
circular forms (Haseloff *et al.*, 198;   Mohamed *et al.*, 1982)
indicating that they differ from the circular form in having a
single site of cleavage.

The primary sequences of the viroids show differences and
similarities.   Thus, PSTV, CSV, CEV and a number of isolates
of ccRNA (Gross *et al.*, 1978; Gross *et al.*, 1982; Haseloff
et al., 1982) have distinct sequences, but each also have
two regions of about 20 nucleotides which are almost identical
for each of these viroids.   When the circular molecules are
drawn with their most probable secondary structures,   as
derived by nuclease sensitivity of the molecules, and thermodynamic considerations (Haseloff   *et al.*, 1982;   Randles *et
al.*, 1982) these two conserved regions of about 20 bases form
a highly base-paired region in the center of the molecule.
This region is shown for ccRNAl in Fig.6, where bases 51-71
are opposite bases 171-194.   This conserved structure is not
found in its entirety in ASBV (Symons, 1981) or in the viroid-like RNAs of VTMoV and SNMV (Haseloff and Symons, 1982),

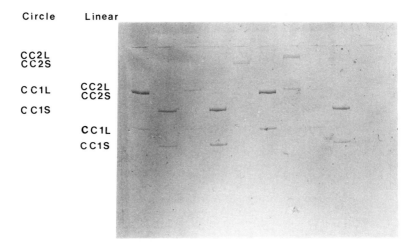

Figure 5.Relative mobilities of circular and linear molecules
of a range of small and large ccRNAs in a 5% denaturing PAGE.

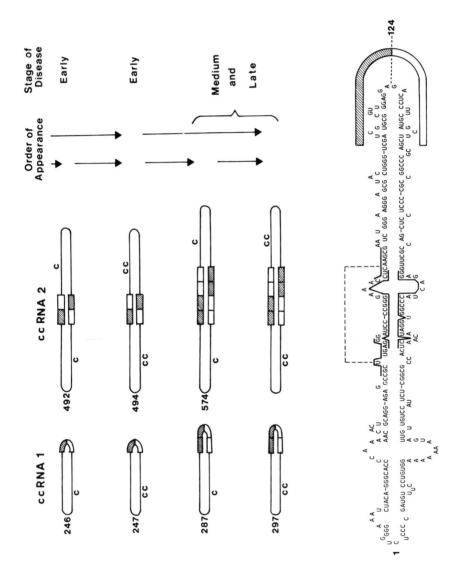

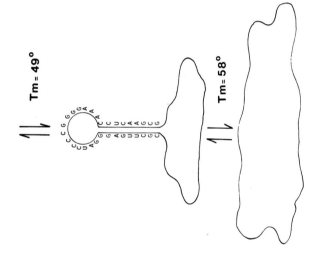

Tm= 49°

Tm= 58°

Figure 6.

but its existence in PSTV, CEV, CSV and ccRNA suggests that
these viroids may have similar mechanisms of replication or
pathogenesis.

B. Dynamic Structural Aspects

Both hydrodynamic and thermodynamic properties of ccRNA
have been studied to check the structural model inferred from
primary sequence data, and to look for possible relationships
between structure and function.

The structural flexibility or "stiffness" of viroids was
compared with that of dsRNA,dsDNA, and viroid-like RNA from
VTMoV and SNMV by analytical ultracentrifugation. PSTV, and
the four ccRNAs (CCIS, CCIL, CC2S, CC2L) all had the same
relationship between molecular weight and sedimentation coefficient, and therefore had the same flexibility (Riesner
et al., 1982). They were more flexible than the dsRNA and
dsDNA, but less flexible than the non-viroid circular RNAs.
It is concluded that on the basis of hydrodynamic properties, these viroid RNAs form a series of homologous native

Figure 6. The basic primary sequence of one isolate of CCCV
(Haseloff *et al.*, 1982) drawn with the secondary structure
interpretation of Randles *et al.*, (1982). The central region
common to other viroids (nucleotides 52-71, 171-194) is marked
with a line within the sequence whereas the complementary
series either side of this conserved region is marked with a
bracketed line above the sequence.

In the diagrams, the loop at the right hand end (105-143)
which is duplicated to give the large forms of ccRNA is shown
by the hatched and clear blocks. The presence of one or two
cytosine residues at position 197-198 is shown diagramatically
by C or CC. The specific pairs of ccRNA1 and ccRNA2 are
shown with one possible arrangement of the duplicated region
for the ccRNA2 molecule. The actual number of nucleotides
for the sequenced representative of each group is shown to
the left (Haseloff *et al.*, 1982).

The relationship between stage of disease development
and the variant observed in the palm is shown, whereby the
minimal CCCV sequence is modified by duplication of the
right-end-sequence, as palms progress from the E to M stage
of disease. Note also the progression from the C to the CC
form (Imperial and Rodgriguez, 1983).

Below the sequence is shown the mechanism of thermal
denaturation of ccRNA. Following the cooperative melting of
internal base pairing at Tm_1 the complementary sequence pairs
to produce a hairpin with a small loop comprising 14 of the
nucleotides in the conserved region. (This is the sequence
involved in the intron hypothesis). The hairpin melts at Tm_2.

structures, which differ from that of the non-viroid circular RNAs. This study also detected rod-shaped native structures only; no cruciform structures were observed even though such structures are possible alternative native forms of CC2S and CC2L (Haseloff et al.m, 1982; Riesner et al., 1982).

Molecular thermodynamics can be studied by equilibrium melting analysis and fast temperature jump techniques.

Equilibrium melting analysis, which is done by slowly increasing the temperature of a solution of viroid in a particular medium while monitoring A_{260} and A_{280} values can provide information on the number and size of structural changes in transitions, the temperature at which they occur, the number of G:C pairs involved in these transitions, and the transitions (and hence whether they are cooperative or non-cooperative). A number of studies on viroids (Riesner et al., 1979) have shown that they undergo common structural changes which can be summarized as follows. Raising the temperature to just below the main melting temperature (Tm_1) results in a negligible increase in UV absorption, indicating that the native molecule has no tertiary folding, and all base pairs are stable to this point. At about 2° below Tm_1, hypochromocity is first observed, and calculations show that this is due to the preliminary opening up of base pairs on the left side of the central conserved region of PSTV, CEV and CSV (Gross et al.,). Further heating completes the dissociation of the more weakly paired left side, and UV absorption increases rapidly over a 2-3° interval as a result of the dissociation of all the native base pairs in a single highly cooperative main transition coupled with the formation of very stable hairpins not originally present (Riesner et al.,1979). Tm_1 occurs at about 50°C in 10 mM Na^+. Further heating to approx. 20° above Tm_1 leads to the consecutive denaturation of the stable hairpins through two less well defined thermal transitions in the case of PSTV (Gross et al., 1981) until the fully denatured open circle is obtained.

To analyse the two less well defined transitions, the kinetics of their melting was studied by the fast temperature jump technique (Henco et al., 1979. The G + C content of the base paired region of the hairpins, and the size of the small loops subtended by the base paired region could be estimated from the relative hypochromicities at 260 and 280 nm and the speed of the thermal denaturation following a sharp increase in temperature. The sequence of structural changes described is consistent with these observations.

The equilibrium melting profiles of ccRNA1 showed a sharp cooperative first transition at around 49°C which accounted for about 80-90% of the hypochromicity and a minor

second transition at about 10°C higher (Randles *et al.,*
1976: Randles *et al.,* 1982). This second transition was
more obvious than observed with other viroids, and temperature jump studies showed that this second transition represented an intermediate hairpin structure which occurred
before the molecule was completely dissociated. This hairpin
melted more rapidly than for PSTV, and the data obtained were
consistent with a base paired region comprising about 70% G +
C, subtended by a single stranded loop of around 20 nucleotides. Fig. 6 shows the interpretation of the thermal dissociation reaction. The first transition (Tm c.49°C) arises
from the cooperative melting of the native base paired structure coupled with the association of 9 bases on the left of
the conserved central region with 9 bases on the right of the
conserved central region. These bases, although completely
complementary, are unable to pair until the basic native
structure is dissociated at about Tm_1. When this new base
paired region forms, a small single-stranded loop of 14
nucleotides is created, and this comprises a sequence common
to the other viroids. At Tm_2 (about 58°C), the data agrees
with the single step melting of the base paired region to
produce a single stranded circle. The exposure of this short
sequence as a single stranded loop in such an intermediate
structure has generated interest because it supports a hypothesis that viroids may interact with their host by inter-
fering with the splicing of exons. The sequence exposed
occurs in the central conserved region, and this and the
complementary region on the opposite side of the molecule
show homology either with introns or the small nuclear Ula
RNA. Thus, these sequences could associate with introns, or
Ula RNA, and thus interfere with the splicing of exons in
heteronuclear RNA (Randles *et al.,* 1982:   Riesner *et al.,*
1983).

The similarities between ccRNA1 and PSTV, CEV, and CSV
in their dissociation-reassociation properties suggest that
is is reasonable to conclude that ccRNA1 resembles other
known viroids not only in structure, but function. It is
noteworthy (Randles *et al.,* 1982) that CC1S AND CCIL have the
same Tm_1 and Tm_2, so additional length of CCIL does not affect its thermal dissociation properties. CC2S and CC2L melt
about 2°C below CC1, but still appear to retain a second
transition. The linear forms of CC1 are less stable than the
circular, with a lower Tm_1, a broader transition, lower hypochromicity, and a less well defined second transition. The
single break may allow different regions of the molecule to
base pair compared with the circular form, thus producing a
different native structure of lower thermal stability.

VIII. UNIQUE AND UNUSUAL FEATURES OF CCCV

Although the foregoing has shown that CCCV has properties typical of the viroids, it differs from the 'type'
viroids, PSTV, CEV and CSV in its epidemiological, biological
and molecular properties. This section emphasizes these
differences to illustrate the range of properties attributa-
ble to this still small group of pathogens.

A. Biological Aspects. CCCV has a narrow host range.
No herbaceous hosts are known despite a number of attempts to
infect species susceptible to PSTV (unpublished results).
The few known hosts are all members of the *Palmae.* The
symptoms in these hosts resemble each other in the production
of leaf spots, stunting, and in the case of oil and coconut
palm at least, sterility. However, in the absence of a
common host comparison of symptoms produced by CCCV and other
viroids is not meaningful.

Unlike PSTV, CEV and CSV (Diener, 1979) CCCV appears not
to be closely associated with cell organelles or membranes.
Whereas the former sediment with tissue debris and appear to
be associated with chromatin, CCCV is not sedimented from sap
extracts at centrifugal forces sufficient to sediment particles down to 130S (Randles *et al.,* 1976). Nevertheless, the
association of CCCV with material precipitated from tissue
extracts with either PEG or amonium sulfate (Randles *et al.,*
1976) indicates that CCCV is associated with some cell
component. Neither purified CCCV (Randles *et al.,* 1976)
nor PSTV in tomato leaf extracts (T.O. Diener and J.W.
Randles, unpublished results) are precipitated with PEG, so
the component is not covalently bound, and it seems to be
unique to the CCCV-coconut system. Whatever is associated
with CCCV is small because the 'complex' recovered by PEG
precipitation has a sedimentation coefficient below about
40S, and it appears to be tenacious because CCCV can be
resuspended and precipated with PEG through at least 3
cycles, Its composition is unknown, but it is removed by
phenol-SDS deproteinization. A study of its nature may
provide evidence on the cellular site of accumulation of
CCCV.

The most efficient transmission of PSTV, CEV and CSV in
crops where they are important occurs through vegetative
propagation. PSTV and ASBV are also transmitted through true
seed, but little is known of the role of vectors in natural
transmission except that aphid transmission of PSTV has been
reported (De Bokx and Piron, 1981). Coconut palms cannot be
vegetatively propagated and there is no evidence that seed
transmission is important in natural spread of CCCV. Unlike
the other viroids, the ability of CCCV to spread naturally is

important in determining its economic impact.   Cadang-cadang
is the only viroid disease whose epidemiology has been extensively investigated.

        B. Molecular Aspects
        CCCV is distinct from the other viroids because of its
size, unique sequence, and molecular variation. The molecular
variation was first apparent with the detection of two unique
disease-associated ccRNA, CC1 and CC2 (Randles, 1975).   The
dimeric CC2 is always isolated with CC1, but always in lower
amounts. It is probable that CC2 is synthesized simultaneously with CC1, as the size of the CC2 present is always
correlated with the size of the CC1.   For example, if both
CC1S and CC1L are found together in nucleic acid extracts,
both CC2S and CC2L are seen.   If CC1S only is found, CC2S is
the only dimer found. Fig. 7 shows an example of a palm in
which a transition from CC1S to CC1L occurs in a sequence of
fronds of different ages, and demonstrates the correlation
between the appearance of monomeric CC1 and its dimeric CC2.
No higher order oligomers of CCCV have been detected by
staining or molecular hybridization (Randles and Palukaitis,
1979)but there has been a recent report that ASBV has a meric
series of + sense viroid up to an 8-mer (Bruening *et al.*,

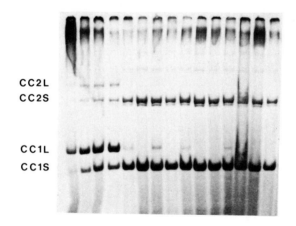

Figure 7.   S and L forms of CC1 and CC2 in a succession of
fronds in an infected palm.   The oldest fronds (right) have S
forms only, the youngest (left) have L only, the intermediate
fronds have both;   this series demonstrates the transition
from small to large as the disease develops.   Analysis by non-
denaturing PAGE according to Imperial *et al.*, (1981).

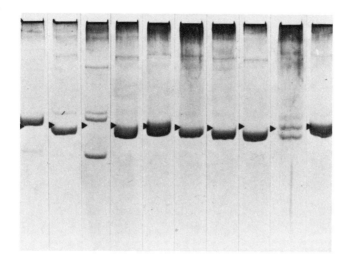

Figure 8.   Variation in the electrophoretic mobility of
10 isolates of ccRNA 1 (lower band), and ccRNA 2 (upper band)
in a non-denaturing polyacrylamide gel (Randles and Salabao,
unpublished). The arrow shows the mobility of a marker ccRNA
1 band.

1982). Sensitive blot hybridization techniques may soon show
that other viroids have oligomers. It is noteworthy that CC2
is infectious (Table 2) and it will be interesting to see
whether other viroid oligomers are infectious .
     The next examples of multiple molecular forms were
obtained with the electrophoretic analysis of CCCV isolates
from a number of palms. CC1 bands with different electrophoretic mobilities were observed, and double or triple bands
were occasionally seen (Fig. 8). Recent studies (Imperial
et al., 1981; Mohamed et al., 1982; Imperial and Rodriguez,
1983) explain some of this variation. Imperial and her co-
workers defined two main classes of CC1; the fast and slow
(CC1L) electrophoretic forms. Working with a collection of
inoculated, recently infected, and older infected palms, a
relationship was discovered between the form of CC1 and the
stage of the disease. This phenomenon was investigated
further by taking advantage of the age-related positioning of
the fronds of palms, and analysing each frond of a number of
early stage palms for CC1. In palms containing both forms of
CCRNA a transition from CC1S to CC1L occurred. The older (or
first infected) fronds contained CC1S, some fronds of intermediate age contained decreasing amounts of CC1L, while the
youngest or more recently infected fronds contained CC1L only
(Fig. 7). It was shown by Mohamed et al., (1982)that CCCV
did not move down the canopy into successively older fronds,

and so it can be concluded that the form of CC1 found in each
frond was probably that which appeared in that frond.   At
later stages of the disease, all fronds contained the CC1L
form only, a result of the upper fronds with CC1L maturing
and moving down through the canopy, while the fronds with
CC1S senesced and abscissed.

The sequencing data of the small and large forms of CC1
and CC2 (Haseloff *et al.*, 1982) shows that CC1S becomes CC1L
by the repetition or duplication of between 41 and 55 nucleotides at the right hand end of CC1S.   Imperial *et al.*, (1981)
and Mohamed *et al.*, (1982)have shown the correlation between
the appearance of CC1L and the onset of reduced nut production, sterility, and the development of prominent leaf spots
in infected palms.   It is tempting to speculate that this sequence repetition may be involved in the onset of the later
more severe stages of sterility and death.   Nevertheless,
palms can be infected by artificial inoculation with either
CC1S or CC1L, and in some palms CC1L is the only form isolated within 2 yrs of inoculation (Imperial *et al.*, 1981).   An
alternative hypothesis could be that the CC1S predominates
early in infection because it is the form transmitted by the
putative vector;   the large forms may then result from faulty
CC1S synthesis as symptoms appear and cell RNA metabolism is
deranged.

ccRNA shows another minor variation, in the presence or
absence of a cytosine residue at position 198 (of CC1S;
Fig. 6).   Isolates sequenced by Haseloff *et al.*, (1982) were
of either form, and some palms contained both c and cc forms.
Imperial and Rodriguez (1983) found that the c and cc variants
could be separated by electrophoresis in non-denaturing 20%
polyacrylamide gels, apparently because they adopted a different native conformation. They were therefore able to follow
the appearance of the c and cc variants in relation to stage
of disease development by analyzing consecutive fronds of
many palms.   They found (Fig. 6) that if CC1S(c) first appears, the sequence of development is then CC1S(cc), CC1L(c),
CC1L(cc).   If CC1S(cc) first appears, it is replaced by CC1L
(cc).

These systematic studies have been possible because of
the phyllotaxis of palms and the duration of the disease.
They have allowed structural changes in viroid to be monitored
according to time, and stage of disease.   They have shown
that the basic nucleotide sequence in CC1S is sufficient to
initiate infection, predictable changes occur in the sequence
as the disease develops, and these are correlated with the
stage of disease.   Such a correlation between a programmed
change in the structure of a pathogen and the stage of disease
development has not previously been observed.   These observations with CCCV now show that it is possible for RNA

molecules to be modified systematically from an original sequence with time, and it is interesting to speculate that this may be correlated with a change in function.

Further variation in CCCV electrophoretic mobility will arise from variation in the length of the sequence which is reiterated to give CC1L from CC1S. Since Haseloff *et al.*, showed that this reiterated sequence could range in length from 41 to 55 nucleotides, multiple bands may result from mixtures of CC1L forms.

C. Possible Taxonomic Groups of the Viroids

Viroids can be separated into three main groups. The first comprises PSTV, CEV and CSV. They share about 50% sequence homology, are about the same size (356–371 nucleotides) (Gross *et al.*, 1982; Haseloff *et al.*, 1982), they infect common species (notably Rutgers tomato, chrysanthemum and *Gynura)* and show a degree of interference with each other when co-inoculated (Niblett *et al.*, 1978).

The second group would consist of CCCV which is smaller than the members of the first group, and has sequence homology only with the central region of about 20 nucleotide pairs. Its known host range includes no herbaceous species, only several species of the *Palmae*.

The third group includes ASBV which is as small as CCCV, but differs from the other two groups in having a sequence of only 6 nucleotides in common with them. Its host range is very narrow.

The viroid-like RNA's of VTMoV and SNMV (Randles *et al.*, 1981; Gould and Hatta, 1981) show no extensive homology with the viroids, and have only 5 nucleotides in the central region homologous with those in ASBV and the other viroids (Haseloff and Symons, 1982). They may be regarded as having a virus host (Gould *et al.*, 1981). At present they are not included with the viroids.

Determination of the primary sequences of all of the viroids may eventually allow a general scheme of classification to be established on the basis of molecular properties only.

VIII.   STRATEGIES FOR CONTROL

Cadang-cadang is the most important of the viroid diseases because of its lethality and economic impact in a country largely dependent on coconut products for export earnings. The main objective of research on the disease has always been to obtain sufficient information on disease etiology, epidemiology, and host reaction to allow control measures to be developed. Clearly, the investigations of CCCV have opened up an intriguing new dimension on the nature of viroids and some of the molecular aspects are relevant to control. The nature of the coconut industry requires that

control measures be simple, reliable, and cost efficient.
While such measures are not yet available some current and
potential methods for the control of cadang-cadang are discussed.
      A. Replanting
      The replanting of infected palms, or infected planta-
tions appears to be the earliest recommended means of reducing the losses due to cadang-cadang (Bigornia, 1977). This
recommendation was based on the observation that the rate of
spread in new plantings was not influenced by the proximity
of infected palms. While having an economic cost in lost
production and cost of planting, this practice has allowed
production to continue in the cadang-cadang area.
      B.   Eradication
      Control by removal of diseased palms has been attempted
in two series of trials (Anon, 1982; Zelazny *et al.*, 1982).
In 1952-1955, diseased palms were removed every 3 mos., and
after 2 yrs., the rate of spread was reported to be about
1/10th that in the untreated area (J.L. Naron; in Zelazny
et al., 1982). A trial commenced in 1979 on an isolated
island with about 300,000 palms in which all diseased palms
were cut annually, showed that there was a marked decline in
new cases of disease during the first two years, but in the
third year, as many new cases occurred as at the beginning of
the trial (Zelazny *et al.*, 1982). This trial is continuing,
but it is noteworthy that early attempts to eradicate cadang-
cadang from apparently new outbreak sites have not succeeded
- infected palms still appear in these areas (Anon, 1982;
Zelazny *et al.*, 1982.
      While at first observation eradication appears to be in-
effective for controlling cadang-cadang, two points must be
considered. Firstly, the latent period of CCCV in mature
coconut palms is not known, although it is known that from
the first detection of CCCV in fronds, 1-2 years may elapse
before symptoms are first seen (Mohamed *et al.*, 1982).
Secondly, CC1S, which predominates in early stage palms before symptoms are recognizable, appears to be the more infectious form of CCCV (Imperial *et al.*, 1981). Early (E_0, E_1,
E_2) stage palms are unlikely to be removed in an eradication
program, even though the above indicates that they may be the
major source of infection. Consequently, eradication as a
means of control may not be properly tested until very early
diagnosis is achieved. If cadang-cadang is eventually controlled by the removal of very early stage infected palms,
the question of the source of infection will finally be
answered.

C. Resistance

Resistance and tolerance are currently being sought in field populations exposed to cadang-cadang for many years (Bigornia and Infante, 1965) and by the inoculation of specific seedlines (Imperial, 1980b). The development of field resistance relies on selecting and breeding from survivor palms in high incidence areas, and preliminary results suggest that disease incidence is lower in selected plants, and that they may also be less readily infected by inoculation (Imperial, 1980b). The current hypothesis that cadang-cadang has been present in the Bicol region for several centuries suggests that much of the selection for field resistance may have already occurred in populations established in the region. Nevertheless, several generations of selection are required to ensure that apparent survivors are not merely escapes, and that development of field resistance is a practical goal.

The current interest in the heterosis obtained with dwarf x tall hybrids has meant that parent material of un - known susceptibility to cadang-cadang is being used to produce F1 seed. Inoculation of CCCV is now used routinely to seek resistance or tolerance in these parent lines for future breeding programs.

D. Vector Control

Although the search for a vector has been unsuccessful, the probability that one or more exists means that control measures may eventually be directed towards vectors.

E. Mild Strain Protection

Mild strains of viroids can cross protect against severe strains (Horst, 1975; Niblett *et al.,* 1978). The long term nature of coconut plantations, and the natural spread of CCCV, are factors which would favor the use of mild strain protection.   The mild strain of PSTV differs only slightly in its nucleotide sequence from the severe strain (Gross *et al.,* 1981) and it seems likely that eventually the sites on viroid molecules where changes in sequence can be induced so as to modify pathogenicity will be defined. CCCV can show considerable variation at the right end of the molecule, by duplicating sequences of different length, and apparently without affecting the ability of variants to infect and produce a typical early disease symptom. Variation at the left end of the molecule has not been reported by Haseloff *et al.,* (1982) and it may be that variations in this region of the molecule could influence severity of disease.

If mutants can be found, or induced, long term experiments will be needed to determine their stability and degree of pathogenicity. The use of mild variants may also be determined by the degree of uniformity of coconut varieties and hybrids in the future.

IX. CONCLUSIONS

The cause of the economically important cadang–cadang disease has been determined, and shown to be the smallest known pathogen with a number of unique properties. It will be interesting to see whether knowledge of the molecular structure of CCCV will allow structural modifications to be obtained in CCCV for use in mild strain protection. Some immediate goals in the cadang–cadang program are the development of simple, sensitive, early diagnostic methods; improving the efficiency of inoculation; developing methods for inoculating mature palms; determination of the mode of natural spread; and the selection of resistant or tolerant breeding lines. No specific or direct control measures can be recommended at present, but achievement of some of the above goals should allow their early development.

ACKNOWLEDGMENTS

The following are thanked for enthusiastic help, discussion, and scientific collaboration in the more recent investigations on cadang–cadang: at the Albay Research Center; W.C. Price, A.E. Bigornia, D.J. Meadows, M.L. Retuerma, E.P. Rillo, G.Boccardo, B.Zelazny, J.S.Imperial, M.J.B. Rodriguez, N.A. Mohamed: at the University of Adelaide; R.I.B. Francki, P. Palukaitis, T.Hatta, C.Davies, J. Haseloff, R. H. Symons: at Universität Düsseldorf; D.Riesner, G.Steger, J.Schumacher.

B. Zelazny and J.S. Imperial are thanked for critical reading of the manuscript, and L. Wichman and B. Palk are thanked for preparation of figures. The Food and Agriculture Organization under the United Nations Development Program, the Australian Research Grants Committee, and the Alexander von Humboldt Stiftung have sponsored or financed aspects of work on cadang–cadang reviewed here.

REFERENCES

Anonymous (1982). Research on the cadang–cadang disease of coconut palm. Food and Agriculture Organization of the United Nations, Manila and Rome. Mimeographed, 75 pp.
Beakbane, B.A., Slater, C.H.W., and Posnette, A.F. (1972). Mycoplasmas in the phloem of coconut, *Cocos nucifera L.,* with lethal yellowing disease. Journal of Horticultural Science 47, 265.

Bigornia, A.E. (1977). Evaluation of trends of researches on the coconut cadang-cadang disease. *Philippine Journal of Coconut Studies* 2, 5-36.

Bigornia, A. E., and Infante, N.A. (1965). Progress report on selection and breeding program for cadang-cadang resistant coconut in the Bicol region. *Philippine Journal of Plant Industry 29*, 103-114.

Boccardo, G., Beaver, R. G., Randles, J. W., and Imperial, J.S. (1981). Tinangaja and bristle top, coconut diseases of uncertain etiology in Guam, and their relationship to cadang-cadang disease of coconut in the Phillippines. *Phytopathology 71*, 1104-1107.

Bruening, G., Gourl, A. R., Murphy, P.J., and Symons, R.H. (1982). Oligomers of avocado sunblotch viroid found in infected avocado leaves. *FEBS Letters 148*, 71-78.

Calica, C.A., and Bigornia, A.E. (1962). Salient and most characteristic symptoms of the coconut cadang-cadang disease. *Proceedings Symposium on cadang-cadang of coconut.* Cadang-cadang Research Foundation, Inc. National Science Development Board, Mainila, pp. 111-114.

Celino, M.S. (1946). The cadang-cadang disease of coconut in Laguna and suggestions for its control. *Plant Industry Digest 9*, 10-14.

Celino, M.S. (1947). A preliminary report on a blight disease (cadang-cadang) of coconut in San Miguel estate, Albay Province, *Philippine Journal of Agriculture 13*, 31-35.

De Bokx, J.A., and Piron, P.G.M. (1981). Transmission of potato spindle tuber viroid by aphids. *Netherlands Journal of Plant Pathology 87*, 31-34.

De Leon, D., and Bigornia, A.E. (1953). Coconut cadang-cadang disease in the Philippines and experimental control program. *United States Operations Mission to the Philippines*, 17 pp.

Diener, T.O. (1979). Viroids and viroid diseases. John Wiley & Sons, N.Y.

Gould, A.R., Francki, R.I.B., and Randles, J.W. (1981). Studies on encapsidated viroid-like RNA IV. Requirement for infectivity and specificiity of RNA components from velvet tobacco mottle virus. *Virology 110*, 420-426.

Gross, H.J., Domdey, H., Lossow, C., Jank, P., Raba, M., Alberty, H., and Sänger, H.L. (1978). Nucleotide sequence and secondary structure of potato spindle tuber viroid. *Nature 273*, 203-208.

Gross, H.J., Krupp, G., Domdey, H., Raba, NM., Jank, P.,
    Lossow, C., Alberty, H., Ramm, K., and Sänger, H.L.
    1982). Nucleotide sequence and secondary structure
    of citrus exocortis and chrysanthemum stunt
    viroid. *European Journal of Biochemistry 121,* 249-
    257.
Gross, H.J., Krupp, G., Domdey, H., Steger, G., Riesner, D.,
    and Sänger, H.L. (1981). The structure of three
    plant viroids. *Nucleic Acids Research Symposium
    Series* No. 10, 91-98.
Gross, H.J., Liebl, U., Alberty, H., Krupp, G., Domdey,
    H., Ramm, K., and Sänger, H.L. (1981). A severe
    and a mild potato spindle tuber viroid isolate
    differ in three nucleotide exchanges only.
    Bioscience Reports 1, 235-241.
Gould, A.R. and Hatta, T. (1981). Studies on encapsidated
    viroid-like RNA III. Comparative studies on
    RNAs isolated from velvet tobacco mottle virus and
    Solanum nodiflorum mottle virus. *Virology 109 ,*
    137-147.
Haseloff, J., Mohamed, N.A., and Symons, R.H. (1982). Viroid
    RNAs of cadang-cadang disease of coconuts. *Nature
    299,* 316-321.
Haseloff, J., and Symons, R.H. (1982). Comparative sequence
    and structure of viroid-like RNAs of two plant
    viruses. *Nucleic Acids Research 10,* 3681-3691.
Heinze, K., and Robinson, R.A. (1972). Report of FAO mission
    to the Philippines on cadang-cadang disease of coco-
    nut. *FAO,* Rome, 12 pp.
Hell, A., Young, D.B., and Birnie, G.D. (1976). Synthesis of
    DNAs complementary to human ribosomal RNAs polyadenyl-
    ated in vitro. *Biochemica et Biophysica Acta 442,* 37-
    49.
Henco, K., Sänger, H.L., and Riesner, D. (1979). Fine struc-
    ture melting of viroids as studied by kinetic methods.
    Nucleic Acids Research 6, 3041-3059.
Holmes, F.O. (1961). Does cadang-cadang spread from diseased
    to healthy coconut trees. *FAO Plant Protection Bulle-
    tin, 9,* 139-143.
Horst, R.K. (1975). Detection of a latent infectious agent
    that protects against infection by chrysanthemum
    chlorotic mottle viroid. *Phytopathology 65,* 1000-1003.
Imperial, J.S. (1980a). Study on the effect of tetracycline
    on coconut palm infected with cadang-cadang. *In* "PCA
    Albay Research Center Annual Report, 1980". 58 pp.
Imperial, J.S. (1980b). Resistance and susceptibility of
    coconut populations and hybrids to experimental inocu-
    lation. *In* "Philippine Coconut Authority Annual
    Report 1980". 188 pp.

Imperial, J.S., Buenaflor, G.G., and Rodriguez, J.B. (1980). Various studies on the cadang-cadang associated ribonucleic acids (ccRNA). The host range of ccRNA. *In* "Philippine Coconut Authority Annual Report, 1980". 188 pp.

Imperial, J.S., and Rodriguez, M.J.B. (1983). Variation in the coconut cadang-cadang viroid: evidence for single-base additions with disease progress. *Philippine Journal of Crop Science 8* (in press).

Imperial, J.S., Rodriguez, M.J.B. and Randles, J.W. (1981). Variation in the viroid-like RNA associated with cadang-cadang disease: evidence for an increase in molecular weight with disease progress. *Journal of General Virology 56,* 77–85.

Kent, G.C. (1953). Cadang-cadang of coconut. *The Philippine Agriculturist 37,* 228–240.

Mohamed, N.A., and Imperial, J.S. (1983). Infectivity of the coconut cadang-cadang viroid. Proceedings, 4th International Congress of Plant Pathology, Melbourne.

Mohamed, N.A., Haseloff, J., Imperial, J.S., and Symons, R.H. (1982). Characterization of the different electrophoretic forms of the cadang-cadang viroid. *Journal of General Virology 63,* 181–188.

Nagaraj, A.N., Pacumbaba, R.P., and Pableo, G.O. (1965). Diagnostic symptoms of cadang-cadang disease of coconuts. *FAO Plant Protection Bulletin 13,* 1–8.

Niblett, C.L., Dickson, E., Fernow, K.H., Horst, R.K., and Zaitlin, NM. (1978). Cross protection among four viroids. *Virology 91,* 198–203.

Ocfemia, G.O. (1937). The probable nature of cadang-cadang disease of coconuts. *The Philippine Agriculturist 26,* 338–340.

Owens, R.A., and Cress, D.E. (1980). Molecular cloning and characterization of spindle tuber viroid cDNA sequences. *Proceedings National Academy of Science U.S.A. 77,* 5302–5306.

Owens, R.A., and Diener, T.O. (1981). Sensitive and rapid diagnosis of potato spindle tuber viroid disease by nucleic acid hybridization. *Science 213,* 670–672.

Parthasarathy, M.V. (1973). Mycoplasma-like organisms in the phloem of palms in Florida affected by lethal yellowing. *Plant Dis. Rep. 57,* 861–862.

Plavsic-Banjac, B., Hunt, P., and Maramorosch, K. (1972). Mycoplasma-like bodies associated with lethal yellowing disease of coconut palms. *Phytopathology 62,* 298–299.

Price, W. C. (1957). Report to the government of the Philippines on the yellow mottle decline (cadang-cadang). of coconuts. *FAO Report (850)*, 1-56.

Price, W.C. (1971). Cadang-cadang of coconut - a review. *Plant Science 3*, 1-13.

Price, W.C., and Bigornia, A.E. (1971). Incidence of cadang-cadang in varieties of coconut trees of different ages. *FAO Plant Protection Bulletin 19*, 136-137.

Price, W.C., and Bigornia, A.E. (1972). Evidence for spread of cadang-cadang disease of coconut from tree to tree *FAO Plant Protection Bulletin 20*, 133-135.

Randles, J.W. (1975a). Detection in coconut of rod-shaped particles which are not associated with cadang-cadang disease. *Plant Disease Reporter 59*, 349-352.

Randles, J.W. (1975b). Association of two ribonucleic acid species with cadang-cadang disease of coconut palm. *Phytopathology 65*, 163-167.

Randles, J.W., Boccardo, G., and Imperial, J.S. (1980). Detection of the cadang-cadang RNA in African oil palm and buri palm. *Phytopathology 70*, 185-189.

Randles, J.W., Boccardo, G., Retuerma, M.L., and Rillo, E.S. (1977). Transmission of the RNA species associated with cadang-cadang of coconut palm, and insensitivity of the disease to antibiotics. *Phytopathology 67*, 1211-1216.

Randles, J.W., Davies, C., Hatta, T., Gould, A.R., and Francki, R.I.B. (1981). Studies on encapsidated viroid-like RNA. I. Characterization of velvet tobacco mottle virus. *Virology 108*, 111-122.

Randles, J.W., and Hatta, T. (1979). Circularity of the ribonucleic acids associated with cadang-cadang disease. *Virology 96*, 47-53.

Randles, J.W., and Palukaitis, P. (1979). In vitro synthesis and characterization of DNA complementary to cadang-cadang-associated RNA. *Journal of General Virology 43*, 649-662.

Randles, J.W., Rillo, E.P., and Diener, T.O. (1976). The viroid-like structure and cellular location of anomalous RNA associated with cadang-cadang disease. *Virology 74*, 128-139.

Randles, J.W., Steger, G., and Riesner, D. (1982). Structural transitions in viroid-like RNAs associated with cadang-cadang disease, velvet tobacco mottle virus and *Solanum nodiflorum* mottle virus. *Nucleic Acids Research 10*, 5569-5586.

Rasa, E.A. (1968). Anatomic effects of cadang-cadang disease on coconuts. *Plant Disease Reporter 52*, 734-737.

Reinking, O.A. (1950). Preliminary report on the cadang-cadang disease and on soil deficiency troubles of coconuts in the Philippines. *Plant Disease Reporter* *34*, 300–304.

Riesner, D., Henco, K., Rokohl, U., Klotz, G., Kleinschmidt, A.K., Domdey, H., Jank, P., Gross, H.J., and Sänger, H.L. (1979). Structure and structure formation of viroids. *J. Mol. Biol. 133*, 85–115.

Riesner, D., Kaper, J.M., and Randles, J.W. (1982). Stiffness of viroids and viroid-like RNA in solution. *Nucleic Acids Research 10*, 5587–5598.

Riesner, D., Steger, G., Schumacher, J., Gross, H.J., Randles, J.W., and Sänger, H.L. (1983). Structure and fuction of viroids. *Biophys. Struct. Mech. 9*, 145–170.

Rillo, E.P., Pableo, G.O., and Price, W.C. (1972). An anatomical study of coconut leaves from healthy trees and those affected by cadang-cadang. *Bulletin Torrey Botanical Club 99*, 271–277.

Rillo, E.P., and Rillo, A.R. (1981). Abstracts on the cadang-cadang disease of coconut 1937-1980. *Philippine Coconut Authority*, 50 pp.

Schumacher, J. Randles, J.W., and Riesner, D. (1983). Viroid and virusoid detection: an electrophoretic technique with the sensitivity of molecular hybridization. *Analytical Biochemistry 135*, 288–295.

Sill, W.H., Bigornia, A.E., and Pacumbaba, R.P. (1964). Incidence of cadang-cadang disease of coconut trees of different ages and its relationship to practical control. *Philippine Journal of Plant Industry 29*, 87–100.

Symons, R.H. (1981). Avocado sunblotch viroid: primary sequence and proposed secondary structure. *Nucleic Acids Research 9*, 6527–6537.

Velasco, J.R. (1961). A re-examination of the coconut cadang-cadang question. *The Philippine Agriculturist 45*, 145–164.

Velasco, J.R. (1982). Review of studies tending to link the rare earths with coconut cadang-cadang. *Scientia Filipinas 2*, 64–76.

Zelazny, B. (1979). Distribution and spread of the cadang-cadang disease of coconut palm. *Acta Phytopathologica Academiae Scientiarum Hungaricae 14*, 115–126.

Zelazny, B. (1980). Ecology of cadang-cadang disease of coconut palm in the Philippines. *Phytopathology 70*, 700–703.

Zelazny, B., and Niven, B.S. (1980). Duration of the stages of cadang-cadang diseases of coconut palm. *Plant Disease 64* 841–842.

Zelazny, B., and Pacumbaba (1982a). Phytophagous insects associated with cadang-cadang infected and healthy coconut palms in south-eastern Luzon, Philippines. *Ecological Entomology 7,* 113-120.

Zelazny, B., and Pacumbaba, E. (1982b). Incidence of cadang-cadang of coconut palm in the Philippines. *Plant Disease 66,* 547-549.

Zelazny, B., Randles, J.W., Boccardo, G., and Imperial, J.S. (1982). The viroid nature of the cadang-cadang disease of coconut palm. *Scientia Filipinas 2,* 45-63.

Chapter 4

VIROID ETIOLOGY OF TINANGAJA AND ITS RELATIONSHIP
WITH CADANG-CADANG DISEASE OF COCONUT

Guido Boccardo

Laboratorio fi Fitovirologia Applicata
C. N. R.
Universita di Torino
10135 Torino, Italy

I. HISTORICAL

In 1917 Weston (1918) reported a destructive disease
of coconut palm *(Cocos nucifera)* on Guam, Marianas Islands.
At that time no reports of similar disorders were available
from other Pacific Islands. The disorder was called 'tinangaja', a name possibly derived from local Chamorro dialect,
though at present it is meaningless to the islanders themselves. About ten years later (Anonymous, 1927) the hypothesis was advanced that tinangaja might be an infectious disease. It is not known where on the island disease symptoms
were first observed, but later (Reinking, 1961) the most
severly affected plantations were found in the
Malojloj-Inarajan area and on Cocos Island (Fig. 1; see also
Section III B).
In 1931, a new disease of coconut palm came to the

Copyright © 1985 by Academic Press, Inc.
All rights of reproduction in any form reserved.
ISBN 0-12-470230-9

SUBVIRAL PATHOGENS
OF PLANTS AND ANIMALS:
VIROIDS AND PRIONS

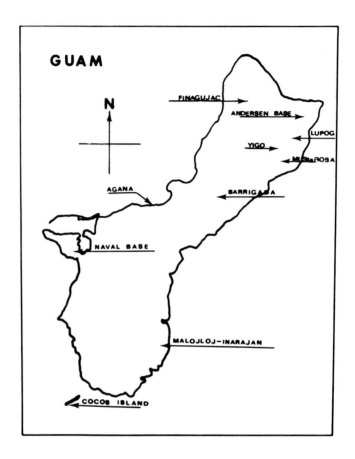

Figure 1.   Map of Guam Island with indication of some localities with various tinangaja incidences (see Section III B).

attention of a Philippine plant pathologist (Ocfemia, 1937)
when coconut plantations in the Bicol area (south-eastern
Luzon) were seriously damaged and sometimes completely destroyed by the disease called cadang-cadang (English pro-
onunciation of the local work gdang or kdang, meaning dying).   Owing to the importance of the coconut industry in the
Philippines,considerable attention was paid to cadang-cadang,
which was later reported as having been present in the area
possibly since 1900-1910 (Price, 1958).   Cadang-cadang, on
the basis of its symptoms and distribution in the fields, was
judged an infectious disease of probable virus etiology
(Ocfemia, 1937), and was first believed to have originated on

San Miguel Island (Ocfemia, 1937; Price, 1958; Maramorosch, 1961; Bigornia, 1977), but more recent studies on the distribution of the disease and its rate of spread suggest a multifocal origin and possible endemic nature of cadang-cadang (Anonymous, 1982; Zelazny *et al.*, 1982; Randles, 1984).

However, while observations and information on cadang-cadang were constantly increasing (see Rillo and Rillo,1981), nothing more was heard of tinangaja until Reinking (1961), reviewing the reasons responsible for the decline of coconuts on Guam called the disease 'yellow mottle decline', adopting for tinangaja the name he also applied to cadang-cadang (Reinking, 1950). However, the suggested English name never became current and the two diseases continued to be known under their original locally derived names. Reinking (1961) considered the two diseases of Guam and the Philippines identical on the basis of their symptoms, and a possible nematode-mediated virus etiology for tinangaja was suggested (Reinking and Radewald, 1961).

Later, Holmes (1962) stated that tinangaja and cadang-cadang were only similar in that sterility was induced and affected palms eventually died (see Section II). Furthermore, he also suggested that tinangaja could be of the same nature as frond-drop, a disease of unknown origin first reported from Jamaica (Nutman and Roberts, 1955) and described later also from the Bicol region in the Philippines (Bigornia *et al.*, 1967), but clearly distinct from cadang-cadang. On the basis of nut symptoms (see Section II), Holmes (1962) considered that tinangaja resembled another disorder of the coconut palm present in an area free of cadang-cadang in the Philippines (Southern Mindanao), the so-called 'boang' or 'empty nut' disease, which Castillo and Maramorosch (1960) had suggested was the result of insect injury. Other authors were less convinced of a clear distinction between cadang-cadang and tinangaja diseases of coconut palm, for we can read that"the yellow mottle of tinangaja is indistinguishable from that of cadang-cadang, and the general appearence of a severely affected tree also resembles that of cadang-cadang. However, the oblong, distorted nuts and finally the dense cluster of very small, badly distorted nuts are different from the nuts produced in cadang-cadang affected palms" (Maramorosch, 1964).

This debate however, was conducted merely on an examination of symptoms, and it has now proven to be of little consequence. Only after the discovery that two viroid-like ribonucleic acid species (ccRNAs) were uniquely associated with cadang-cadang affected coconuts (Randles, 1975; Randles *et al.*, 1976, 1977) and the development of very sensitive methods for the detection of ccRNAs (Randles and Palukaitis,

1979; Randles *et al*, 1980)(see Section IV and Randles 1984 for a review) was the co-identity of cadang-cadang and tinangaja diseases finally demonstrated (Boccardo *et al.*, 1981).

II.   SYMPTOMS

In this section, the comparative symptoms of the two diseases will be briefly reviewed. One must, however, consider that cadang-cadang has been the object of constant observations and investigations for the last fifty years which have resulted in the production of about 240 reports and publications (Rillo and Rillo, 1981; Zelazny *et al.*, 1982), while tinangaja has been studied only sporadically, and few reports are available (Weston, 1918; Reinking, 1961; Reinking and Radewald, 1961; Holmes, 1962; Maramorosch, 1964; Bigornia, 1977; Boccardo *et al.*, 1981). This difference in information obviously reflects the different concern and attention for the coconut industry in the two areas. While early in this century dried copra was exported from Guam, the 1917 epidemics severely depleted the number of palms on the island, and after World War II coconuts are used only locally for livestock feed and limited human consumption, whereas copra has always been and still is a major source of revenue for the Philippines.

A. Field Symptoms of Cadang-Cadang.

In the original symptom description, Ocfemia (1937) stated that the affected palms were stunted and showed yellowing of older leaves, reduction in size and number of the newly emerging ones, reduction of the width of leaflets, bending over and breaking of the pinnae, reduction and finally suppression of nut production, and discoloration and death of roots. On the leaves of affected palms he observed a large number of yellowish spots 1 to 4 mm in diameter, which in reflected light appear 'water-soaked' (Ocfemia, 1937; Price *et al.*, 1973; Bigornia, 1977; Zelazny *et al.*, 1982).

Unlike spots resulting from insect injury or fungus infection these have no brown center and are considered of diagnostic value (Nagaraj *et al.*, 1965). However, for convenience, diagnosis in the field is based largely on the effect on fruit production, for the disease is said to occur almost exclusively in bearing palms, though coconuts in pre-bearing age can occasionally be found infected (Zelazny and Niven, 1980; Zelazny *et al.*, 1982). After leaf spots appear, the nuts become more rounded than normal and are scarified chiefly around the equator. Nuts at the beginning of the disease are more numerous than are those on healthy trees and have almost normal kernels, but reduced husk thickness (Fig. 2).

Figure 2. Nuts from healthy (left) and CCCV-infected coconuts from the Philippines (domesticated type or "niu vai";
Harries, 1979).

In time, inflorescences production decreases and eventually
ceases, thus characterizing the disease through early, medium and late stages. In the instances of pre-bearing coconuts believed to be cadang-cadang affected, diagnosis was
based on the type and distribution of leaf spotting and on
the reduction in size and number of the fronds, resulting in a
stunted appearance. Of course, after the discovery of ccRNAs
and subsequent work (see Section IV; and for a more complete
review Randles 1984), diagnosis has relied more on biochemical methods than on the comparison of symptoms, especially
for doubtful cases.

B. Field Symptoms of Tinangaja.

Weston's original description of the disease ran in
part: "The symptoms showed by this disease involved first the
withering and hanging down of the lower leaves, followed
gradually by others near the tip, until finally the whole top
dies and the dead stub remains with a few dead leaves still
hanging to it. The activity of the growing point is seemingly lessened some time before the top begins to die, for in
affected trees the diameter tapers with abnormal rapidity
just below the top". No cadang-cadang-like nut symptoms
have been reported for tinangaja-affected trees by various
authors (Weston, 1918; Reinking, 1961; Holmes, 1962; Maramorosch, 1964; Bigornia, 1977). Instead, all described
severe distortion and crinkling of the nuts (see Figs. 3B

Figure 3. Nut bunches on healthy (A) and tinangaja-affected
(B) palms (elongated type or "niu Kafa"; Harries, 1979), showing small rounded nuts on the oldest bunches and typical mummified husks on the later inflorescences.

and 7A), which are often reduced to mummified husks with no
meat inside (hence the suggestion that tinangaja could corre-
correspond to the 'boang' or 'empty nut' disorder reported
from southern Mindanao (Holmes, 1962)). Nut production also
ceases, but apparently over a longer period than in cadang-
cadang affected trees, and infected coconuts continue to
bear numerous clusters of mummified husks (Reinking, 1961;
Maramorosch, 1964). After nut production ceases the palms
soon die, contrary to those palms affected by cadang-
cadang in the Philippines, where sterility is induced much
earlier and the late stage can last for years (Zelazny and

Figure 4.   Mottling on leaflets from a tinangaja-affected
coconut, compared with healthy leaflets on the sides (note
beetle damage, arrowed).

Niven, 1980).
        During a recent survey on Guam Island Boccardo *et al.*,
(1981) noted that coconuts were neglected and seriously damaged by the indiscriminate use of weed killers and extensive
attack by *Brontispa* beetles *(B. marianensis* and especially
the newly introduced *B. palauensis)*. These factors hamper the
study of tinangaja and its true effect on the palms, because
symptoms can be mimicked, masked or obscured. However, as
expected, coconut palms bearing characteristic tinangaja-
mummified husks were observed throughout the island, together
with others with yellowish and reduced crowns, no nuts and
leaflets showing severe mottling (Fig. 4). These appeared
indistinguishable from cadang-cadang affected coconuts in the
late stage of the disease (Fig. 5)(Boccardo *et al.*, 1981).
Like cadang-cadang, tinangaja seems to affect most prevalently
trees of 25-30 years of age or older, though Reinking (1961)
reported that pre-bearing coconuts about 6 years old were
affected by the disease. It is certainly possible for young
palms to be affected by tinangaja, similarly to what happens
in the case of cadang-cadang in the Philippines (Zelazny,
1979, 1980; Zelazny *et al.*, 1982); but it should be remem-
bered that some confusion arose in the past regarding the
final stage of tinangaja, the appearence of young infected
coconuts and what was later called bristle top, a disorder

Figure 5. Coconuts showing tinangaja symptoms at various stages of the disease (the one on the right is healthy). Note extensive beetle damage on the crowns. Photograph taken in Yigo.

probably caused by excess fertilizer or weed killers (Maramorosch, 1964), and not related to tinangaja (Boccardo *et al.*, 1981) (see Section II C).

In their survey, Boccardo *et al.*, (1981) observed in two instances coconut palms, about 30 years of age, one from Andersen base and the second from Agaña Heights, far from the first locality (see Fig. 1), bearing on their medium and young inflorescences typical tinangaja—mummified nut clusters (Fig. 3B), but having as well on their lowest (=oldest) inflorescences smaller than normal, rounded nuts, scarified around the equator, with much reduced husk, but with almost normal meat thickness, typical of cadang-cadang disease Figs.6 and 7 A,B). The fact that such a syndrome had long escaped recognition and that it had been observed on two coconuts only across the island could be explained by assuming that rounded nuts were produced at the very early stage of the disease and for only a very short time (Boccardo *et al.*, 1981). As successive inflorescences are normally produced every 4-6 weeks (Randles *et al.*, 1977), and only the two oldest showed rounded nuts, the early stage of the disease conceivably could last three or four months only. If this were true, then the medium stage of the disease, which seems to be the longest(Reinking, 1961; Maramorosch, 1964), would be characterized by the mummified husks. Table I summarized comparatively the major features of tinangaja and cadang-cadang diseases.

Figure 6.   Two bunches of rounded nuts and mummified husks
from the same coconut in the early stage of tinangaja.

Table 1. Comparative Features of Coconuts Affected by Cadang-
         Cadang and Tinangaja at various stages.

Stage	Disease	
	Cadang-Cadang	Tinangaja
early	Mottled leaflets, large number of smaller than normal rounded nuts with reduced husks, normal kernels (Fig. 2). Duration: 2-4 years (a,b).	Mottled leaflets, a few inflorescences with rounded nuts (Fig. 3B). Husks severely reduced, normal kernels. (c) Duration: 3-4 months (?).
medium	decreasing number of rounded nuts, crown becoming yellowish. Duration: 2 years (a,b).	numerous clusters of mummified husks. Duration: undetermined, said to be long (d).
late	much reduced yellow crown. No nuts. Duration: 5 years (a,b).	same as cadang-cadang Duration: undetermined, said to be very short (d).

(a) Zelazny and Niven, 1980: (b) Anonymous, 1982;(c) Boccardo
et al., 1981; (d) Reinking, 1961.

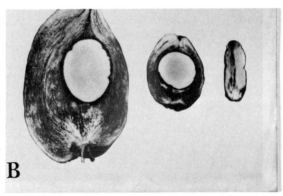

Figure 7. A normal elongated, thick-husked nut from a healthy coconut (left), a nut from a tree in the early stage of the disease (center) and a mummified husk (medium stage). A: entire nuts. B: the same, opened to show relative husk and meat thickness.

C.   Coconut Diseases of Obscure Origin Reminiscent of Tinangaja and Cadang-Cadang.

As previously noted, the bristle top disorder of coconut palm apparently co-exists with tinangaja on Guam. It was not detected as such by Reinking (1961), but Maramorosch (1964) reported it from Anahatan and Guam Islands of the Marianas archipelago. Fronds of affected palms are much shortened, stiffened and they remain erect, thus leaving an upright tuft at the top of the trees, but there is no sign of mottling on the leaflets, which remain green and show a juvenile character in that they do not separate normally but remain fused. With both tinangaja and cadang-cadang, leaflets are always mottled (at least from the fourth full opened frond down;   Price,

1958), and once mottling has started, the leaflets never recover and fronds do not remain erect (Price, 1958; Price *et al.*, 1973; Bigornia, 1977; Randles *et al.*, 1977). On the basis of these differences, Maramorosch (1964) questioned the original interpretation of the appearance of young pre-bearing affected palms, and therefore the doubt remains that the young coconuts described as tinangaja-affected (Reinking, 1961) might have been suffering from bristle top.

The development of diagnostic methods for cadang-cadang (see Randles (1984) for a review) has shown that it and tinangaja have the same cause (see Section IV B). The same methods (polyacrylamide gel electrophoreis of nucleic acid extracts and molecular hybridization assays; see Section IV, and Randles, 1984, for a review) have been applied to bristle top and three other lethal diseases of coconut palm of unknown etiology occurring in Asia and the South Pacific. These diseases are: Kerala wilt and tatipaka, occurring in the state of Kerala and in the East Godavari district of Andhra Pradesh, India (Anonymous, 1976) and the die-back of coconut present in Vanuatu, New Hebrides (Dollet and De Taffin, 1979). Of all these, the symptomatology of tatipaka disease is somewhat similar to that of cadang-cadang and tinangaja, in that leaflets are mottled and deformed. Moreover, tatipaka-affected coconuts produce distorted and narrowed nuts with much reduced or no kernels, resembling the mummified husks of tinangaja (Anonymous, 1976; Boccardo *et al.*, 1981). Both Kerala wilt and the Vanuatu disease induce sterility in time and eventually death of the affected palm, though in a much shorter time than do tinangaja and/or cadang-cadang (Anonymous, 1976; Dollet and De Taffin, 1979); but symptom development (necrosis of the inflorescences and leaf bronzing) appears rather distinct from that of tinan-gaja and/or cadang-cadang.

However, none of the nucleic acid samples from coconuts suffering from any of the four above disorders could be shown to contain low molecular weight RNA species with nucleotide sequences in common with ccRNAs (J.W. Randles, unpublished; Boccardo *et al.*, 1981; Dollet *et al.*, 1981; Randles, 1984).

III. ECOLOGY

Cadang-cadang and tinangaja are now known to be caused by the same agent (see Section IV), but how the disease spread in the field remains obscure in spite of intensive investigations conducted in the Philippines on cadang-cadang (Zelazny *et al.*, 1982, Randles, 1984), and the one report available on the ecology of tinangaja.

A. Cadang-Cadang.

The duration of the different stages of the disease and its incidence in the field have been determined (Zelazny, 1979; Zelazny and Niven, 1980; Zelazny and Pacumbaba, 1982a). According to present evidence the disease develops in a gradual progression within rather stable boundaries, though exceptionally cadang-cadang-affected coconuts can suddenly appear or perhaps can suddenly become recognized as such, in small localized areas far from the Bicol region where the disease is endemic (Bigornia *et al.*, 1960; Price and Bigornia, 1969; Zelazny and Pacumbaba, 1982a). Recent estimates put yearly losses at about half a million palms, which would translate into about 6 million U.S. dollars (Anonymous, 1982: Zelazny *et al.*, 1982; Randles, 1984).

The relationship between incidence of the disease and different environments has also been studied (Zelazny, 1979, 1980). The available data suggest that environmental factors may have some influence on the spread of the disease. However, while the known correlation between age of the palms and cadang-cadang symptoms (Sill *et al.*, 1965) was found most significant in explaining variations in the incidence of the disease, no suggestion of an alternative weed host, as put forward by Holmes (1961) was confirmed (Zelazny, 1980). To ascertain whether the potential inoculum was confined to coconut palm or if other palms could harbor the disease, studies on the natural host range of cadang-cadang have been conducted (see also Randles, 1984). Two palm species other than coconut, displaying cadang-cadang-like symptoms and coming from within the area of distribution of the disease have been found to contain viroid-like RNAs with nucleotide sequences in common with ccRNAs. These palms are the African oil palm *(Elaeis guineensis)* and the buri palm *(Corphya elata)* (Randles *et al.*, 1980; Randles, 1984).

The scattered distribution of cadang-cadang infected palms in the field does not suggest that factors in the soil (fungi, nematodes or essential element deficiencies) could be responsible for causing or transmitting the disease (Anonymous, 1982; Zelazny *et al.*, 1982). Spread of the disease through an insect vector always seemed the most likely mechanism. However, so far, all attempts to transmit cadang-cadang with leaf eating or sucking insects have been unsuccessful (Bigornia, 1977; Zelazny *et al.*, 1982), though field surveys have revealed conspicous associations of certain insect species, especially beetles, with cadang-cadang affected coconut and buri palms (Zelazny and Pacumbaba, 1982b; Zelazny *et al.*, 1982). This topic is also further discussed by Randles(1984). Vertical transmission of cadang-cadang has been considered possible and *ad hoc* experiments planned to test for its existence (Randles, 1977). However, though such a mechanism is known to contribute to the field spread of potato spindle tuber viroid (Fernow *et al.*, 1970), the evidence that pollen and/ or seed transmission occurs in the case of other viroid diseases is questionable or negative (Diener, 1979). Furthermore, in the case of cadang-cadang, this could not be the only mechanism contributing to the spread of the disease. In fact, while vertical transmission might occur through bearing coconut or oil palms, it could not be effective in causing the disease in young pre-bearing coconuts or buri palms. The buri palms in fact blossom only once in their lives, after which they die, and the infected ones always die before blossoming (Randles *et al.*, 1980). Coconut palms infected at a prebearing age behave similarly.

    B. Tinangaja.

Reinking (1961) reported that all available evidence indicated that the disease took some forty years to wipe out completely the coconut industry throughout Guam Island, and therefore concluded that the spread of the disease must have been slow and gradual. Reinking (1961) also reported that tinangaja occurred more often in the southern than the northern half of the island: in the Malojloj-Inarajan and Merizo areas and on Cocos Island (Fig. 1)nearly 100% of the coconuts showed disease symptoms, while the north-eastern tip of Guam (Andersen Base) was practically free of the disease. In the northern part of the island as a whole, the incidence was as low as 2-5% (Lupog, Mount Santa Rosa; Fig.1), though in some isolated foci about 80% of the coconut palms showed symptoms (Yigo, Fig. 1). Reinking (1961) also reported that disease incidence increased southwards on the western coast of the island (from 50% in Finagujac up to 100% north of Agaña and in Barrigada; Fig. 1), while newly planted areas (west of Lupog) were apparently disease-free.

The economy of the Trust Territory changed after World War II and as consequence coconuts are now almost completely neglected. At present it would be extremely difficult to conduct accurate and detailed epidemiological surveys to establish incidence and rate of spread of the disease such as those reported for cadang-cadang (Zelazny, 1979,1980; Zelazny and Pacumbaba, 1982a,b; Zelazny *et al.*, 1982). No studies on the possible natural host-range of tinangaja have been conducted, nor transmission experiments of any kind attempted.

Reinking (1961), at a time when virus etiology was

strongly suspected for the disease, pointed out that at least
five different species of nematodes were present in soils
sampled from areas where tinangaja had a high incidence.
Reinking and Radewald (1961) suggested that dagger nematodes
(*Xiphinema americanum* and *X. diversicaudatum*) could play
an active role in the spreading of the disease. He had
observed that in many instances, seedlings newly planted in
areas where tinangaja had been very active, developed disease
symptoms, and apparently the 'disease' follows a regular
pattern in spreading slowly from tree to tree. However,
nothing more than this rather circumstantial evidence was put
forward to substantiate the nematode hypothesis and no transmission experiments have been attempted. Moreover, even
discounting the possible confusion between the appearence of
young tinangaja-affected coconuts and bristle top effect
(Maramorosch, 1964; and above Sections II B and C),appropri-
ate experiments failed to associate nematode activity with
cadang-cadang in the Philippines(Bigornia,1977),and therefore
their primary involvement in natural transmission of tinangaja appears unlikely.

IV. EVIDENCE FOR VIROID ETIOLOGY

Both for cadang-cadang and tinangaja, theories favoring
virus etiology (at a time when viroids were unheard of) have
always been preeminent (Anonymous, 1927: Ocfemia, 1937:
Reinking, 1950, 1961; Price, 1958; Holmes, 1961, 1962;
Maramorosch, 1964). Other factors have also been considered
responsible for cadang-cadang, whereas tinangaja until recently has been neglected. Though inconclusive data have
been obtained and attempts to obtain symptom remission by
applying various fertilizers have invariably failed (Zelazny
et al., 1982), a large number of experiments attempting to
link various soil deficiencies or toxic levels of rare earths
with cadang-cadang symptoms have been conducted (see Velasco,
1982, for a review). Mycoplasma- and rickettsia-like bodies
have also been considered as possible disease agents, but
treatments of cadang-cadang affected coconuts with either
tetracycline or penicillin did not alter the course of the
disease (Randles *et al.*, 1977; Imperial, 1980). Electron
microscopical examinations always failed to reveal the presence of mycoplasma-like organisms in the phloem of diseased
coconuts (Plavsic-Banjac *et al.*, 1972; Randles *et al.*, 1977),
however there is one report of rickettsia-like organisms
harbored in diseased coconuts (Petzhold *et al.*, 1974). In the
light of subsequent work (see below, and Randles, 1984) no
further doubt should exist on the causal agent of cadang-
cadang, and the microorganisms occasionally observed in the

phloem of affected coconuts can be interpreted as a secondary
phenomenon (cf. Randles, 1984).

A. Cadang-Cadang.

For detailed information on the causative agent of
cadang-cadang, one should refer to the papers by Zelazny *et
al.*, (1982) and Randles (1984). Here, it is sufficient to
say that two RNA species (ccRNA$_1$ and ccRNA$_2$), which share
many properties in common with other viroids (Randles *et
al.*, 1976, 1982; Randles and Hatta, 1979; Haseloff *et
al.*, 1982) have been demonstrated, by polyacrylamide gel
electrophoretic analysis of nucleic acid extracts from coconut palms to be uniquely associated with cadang-cadang af-
fectted trees (Randles, 1975). Recently evidence has been
presented that both ccRNAs can vary in size and electrophoretic mobility, with molecular weights increasing and relative
infectivity decreasing with the progression of the disease
(Imperial *et al.*, 1981; see also Randles, 1984). The complete sequences (from 246 to 574 residues) of all'fast' and
'slow' ccRNA variants have been determined and shown to share
structural homologies with those of other viroids (Haseloff
et al., 1982; see also Symons *et al.*, 1984).

Tritium-labelled deoxyribonucleic acid complementary to
ccRNA$_1$ (cDNA), synthesized using S$_1$-cleaved polyadenylated
ccRNA$_1$ as the template for avian myeloblastosis virus reverse
transcriptase (Randdles and Palukaitis, 1979), has been used
as a probe in molecular hybridization assays for the detection
of ccRNAs in crude nucleic acid extracts of coconut, oil and
buri palms (Randles *et al.*, 1980; Randles, 1984). The availability of very sensitive detection methods for the ccRNAs,
helps greatly in epidemiological studies, and combined with
improved mechanical inoculation techniques (Imperial *et al.*,
1981) certainly represents a great step forward in screening
for varietal resistance (Zelazny *et al.*, 1982; Randles,1984).

B. Tinangaja.

As mentioned, this disease has long been neglected, not
only because Guam is rather isolated geographically, but
especially because of the lack of economic concern for the
damaged crop. Considering that all evidence pointed to a
viroid etiology of cadang-cadang, and that the overalll
symptomatology of tinangaja had prompted one author to describe it as identical to cadang-cadang (Reinking, 1961),
Boccardo (1976) proposed that the two diseases should be
compared by the same analytical techniques.

The routine diagnostic polyethyleneglycol-mediated extraction of ccRNAs (Randles, 1975, 1984; Randles *et al.*,
1976, 1977) was used to concentrate nucleic acids of healthy
and tinangaja-affected coconuts on Guam. Typically, samples
(50 grams of leaflet tissue) were collected from the sixth

fully opened frond of chosen trees (Table 2). Nucleic acids,
fractionated in 2 *M* LiCl and further purified with half volume
of 0.1% (w/v) cetyltrimethylammonium bromide (Randles *et al.*,
1980) were subjected to electrophoretic analysis in 5% aqueous
polyacrylamide gels, along with standard preparations of
'slow' and 'fast' moving ccRNA variants extracted from cadang-
cadang affected coconuts. Irrespective of the stage of the
disease, coconut palms showing tinangaja symptoms were shown
to contain 2 low molecular weight RNAs of the same apparent
electrophoretic mobility as those of the 'fast' variant of
ccRNAs (Fig. 8; Boccardo *et al.*, 1981). Furthermore,

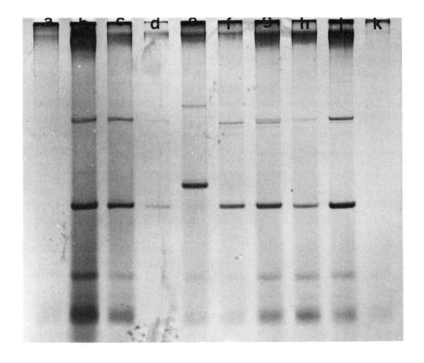

Figure 8. Polyacrylamide (5% aqueous gel slab buffered in 90
mM Tris, 90 mM borate and 3 mM EDTA, pH 8.3) co-electrophoresis (5 hr at a constant current of 10 mA) of nucleic acid
extracts from coconuts (i) showing bristle top symptoms (lanes
a and k); (ii) CCCV-infected (lanes e and f, 'slow' and
'fast' moving variants, respectively); and (iii) tinangaja-
affected in the early (lanes b and c), middle (lanes d,g and
h), and late (lane j) stages of the disease (from Boccardo
et al., 1981).

Table 2. List of some of the samples (from Boccardo, 1980) collected on Guam with indication of the localities (Fig.1), syndromes, and results of the analysis (Section IV).[a]

Sample	Locality	Syndrome	ccRNAs[b]
1	Malojloj	30-40 yr old, no nuts reduced yellow crown (late stage)	Present
2	"	30-40 yr old, bearing well (healthy)	Absent
3	"	20-30 yr old, bearing well (healthy)	Absent
4	"	40-50 yr old, no nuts reduced yellow crown (late stage)	Present
5	Yigo	20 yr old, bearing well (healthy)	Absent
6	"	20 yr old, no nuts, brownish crown, beetle damaged	Absent
7	Barrigada	40-50 yr old, no nuts reduced yellow crown (late stage)	Present
8	"	40-50 yr old, bearing well (healthy)	Absent
9	"	25-30 yr old, bearing mummified husks (medium stage)	Present
10	Paseo de Oro (Agana)	25-30 yr old, bearing mummified husks and rounded nuts (early stage)	Present
11	"	25-30 yr old, infloresences heavily damaged by beetles	Absent
12	Andersen Base	60 yr old, bearing mummified husks (medium stage)	Present
13	"	as No. 10 from Agana	Present

[a]All trees positive for ccRNAs were dead one year after sampling (R.G. Beaver, *private communication*) ,with the exception of No. 13 (No. 10 was felled to ascertain the distribution of CCCV in various fronds; see Section IV B).

samples (20-30 g) taken from all opened fronds of three coconuts (numbers 4, 9 and 10 in Table 2) in the early, medium and late stages of tinangaja, were processed in order to ascertain whether any variation in electrophoretic mobility occurred with the viroid-like tinangaja RNAs with the progres-

sion of the disease. Contrary to experience with cadang-
cadang (Imperial *et al.*, 1981;   Randles, 1984),   only the
species corresponding to the 'fast' electrophoretic variant
of ccRNAs could be detected (G. Boccardo and R.G.   Beaver,
unpublished). Aliquots of the nucleic acid preparations showing the viroid-like RNAs upon electrophoretic analysis, were
fractionated on   sucrose   density   gradients,   and   the   zones
containing nucleic acid of approximately the size of ccRNAs
(Randles *et al.*, 1980)were recovered and probed with ccRNA$_1$
cDNA. In molecular hybridization assays, ccRNA$_1$ and RNAs of
the same size from tinangaja-affected coconuts were shown to
have the same ability to form homologous hybrids with ccRNA$_1$
cDNA (Boccardo *et al.*, 1981, and therefore to contain indistinguishable nucleotide sequences (see also Randles, 1984).

Hence, palms from the Philippines *(Cocos nucifera,*
Elaeis guineensis and *Corypha elata)* naturally infected with
cadang-cadang, and from Guam *(C. nucifera),* showing tinangaja
symptoms, contain an essentially identical RNA which has been
shown to have the properties of a viroid (see Randles,1984).
There is thus convincing evidence that the two diseases are
caused by the same pathogen, the coconut cadang-cadang viroid
(CCCV).

V.   CONCLUSIONS

Overall symptomatologies led one author (Reinking, 1961)
to consider that cadang-cadang and tinangaja were strictly
related if   not   identical,   but   others   questioned this in-
interpretation (Maramorosch, 1964) or believed them to be
different on the basis of nut symptoms (Holmes, 1962; Bigornia, 1977).   The observation that rounded nuts,   scarified along the equator, considered 'typical' of cadang-cadang
disease, can also be found, albeit rarely and very likely for
a short period only during the development of the disease
(Section II B), on tinangaja-affected coconuts suggests that
nut symptoms can not be relied upon for distinguishing these
diseases.   In fact, tinangaja-like nuts are also found on
coconuts suffering from tatipaka, a disorder of palms   not
caused by CCCV (Section II C).   And in two instances on San
Miguel Island(the Philippines), J.S. Imperial, *(unpublished)*
observed cadang-cadang affected coconuts with elongated and
distorted nuts,   such   as   those   in   Fig.   9.   This   could   be
explained by a varietal difference (indeed all nuts in Fig. 9
appear elongated if compared with the usual varieties cultivated in that area) a point which may have been overlooked in
the past.   On the other hand, it is also possible that such a

Figure 9. A CCCV-infected coconut from San Miguel Island
(the Philippines) showing elongated and distorted tinangaja-
like nuts (courtesy of J.S. Imperial.

reaction could be the result of some mineral imbalance in the
soil (Velasco, 1982), and tinangaja-like nuts on a cadang-
cadang-affected coconut may well be the result of different
combined factors.

The different rates of progress of the diseases in the
Philippines and Guam can be explained possibly by the reaction of the different varieties of coconuts to CCCV. The
fact should be stressed that CCCV can attack coconuts of
totally different kinds, such as the 'elongated' type present
on Guam ('wild type' or niu-kafa; Harries, 1979) and the
spherically-fruited type cultivated in the Philippines('domesticated type' or niu vai; Harries,1979). This poses un-
answerable questions as to the origin of a pathogen which
seems equally able to affect coconuts of the ancient naturally evolved and disseminated type (niu-kafa), as well as
coconuts said to have been developed through selection by man
(niuvai). Also, it remains to be explained why various electrophoretic variants are normally found in CCCV-infected coconuts in the Philippines (Imperial *et al.*, 1981), and only
the corresponding 'fast' form can be detected in CCCV-infected

coconuts from Guam, irrespective of the stage of the disease
and position of the sampled frond (Section IV B). Someone
needs to establish that these differences are real ones
bearing in mind that in the Philippines the 'slow' electrophoretic variant appears to originate from the 'fast' one with
the progression of the disease (Imperial *et al.*, 1981), probably by processing and/or transcription mechanisms with
the insertion of a single repeated sequence which may vary in
size (Haseloff *et al.*, 1982; Symons *et al.*, 1984). If this
is done the case may be made on Guam a more 'stable' strain
of CCCV actually does exist. On the other hand, if the
CCCV'fast' variant is in fact more infectious than the 'slow'
one (Imperial *et al.*, 1981; Zelazny *et al.*, 1982), the tinangaja variant of CCCV may represent a 'severe' strain. However, far more work should be done on tinangaja CCCV to
substantiate this hypothesis, and ultimately sequences should
be compared to ascertain whether biological differences between the Guam and the Philippines variants also reflect
chemical and structural differences.

   CCCV is seriously threatening a large area in the
Philippines (Zelazny, 1979, 1980; Zelazny *et al.*, 1982),
and has destroyed the coconut industry on Guam, 1,500 miles
east of the Philippines (Reinking, 1961; Boccardo *et al.*,
1981). At present to establish which way the pathogen has
migrated would be difficult and meaningless unless we hypo-
thesize independent origins and convergent evolutions of
CCCV in Guam and in the Philippines. In the latter case, the
differences in electrophoretic variants and in the progression of the diseases would be easier to explain. Cultural
interchanges among the Marianas Islands may have allowed CCCV
to have escaped somewhere else and be at present undetected
in other islands in the South Pacific and to pose a considerable threat to the area. In fact, coconut palms with tinangaja like nut symptoms have been observed on Rota and Tinian,
two of the Marianas near Guam (R.G. Beaver, *unpublished*),
but no analysis has been made to ascertain if those palms
were really CCCV-infected. Of obvious interest would be to
ascertain whether the tinangaja variant of CCCV occurs also
somewhere else in the Marianas or even east of the archipelago. Not only would its presence elsewhere be of epidemiological value and of interest for the coconut industry of
that region, it might also lead to the discovery in geographically isolated areas of new molecular variants of CCCV or
new manifestations of the pathogen. Whether or not the
distribution patterns, the rates of spread in the field and
the natural hosts are the same for CCCV in causing both
tinangaja and cadang-cadang should also be established to
allow full comparison of the two diseases.

In the absence of reports of obscure or unidentified coconut diseases from the Pacific area which could be under threat, it is difficult to enforce appropriate quarantine measures or controls, but extreme care should be taken when interchanging materials from and within the Marianas, for once CCCV-induced disease is established, even only in isolated spots, eradication of infected palms seems an ineffectual measure of control. (Anonymous, 1982; Zelazny *et al.*, 1982; Randles, 1984).

ACKNOWLEDGEMENTS

I thank J.W. Randles (Department of Plant Pathology, Waite Agriculture Research. Institute, Australia), B. Zelazny and J.S. Imperial (Albay Research Center, Banao, The Philippines) for helpful discussion and scientific cooperation; M. d'Aquilio and A. Sn. J. Namia for some technical assistance; R.G. Milne for revising the English text. The support of D.J. Meadows, formerly FAO/UNDP Coconut Research and Development Project project manager has been essential in conducting this study.

VI.   REFERENCES

Anonymous, 1927. Report of the Guam Experiment Station, 14. (mimeographed)

Anonymous, 1976. Coconut diseases of uncertain etiology. In *Central Plantation Crop Res. Inst. Tech. Bull.* I. Kasaragod, Kerala, India, p.16 - 21.

Anonymous, 1982. Research on the cadang-cadang disease of coconut palm. Food and Agriculture Organization of the United Nations, Manila and Rome, 75pp. (mimeographed).

Bigornia, A.E. (1977). Evaluation and trends of researches on the coconut cadang-cadang disease. *Philipp. J. Coconut Stud.* 2, 5-33

Bigornia, A.E., Calica, C.A., and Pableo, G.O. (1960). Epidemiological studies on the coconut cadang-cadang disease. *DARN, Bureau of Plant Industry,* 11 pp.

Bigornia, A.E., Price, W.C., and Rillo, E.P. (1967). Fronddrop: an unrecorded disease of coconut of unknown etiology in the Bicol region of the Philippines. *FAO Plant Prot. Bull. 15,* 1-4

Boccardo, G. (1976). Report to the Government of the Philippines on the cadang-cadang disease of coconut. Manila, March 1976, 47 pp. (mimeographed).

Boccardo, G. (1980). Report to the Government of the Philippines on the cadang-cadang disease of coconut. Manila, April 1980, 15 pp. (mimeographed).

Boccardo, G., Beaver, R.G., Randles, J., and Imperial, J.S. (1981). Tinangaja and bristle top, coconut diseases of uncertain etiology in Guam, and their relationship to cadang-cadang disease of coconut in the Philippiines. *Phytopathology 71*, 1104-1107.

Castillo, B.S., and Maramorosch, K. (1960). Preliminary report on the boang disease of coconut in Mindanao, the Philippines. *FAO Plant Prot. Bull. 9*, 148-152.

Diener, T.O. (1979). Viroids and viroid diseases. 252 pp. John Wiley & Sons.

Dollet, M., and De Taffin, G. (1979). Progress report on the virological study of the New Hebrides coconut disease. Coc. N. 1437 I.R.H.O., March 1979, 15 pp. mimeographed.

Dollet, M., Gargani, D., and Boccardo, G.,(1981). Recherches sur l'etiologie d'un deperissement des cocotiers au Vanuatu. *Intl. Conf. Tropical Plant Prot.*, Lyon (France) 8-10 July, 1981, p.65 (Abstract).

Fernow, K.H., Peterson, L.C., and Plaisted, R.L. (1970). Spindle tuber virus in seeds and pollen of infected potato plants. *Am.Potato J. 47*, 75-80

Harries, H.C. (1979). The evolution, dissemination and classification of *Cocos nucifera* L. *Bot. Rev. 44*, 265-319.

Haseloff, J., Mohamed, N.A., Symons, R.H. (1982). Viroid RNAs of cadang-cadang disease of coconuts. *Nature, London 299*, 316-321.

Holmes, F.O. (1961). Does cadang-cadang disease spread from diseased to healthy coconut trees? *FAO Plant Prot. Bull. 9*, 133-135.

Holmes, F.O. (1962). The Guam disease of coconut plams. *FAO Plant Prot. Bull. 10*, 25-28.

Imperial, J. S. (1980). Study on the effect of tetracycline on coconut palm infected with cadang-cadang. PCA Albay Research Center, Annual Report, 58 pp. (mimeographed).

Imperial, J.S., Rodriguez, Ma.J.B., and Randles, J.W. (1981). Variation in the viroid-like RNA associated with cadang-cadang disease: evidence for an increase in molecular weight with disease progress. *J. Gen. Virol. 56*, 77-85.

Maramorosch, K. (1961). Report to the Government of the Philippines on the cadang-cadang disease of coconut. FAO ETAP Bull. 1333. Rome. mimeographed

Maramorosch, K. (1964). A survey of coconut diseases of unknown etiology. FAO, Rome, 39 pp. (mimeographed).

Nagaraj, A.N., Pacumbaba, R.P., and Pableo, G.O. (1965). Diagnostic symptoms of cadang-cadang disease of coconuts. *FAO Plant Prot. Bull. 13*, 1-8.

Nutman, F.J., and Roberts, F.M. (1955). Frond-drop. A note on an abnormal condition of coconut palm in Jamaica. *Empire J. Exp. Agr.23*, 268-270.

Ocfemia, G.O. (1937). The probable nature of cadang-cadang disease of coconut. *Philipp. Agriculturist,26,* 338-340.

Petzhold, H. Marwitz, R., and Heinze, K. (1974).Elektronenmikroscopische Untersuchungen als Beitrag zur Klärung der Aetiologie der Cadang-Cadang Krankheit bei Kokospalmen. Jahresbericht 1973 Biol. Bundesanst. für Land- u. Forstwirtsch. 57-58, Berlin und Braunschweig.

Plavsic-Banjac, B., Maramorosch, K., and von Uexküll, H.R. (1972). Preliminary observations of cadang-cadang disease of coconut palm leaves by electron microscopy. *Pl. Dis. Reptr. 56,* 643-645.

Price, W. C. (1958). Yellow mottle decline (cadang-cadang) of coconut. *Fla. Agric. Exp. Stn. J. Series,No.839,* 1-7.

Price, W. C., Bigornia, A.E., (1969). Further studies on the epidemiology of coconut cadang-cadang. *FAO Plant Prot. Bull. 17,* 11-16.

Price, W.C. Rillo, A.E., and Pableo, G.O. (1973). A statistical study of the yellow or olivaceous spots characteristic of cadang-cadang. *Philipp. J. Plant Ind. 38,* 13-31.

Randles, J.W. (1975). Association of two ribonucleic acid species with cadang-cadang disease of coconut palm. *Phytopathology 65,* 163-167.

Randles, J.W. (1977). UNDP/FAO Coconut Research and Development Project. Report on the ninth visit, 9 pp. (mimeographed).

Randles, J. W. (1984). Coconut cadang-cadang viroid. In: "Subviral pathogens of plants and animals: Viroids and prions". (K. Maramorosch and J.J. McKelvey,Jr.,eds.) Academic Press.

Randles,J.W., and Hatta, T. (1979). Circularity of the ribonucleic acids associated with cadang-cadang disease. *Virology 96,* 47-53.

Randles, J.W., and Palukaitis, P. (1979). *In vitro* synthesis and characterization of DNA complementary to cadang-cadang associated RNA. *J. Gen. Virol. 43,* 649-662.

Randles, J.W., Rillo, A.E., and Diener, T.O. (1976). The viroid-like structure and cellular location of anomalous RNAs associated with cadang-cadang disease. *Virology 74,* 128-139.

Randles, J.W., Boccardo, G., Retuerma, M.L., and Rillo, A.E. (1977). Transmission of the RNA species associated with cadang-cadang of coconut palm and the insensitivity of the disease to antibiotics. *Phytopathology 67,* 1211-1216.

Randles, J.W., Boccardo, G., and Imperial, J.S. (1980). Detection of the cadang-cadang associated RNAs in African oil palm and buri palm. *Phytopathology 70*, 185-189.

Randles, J.W., Steger, G., and Riesner, D. (1982). Structural transition in viroid-like RNAs associated with cadang-cadang disease, velvet tobacco mottle virus, and Solanum nodiflorum mottle virus. *Nucleic Acid Res. 10*, 5569-5586.

Reinking, O.A. (1950). Preliminary report on the cadang-cadang disease and soil deficiency troubles of coconuts in the Philippines. *Plant Dis. Reptr. 34*, 300-304.

Reinking, O.A. (1961). Yellow mottle decline of coconuts in the territory of Guam. *Plant Dis. Reptr. 34*, 599-604.

Reinking, O.A., and Radewald, J.D. (1961). Cadang-cadang disease of coconuts in Guam may be caused by a soil-borne plant virus spread by dagger nematodes (Xiphinema spp.). *Plant Dis. Reptr. 45*, 411-412.

Rillo, E.P., and Rillo, A.E. (1981). Abstracts on the cadang-cadang disease of coconuts, 1937-1980. *Philippine Coconut Authority*, Manila, 50 pp.

Sill, W.H., Bigornia, A.E., and Pacumbaba, R.P. (1965). Incidence of cadang-cadang disease of coconut in trees of different ages and its relationship to practical control. *Philipp. J. Plant. Ind. 29*, 87-101.

Symons, R. H., Haseloff, J., Visvader, J.E., Keese, P., Murphy, P.J., Gill, D.S., Gordon, K.H.J., and Bruening, G. (1984). On the mechanism of replication of viroids, virusoids and satellite RNAs. In: "Subviral pathogens of plants and animals: Viroids and prions". (K. Maramorosch and J.J. McKelvey, Jr.,eds.)

Velasco, J.R. (1982). Review of studies tending to link the rare earths with coconut cadang-cadang. *Scientia Filipinas 2*, 64-76.

Weston, W.H., Jr. (1918). Report on the plant disease situation in Guam, pp.45-62, *In:* Guam. Agricultural Experiment Station Report for 1917, 89 pp (memeographed).

Zelazny, B. (1979). Distribution and spread of the cadang-cadang disease of coconut palm. *Acta Phytopath. Acad. Scient. Hung. 14*, 115-126.

Zelazny, B. (1980). Ecology of cadang-cadang disease of coconut palm in the Philippines. *Phytopathology 70*, 700-703.

Zelazny, B. and Niven, B.S. (1980). Duration of the stages of cadang-cadang disease of coconut palm. *Plant Dis. 64*, 841-842.

Zelazny, B., and Pacumbaba, E. (1982a). Incidence of cadang-cadang of coconut palm in the Philippines. *Plant Dis. 66*, 547-549.

Zelazny, B., and Pacumbaba, E. (1982b). Phytophagous insects
    associated with cadang-cadang infected and healthy
    coconut palm in south-eastern Luzon, Philippines.
    Ecol. Entomol. 1, 113-120.
Zelazny, B., Randles, J.W., Boccardo, G., and Imperial, J.S.
    (1982). The viroid nature of the cadang-cadang disease
    of coconut palm. *Scientia Filipinas 2*, 45-63.

Chapter 5

HOP STUNT VIROID AND HOP VIROID DISEASE

Eishiro Shikata

Department of Botany
Faculty of Agriculture
Hokkaido University
Sapporo, Japan

I. INTRODUCTION

Hop plants are cultivated in many regions of the world in relation to beer production. The plants cultivated in Japan originated from European cultivars. However, hop stunt disease, so far as we are aware, has been reported only in Japan and thus it appears to be a specific disease indigenous to this country.

Most Japanese commercial hops *(Humulus lupulus L.)* are infected with a complex of several viruses, causing mosaic or latent symptoms. These viruses probably affected more or less the growth of the plants, and since 1952, the plants showing abnormal growth have attracted the attention of the hop growers in Japan (Yamamoto *et al.* 1970,1973).

In 1970, Yamamoto *et al.* reported that the disease agent was mechanically transmissible to cultivated and wild hop *(Humulus japonicus* Sieb. et Zucc.), and spread along the ridges of hop gardens. Following the experiments involving

SUBVIRAL PATHOGENS
OF PLANTS AND ANIMALS:
VIROIDS AND PRIONS

101

Copyright © 1985 by Academic Press, Inc.
All rights of reproduction in any form reserved.
ISBN 0-12-470230-9

grafting, sap transmission, symptomatology and epidemiology, they concluded that a virus causes the disease, although no causal virus particles have been detected in the diseased plants.

II HOP STUNT DISEASE

1) Symptoms on hop: Typical symptoms of abnormal growth are shortening of the internodes of the main and lateral vines, and curling of the upper leaves. The plants become stunted and thus the disease is named "hop stunt disease" (Yamamoto *et al.*, 1970,1973).

The main vines of the plants which are free from the hop stunt disease usually grow about 8 meter high, whereas those infected by the disease with the same number of nodes grow only 5 meter high. The main vines become thinner, and hooked hairs and ridges on the under parts of the vines develop poorly. The leaves are smaller and more yellowish than those of the stunt-free hops. Some of the upper leaves curl out- wards. (Fig. 1).

Figure 1. Symptoms on hops caused by HSV. a. Note that two plants at right hand (arrows) are extremely stunted by HSV infection, but the vines of healthy plants at left have al- ready reached to the highest wire. b. Close up of the upper leaves of a HSV-infected hop. Note that the upper leaves curled downwards.

The cone yields of the diseased hops were reduced to approximately half of those of the stunt-free hops (which might be infected with some of the hop viruses). In addition, the α-acid content in the bitter substances in cones from the diseased hop plants was reduced to about one half to one third of that from the stunt-free hops (Yamamoto *et al.*, 1973).

2) Distribution: In Japan, commercial hop cultivation is mostly distributed in the northern part of mainland Japan such as Tohoku District and Hokkaido. Since approximately 1952 hop plants showing dwarf symptom were observed in several hop gardens in Fukushima Prefecture of Tohoku District. The disease spread widely and caused significant damage in the early 'sixties (Yamamoto *et al.*, 1973).

Following investigation of the disease since 1965, the disease was found to be prevalent in almost all commercial hop gardens in Tohoku District.

When Sasaki and Shikata found the agent of this disease to be a viroid, the practical procedures for detecting the infected plants were established using cucumber as a test plant in combination with analysis of α-acid contents of the cones. Since then, the number of diseased plants in this area has rapidly decreased as a result of the eradication of diseased stocks and of replanting with stunt-free plants.

No report has been published so far concerning the stunt disease of hop or its related diseases in the world except Japan. Therefore, one may assume that the disease is an indigenous one occuring in Japan, although most commercial hop plants cultivated in Japan were introduced from European cultivars .

3) Host ranges and their symptoms. In 1977, Sasaki and Shikata (1977a) found that hop stunt disease was able to infect cucumber plants by mechanical inoculation, and it produced severe symptoms in cucumber plants. Among cucumber *(Cucumis sativus L.)*, melon *(C.melo L.)*, Oriental pickling melon *(C. melo* var. Conomon (Thunb.) Makino), bottle gourd *(Lagenaria siceria* var. *clavata* Hara, var. Gourda Hara and var. *microcarpa* Hara), sponge gourd "Hechima" *(Luffa cylindrica* Roem.), wax gourd *(Benincasa hispida* (Thunb.) Cogn.), tomato *(Lycopersicon esculentum* Mill.) and wild hop *(Humulus japonicus* Sieb. et Zucc.)demonstrated susceptibility to the disease. Usually the infected cucurbitaceous plants showed stunted growth two to four weeks after inoculation. Tomato was a symptomless carrier. Wild hop showed symptoms of stunted growth and leaf curl about three months after inoculation. HSV was detected by cucumber test 2 months after inoculation to HSV-free hops without any outer symptoms (Sasaki and Shikata, 1978 a,c). In the fields, a period of

Table I.   Properties of the Viroids

		PSTV	CSV	CEV	HSV
1.	electron microscope	−	−	−	−
2.	centrifugation	top	top	top	top
	rpm	40.000	50.000	10.000	45.000
	(hr)	(3)	(2)	(2)	(2)
3.	buffer extraction	0.5M +	0.5M +	0.3M +	0.5M +
4.	chloroform-butanol	no	no	no	no
	extract				
5.	phenol extract	+	+	+	+
6.	ethanol precipitation	+	+	+	+
7.	RNase	lost	lost	lost	lost
8.	DNase	no	no	no	no
9.	sucrose density	top	top	top	top
	gradient centrifugation				
	rpm	24.000	24.000	45.000	45.000
	(hr)	(16)	(26)	(4.5)	(4)
10.	sedimentation	10S	5–7.5S	10S	7S
11.	molecular weight	11.500	12.000	12.500	10.000
12.	thermal inactivation	75°C			84°C
13.	incubation period	tomato	chrys.	petunia	cucumber
	(days)	(10–21)	(60)	(30)	(20–30)
14.	symptom	stunt	stunt	stunt	stunt

at least one year of incubation was required before the
symptoms on the field grown hops would appear (Sasaki *et
al*, 1982). No infection occurred in squash *(Cucurbita
maxima* Duch.), pumpkin *(C.pepo* L.) and water melon
(Citrullus vulgaris Schrad.).

III ETIOLOGY OF HOP STUNT DISEASE

Using cucumber plants, Sasaki and Shikata (1977b,d,
1980) indicated that HSV infectivity was closely associated
with a low molecular weight RNA, about 7S RNA fraction, and
the disease agent was extractable in phenol and precipitated
in ethanol; it was DNase insensitive but RNase digestive.
Finally they concluded that the causal agent of the disease
was a viroid (Table 1). Takahashi (1981 confirmed these
results later.

IV   DIAGNOSIS AND CONTROL MEASURES

Diagnosis of hop stunt disease can usually be made either
by observation of symptom appearance of the plants (Yamamoto
et al, 1970), by analysis of α–and β–acid contents in cones
(Yamamoto *et al*, 1973),or by bioassay of cucumber plants

(Sasaki and Shikata, 1977a,b,1978a,b,c,d, Takahashi and Tak-usari, 1979a,b). Alpha-acid analysis is a rapid and reliable diagnosis for hop stunt disease. However, HSV was sometimes detected by cucumber bioassay in the plants shown to be HSV free either by symptom diagnosis or by α-acid analysis (Table 2). This indicates that HSV is more reliably detected by bioassay using cucumber plants. (Sasaki and Shikata, 1980). This method, however, requires the use of a temperature controlled greenhouse or plastic house at 30°C and approximately one month of observation (Sasaki, and Shikata, 1977a, 78b, Takahashi and Takusari, 1977b). HSV was detected by cucumber bioassay in the preparations of a mixture of one HSV-infected leaf disc and 200 HSV-free leaf discs collected in August (Sasaki, Sano and Shikata, 1980, Sasaki and Shikata 1980). Practical use of such a mass diagnostic method has been employed in the fields (Sasaki and Shikata, 1980, Sasaki *et al*, 1981).

To avoid further dispersal of the disease, it is most important to distribute only those HSV-free cuttings which were taken from HSV-free stocks after careful investigation of cucumber bioassay and α-acid analysis.

As the disease agent is mechanically transmitted by hands, sicles, scissors and other direct contact with the vines (Yamamoto *et al.*, 1970,1973), cleaning ones hands and the instruments used after contact with individual plants is absolutely essential.

Partial replanting by removing and replacing diseased

TABLE 2. Comparison of Three Different Diagnostic Methods for Hop Stunt Disease (Sasaki, Shikata, Fukamizu & Yamamoto, unpublished data)

Date	Method	Hop plants tested[a]				
		A	B	C	D	E
June, 1977	Symptom-diagnosis	+	−	−	−	−
May, 1978	Cucumber-bioassay	+ (4/4)[b]	+ (4/4)	− (0/4)	− (0/4)	− (0/4)
july	Symptom-diagnosis	+	+	−	−	−
Aug.	α-acid analysis	+ (1.8)[c]	+ (2.9)	− (6.2)	− (5.5)	− (7.3)
Sept.	Cucumber-bioassay	+ (4/4)[b]	+ (4/4)	+ (4/4)	− (0/4)	− (0/4)
July, 1979	Symptom-diagnosis of cuttings collected in May, 1978	+	+	−	−	−
	Symptom-diagnosis of cuttings collected in Sept., 1978	NT[d]	NT	+[e]	−	+[e]

a) Hop plants (cv. Kirin II) from A to E were planted in the same ridge.
   +; HSV-infected, −; HSV-free.
b) Number of cucumber plants infected/plants inoculated.
c) Percent α-acid content.
d) Not tested.
e) Hop plants C and E may have been infected after May, 1978, because cuttings collected from hop C and E, in Sept., 1978, showed HSD symptoms, unlike those collected in May.

plants including 5-10 plants adjacent to the diseased ones was not always successful. The most satisfactory method of eradication of the disease was the removal of all the stocks in a field and replanting with HSV-free plants. In any case, careful treatment to destroy the root stocks and deep roots is definitely required (Sasaki and Shikata, 1980).

V. PURIFICATION

A rapid purification of HSV from the infected cucumber plants has been accomplished on 7.5% polycrylamide gel electrophoresis by a modified procedure of potato spindle tuber viroid purification described by Diener *et al* (1977) (Yoshikawa and Takahashi, 1982). They obtained 30-40 μg HSV from 1 Kg infected leaves. Infectivities were equally recovered from the two bands obtained on 5,7.5 and 10% polyacrylamide gel electrophoresis under 8M urea denaturing condition.

Ohno *et al.* (1982) succeeded in purifying HSV on 10% polyacrylamide gel electrophoresis and showed electron micrographs of the viroid molecules under non-denaturing and denaturing conditions. The viroid RNA molecules under denaturing condition showed typical circular form. The molecular length of circular form was estimated to be 77 ± 10nm, and 290-300 nucleotides, and 0.99×10^5 daltons by electron microscopy and polyacrylamide gel electrophoresis when potato spindle tuber viroid (PSTV) was used as a standard. Both circular and linear forms have been shown to be infectious.

Uyeda, Sano and Shikata (1982, 1983) performed further purification of HSV and cucumber pale fruit viroid (CPFV from the infected cucumber plants and of PSTV from tomato plants. *Extraction of low molecular weight RNAs* ; Combined procedures described by Raymer and Diener (1969) and Singh and Sänger (1976) were employed. Total nucleic acids were extracted from 200g of frozen tissues by blending them with 1M K_2HPO_4 (300ml), SDS (4g), bentonite (0.4g) and water saturated phenol (40ml). The supernatants obtained by centrifugation were reextracted by blending them with water saturated phenol (200ml) and $CHCl_3$ (200ml). The supernatants were collected by centrifugation and the nucleic acids were precipitated twice by adding 2.5 volumes of 95% ethanol containing 0.2M sodium acetate. The nucleic acids were dissolved in 50ml of TES buffer (0.1M Tris, 0.001M EDTA, 0.1M Nacl, pH 7.5), and then polysaccharides were removed by blending in 1 volume of ethylene glycol monomethyl ether and 1 volume of 2.5M K_2HPO_4, pH 8.3. The upper phase which contained nucleic acids, was collected by centrifugation and diluted to make 0.2M K_2HPO_4 solution with distilled water. Then 10ml of 2%

cetyltrimethyl ammonium bromide (CTAB) was added. After
standing for 30 min. at 6°C, CTA-nucleic acid complex was
precipitated by centrifugation. The precipitates were washed
twice with 70% ethanol containing 0.2M sodium acetate and
dissolved in TES buffer at pH 7.5. To remove ribosomal RNA,
1 volume of 4M LiCl solution was added and incubated on ice
for 4 hr. The supernatant, which contained 2M LiCl soluble
low molecular weight RNAs and DNA, were collected by centrifugation. DNA was digested by DNase I (Worthington Biochem.)
solution containing 25 µg/ml of DNase I in 0.15M NaCl, M
Tris, 0.005M $MgCl_2$, pH7.5 (Erikson, 1969). After incubation
for 30 min. at 37°C, reaction was stopped by adding water
saturated phenol and $CHCl_3$ mixture (1:1), and the mixture was
shaken for 5 min. The aqueous phase was collected by centrifugation and re-extracted with water saturated phenol and
$CHCl_3$ mixture. The resultant aqueous phase contained 2M LiCl
soluble"low molecular weight RNAs". *Column chromatography*
The viroids were further purified by CF-11 cellulose column
chromatography, according to the procedures of Franklin
(1966). Column size was 1.0 x15 cm and flow rate was 30ml/hr.
The low molecular weight RNAs were fractionated by stepwise
elution using 35% and 15% ethanol,followed by an ethanol
free buffer. The fraction eluting in 15% ethanol contained a
small amount of t-RNA, 5S RNA, the viroid RNA and some minor
species of cellular RNA; it was designated as a "partially
purified preparation". *Purification of the viroids;* The
partially purified preparations of HSV and CPFV were electr -
ophoresed on 15% polyacrylamide Slab gel (20cm x 15 cm x 1.5mm)
under nondenaturing conditions in Tris-acetate EDTA buffer at
pH 7.2 (Loening, 1967) in a cold room at 6°C for about 20 hr
at 15 mA, 40-50 V. Then the gel was stained with 0.02%
toluidin blue 0 and destained by distilled water. The viroid
bands were cut out and homogenized in 0.5M ammonium acetate,
0.01M magnesium acetate, 0.1% SDS.

After stirring with a magnetic stirrer overnight at room
temperature, gel slurries were pelleted by centrifugation and
resultant supernatants were collected. The viroids were
sedimented by adding 2.5 volumes of 95% ethanol containing
0.2M sodium acetate and dissolved in 0.3M NaCl,0.02M Tris-HCl
at pH 7.6 The viroids were then absorbed to DEAE cellulose
(DE-32, Whatman) equilibrated with 0.3M NaCl.,0.02M Tris-HCl,
pH 7.6 and washed with the same buffer and eluted in 0.6M
NaCl, 0.02M Tris-HCl, pH 7.6 to obtain the "purified viroid
preparations".

The use of 15% polyacrylamide gel electrophoresis was
found to be effective to separate the viroids from the cellular RNAs of the similar size.

VI. COMPARATIVE STUDIES ON HOP STUNT VIROID, CUCUMBER
PALE FRUIT VIROID AND POTATO SPINDLE TUBER VIROID

The host plants of hop stunt viroid (HSV) are restricted
to hops, Cucurbitaceous plants and tomatoes. Symptoms expressed on the infected plants seemed to be identical with
those infected with cucumber pale fruit viroid (CPFV) in the
Netherlands,as far as we know from the literature as described by van Dorst and Peters (1974).

Therefore, we carried out comparative studies with hop
stunt and cucumber pale fruit viroid, as well as with potato
spindle tuber viroid. Comparison of HSV, CPFV and PSTV was
made as follows:

A.   Biological properties in host range and symptomatology.
B.   Cytopathic changes in ultrathin sections.
C.   Co-electrohporesis of the partially purifed preparations.
          1)   15% PAGE, non-denaturing condition
          2)   7.5% PAGE,   denaturing condition
          3)   5% Page,   denaturing condition
D.   Estimation of number of nucleotides of the purified
      viroid preparations.
E.   Electron microscopy of the purified viroid preparations.
          1)   no-denaturing condition
          2)   denaturing condition

A.   Biological properties in host range and symptomatology.
Eleven test plants in Cucurbitaceae, Solanaceae and
Compositae were inoculated with HSV, CPFV and PSTV (Table 3;
Sano *et al.*, 1981.

Both HSV and CPFV produced symptoms on cucumber *(Cucumis
sativus),(C. melo), Benincasa hispida, Lagenaria siceraria*
var. *clavata* and *L.siceraria* var. *microcarpa (Fig.2.)*
Cucumber plants infected with HSV and CPFV showed stunting, vein clearing and leaf curling 14-17 days after inoculation. The other 4 plants in Cucurbitaceae also showed
stunting, leaf curling and top necrosis 16-22 after inoculation, and the severely infected plants sometimes died.
Tomato plants failed to show symptoms from infection of HSV
and CPFV. Watermelon *(Citrullus vulgaris)*, squash *(Cucurbita
maxima)* and *Gynura aurantiaca* were not infected with HSV and
CPFV. The host ranges of HSV and CPFV were almost identical.
Moreover, the symptoms on each test plant were similar and
thus differentiation between HSV and CPFV by their biological
properties was impossible.

Table 3. Sap inoculation experiments

Plants	Symptoms[a]		
	HSV	CPFV	PSTV
Bonincasa hispida	LC, M, St, TN, D	LC, M, St, TN, D	-(0/2)[c]
Citrullus vulgaris (Shimatama suika)[b]	-(0/6)	-(0/6)	-(0/2)
Cucumis melo (Yubari melon)	LY, N, St, D	LY, N, St, D	-(0/2)
C. sativus (Suyo)	LC, VC, St	LC, VC, St	-(0/2)
(Sporu)	LC, VC, St	LC, VC, St	-(0/2)
Cucurbita maxima (Ebis)	-(0/6)	-(0/6)	-(0/2)
Lagenaria siceraria var. *clavata* (Daimaru)	LC, St, M, TN, D	LC, St, M, TN, D	-(0/2)
L. siceraria var. *microcarpa* (Sennari hyoutan)	LC, St, M, TN, D	LC, St, M, TN, D	-(0/2)
Lycopersicon esculentum (Rutgers)	l (3/3)	l (3/3)	St, Ep
(Rentita)	l (3/3)	l (3/3)	St, Ep
Gynura aurantiaca	-(0/3)	-(0/3)	l (2/2)

a) LC: leaf curling. M: mosaic. St: stunting. TN: top necrosis. D: plant death. LY: leaf yellowing.
N: necrosis. VC: veinclearing. l: symptomless. Ep: epinasty.
b) cultivar name.
c) results of back-inoculation; numbers of plant infected/inoculated.

Figure 2. Similarity of the symptoms on cucumber plants(cv. Suyo) inoculated by HSV and CPFV. Right: healthy; middle: CPFV; left: HSV. a. whole plants, b. leaves, c. flowers.

TABLE 4. Cytopathic changes in cucumber and tomato plants infected by viroids

Host	Cucumber (Suyo)			Tomato (Rentita)				
Viroid	HSV	CPFV	control[†]	HSV	CPFV	PSTV	CEV	control[†]
External symptom	++	++	—	—	—	++	+++	—
Papamural body	+	+	+	+	+	+	+	+
Aberration of cell wall	++	++	—	—	—	++	++	—
Chloroplast disintegration	++	++	—	+	+	+++	+++	—
Disappearance of tonoplast	+	+	—	+	+	+	+	—

† healthy plants

On the other hand, tomato plants infected with PSTV developed severe stunting and epinasty about 14 days after inoculation, but cucumber, melon, B. hispida, L. siceraria var. clavata, L. siceraria var. microcarpa, watermelon and squash were not infected with PSTV or remained symptomless. Thus PSTV was apparently biologically different from HSV and CPFV.

B. Cytopathic changes in ultrathin sections.

1) Cucumber plants infected with HSV and CPFV.

As indicated in Section VI, A, symptoms caused by HSV were quite similar to those caused by CPFV in cucumber plants. The electron microscopic examinations of the infected plants with HSV, CPFV and PSTV indicated that their internal symptoms were almost identical, as shown in Table 4. (Kojima, Murai and Shikata, 1983). One of the typical alterations was aberration of cell walls in all tissues, such as epidermis, palisade parenchyma, spongy parenchyma cells and in vascular bundles. The cell walls of HSV – and CPFV – infected cucumber leaves were extremely distorted. These areas were characterized by cell walls with corrugated profile and irregular thickness (Fig. 3). These aberrations appear to lead to a deformation of the tissues themselves, resulting in external symptoms such as stunting, vein clearing and leaf curling(Momma and Takahashi,1982). Another alteration in the infected leaf cells was disintegration of the chloroplasts (Fig. 4). Futhermore, these cells were usually accompanied with breakdown of tonoplast and the production of granules within the cytoplasm. These structural changes were almost the same as those which occur in tomato plants infected with PSTV or citrus exocortis viroid (CEV).

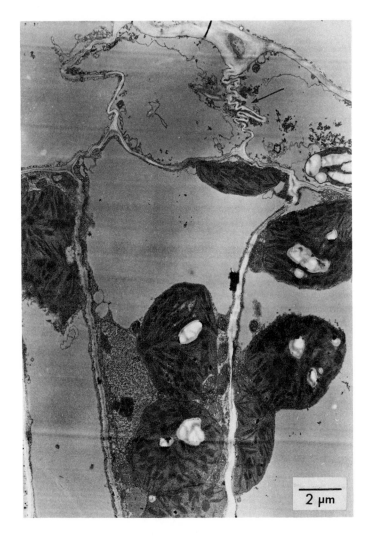

Figure 3. Cell wall abberation (arrow) occurring in the epidermal cells of a cucumber plant infected with CPFV. The palisade cells below abnormal epidermis look normal.

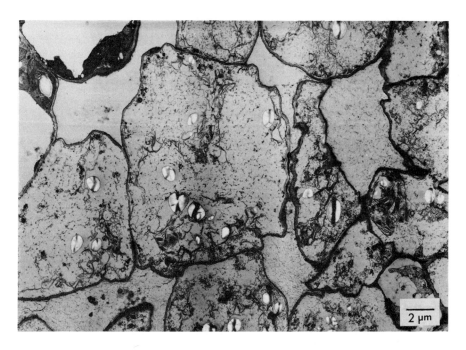

Figure 4.   Spongy parenchymatous cells of a cucumber plant
infected with HSV, showing disintergrated chloroplast and
aberration of membrane systems.

     Remarkable changes of the membrane systems within cells
of viroid infected plants may be related to the subcellular
location of HSV in that the viroid fractions are associated
with the nuclear and plasma membrane fractions (Takahashi
et al., 1982).
               2)   Tomato plants infected with HSV and CPFV
     Tomato plants showed no symptom when infected with HSV
and CPFV, but were proved to be capable of carrying these
agents.   Therefore, it was rather difficult to find distinctive alterations of leaf cells in the infected tomato plants
However, disintegration of chloroplasts, sometimes, but not
often, occurred in these systems.
C.   Co-electrophoresis of the partially purified preparations.
     In the preliminary experiments using the nucleic acid
extracts from HSV-, CPFV-, and PSTV-infected tomatoes, the
migration rates of HSV and CPFV were almost identical on 5%
polyacrylamide gel.   In addition, HSV and CPFV displayed
identical migration rates with cellular RNA (7S RNA) and thus
no specific viroid band was observed, but the extract from
PSTV infected tomatoes displayed a specific band associated

with infectivity (Sano, Sasaki and Shikata, 1981).

    Co-electrophoresis was carried out on polyacrylamide Slab
gel under non-denaturing or denaturing conditions (Sano,
Uyeda and Shikata, 1983). Electrophoresis under non-denaturing condition was carried out in 15% gel in Tris-acetate-EDTA
buffer at pH 7.2 (Loening, 1967). Electrophoresis was carried out in a cold room at 6°C for about 20 hrs at 15mA,
40-50V. For electrophoresis under 7M urea denaturing condition, samples were dissolved in 0.01M EDTA, pH 7.0 (10μl),
dimethylsulfoxide (5 1), 40% sucrose containing bromophenol
blue (10μl) and heated at 50°C for 10 mins. The gel containing 7M urea was made in 74.5 mM Tris-44.5mM boric acid-1.25mM
EDTA, pH 8.3 (Maniatis and Efstratiadis, 1980).

    1) Electrophoresis on 15% polyacrylamide gel
under non-denaturing condition: The partially purified preparations of HSV, CPFV and PSTV were electrophoresed on a 15%
polyacrylamide Slab gel. The migration rates of HSV, CPFV
and PSTV were almost identical under this condition (Sano,
Uyeda and Shikata, 1983).

    2) Electrophoresis on 7.5% polyacrylamide gel
under a 7M urea denaturing condition: The partially purified
preparations of HSV, CPFV, PSTV and healthy cucumber plants
were electrophoresed on 7.5% polyacrylamide Slab gel under a
7M urea denaturing condition (Sano, Sasaki and Shikata, 1983).
Two extra bands were detected from PSTV preparation, the
upper band for circular molecules and the lower band for
linear molecules. On the other hand, only one extra band,
which we assumed to be circular molecules, was detected from
both HSV and CPFV preparations. The migration rates of
circular molecules of both HSV and CPFV were apparently faster
than that of PSTV. Furthermore, the migration rate of the
upper band of HSV seemed to be slightly faster than that of
CPFV.

    Then the gels of HSV and CPFV were sectioned into 5
slices, bioassayed on cucumber plants, and the infectivity
index was calculated according to Raymer and Diener (1969).
Two peaks of infectivity were detected in both viroid preparations. One of them in fraction 2 was closely associated
with the upper bands of HSV and CPFV which we assumed to be
circular molecules. The other in fraction 4 and 5 for HSV
and fraction 4 for CPFV, the lower bands, seemed to be associated with linear molecules (although no extra visible band
was detected in fractions 4 and 5, and 4 respectively)
because a band with the same migration rate of those fractions seemed to be 9S RNA and it also appeared in the healthy
plant preparations.

    3) Electrophoresis on 5% polyacrylamide gel
under 7M urea denaturing condition: In order to ascertain

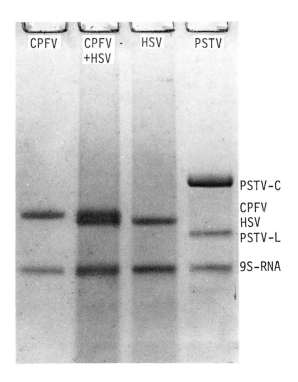

Figure 5. Co-electrophoresis of the partially purified viroids on 5% polyacrylamide Slab gel electrophoresis under
7M urea-denaturing condition. HSV and CPFV were prepared
from cucumber, PSTV was prepared from tomato.

the difference between HSV and CPFV, both viroid preparations
were mixed and arranged in the same well and electrophoresed
on 5% polyacrylamide gel (Sano, Uyeda and Shikata, 1983). The
slowest moving component in the mixed preparation appeared
finely separated into two bands. The upper band corresponded
with the circular form of CPFV and the lower band corresponded
with that of HSV. The fastest moving component, the linear
forms of HSV and CPFV, showed the same migration rate and
corresponded with 9S RNA (Fig. 5). This experiment showed
the migration rate of HSV was apparently faster than that of
CPFV. The result suggested that the difference between the
number of nucleotides of HSV and CPFV was quite small.

D. Estimation of number of nucleotides of the purified viroid
   preparations.
      The purified viroid preparations of HSV, CPFV and PSTV
were dissolved in 8M urea (20μl), heated at 65°C for 5 min.
and mixed with 40% sucrose containing bromophenol blue(10μl).
The gel containing 8M urea was made in 22.5mM Tris-22.5mM

boric acid–0.5mM EDTA, pH 8.3 (Sänger *et al.*, 1979). Electrophoresis was carried out for 15 hrs. at 40V, 4–5mA at
50–60°C.

     After electrophoresis, each of the viroid preparations
was separated into two components, the slowest–moving component and the fastest–moving component. The result of the
bioassay from the two components of each viroid preparation
indicated that both components were highly associated with
infectivity. These two components were assumed to be circular and linear molecules of the respective viroids (Sänger
et al., 1979; Ohno *et al.*, 1982). The number of nucleotides
of linear molecules of HSV and CPFV was estimated. Based on
the use of PSTV, 5S rRNA and tRNA as markers they were calculated to be about 315 nucleotides and about 320 nucleotides
for HSV and CPFV, respectively (Sano, Uyeda and Shikata,
1983).
E.   Electron microscopy of the purified viroid preparations:
     An attempt to compare the size of the viroids by elec-
tron microscopy under non–denaturing and denaturing conditions was performed (Sano, Uyeda and Shikata, 1983).
          1)   Non–denaturing condition: The preparations
for electron microscope examinations were made according to
the method described by Sogo *et al.*, (1973). The purified
preparations of HSV and CPFV (0.2µg/2 1) were dissolved in 4M
sodium acetate(18µl) and 0.05% cytochrome C–4M sodium acetate
(20µl). The mixture was spread on water hypophase at room
temperature, and picked up on carbon coated grids. After
they were washed in 30% ethanol for 10 min., the grids were
stained in 0.05mM uranyl acetate in 90% ethanol for 30
seconds, and rotary shadowed with platinum–paladium at an
angle of 8°.
     Under non–denaturing condition as shown in Fig. 6–A
short rod like molecules about 50nm long were observed, which
seemed to be native viroid molecules. In this condition,
some viroid molecules were aggregated upon each other.
          2)   Denaturing condition: The purified prepara-
tions of HSV and CPFV were spread on water hypophase according
to the method described by Randles and Hatta (1979) with some
modifications. The viroids (2µg/10 1) were dissolved in 90µl
of a formamide solution (99% formamide–10mM Tris, pH8.5–1mM
EDTA). The mixture was then heated at 60°C for 15 mins.
Immediately after heating, cytochrome C (4µg/4–1) was added
and the mixture was spread on hypophase (1.5mM Tris, pH8.5–
0.15mM EDTA) preheated at 60°C, picked up on the grids and
stained.
     Under denaturing condition, most of the molecules obser-
ved were closed circular forms (Fig. 6–B). The linear forms
were scarcely observed in both HSV and CPFV preparations.
The result coincided with that of Sänger *et al.* (1976).

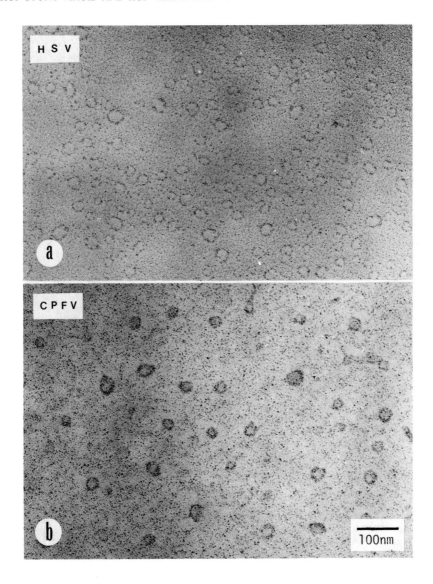

Figure 6. Electron micrographs of (a) HSV and (b) CPFV under 90% formamide denaturing condition. Pt-Pd shadowed.

They examined PSTV by electron microscopy under strongly denaturing condition, and indicated that most of the viroid molecules were closed circular in form; linear ones accounted for less than 1% of the viroid molecules.

The length of viroid molecules were calculated from

circular molecules under denaturing condition. The mean
length of HSV and CPFV were 80-100 nm and 90-100 nm, respectively (Sano, Uyeda and Shikata, 1983). It was difficult to
distinguish both viroids by electron microscope examinations.

VII   CONCLUSIONS

The number of the nucleotides of the viroids so far
known are listed in Table 5. The present investigation

Table 5. The number of nucleotides of the viroids

Viroids	Nucleotides	M.W.	References
Citrus exocortis	371	125.000	Gross *et al.* (1982)
Potato spindle tuber	359	120.000	Gross *et al.* (1978)
Chrysanthemum stunt	354	120.000	Gross *et al.* (1982)
Cucumber pale fruit	330	110.000	Sänger (1976)
	320		Sano, Uyeda and Shikata(1983)
Hop stunt	297		Ohno *et al.* (in press)
	315		Sano, Uyeda and Shikata (1983)
Avocado sunblotch	247		Symons (1981)
Coconut cadang-cadang	246-574		Mohamed *et al.* (1982)

revealed that the size of CPFV and HSV is quite similar, 320
nucleotides for CPFV and 315 nucleotides for HSV, only 5
nucleotides difference.   Quite recently, Ohno *et al.*, (in
press) estimated the nucleotide sequence of the full length
of HSV molecules at 297 nucleotides.

As mentioned in this paper, HSV and CPFV are biologically indistinguishable. Therefore, it is important to know the
similarities and differences of sequence of both viroids.

Preliminary studies on molecular hybridization between
purified CPFV and cloned cDNA with HSV was performed (Sano,
Uyeda, Shikata, Ohno and Okada, 1983). The viroid suspensions
were blotted onto nitro-cellulose paper and dried. After pre-
hybridization, the nick-translated probe of the cloned cDNA
to HSV was denatured at 100°C for 10 minutes. Then the blots
were hybridized over night at 42°C, and autoradiographed.

The result of the spot hybridization indicated that the
cDNA to HSV was fairly well hybridized with CPFV as well as
with HSV in our experimental conditions. On the other hand,
cDNA to HSV did not hybridize with PSTV and CEV. One may
therefore assume that the sequence homology between HSV and
CPFV is very high. Further studies on the molecular hybridization of the viroids and the sequencing of CPFV are under
way.

VIII   REFERENCES

Erikson, R.L. (1969). Procedures for the purification of intermediate forms of viral RNA from RNA-virus infected cells. *In* "Fundamental techniques in Virology. " Academic Press, New York. pp 451-459.

Franklin, R.M. (1966). Purification and properties of the replicative intermediate of the RNA bacteriophage R 17. *Proc. Natl.Acad.Sci.USA.55* ,1504-1511.

Kojima, NM., Murai. M., and Shikata, E. (1983). Cytopathic changes in viroid-infected leaf tissues. *J. Fac. Agr. Hokkaido Univ. 61*, 219-223.

Loening, U.E. (1967). The fractionation of high-molecular-weight ribonucleic acid by polyacrylamide-gel electrophoresis. *Biochem.J.102*, 251-257.

Maniatis, T., and Efstratiadis, A. (1980). Fractionation of low molecular weight RNA or DNA in polyacrylamide gels containing 90% formamide or 7M urea. *In* "Methods in Enzymology." 65, 299-305. Academic Press,New York.

Momma, T., and Takahashi, T. (1982). Ultrastructure of hop stunt viroid-infected leaf tissue. *Phytopath. Z.104*, 211-221.

Ohno, T., Akiya, J., Higuchi, M., Okada, Y., Yoshikawa, N., Takahashi, T., and Hashimote, J. (1982). Purification and characterization of hop stunt viroid. *Virology 118*, 54-63.

Ohno, T., Takamatsu, N. Meshi, T., and Okada, Y. (1983). Hop stunt viroid: Molecular cloning and nucleotide sequence of the complete cDNA copy. *Nucleic Acid Res.* , 6185-6197.

Sasaki, M, Fukamizu, T., Yamamoto, K., Ozawa, T., Kagami, Y., and Shikata, E. (1981). Detection of HSV in the latent- infected hops by mass diagnosis and its application. *Ann. Phytopath.Soc. Japan 47*, 416 (abstr. in Japanese).

Sasaki, M., Fukamizu, T., Yamamoto, K., Ozawa, T., Kagami, Y. (1982). Biological detection of hop stunt viroid. Rept. Grant-in-Aid for Co-operative Res. A. 1981, Ministry of Education, Japan. pp.1-7. (In Japanese).

Sasaki, M., Sano, T., and Shikata, E. (1980). Relation of hop stunt viroid and other viroids, and mass diagnosis of hop stunt disease. *Ann. Phytopath. Soc. Japan 46* 418. (abstr. in Japanese).

Sasaki, M., and Shikata, E. (1977a). Studies on the host range of hop stunt disease in Japan. *Proc. Japan Acad. 53B*, 103-108.

Sasaki, M., and Shikata, E. (1977b). On some properties of hop stunt disease agent, a viroid. *Proc. Japan Acad. 53B*, 109-112.

Sasaki, M., and Shikata, E. (1978a) Studies on hop stunt disease I. Host range. *Ann.Phytopath.Soc.Japan 44*, 465-477. (in Japanese with English summary).

Sasaki, M., and Shikata, E. (1978b). Studies on hop stunt disease II. Properties of causal agent, a viroid. *Ann. Phytopath. Soc. Japan 44*, 570-577.

Sasaki, M., and Shikata, E. (1978c). Studies on hop stunt disease I. Host range. *Rept. Res. Lab. Kirin Brewery Co. Ltd. No. 21*, 27-39

Sasaki, M., and Shikata, E. (1978d). Studies on hop stunt disease II. Properties of the causal agent, a viroid. *Rept. Res. Lab. Kirin Brewery Co. Ltd. No. 21*, 41-48.

Sasaki, M., and Shikata, E. (1980). Hop stunt disease, a new viroid disease occurring in Japan. *Rev. Plant Protect. Res. 13*, 97-113.

Randles, J.W., and Hatta, T. (1979). Circularity of the ribonucleic acids associated with cadang-cadang disease. *Virology 96*, 47-53.

Raymer, W.B., and Diener, T.O. (1969). Potato spindle tuber viroid: A plant virus with properties of a free nucleic acid. I. Assay, extraction and concentration. *Virology 137*, 343-350.

Sänger, H.L.,Klots, G., Riesner, D., Gross, H.J., and Klein-schmidt, A.K. (1976). Viroids are single-stranded covalently closed circular RNA molecules existing as highly base-paired rod-like structures. *Proc. Natl. Acad. Sci. U.S.A. 73*, 3852-3856.

Sänger, H.L., Ramm, K., Domdey, H., Gross, H.J. Henco, K., and Riesner, D. (1979). Conversion of circular viroid molecules to linear strands. *FEBS letters 99*, 117-122.

Sano, T., Sasaki, M., and Shikata, E. (1981). Comparative studies on hop stunt viroid, cucumber pale fruit viroid and potato spindle tuber viroid. *Ann. Phytopath. Soc. Japan 47* 599-605.

Sano. T., Uyeda, I., and Shikata, E. (1983). Comparative studies of hop stunt viroid and cucumber pale fruit viroid by polyacrylamide gel electrophoresis. Rept. Grant-in-Aid for Co-Operative Res. B, 1982, Ministry of Education, Japan, pp 26-36.

Sano, T., Uyeda, I., Shikata, E., Ohno, K., and Okada, Y. (1983). Molecular hybridization of cDNA to HSV and CPFV. *Abstr.Papers 6th Ann. Meet. Mol. Biol. Soc. Japan, Aug. 22-25, 1983, Sapporo*, p. 57.

Singh, A., and Sänger, H.L. (1976). Chromatographic behavior of the viroid of the exocorotis disease of citrus and the spindle tuber disease of potato. *Phytopath. Z. 87*, 143-160.

Sogo, J.M., Koller, T., and Diener, T.O. (1973). Potato spindle tuber viroid X. Visualization and size determination by electron microscopy. *Virology 55*, 70-80.

Takahashi, T., (1981). Evidence for viroid etiology of hop stunt disease. *Phytopath.Z 100*, 193-202.

Takahashi, T., and Takusari, H. (1979a). Detection of the causal agent associated with hop stunt disease in Japan. *Phytopath. Z. 95*, 6-11.

Takahashi, T. and Takusari, H. (1979b). Some factors affecting mechanical transmission of hop stunt disease agent. *Phytopath. Z. 96*, 352-360.

Takahashi, T., Yaguchi, S., Oikawa, S., and Kamita, N. (1982) Subcellular location of hop stunt viroid. *Phytopath. Z. 103*, 285-293.

Uyeda, I., Sano, and Shikata, E. (1982). Purification of cucumber pale fruit viroid. Rept. Grant-in-Aid for Co-operative Research A, 1981, Ministry of Education, Japan. pp 23-28. (in Japanese).

Uyeda, I., Sano. T., and Shikata, E. (1983). Purification of cucumber pale fruit viroid and hop stunt viroid. Rept. Grant-in-Aid for Co-operative Res. B, 1982, Ministry of Education, Japan. pp 13-25.

Van Dorst, H.J.M., and Peters, D. (1974). Some biological observations on pale fruit, a viroid-induced disease of cucumber. *Neth. J. Pl. Path. 80*, 85-96.

Yamamoto, H., Kagami, Y., Kurokawa, M., Nishimura, S., Kubo, S., Inoue, M., and Murayama, D. (1970). Studies on hop stunt disease. I. *Mem.Fac. Agr. Hokkaido Univ. 7*, 491-515. (in Japanese with English summary).

Yamamoto, H., Kagami, Y., Kurosawa, M., Nishimura, S., Ukawa, S.,and Kubo,S.(1973). Studies on hop stunt disease in Japan. *Rept. Res. Lab. Kirin Brewery Co. Ltd. 16*, 49-62

Yoshikawa,N., and Takahashi,T., (1982). Purification of hop stunt viroid. *Ann. Phytopath.Soc. Japan 48*, 182-191.

Chapter 6

VIROIDS AND VIROID DISEASES IN CHINA

Tien Po

Institute of Microbiology
Academia Sinica
Beijing, People's Republic of China

INTRODUCTION

Viroids, the smallest known agents of infectious disease, were discovered in China in 1972 (Tien, 1973). Surveys and investigations of viroid diseases were started at that time and have continued since. Being disease-causing agents of several economically important crops, viroids have become exceedingly important objects in agricultural and molecular biological research. A recent review of the literature on viroids has appeared in Chinese (Tien and Xia, 1982). The present article is concerned chiefly with studies of viroids and viroid diseases in China.

II. OCCURRENCE OF WELL KNOWN VIROIDS IN CHINA

A. Potato spindle tuber viroid (PSTV): The disease caused by PSTV occurs in the potato-growing regions of

SUBVIRAL PATHOGENS
OF PLANTS AND ANIMALS:
VIROIDS AND PRIONS

Copyright © 1985 by Academic Press, Inc.
All rights of reproduction in any form reserved.
ISBN 0-12-470230-9

northern, northeastern and northwestern China, such as
Heilungkang, Inner Mongolia and Chinghai. PSTV was identified
by means of indicator plants and polyacrylamide gel electrophoresis. When PSTV isolated from diseased potato was inoculated onto Rutgers tomato and *Scopolia sinensis,* it caused
typical epinasty in the former and local lesions in the
later. The RNA samples extracted from diseased tomato leaves
and layered on 5% polyacrylamide gel in electrophoresis,
revealed the presence of an infective specific PSTV band
(Tien and Chang, 1979).

Decreases of tuber yield by PSTV depend on the cultivars used. Datong 8, New Keshan (local cultivars), Saco and
Schwalbe were susceptible,while Red Warba,Chippewa, Katahdin,
Kennbec and Apta were less susceptible. The disease incidence
of Datong 8 was above 80% and the tuber yield was decreased
by 60-70%. One should be extremely careful when using true
seeds as planting materials because PSTV produces a high
proportion of infected seed from infected plants. For example
the percentage of seed transmission of PSTV in Cultivar Datong 8 was 15-20% in the first season (Tien *et al.,* 1982).

The control measure used today in China is to produce
virus and viroid-free potato stocks (Tao and Tien, 1978). A
number of potato stock farms have been set up in several
provinces. Indexing of seed stocks on Rutgers tomato and by
polyacrylamide gel electrophoresis has been used for seed in-
spection. Using E. coli cloned ^{32}P-PSTV-cDNA provided by Dr.
L.F. Salazar of International Potato Center, Lima, Peru, as
a probe, the presence of PSTV in Beijing was confirmed by
molecular hybridization analysis in the form of a dot blot.

B.   Citrus exocortis viroid (CEV): Citrus exocortis
disease, which is thought to have been introduced from abroad
prior to 1950, has now been found in Sichuan, Guangxi, Hunan
and Guangdong provinces. Zhao *et al.,* (1983) reported indexing for the infection of CEV using grafting onto the sensitive Etrog Citron Arizona 861-S1. Seventeen of the 19 cultivars introduced from America, Morocco, Albania and Cuba were
infected with CEV. Seedling propagations of three of these
cultivars and of the Satsuma introduced from Japan were free
of CEV. Six of the 27 native cultivars of sweet orange and
mandarin were infected. Native sweet orange and six sources
of Anliucheng were also all infected.

The existence of CEV in China has also been demonstrated
by infection tests and polyacrylamide gel electrophoresis.
Sap or RNA extracted from diseased or healthy citrus was
dropped on to the surface of petiole excisions as on the
stem. The dropped positions were then punctured with needles.
The top leaves of *Gynura aurantiaca* inoculated with inocula

from diseased plant became small and epinasty and severe syndrome appeared on new leaves. On the contrary, the *G. aurantiaca* inoculated with extracts from a healthy plant grew normally. The nucleic acid from diseased citrus gave a significant CEV band on the polyacrylamide gel electrophoresis (Tien *et al.*, 1979; Mi *et al.*, 1983).

Zhao *et al.*, (1983) recommended grafting buds from healthy trees as a control measure against citrus exocortis. Therefore, a faster and more reliable means of detecting CEV infection became necessary. The ^{32}P-cDNA probes of CEV were synthesized by two different methods.

1) Using recombinant M_{13} phage containing CEV fragment inserts of the appropriate polarity (provided by Dr. Symons and Haseloff of Department of Biochemistry, Adelaide University, Australia) to produce a single stranded ^{32}P-cDNA probe.

2) Synthesizing the ^{32}P-cDNA with CEV for template and oligo (dT) as a primer. The CEV samples from Sichuan and Hunan provinces were spotted to the nitrocellulose filter and hybridized with a ^{32}P-CEV-cDNA probe. The autoradiogram showed a strong hybridization spot with the diseased samples, but not with the healthy samples. (Chang *et al.*,1983).

C. Chrysanthemum stunt viroid (CSV): Symptoms similar to that of CSV were observed on chrysanthemum in Beijing and Guangzhou. The existence of CSV in China has been demonstrated through infection tests, molecular hybridization analysis using complementary DNA and polyacrylamide gel electrophoresis.

Using ^{3}H-CSV-cDNA provided by Dr. P. Palukaitis and J. Randles of the University of Adelaide, Australia as a probe, we have detected the presence of CSV. Six samples from diseased plants hybridized with ^{3}H-CSV-cDNA with a hybridization ratio of more than 70%, against 10% for samples from healthy plants (Table 1). (Chen *et al.*, 1982).

III. EFFECT OF ACTINOMYCIN D, GIBBRELLIC ACID AND
NUTRIENT ELEMENTS ON VIROID SYNTHESIS AND
SYMPTOM EXPRESSION

A. Effect of actinomycin D and gibberellic acid on CSV synthesis: Leaves from healthy or CSV-infected chrysanthemum were incubated in solutions containing ^{3}H-uridine. Extraction of nucleic acid and analysis by polyacrylamide gel electrophoresis were performed according to the methods of Palukaitis and Symons (1980). Viroid infection caused reduction of cellular DNA,7S RNA, 5S RNA and tRNA synthesis by about 40%. The leaves were pretreated with actinomycin D or gibberellic acid (GA). AMD at a concentration of 50 μg/g leaves inhibited

Table 1.
Hybridization Ratio of Nucleic Acid Extracts From Stunted
and Healthy Chrysanthemum Leaves with ^{3}H–CSV–cDNA

Samples		Plus nuclease S_1	Without nuclease S_1	Hybridization Percentage(%)
		cpm		
	CD–1	424	430	99
	CD–2	370	525	70
Diseased	CD–3	343	444	77
leaves	CD–4	311	416	75
	CD–5	301	340	72
	CD–6	235	256	92
Healthy	CH–1	35	342	10
leaves	CH–2	40	342	12
Purified 35) as a standard	CSV(V	201	215	93

synthesis of host DNA, 7S RNA and 5S RNA by 79%, 43% and 70%, respectively, but synthesis of viroid and tRNA were not inhibited. With 100 μg/g leaves AMD, syntheses of the DNA, 7S RNA, 5S RNA and tRNA were inhibited by 75%, 64%, 86% and 43%, respectively, but viroid synthesis was reduced only by 15%. GA (60 μg/g leaves) did not increase viroid synthesis but increased synthesis of cellular DNA by 300% and 7S RNA, 5S RNA and tRNA by 10-30% in CSV-infected leaves. These results suggest that viroid synthesis is unlikely to be mediated through a DNA intermediate. Therefore, the author assumes a more reasonable scheme of RNA directed RNA synthesis in viroid replication. (Xia, 1981)(Table 2).

B. Effect of nutrient elements on symptom expression of viroid: Lee & Singh (1972) and Singh *et al.*, (1974)studied the effect of manganese on symptoms induced by PSTV in tomato (cultivar Allerfrüheste Freiland) and *Scopolia sinensis*. The effect of boron, cobalt, copper, ferric, manganese and zinc on symptoms of PSTV in Rutgers tomato and of CEV in Gynura have been investigated in China since 1980. Tomato or Gynura plants were grown in soil or sand cultures. Increase of Mn, Zn and B in the soil (by watering 100 μg/ml solution) strengthened stunting and epinasty symptoms, while increase of Fe and Cu weakened the symptoms (Fig. 1). Fe was the most effective element for inhibiting the expression of viroid symptoms.At a concentration of 50-100 μg/ml , the symptoms of PSTV in Rutgers tomato and of CEV in Gynura were inhibited. The results

Table 2. Effect of actinomycin D (AMD) and gibberellic acid (GA) on incorporation of ^{3}H-Uridine into nucleic acids and CSV in leaf tissues of chrysanthemum.(Xia, Y.N. 1981)

Treatment	Total nucleic acids	cpm DNA	CSV	7S RNA	5S RNA	tRNA
Healthy	115998	56751	---	941	6061	38397
CSV-infected	65342	30368	264	549	3992	15933
Decrease (%)	43.7	46.5	---	42.1	34.1	49.1
Medium AMD 50μg/ g tissue	149660 59876	66384 18017	--- ---	1240 676	7937 1973	52230 31260
Decrease (%)	60.0	72.9	---	45.5	25.1	40.1
Medium AMD 50μg /g tissue	41115 30573	13921 2888	140 210	338 191	2585 767	19654 24360
Decrease (%) AMD 100μg /g tissue	25.6 16823	79.2 3388	118	43.5 122	70.3 359	11188
Decrease (%)	59.8	75.7	15.7	64.0	86.1	43.1
Medium GA 60 μg /g tissue	82336 97026	47117 51630	--- ---	641 859	4192 4437	24527 28917
Increase (%)	17.8	9.6	---	34.0	5.8	17.9
Medium GA 60μg /g tissue	26514 42088	4465 18020	205 200	180 238	1574 1970	16024 17751
Increase	58.7	303.6		32.2	25.2	10.8

of viroid assay by polyacrylamide gel electrophoresis indicated that the symptomless plants treated by increasing Fe, Cu or Co contained about the same amount of viroids as did the untreated ones. (Tien, *et al.*, 1983).

IV.
VIROID-LIKE RNAs ASSOCIATED WITH
BURDOCK STUNT DISEASE

A.   The burdock stunt disease: The burdock, *Arctium tomentosa* and *A. lappa,* which are grown as biennial or perennial medicinal plants in Beijing, are afflicted with burdock stunt disease (BSD). The symptoms of this disease involve plant stunting and leaf mottling. The diseased plant cannot elongate and produce a head. Therefore no seeds can be ob-

Figure 1. Effect of nutrient elements on symptom expression of viroids. A-E, PSTV on Rutgers tomato (A, increasing Mn; B, increasing B; C, increasing Zn; D, increasing Cu; E, increasing Fe). Right, PSTV-infected. Middle, PSTV-infected and increasing an element. Left, Healthy and increasing an element. F, CEV on Gynura (a, Healthy; b, CEV-infected; c, CEV-infected and increasing Mn; d, CEV-infected and increasing Fe; e, CEV-infected and increasing Mn + Fe.

tained. Neither virus-like particles nor mycoplasma-like organisms have been detected in the extracts and thin sections of diseased leaves, but two disease-specific RNAs, RNA-1 or RNA-2 were found to be associated with BSD. Since 1980 transmission tests have been conducted which depended for transmission on aphids and mechanical inoculation. Some of the mechanically inoculated burdock seedlings developed ambiguous symptoms of BSD, but when nucleic acids were extracted from the leaves developing symptoms,and subjected to electrophoresis, on analytical gels, no specific bands could be detected. On *Gynura aurantiaca* and Rutgers tomato no definite symptoms developed. Further transmission studies are necessary. (Chen *et al.*, 1982).

B. Specific low-molecular weight RNAs associated with BSD. Nucleic acids were extracted from either diseased or healthy leaf tissue by three methods (Chen *et al.*, 1983). The resultant preparation was subjected to 4-5% polyacrylamide gel electrophoresis. Two low-molecular weight RNA species were found by analytical non-denatured gel in preparations from diseased leaf tissues of *A. tomentosa* or *A. lappa* but not in preparations from healthy ones. The two bands, BSD RNA-1 and RNA-2 had an electrophoretic mobility between that of DNA and 5S RNA. The ratio of RNA-1 to RNA-2 varied with different batches of the sample. The electrophoretic mobility of *A. tomentosa* BSD RNA-1 was less than that of the *A. lappa* BSD RNA-1, while the mobilities of the two RNA-2 were the same.

The BSD RNAs are resistant to 20 µg/ml DNase I and 80 µg/ml DNase II, but sensitive to 20 µg/ml RNAase in low-ionic strength (0.01 x SSC). This indicates that the BSD RNAs are ribonucleic acids.

C. Purification and UV absorption of BSD RNAs: The semi-purified nucleic acids from diseased leaves were further purified by a cellulose CF-11 column and by preparative gel electrophoresis. In the analysis of purified BSD RNA-1 or RNA-2 on 4-5% polyacrylamide gel only a single nucleic acid component was observed. (Chen *et al.*, 1983 a,b).

Although no systematic investigation on the yields of BSD RNAs from diseased leaves was done, the yields of BSD RNAs were obviously higher than those of other viroids. For example, from 200g of leaves, about 100 g purified BSD RNA-1 was obtained.

For detection of UV absorption spectra, the BSD RNA-1 or RNA-2 was dissolved in 0.01 x SSC or in 0.01M sodium cacodylate. Fig. 2 shows UV absorption spectra for BSD RNA-1 and RNA-2. From this figure, it follows that, purified BSD RNA-1 or RNA-2 had typical nucleic acid spectra. The maximum absorbance of BSD RNA-1 is 260 nm and the minimum is 230 nm. The maximum of BSD RNA-2 is 259 nm and the minimum is 229 nm.

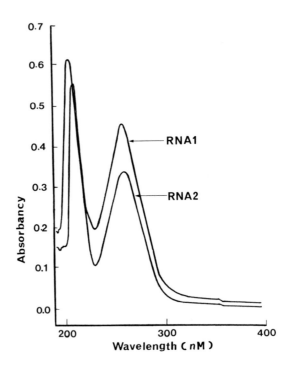

Figure 2. UV absorption spectra of purified BSD RNA-1 and
RNA-2 in 0.01M sodium cacodylate, 0.1M NaCl and 1mM EDTA,
pH 6.8.

   D. Occurence of BSD RNA-1 and RNA-2 in separate plants:
RNA extracted from individual diseases plants gave only one
specific viroid-like RNA, RNA-1 or RNA-2. No plants have yet
been detected to contain both. No variation whatsoever in
the electrophoretic mobility was observed for BSD RNA-1 or
RNA-2 even over a period of two and half years. (Table 3)
   Diseased plants, which were derived from specific paren-
tal plants, contained the same species of BSD RNSs as the
original.
   The occurence of BSD RNA-1 and RNA-2 in separate plants
is obviously different from that of the usual viroids which
have only one viroid RNA component. Imperial *et al.*, (1981)
reported that RNAs of coconut cadang-cadang (ccRNAs) have at
least four components. The variation in electrophoretic mobility of the ccRNAs was observed in gels. The fast and slow
forms can occur separately or together in the same plants and
their occurence is related to the stage of disease development in coconut palms. In the case of the RNAs of avocado
sunblotch viroid (ASBV) the extracts of leaf tissue contained
an oligometric series of RNAs which are integral multiples of
the unit length of ASBV. (Bruening *et al.*, 1982). The BSD
RNAs are also different from ccRNAs and ASBV RNAs.

Table 3. Occurrence in separate plants of the viroid-like RNA 1 and 2 associated with burdock stunt disease.

Number of burdock plants	Viroid-like RNA	Detected in the year			
		1980	1981	1982	1983
1	RNA 1	+	+	Died	
	RNA 2	−	−		
2	RNA 1	−	−	Died	
	RNA 2	+	+		
3	RNA 1	−	−	Died	
	RNA 2	+	+		
4	RNA 1	+	+	+	
	RNA 2	−	−	−	
5	RNA 1	+	+	Died	
	RNA 2	−	−		
6	RNA 1	−	−	Undetected	
	RNA 2	+	+		
7	RNA 1	−	−	Undetected	
	RNA 2	+	+		
8	RNA 1	−	−	Undetected	
	RNA 2	+	+		
9	RNA 1	+	+	Undetected	
	RNA 2	−	−		
10	RNA 1	−	−	−	Undetected
	RNA 2	−	−	−	
11	RNA 1	−	−	−	Undetected
	RNA 2	−	−	−	

E. Tissue culture of diseased burdock leaves and ex-traction of BSD RNAs from the callus: The burdock leaves from healthy and diseased plants were cultured on solid MS media, calli were transferred to B-5 medium. The calli from diseased leaves developed and grew rather slowly as compared with those from the healthy ones. In the case of healthy leaves, one and half months after placing leaf pieces on MS medium, the callus tissues developed. After that newly formed callus tissue was transferred to new medium at intervals of 30-60 days, then transferred to B-5 medium. The calli grew exuberantly; they were white in color.

After two months in the case of diseased leaves, only a few of the leaf pieces developed small calli in MS medium. The growth of diseased calli was slow and showed a dark brown color.

Figure. 3 shows the polyacrylamide gel patterns of nucleic acids of calli from healthy and diseased(containing BSD RNA-1) leaves. The presence of BSD RNA-1 in diseased calli which had grown continously for 6-8 months was evidenced by the distinct bands of BSD RNA-1 in the gel. The migration of the specific bands of BSD RNA-1 from diseased calli was

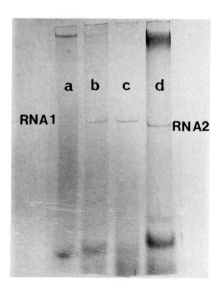

Figure 3. 5% polyacrylamide slab gel electrophoresis of nucleic acids from healthy burdock calli (a), diseased calli containing BSD RNA-1 (b), diseased leaves containing BSD RNA-1 (c) and diseased leaves containing BSD RNA-2 (d).

the same as that of BSD RNA-1 from the diseased leaves. No specific band was detected in the gel from healthy callus.

Our investigation on callus culture shows continous re-plication of BSD RNA-1 in permanent cell cultures of burdock over a period of eight months. This property is similar to other viroids. The replication of PSTV persisted through at least 14 subculture passages corresponding to a period of more than one year(Mühlbach *et al.*, 1981). The relative yield of BSD RNAs in the callus was so high, that RNA-1 extracted from 0.5 g calli could be seen clearly on the gel after it was stained. It is well known in the case of conventional plant viruses that during continous replications viruses are often eliminated from continously dividing meristematic tissues (Hollings, 1965). Thus, our investigations provided addition-al evidence of fundamental differences between the mechanisms of replication of conventional plant viruses and viroid RNA.

The calli from our leaf pieces of healthy plant grew rather rapidly as compared with those from diseased ones; This is apparently different from the calli of PSTV.(Mühlbach *et al.*, 1981).

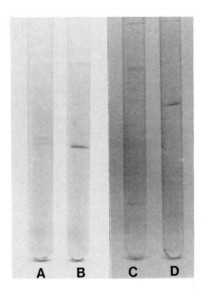

Figure 4. 4% polyacrylamide tuber gel electrophoresis patterns of BSD RNA-1 under denaturing conditions. A and C,
after treatment with 50% formamide at 80°C for 1 min. B
and D, without treatment.

  F. Preliminary studies on structure of BSD RNAs: Numerous assays demonstrate that BSD RNAs have properties intermediate between those of double-stranded RNA (dsRNA) and
single-stranded RNA(ssRNA). They are resistant to S_1 nuclease
and found to be more resistant to pancreatic RNase treatment
in buffers of high ionic strength (2.5 x SSC) as would be
expected for the known viroids with a high degree of base-
pairing. BSD RNSs elute from cellulose CF_{11} columns with the
ssRNAs (14% ethanol fraction).

  On 4% polyacrylamide gels containing 7M urea, after the
treatment with 50% deionizated formamide at 80°C for 1 min,
BSD RNA-1 was separated into two to five bands on the gels.
Among these bands the slowest migrating band had the same
electrophoresis mobility as in the sister gels, in which a
similar sample had been subjected, but without formamide
treatment. Other bands migrated more slowly (Fig. 4).

  The multiple bands of BSD RNAs occurred under denaturing
conditions. This may be accounted for by the fact that during

denaturing and renaturing processes multiple state intermediates were formed. (Sänger *et al.*, 1976).

Denatured BSD RNA-1 and RNA-2 by 90-95% formamide were
spread, stained, shadowed and observed by electron microscopy
as described by Randles and Hatta (1980). Circular molecules
were observed in both BSD RNA-1 and RNA-2, respectively.
This and other experiments suggest that BSD RNA-1 and RNA-2
have single-stranded covalently closed circular structures.

One of the most interesting questions centers around the
possible existence of viroids or viroid-like pathogens as
causative agents of certain unconventional diseases of other
forms of life, including microbes. Until now, no studies
have been undertaken to study this possibility.

V. CONCLUSIONS

Viroid diseases are of great importance to agriculture,
horticulture and the culture of medicinal plants in China,
because of their potential threat to crop plants for the
economically important losses they may cause. Three viroids
and one viroid-like pathogen have ben found in China, and
other plant diseases may also be recognized as being of viroid
origin. Potato spindle tuber viroid (PSTV), citrus exocortis
viroid (CEV), chrysanthemum stunt viroid (CSV)and the viroid-
like RNAs associated with burdock stunt disease have been
studied in detail. The action of actinomycin D and gibberellic acid were tested on viroid synthesis and the results
indicated that viroid synthesis in unlikely to be mediated
through a DNA intermediate.

The effects of nutrient elements, such as manganese,
boron, cobalt, copper, iron, and zinc were tested on the
symptom expression of potato spindle tuber and citrus exocortis. It was found that Fe and Cu were most effective in
inhibiting viroid symptom expression, although the viroid
concentration in treated plants did not differ from that of
untreated ones.

The study of burdock stunt-affected plants revealed the
presence of two specific low molecular weight RNAs. Since
either one or the other, RNA-1 or RNA-2 viroid-like nucleic
acids, but never both together were detected in individual
plants, it was concluded that they represented separate
viroids, rather than two viroid components.

Burdock stunt-derived callus, grown in tissue culture
media, retained its viroid through 14 subcultures, indicating
a difference between the retention of viroids and lack of
retention of viruses in plant cells *in vitro*.

ACKNOWLEDGEMENTS

The author wishes to express sincere thanks to Prof. Dr. Lu S.I. for his invaluable help in writing this manuscript, to Drs. J. Randles, P. Palukaitis, J. Haseloff and L.F. Salazar for teaching him viroid techniques and to Prof. C.C. Cheo for his encouragement during the investigation.

REFERENCES

Bruening, G., Gould,A.R., Murphy, P.J.and Symons, K.H.(1982). Oligomers of avocado sunblotch viroid are found in infected avocado leaves. *FEBS Letters 148*, 71-78.

Chang, O.Y. and Liu, Y. (1983). Synthesis of complementary DNA of citrus exocortis viroid and their use for diagnosis. (submitted).

Chen, W., Tien, Y.C., Liu, Y., Peng, B., Xia, Y.N. and Tien P. (1982). Detection of chrysanthemum stunt viroid by molecular hybridization analysis and polyacrylamide gel electrophoresis. *Kexue Tongbao 27*, 660-664.

Chen, W., Tien, P., Zhu, Y.X. and Liu, Y. (1982). Asociation of two viroid-like RNAs with stunting disease of burdock: I. Isolation and properties of anomalous RNAs. *Acta Microbiologica Sinica 22*, 241-247.

Chen, W., Tien, P., Yang, X.C., Zhu, Y.X. and Sun, G.D. (1983) Occurence of viroid-like RNA-1 and RNA-2 in separate burdock plants and their preliminary characterization. (submitted for publication).

Chen, W., Tien, P., Zhu, Y.X. and Liu, Y. (1983). Viroid-like RNAs associated with burdock stunt disease. *J. Gen. Virol. 64*, 409-414.

Editorial Committee, (1981). "Diseases and pests of crops in China. 2, 1804-1805. Agriculture Press, Beijing.

Hollings,M. (1965). Disease control through virus-free stock. *Annu. Rev. Phytopathol. 3*, 367-396.

Imperial, J.S., Rodrigues, J.B. and Randles, J.M. (1981). Variation in the viroid-like RNA associated with cadangcadang disease: evidence for an increase in molecular weight with disease progress. *J.Gen.Virol. 56*, 77-85.

Lee, C.R., and Singh, R.P. (1972). Enhancement of diagnostic symptoms of potato spindle tuber virus by manganese. *Phytopathology 62*, 516-520.

Mi, K.Y., Yong, Y.P. Yong,P., Xu, Y.Z., Un, M.N. and Liu, Y. (1983). The isolation and preliminary identification of citrus exocortis in China. *Acta Virologica Sinica* (in press).

Mühlbach, H.P. and Sänger, H.L. (1981). Continuous replication of potato spindle tuber viroid in permanent cell-culture of potato and tomato. *Biosci. Rep.1*, 79-87.

Palukaitis, P. and Symons, R.H. (1980). Purification and characterization of circular form of chrysanthemum stunt viroid. *J.Gen.Virol. 46*, 477-489.

Randles, J.W. and Hatta, T. (1979). Circularity of the ribonucleic acids associated with cadang-cadang disease. *Virology 96*, 47-53.

Sänger, H. L., Riesner, K.G., Gross, H.J. and Kleinschmidt, A.K. (1976). Viroids are single stranded covalently closed circular RNA molecules existing as highly basepaired rod like structure. *Proc.Natl.Acad.Sci. U.S.A. 73*, 3852-3856.

Singh, R.P., Lee C.R. and Clark M.C. (1974). Manganese effect on the local lesion symptom of potato spindle tuber virus in *Scopolia sinensis. Phytopathology 64*, 1015-1018.

Tien, P. (1973). The discovery of viroid. *Applied Microbiology 1973*, 1-4.

Tien, P. and Chang, X.H. (1979). Surveys and identification of viroids in China. *Abstracts Annu.Meeting Chinese Soc. Microbiol.*, 95-96.

Tien, P., Chang, X.H. and Xia, Y.N. (1982). Preliminary studies of potato spindle tuber viroid in China. *Acta Virologica Sinica 1*, 119-122.

Tien, P. and Xia, Y.N. (1982). Advances and prospects of viroid research. *Acta Virologica Sinica 2*, 5-14.

Tien, P.,Zhao, J.Y., Xia,Y.N. and Wang, Y.X. (1983). Effects of nutrient elements on symptom expression of viroids. (submitted for publication).

Xia, Y.N. (1981). The relationship between chrysanthemum stunt viroid synthesis and host DNA. Ph.D. Thesis.

Zhao, X.Y., Jiang, Y.H., Qiu, Z.S. and Su, W.F. (1983). Indexing for the infection of citrus exocortis viroid. *Acta Phytopath. Sinica* (in press).

Chapter 7

ELIMINATION OF POTATO SPINDLE TUBER VIROID
FROM POTATO BY COLD TREATMENT
AND MERISTEM CULTURE

L. F. Salazar
L. Schilde-Rentschler
R. Lizarraga

The International Potato Center
Apartado 5969
Lima, Peru

I. INTRODUCTION

The potato spindle tuber disease has been recognized as a serious threat for potato production since 1922 (Schultz and Folsom, 1923) but the nature of the pathogenic agent, the potato spindle tuber viroid (PSTV), remained obscure for many years (Diener, 1979; Diener and Raymer, 1969). Spindliness and uprightness of vines, more erect and often somewhat darker green leaves than those on healthy plants, and spindling of tubers were characteristic symptoms on potato that helped to identify the disease (Schultz and Folsom 1923). However, it is now well known that symptoms vary considerably depending on the potato cultivar and on environmental conditions (Diener and Raymer, 1971).

PSTV is known to be transmitted primarily by foliar or mechanical contact (Merriam and Bonde, 1954) or through the

SUBVIRAL PATHOGENS
OF PLANTS AND ANIMALS:
VIROIDS AND PRIONS

Copyright © 1985 by Academic Press, Inc.
All rights of reproduction in any form reserved.
ISBN 0-12-470230-9

seed of many of its hosts (Singh, 1966).

Its ease of transmission makes PSTV spread rapidly through valuable germplasm during stock multiplication and handling of plants, and, therefore, becomes of great concern to seed production programs, genetic resources' centers, and breeding programs around the world.

Yield depression can be dramatic depending on the susceptibility of the cultivars and environmental conditions prevailing during the growing period. Yield reductions amounting to 64% were obtained in a crop totally infected with a severe strain whereas yield reductions up to 24% were obtained with mild strains (Singh *et al*, 1971).

The most effective measure to control PSTV on potatoes relies on the production of "seed" stocks free of PSTV (Bonde and Merriam, 1951; Diener, 1979). However, development of nuclear potato stocks free of PSTV was in the past limited by two factors:

a)   Non-existence of sensitive diagnostic methods suitable for large scale application.

b)   lack of an effective method of eliminating PSTV from infected cultivars.

The relatively recent development of electrophoresis in polyacrylamide gels (Morris and Wright, 1975; Pfannenstiel *et al.*, 1980) and the nucleic acid hybridization technique (Owens and Diener, 1981) have provided us with sensitive tools for diagnosing infections; however, the production of PSTV-free cultivars or clones remained an unsolved question since procedures effective in eradicating viruses e.g. thermotherapy followed by meristem culture, proved to be ineffective in eradicating PSTV (Stace-Smith and Mellor, 1970).

II.   EARLY ATTEMPTS TO ERADICATE PSTV

In spite of its importance, eradication of PSTV has only been attempted in few occasions. This situation may have resulted from the scarcity of knowledge on the properties of the causal agent in the past and on the difficulty of diagnosing infections. A rather similar situation is found with other viroid-incited diseases although Hollings and Kassanis (1957) reported "cure" of Chrysanthemum plants infected with the "English stunt" isolate (Chrysanthemum stunt viroid) in "minicuttings" of plants grown at 37°C for 4 weeks. Heat treatment followed by meristem culture allowed Hollings and Stone (1970) to obtain only two healthy plants from 139 that developed.

Goss (1931) claimed eradication of PSTV from infected tuber "plugs" heated at 65°C before grafting them to healthy tubers. These results, however, might have been due to unsuccessful transmission of PSTV by tuber grafting. Fernow *et al.* (1962) also attempted eradication of PSTV from infected tubers while trying to eliminate potato leafroll virus by heat treatment. They subjected tubers of nine infected cultivars to 35°C for varying periods but PSTV survived the 39 days treatment. On the contrary, a similar treatment eliminated potato leafroll virus.

Stace-Smith and Mellor (1970) claimed that a severe strain of PSTV was eradicated by *in vitro* culture of axillary buds excised from PSTV-infected plants and treated to air temperatures between 33 to 36°C. However, their percentage of eradication was very low since only four plants out of 66 that developed were free of the severe strain, although all were infected with a mild strain. Subsequent similar treatment of one of such plants infected with the mild strain revealed that only six plants of 248 were free from both mild and severe strains.

III. EFFECT OF TEMPERATURE AND LIGHT INTENSITY ON THE REPLICATION OF PSTV

Early work on the detection of the viroid suggested that temperature affected PSTV replication and accumulation in plant tissues. Many researchers found it necessary to grow infected potato plants under high temperature regimes in order to obtain "rich" inoculum or have stronger and more rapid symptom development (Goss and Peltier, 1925; Goss, 1930; Gratz and Schultz, 1931). Raymer and O'Brien (1962) also demonstrated that development of symptoms on tomatoes required only 10 days under greenhouse conditions during early fall whereas 42 days or more were needed during winter months. More detailed work by Sänger and Ramm (1975) clearly demonstrated the effect of temperature on accumulation of PSTV in the foliage of infected tomato. Their experiments showed that PSTV-RNA starts to accumulate in concentrations descernible in gels as UV-absorbing peaks only at temperatures above 24°C and that above 30°C PSTV-RNA is synthesized at unusally high concentrations (Fig. 1). The recovered PSTV from tomato plants increased approximately 300-fold relative to the amount of t-RNA recovered when greenhouse temperatures were increased from 18-20°C to 30-32°C. Their work also implies that the time required for symptom development is related to the concentration of PSTV. The higher the concentration the shorter the time needed for symptom development. Reduction of incubation period at higher temperatures as has also been demonstrated with cucumber pale fruit (Van Dorst and Peters, 1974) in cucumbers and chrysanthemum chlorotic mottle viroid in chrysanthemum (Horst, 1975) suggests similarities among these viroids on temperature requirements for replica-

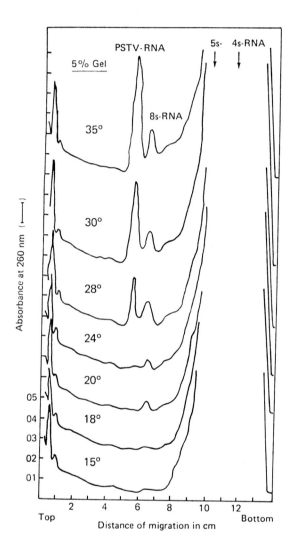

Figure 1. Electrophoretic analysis of a 5% polyacrylamide gel of "2 M LiCl-soluble RNA" from PSTV-infected tomatoes grown for four weeks at different temperatures. From Sänger and Ramm (1975). Reprinted by permission North-Holland Publishing Co., Amsterdam.

tion. Similar results with PSTV were obtained by Morris and Smith (1977) and Harris and Browning (1980). On the other hand, the fact that low temperature does not eliminate PSTV from living tisue but that it only affects its rate of multiplication was implicated by Lizárraga *et al.* (1980). They were unable to detect PSTV by inoculation to tomato when potato plantlets were kept at 5°C for varying periods, but viroid was present in the tissue as evidenced by their ability to readily detect PSTV when these plantlets were transferred to 25°C for one month (Table 1).

Table 1
Effect of Temperature on Detection of Potato
Spindle Tuber Viroid
(PSTV)

Treatment[a]	Temperature (C)	Incubation Period(mo)	Ratio[b] (positive sample/total sample tested)
A	30/36	1	8/8
B	24	1	8/8
C	5	3	0/8
D	5	6	0/8
E	(5)25	(3)1	8/8

[a]Plantlets of clone BR 63.5 for all treatments were obtained from nodal cuttings infected with a severe strain of PSTV. For treatment E, nodal cuttings were obtained from negative plantlets of treatment D and grown to plants at 25°C for 1 month.
[b]Tests were carried out by inoculation onto tomatoes.
(From Lizarraga *et al.* ,1980. Phytopathology *70* :754-755).

Sänger and Ramm (1975) also suggested that illumination has an effect, although less pronounced than temperature, on the period of incubation and the severity of the disease symptoms. In plants grown under a constant greenhouse temperature of 20°C -22°C, incubation period and time required for symptom development of PSTV on tomato was reduced at an illumination of *c.* 36,000 lux daylength equivalent. Harris and Browning (1980) obtained similar results. This effect, however, was more dramatic with citrus exocortis viroid in *Gynura aurantiaca* than with PSTV on tomato.

The effect of high temperature and, less conspicuously, that of illumination explain why early attempts to eradicate PSTV from infected potato tubers or plants were not successful and it is rather surprising that under these conditions any success has been achieved.

The above research dealt only with the effect of temperature and illumination on viroid replication and in no case have those factors been related to their effect on the host. Any factor affecting host metabolism will undoubtedly cause an effect on viroid replication.

Since temperature is prominent among the major ecological variables that determine the natural distribution of plants (Berry and Björkman, 1980) one would expect to find plants with genotypic adaptation to lower temperatures. Potato is one of such plants. Because it originated in the cooler areas of the Andean region it shows optimum growth and tuber production at cool temperatures around 15-20°C during daytime with some variation depending on the genotype.

Almost all growth processes of potato plants are strongly affected by temperature e.g. photosynthesis, respiration (Lundegardh, 1949), chlorphyll synthesis or rRNA metabolism (Oslund *et al.*, 1972). Similarly, transport processes in the plant are also markedly temperature-dependent(Swanson, 1959). Some of these processes are reversible over a considerable range of temperatures (commonly 10 to 35°C) but exposures to temperatures below or above these limits may cause irreversible injury to the system.

Little information exists about the mechanisms by which growth processes in potato plants become affected by lower temperatures before chilling injury occurs. However, these will not be discussed further because they fall beyond the scope of the review.

IV.   LOW-TEMPERATURE TREATMENT AND MERISTEM CULTURE FOR ELIMINATION OF PSTV

As mentioned previously concentration of PSTV in plants appeared to increase at higher temperatures, consequently lower temperatures should cause the opposite effect. This corollary was the basis for the work of Lizárraga *et al.*, (1980) in their attempt to eradicate a severe strain of PSTV from infected potato. In a typical experiment they treated infected plants in four different ways to wit:

   a)   Growing infected plantlets in culture medium at 5-6°C under diffused light (500 lux) for six months.

   b)   Growing infected plantlets in culture medium at 25°C for two months under 1,500 lux light intensity.

   c)   Growing plants from infected tubers at 8°C and 5,000 lux 16 hr/day for four months.

   d)   Growing plants from infected tubers under normal greenhouse conditions (20-25°C and 12 hr daylight) for four months.

Meristems containing only apical domes without leaf primordia (herein called apical domes) were excised from

Table 2.
Elimination of a severe strain of potato spindle tuber viroid (PSTV) from infected potato by low-temperature treatment followed by meristem culture

Treatment	Temp. (°C)	Light Intensity (lux)	Incubation Period (mo)	Ratio (PSTV-free plants/total plants)
A	5-6	500	6	7/13 (53%)
B	25	1,500	2	0/16 (0)
C	8	5,000	4	5/17 (30%)
D	22	5,000	4	0/16 (0)

Adapted from: Lizárraga *et al.* 1980. Phytopathology *70* 754-755.

plants of above treatments and calli developed in medium N#6 of Kao and Michayluk (1975). These were transferred to a liquid medium that contained the inorganic salts and vitamin components of the medium of Murashige and Skoog (1962) and the various hormonal supplements developed by Roca *et al.* (1978) for differentiation of multiple shoots in shake culture. Plantlets that developed were transferred to pots and grown under conditions suitable for PSTV replication (25 ± 2°C and normal daylength) and tested for PSTV infection by inoculation to tomatoes (Yang and Hooker, 1977) checked by electrophoresis. Potato plants were allowed to produce tubers which were then sprouted, planted and retested for PSTV.

The results of this experiment appear in Table 2. Seven out of 13 plants in treatment A (5-6°C) and 5 out of 17 in treatment C (8°C) were viroid-free whereas no viroid-free plants were obtained in plants or tubers grown at 25° or 22°C. Since plants were tested in two generations by a combination of the two most reliable methods of detection at that time Lizárraga *et al.* felt that they were indeed free of PSTV. Furthermore, two of such free plants were also tested by Drs. R.A. Owens and T. O. Diener at Beltsville, USA by the nucleic acid spot hybridization (Owens and Diener, 1981) and freedom from PSTV was confirmed. The above results indicate clearly that PSTV is indeed efficiently eliminated from infected tissue by a combination of cold treatment and meristem culture.

A. Effect of temperature and incubation period: The above experiments of Lizárraga *et al.* (1980) revealed that 5-6°C and 8°C for 6 and 4 months, respectively, were effective for PSTV eradication whereas 22°C or 25°C did not eliminate the viroid. In a second experiment Lizárraga *et al.* (1982)

found that potato plants grew better and faster at 10°C than
at 8°C and the percentage of eradication was still high. As
a compromise this new temperature treatment was preferred
since sprouting of tubers and growing of potato plants was
more likely to proceed at higher rates. No detailed experiments have been carried out to determine even higher temperatures and incubation periods for successful eradication of
PSTV. Should efficiency of PSTV eradication remain the same,
we can assume that an increase in temperature will induce
more rapid growth of potato and, therefore, incubation periods
will need to be accordingly reduced.

    B.   Effect of size of explant (PSTV free plantlets ex-
cised from PSTV infected plants): The work of Stace-Smith and
Mellor (1980) implied that the size of the apical tissue
excised was one factor favoring eradication since the viroid-
free plantlets they obtained were derived from the smallest
excised axillary buds. However, Hollings and Stone (1970)
attempting eradication of Chrysanthemum stunt did not find any
correlation between the size of tissue excised and eradication of the viroid. Further work of Lizárraga *et al.* (1982)
clearly showed that eradication of PSTV was higher in the
smaller tissue sections. In their experiments, apical domes
(around 0.1 mm long), meristem tips consisting of apical dome
plus 1 or 2 leaf primordia and shoot tips containing in addition 2-3 leaflets (Quak, 1977) (see Fig.3) from PSTV-infected
plants grown at 10°C were compared for efficacy in viroid
eradication and regeneration of explants. As seen in Fig. 2,

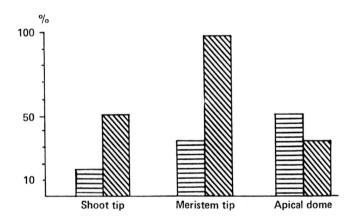

Figure 2. Comparison of efficiency of eradication three explant sizes from infected plants after low-temperature treatment (10°C) (▤), and regeneration onto plantlets (▨).
(Adapted from Lizarraga et al. [1982].)

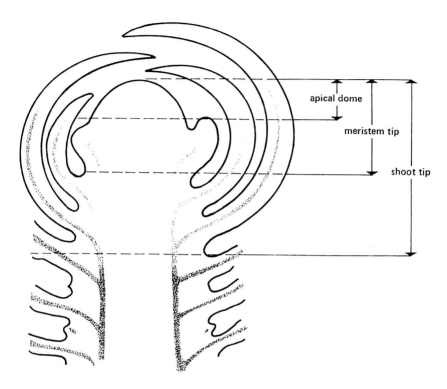

Figure 3. A diagrammatic representation of uppermost shoot portion from a potato plant showing vascular connections and explant's constitution. Ve, vascular elements; VS, vascular system; Lp, leaf primordium; and Lf, leaflet.

higher percentage of eradication was obtained from apical domes, followed by meristems and in lower percentage from shoot tips. The difference in elimination of PSTV appears to be in close correlation to the stage of organization of vascular tissue in these three types of apical tissue. On the contrary, regeneration of plants is more easily accomplished in shoot tips than in meristems or apical domes although in the experiment of Lizárraga *et al.* (1982) contamination of shoot tip cultures with bacteria prevented a clear observation of this relationship. The preferential localization of bacteria in vascular tissue makes shoot tip cultures prone to contamination. In spite of being more effective for eradicating PSTV, the authors do not recommend using apical domes since to induce growth of small meristematic tissue an enriched culture medium leading to callus formation has to be used. This procedure may induce genetic variation in plants

(D'Amato, 1975). Furthermore, it is difficult to regenerate plants from callus in some genotypes.

C. The combined effect of temperature and meristem culture: The effect of temperature on the overall multiplication and distribution of PSTV in the plant cannot be explained as a single event. It rather seems to affect some specific processes in viroid multiplication perhaps with different intensity. The processes for which some evidence appears to exist are replication, long-distance movement and cell to cell movement.

The mechanism by which high temperature preferentially increases PSTV replication is not known and will not probable be elucidated before the mechanism of viroid replication is fully understood. At this stage, we can only adhere to Sänger and Ramm's (1975) speculation, " that this behavior might be related to some regulatory mechanism acting at higher temperatures in favor of viroid-RNA replication". Conversely, at lower temperatures this mechanism, whatever its nature, is impaired reducing or stopping viroid replication. Long distance translocation of viroid-RNA more probably occurs via phloem tissue as is the case for most plant viruses (Helms and Wardlaw, 1976; Bennet,1940). Translocation in the phloem bundle is the first process affected at chilling temperatures (below 10°C for most plants) probably due to physical blockage of sieve plates (Giaquinta and Geiger, 1973). As virus translocation follows the directional nature of protoplasmic streaming in the phloem bundle (Worley, 1965) the velocity of viroid translocation will be consequently reduced or stopped as a consequence of a reduced transport system in the plant.

Viroid synthesized in the cell has to reach the phloem for fast distribution. This is possible by cell to cell movement which is probably due to passive transport by diffusion and by protoplasmic streaming. As in long-distance transport reduction of translocation velocity may be related to lower temperature. In addition, passage of viroid-RNA through plasmodesmata may be related to the permeability of those membranes which show a strong temperature dependence.

Cell to cell movement is particularly important to explain slow or no invasion of PSTV in meristematic cells since no phloem elements are found in apical domes and phloem elements disconnected from the rest of the plant vascular system are present in meristem tips. Larger portions of apical tissue (like shoot tips) already contain well-organized sieve tubes which are connected to the main vascular system of the plant.

It is extremely difficult to allocate an order of importance to each process contributing to successful eradication because all factors are interrelated. One can assume,however, that a reduced or ceased viroid replication is the key factor in eradication since translocation in the potato plant has been reported to proceed even at temperatures around freezing injury (0.2°C).

V.   CONCLUDING REMARKS

Even though low-temperature treatment followed by *in vitro* culture provides an extremely valuable procedure for eradication of PSTV we feel that on practical grounds the method will be more useful to free plants harboring PSTV from infection in situations where valuable cultivars on clones are universally infected under conditions of commercial plantings. Genetic resources' centers and breeding programs might use this method advantageously since only a few plants may constitute their source of valuable germplasm.

Although this procedure, or its principle, can also be used to free hosts other than potatoes from viroid infection, the unique situation of potato/PSTV in which the host is well adapted to stand rather low temperatures and the viroid requires higher temperatures for replication is not a common feature for all viroids and their main hosts. This contrasting temperature adaptation tempts us to believe that PSTV is a pathogenic agent adapted to the potato outside its center of origin. Should PSTV have evolved or coexisted with the potato in its center of origin its optimum temperature for replication would have been closer to that of the potato. This assumption seems to be reinforced by the fact that PSTV has not been found in wild potato species or native cultivars in the Peruvian Andes (CIP, 1982).

This procedure of low temperature treatment followed by *in vitro* culture might also find an application in studies leading to understand the seemingly complex replication system in viroids.

LITERATURE CITED

Bennet, C.W. (1940). The relation of viruses to plant tissues. *Bot. Rev.6*, 427-473.

Berry, J. and Björkman, O. (1980). Photosynthetic response and adaptation to temperature in higher plants. *Ann. Rev. Plant Physiol. 31*, 491-543.

Bonde, R., and Merriam, D. (1951). Studies on the dissemination of the potato spindle tuber virus by mechanical inoculation. *Am. Potato J. 28p* 558-560.

CIP (1982). Annual Report (In press).

D'Amato, F. (1975). The problem of genetic stability in plant tissue and cell cultures. *In:* O.H. Frankel and J.G. Hawkes (eds.) Crop Genetic Resources for Today and tomorrow. pp. 338-348. Cambridge Univ. Press, England.

Diener, T. O. and Raymer, W. B. (1967). Potato spindle tuber virus. A plant virus with properties of a free nucleic acid. *Science 158*, 378-381.

Diener, T.O., and Raymer, W.B. (1969). Potato spindle tuber virus: a plant virus with properties of a free nucleic acid. II. Characterization and partial purification. *Virology 37*, 1347-1352.

Diener, T.O., and Raymer, W.B. (1971). Potato spindle tuber "virus". CMI/AAB descriptions of plant viruses, N°64, 4 pp.

Diener, T.O. (1979). Viroids and Viroid Diseases. John Wiley & Sons, New York, N.Y. 252 pp.

Fernow, K.H., Peterson, L. C., and Plaisted, R.L. (1962). Thermotherapy of patato leafroll. *Amer.Potato J.39*, 445-451.

Giaquinta, R. T., and Geiger, D.R. (1973). Mechanism of inhibition of translocation by locallized chilling. *Pl. Physiol.,Lancaster 51*, 372-377.

Goss, R. W., and Peltier, G.L. (1925). Further studies on the effect of environment on potato degeneration diseases. *Neb. Agric. Expt. Sta. Res. Bull.29*, 32 pp.

Goss, R. W. (1930). The symptoms of spindle tuber and unmottled curly dwarf of the potato. *Neb. Agric. Expt. Sta. Res. Bull. 47*, 39pp.

Goss, R. W.(1931). Infection experiments with spindle tuber and unmottled curly dwarf of the potato. *Nebr. Agric. Exp. Sta. Bull.53*, 1.

Gratz, L. O., and Schultz, E. S. (1931). Observations on certain virus diseases of potatoes in Florida and Maine. *Am. Potato J. 7*, 187-200.

Harris, P. S., and Browning, I.A. (1980). The effects of temperature and light on the symptom expression and viroid concentration in tomato of a severe strain of potato spindle tuber viroid. *Potato Res.23*, 85-93.

Helms, K., and Wardlaw, I.F. (1976). Movement of viruses in plants: long distance movement of tobacco masaic virus in *Nicotiana glutinosa*. In: Wardlaw, I.F. and J. B. Passioura (eds.) Transport and transfer processes in plants. Academic Press, New York. p. 283-294.

Hollings, M., and Kassanis, B. (1957). The cure of Chrysanthemums from some virus diseases by heat. *Fl.R.Hort. Soc. 82*, 339.

Hollings, M., and Stone, O.M. (1970). Attempts to eliminate

Chrysanthemum stunt from Chrysanthemum by meristem-tip culture after heat treatment. *Ann.Appl.Biol.65*, 311-315.

Horst, R. K. (1975). Detection of a latent infectious agent that protects against infection by Chrysanthemum chlorotic mottle viroid. *Phytopathology 65*, 1000.

Kao, K. N., and Michayluk, H. R. (1975). Nutritional requirements for growth of *Vicia hajastana* cell and protoplasts at a very low population density in liquid media. *Planta (Berl.) 126*, 105-110.

Lizàrraga, R. E., Salazar, L. F., Roca, W.M., and Schilde-Rentschler, L. (1980). Elimination of potato spindle tuber viroid by low temperature and meristem culture. *Phytopathology 70*, 754-755.

Lizàrraga, R. E. , Salazar, L.F., and Shilde-Rentschler, L. (1982). Effect of meristem size on eradication of potato spindle tuber viroid. *In:* Hooker, W.J. (ed.) Research for the Potato in the Year 2000. Proc. Int. Congress 10th Anniv. Int. Potato Center, February 1982, Lima, Peru. pp.118-119.

Lundegardh, H. (1949). Klima und Boden. Fischer Verlag, Jena.

Merriam, D., and Bonde, R. (1954). Dissemination of spindle tuber by contaminated tractor wheels and by foliage contact with diseased potato plants. *Abstract Phytopathology 44*, 111.

Morris, T. J., and Wright, N. S. (1975). Detection on polyacrylamide gels of a diagnostic nucleic acid from tissue infected with potato spindle tuber viroid. *Am. Potato J. 52*, 57-63.

Morris, T. J., and Smith, E.M. (1977). Potato spindle tuber disease. Procedures for the detection of viroid RNA and certification of disease-free potato tuber. *Phytopathology 67*, 145-150.

Murashige, T., and Skoog, F. (1962). A revised medium for rapid growth and bioassays with tobacco tissue culture. *Physiol. Plant 15*, 473-497.

Oslund, C. R., Li, P.H. and Weiser, C.J. (1972). Quantitative changes in ribonucleic acids of potato plants in response to photoperiod and temperature. *Amer.Soc. Hort. Sci. 97*, 93-96.

Owens, R. A., and Diener, T.O. (1981). Sensitive and rapid diagnosis of potato spindle tuber viroid disease by nucleic acid hybridization. *Science 213*, 670-672.

Pfannenstiel, M. A., Slack, S.A., and Lane, L.C. (1980). Detection of potato spindle tuber viroid in field-grown potatoes by an improved electrophoretic assay. *Phytopathology 70*, 1015-1018.

Quak, F. (1977). *In:* J. Reinert and Y.P.S. Bajaj (eds.)

Plant cell, tissue and organ culture. pp. 589-615.
Springer Verlag, Berlin, Heidelberg, New York.

Raymer, W. B., and O'Brien, M.J. (1962). Transmission of
potato spindle tuber virus to tomato. *Amer. Potato J.*

39, 401-408.

Roca, W. M., Espinoza, N.O., Roca, M.R., and Bryan J.E. (1978)
A tissue culture method for the rapid propagation of
potatoes. *Am. Potato J. 55*, 691-705.

Sänger, H.L., and Ramm, K. (1975). Radioactive labelling
of viroid RNA. Pages 250-253. *In:* Markham *et al.*
(eds.). Modification of the information content of
plant cells. Proc. 2nd John Innes Symposium, July
1974, Norwich, England.

Schultz, E. S., and Folsom, D. (1923). Spindling tuber and
other degeneration disease of Irish potatoes.
Phytopathology 13, 40.

Singh, R. (1966). Studies on potato spindle tuber virus.
Ph. D. Thesis, North Dakota State University,
Fargo, 89 pp.

Singh, R., Finnie, R. E., and Bagnall, R. H. (1971). Losses
due to the potato spindle tuber virus. *Am. Potato
J. 48*, 262-267.

Stace-Smith, R., and Mellor, F.C. (1970). Eradication of
potato spindle tuber virus by thermotherapy and
axillary bud culture. *Phytopathology 60*, 1857-1858.

Swanson, C. A. (1959). Translocation of organic solutes.
In: Stewart, F. C. Plant Physiol. Vol. II,
Academic Press, New York, p. 481-551.

Van Dorst, M.J.M., and Peters, D. (1974). Some biological
observations on pale fruit, a virus-incited disease
of cucumber. *Neth. J. Plant Pathol. 80*, 85.

Chapter 8

CONTROL OF VIROID DISEASES

Karl Maramorosch

Waksman Institute of Microbiology

Rutgers - The State University of New Jersey

P.O. Box 759, Piscataway, NJ 08854

I.   INTRODUCTION

Control of plant diseases is primarily aimed at reducing or eliminating losses to affected crops. In addition, control measures can be aimed at preventing the spread of pathogens from reservoirs, such as weeds or vector reservoirs, to cultivated plants. At present, 12 viroid diseases are known. The chronology of their discovery or recognition as viroid-caused diseases is presented in the first chapter (Diener and Prusiner, 1984). Before 1969 all of these diseases have been believed to be caused by viruses. Most plant virus diseases require vectors for transmission from plant to plant, but some can be transmitted by seed and by pollen (Mandahar, 1981; Carroll, 1981). Transmission can also occur through cultural practices, including grafting and manual handling. Before the existence of viroids became known, it was commonly assumed that the detection of a vector and subsequent vector

SUBVIRAL PATHOGENS
OF PLANTS AND ANIMALS:
VIROIDS AND PRIONS

Copyright © 1985 by Academic Press, Inc.
All rights of reproduction in any form reserved.
ISBN 0-12-470230-9

control would help in preventing the spread of the causative
viral pathogens of these diseases.

In 1980, at the request of the Food and Agriculture
Organization of the United Nations (FAO) and the Philippine
Government, I undertook a 6-mo. study of the coconut palm
disease in the Philippines (Maramorosch, 1960, 1961). In
1963, as FAO Consultant, I made a world-wide survey of coconut palm diseases of uncertain etiology, including cadang-
cadang in the Philippines and Tinangaja of Guam (Maramorosch,
1964). At the time of these assignments the existence of
viroids was not yet suspected and I worked under the assumption that both cadang-cadang and Tinangaja were caused by
viruses.

Several years earlier DeLeon and Bigornia (1953) out-
lined the methodology required to find the insect vector
responsible for the spread of cadang-cadang. At the time,
neither eriophyid mites, nematodes, nor lower fungi were
known as virus vectors, but during my assignments the vectors
of "soilborne" viruses had been recognized and their possible
involvement was being considered. I studied the pattern of
spread of cadang-cadang in the Bicol area of Luzon, in the
provinces of Sorsogon, Camarines Sud and Camarines Norte, the
small offshore island San Miguel, and on the Bondoc peninsula, hoping to find a clue to the vector of the causative
"virus" (Maramorosch, 1960). There was no clear-cut or defined pattern of infection, as trees succumbed not only in
isolated spots but also in clusters, sometimes at edges of
plantations and at other times starting in the middle of a
plantation. In one 80-year-old plantation where four nuts
were originally planted at each spot, occasionally only one
of the four old palms became affected, while in other parts
of the same plot 3 or all 4 trees were slowly dying. One
puzzling observation, inconsistent with any known vectors,
and, in fact, illogical at first, became apparent during the
extensive study performed in 1960. By that year certain
villages and plantations in Bicol and Sorsogon had lost
nearly all coconut palms and presented a picture of complete
disaster, while adjoining plantations with palms of the same
age and variety sometimes appeared completely healthy! The
only difference that could be detected between destroyed and
healthy plantations was that the owners of the destroyed ones
spoke Bicolano, while those that had healthy palms spoke
Tagalog. This observation defied not only known principles
of plant pathology but also defied logic and, at the time,
was so absurd that I did not dare to present it in my reports
to the Philippine Government and to the United Nations FAO
(Maramorosch, 1961).

I returned to the Philippines for shorter visits in 1963,

1965, 1967 and 1971. The main coconut growing area around San Pablo in Laguna Province remained almost completely free from cadang-cadang disease and even today this Tagalog-inhabited area is apparently free from disease. Small pockets of cadang-cadang have appeared at several other locations on Luzon Island in the meantime. The disease has also spread to other islands — Catanduanes, Leyte, Masbate and Samar, but it did not affect palms on Mindoro, Cebu, Negros or Mindanao (Maramorosch, 1969; Randles, 1984).

When Randles (1975) analyzed the nucleic acids of healthy and diseased coconut palms in the Philippines and concluded that the disease was caused by viroids, the mysterious predilection of cadang-cadang to Bicolano-owned palms could be explained finally. All viroids known today can be transmitted to plants mechanically and, with but one or two exceptions (Van Dorst and Peters, 1974), viroids seem to depend solely on man's intervention for their movement from plant to plant. The possibility of insect vectors or of pollen transmission has not been excluded entirely, but mechanical transmission seems to be efficient and, as far as known, is the normal and usual way of transmission.

Apparently the cadang-cadang viroids are being transmitted from diseased to healthy coconut palms by plantation workers. Their contaminated tools, bolo knives (machetes), used to cut steps at the base of palms before climbing the trees to remove the nuts, or to cut inflorescences in the tree tops for the collection of flower sap, are the actual means of cadang-cadang viroid transmission. It is customary for Bicolano plantation owners to hire Bicolanos, and for Tagalog owners to hire Tagalogs for work on their plantations.

The first scientifically verified occurrence of the disease in the Philippines was from San Miguel island, where coconut palms began to die in the late 1920s. The American-owned plantation on this small offshore island used Bicolano workers from nearby localities on Luzon. It is not known wherefrom the disease came to San Miguel island but we now know that it certainly existed earlier on Guam where it was known under the name of Tinangaja disease (Weston, 1918; Maramorosch, 1964; Boccardo, 1984). Perhaps it was introduced from Guam with other plant material, via Legazpi, to Luzon, or by the Taylor family that owned the San Miguel plantation, with any palms that might have been brought as ornamentals. There have been speculations that the disease has been present on Luzon Island some years earlier but these accounts cannot be verified. The U.S.-trained Philippino plant pathologist, Professor G.O. Ocfemia, a native of Guinobatan in the Bicol area near Legazpi, who visited his home town every year, did not notice the disease until the 1930s, when he was requested to inspect the dying coconut palms on San Miguel island. Shortly thereafter he observed the first outbreaks on the mainland of Luzon, across San Miguel island (Ocfemia, 1937). Thereafter the disease continued its spread in and around Guinobatan and Legazpi in Bicol, Sorsogon, and adjacent provinces, sometimes at considerable distance from where it was first observed.

The spread of cadang-cadang along "linguistic perimeters" suggests one method of viroid disease prevention and control – by decontamination of the tools used by plantation workers. Dipping the bolos in a solution of sodium hydroxide after each use would most likely prevent the mechanical transmission and further spread. While this seems simple in theory, it is rather complicated on location, especially in the case of workers engaged in the collection of flower sap in the crowns of the palms. Bamboo planks there connect adjacent trees and collectors of "tuba", the sap from which the inexpensive alcoholic beverage is made, move from tree to tree without descending.

II. SPECIFIC CONTROL METHODS

Table I lists the main control methods that might be recommended for viroid diseases. These methods have been based on measures used to control plant diseases caused by other pathogens, such as viruses, bacteria and fungi. Some have already been tried and found promising, while others have been listed either as possible avenues of approach, or as unlikely candidates for practical control.

Table I.

CONTROL OF VIROID DISEASES

1. Use of viroid-free stock (seed)
2. Selection and breeding for resistance
3. Decontamination of tools and hands
4. Rapid indexing procedures
5. Cross-protection by mild strains
6. Vector control
7. Chemical protectants
8. Eradication
9. Replanting
10. Tissue culture
11. Quarantine enforcement

a). Use of Viroid-Free Stock (Seed)

The use of healthy, viroid-free seed or planting material is one of the best means of preventing diseases that are known, or might possibly be seedborne or vegetatively propagated. It is not known whether any of the viroids known at present can be transmitted through the seed, but, besides the botanical meaning of the word "seed", the term is also used for vegetative parts, such as potato bulbs, that are called "seed potatoes". In such instances the use of viroid-free material is one of the best means of preventing the dissemination and further spread of viroid diseases. In order to assure freedom from viroid infection, often elaborate and time-consuming tests are required. The problem can be illustrated with potato spindle tuber viroid disease. In recent years healthy-appearing "seed potatoes" have been shipped to various areas around the world, only to be proven later to have been contaminated by the spindle tuber pathogen.

The viroid disease citrus exocortis has been dispersed widely by unintentionally using infected material as root stock, unto which healthy material was being grafted.

b).Selection and Breeding for Resistance

The best and most reliable control method available for viroid diseases, as well as for other plant diseases, is the selection and breeding for disease resistance. Efforts are under way to find coconut palm varieties resistant to cadang-cadang. At first, it was hoped that the small number of palms not killed during the past 50 years, would prove resistant. Nuts from these palms are now being propagated in the hope that the progeny of the San Miguel survivors will resist infection. The results will be available in a few years and only then will it become known whether the surviving palms were actually resistant, or whether they merely escaped infection. Testing other types and varieties, imported from different areas of the world, is also under way in the Philippines. The challenging with viroids can now be carried out more effectively and no longer left to chance infection, as high pressure infusion of viroid-containing extracts eliminates the need for prolonged natural exposure in the field (Randles, 1984).

It is not surprising that the search for viroid-resistant potatoes, tomatoes, hops, chrysanthemums, cucumbers, avocado, coconut or citrus has not yet yielded results. After all, the recognition of the existence of viroids is of very recent date. If the assumption is correct that most, if not all, viroid diseases are of recent origin (Diener, 1979) chances of finding preexisting resistance to these diseases would be remote, as plants were not exposed to viroid diseases for adequate time to develop such resistance. The time needed to evolve natural resistance is believed to be of considerable length.

c). Decontamination of Tools and Hands

Viroids can be destroyed by dipping tools in a sodium hydroxide solution (2%). Grafting utensils, such as knives, could be decontaminated in the same manner. Theoretically this appears rather simple but in tropical, developing countries the decontamination might encounter formidable difficulties. A large, heavy container with sodium hydroxide would have to be moved from place to place in a coconut plantation to enable the workers to dip their large bolos in the solution each time they were starting work on a different palm. While this could be carried out and properly supervised, the implementation of the method in tuba collection would be much more difficult. Crowns of several palms are usually linked with planks and bamboo sticks or ropes, to enable workers to move from crown to crown without descending each time. The risk of accidents in this work is notoriously high and the morbidity and mortality among tappers is staggering. This risk would increase if the workers were required to lower their knives on strings so others on the ground could decontaminate them after every tree has been tapped. It would also increase the cost of tapping and of the final product.

It would seem even more difficult, if not impossible, to prevent dissemination of potato spindle tuber viroids from plant to plant by a mechanically operated cultivator, whose blades come in contact with roots and bulbs of numerous potato plants in a field. Even decontamination of hands of workers presents a problem. It would not be feasible to require washing hands after touching every tomato plant when thousands of seedlings were being handled and planted, sorted, or otherwise touched. Decontamination procedures would seem feasible in but limited instances, such as harvesting hops in Japan and harvesting coconuts in the Philippines.

d). Rapid Indexing Procedures

The need for rapid indexing procedures can hardly be overemphasized. Earlier indexing for the detection of citrus exocortis required grafting onto indicator plants, a procedure that is very slow in providing results. A few years have to pass before a positive viroid detection can be made this way. In cadang-cadang the detection of viroids by gel electrophoresis is comparatively fast, but it requires proper equipment and laboratory personnel, thus limiting the usefulness of the procedure. Development of rapid indexing has been given high priority both in spindle tuber viroid studies and in citrus exocortis work, and new, promising approaches are now being tried.

e). Cross-Protection

The term cross-protection is usually used by plant pathologists to describe the interference in the expression of signs of viroid disease by preinoculation with a "mild" viroid strain. In plant pathology publications terms such as "cross-immunity" were earlier used and, until today, the term "symptom" is used for what medical science defines as signs of disease.

The mechanism of cross-protection in viroids is unknown. The occurrence of cross-protection with viroids of potato spindle tuber has been discovered by Fernow (1967). He demonstrated that preinoculation of tomatoes with a mild strain of potato spindle tuber protected the plants from developing severe signs of the disease when experimentally inoculated with a severe strain. Although no signs of the severe strain infection were observed in these plants, the severe strain could be isolated from inoculated, "protected" plants.

The viroids of potato spindle tuber and exocortis of citrus can infect tomato plants. Chrysanthemum plants can be infected with chrysanthemum stunt and chrysanthemum chlorotic mottle viroids, as well as with potato spindle tuber and citrus exocortis viroids. By performing cross-protection tests in tomato and chrysanthemum plants, Niblett *et al.* (1978) showed that crossprotection occurred among viroids that differ significantly in nucleotide sequence. The authors suggested that the mechanism of viroid protection is based on the establishment of infection by the first-inoculated viroid and that this infection delays, or prevents, the appearance of signs of disease ("symptom expression") by the challenge-inoculated viroid. Irrespective of the nature of the mechanism by which cross-protection is achieved, the fact that plants can be protected is of considerable importance (Van der Want and Peters, 1981). In the case of viruses, cross-protection has been exploited commercially to control tobacco mosaic virus infection (Rast, 1972). A "mild strain" has been patented more than a decade ago and it is now being used widely in Europe. Tristeza of citrus can also be controlled by cross-protection, as demonstrated in Brazil by Müller and Costa (1977). It can be expected that cross-protection against several viroids might eventually become feasible as well. Therefore the search for mild viroid strains ought to be intensified. In several instances strains have already been detected. Citrus exocortis strains have been reported by several authors (Diener, 1981) and they might eventually be employed to protect citrus species against exocortis-induced losses. Chrysanthemum chlorotic mottle viroid strains were implicated by Horst (1975) when he observed protection in plants infected by a latent viroid strain.

f). Vector Control

Early studies of cadang-cadang disease were concentrated on finding a vector, or vectors, responsible for the spread of the disease. As already mentioned, it was hoped that finding the vector would permit disease control through vector control. The outcome of more than two decades of studies was very frustrating, as no aphids, leafhoppers, planthoppers, mites, whiteflies, mealybugs, beetles, nematodes or lower fungi could be linked to candang-cadang transmission. Entomologists who were experts in the above groups of virus vectors found various species of suspected carriers but were unable to obtain experimental transmission. After Randles (1975) discovered the association of cadang-cadang with viroids, the search for vectors came to an end.

Experimental transmission of viroids by aphids has been achieved (Van Dorst and Peters, 1974) but whether such transmission actually occurs in nature and whether it does account for the spread of any of the 12 viroids known at present is doubtful.

g). Chemical protectants

No chemical protectants have been found as yet for the control of viroid diseases. It is unlikely that systemic or topical applications of chemicals could control viroid infection. Antiviral compounds, such as the interferon like factor (Sela, 1981) can protect against viruses that are mechanically transmissible. Surprisingly, human interferon can protect a plant against tobacco mosaic infection, but the reverse, animal protection against a virus by the plant interferon-like factor could not be demonstrated. No data are available on antiviroid factors. From a practical viewpoint chemical protectants have little if any prospects of being useful in the foreseeable future.

h). Replanting

Replanting is not a control method per se, but it has been recommended as a stop-gap method in the Philippines since 1953 (Erquiaga, 1959) because newly planted coconut palms usually produce nuts for several years before succumbing to cadang-cadang. Replanting enabled the continuous production of coconuts in areas where the disease was rampant. From an economic point of view replanting proved feasible in preventing losses, even though the cost of replanting and the lag of several years in nut production resulted in lower returns. This form of "disease control" is limited to cadang-cadang disease and it has no practical application to other viroid diseases.

i). Eradication

Plant diseases caused by fungi, bacteria or viruses can

often be controlled by eradication of diseased plants, thus eliminating the source of the pathogen and preventing further infection. In one viroid disease eradication has been ineffective, as documented in the Philippines (Zelazny *et al.*, 1982). The reason in the case of cadang-cadang disease might be the long latent period during which the infection of the viroids takes place. During eradication carrier plants may be left, unrecognized, in a plantation, thus providing a source of the pathogen. If viroids affect other hosts, such as weeds, the eradication of the affected cultivated plants would also have little if any effect. Nevertheless, the idea of removing diseased plants is deeply ingrained in all who have studied plant pathology and it is sometimes carried out with viroid diseases simply as a routine method, irrespective of the final result.

j). Tissue Culture

Usually the word "cure" implies that a diseased individual is being restored to the disease-free state. Such cure has not been achieved in plants infected by viroids. Neither chemical nor physical treatments, such as heat treatment or irradiation, could destroy selectively viroids in systemically infected plants. However, in a broader sense, the elimination of viroids from the vegetatively propagated progeny of infected plants can be considered a cure from a practical point of view. A detailed description of such a cure in potato spindle tuber-infected potatoes is presented in this volume by Salazar *et al.* (1984). The successful cure combines exposure to low temperature with subsequent tissue culture propagation. Whether similar approaches could provide a means for the elimination of citrus exocortis, hop stunt, avocado blotch and other viroids remains to be tested.

k). Quarantine enforcements

Many countries enforce plant quarantine regulations and specify that certain species cannot be imported or introduced at all, or that such species can be imported only from countries where specific diseases do not occur. A survey of quarantine regulations (Kahn, 1980) showed that coconuts, citrus and potatoes are among the 40 most frequently prohibited crops. Potato spindle tuber viroid was among the 10 most frequently mentioned pathogens (Kahn, 1981). Strict quarantine, prohibiting and excluding the movement of potential hosts of viroids into new viroid-free areas would seem to provide an efficient control measure, but effective regulatory control is limited today to highly developed countries. It is in its infancy or nonexistent in less developed regions of the world. The lack of simple, rapid identification methods for viroids further complicates regulatory control measures. Since man can be an efficient carrier of viroids from one region to another, both short distance and long distance movements of viroids take place.

There is no doubt that viroids can be present, and carried to other locations in living plant material such as propagative tubers, roots, stems or bulbs, but it is uncertain whether viroids are seed borne or pollen-borne. Nevertheless, quarantine restrictions have been imposed by some countries to import avocado fruit from sunblotch-infected areas, in the assumption that viroids might be carried in avocado seed. One such quarantine restriction, in Australia, where avocado sunblotch disease already occurs, might have been imposed not so much to prevent the importation of possibly infected material, as to eliminate the competition of imported fruit.

There is no evidence that cadang-cadang viroids can be carried in coconuts, but until otherwise proven, caution has to be taken because this possibility has not yet been ruled out completely.

III. SUMMARY AND CONCLUSIONS

At present control of viroid diseases relies primarily on prevention, specifically on the use of viroid-free seed and planting material, prevention of mechanical transmission, and, hopefully, use of resistant varieties. Since cross-protection appears to be effective in chrysanthemum and citrus viroid diseases, the search for "mild strains" of other viroids should be intensified and their effectiveness for cross-protection established. Quarantine enforcement ought to be strengthened and rapid identification tests developed to prevent further spread and major disasters. The ingenious cure of the progeny of potato spindle tuber-infected plants indicates new avenues of approach in the control of viroid diseases.

REFERENCES

Boccardo, G. (1984). Viroid etiology of Tinangaja and its relationship with cadang-cadang disease of coconut. In *"Subviral Pathogens of Plants and Animals: Viroids and Prions"*. K. Maramorosch and J.J. McKelvey, Jr., eds. Academic Press, Chapter 4.

Carroll, T.W. (1981). Seedborne viruses: virus-host interactions. In *"Plant Diseases and Vectors: Ecology and Epidemiology."* K. Maramorosch and K.F. Harris, eds. Academic Press, 293-317.

DeLeon, D., and Bigornia, A.E. (1953). Coconut kadang-kadang disease in the Philippines and experimental control progress. *USA Operations Mission to the Philippines* (Mimeographed).

Diener, T.O. (1979). *Viroids and Viroid Diseases.* 252 pp. Wiley Interscience, New York.

Diener, T.O. (1981). Viroids. In *"Handbook of Plant Virus Infections: Comparative Diagnosis".* E. Kurstak, ed. Elsevier, North Holland: 913-934.

Diener, T.O., and Prusiner, S.B. (1984). The recognition of subviral pathogens. In *"Subviral Pathogens of Plants and Animals: Viroids and Prions."* K. Maramorosch and J.J. McKelvey, Jr. eds. Academis Press Chapter 1.

Erquiaga, B. de. (1959). A practical approach to "Kadang-Kadang" *(Mimeographed).*

Fernow, K.H. (1967). Tomato as a test plant for detecting mild strains of potato spindle tuber virus. *Phytopathology 57,* 1347-1352.

Horst, R.K. (1975). Detection of a latent agent that protects against infection by chrysanthemum chlorotic mottle viroid. *Phytopathology 65,* 1000-1003.

Kahn, R.P. (1980). The host as a vector: exclusion as a control. In *"Ecology and Control of Vector-borne Pathogens".* Academic Press, New York.

Kahn, R.P. (1981). Trees as vectors of spiroplasmas and mycoplasma and rickettsia-like organisms. In: *"Mycoplasma Diseases of Trees and Shrubs".* K. Maramorosch and S.P. Raychaudhuri, eds. Academic Press, 281-298.

Mandahar, C.L. (1981). Virus transmission through seed and pollen. In: *Plant Diseases and Vectors: Ecology and Epidemiology".* K. Maramorosch and K.F. Harris, eds. Academic Press, 241-292.

Maramorosch, K. (1960). New experimental approaches to the study of cadang-cadang disease of coconut. *Coconut Briefs* (Bureau Plant Ind., Manila), 11.

Maramorosch, K. (1961). Report to the Government of the Philippines on the cadang-cadang disease of coconut. *FAO ETAP Bull.* #1333. Rome. 26 pp.

Maramorosch, K. (1964). *A survey of coconut diseases of unknown etiology. FAO.* Rome. 38 pp.

Maramorosch, K. (1969). The riddle of cadang-cadang. *Plants and Gardens 24:* 27-28.

Müller, G.W., and Costa A.S. (1977). Further evidence on protective interference in citrus tristeza. In: *"Proceedings th Conf. Intern. Organization Citrus Virologists".* J.F.L. Childs, ed. U. Florida Press, Gainesville: 71-82.

Niblett, C.L., Dickson, E., Fernow, K.H., Horst, R.K., and Zaitlin, M. (1978). Cross-protection among four viroids. *Virology, 91,* 198-203.

Ocfemia, G.O. (1937). The probable nature of "cadang-cadang" disease of coconut. *Philippine Agriculturist* 26, 338-340.

Rast, A.T.B. (1972). MII-16, an artificial symptomless mutant of tobacco mosaic virus for seedling inoculation of tomato crops. *Neth. J. Plant Pathol.* 78, 110-112.

Randles, J.W. (1975). Association of two ribonucleic acid species with cadang-cadang disease of coconut palm. *Phytopathology* 65, 163-167.

Randles, J.W. (1984). Coconut cadang-cadang viroid. In: *"Subviral Pathogens of Plants and Animals: Viroids and Prions"*. K. Maramorosch and J.J. McKelvey, Jr., eds. Academic Press, Chapter 3.

Salazar, L.F., Schilde-Rentschler, L., and Lizarraga, R. (1984). Elimination of potato spindle tuber viroid from potato by cold treatment and meristem culture. In: *"Subviral Pathogens of Plants and Animals: Viroids and Prions"*. K. Maramorosch and J.J. McKelvey, Jr., eds. Academic Press, Chapter 7.

Sela, I. (1981). Plant virus interactions related to resistance and localization of viral infections. In: *"Advances Virus Res."* M.A. Lauffer, F.B. Bang, K. Maramorosch, and K.M. Smith, eds. Academic Press, *26*, 201-237.

Van der Want, J.P.H., and Peters, D. (1981). Perspectives of virus-induced protection in the control of plant viral diseases. In: *"Vectors of Disease Agents: Interactions with Plants, Animals, and Man"*. J.J. McKelvey, Jr., B.F. Eldridge and K. Maramorosch, eds. Prager, New York, 179-188.

Van Dorst, H.J.M., and Peters, D. (1974). Some biological observartions on pale fruit, a viroid-incited disease of cucumber. *Neth. J. Plant Pathol.* 80, 85-96.

Weston, W.H., Jr. (1918). Report on the plant disease situation in Guam. *Guam Agr. Expt. Sta. Rept.* 1917, 45-62.

Zelazny, B., Randles, J.W., Boccardo, G., and Imperial, J.S. (1982). The viroid nature of the cadang-cadang disease of coconut palm. *Scientia Filipinas* 2, 45-63.

PART III

Viroid Structure and Replication

Chapter 9

VIROIDS: THEIR STRUCTURE AND POSSIBLE ORIGIN

Hans J. Gross

Institut Für Biochemie,Universität Würzburg
Rötgenring 11, D-8700 Würzburg, FRG

INTRODUCTION

Viroids are unique nucleic acid molecules: They are the smallest known infectious agents (Fig.1) which consist of a single-stranded, covalently closed circular RNA molecule. The nucleotide number of the sequenced viroids ranges from about 250 for Avocado Sunblotch Viroid (Symons, 1981) and the smallest form of Coconut Cadang-Cadang Viroid to almost 600 for the largest isolate of CCCv (Haseloff *et al.*, 1982)

Viroids differ from conventional viruses by several properties: They are protein-free RNA molecules which are in no way encapsidated; they do not seem to code for any proteins; they appear to depend completely and absolutely on host enzymes for their replication and circularization.

Finally, there is the enigma of their exclusive occurrence in higher plants, and their predilection for producing symptoms preferentially in cultivated plants (Table 1). In contrast

Copyright © 1985 by Academic Press, Inc.
All rights of reproduction in any form reserved.
ISBN 0-12-470230-9

TABLE I
Known viroids and viroid diseases

Viroid (Abbr.)	Viroid disease	References
1. PSTV	Potato spindle tuber	(Diener 1971; Singh and Clark 1971).
2. CEV	Citrus exocortis	(Sänger 1972; Semancik and Weathers, 1972)
3. CSV	Chrysanthemum stunt	(Hollings and Stone, 1973; Diener and Lawson, 1973)
4. CCMV	Chrysanthemum chlorotic mottle	(Romaine and Horst, 1975; Horst and Romaine,1975)
5. CPFV	Cucumber pale fruit	(van Dorst and Peters,1974; Sänger *et al.*, 1976.
6. CCCV	Coconut"Cadang-Cadang"	(Randles,1975; Randles *et al.* 1976)
7. HSV	Hop stunt	(Sasaki and Shikata,1977a; Sasaki and Shikata,1977b)
8. ASBV	Avocado sunblotch	(Thomas and Mohamed,1979)
9. TBTV	Tomato bunchy top	(Walter, 1981)
10.TPMV	Tomato"planta macho"	(Galindo *et al.*, 1982)
11.BSV	Burdock stunt	(Chen *et al.*, 1982)

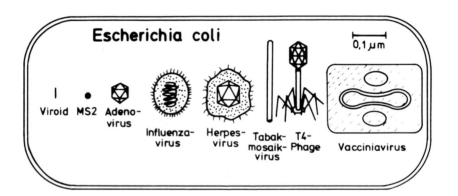

Figure 1.   The relative size of viroids.

to viroids, conventional pathogens like viruses, protozoa, bacteria and fungi cause diseases in all types of eukaryotic organisms. Therefore, it is a disquieting challenge that viroids or viroid-like infectious RNSs have not yet been detected in other organisms than higher plants . If viroid-like pathogens would actually be restricted to higher plants only , then possible for two reasons: (i) Certain essential properties of the higher plant as a viroid host, and/or (ii) the way from where and how viroids have evolved.

I. THE STRUCTURE OF VIROIDS

Early studies on purified viroid species had indicated that the following features should be common properties of the known viroids: Circular, covalently closed rings form an extended, rod-like secondary structure, which is character-ized by an alternating arrangement of short double-helical regions and single-stranded loop. These conclusions were deduced from electron microscopic, hydrodynamic and thermody-namic studies (Sänger *et al.*, 1976), and from model calcula-tions based on the physical properties of several viroids (Langowski *et al.*, 1978). The first complete viroid struc-ture, that of Potato Spindle Tuber Viroid was established in 1978 (Gross *et al.*, 1978). A ring of 359 ribonucleotides was found to form an extended, rod-like secondary structure expected from the early studies.

The experimental evidence for this secondary structure as shown in Fig. 2 comes from the location of enzymatic cleavage sites in single-stranded regions (Gross *et al.*, 1978), acessibility of unpaired sequences to chemical mod-ification (Domdey *et al.*, 1978) and calculation of the opti-mal energy of base pairing and quantitative evaluation of thermal denaturation curves (Riesner *et al.*, 1979).

The primary and secondary structures of Citrus Exocortis Viroid, Chrysanthemum Stunt Viroid, Fig.2(Gross *et al.*, 1981a, 1982; Haseloff and Symons, 1981; Visvader *et al.*, 1982), of Avocado Sunblotch Viroid (Symons, 1981) and of the differ-ent size variants of Coconut Cadang-Cadang Viroid (Haseloff *et al.*, 1982) published later also fully confirmed the early conclusions about the common features of viroid secondary structure.

Other general properties of viroids, by which they dif-fer from random sequences of similar size and base compos-tions, are:

(i) The complete absence of tertiary structure, as evidenced by studies with dye binding to helical regions (Riesner *et al.*, 1979) and tRNA anticodon binding to unpair-ed regions (Wild *et al.*, 1980), in complete agreement with

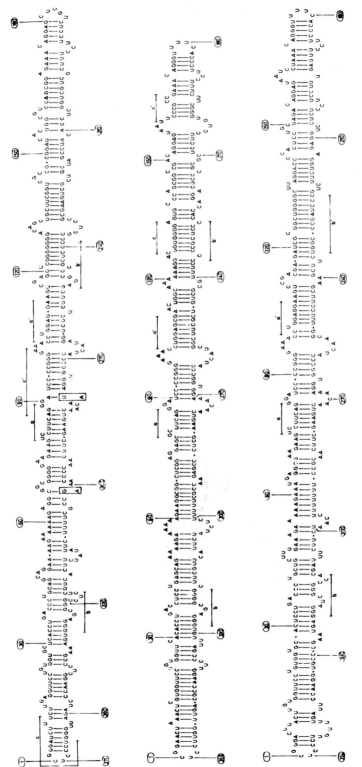

Figure 2.

chemical modification of unpaired cytosines (Domdey *et al.*, 1978) and enzymatic digestion in loops (Gross *et al.*, 1978).

(ii) A complex mechanism of thermal denaturation, which involves the formation of branched intermediates with new, more stable hairpin structures before complete denaturation. These and the other principles of viroid structure and structure formation have been reviewed by Riesner *et al.*, 1979, Gross and Riesner(1980), Sänger (1980) and Riesner *et al.*, (1983). Avocado Sunblotch Viroid, however, seems to differ from the other viroids in this respect and may therefore belong to a completely different class of viroids which evolved separately (Symons, 1981).

II. THE POSSIBLE ORIGIN OF VIROIDS

The most important fact concerning the origin of viroids is, that there are no real facts. Therefore, only speculations can be offered. In the following I want to give a review of the different observations and ideas which may contribute to this complex question. Many of these notions and concepts have been formed by Dr. Diener (Diener and Hadidi, 1977; Diener, 1979a) and have been discussed and extended by others (Sänger, 1982). At the end I hope to be able to offer some conclusions about viroid evolution.

(1) The early idea that viroids might have originated from conventional viruses by degeneration (Diener, 1974) was given up when the unique structure of viroids became clear.

(2) It also became unlikely that viroids are primitive viruses that had not yet developed the ability to form a capsid protein (Diener 1979 a,b).

(3) An important observation with respect to the evolution of viroids is related to their discovery (summa-

---

Figure 2. Primary and secondary structures of CEV, PSTV and CSV (from top to bottom). The sequences are folded in a way which results in a maximum number of base pairs and shows the typical rod-like structure. The first possible A:U or G:C pairs in the end loops are regarded as non-hydrogen-bonded on the basis of their reactivity (Gross *et al.*, 1978; Domdey *et al.*, 1978). The segments which can form "secondary" hairpin structures (Riesner *et al.*, 1979; Gross and Riesner, 1980) upon thermal denaturation are indicated by lines indexed I,I'; II, II' and III, III'. Segments I and I' form one new hairpin, etc. Hairpins I and III in CEV can not exist simultaneously; the low stability of hairpin III in CEV can not exist simultaneously; the low stability of hairpin III eliminates the possibility of its occurrence (from Gross *et al.*, 1982, with permission from Eur. J. Biochem.).

rized by Diener, 1979a): All viroid diseases have been
detected in the 20th century, some of them only quite recently, very much in contrast to plant diseases caused by conventional plant viruses or other plant pathogens. It appears
reasonable to follow Diener's argument, that all or most of
the known viroid diseases did not exist earlier, since after
their discovery, often in single greenhouses (CPFV) or on a
small isolated island (CCCV), the diseases spread rapidly
and were then observed all over the country. In summary, the
viroid diseases of cultivated plants seem to be of recent
origin (Diener, 1979a) Hence it was postulated that human
activities have contributed to the propagation of viroid
diseases in cultivated plants, because viroids often do not
cause symptoms when introduced into wild host plants. They
may therefore be latent in their unknown natural wild host
plants and become pathogenic through transfer to other species, or to cultivated plants, e.g., by grafting, or accidentally. Hence the huge monocultures planted in our century
may have contributed to the dissemination and discovery of
viroid diseases.

Alternatively, viroids were thought to have evolved from
normal, regulatory (nuclear) RNAs in their natural cultivated
host - or as a consequence of their introduction from the wild
host into the cultivated plant - into structures of high
stability with the capacity of self-replication and intercellular and interorganismal mobility. Consequently, Diener
(1979a) predicted, that:

i) new viroid diseases of cultivated plants will
continue to develop and to appear unexpectedly, and   -

ii) viroid-like RNAs will be found in many apparently healthy plants of diverse species, and some of these RNAs
will be pathogenic in certain cultured plants (Diener,1979a).

(4) More recently, the possibility has been discussed
that viroids may have evolved from intervening sequences
excised during RNA splicing (Roberts, 1978; Crick, 1979;
Diener, 1981; Dickson, 1981; Gross et al., 1982, Kiss and
Solymosy, 1982). This hypothesis is based on the surprising
sequence homology between all sequenced viroids and the 5'-
end of U1 RNA (Fig. 3), a small nuclear RNA which is believed
to be involved in mRNA splicing (Lerner et al., 1980; Rogers
and Wall, 1980). During the splicing process, the 5' end of
U1 RNA is thought to form base-pairs with both ends of the
intron to be excised. Circularization of an intervening
sequence by plant ligase (Konarska et al., 1981, 1982;
Branch et al., 1982; Kikuchi et al., 1982; Tyc et al.,
1983) could accidentally have created a RNA of viroid-like
secondary structure, an "escaped intron", which had or acquired the ability of intercellular and interorganismal mo-

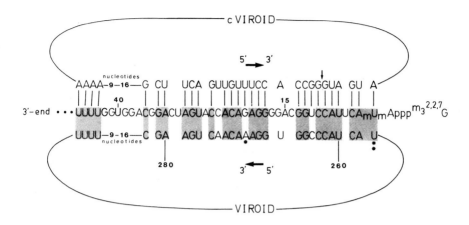

Figure 3.   Sequence homology of a highly conserved viroid sequence with, and complementarity of the corresponding complementary viroid (cVIROID) to, the 5'-terminal sequence of U1a RNA of chicken.
Nucleotide numbers in the viroid sequence refer to PSTV (Fig. 2 and 4).   Shaded nucleotides indicate homology between the three viroids and the 5'end of U1a RNA are indicated by vertical bars.   The arrow points to a hypothetical splice junction. *Indicates that a CEV mutant contains U in this position; *indicates that CSV contains A in this position (from Gross *et al.*, 1982, with permission from Eur. J. Biochem.).

bility, stability against host RNases, and replicability. The sequence homology between a conserved region of three viroids (Fig. 3) with the 5'-end of U1 RNA would imply that not the viroids as they are isolated from infected plants, but their complementary replication intermediates, would derive from an "escaped intron". Moreover, the sequence homology shown between U1, U5 and U3 RNA and viroids (Solymosy, 1984) could even indicate a direct phylogenetic relation betwen viroids and small nuclear RNAS. However, nothing is known yet about U1-like RNAs in plants.
     (5) Viroids may have evolved from "virusoids", small circular RNAs recently found encapsidated in plant viruses with multipartite genomes (Randles *et al.*, 1981; Gould,1981; Gould and Hatta, 1981; Gould *et al.*, 1981; Tien *et al.*, 1981; Francki *et al.*, 1983). At the moment a direct relationship between viroids and the two virusoids studied so far (Haseloff and Symons, 1982) appears unlikely, since there

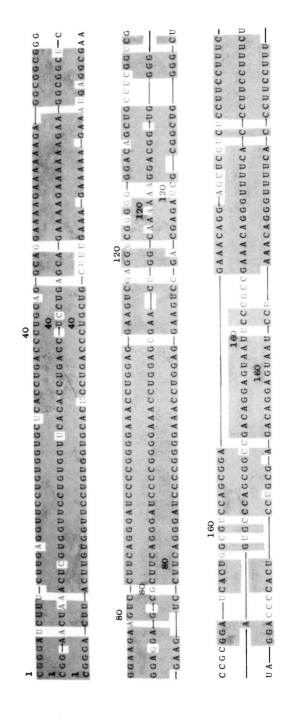

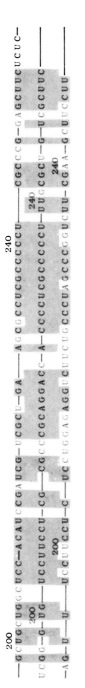

Figure 4. Primary structure of CEV, PSTV, and CSV (from top to bottom) and sequence homology between the three viroids. Sequences are aligned for maximum homology; numbering
is as in Fig. 2. Homologous sequences are indicated by shaded areas. Although CEV, PSTV
and CSV differ in base composition and length (371, 359 and 354 nucleotides, respectively),
a considerable homology is found: CEV-PSTV, 73%; CSV-PSTV, 73%; CEV-CSV, 67% CEV-PSTV-CSV,
59% (from Gross et al 1982, with permission from Eur. J. Biochem.).

is no sequence homology between both types of RNAs, except a GAAAC pentanucleotide in the central region of the native secondary structure. Also, virusoids differ considerably from viroids in their thermodynamic and hydrodynamic properties in that they closely resemble random sequences with the length, base-composition and circularity of viroids. Their secondary structure denatures at least 10°C lower than that of viroids, they do not form branched intermediates during thermal denaturation (Randles *et al.*, 1982), and their rod-like secondary structure is significantly more flexible than that of viroids (Riesner *et al.*, 1982, 1983).

(6) According to a highly speculative hypothesis of Zimmern (1982), viroids (and RNA viruses) may have originated from a system that exchanges genetic information between eukaryotic cells and cell organelles. It is postulated that viroids are able to infect a plant systemically, that they can rely on host mechanisms for intercellular transportation (from nucleus to nucleus via the cytoplasm) and for their replication (in the nucleus) only because normal cells contain structurally related RNAs which are also transportable and replicable in order to facilitate their amplification and/or extrachromosomal inheritance. Two novel types of functionally incomplete RNAs are proposed to exist: "signal RNAs", which may be excised from other RNAs. e.g., through a splicing process in the nucleus followed by their transportation into the cytoplasm or into cell organelles, where they may be (perhaps reversibly) integrated into the other hypothetical class of "antenna" RNAs. The fusion of "signal" and "antenna" RNAs, called a "fuson", is postulated to be translated and replicated, and to operate as independently of chromosomal DNA as a viroid. It is evident that any such system involving RNA recombination and amplification – if it exists – would be a source for the evolution of RNA viruses. According to this hypothesis viroids would represent aberrant "signal" RNAs or small, extremely deleted "fusons" which just contain an origin of replication and a splice junction, and which are no more under copy number control.

(7) Viroids might have evolved through the infection of higher plants with prokaryotic pathogens. This hypothesis on the origin of viroids is based on the finding that not only eukaryotic DNA-dependent RNA polymerase, but also the prokaryotic counterpart as well as DNA-dependent DNA-polymerase from *E. coli* are able to transcribe viroid RNA *in vitro* into viroid-complementary RNA and DNA copies, respectively (Rohde *et al.*, 1982). However, viroid-related sequences have not yet been found in prokaryotes.

III. CONCLUSIONS

So far, the different hypotheses on viroid evolution are not supported by reliable experimental data. However, there are three important facts which have not yet been discussed. These are *(a)*, the evident relation among the three viroids shown in Fig. 2; *(b)*, the absence of viroid sequences in host plant DNA, and *(c)*, the total dependence of viroid replication and circularization on host enzymes.

(a) As illustrated in Fig. 4, CEV, PSTV and CSV show a considerable amount of sequence homology, i.e., between 60 and 73%, although the three viroids differ in the number of nucleotides and in their base composition (Gross *et al.*, 1982). It seems reasonable to assume that they belong to a group of related viroids, albeit there is no evidence that they derive from a common ancestor. Their structural relation can either come from a divergent evolution in case that they descend from a common non-viroid ancestor RNA or by separated evolution if each of them originates from different, although related non-viroid RNAs, or finally by convergent evolution in case that they are offsprings of different, rather unrelated non-viroid RNAs. Comparing the group of CEV, PSTV and CSV with ASBV (Symons, 1981) and CCCV (Haseloff *et al.*, 1982), we find about 18% and 11% sequence homology, respectively. We should therefore assume that at least three "families" of viroids evolved independently in geographically separated events, the CEV/PSTV/CSV-group, ASBV and CCCV. Since, as mentioned above all viroid diseases seem to have originated only recently during our lifetime (Diener, 1979a), it even appears rather unlikely that the structurally related viroids CEV, PSTV and CSV can have evolved from a common viroid or non-viroid ancestor. This is supported by the observation that viroids do not seem to have an extraordinarily high mutation rate: Isolates of the same viroid from different geographic origin (Gross *et al.*, 1981a, 1982; Haseloff and Symons, 1981; Visvader *et al.*, 1982) or "mutants" which differ in symptom expression (Gross *et al.*, 1981b; Sänger, 1982), and which have been propagated experimentally for years, differ in their sequence by a few point mutations only. These considerations justify the assumption that CEV, PSTV and CSV may have evolved from different, although related, non-viroid ancestors. ASBV and CCCV would then be descendants of unrelated non-viroid precursors. Now the following observations become very important.

(b) Host plant DNA does not contain viroid-specific sesequences(Zaitlin *et al.*, 1980;Branch and Dickson,1980; Rohde and Sänger, 1981: Hadidi *et al.*, 1981; Branch *et al.*, 1981). Until now the value of this observation with respect to vi-

roid evolution has been underestimated. The consequent application of this finding, together with the recent origin of
viroid diseases, would rule out all ideas about viroids being
offsprings of regulatory, nuclear or intron-derived RNA coded
for by the host plant or a related species.

(c) Viroid replication (reviewed by Sänger, 1982), although far from being understood, and circularization of
linear viroid RNA (Branch et al., 1982; Kikuchi et al., 1982)
seem to depend completely on host enzymes. This would strongly indicate that viroids derive directly from their hosts or
from related species, however, this seems impossible since
viroid-specific sequences are not present in host plant DNA.
As a consequence I would like to conclude that only three
alternatives for the origin of viroids remain:

(i) Viroids derive from host RNA which multiplies
extrachromosomally, and for which no DNA sequences exist any
more because it became self-replicative long ago during
evolution, and which became a pathogen by some accidental
event very recently. However, I propose to reject this idea
since it requires several speculative assumptions.

(ii) If we accept the sequence homology with U1, U5
and U3B RNA as being significant, at least as far as CEV,
PSTV and CSV are concerned, the absence of viroid sequences
in host plants rather indicates that viroids may derive from
RNA of unrelated eukaryotic organisms. Any unrelated plants,
insects, fungi, protozoa, any eukaryotic symbiont or pathogen, whose close contact with the affected host plant is
favored by human activities or mass propagation of certain
plants in monoculture, should hence be the cryptic carrier of
potential viroid RNA. Such viroid-like or not viroid-like,
nuclear or nucleolar, non-replicative, perhaps non-regulatory
or non -functional and harmless RNAs, would give rise to
replicable molecules when introduced into a susceptible host
plant, because this foreign RNA accidentally mimics a natural
substrate of host replicases and ligases.

(iii) Wild plants may exist which (a) produce viroid
like RNAs or (b) carry self-replicative RNAs of this type,
which both may be called proviroids, because they do not
cause symptoms in their natural hosts. It is not unreasona-
ble to speculate that such a yet hypothetical symbiosis
between a symptomless proviroid and its host, or the production of a symptomless proviroid by a plant, may have evolved
early during plant evolution. The selective advantage of a
plant carrying such a proviroid would become evident as soon
as this plant is in danger to be overgrown by unrelated
competing plant species: Mechanical contact or biting insects would then transfer the proviroid into the aggressor,
in which it causes symptoms and replicates autonomously, i.e.

becomes a true viroid, which thus guarantees the survival of its natural host.

I am personally convinced that at the moment the latter two hypotheses are the most plausible concepts for viroid evolution, or better, viroid devolution. The search should now be open for the unknown viroid ancestor, which may have the properties and functions of a proviroid.

ACKNOWLEDGEMENTS

The author's experimental work described here has been supported by the Deutsche Forschungsgemeinschaft and by Fonds der Chemischen Industrie.

REFERENCES

Branch, A.D. and Dickson, E. (1980) Tomato DNA contains no detectable regions complementary to potato spindle tuber viroid as assayed by Southern hybridization. *Virology 104,* 10-26.

Branch, A.D., Robertson, H.D. and Dickson, E. (1981) Longer-than-unit-length viroid minus strands are present in RNA from infected plants. *Proc.Natl.Acad.Sci.U.S.A. 78,* 6381-6385.

Branch, A.D., Robertson, H.D., Greer, C., Gegenheimer, P., Peebles, C. and Abelson, J. (1982) Cell-free circularization of viroid progeny RNA by an RNA ligase from wheat germ. *Science 217,* 1147-1149.

Chen, W., Tien, P., Zhu, Y.X. and Liu, Y., (1983) The viroid-like RNAs associated with Burdock stunt desease. *J. Gen. Virol. 64,* 409-414.

Crick, F. (1979) Split genes and RNA splicing *Science 204,* 264-271.

Dickson, E. (1981) A model for the involvement of viroids in RNA splicing. *Virology 115,* 216-221.

Diener, T.O. (1971) Potato spindle tuber virus. IV. A replicating, low molecular weight RNA. *Virology 45,* 411-428.

Diener, T.O. (1974) Viroids: The smallest known agents of infectious disease. *Ann. Rev. Microbiol. 28,* 23-39.

Diener, T.O. (1979a) "Viroids and Viroid Diseases", J. Wiley and Sons, New York, Chichester, Brisbane, Toronto.

Diener, T.O. (1979b) Viroids: Structure and function. *Science 205,* 859-866.

Diener, T.O. (1981) Are viroids escaped introns? *Proc.Natl. Acad.Sci. U.S.A. 78,* 5014-5015.

Diener, T.O. and Lawson, R.H. (1973) Chrysanthemum stunt: A
    viroid disease. *Virology 51*, 94-101.
Diener, T.O. and Hadidi, A. (1977) Viroids, *In* "Comprehensive
    Virology", (H. Fraenkel-Conrat and R.R. Wagner,eds.)
    11, 285-337.
Domdey, H., Jank, P., Sänger, H.L. and Gross, H.J. (1978)
    Studies on the primary and secondary structure of
    potato spindle tuber viroid: Products of digestion
    with ribonuclease A and ribonuclease T₁, and mod-
    ification with bisulfite. *Nucleic Acids Res.5*, 1221-
    1236.
Francki, R.I.B., Randles, J.W., Hatta, T, Davies, C., Chu,
    P.W.C. and McLean, G.D. (1983) Subterranean clover
    mottle virus - another virus from Australia with
    encapsidated viroid-like RNA. *Plant Pathol.32*, 47-59.
Galindo, J.,Smith, D.R. and Diener, T.O. (1982) Etiology of
    planta macho, a viroid disease of tomato.
    Phytopathology 72, 49-54.
Gould, A.R. (1981) Studies on encapsidated viroid-like RNA
    II. Purification and characterization of a viroid-
    like RNA associated with velvet tobacco mottle virus
    (VTMoV). *Virology 108*, 123-133.
Gould, A.R. and Hatta, T. (1981) Studies on encapsidated
    viroid-like RNA. III. Comparative studies on RNAs
    isolated from velvet tobacco mottle virus and
    Solanum nodiflorum mottle virus. *Virology 109*,
    137-147.
Gould, A.R., Francki, R.I.B. and Randles, J.W. (1981) Studies
    on encapsidated viroid-like RNA. IV. Requirement
    for infectivity and specificity of 2 RNA components
    from velvet tobacco mottle virus. *Virology 110*,
    420-426.
Gross, H.J., Domdey, H., Lossow, C., Jank, P., Raba, M.,
    Alberty, H. and Sänger, H.L. (1978) Nucleotide
    sequence and secondary structure of potato spindle
    tuber viroid. *Nature (London) 273*, 203-208.
Gross, H. J. and Riesner, D. (1980) Viroids: A class of
    subviral pathogens. *Angew.Chem.Int.Ed.Engl.19*,
    231-243.
Gross, H.J., Krupp, G., Domdey, H., Steger, G., Riesner, D.
    and Sänger,H.L. (1981a) The structure of three plant
    viroids. *Nucleic Acids Res. Symp. Ser.No.10*,
    91-98.
Gross, H.J., Liebl, U., Alberty, H., Krupp, G., Domdey, H.,
    Ramm, K. and Sänger, H.L. (1981b) A severe and a mild
    potato spindle tuber viroid isolate differ in three
    nucleotide exchanges only. *Biosci.Rep.1*, 235-241.
Gross, H.J., Krupp, G., Domdey, H., Raba, M., Alberty, H.,

Lossow, C., Ramm, K. and Sänger, H.L. (1982)
Nucleotide sequence and secondary structure of
citrus exocortis and chrysanthemum stunt viroid.
Eur. J. Biochem.121, 249–257.

Hadidi, A., Cress, D.E. and Diener, T.O. (1981) Nuclear
DNA from uninfected or potato spindle tuber viroid-
infected tomato plants contains no detectable
sequences complementary to cloned double-stranded
viroid cDNA. *Proc. Natl. Acad. Sci.U.S.A.78,*
6932–6935.

Haseloff, J., Mohamed, N.A. and Symons, R.H. (1982) Viroid
RNAs of the cadang-cadang disease of coconuts.
Nature (London) 299, 316–322.

Haseloff, J. and Symons, R.H. (1981) Chrysanthemum stunt
viroid – primary sequence and secondary structure.
Nucleic Acids Res.9, 2741–2752.

Haseloff, J. and Symons. R.H. (1982) Comparative sequence and
structure of viroid-like RNAs of two plant viruses.
Nucleic Acids Res. 10, 3681–3691.

Hollings, M. and Stone, O.M. (1973) Some properties of
chrysanthemum stunt, a virus with the characteristics
of an uncoated ribonucleic acid. *Ann.Appl.Biol.74,*
333–348.

Horst, R.K. and Romaine, C.P. (1975) Chrysanthemum chlorotic
mottle: A viroid disease. *N.Y. Food Life Sci.Q.8,*
11–14.

Kikuchi, Y., Tyc, K., Filipowicz, W., Sänger, H.L. and Gross,
H.J. (1982) Circularization of linear viroid RNA
via 2'-phosphomonoester, 3', 5'-phosphodiester bonds
by a novel type of RNA ligase from wheat germ and
Chlamydomonas. Nucleic Acids Res.,10, 7521 –7529.

Kiss, T. and Solymosy, F. (1982) Sequence homologies between
a viroid and a small nuclear RNA (snRNA) species of
mammalian origin. *FEBS Lett. 144,* 318–320.

Konarska, M., Filipowicz, W., Domdey, H. and Gross, H.J.
(1981) Formation of a 2'-phosphomonoester, 3',5'-
phosphodiester linkage by a novel RNA ligase in wheat
germ. *Nature (London)293,* 112–116.

Konarska, M., Filipowicz, W. and Gross, H.J. (1982) RNA
ligation via 2'-phosphomonoester, 3', 5'-phosphodi-
ester linkage: Requirement of 3',5"-cyclic phosphate
termini and involvement of a 5"-hydroxyl polynucleotide kinase. Proc. *Natl.Acad.Sci.USA 79,* 1474–1478.

Langowski, J., Henco, K., Riesner, D. and Sänger, H.L.
(1978) Common structural features of different viroids: Serial arrangement of double helical sections
and internal loops. *Nucleic Acids Res. 5,* 1589–1610.

Lerner, M.R., Boyle, J. A., Mount, S.M., Wolin, S.L. and Steitz, J.A. (1980) Are snRNPs involved in splicing? *Nature (London) 283*, 220-224.

Randles, J.W. (1975) Association of two ribonucleic acid species with cadang-cadang disease of coconut palm. *Phytopathology 65*, 163-167.

Randles, J.W., Rillo, E.P. and Diener,T.O. (1976) The viroid-like structure and cellular location of anomalous RNA assscoiated with the cadang-cadang disease. *Virology 74*, 128-139.

Randles, J.W., Davies, C., Hatta, T., Gould, A.R. and Francki, R.I.B. (1981) Studies on encapsidated viroid-like RNA. I. Characterization of velvet tobacco mottle virus. *Virology 108*, 111-122.

Randles, J. W., Steger, G. and Riesner, D. (1982) Structural transitions in viroid-like RNAs associated with ca-dang-cadang disease, velvet tobacco mottle virus, and *Solanum nodiflorum* mottle virus. *Nucleic Acids Res. 10*, 5569-5586.

Riesner, D., Henco, K., Rokohl, U., Klotz, G., Kleinschmidt, A.K., Gross, H.J., Domdey, H. and Sänger,H.L. (1979) Structure and structure formation of viroids. *J. Mol. Biol.133*, 85-115.

Riesner, D., Kaper, J.M. and Randles, J.W. (1982) Stiffness of viroids and viroid-like RNA in solution. *Nucleic Acids Res. 10*, 5587-5598.

Riesner, D., Steger, G., Schumacher, J., Gross, H.J., Randles, J.W. and Sänger, H.L. (1983) Structure and function of viroids. *Biophys. Struct.Mech.9*, 145-170.

Roberts, R. J. (1978) Intervening sequences excised *in vitro*. *Nature (London) 274*, 530.

Rogers, J. and Wall, R. (1980) A mechanism for RNA splicing. *Proc. Natl. Acad.Sci. U.S.A.77*, 1877-1879.

Rohde, W. and Sänger, H.L. (1981) Detection of complementary RNA intermediates of viroid replication by northern blot hybridization. *Biosci.Rep.1*, 327-336.

Rohde, W., Rackwitz, H.-R, Boege, F. and Sänger, H.L. (1982) Viroid RNA is accepted as a template for in vitro transcription by DNA-dependent DNA poly-merase I and RNA polymerase from *Escherichia coli*. *Biosci. Rep.2*, 929-939.

Romaine, C.P. and Horst, R.K. (1975) Suggested viroid etiolo-gy for chrysanthemum chlorotic mottle disease. *Virology 64*, 86-95.

Sasaki, M. and Shikata, E. (1977a). Studies on the host range of hop stunt disease in Japan. *Proc. Jpn. Acad. 53B*, 103-108.

Sasaki, M. and Shikata, E. (1977b). On some properties of

hop stunt disease agent, a viroid. *Proc. Jpn. Acad.* *53B*, 109-112.

Sänger, H.L. (1972) An infectious and replicating RNA of low molecular weight: The agent of the excortis disease of citrus. *Adv. Biosci. 8*, 103-116.

Sänger, H.L., Klotz, G., Riesner, D., Gross, H.J. and Klein-schmidt, A.K. (1976) Viroids are single-stranded co-valently closed circular RNA molecules existing as highly base-paired rod-like structures. *Proc. Natl. Acad. Sci. U.S.A. 73*, 3852-3856.

Sänger, H.L. (1982) Biology, structure, functions and possi-ble origin of viroids, *In* "Encyclopedia of Plant Phy-siology", New Series, Vol. *14B*, Nucleic Acids and Proteins in Plants, II (B. Parthier and D. Boulter, eds.) pp. 368-454. Springer-Verlag, Berlin, Heidel-berg, New York.

Semancik, J.S. and Weathers, L.G. (1972). Exocortis disease: Evidence for a new species of "infectious" low mole-cular weight RNA in plants. *Nature (New Biol.) 237*, 242-244.

Singh, R.P. and Clark, M.C. (1971) Infectious low-molecular-weight ribonucleic acid. *Biochem. Biophys. Res. Commun. 44*, 1077-1082.

Symons, R.H. (1981) Avocado sunblotch viroid - primary se-quence and proposed secondary structure. *Nucleic Acids Res. 9*, 6527-6537.

Thomas, W. and Mohamed, N.A. (1979) Avocado sunblotch - a viroid disease? *Aust. Plant Path. Soc.Newslett.* 1-2.

Tien, P., Davies, C., Hatta, T. and Francki, R.I.B. (1981) Viroid-like RNA encapsidated in lucerne transient streak virus. *FEBS Lett.132*, 353-356.

Tyc, K., Kikuchi, Y., Konarska, M. Filipowicz, W. and Gross, H.J. (1983) Ligation of endogenous tRNA 3'half mole-cules to their corresponding 5' halves via 2'-phos-phodiester bonds in extracts of *Chlamydomonas*. *EMBO J. 2*, 605-610.

Van Dorst, H.J.M. and Peters, D.(1974) Some biological obser-vations on pale fruit, a viroid-incited disease of cucumber. *Neth. J. Plant Path.80*, 85-96.

Visvader, J.E., Gould, A.R., Bruening, G.E. and Symons, R.H. (1982) Citrus exocortis viroid - nucleotide sequence and secondary structure of an Australian isolate. *FEBS Lett.137*, 288-292.

Walter, B. (1981) Un viroide de la tomate en Afrique de L' Ouest: identité avec le viroide du "potato spindle tuber"? *C.R. Acad.Sci.Paris 292 III*, 537-542.

Wild, U., Ramm, K., Sänger, H.L. and Riesner, D. (1980) Loops in viroids. *Eur. J. Biochem.103*, 227-235.

(1980) Tomato DNA contains no detectable regions complementary to potato spindle tuber viroid as assayed by solution and filter hybridization. *Virology 104,* 1-9.

Zimmern, D. (1982) Do viroids and RNA viruses derive from a system that exchanges genetic information between eukaryotic cells? *Trends Biochem.Sci.* 205-207.

Chapter 10

VIROIDS AND snRNAs

F. Solymosy and T. Kiss

Institute of Plant Physiology
Biological Research Center
Hungarian Academy of Sciences
Szeged, Hungary

I.   INTRODUCTION

Viroids (Diener, 1971b), a distinct class of plant pathogenic agents, are covalently closed circular single-stranded RNA molecules (Gross *et al.*, 1978) with a particular, DNA-like secondary structure (Riesner *et al.*, 1979). A number of them have been sequenced and fitted into a uniform model of secondary structure: potato spindle tuber viroid (PSTV) by Gross *et al.* (1978), the Californian isolate of citrus exocortis viroid (CEV) by G r o s s *et al.* (1982), the Australian isolate of CEV by Visvader *et al.* (1982), the Australian isolate of chrysanthemum stunt viroid (CSV) by Haseloff and Symons (1981), the English isolate of CSV by Gross et al. (1982), avocado sunblotch viroid (ASBV) by Symons (1981) and coconut cadang-cadang viroid (CCCV) by Haseloff *et al.* (1982). In spite of this firm knowledge of their primary and secondary structure and rapidly accumulat-

Copyright © 1985 by Academic Press, Inc.
All rights of reproduction in any form reserved.
ISBN 0-12-470230-9

ing information about their mode of replication (Sänger, 1982), practically nothing is known about their biochemical function in the plant.

One of several approaches towards an understanding of viroid function consists in looking for normal cell constituents that are structurally related to viroids and in assuming that, on the basis of eventual structural similarities, a functional relation also exists.

The most likely candidates for such a comparison, as suggested by Diener as early as 1974 (Diener, 1974) are small nuclear RNAs (snRNA).

Eukaryotic snRNAs are linear single-stranded RNA molecules with experimentally supported models of secondary structure (Busch *et al.*, 1982; Branlant *et al.* 1982; Bernstein *et al.*, 1983). All of the snRNAs of the U series (U1 to U6) have been sequenced from one source or another and shown to contain a cap structure at their 5' end and modified bases (Busch *et al.*, 1982). They are very conserved molecular species in nature, from dinoflagellates to man (Busch *et al.*, 1982).

The following criteria seem to justify a systematic search for structural (and functional) relationships between viroids and snRNAs:

1. Both have been found so far only in eukaryotes.

2. Both are localized and synthesized (replicated) in the cell nucleus (Busch *et al.* 1982) for U snRNAs and Diener (1971a), Takahashi and Diener (1975), Semancik *et al.* (1976) for viroids).

3. In the synthesis (replication) of both of them an enzyme whose sensitivity to   -amanitin corresponds to that of DNA-dependent RNA polymerase II is involved (Frederiksen *et al.* (1978), Gram-Jensen *et al.* (1979) for U1, U2 and U3 snRNAs and Mühlbach and Sänger (1979), Rackwitz *et al.* (1981) Flores and Semancik (1982) for viroids).

4. Both are small single-stranded RNA molecules comprising 107 to 214 (Busch *et al.*, 1982) and 246 to 371 (Sänger, 1982) nucleotide residues, depending on the individual species of U snRNA and viroid, respectively.

5. Both seem to be devoid of tRNA and mRNA activities in the appropriate *in vitro* systems (Hellung-Larsen (1977), for snRNAs and Davies *et al.* (1974), Hall *et al.* (1974), Semancik *et al.* (1977) for viroids).

It will be shown in the present paper that there is a striking sequence homology between U3B snRNA from Novikoff hepatoma cells and unique stretches of the PSTV, CEV and CSV molecules. Also, homologous stretches in a colinear arrangement were found in U5 snRNA from Novikoff hepatoma cells and ASBV.

II.   MATERIALS AND METHODS.

Computer analysis was based on a program described by Goad and Kanehisa (1982). The nucleotide sequences of PSTV, CEV and CSV were taken from Gross *et al.* (1982), that of ASBV from Symons (1981) and those of the snRNAs of Novikoff hepatoma cells from Busch *et al.*, (1982). As the secondary structure of PSTV the experimentally proved (Domdey *et al.*, 1978; Riesner *et al.*, 1979; Wild *et al.*, 1980) model originally proposed by Gross *et al.* (1978), as that of U3B snRNA the closed form proposed by Bernstein *et al.* (1983) were used.

III. RESULTS.

Screening of the extent of sequence homologies between PSTV, CEV, CSV and ASBV on the one hand and the six U snRNAs (U1 to U6) on the other, showed that the maximum number of the longest homologous stretches located in a colinear way occurred in U5 snRNA with respect to ASBV and in U3B snRNA with respect to PSTV, CEV and CSV.

A. Sequence homologies between U5 snRNA of Novikoff hepatoma cells and ASBV.

Fig. 1 shows sequence homology between stretches of ASBV and stretches of U5 snRNA from Novikoff hepatoma cells. These stretches are colinear in arrangement and involve 53 per cent of the U5 snRNA molecule. The sequence between nucleotide residues 13-21 in U5 snRNA is also present in the form of an uninterrupted stretch of 9 nucleotide residues between residues 164-172 of ASBV (not shown). This increases the length of the U5 snRNA molecule involved in sequence homology with ASBV to 61%.

B. Sequence homologies between U3B snRNA of Novikoff hepatoma cells and PSTV.

Fig. 2 presents sequence homology between PSTV and U3B snRNA of Novikoff hepatoma cells. It can be seen that this homology (i) is colinear in arrangement and (ii) extends in U3B snRNA to 81% (174 nucleotide residues) of the length of the entire U3B snRNA molecule. Sixty eight per cent (119 nucleotide residues) of this region are actually involved in the formation of *bona fide* homologies with PSTV.

These nucleotide residues are depicted in Fig. 3 in terms of the proposed secondary structure of U3B (Bernstein *et al.*, 1983). It can be seen that one (nucleotide residues 25-53) out of the two (nucleotide residues 25-53 and 187-195) regions in U3B that are not involved in sequence homology with PSTV, forms a well defined arm in the U3B snRNA molecule.

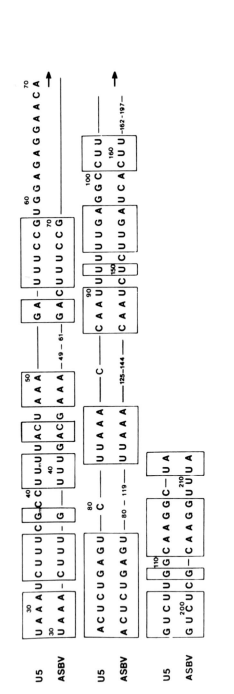

Figure 1. Sequence homologies (boxed areas) between stretches of the 118 nucleotide residue-long Novikoff hepatoma U5 snRNA molecule and those of the 247 nucleotide residue-long ASBV molecule. Sequences are aligned for maximum homology. The figures refer to the positions of nucleotide residues in the linear U5 snRNA (Ψ indicated as U) or to those in the circular ASBV. (From Kiss and Solymosy, 1982.)

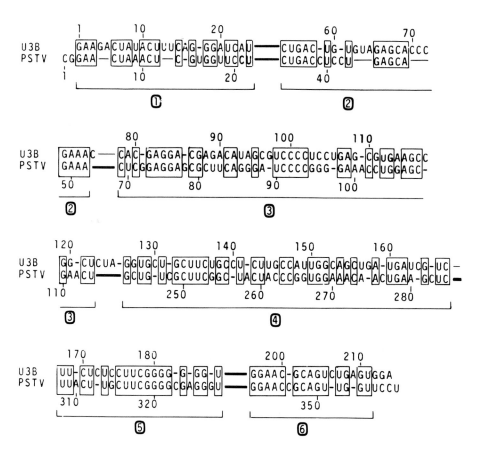

Figure 2.   Sequence homologies (boxed areas) between regions of the 214 nucleotide residue-long Novikoff hepatoma U3B snRNA molecule and those (①)to ⑥ as indicated) of the 359 nucleotide residue-long PSTV molecule. Sequences are aligned for maximum homology.   The figures above and below the characters refer to the positions of nucleotide residues in the linear U3B snRNA (modified nucleotides not marked and Ψ indicated as U) and to those in the circular PSTV, respectively. Non-homologous regions are indicated by **fat** lines in the respective sequences.   Thin lines mean continuity in sequence. (From Kiss *et al.*, 1983)

In PSTV the regions that are homologous with U3B snRNA involve unique sites which, if depicted in terms of the secondary structure of the circular PSTV molecule, reveal a conspicuous regularity in their location, as shown in Fig. 4.

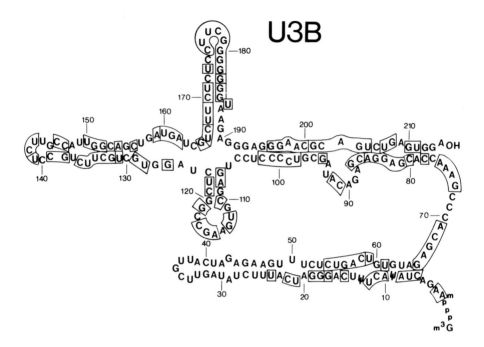

Figure 3. Proposed secondary structure of U3B snRNA (Bern-stein *et al.*, 1983). Nucleotide residues, individual or in blocks, that are homologous in a colinear arrangement with nucleotide residues in PSTV are boxed. Between individual boxes there is mismatch in the corresponding part of the PSTV molecule.

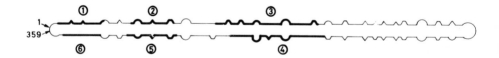

Figure 4. Schematic diagram of the secondary structure of PSTV. The regions (① to ⑥ as in Fig. 2) that show sequence homologies with stretches of U3B snRNA are drawn in **fat**. The figures with the arrows indicate the first and last nucleotide residues in the circular molecule according to the convention-al numbering system (Gross *et al.* 1978).

C.   Sequence homologies between U3B snRNA of Novikoff
     hepatoma cells and CEV as well as CSV.

Fig. 5 shows the regions of homology with U3B snRNA in
CEV and CSV in comparison with those in PSTV. In view of the
high degree of sequence homology between the above three
viroids, sequence homology of CEV and CSV with U3B snRNA is
of about the same extent as that of PSTV and extends to identical regions of the viroid molecules in question.

IV   DISCUSSION

The results presented show that there are sequence
homologies between the viroids and the snRNAs examined.
With ASBV and U5 snRNA sequence homology is quite weak
and comprises distant blocks in the ASBV molecule, that do
not fit well into the secondary structure of ASBV (not shown).
The fact, however, that it includes more than 50 per cent in
length of the U5 snRNA molecule and is colinear in arrangement
favors the view that sequence homology between these two
molecular entities is not accidental.
With PSTV and U3B snRNA (i) the colinear arrangement of
the homologous blocks, (ii) the participation of about four
fifth of the U3B snRNA molecule in the formation of homologous
stretches, (iii) the regularity in the location of the
homologous blocks in the left half of the circular PSTV
molecule, and (iv) the fact that at least one of the stretches
which lack homology with PSTV form a well defined arm in the
secondary structure of U3B snRNA, strongly support the notion
that this sequence homology can be regarded as a true sign of
structural relationship between these two molecular entities.
Practically the same is true of CEV and CSV. It is
worth mentioning that although the number of nucleotide
residues taking part in the formation of homologies with U3B
snRNA is less in CEV and CSV than in PSTV (103 and 102,
respectively, compared to 119), there are some nucleotide

Figure 5. Nucleotide sequences of CEV, PSTV and CSV, aligned
for maximum homology after Gross *et al.* (1982). Homologous
sequences are indicated by shaded areas as in Gross *et al.*
(1982). Nucleotide residues, individual or in blocks, that
are homologous in a colinear arrangement with nucleotide residues in U3B snRNA (cf. Fig. 2) are boxed. Nucleotide residues in CEV and CSV, which are missing in homologous
positions from the PSTV molecule, but are present in homologous positions in U3B snRNA are encircled. Between individual
boxes or boxes and circles there is mismatch in the corresponding part of the U3B snRNA molecule. Regions ① to ⑥ are
indicated as in Figs 2 and 4.

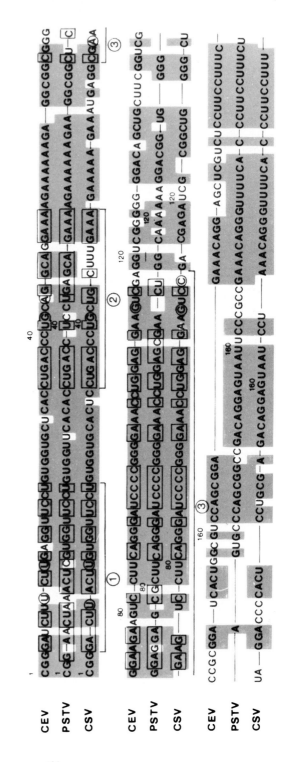

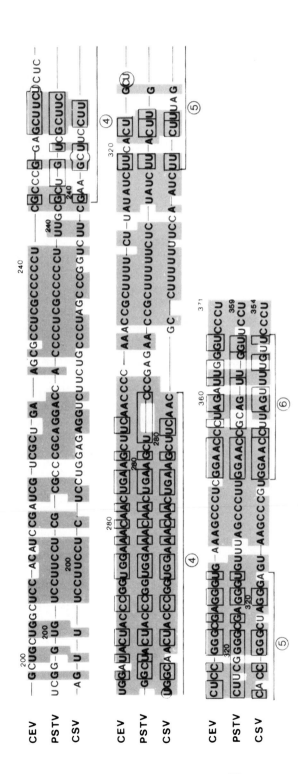

191

residues both in CEV (positions 10, 13, 42, 114, 156, 325, and 326) and CSV (positions 8, 12, 41, 70, 109, 112, 243, and 250) which are missing in homologous positions from the PSTV molecule, but are present in homologous positions in U3B sn-RNA.

The above results and arguments strongly suggest that PSTV, CEV and CSV are phylogenetically related to U3B snRNA. A similar relation may exist between ASBV and U5 snRNA. They also favor the view that elucidation of the function(s) of snRNSs might be a workable way to the understanding of viroid function.

As far as the phylogenetic process by which viroids evolved from U snRNAs is concerned, it might have taken place at both the transcriptional (transcription from an snRNA pseudogene) and the post-transcriptional (circularization) level. Whether such a process took its origin from an alleged plant equivalent of vertebrate snRNAs or from an snRNA of some eukaryote other than plants, cannot be answered at present. Unfortunately, from plants no U-type snRNAs have been isolated so far[1]. There is, however, indication of their existence (Blin et al., 1983). Isolation and sequencing of plant snRNAs, their genes and pseudogenes, as well as a systematic study of sequence homologies between viroids other than the ones described here and snRNAs of different sources, may yield more evidence for the support or rejection of this hypothesis of interrelated phylogenesis of viroids and sn-RNAs. Circularity of viroids versus linearity of U snRNAs as well as the absence of modified bases and a cap structure in viroids versus their presence in U snRNAs are of limited value as arguments against a possible phylogenetic relation-ship between the two, because these differences might have arisen later in evolution.

As far as functional implications of our findings are concerned, one can only speculate without too much experi-mental background. One of the main problems is that at present very little is known about the function of snRNAs themselves. There is, however, one thing worth stressing in this respect: Sequence homology with U3B snRNA is found in the left halves of the circular PSTV, CEV and CSV molecules. This left domain is of decreased stability in all three viroids (Gross et al., 1982), compared to the right domain, as supported by thermal denaturation experiments with PSTV (Henco et al., 1979). One could expect, therefore, that in vivo too, this distinct half of the viroid molecule is functionally exceptionally active. If, in this particular

------

[1] cf. Addendum.

case, primary structure has anything to do with function, one could argue that PSTV, CEV and CSV may interfere with the nuclear events in which U3 snRNA is involved. U3 snRNA is the only snRNA species of nucleolar origin and has been implicated, with some experimental evidence (Prestayko *et al.*, 1970; Zieve and Penman, 1976), to play a role in the processing of ribosomal RNA. PSTV has recently been shown by Schumacher *et al.* (1983) to be preferentially localized in the nucleoli of PSTV-infected tomato plants.

A probably more generally applicable alternative to this hypothesis comes from an original observation by Diener (1981). He noticed, by comparing published sequences, that in PSTV there is a stretch of nucleotide residues (positions 257-279) that shows sequence homology, including some mismatches, with the 5' end of vertebrate U1 snRNA (Fig. 6), supposed to play a vital role in the splicing of pre-mRNA by aligning, through base pairing with the 5' - and 3' - ends of introns, the intron-exon junctions to be spliced (Lerner *et al.*, 1980; Knowler and Wilks, 1980). Such a stretch has later been found also in CEV, CSV (Gross *et al.*, 1982) and CCCV (Haseloff *et al.*, 1982) by actual sequencing work, as well as in ASBV (Kiss and Solymosy, 1982), by comparing published sequences (Fig.6). This means that all viroids tested so far do contain a stretch of nucleotide residues homologous (including some mismatches) with the 5' end of U1 snRNA. Although this region is part of a very stable double-stranded segment in the secondary structure of PSTV, CEV and CSV *in vitro*, its availability as a mainly single-stranded structure under *in vivo* conditions seems feasible (Gross *et al.*, 1982). It would be interesting to know how CCCV and ASBV would behave from this point of view. According to this hypothesis, then, viroids, owing to sequence homology with the 5' end of U1 snRNA, may interfere with the splicing of pre-mRNA. It should be noted that by aligning sequences of PSTV and U1 snRNA for maximum homology, at least three additional stretches can be found in PSTV that are homologous (including some mismatches) with the 5'end of U1 snRNA (Fig. 7). Interestingly, these stretches, if aligned for maximum homology in a different way, will partially fit into the sequences homologous with stretches of U3B snRNA (compare Fig. 2 and Fig. 7). In this case, however, there is no colinearity in arrangement between the two molecules.

To conclude, sequence homologies between viroids and snRNAs (i) suggest that there is a phylogenetic relationship between these two molecular entities and (ii) seem to be in line with a hypothesis according to which viroids may interfere with any of those nuclear and/or nucleolar events in which snRNAs are involved, whatever these events are.

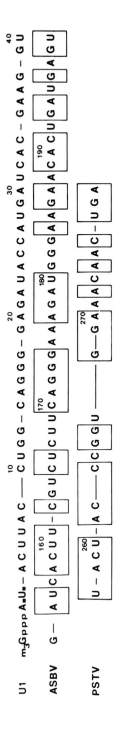

U1   m₃GpppA.U.—ACUUAC——CUGG—CAGGG—GAGAUACCAUGAUCAC—GAAG—GU

ASBV G— AUCACUU-CGUCUCUUCAGGGAAAGAUGGGAAGAACACUGAUGAGU

PSTV U—ACU—AC——CCGGU——G—GAAACAAC—UGA

Figure 6. Sequence homology between the 5' end of Novikoff hepatoma U1 snRNA and a stretch of the ASBV molecule. For comparison, the region of PSTV found by Diener (1981) to be homologous with the 5' end of chicken U1 snRNA is also included. The sequences were aligned for maximum homology. The boxed areas in the sequences of the viroids are homologous with the corresponding segments in U1 snRNA. The figures above the characters refer to the positions of nucleotide residues in the linear U1 snRNA or to those in the circular viroids. (From Kiss and Solymosy, 1982.)

194

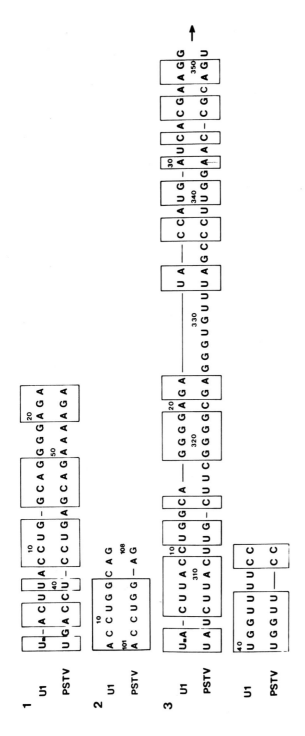

Figure 7. Sequence homologies (boxed areas) between Novikoff hepatoma U1 snRNA stretches of different lengths, all comprising the 5' end region, and three regions (1 to 3) of the PSTV molecule. Sequences are aligned for maximum homology. The figures above the characters refer to the positions of nucleotide residues in the linear U1 snRNA molecule or to those in the circular PSTV molecule. (Modified from Kiss and Solymosy, 1982.)

195

The remote possibility, however, cannot be ruled out that sequence homology between a viroid and an snRNA may just be a reflection of some common structural requirement for biosynthesis and thus be the result of structural convergence.

ACKNOWLEDGEMENTS

Thanks are due to Dr.J. Pósfai (Institute of Biophysics, Biological Research Center, Hungarian Academy of Sciences, Szeged) for helping us write a computer program This work has been supported by grant 363/82/1.6 of the Hungarian Academy of Sciences.

REFERENCES

Bernstein, L. B., Mount, S.M., and Weiner, A.M. (1983). Pseudogenes for human small nuclear RNA U3 appear to arise by integration of self-primed reverse transcripts of the RNA into new chromosomal sites. *Cell* *32*, 461-472.

Blin, N., Weber, T., and Alonso, A. (1983). Cross-reaction of snRNA and an Alu I-like sequence from rat with DNAs from different eucaryotic species. *Nucl. Acids Res.* *11*, 1375-1388.

Branlant, C., Krol, A., Ebel, J.-P., Lazar, E., Haendler, B., and Jacob, M. (1982). U2 RNA shares a structural domain with U1,U4,and U5 RNAs. *EMBO J.* *1*, 1259-1265.

Busch, H., Reddy, R., Rothblum L., and Choi, Y.C. (1982). SnRNAs,SnRNPs,and RNA processing. *Ann. Rev. Biochem.* *51*, 617-654.

Davies, J.W., Kaesberg, P., and Diener, T.O. (1974). Potato spindle tuber viroid. Xll. An investigation of viroid RNA as a messenger for protein synthesis. *Virology 61*, 281-286.

Diener, T.O. (1971a). Potato spindle tuber virus: A plant virus with properties of a free nucleic acid. III. Subcellular location of PSTV-RNA and the question of whether virions exist in extracts or in situ. *Virology 43*, 75-89.

Diener, T.O. (1971b). Potato spindle tuber "virus". IV. A replicating, low molecular weight RNA. *Virology 45*, 411-428.

Diener, T.O. (1974). Viroids: The smallest known agents of infectious disease. *Ann. Rev. Microbiol. 28*, 23-39.

Diener, T.O. (1981). Are viroids escaped introns? *Proc. Natl.Acad.Sci.U.S.A. 78*, 5014-5015.

Domdey, H., Jank, P., Sänger, H.L., and Gross, H. J. (1978). Studies on the primary and secondary structure of potato spindle tuber viroid: Products of digestion

with ribonuclease A and ribonuclease T_1 and
modification with bisulfite. *Nucl. Acids Res. 5,*
1221-1236.

Flores, R., and Semancik, J. S. (1982). Properties of a
cell-free system for synthesis of citrus exocortis
viroid. *Proc. Natl. Acad. Sci. U.S.A.79,* 6285- 6288.

Frederiksen, S., Hellung-Larsen, P., and Gram-Jensen, E.
(1978). The differential inhibitory effect of
α-amanitin on the synthesis of low molecular weight
RNA components in BHK cells. *FEBS Lett. 87,* 227-231.

Goad, W. B., and Kanehisa, M.I. (1982). Pattern recognition
in nucleic acid sequences. I. A general method for
finding local homologies and symmetries. *Nucl. Acids
Res. 10,* 247-263.

Gram-Jensen, E., Hellung-Larsen P., and Frederiksen, S.
(1979). Synthesis of low molecular weight RNA components A, C and D by polymerase II in α-amanitin-re-
sistant hamster cells. *Nucleic Acids Res. 6,* 321-330.

Gross, H. J., Domdey, H., Lossow, C., Jank, P., Raba, M.,
Alberty, H., and Sänger, H.L. (1978). Nucleotide
sequence and secondary structure of potato spindle
tuber viroid. *Nature (London)273,* 203-208.

Gross, H.J., Krupp, G., Domdey, H., Raba, M., Alberty, H.,
Lossow, C.H., Ramm, K., and Sänger, H.L. (1982).
Nucleotide sequence and secondary structure of ci-
trus exocortis and chrysanthemum stunt viroid.
Eur. J. Biochem.121, 249-257.

Hall, T.C. Wepprich, R.K., Davies, J. W., Weathers, L.G.,
and Semancik, J.S. (1974). Functional distinctions between the ribonucleic acids from citrus
exocortis viroid and plant viruses: Cell-free translation and amino-acylation reactions. *Virology 61,*
486-492.

Haseloff, J., and Symons, R.H. (1981). Chrysanthemum stunt
viroid - primary sequence and secondary structure.
Nucl. Acids Res. 9, 2741-2752.

Haseloff, J., Mohamed, N.A., and Symons, R.H. (1982). Viroid
RNAs of the cadang-cadang disease of coconuts. *Nature
(London) 299,* 316-322.

Hellung-Larsen, P. (1977). "Low Molecular Weight RNA Components in Eukaryotic Cells." FADL's Forlag,
Copenhagen.

Henco, K., Sänger, H.L., and Riesner, D. (1979). Fine
structure melting of viroids as studied by kinetic
methods. *Nucl. Acids Res. 6,* 3041-3059.

Kiss, T., and Solymosy, F. (1982). Sequence homologies
between a viroid and a small nuclear RNA (snRNA)
species of mammalian origin. *FEBS Lett. 144,* 318-320.

Kiss, T., Pósfai, J., and Solymosy, F. (1983). Sequence
     homology between potato spindle tuber viroid and U3B
     snRNA. *FEBS Lett. 163*, 217-220.
Knowler, J. T., and Wilks, A.F. (1980). Ribonucleoprotein
     particles and the maturation of eukaryote mRNA.
     Trends Biochem. Sci. 5, 268-271.
Lerner, M.R., Boyle, J.A., Mount, S.M., Wolin, S.L., and
     Steitz, J.A. (1980). Are snRNPs involved in splicing?
     Nature 283, 220-224.
Mühlbach, H.-P., and Sänger, H.L. (1979). Viroid replication
     is inhibited by α-amanitin. *Nature (London)278*,
     185-188.
Prestayko, A.W., Tonato, M., and Busch, H. (1970). Low
     molecular weight RNA associated with 28S nucleolar
     RNA. *J. Mol. Biol.47*, 505-515.
Rackwitz, H.-R., Rohde, W., and Sänger, H.L. (1981).
     DNA-dependent RNA polymerase-II of plant origin
     transcribes viroid RNA into full-length copies.
     Nature (London) 291. 297-301.
Riesner, D., Henco, K., Rokohl, U., Klotz, G., Kleinschmidt,
     A.K., Gross, H.J., Domdey,H., and Sänger,H.L. (1979).
     Structure and structure formation of viroids. *J. Mol.
     Biol. 133*, 85-115.
Sänger, H.L. (1982). Biology, structure, functions and pos-
     sible origin of viroids. *In* "Encyclopedia of Plant
     Physiology". New Series Vol. 14B (B. Parthier and D.
     Boulter eds.), pp. 368-454.
Schumacher, J., Sänger, H.L., and Riesner, D. (1983) Subcellu-
     lar localization of viroids in highly purified nuclei
     from tomato leaf tissue. *EMBO J. 2*, 1549-1555.
Semancik, J. S., Tsuruda, D., Zaner, L., Geelen, J.L.M.C.,
     and Weathers, J.G. (1976). Exocortis disease:
     Subcellular distribution of pathogenic (viroid) RNA.
     Virology 69, 669-676.
Semancik, J.S., Conejero, V., and Gerhart, J. (1977). citrus
     exocortis viroid: Survey of protein synthesis in
     Xenopus laevis oocytes following addition of viroid
     RNA. *Virology 80*, 218-221.
Symons, R.H. (1981). Avocado sunblotch viroid - primary se-
     quence and proposed secondary structure. *Nucl. Acids
     Res. 9*, 6527-6537.
Takahashi, T., and Diener, T.O.(1975). Potato spindle tu-
     ber viroid. XIV. Replication in nuclei isolated from
     infected leaves. *Virology 64*, 106-114.
Visvader, J.E., Gould, A.R., Bruening, G.E., and Symons,
     R.H. (1982). Citrus exocortis viroid: Nucleotide
     sequence and secondary structure of an Australian
     isolate. *FEBS Lett. 137*, 288-292.

Wild, U., Ramm, K., Sänger, H.L., and Riesner, D. (1980)
     Loops in viroids. *Eur. J. Biochem. 103,* 227-235.
Zieve, G.W., and Penman, S. (1976).   Small RNA species of
     the HeLa cell: Metabolism and subcellular location.
     Cell 8, 19-31.

[1]ADDENDUM

     Very recently, Krol *et al.* reported in *Nucl. Acids Res.*
(Vol. 11, pp. 8583-8594, 1983) the isolation of U1, U2 and U5
snRNAs from pea nuclei, with the nucleotide sequence of the
3'-terminal halves of U1 and U2 and the complete sequence of
five out of the six U5 snRNA variants determined.

Chapter 11

IN VIVO INTERMEDIATES AND THE ROLLING CIRCLE
MECHANISM IN VIROID REPLICATION

Andrea D. Branch
Laboratory of Genetics
The Rockefeller University

Kerry K. Willis
New York University Medical Center
550 First Avenue
New York, New York, 10016

George Davatelis
Memorial Sloan-Kettering Cancer Center
425 East 68th Street
New York, N.Y. 10021

Hugh Robertson
Laboratory of Genetics
The Rockefeller University
New York, N.Y. 10021

I.   INTRODUCTION

Plant viroids are among the most intriguing and mysterious agents of disease; however, during the past several
years, many details of their biochemical makeup have emerged
(for a review, see Diener, 1979; Dickson, 1979 and Sänger,
1982). The assays applied to early viroid studies have
subsequently been used by those seeking infectious agents
associated with other diseases (Rizetto *et al.*, 1980; Randles
et al., 1981); a more complete description of the viroid life
cycle would make viroids even more useful as prototype systems. Thus, we and others have carried out numerous experiments to determine the mode of viroid replication. Our
approach to studying viroid replication has been to identify
viroid-specific nucleic acids which accumulate in infected
tomato plants. The nucleic acids have been studied both as
isolated molecules and as complexes. These data have been
combined with information from other groups to yield the
model of the potato spindle tuber viroid (PSTV) replication
cycle shown in Fig.1.

SUBVIRAL PATHOGENS
OF PLANTS AND ANIMALS:

Copyright © 1985 by Academic Press, Inc.
All rights of reproduction in any form reserved.
ISBN 0-12-470230-9

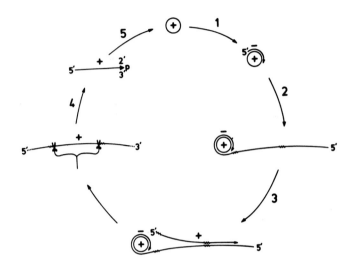

Figure 1.Hypothetical pathway of potato spindle tuber viroid
replication.   See text for details.

II.   A ROLLING CIRCLE MODEL FOR PSTV REPLICATION

A.   Outline of a possible replication cycle.

The hypothetical PSTV replication cycle begins at the
top of Figure 1 with the entrance of an infecting circular
plus strand (marked "+") into the cell and the initiation of
minus strand synthesis (Step 1).   The plus strand is copied
by a rolling circle mechanism into a multimeric complementary
strand (marked"-") composed of RNA (Step 2).   The multimeric
minus strands, with each viroid repeat delineated by short
dividers, then serve as the template for the production of
multimeric plus strands (Step 3), which must be cleaved to

lane (c), 4000 dpm of ^{125}I-labeled PSTV size marker [359
bases (Gross *et al.*, 1978]; lane (d),3000 dpm of pBR322 ^{32}P-
labeled DNA restriction fragments with sizes of 4362 (1),
1631 (2), 516 (3), 506 (3), 396 (4), 344 (5), 298 (6),
221 (7), 220 (7), 154 (8), and 75 (9) bases (Sutcliffe, 1979).
"0" marks the origin of electrophoresis;   the arrowhead marks
the position of the bromphenol blue dye marker;   dots indicate the positions of the four major minus strand bands.
Note: This figure originally appeared in   Branch, A.D.,
Robertson, H.D., and Dickson, E. (1981).   Longer-than-unit-
length viroid minus strands are present in RNA from infected
plants. *Proc. Natl. Acad. Sci. USA 78,* 6381-6385.

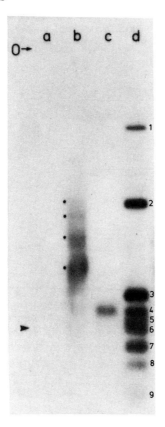

Figure 2. Detection of multimeric PSTV minus strands by Northern hybridization. Samples were treated with glyoxal and dimethyl sulfoxide (McMaster and Carmichael, 1977) and then fractionated by electrophoresis in a 1.6% agarose gel, 10mM phosphate buffer, pH 7.1 (Thomas, 1980). Nucleic acids were transferred to nitrocellulose (Southern,1975). Filters were incubated with 2 X TESS--1 X TESS is 5 mM 2- [tris (hydroxymethyl) methyl] amino ethanesulfonic acid; 5 mM EDTA; 0.15 M NaCl; 0.25% sodium dodecyl sulfate (pH 7.4)--(0.016 ml/cm^2 of nitrocellulose) containing ^{125}I-labelled PSTV at 200,000 dpm/ml and RNA extracted from uninfected tomato plants at 2 g/ml, washed, and prepared for autoradiography. Lane (a) depicts nucleic acids from uninfected tomato plants; lane (b), nucleic acids from PSTV-infected tomato plants;

produce unit length molecules with characteristic endgroups (as in Step 4) and circularized (Step 5) to yield progeny circles. It is interesting to note that the combined steps of cleavage and ligation, required for viroid replication as depicted here, make this process reminiscent of RNA splicing (Chow *et al.*, 1977; Peebles *et al.*, 1979). Certain features of this PSTV replication pathway may apply to other systems as well, such as some of the virus satellites (Schneider and Thompson, 1977: Sogo and Schneider, 1982; Kiefer *et al.*, 1982) and the virusoids (Randles *et al.* 1981; Gould, 1981; Chu *et al.*, 1983; Haseloff, 1983).

   B. Evidence for the involvement of multimeric RNA's in viroid replication.
      1) Detection and analysis of multimeric minus strands.
   The first data suggesting that viroid replication might proceed via a rolling circle mechanism came from Northern hybridization studies. In these experiments, nucleic acids were extracted from infected plants by standard procedures and then chemically denatured, fractionated by electrophoresis in agarose gels, transferred to nitrocellulose and hybridized to ^{125}I-labeled PSTV RNA. An array of minus strand RNAs was detected ranging in size up to at least 2000 bases in length (see Figure 2, lane b). Molecular weight analysis was carried out, using ^{32}P-labeled pBR322 restriction fragments (Figure 2, lane d) and ^{125}I- labeled PSTV plus strands (Figure 2, lane c) as standards. Complementary strand nucleic acids were heterogeneous in size, with four discrete bands containing molecules approximately 700, 1050, 1500, and 1800 nucleotides long (see Branch and Robertson, 1984, Figure 1).One straight-forward mechanism for production of long minus strands is based on the rolling circle model for viral RNA synthesis (Brown and Martin, 1965) and for plus strand synthesis of the DNA bacteriophage ϕx174 (Gilbert and Dressler, 1968). Thus, we proposed that the template for PSTV minus strand synthesis is the circular form of the viroid, and that pauses between successive rounds of synthesis account for the favored size classes, which are multiples of unit length (Branch *et al.*, 1981.

   The high specific activity probes (10^8 dpm/ g) used in this study were obtained by application of the Commerford technique (Commerford, 1971) as previously modified (Robertson *et al.*, 1973; Prensky, 1976; Dickson *et al.*, 1979a). Appropriate controls carried out using RNA duplexes composed of influenza virus plus and minus strands proved that both of the chemical treatments used in the viroid studies were fully denaturing (Branch *et al.*, 1981). Stringent hybridization

conditions were selected which resulted in no labeling of
nucleic acids from uninfected plants (Figure 2, 1and a) and
no labeling of viroid plus strands (note the absence of
hybridization to the unit length position, Figure 2,lane b).
Moreover, to test the specificity of the hybridization conditions, ^{125}I-labeled RNA was recovered following hybridization,
and analyzed. The characteristic RNase T1 fingerprint of
PSTV was obtained (see Branch *et al.*, 1981, Figure 2).

To determine whether multimeric minus strands could be
detected in a different viroid system, we examined RNA from
tomato plants infected with citrus exocortis viroid (CEV),
the first viroid for which minus RNA strands were detected
(Grill and Semancik, 1978). The pattern of complementary
strand nucleic acids associated with CEV was strikingly
similar (see Branch and Robertson, 1984, Figure 1) to the
multimeric minus strands of PSTV. It is now widely accepted
that longer than unit length minus strands are present in
extracts of viroid-infected plants; they have been detected
by other groups in studies of PSTV (Owens and Diener,1982;
Rohde and Sänger,1981), CEV (Grill *et al.*, 1980), and avocado
sunblotch viroid (ASBV) (Bruening *et al.*, 1982). In addition,
the complementary strand nucleic acids found in association
with replication of the virusoid of velvet tobacco mottle
virus (VTMoV) are much longer than the encapsidated form of
the circular plus strand (Chu *et al.*, 1983). Perhaps the
most impressive demonstration of multimeric minus strands was
provided by the study of RNA's associated with tobacco ringspot virus satellite (TobRV-sat) carried out by Bruening and
co-workers (Kiefer *et al.*, 1982). As shown in Figure 3,
twelve distinct minus strand RNA's can be detected; the
longest species are about 4500 bases long.

Despite the widespread occurrence of multimeric minus
strands, it is possible that such RNA's are side-products
which accumulate during the course of viroid infection and
that the actual template for plus strand synthesis is a unit
length species. In fact, a model for viroid replication
based on a circular unit length minus strand is discussed in
Chapter 12 of this volume by Symons *et al.* However, as
illustrated by Figure 2 (lane b), unit length minus strands
are not evident in Northern hybridization experiments.
Indeed, a slight gap is present at this region of the blot.
To test our ability to detect unit length minus strands, a
reconstruction experiment was carried out. The unit length
minus strands needed for this experiment were prepared by
treating nucleic acids of infected plants with pancreatic
RNase (under conditions which lead to the digestion of single
but not double-stranded RNA's) as described previously

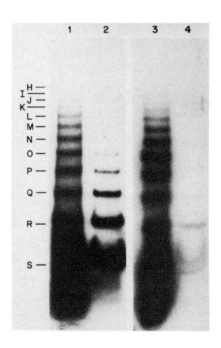

Figure 3. Slowly migrating forms of satellite RNA from
virions and from extracts of infected tissue. Double-
stranded RNA from tissue infected with TobRV plus TobRV-
sat (lanes 1,3) and RNA from virus particles (lanes 2, 4)
derived from a similar infection were denatured in formaldehyde and applied to a 1.5% agarose, 2 M formaldehyde gel.
After electrophoresis the zones were transferred to a nitrocellulose sheet. The molecular hybridization probes were
[^{32}P] cDNA transcribed from electrophoretically purified Tob-
RV-sat RNA S (lanes 1,2) and [5'-^{32}P]RNA S (lanes 3, 4).

Note: This figure originally appeared in Kiefer, M.C.,
Daubert, S.D., Schneider, I.R., and Bruening, G. (1982).
Multimeric forms of satellite of tobacco ringspot virus
RNA. *Virology 121,* 262-273.

(Branch *et al.,* 1981). This treatment is accompanied by the
appearance of duplexes ("cores") containing unit length minus
strands (Owens and Cress, 1980; Branch *et al.,1981*). As
shown in Figure 4, unit length minus strands could be readily
detected in this preparation (as in lanes d,f,h, and j).
However, the ability to detect minus strands was abolished by

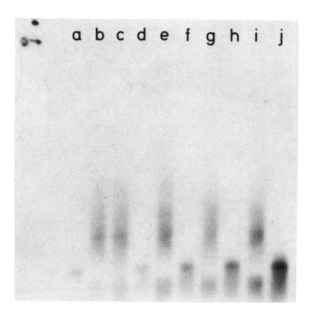

Figure 4. A large accumulation of plus strands can prevent detection of minus strands by Northern hybridization. Nucleic acids were denatured by treatment with glyoxal and dimethyl sulfoxide, fractionated by electrophoresis, transferred to nitrocellulose and hybridized to ^{125}I-labeled PSTV RNA in 2 X TESS at 73° as described before (Branch *et al.*, 1981). To generate unit length minus strands, nucleic acids from infected plants were digested with pancreatic RNase (under conditions favoring cleavage of single-stranded RNA's) and then repurified by phenol extraction and CF11 cellulose chromatography as described before (Branch *et al.*, 1981). Such preparations contain mostly DNA, with a small amount of double-stranded RNA (Branch, 1981)--including viroid-specific RNA's of approximately unit length. Samples contained the following: 4000 dpm of ^{125}I-labeled PSTV (lane a); 5 μg of nucleic acids from PSTV-infected tomato plants either alone (lane b) or mixed with 1 μg (lane c), 2 μg (lane e), 3 μg (lane g), or 4 μg (lane i) of nucleic acids pre-treated with pancreatic RNase; 1 μg (lane d), 2 μg (lane f), 3 μg (lane h), or 4 μg (lane j) of pancreatic RNase-resistant nucleic acids. "0" denotes the origin of electrophoresis of the gel.

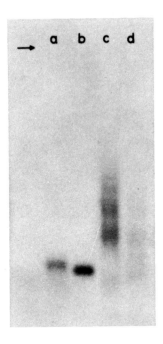

Figure 5. Northern hybridization analysis of PSTV minus strand RNA's following treatment with RNase T1 or chromatography on cellulose CF11. Nucleic acids of PSTV-infected tomato plants, pre-treated as described below, were denatured with glyoxal and dimethyl sulfoxide (McMaster and Carmichael, 1977), fractionated by electrophoresis, transferred to nitrocellulose and hybridized to ^{125}I-labeled PSTV RNA. The sample shown in lane (a) contained 5 μg of plant nucleic acids which had been incubated with 5 μg/ml RNase T1 in 0.01 M Tris, pH 7.6; 0.001 M EDTA at 37° for 40 min and then prepared for Northern analysis as described before (Branch *et al.*, 1981). Lane (b) indicates the position of a ^{125}I-labeled PSTV size marker (4000 dpm). Lane (c) contained 5 μg of total nucleic acids; while lane (d) contained 0.1 μg of nucleic acids eluting in the double-stranded RNA fraction following two sequential rounds of cellulose CF11 chromatography (Franklin, 1966). Samples fractionated in lanes (b) and (d) contained 1 μg of *E. coli* tRNA (carrier). An arrow denotes the origin of electrophoresis of the gel.

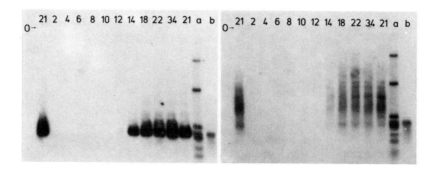

Figure 6. Northern blot analysis of PSTV multimeric plus and minus strands present at various times following infection. Nucleic acids were extracted from PSTV-infected plants at various times following inoculation. Aliquots of the LiCl supernatant fraction of these extracts were denatured by treatment with glyoxal (McMaster and Carmichael, 1977), fractionated by electrophoresis in 1.6% agarose gels, transferred to nitrocellulose (Thomas, 1980) and then hybridized to either ^{32}P-labeled PSTV cDNA (panel A--to detect plus strands) or ^{125}I-labeled PSTV (panel B--to detect minus strands). Numerals across the top of the figure indicate the number of days which elapsed between inoculation and extraction of the tomato plants. In each panel, a sample containing nucleic acids extracted on day 21 was fractionated on the left-hand side of the gel so that the transfer and binding of nucleic acids to this region of the filters could be monitored. Lanes (a) and (b) indicate the positions of pBR322 restriction fragment size markers (see legend to Figure 2) and a ^{125}I-labeled PSTV size marker, respectively. "0" denotes the originof electrophoresis of the gels.
Note: This figure originally appeared in Branch, A.D., and Robertson, H.D., 1984. A replication cycle for <u>viroids and</u> other small infectious RNA's. *Science.*

the addition of 5 μg of nucleic acids extracted from PSTV-infected plants (lanes c, e, g, and i)--presumably because the (relatively) large quantity of plus strands present in the nucleic extract took all the available minus strands and made hybrids with them, outcompeting the probe. To eliminate the free progeny plus strands (whose presence might interfere with detection of unit length minus strands), cellulose CF11 chromatography (Franklin, 1966) was applied to extracts of nucleic acids of infected plants. In this procedure, mature viroid RNA chromatographs as single-stranded RNA, while duplexes containing viroid-specific RNA's chromatograph as typical double-stranded RNA's (Zelcer *et al.*, 1982). Fractions enriched for double-stranded RNA's (which would be expected to contain viroid replication complexes) were studied by Northern hybridization. In this material, predominantly multimeric minus strands were detected, while unit length minus strands (although detectable) did not form a particularly prominent band (see Figure 5, lane d). The presence of multimeric minus strands in the double-stranded RNA fraction supports the hypothesis that they are involved in replication.

To investigate further the potential for the multimeric minus strands to serve as templates for plus strand synthesis, we examined the profile of PSTV-specific RNAs present in plants at various times after infection. As shown in Figure 6 (compare panels A and B), as soon as plus strands could be detected (day 14), multimeric minus strands were also present. Thus, the time course of multimeric minus strand synthesis indicates that they are present at the appropriate times to play a direct role in replication. If these minus strands were copied, they could give rise to plus strands ranging in size up to at least 2000 bases.

2). Properties of longer than unit length plus strands suggesting a precursor function.

We have detected multimeric plus strands of PSTV using several experimental approaches (Branch, 1981). For example, in the Northern hybridization analysis shown in Figure 7, multimeric plus strands were evident following hybridization to ^{32}P-labeled PSTV cDNA. As in our studies of minus strands, the nucleic acids were fully denatured with glyoxal prior to electrophoresis. Additional experiments were carried out in which the samples were denatured with formaldehyde/formamide (Branch, 1981). Samples were compared before (see Figure 7, lane a) and after fractionation by LiCl (lane b) and following chromatography on cellulose CF11(lane c); the double-stranded RNA fraction was enriched for longer than unit length plus strands (see lane c). Other approaches have also been used for obtaining fractions enriched in multimeric PSTV strands. In one series of experiments, a typical non-denaturing viroid preparative gel was run according to Morris and Smith (1977) and then cut up into slices (see Figure 8). RNA was recovered from each gel band and then analyzed by Northern hybridization. PSTV-specific RNAs from such gel bands are shown in lanes (a)-(f) of Figure 9; certain fractions (see lanes a and c, for example) contain a high proportion of longer than unit length plus strands. Lane (h) depicts ^{32}P-labeled pBR322 size markers that were run in the gel

Figure 7.   Enrichment of multimeric viroid plus strands in
double-stranded RNA-containing fractions from PSTV-infected
tomato plants.   Total nucleic acids from PSTV-infected tomato
plants (lane a), extracted as described before (Dickson,
1979), were fractionated by precipitation in 2 M LiCl at 0°
(land b) and then enriched for double-stranded RNA (lane c)
by two successive purifications on cellulose CF11 columns
(Franklin, 1966).   Aliquots of each preparation (0.5   g of
plant nucleic acids plus 2.0   g of *E. coli* tRNA) were
glyoxalated (McMaster and Carmichael, 1977), subjected to
electrophoretic separation in a 1.6% agarose gel, blotted to
nitrocellulose (Thoma, 1980) and hybridized to ^{32}P–labeled
PSTV cDNA (Branch, 1981).   An arrow marks the origin of
electrophoresis; an arrowhead denotes the position of the
bromphenol blue dye marker.

along with the unlabeled plant RNA's and then transferred to
nitrocellulose.   Additional RNA size markers were fractionated in the same gel (data not shown).   The log of the molecular weights of the RNA and DNA size markers (marked with open
circles in Figure 10) were plotted against the distance they
migrated in the gel and used to estimate the sizes of the

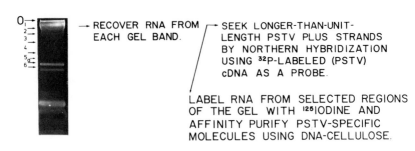

Figure 8. Fractionation of nucleic acids from PSTV-infected
tomato plants in a 5% non-denaturing polyacrylamide gel.
Nucleic acids from PSTV-infected plants were extracted as
described before (Dickson, 1979) and then an aliquot (250 μg)
of the LiCl supernatant fraction was subjected to electrophoresis in a 5% non-denaturing polyacrylamide gel (Morris
and Smith, 1977). After staining with ethidium bromide, the
gel was sliced at the positions indicated in the figure.
Nucleic acids were recovered from each gel band by standard
techniques (Dickson, 1979) and then studied by Northern blot
analysis (see Figure 9) and DNA-cellulose affinity chromatography (see Figure 12). Gel band number 6 contains a mixture
of circular and linear PSTV RNA. "0" marks the origin of
electrophoresis of the gel.

PSTV plus strand RNAs depicted in Figure 9. Three PSTV specific RNAs were detected which appear to be part of a multimeric series;   their sizes were 365, 700 and 1020 bases
(exact multiples of PSTV would be 359 (Gross *et al.*, 1978),
718, and 1077 bases). An additional band (estimated to be
about 520 bases in length) was observed in certain fractions
(see Figure 9, lane a). A possible mechanism to explain its
origin is presented below.
      For multimeric plus strands to yield mature circular
progeny, RNA cleavage and ligation are required. If these
processing steps do not keep pace with replication, the
precursor forms will accumulate. Although the processing of
PSTV plus strands appears to be highly efficient under our
growth conditions, in other systems (such as avocado sunblotch viroid) plus strand dimers can be readily detected as
major RNA bands even in gels stained with ethidium bromide
(Bruening *et al.*, 1982). Highly purified dimer-length plus
strands of cadang-cadang RNA have been obtained and sequenced
(Haseloff *et al.*, 1982). Prominent multimeric plus strands

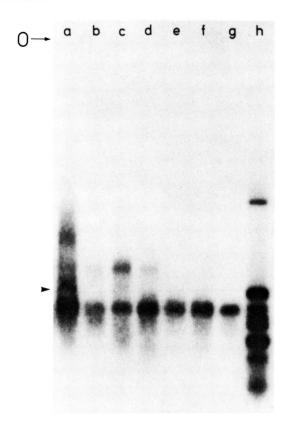

Figure 9. Detection of PSTV plus strand multimers by Northern hybridization analysis of nucleic acids recovered from
slices of a 5% non-denaturing polyacrylamide gel. Nucleic
acids of PSTV-infected tomato plants,fractionated by electrophoresis and eluted from gel bands as described in the legend
to Figure 8, were glyoxalated(McMaster and Carmichael,1977),
separated by electrophoresis in an agarose gel, blotted to
nitrocellulose (Thomas, 1980), and hybridized to ^{32}P-labeled
PSTV cDNA as described before (Branch *et al.*, 1981). Lane
(a) contained RNA from the origin of the 5% non-denaturing
gel [gel band (1); see Figure 8]. All samples (lanes a-f)
contained 2 g of *E. coli* tRNA plus an equal aliquot (one-
third of the total) of the nucleic acid eluted from a given
gel band. Lane (g) contained ^{125}I-labeled PSTV marker RNA,
while lane (h) contained ^{32}P-labeled restriction fragment
size markers produced by digestion of pBR322 DNA by *Hin*fI
(see legend to Figure 2.)"0" marks the origin of electrophoresis, while the arrowhead indicates the position of a bromphenol blue dye marker.

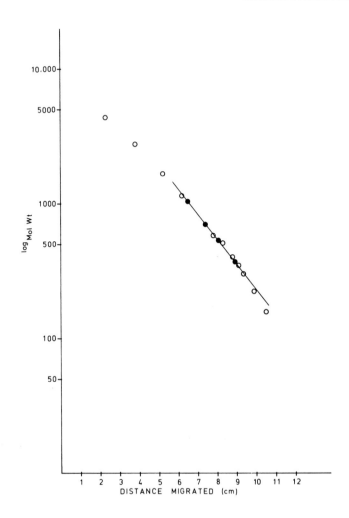

Figure 10. Size estimates for PSTV plus strands. The log of the molecular weights of a series of fully denatured RNA and DNA size markers were plotted against the distance of migration and used to estimate the molecular weights of PSTV plus strands fractionated in the same gel. Marker species (indicated by open circles) included ^{32}P-labeled *Hin*fI restriction fragments of pBR322 (ranging in size from 75–1631 bases; see legend to Figure 2) and the ^{32}P-labeled RNase III cleavage products of the bacteriophage T7 early mRNA precursor [ranging in size from 392 to 2740 bases (Dunn and Studier, 1981)]. PSTV plus strands (detected by Northern hybridization; see Figure 9) are indicated by closed circles.

accumulate in plants replicating TobRV-sat (see Kiefer *et al.*, 1982 and Figure 5, lanes 1 and 2); longer than unit length plus strands of the circular virusoid RNA have been found in extracts from plants infected with VTMoV (Chu *et al.*, 1983; Haseloff, 1983) and Solanum nodiflorum virus (Haseloff, 1983). In addition to multimeric plus strands, viroid-specific plus strands of fractional length have also been detected by analysis of nucleic acids from plants infe - cted by a number of viroids. In addition to the 520 baselong PSTV RNA mentioned above, a series of fractional length RNAs associated with ASBV have been described (Bruening *et al.*, 1982). Furthermore, late in infection, cadang-cadang-infected palms accumulate RNAs which contain small duplications (and, thus, migrate between monomeric and dimeric forms). Although it is not known how any of these RNAs of intermediate size are generated, it is interesting to speculate that they may arise via post-transcriptional processing events whereby incorrect cleavage takes place beyond the position in the multimeric precursor appropriate to give unit length molecules. Such incorrect cleavage could give rise to "dead end" products, or if it generated molecules capable of circula - rization and replication, cleavage at cryptic sites could lead to the accumulation of molecules containing internal duplication. Multiple rounds of cryptic cleavage and replication could give rise to species such as the "slow" forms of cadang-cadang (Haseloff *et al.*, 1982).

       3). Discussion.

    There is widespread agreement in the field that multimeric viroid plus strands exist and play an important role in replication, although debate continues regarding the pathway leading to the production of long plus strands. Symons and collaborators (Bruening *et al.*, 1982) propose that multimeric plus strands are synthesized by a rolling circle mechanism from a unit length circular minus strand in a process which is directly analogous to the original rolling circle model presented by Brown and Martin (1965). Favoring this model is the observation that prominent multimeric minus strands were not detected by Northern analysis of ASBV-specific RNA's (Bruening *et al.*, 1982). However, since multimeric ASBV *plus* strands accumulate to high levels in infected tissues, it is possible that multimeric ASBV minus strands were present, but not detectable. As noted above (see Figure 4), whenever one member of a pair of complementary strands is present in large excess over the other, the minority strand is difficult, or impossible, to detect by Northern hybridization analysis.

Final conclusions regarding the nature of the viroid minus strand may depend upon future pulse labeling studies coupled with direct analysis of purified viroid-specific RNAs. However, for the moment, we favor a model based on multimeric minus strands for the following reasons: (i) longer-than-unit length minus strands have been found in association with each viroid system in which they have been carefully sought--including ASBV (see Bruening *et al.*, 1982); (ii) multimeric minus strands can be detected as soon after infection as plus strands can be identified by Northern hybridization analysis (see Figure 6); (iii) multimeric minus strands are isolated in complexes which contain extensive regions of regular RNA:RNA duplex structure--a property characteristic of molecules involved in replication. Besides acting directly as templates for plus strand synthesis, multimeric minus strands could also function as precursors, giving rise to unit length minus strands.

      C.   Pathways for converting plus strand precursors to mature progeny circles.

However they are generated (whether their template is multimeric and/or circular) precursor plus strands must be cleaved to produce unit length progeny. If cleavage and circularization are not tightly coupled processes *in vivo*, unit length linear plus strands might accumulate in infected plants (see Tyc *et al.*, 1983, for evidence that tRNA "half" molecules can be isolated from extracts of *Chlamydomonas* and wheat germ). In fact, unit length linear plus strands have been widely detected and studied (Owens *et al.*, 1977; Palukaitis and Symons, 1980), although their biological role and biochemical composition remain obscure. The apparent formal similarity between viroid circularization and RNA splicing suggested that at least some of these molecules might possess characteristics of RNAs which are intermediates in the splicing reaction. Thus, in collaboration with members of Dr. J. Abelson's laboratory, we incubated ^{125}I-labeled linear viroid RNA molecules obtained from extracts of infected plants in the presence of an RNA ligase purified from wheat germ (Branch *et al.*, 1982). This enzyme activity, originally identified because of its ability to ligate tRNA exons, was capable of ligating the PSTV RNA to produce circular molecules (see Figure 11). In the case of yeast tRNA, whose splicing mechanism has been studied in detail (Greer *et al.* 1983),the RNA splicing intermediates have highly characteristic 2', 3' cyclic phosphate termini. As first shown

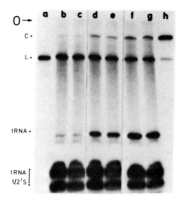

Figure 11. Viroid circularization by the RNA ligase from wheat germ. ^{125}I-labeled PSTV natural linear RNA molecules and ^{32}P-labeled tRNA half-molecules (knapp *et al.*, 1979) were incubated with increasing concentrations of wheat germ RNA ligase. Lanes (a) and (h) show PSTV linear and circular size markers, respectively. Lanes (b) to (g) show reaction mixtures including ligase, diluted 1:50 (b and c); 1:25 (d and e); 1:12.5 (f and g). Incubations were for 20 minutes (b, d, and f) or 40 minutes (lanes c, e, and g) at 30° under conditions used before (Knapp *et al.*, 1979). The positions of the tRNA half-molecules and the mature sequence tRNA are indicated.

Note: This figure originally appeared in Branch, A.D., Robertson, H.D., Greer, C., Gegenheimer, P., Peebles, C., and Abelson, J. (1982). Cell-free circularization of viroid progeny RNA by an RNA ligase from wheat germ. *Science 217* , 1147-1149.

by Filipowicz and co-workers (Konarska *et al.*, 1981; Konarska *et al.*, 1982), such cyclic phosphate termini are also required by the RNA ligase of wheat germ. To prove that cyclic termini were present on the naturally occurring viroid RNA acted upon by the wheat germ ligase, we tested the susceptibility of the ligation reaction to pre-treatment of the viroid RNA with calf alkaline phosphatase (CAPase). Cyclic phosphate termini are not removed by treatment with CAPase (Konarska *et al.*, 1982); ligation of the viroid RNA was not inhibited by treatment with CAPase (Branch *et al.*, 1982).

To show that the conditions used for phosphatase treatment were capable of removing a conventional phosphate, a control experiment was carried out using linear molecules produced by mild digestion of PSTV circles with nuclease S1. This treatment produces molecules which have 5' terminal phosphates and which can be circularized by the RNA ligase from *E. coli* infected by bacteriophage T4. CAPase pretreatment of the S1 derived linear viroid RNA's completely inhibited ligation, indicating that CAPase was able to remove efficiently conventional phosphates present at the termini of full-length RNA's.

To determine whether the viroid circularization followed the mechanism described by Filipowicz and co-workers in detail, viroid RNA was incubated with highly purified RNA ligase from wheat germ in a reaction mixture containing gamma ^{32}P-labeled ATP. ^{32}P-labeled viroid RNA's with the mobilities of circular and linear viroid size markers were produced (Branch and Robertson, 1984). Previous studies of both Konarska *et al.*, (1982) and Greer *et al.*, (1983) had demonstrated that the phosphate incorporated into the new 3', 5' phosphodiester bond is provided by ATP, while the phosphate originally present as a 2', 3' cyclic moiety is shifted onto the 2' position. Thus, when the ligation of tRNA half-molecules was carried out in the presence of ^{32}P-labeled gamma ATP, label was incorporated exclusively into the junction site. This observation suggests a procedure which might be used to determine the point in the viroid molecule at which ligation takes place *in vivo*. A similar approach has been previously applied by Kikuchi and co-workers (1982) to study PSTV RNA's which had been labeled at their 5' ends by the action of bacteriophage T4 polynucleotide kinase prior to ligation.

To seek further information about the position of the PSTV junction point, progeny plus strands could be rigorously scrutinized for evidence of the 2' monophosphate moiety. Alternatively, labeling could be carried out on chemically denatured RNA's to reduce the marked tendency of kinases, such as polynucleotide kinase from *E. coli* infected by bacteriophage T4, to label certain 5' ends in preference to others (when all are present at equimolar concentration).

A mechanism in which multimeric viroid plus strands are enzymatically cleaved to linear monomers by a specific RNA precessing endonuclease, and subsequently ligated to give mature viroid circles, is only one possible scenario for viroid maturation. Another involves RNA self-cleavage and ligation along the lines demonstrated by Cech and his colleagues (Grabowski *et al.*, 1981; Zaug *et al.*, 1983) for the maturation of *Tetrahymena* ribosomal RNA. According to this mechanism, folding of the RNA precursor (in this case, the multimeric viroid plus strand) allows correct termini to be aligned. Concerted cleavage and ligation events occur in a non-enzymatic fashion. Additional experiments on multimeric PSTV plus strands following their isolation by DNA-cellulose chromatography will be carried out to test this possibility.

To permit affinity purifcation of viroid RNA's, strand-specific DNA clones carrying viroid sequences are needed. As a first step toward obtaining such clones, Joan T. Odell constructed viroid cDNA/pBR322 hybrid clones in our laboratory. The RNA template for these clones was purified from plants infected by the severe strain of PSTV (which was originally isolated by Karl H. Fernow and is described in Dickson *et al.*, 1979b). Oligo (dT)$_6$, a synthetic oligonucleotide, was used as a primer for reverse transcriptase copying of the RNA (Branch, 1981). Two PSTV/pBR322 hybrid clones were obtained: pJ08, which contains a 228 base-long insert of viroid cDNA and spans the region from residue 191 to 359 and 1 to 60 [according to the numbering scheme established by Gross and colleagues (1978)] and pJ018, which contains a 164 base-long insert and spans the region from residue 318 to 359 and 1 to 123. Subsequently, cloned inserts of pJ018 were excised from pBR322 by cleavage with *Pst* I and introduced into the *Pst* I restriction site of the strand-specific vector M13 mp8 (BRL). Recombinant phage were isolated which package viroid-specific DNA of either the plus (phage #2) or minus (phage #47) polarity. For use in plus strand purification, single-stranded DNA was extracted from phage #47 and then covalently attached to activated cellulose (Noyes and Stark, 1975).

The power of the DNA affinity method for purifying viroid RNA is demonstrated in Figure 12. Nucleic acids from infected plants were hybridized to the viroid-DNA-cellulose, under conditions described by Nicholson *et al.* (in preparation). RNA binding to the DNA-cellulose was recovered, iodinated in vitro (Prensky, 1976) and analyzed by gel electrophoresis. Readily detectable viroid bands are visible (see lane c; compare to lanes a and b, which depict pBR322 and viroid size markers, respectively). For greater purification of the viroid RNAs, an aliquot of the sample shown in lane (c) was hybridized to the DNA-cellulose a second time. A rather pure preparation of PSTV was obtained as evidenced by the prominent viroid bands (see lane d). RNase T1 fingerprint analysis indicated that viroid RNA was the major component of this fraction (data not shown). Affinity purification can also be applied to samples eluted from polyacrylamide gels. Thus, RNA migrating near the top of a 5% non-denaturing polyacrylamide gel [see Figure 8, gel band (3)] was eluted, iodinated in vitro (Prensky, 1976) and then analyzed either before or after hybridization to DNA-cellulose. RNA from gel band (3) was chosen for affinity purification and detailed analysis because Northern hybridization experiments (see Figure 9)

indicated that it contained longer than unit length plus
strands. Although direct analysis of the ^{125}I-labeled RNAs
from gel band (3) did not reveal any detectable viroid bands
(see Figure 12, lane e), when this sample was affinity purified, the viroid bands became prominent components (see lane
f). The faint band in lane (f) marked with the open arrowhead may be the longer than unit length plus strand expected
from the Northern hybridization data. This procedure is now
being repeated to obtain high molecular weight PSTV RNA for
further analysis.

It is clear from the data presented here that affinity
hybridization can be used to purify viroid plus strand RNA's
from complex mixtures. This procedure is relatively easy to
use, and provides material suitable for subsequent analysis--
such as fingerprinting. Furthermore, additional experiments
indicate that affinity hybridization is also effective at
purifying PSTV minus strands (data not shown). We hope to
couple affinity purification of PSTV minus strands with
sequence analysis in order to determine whether the minus
strands contain any bases not predicted from the sequence of
the plus strand. Such information about the composition of
the PSTV minus strand could shed light on the final steps of
plus strand maturation. There are numerous examples in other
systems of product strands which do not contain the exact
complementary sequence of their corresponding templates
[e.g.,the sequence of a spliced mRNA as compared to its
genomic DNA (Chow *et al.*, 1977); or more drastically--the
insertion of the Q-base into tRNA following transcription
(Farkas and Singh, 1973), and the insertion of oligo(A)
tracts into viral transcripts (Iverson and Rose, 1980)].
Thus, it may not be surprising that our Northern hybridization analysis of RNase Tl-resistant "cores" (prepared as

---

bases (Sutcliffe, 1979). Lane (b) contained 15,000 dpm of
[125]I-labeled PSTV circular (upper) and linear (lower) size
markers. Lane (c) contained 15,000 dpm of nucleic acids from
the LiCl supernatant fraction of PSTV-infected tomato plants
(Dickson, 1979), which was purified by one round of affinity
hybridization (prior to *in vitro* iodination; Prensky,1976).
Lane (d) contained 8,000 dpm of the ^{125}I-labeled RNA shown in
lane (c) which was further purified by affinity hybridization.
Lane (e) contained a 15,000 dpm aliquot of ^{125}I-labeled RNA
from gel band (3) (see Figure 8); while lane (f) contained
8,000 dpm of the RNA from gel band (3) after purification by
affinity hybridization. The open arrowhead to the left of
lane (f) indicates the position of a band which may represent
longer than unit length plus strands; "0" marks the origin of
electrophoresis; the closed arrowhead denotes the position of
a xylene cyanol dye marker.

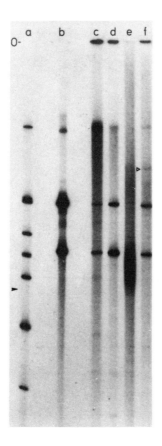

Figure 12. Gel electrophoresis of [125] I-Labeled PSTV RNA's following purification by affinity hybridization. Various nucleic acid preparations from PSTV-infected plants were labeled *in vitro* with [125]I (Prensky, 1976) and then hybridized to DNA cellulose (Nicholson *et al.*, in preparation). Following elution samples were prepared for analysis by ethanol precipitation and then fractionated by electrophoresis in a 0.3 mm x 40 cm 3% polyacrylamide gel containing 7 M urea (Sanger and Coulson, 1978). The DNA used here was obtained from an M13/PSTV hybrid clone containing a 164-base insert of viroid-specific DNA oriented so that the packaged single-stranded DNA in the bacteriophage had sequences complementary to plus strand PSTV. Lane (a) contained 5000 dpm of ^{32}P-labeled pBR322 restriction fragment markers with sized of 1631, 516-506 (doublet), 396, 344, 298, 221-220, and 154

described in Branch *et al.*, 1981) suggests that PSTV minus
strands may contain inserts. As shown in Figure 5, lane (d),
RNase Tl-resistant minus strands migrate more slowly than the
mature plus strand size marker. Besides non-viroid inserts,
this mobility difference could reflect either the sequence
difference between the plus and minus strands or the presence
of a terminal repeat or other unusual structure in the minus
strand.

D. Properties of the PSTV replication complex.

In the earlier sections of this chapter we have empha-
sized the various steps which may be required to synthesize
viroid progeny RNA, such as the synthesis of multimeric minus
and plus strands, and the possibility that such multimers may
be processed by host enzymes to yield mature progeny RNA
circles. During viroid replication taking place in infected
plants, these strands are part of complicated multi-stranded
structures containing RNA's of positive and negative polari-
ties, host proteins and (possibly) other factors. As a step
toward defining the components of the elaborate replication
complex, we have carried out a series of studies on the
viroid-specific RNA's ("cores") which remain following digestion of nucleic acids of PSTV-infected plants with RNase Tl.

We found that the RNase Tl-resistant "cores" do not have
the characteristic response of double-stranded RNA to treatment with *E. coli* RNase III (see Figure 13), an enzyme which
can be used to digest regular RNA:RNA duplex molecules
(Robertson *et al.*, 1968; Robertson and Dunn, 1975). In this
experiment,nucleic acids of PSTV-infected plants were digested with RNase Tl (to digest single-stranded RNAs such as the
free progeny PSTV plus strands), treated with RNase III, purified by phenol extraction and CF11 cellulose chromatography
(Franklin,1966) and probed by Northern hybridization using
^{125}I-labeled PSTV to detect minus strands and ^{32}P-labeled
PSTV cDNA to detect plus strands. Following RNase Tl digestion, both plus and minus strands are approximately the size
of unit length PSTV (see lanes a and c). However, after
digestion by RNase Tl followed by treatment with RNase III,
no minus strands can be detected (lane b), while full length
plus strands remain (lane d). Thus, it appears that RNase
III is cleaving only one strand of the RNA:RNA duplex present in PSTV replication complexes instead of cleaving both
strands as it does in all other naturally occurring RNA:RNA
duplexes studied to date (Robertson *et al.*, 1968; Robertson
and Dunn, 1975; Robertson and Barany, 1979; Robertson, 1982).

Through additional experiments, we found that the RNase

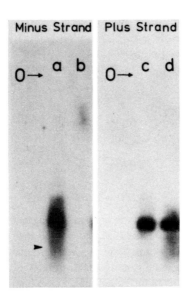

Figure 13. E. coli ribonuclease III digests the minus strand of RNase T1-resistant "cores". Nucleic acids of PSTV-infected plants, treated as described below,were denatured with glyoxal and dimethyl sulfoxide (McMaster and Carmichael, 1977), fractionated in 2.5% agarose gels, transferred to nitrocellulose (Thomas, 1980) and then hybridized to either ^{125}I-labeled PSTV (to detect minus strands) or ^{32}P-labeled PSTV cDNA (to detect plus strands). To prepare starting material for this experiment, total nucleic acids (at a final concentration of 5 mg/ml) were incubated with 1 mg/ml RNase T1 for 40 min at 37°, extracted with phenol, chromatographed on CF11 cellulose (Franklin, 1966) and precipitated with ethanol. Subsequently, the RNase T1-resistant nucleic acids were digested with RNase III under conditions described before (Branch *et al.*, 1981). Lanes (a) and (c) contained 5 µg of the RNase T1-resistant nucleic acids. Lanes (b) and (d) contained 5 µg of the RNase T1-resistant nucleic acids recovered following treatment with RNase III. "0" marks the origin of electrophoresis of the gel; the arrowhead denotes the position of the bromphenol blue dye marker.

T1-resistant plus strands could be rendered RNase T1-sensitive by prior treatment with RNase III (see Figure 14, panel A, lane h), but not by prior treatment with buffer (lane g). This suggests that RNase III cleaves the minus strand of the viroid "core," leaving an exposed plus strand (which is susceptible to RNase T1 digestion, Post hybridization of the

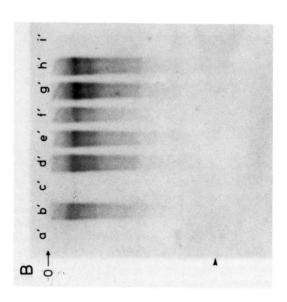

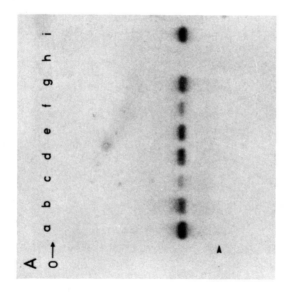

nitrocellulose filter shown in Figure 14 panel A to a probe
containing ^{125}I-labeled tomato nucleic acids demonstrated conclusively that although the sample in lane (h) contained no
detectable plus strand, it did contain the expected amount of
plant nucleic acids (see Figure 14, panel B, lane h), indicating that the numerous steps of this experiment had been
completed successfully. It is not clear what this extra-
ordinary resistance of viroid plus strands (remaining in
replicating complexes after RNase Tl digestion) to cleavage

Figure 14A.& 14B. Northern blot analysis of asymmetric RNase
III cleavage of RNase Tl-resistant PSTV "cores". Nucleic
acids of PSTV-infected plants, treated as described below
were denatured with glyoxal and dimethyl sulfoxide (McMaster
and Carmichael, 1977), fractionated by electrophoresis in a
2.5% agarose gel, transferred to nitrocellulose (Thomas,
1980) and then hybridized to ^{32}P-labeled PSTV cDNA (panel A).
After autoradiography the filter was post-hybridized to [125]I
-labeled plant nucleic acids (panel B). Lane (a) contained
[125]I-labeled PSTV circular RNA. Lane (b) contained RNase
Tl-resistant nucleic acids from PSTV-infected plants, prepared
as described in the legend to Figure 13. Lane (c) contained
[125]I-labeled PSTV linear RNA. Lanes (d) and (e) depict RNase
Tl-resistant nucleic acids digested by two different preparations of RNase III under conditions described before (Branch
et al., 1981); each lane contained 5.0 μg. Lane(f) contained
2.0 μg of the preparation shown in lane(e). Lane (g)contained
RNase Tl-resistant nucleic acids which were incubated in NEB
(the buffer for RNase III digestion: 0.03 M Tris-HCl, pH 8.0;
0.1 M NaCl; 0.005 M $MgCl_2$; 0.1 mM dithiothreitol) for 30 min
at 37°, purified by phenol extraction and cellulose CF11
chromatography, and then incubated with 1 mg/ml RNase Tl for
40 min at 37°. Lane (h) contained RNase Tl-resistant nucleic
acids which were digested with RNase III, repurified and then
incubated with 1 mg/ml RNase Tl for 40 min at 37°. Lane (i)
contained [125] I-labeled PSTV circular RNA. "0" marks the
origin of electrophoresis of the gel; the arrowhead denotes
the position of the bromphenol blue dye marker.

by RNase III might mean for the viroid in terms of survival, since no RNase III activity has been reported in plants thus far. However, it is interesting to speculate that viroids have evolved a genome which takes full advantage of the host RNA processing enzymes required for replication, while escaping any activities designed to hold double-stranded RNA pathogens in check.

Future investigations of the RNase Tl-resistant "cores" will be aimed at determining whether the plus strands present in these complexes have common termini. Preliminary fingerprinting analysis carried out on viroid "cores" which were purified by two rounds of CF11 cellulose chromatography and then labeled at their 5' ends by polynucleotide kinase and ^{32}P-labeled gamma ATP suggested that non-random terminal sequences are present (data not shown); however, more detailed study [perhaps including nuclease Sl-protection of cloned viroid-specific DNA fragments (Berk and Sharp, 1977)] is needed to confirm this impression.

III. IMPLICATIONS OF THE PSTV REPLICATION PATHWAY.

The proposed PSTV replication cycle shown in Figure 1 gives rise to a number of characteristic RNA structures which (once identified) can be sought in other systems as well. As already mentioned, other viroids, virusoids, and certain virus satellite RNAs have all begun to show signs of following a pathway of replication with many similarities to that of PSTV. Since viroids encode no proteins (Davies *et al.*, 1979), it is evident that all activities required for their replication must exist in host cells. In fact, it is tempting to speculate that all three classes of circular pathogenic RNA just mentioned use similar host components. An equally interesting point to consider is the possible functions of such a host pathway—is it possible, for example, that plant cells encode and replicate small circular RNA's as part of their normal gene expression? If so, could such RNA's play a regulatory role which viroids and other pathogenic circular RNA's can interrupt, thus causing the observed disease symptoms? The association of a characteristic RNA replication pathway for circular RNA's with the presence of disease symptoms raises two additional questions: Are the components needed to carry out viroid replication limited to plant cells? Which maladies currently without an identified pathogenic agent should be considered as candidates for a viroid-like causative agent?

With regard to the first question, we have recently found that PSTV can be stably introduced into *Drosphila* tissue culture cells (unpublished observations). These experiments, which make use of liposome fusion (Szoka and Papahadjopoulos, 1978; Fraley *et al.*, 1980; Gross and Ringler, 1979), were carried out in collaboration with R. Gross and D. Rosen of Dartmouth Medical College. We will now seek greater than unit length minus and plus strands in extracts of these cells. The presence of such RNA species would suggest that the host components required for viroid replication are not limited to plant cells.

With regard to the second question (concerning disease agents), the recent evidence obtained by Coggin and coworkers (1981, 1983) linking a viroid-like agent to an epidemic of infectious lymphoma in hamsters is highly suggestive. With this finding in mind, it would also seem prudent to apply the techniques of viroid detection to other diseases of unknown etiology, of which acquired immune deficiency syndrome [AIDS (Curran, 1983; Harris *et al.*, 1983)], has served as an example.

In the initial stages of investigation, several lines of evidence have suggested that a search for an AIDS-specific viroid might be fruitful. First, although a number of familiar viruses were identified in AIDS patients, no AIDS-specific micro-organism (viral or bacterial) was identified in initial screening studies, despite extensive examination of tissues from affected individuals. Viroids do not form particles (Diener, 1979). Thus, a viroid-like agent associated with any disease would escape detection in all of the usual assays employed to identify conventional viruses. Second, viroids cause elaborations of cellular membranes (Semancik and Vanderwoude, 1976; Sänger 1982) which could be compared to the vesicular rosettes recently described in lymphoid cells of AIDS patients (Ewing *et al.*, 1983). Third, the agent studied by Coggin and co-workers (1981, 1983) was shown to affect cells of the immune system--the target for AIDS. Fourth, like AIDS, viroid diseases are known to arise suddenly and spread rapidly, often with disastrous consequences for the host (Hollings and Stone, 1970; Randles, 1975). Furthermore, a pathogenic agent containing a comparatively small RNA molecule (the delta agent) with certain properties expected of a sub-viral pathogen has recently been found in the bloodstream of patients suffering from fulminant hepatitis B (Bonino *et al.*, 1981; Arico *et al.*, 1978; Rizzetto *et al.*, 1980).

Since it is becoming increasingly clear that subviral agents such as viroids are responsible for serious diseases in various higher eukaryotes, perhaps it is time to redouble efforts to identify viroid-like pathogens associated with human diseases as well.

ACKNOWLEDGEMENTS

We thank David D. Elliman, Louise K. Pape, Edmond Chin, J.F. Shaw, Nancy Donovan, and Bonnie J. Benenfeld for their dedicated and excellent technical assistance and Dr. George Bruening (University of California, Davis) for many interesting discussions and for permitting us to reproduce one of his figures. This research was supported by grants from the National Science Foundation, the Science and Education Administration of the U.S. Department of Agriculture, the National Institutes of Health and the McKnight Foundation.

REFERENCES

Arico, S., Rizzetto, M., Crivelli, O., *et al.*, (1978). The clinical and immunological significance of a new antigen/antibody system (delta/anti-delta) in chronic carriers of the HBsAg. *Ital. J. Gastroent.* 10, 146–151.

Bonino, F., Hoyer, B., Ford, E., Shih, J.W.-K, Purcell, R.H., and Gerin, J.L. (1981) The delta agent: HBsAg particles with delta antigen and RNA in the serum of an HBV carrier. *Hepatology 1,* 127–131.

Berk, A. J. and Sharp, P.A. (1977) Sizing and mapping of early adenovirus mRNAs by gel electrophoresis of S1 endonuclease-digested hybrids. *Cell 12,* 721–732.

Branch, A.D. (1981) Characterization of potato spindle tuber viroid-specific nucleic acids in tomato plants. Doctoral Dissertation, The Rockefeller University Press, New York, New York.

Branch, A. D. and Robertson, H.D. A replication cycle for plant viroids and other small pathogenic RNA molecules. *Science,* in press.

Branch, A. D., Robertson, H.D., and Dickson, E. (1981) Longer than unit length viroid minus strands are present in RNA from infected plants. *Proc.Natl.Acad.Sci. U.S.A. 78,* 6381–6385.

Branch, A.D., Robertson, H.D., Greer, C., Gegenheimer, P., Peebles, C., Abelson, J. (1982) Cell-free circularization of viroid progeny RNA by an RNA ligase from wheat germ. *Science 217,* 1147–1149.

Brown, F. and Martin, S.J. (1965) A new model for virus ribonucleic acid replication. *Nature (London) 208,* 861–863.

Bruening, G., Gould, A.R., Murphy, P.J., and Symons, R.H. (1982) Oligomers of avocado sunblotch viroid are found in infected avocado leaves. *FEBS Letters 148,* 71–78.

Chow, L.T., Gelinas, R.E., Broker, T.R., and Roberts, R.J.
    (1977) An amazing sequence arrangement at the 5'
    ends of adenovirus 2 messenger RNA. *Cell 12*, 1-8.
Chu, P. W. G., Francki, R.I.B., and Randles, J.W. (1983)
    Detection, isolation and characterization of high
    molecular weight double-stranded RNAs in plants
    infected with velvet tobacco mottle virus. *Virology
    126* 480-492.
Coggin, J. H. Jr., Oakes, J.E., Huebner, R.J., and Gilden,
    R. (1981) Unusual filterable oncogenic agent
    isolated from horizontally transmitted Syrian hamster
    lymphomas. *Nature (London) 290*, 336-338.
Coggin, J.H. Jr., Bellomy, B.B., Thomas, K.V., and Pollock,
    W.J. (1983) B-cell and T-cell lymphomas and other
    associated diseases induced by an infectious
    DNA viroid-like agent in hamsters. *Am. J. Pathol.
    110*, 254-266.
Commerford, S.L. (1971) Iodination of nucleic acids in vitro.
    Biochemistry 10, 1993-1999.
Conejero, V., Picazo, I., and Segado, P. (1979) Citrus
    exocortis viroid (CEV): Protein alterations in
    different hosts following viroid infections.
    Virology 97, 454-456.
Curran, J.W. (1983) AIDS--two years later. *N.Engl.J.Med.309*,
    609-610.
Davies, J.W., Kaesberg, P., and Diener, T.O. (1974) Potato
    spindle tuber viroid. XII. An investigation of
    viroid RNA as messenger for protein synthesis.
    Virology 61, 281-286.
Dickson, E. (1979) Viroids: infectious RNA in plants.
    In: Nucleic Acids in Plants, Vol. II (Hall, T.C.
    and Davies, J.W., eds.) CRC press,Inc., Boca
    Raton, Florida, pp. 153-193.
Dickson, E. Diener, T.O., and Robertson, H.D. (1978) Potato
    spindle tuber and citrus exocortis viroids undergo
    no major sequence changes during replication in
    two different hosts. *Proc. Natl. Acad. Sci. U.S.A.
    75*, 951-954.
Dickson, E., Pape, L. K., and Robertson, H. D. (1979a)
    Approaches to sequence analysis of ^{125}I-labeled
    RNA. *Nucleic Acids Res. 6*, 91-109.
Dickson, E., Robertson, H.D., Niblett, C.L., Horst, R.K.,
    and Zaitlin, M. (1979b). Minor differences between
    nucleotide sequence of mild and severe strains of
    potato spindle tuber viroid. *Nature (London) 277*,
    60-62.
Diener, T.O. (1979) Viroids and Viroid Diseases. Wiley, T.J.
    and Sons, New York, New York.
Dunn, J.J. and Studier, F.W. (1981) Nucleotide sequences
    from the genetic left end of bacteriophage T7 DNA to

the beginning of gene 4. *J. Mol. Biol. 148,* 303-330.

Ewing, E.P., Spira, T.J., Chandler, F.W., Callaway, C.S., Brynes, R.K., and Chan, W.C. (1983) Unusual cytoplasmic body in lymphoid cells of homosexual men with unexplained lymphadenopathy. *N. Engl. J. Med. 308,* 819-822.

Farkas, W.R. and Singh, R. (1973) Guanylation of transfer ribonucleic acid by a cell-free lysate of rabbit reticulocytes. *J. Biol. Chem.248,* 7780-7785.

Fraley, R., Subramani, S., Berg, P., Papahadjopoulos, D. (1980) Introduction of liposome-encapsulated SV40 DNA into cells. *J. Biol Chem. 255,* 10431-10435.

Franklin, R.M. (1966) Purification and properties of the replicative intermediate of the RNA bacteriophage R17. *Proc. Natl. Acad. Sci. U.S.A.55,* 1504-1511.

Gilbert W. and Dressler, D. (1968) DNA replication: The rolling circle model. *Cold Spring Harbor Symp.Quant. Biol. 33,* 473-484.

Gould, A.R. (1981) Studies on encapsidated viroid-like RNA. II. Purification and characterization of a viroid-like RNA associated with velvet tobacco mottle virus (VTMoV). *Virology 108,* 123-133.

Grabowski, P. J., Zaug, A.J., and Cech, T.R. (1981) The intervening sequence of the ribosomal RNA precursor is converted to a circular RNA in isolated nuclei of *Tetrahymena. Cell 23,* 467-476.

Greer, C.L., Peebles, C.L., Gegenheimer, P., and Abelson, J. (1983) Mechanism of action of a yeast RNA ligase in tRNA splicing. *Cell 32,* 537-546.

Grill, L.K., and Semancik, J.S. (1978) RNA sequences complementary to citrus exocortis viroid in nucleic acid preparations from infected *Gynura aurantiaca. Proc. Natl. Acad. Sci. U.S.A. 75,* 896-900.

Grill, L.K., Negruk, V.I., and Semancik, J.S. (1980) Properties of the complementary RNA sequence associated with infection by the citrus exocortis viroid. *Virology 107,* 24-33.

Gross, H.J., Domdey, H., Lossow, C., Jank, P., Raba, M., Alberty, H., and Sänger, H.L. (1978) Nucleotide sequence and secondary structure of potato spindle tuber viroid. *Nature (London) 273,* 203-208.

Gross, R.H. and Ringler, J. (1979) Ribonucleic acid synthesis in isolated *Drosophila* nuclei. *Biochemistry 18,* 4923-4927.

Hall, T.C., Wepprich, R.K., Davies, J.W., Weathers, L.G., and Semancik, J.S. (1974) Functional distinctions between the ribonucleic acids from citrus exocortis viroid and plant viruses: Cell-free translation and amino-acylation reactions. *Virology 61*, 486-492.

Harris, C., Butkus Small, C., Klein, R.S., *et al.* (1983) Immunodeficiency in female sexual partners of men with the acquired immunodeficiency syndrome. *N. Eng. J. Med. 308*, 1181-1184.

Haseloff, J., Mohamed, N.A., Symons, R.H.(1982). Viroid RNA's of cadang-cadang disease of coconuts, *Nature, London* 299 316-321.

Haseloff, J. (1983) Comparative structure and properties of viroids, virusoids, and satellites. Doctoral Dissertation, Department of Biochemistry, University of Adelaide, Australia.

Hollings, M. and Stone, O.M. (1970) Attempts to eliminate chrysanthemum stunt from chrysanthemum by meristem-tip culture after heat-treatment. *Ann. Appl. Biol. 65*, 311-315.

Iverson, L.E. and Rose, J.K. (1981) Localized attenuation and discontinuous synthesis during vesicular stomatitis virus transcription. *Cell 23*, 477-484.

Kiefer, M.C., Daubert, S.D., Schneider, I.R., and Bruening, G. (1982) Multimeric forms of satellite of tobacco ringspot virus RNA. *Virology 121*, 262-273.

Kikuchi, Y., Tyc, K., Filipowicz, W., Sänger, H.L., and Gross, H.J. (1982) Circularization of linear viroid RNA via 2'-phosphomonoester, 3',5'-phosphodiester bonds by a novel type of RNA ligase from wheat germ and *Chlamydomonas. Nucleic Acids Res. 10*, 7521-7529.

Knapp, G., Ogden, R.C., Peebles, C.L., and Abelson, J. (1979) Splicing of yeast tRNA precursors: structure of the reaction intermediates. *Cell 18*, 37-45.

Konarska, M., Filipowicz, W., Domdey, H., and Gross, H.J. (1981) Formation of a 2'-phosphomonoester, 3', 5'-phosphodiester linkage by a novel RNA ligase in wheat germ. *Nature (London)293*, 112-116.

Konarska, M., Filipowicz, W., and Gross, H.J. (1982) RNA ligation via 2'-phosphomonoester, 3', 5'-phosphodiester linkage: Requirement of 2', 3'-cyclic phosphate termini and involvement of a 5'-hydroxyl polynucleotide kinase. *Proc. Natl. Acad. Sci. U.S.A. 79*, 1474-1478.

McMaster, G.K. and Carmichael, G.G. (1977) Analysis of single and double-stranded nucleic acids on polyacrylamide and agarose gels by using glyoxal and acridine orange. *Proc. Natl. Acad. Sci. U.S.A.74*, 4835-4838.

Morris, T.J. and Smith, E.M. (1977) Potato spindle tuber disease: procedures for the detection of viroid RNA and certification of disease-free potato tubers. *Phytopath. 67*, 145-150.

Nicholson, A.W., Davis, N.G., Frankfort, H.F., Lamb, R.A., and Robertson, H.D. The cell-free synthesis, purification and characterization of influenza viral NS$_1$ mRNA for use as an RNA processing substrate (in preparation).

Noyes, B.E. and Stark, G.R. (1975) Nucleic acid hybridization using DNA covalently coupled to cellulose. *Cell 5*, 301-310.

Owens, R.A. and Cress, D.E. (1980) Molecular cloning and characterization of potato spindle tuber viroid cDNA sequences. *Proc. Natl. Acad. Sci.U.S.A.77*, 5302-5306.

Owens, R.A. and Diener, T.O. (1982) RNA intermediates in potato spindle tuber viroid replication. *Proc. Natl. Acad. Sci. U.S.A. 79*, 113-117.

Owens, R. A., Erbe, E., Hadidi, A., Steere, R.L., and Diener, T.O. (1977) Separation and infectivity of circular and linear forms of potato spindle tuber viroid. *Proc. Natl. Acad. Sci. U.S.A. 74*, 3859-3863.

Palukaitis, P. and Symons, R.H. (1980) Purification and characterization of the circular and linear forms of chrysanthemum stunt viroid. *J. Gen. Virol. 46*, 477-489.

Peebles, C.L., Ogden, R.C., Knapp, G., and Abelson, J. (1979) Splicing of yeast tRNA precursors: a two-stage reaction. *Cell 18*, 27-35.

Prensky, W. (1976). The radioiodination of RNA and DNA to high specific activities. In: Methods in Cell Biology, Vol. 13. (Prescott, D., ed.) Academic Press, New York, New York, pp 121-152.

Randles, J.W. (1975) Association of two ribonucleic acid species with cadang-cadang disease of coconut palm *Phytopath. 65*, 163-167.

Randles, J.W., Davies, C., Hatta, T., Gould, A.R.,and Francki, R.I.B. (1981) Studies of encapsidated viroid-like RNA. I. Characterization of velvet tobacco mottle virus. *Virology 108*, 111-122.

Rizzetto, M., Hoyer, B., Canese, M.G., Shih, J.W.-K., Purcell, R.H., and Gerin, J.L. (1980) Delta agent: Association of delta antigen with hepatitis B surface antigen and RNA in serum of delta-infected chimpanzees. *Proc. Natl. Acad. Sci. U.S.A. 77*, 6124-6128.

Robertson, H.D.(1982) *Escherichia coli* ribonuclease III cleavage sites. *Cell 30*, 669-672.

Robertson, H.D. and Barany, F. (1979). Enzymes and mechanisms in RNA processing. In: Proceedings of the 12th FEBS Congress, Vol. 51 (Rosenthal, S., Bielka, H., Coutelle, Ch., and Zimmer, Ch.,eds.) Pergamon Press, Oxford, New York, Frankfurt, pp 285-295.

Robertson, H.D. and Dunn, J.J. (1975) Ribonucleic acid processing activity of *E. coli* ribonuclease III. *J. Biol. Chem. 250*, 3050-3056.

Robertson, H.D., Webster, R.E., and Zinder, N.D. (1968) Purification and properties of ribonuclease III from *E. coli. J. Biol. Chem. 243*, 82-91.

Robertson, H.D., Dickson, E., Model, P., and Prensky, W. (1973) Application of fingerprinting techniques to iodinated nucleic acids. *Proc. Natl.Acad. Sci. U.S.A. 70*, 3260-3264.

Rohde, W. and Sänger, H. L. (1981) Detection of complementary RNA intermediates of viroid replication by Northern blot hybridization. *Biosci. Rep. 1*, 327-336.

Sänger, F. and Coulson, A.R.(1978) The use of thin acrylamide gels for DNA sequencing. *FEBS Letters 87*, 107-110.

Sänger, H.L. (1982) 12 Biology, structure, functions and possible origin of viroids. In: Nucleic Acids and Proteins in Plants II, Vol. 14B of the Encyclopedia of Plant Physiology, New Series (Parthier, B. and Boulter, D., eds.) Springer-Verlag,Berlin and Heidelberg, Germany, pp. 368-454.

Schneider, I.R. and Thompson, S.M. (1977) Double-stranded nucleic acids found in tissue infected with the satellite of tobacco ringspot virus. *Virology 78*, 453-462.

Semancik, J.S. and Vanderwoude, W.J. (1976) Exocortis viroid: Cytopathic effects at the plasma membrane in association with pathogenic RNA. *Virology 69*, 719-726.

Semancik, J.S., Conejero, V., and Gerhart, J. (1977) Citrus exocortis viroid: Survey of protein synthesis in *Xenopus laevis oocytes* following addition of viroid RNA. *Virology 80*, 218-221.

Sogo, J.M. and Schneider, I.R. (1982) Electron microscopy of double-stranded nucleic acids found in tissue infected with the satellite of tobacco ringspot virus. *Virology 117*, 401-415.

Sutcliffe, J.G. (1979) Complete nucleotide sequence of the *Escherichia coli* plasmid pBR322. *Cold Spring Harbor Symp. Quant. Biol.43*, 77-90.

Szoka, F. and Papahadjopoulos, D. (1978) Procedure for preparation of liposomes with large internal aqueous space and high capture by reverse-phase evaporation. *Proc. Natl. Acad. Sci. U.S.A. 75*, 4194-4198.

Thomas, P.S. (1980) Hybridization of denatured RNA and small DNA fragments transferred to nitrocellulose. *Proc. Natl. Acad. Sci. U.S.A. 77*, 5201-5205.

Tyc, K., Kikuchi, Y., Konarska, M., Filipowicz, W., and

Gross, H.J. (1983) Ligation of endogenous tRNA 3'half molecules to their corresponding 5' halves via 2'-phosphomonoester 3', 5' phosphodiester bonds in extracts of *Chlamydomonas*. *EMBO J. 2*, 605–610.

Zaug, A. J., Grabowski, P.J. and Cech, T.R. (1983) Autocatalytic cyclization of an excised intervening sequence RNA is a cleavage–ligation reaction.

Zelcer, A., Van Adelsberg, J., Leonard, D.A. and Zaitlin, M. (1981) Plant cell suspension cultures sustain long-term replication of potato spindle tuber viroid. *Virology 109*, 314–322.

Zelcer, A., Zaitlin,M., Robertson,H.D., and Dickson, E.(1982) Potato spindle tuber viroid-infected tissues contain RNA complementary to the entire viroid. *J. Gen. Virol. 59*, 139–148.

Chapter 12

ON THE MECHANISM OF REPLICATION OF VIROIDS, VIRUSOIDS, AND SATELLITE RNAs

Robert H. Symons

Department of Biochemistry
University of Adelaide
South Australia

James Haseloff

M.R.C. Laboratory of Molecular Biology
Cambridge, England

Jane E. Visvader, Paul Keese, Peter J. Murphy

Department of Biochemistry
University of Adelaide
South Australia

Dalip S. Gill

Roche Institute of Molecular Biology
Nutley, New Jersey

Karl H. J. Gordon

Department of Biochemistry
University of Adelaide
South Australia

George Bruening

Department of Biochemistry and Biophysics
University of California
Davis, California

SUBVIRAL PATHOGENS
OF PLANTS AND ANIMALS:
VIROIDS AND PRIONS

235

Copyright © 1985 by Academic Press, Inc.
All rights of reproduction in any form reserved.
ISBN 0-12-470230-9

I. INTRODUCTION

Our understanding of viroids, encapsidated viroid-like RNAs (virusoids) and plant satellite RNAs is now entering a new phase. The nucleotide sequences of many of these have been determined (Table I) and this has allowed the prediction of their secondary structures on the basis of additional physical data as well as on nuclease cleavage studies which indicate which parts of each molecule are single stranded or double-stranded (Gross and Riesner, 1980; Riesner *et al.*, 1983; Sänger, 1982). The sequences and proposed secondary structures permit comparisons, not only between different viroids and virusoids, but also between different naturally occurring isolates of the same infectious agent. Such comparisons will help to define regions of sequence and structure which are important for biological activity and hopefully will allow the correlation of a particular biological parameter with a specific part of each molecule. Although there is still considerable work to be done in these areas, the viroid, virusoid and satellite RNA field is now moving into the much broader and considerably more difficult areas of relating structure to biological activity at the molecular level and of determining the difficulty in unravelling the complex interactions between these small infectious agents and the host plant.

This paper considers the possible mechanisms by which viroids, virusoids and satellite RNAs are replicated. Since there is very little data available in this area, the discussion will be essentially speculative and based on information in the literature as well as on our own published and unpublished data. Emphasis will be given to unexplained aspects which may be providing definite hints for us to follow in our attempts to tackle this complex problem. Readers should refer to the articles by H.J. Gross (Chapter 9) and R.I.B. Francki, *et al.*, (Chapter 13) for more general discussions on viroids and virusoids, respectively.

II. WHAT IS THE ROUTE BY WHICH VIROIDS AND VIRUSOIDS ARE REPLICATED?

The current approach being used in several laboratories to search for possible intermediates in the replication of viroids and virusoids is to fractionate nucleic acid extracts of infected plants by gel electrophoresis in order to detect various sized components of plus and minus polarity by hybridization with appropriate radioactive probes. Any components which vary from the normal plus single-strand monomers found in appreciable amounts in infected plants are assumed to be

TABLE I

Sizes of Viroids, Virusoids and Satellite
RNAs as Determined by Sequencing.

RNA	No. of Nucleotides	References
VIROID		
Avocado sunblotch viroid (ASBV)	247	Symons, 1981
Chrysanthemum stunt viroid (CSV)	356 354	Haseloff and Symons,1981 Gross *et al.*, 1982
Citrus exocortis viroid (CEV)	371	Visvader *et al.*, 1982 Visvader & Symons, 1983 Gross *et al.* 1982
Coconut cadang-cadang viroid(CCCV)		
RNA 1 fast	246-247	Haseloff *et al.* 1982
RNA 1 slow	287-301	
RNA 2 fast	492-494	
RNA 2 slow	574-602	
Potato spindle tuber viroid (PSTV)	359	Gross *et al.*, 1978,1981
VIRUSOID (RNA2)		
Lucerne transient streak virus (LTSV)	324	Keese *et al.*, 1983
Solanum nodiflorum mottle virus (SNMV)	377	Haseloff & Symons,1982
Subterranean clover mottle virus(SCMoV)	327 & 388	Haseloff & Symons,unpub.
Velvet tobacco mottle virus (VTMoV)	365-366	Haseloff & Symons, 1982
SATELLITE RNA		
Cucumber mosaic virus (CMV)	334 335 336	Collmer *et al.*, 1983 Richards *et al.* 1978 Gordon & Symons. 1983
Tobacco necrosis virus (TNV)	1239	Ysebaert *et al.*, 1980
Tobacco ringspot virus(TobRSV)	357	Bruening, unpubl.

either intermediates in, or the end products of, the replication process. However, it is feasible that some components detected may be dead-end products formed by an aberration of the normal replication pathways as a consequence of damage to the cell caused by viroid or virusoid infections. This type of work is only the start to sorting out the mechanism and enzymology of what is likely to be a very complex process.

We first consider here our own work on the various nucleic acid components in plants infected with viroids and virusoids as a basis for developing a simple replication model and for discussion of results published by others. We also consider some unique features of viroids and virusoids which may be important in our understanding of their replication.

    A.   Oligomers of Avocado Sunblotch Viroid are Found in Infected Avocado Leaves.

The one isolate of ASBV sequenced contains 247 residues (Symons, 1981) and has very limited sequence homology with PSTV, CSV, CEV and CCCV. Highly purified preparations of the circular viroid infect avocado and induce the sunblotch disease (Allen *et al.*, 1981). In order to investigate the replication of this viroid, we considered that it was of utmost importance to use rigorously purified single-strand ^{32}P-DNA probes of both plus and minus polarity for this purpose. We, therefore, prepared partial recombinant DNA clones of ASBV in the plasmid vector pBR322 and the cloned insert was then sub-cloned into the single-strand vector M13mp93 (Bruening *et al.*, 1982). By using M13mp93 clones containing either a plus or a minus insert, it was possible to prepare single-strand ^{32}P-DNA probes of high specific activity for the detection of either plus or minus sequences, respectively (Bruening *et al*, 1982).

Partially purified nucleic acid extracts of ASBV-infected avocado leaves were reacted with glyoxal to ensure denaturation of all component nucleic acids. After fractionation of the mixture by electrophoresis on 1.9% agarose gels, the nucleic acids were transferred by blotting to nitrocellulose and then hybridized with ^{32}P-DNA probes prepared from M13mp93 clones containing either plus or minus sequences. The results for one experiment are given in Fig.1. The plus RNA sequences (Figure 1A, lane 2) show a series of bands of increasing M_r-

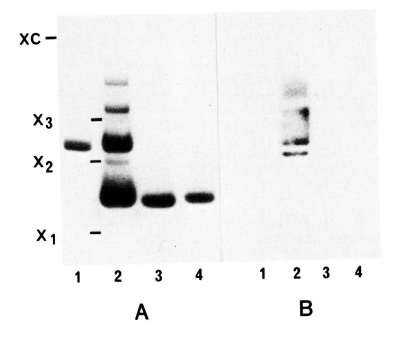

Figure 1. Detection of plus and minus sequences of ASBV in nucleic acid extracts of avocado leaves after electrophoresis in a 1.9% agarose gel (14 x 14 x 0.3 cm) in 10 mM sodium phosphate (pH 6.5) at 30 mA for 3.0 h. Nucleic acid samples were glyoxalated before electrophoresis. After electrophoresis, nucleic acids were transferred to nitrocellulose and probed with single-strand ^{32}P-DNA probes prepared from recombinant DNA clones for plus ASBV sequences (A) or for minus ASBV sequences (B). Autoradiography was for 6 h at room temperature in (A) and for 4 days at −70°C in (B). (1) Marker circular dimer ASBV, (2) nucleic acid extract, (3) marker circular ASBV, (4) marker linear ASBV. For minor bands X_1 − X_3, see text. XC, xylene cyanol FF marker dye, 5.0 cm from origin. Autoradiogram taken from Bruening et al. (1982)

value with the fastest migrating major band corresponding to
the monomer ASBV markers; the circular ASBV (lane A3) migrated slightly faster than the linear ASBV marker (lane A4).
The second fastest major band comigrated with the ASBV dimer
marker (lane A1) which had been purified in small amounts
from infected leaf extracts (Bruening *et al.*, 1981) and shown
to be a true sequence dimer by two-dimensional fingerprinting
of $5'-^{32}$ P-labeled fragments in complete RNase A and RNase T1
digests; identical patterns were obtained for both the ASBV
monomer and dimer (unpublished data).

The series of plus RNA bands, which were sensitive to
RNase digestion, were taken as oligomers of the monomer ASBV
since a plot of the mobility of each band against the logarithm of its putative M_r-value was linear. The minor components labeled X_1, X_2 and X_3 in Fig. 1 also form an oligomeric
series; although we have repeatedly observed these, we have
no further information on their structure and they have not
been fingerprinted or sequenced.

In contrast to the plus ASBV sequences, minus sequences
were present at much lower concentrations (Fig.1B). The main
minus species were two closely migrating bands with mobilities similar to that of the ASBV dimer as well as a blur of
higher M_r material. The total radioactivity hybridized to
the minus sequences was 0.5% of that hybridized to the plus
sequences. Since the plus and minus probes were of the same
specific activity, this value gives an approximate relative
estimate of the two types of sequence detected under the
conditions used. These minus components have not been further characterized.

The nucleic acid extracts used for this work were prepared by a method we developed for the handling of 500 g
batches of infected leaves (Palukaitis and Symons, 1980;
Palukaitis *et al.*, 1981). Recent unpublished work using different extraction procedures which were expected to provide
better extraction of nucleic acids from 5-10 gram quantities
of leaves have allowed the detection of minus sequences of
unit and dimer size at 5 to 10% of the level of the corresponding plus sequences. Further, the analysis of nucleic
acid extracts on non-denaturing as well as denaturing gels is
proving helpful in sorting out the various viroid specific
components in ASBV-infected leaves. Our experience is indicating that it is essential to investigate various extraction
procedures and various types of gel fractionation techniques
in order to document the many species of ASBV present.

            B. Oligomers of CCCV, CEV and of Three Virusoids
                    are Found in Infected Leaves.

Extracts of coconut palms infected with CCCV contain, at
the early stages of infection, high concentrations of the
monomer CCCV (Imperial *et al.*, 1981; Mohamed *et al.*, 1982),

which is usually a mixture of two species, one containing 246 residues and another with one extra residue (Haseloff *et al.*, 1982). As the disease progresses, exact dimers of one or other of the monomers appear and can be readily seen as stainable bands on preparative gel electrophoresis (Imperial *et al.*, 1981; Mohamed *et al.*, 1982). In addition, there are higher molecular weight variants of these monomers and dimers (Imperial *et al.*, 1981) which are considered further in section 2E. Preliminary unpublished experiments on the analysis of extracts of CCCV-infected coconut palms early in infection as for the ASBV-infected avocado leaves in Fig. 1 and using ^{32}P-DNA probes derived from plus and minus M13 clones of CCCV, plus oligomers up to tetramers were found with an oligomeric series of minus sequences present at much lower levels.

The corresponding analysis of nucleic acid extracts of CEV-infected tomato showed, in addition to the plus monomer, plus dimers and low levels of higher oligomers. In contrast, no oligomeric plus sequences were found in extracts of CEV-infected chrysanthemum or *Gynura aurantiaca*. An oligomeric series of minus sequences were at about the same level as the plus dimer (unpublished).

When nucleic acid extracts of *N. clevelandii* infected with VTMoV and SNMV and of *Chenopodium quinoa* infected with LTSV were fractionated by gel electrophoresis under denaturing conditions, the nucleic acids transferred to nitrocellulose and probed with single-strand ^{32}P-cDNA probes prepared from recombinant DNA plus and minus clones of the virusoids (RNA 2), an oligomeric series of plus species was found for the three virusoids. These plus oligomers are encapsidated since the same pattern was obtained when total virion RNA was fractionated in the same way. An autoradiogram for the plus oligomers of VTMoV RNA 2, SNMV RNA 2 and LTSV RNA 2 in extracts of infected plants and in RNA isolated from purified virions is shown in Fig. 2. Oligomers up to 10-mers were usually seen in both extracts and viral RNA.

In contrast to the high levels of plus virusoid oligomers in extracts of infected plants, initial experiments indicated that minus species were present at very low levels for VTMoV and SNMV but at higher levels for LTSV. These preliminary investigations on the plus and minus components of virusoid-infected plants as well as of those infected with CEV and CCCV have further convinced us, as in the case of ASBV (section 2A), that a thorough investigation of the leaf fractionation procedures and of gel analysis techniques is necessary before we can feel confident on what viroid or virusoid-specific components are present and at what concentration.

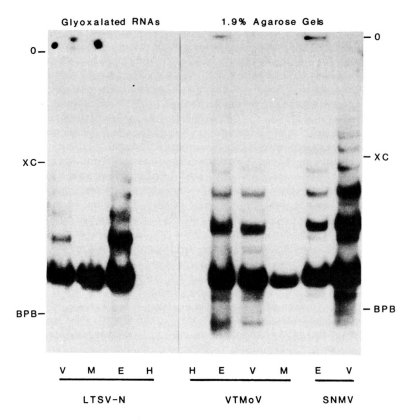

Figure 2. Plus virusoid oligomers in nucleic acid extracts
of plants infected with VTMoV, SNMV and LTSV-N and in total
viral RNA. Electrophoresis of glyoxalated RNAs and autoradiography was as for Fig. 1. Nucleic acid extracts of
infected plants were prepared by a modification of the method
of Laulhere and Rozier (1976) and viral RNA was prepared from
purified virions by phenol–SDS extraction and ethanol precipitation. V - viral RNA; E - nucleic acid extract from infected plants; H –nucleic acid extract from healthy plants;
M, marker RNA 2.

   C. Rolling Circle Model for the Replication of
     Viroids and Virusoids.
  On the basis of our results with ASBV, we proposed a
simple rolling circle model of replication to account for the
production of plus oligomers (Bruening *et al.*, 1982). The
model is really a variation on that originally proposed for
viral RNA replication (Brown and Martin, 1965) and for the
synthesis of single-strand circular bacteriophage DNA (Gilbert and Dressler, 1968; Kornberg, 1980). In this model

(Fig. 3), invading plus circular, single-strand RNA is converted by an unidentified host enzyme to a covalently closed double-strand RNA. At a specific initiation site (S in Fig. 3), the plus strand is nicked and the same, different or modified host enzyme starts polymerizing from the 3'-hydroxyl. As it moves around the covalently closed minus circular RNA, the plus RNA is displaced. When the enzyme has been around once, a specific host processing enzyme cleaves the single-strand RNA which is then ligated to produce the covalently closed single strand circular viroid or virusoid. Appropriate plant enzymes which could carry out this ligation have been described (Konarska *et al.*, 1981, 1982; Branch *et al.*, 1982). It is also feasible that the actual processing event could generate circular RNA products by attack of the 3'-end of the single-strand at the cleavage site. Although this model was developed on the basis of our results for ASBV, it is considered applicable, perhaps with variations, to other viroids and to virusoids.

The plus oligomeric species are considered to arise due to the malfunctioning of this processing event. When synthesis of viroids or virusoids is occurring at a rapid rate, it is feasible that processing may not keep up with synthesis. For example, if processing can only occur when the RNA polymerase is at or near the initiation site, then a dimer could be produced by the processing enzyme only cutting every second round of synthesis. In a similar way, higher oligomers could be produced. It is of interest that the extent of oligomer formation is related to the concentration of monomer usually found in nucleic acid extracts of infected plants. Oligomer concentration is higher for the virusoids, as compared with viroids, where purified virus yields can be about 1 mg/g of leaf material; the virusoids usually constitute at least half of the total encapsidated RNA (Randles *et al.*, 1981; Gould, 1981; Gould and Hatta, 1981). In our experience for viroids, the concentration of ASBV in nucleic acid extracts is higher than that of CCCV with CEV showing the lowest levels. The extent of oligomer formation correlates with this and may reflect the extent of disruption of normal host processes.

The model of Fig. 3 predicts that circular minus RNAs should be present in low concentrations in infected plants, and this is the case for ASBV, CCCV and the virusoids of VTMoV, SNMV and LTSV. Higher levels of minus species are found in CEV-infected tomatoes (section 11B) and a possible explanation for this is given in section 11D. All these results must be considered preliminary. A special search for what minus species are present and in what amounts is obviously necessary and this should provide confirmation, or require modification, of the simple model of Fig. 3.

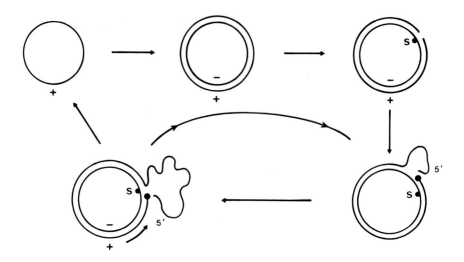

Figure 3.   Rolling circle model for the replication of viroids and virusoids. S. represents the site of initiation of
RNA synthesis. See text for further details. The small filled circle represents the RNA polymerase and the associated
arrow the direction of RNA synthesis.

        D.   Other   Rolling   Circle   Models   for   the   Repli-
            cation of Viroids
    On the basis of results obtained with PSTV infection of
tomato, Branch *et al.,* (1981,1982) and Owens and Diener
(1982) have suggested a rolling circle model of replication
which is a variation of the one considered in Fig. 3.   Thus,
the invading plus circular RNA is copied by a host RNA polymerase to produce a long *minus* linear molecule. The multimeric minus strand then serves as a template for the production of either unit length or multimeric plus strands, the
latter being cleaved to produce unit length linear molecules
or higher oligomers. All linear molecules are then ligated
to circles. Oligomeric minus sequences are presumably
formed by processing of the long minus strand.
    The main difference between this model and that of Fig.3
is the requirement for the synthesis of a multimeric minus
strand as template. It is feasible that any dimer, trimer
and tetramer minus strands found for PSTV (Branch *et al.,*
1981) could just have easily arisen by copying of plus dimers, trimers and tetramers produced in the model of Fig. 3
and that these are essentially dead-end complexes of the

replication machinery. The same explanation could account for our preliminary observation of an appreciable level of oligomeric minus sequences in CEV-infected tomato.

The area of viroid and virusoid replication will undoubtedly be complex and we have probably hardly scratched the surface. Future work requires a very careful analysis and quantitation of the various plus and minus species, both single-and double-stranded, as well as of any intermediate forms. It will also be important to determine the intracellular location of the various intermediates and to develop methods for pulse chase experiments to follow the sequence of events *in vivo*. For much of this work it is considered most important that rigorously characterized DNA probes prepared from cloned viroids and virusoids be used.

> E. What are the Unusual Properties of CCCV and Two Isolates of SCMoV Virusoid Telling Us about Viroid and Virusoid Replication.

CCV is the most unusual of the viroids sequenced so far in that four different species are present in extracts of infected coconut palms, the relative proportion of the different species varying with the stage of the disease. The smallest component of 246 or 247 residues appears first and soon after an exact dimer of 492 or 494 residues which reaches easily detectable levels (Imperial *et al.,* 1981; Mohamed *et al.,* 1982). In addition, from nine separate isolates of CCCV sequenced (Haseloff *et al.,* 1982), three other variants were found which were modifications of the 246 (247) residue monomer. Thus, either 41, 50 or 55 residues at the right hand end of the predicted secondary structure of CCCV were repeated to give the structures shown in Fig. 4. These structures are also found as exact dimers (Haseloff *et al.,* 1982).

Any model for the replication of viroids must account for the production of these unusual variants involving repetition of part of the monomer sequence. They could arise by a complex mechanism in which the RNA polymerase, when it gets to residue 124 of the right hand loop, then returns to continue synthesis from either residue 143, 147 or 150. After continuing synthesis around the end of the molecule to residue 103, 98 or 96, respectively, the RNA polymerase again would have to return to residue 123 to allow completion of synthesis of the variant molecule. The same model would pertain if the variants arose during the copying of a unit length minus rather than a plus template. It is of interest to know if similar variant RNAs occur during infection by other viroids, even in very low amounts.

This type of variation in copying the same template is difficult to envisage and solely on this basis does not seem feasible. What may be more likely is a completely different

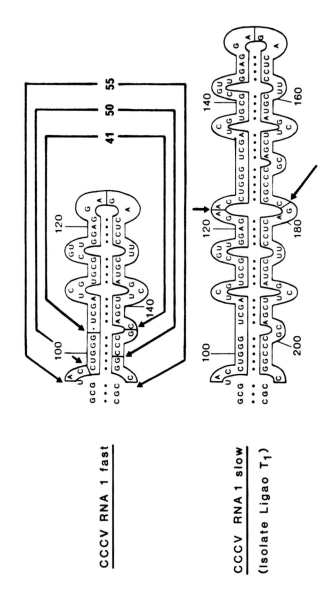

CCCV RNA 1 fast

CCCV RNA 1 slow
(Isolate Ligao T₁)

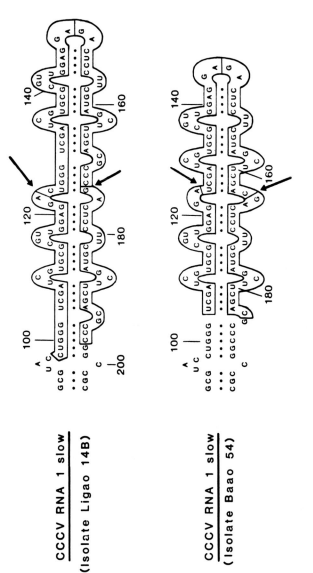

Figure 4. Sequence variation between CCCV RNA 1 slow of three isolates of CCCV. Only the right hand ends of the proposed secondary structures (Haseloff *et al.*, 1982) of CCCV are shown. Boxed regions represent those sequences which are duplicated in the CCCV RNA 1 slow molecules and which are 41, 50, or 55 residues long. All CCCV RNA 1 slow isolates correspond to one of these forms (Haseloff *et al.*, 1982).

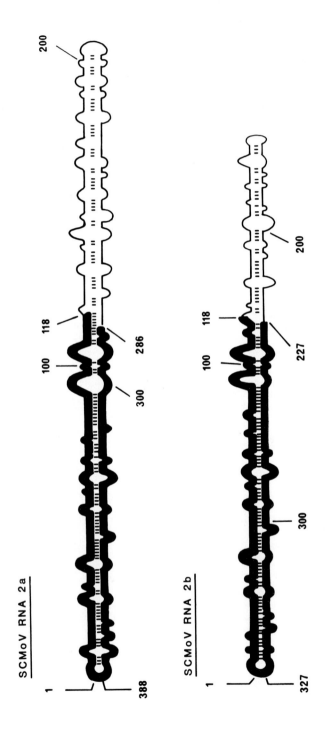

SCMoV RNA 2a

1

118
100
300
286

200

SCMoV RNA 2b

1

118
100
300
227

200

327

━━━ HOMOLOGY BETWEEN TWO RNAs

mixture of species with either an extra residue or with one
or more base substitutions.

Sequence heterogeneity has been found frequently in
viral RNAs which are replicated directly by copying RNA
templates and is considered to result from the lower accuracy
of RNA,as compared to DNA,replication (Holland *et al.*, 1982).
Where no one species has a significant replication advantage,
the sequence heterogeneity persists during later infections,
resulting in a mixed population of RNA pathogens. Another
possibility which must be considered is that two or more
species present in a mixture can provide different functions
of mutual benefit. Such complementation could arise by one
species providing a function absent in the other species or
by a synergistic effect of the same function provided by the
different species.

III.   HOW SIMILAR IS THE REPLICATION OF LINEAR SATELLITE
       RNAs TO THAT OF VIROIDS AND VIRUSOIDS?

A.   Intra-cellular Forms of Linear Satellite RNAs.
Some linear plant virus satellite RNAs are of similar
size to the circular viroids and virusoids (Murant and Mayo,
1982). It is, therefore, of interest to consider if their
replication mechanisms are similar in any way to those of the
viroids and virusoids. The satellite RNA most extensively
studied is that of tobacco ringspot virus (sat-TobRSV;
Schneider, 1971); the budblight strain contains 357 residues, is terminated by a 5'-hydroxyl and a 3'-phosphate and
does not contain a poly(A) tail (Bruening, unpublished).
High molecular weight double-strand RNA forms of this satellite have been isolated from infected tissue (Schneider and
Thompson, 1977; Sogo and Schneider, 1982). When nucleic
acid extracts of infected plants enriched for double-strand
RNA were denatured in formaldehyde and analysed under denaturing conditions by electrophoresis on formaldehyde-agarose
gels, a series of both plus and minus species of increasing
molecular weight was detected after transfer to nitrocellulose and hybridization with ^{32}P-probes for plus and minus
sequences (Kiefer *et al.*, 1982). A plot of mobilities of the
components versus the logarithm of their presumed molecular
sizes was linear and indicated that both the plus and minus
species were integral multiples of the 357 residue monomer

Figure 5.   Diagrammatic comparison of the sequence homology
(Haseloff and Symons, unpublished) between two isolates of
the virusoid of SCMoV (Francki *et al.*, 1983). The thick left
hand parts of the proposed secondary structure models show
almost complete sequence homology, whereas there is no homology between the thin right ends. Residues are numbered from
the lefthand end of each molecule.

(Kiefer *et al.*, 1982). The plus series with oligomers up to
12-mers was, therefore, very similar to that found for viroids, especially ASBV, and for virusoids. In contrast, the
high concentration of oligomeric minus species in sat–TobRSV
infection was not found with either viroids of virusoids.
These results suggest a basic difference in the replication
mechanisms for the circular and linear molecules. An interesting aspect is that when RNA isolated from purified virions
was analysed in the same way, only the plus series of oligomers was found to be packaged (Kiefer *et al.*, 1982) which
means that some mechanism exists for exclusion of the minus
oligomers during encapsidation.

Another plant virus satellite RNA, that of CMV (sat-
RNA), shows a different pattern of presumed replication
intermediates. Double-strand sat-RNA can occur at approximately the same concentration as single-strand plus sat-RNA
in extracts of infected plants but there is only a trace of
higher molecular weight double-strand forms (Diaz-Ruiz and
Kaper, 1978). When we analyzed various nucleic acid extracts
of cucumber seedlings infected with CMV and an Adelaide
isolate of sat-RNA (Gould *et al.*, 1978; Mossop and Francki,
1979; Gordon and Symons, 1983) by gel electrophoresis under
denaturing conditions either before or after treatment with
ribonuclease, transfer to nitrocellulose and hybridization
with specific ^{32}P-DNA probes for plus and minus sequences
derived from clones of cDNA to sat-RNA, the pattern obtained
is given in Fig. 6. Virion RNA contained mainly plus monomer
sat-RNA (lane B1) with small amounts of plus dimer and of a
higher molecular form equivalent in size to a decamer (not
visible in Fig. 6). A trace of minus monomer sat-RNA (lane
A1) was also found. Consistent with the results of Diaz-Ruiz
and Kaper (1978), plant extracts of a particulate fraction
contained large amounts of both monomeric plus and minus
sequences (lanes B2 and A2) much of which was present in a
double-strand form because of its resistance to ribonuclease
(lanes B3 and A3). A purified double-strand fraction showed
the expected resistance to ribonuclease digestion (lanes A4
and A5, B4 and B5). Low levels of plus dimers of sat-RNA
were seen (lane B2); since these were susceptible to ribonuclease (lane B3),they were not present in double-strand
RNA. This is consistent with the lack of a minus dimer band
(lanes A2 and A3).

        B.   Rolling Circle Model for the Replication of
             Satellite RNAs.

A rolling circle type model for the replication of
satTobRSV has been proposed to account for the high molecular
weight double-strand forms of the RNA (Sogo and Schneider,

A – MINUS PROBE   B – PLUS PROBE

PARTICULATE EXTRACT   DS-RNA FRACTION

1. Viral RNA   2. – RNase   4. – RNase

3. + RNase   5. + RNase

Figure 6. Plus and minus forms of CMV satellite RNA (sat-RNA) in nucleic acid extracts of infected cucumber seedlings,. Electrophoresis conditions were essentially as described in Figs. 1 and 2. 1x and 2x indicate the position of monomer and dimer sat-RNA. See text for further details.

1982; Kiefer *et al.*, 1982). Linear sat-TobRSV is converted to a covalent plus circle which is then copied by a rolling circle mechanism to produce a long linear minus strand. This is then copied to produce a long plus strand hydrogen bonded to the minus strand. Processing of this product and/or variation in the replication mechanism produced the single-strand plus monomers in addition to the large amounts of oligomeric double-strand RNAs. The original model postulated that there were non-viral spacers between the monomeric units in the minus strand but this appears to be an unnecessary hypothesis for which there is no evidence.

Although there are appreciable differences between the forms of sat-TobRSV and CMV sat-RNA found *in vivo*, the possibility must be considered that both satellite RNAs are replicated by similar mechanisms and that these may share features with the replication of viroids and virusoids. A model for the replication of satellite RNAs is given in

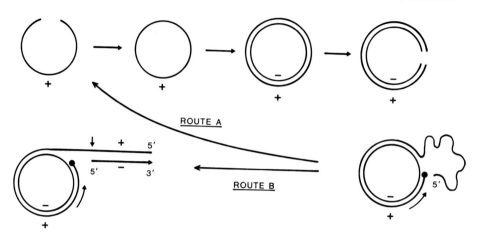

Figure 7. Rolling circle model for the replication of linear satelite RNAs. The small filled circle represents the RNA polymerase and the associated arrow the direction of RNA synthesis. See text for further details.

Fig. 7. The essential difference between this model and that proposed for viroids and virusoids (Fig. 3) lies in the two alternative routes for the fate of the rolling circle. Route A gives the single-strand monomeric linear satellite RNAs found in virions. It could also provide the dimeric CMV sat-RNA and the single-strand encapsidated oligomeric plus sat-TobRSV RNAs (Kiefer *et al.*, 1982) as already considered for the oligomeric plus viroids and virusoids. Route B would provide the double-strand forms of both satellite RNAs. In the case of CMV sat-RNA, processing is considered so efficient that only monomeric double-strand RNAs are found, whereas partially defective processing for sat-TobRSV could provide the observed oligomeric series of double-strand RNAs. The relative extent to which the two routes are followed and variation in the processing of the single-strand and double-strand products allows the flexibility to cater for future observations.

The model of Fig. 7 is obviously very simple but forms the basis for discussion in the essential absence of any data on the replication of satellite RNA. Since the encapsidated circular virusoids form a link between viroids and the encapsidated linear satellite RNAs, serious comparison between them is warranted. In the case of encapsidated satellites, the high molecular weight RNA of the helper virus is considered to code for at least part of the replication machinery necessary for the replication of the viral RNA and of the satellite. Since there is no helper virus in the case of viroids, it could be argued that this would mean different replication strategies for viroids and for virusoids and satellite RNAs. A novel possibility is that the assumption that linear satellite RNAs make use of the same replication machinery as that of the helper viral RNA is not correct but rather the viral RNA specifically stimulates the formation of a completely host-encoded system for the replication of these satellite RNAs and that this is independent of the viral RNA replication system. The latter suggestion should be kept in mind when we compare the replication of viroids with the circular virusoids, all four of which are probably satellite RNAs (Jones *et al.*, 1983; our unpublished data).

There is little data to support the model of Fig. 7 for sat-TobRSV replication and there is even less for sat-RNA of CMV. Circular structures have been seen in plants infected with sat-TobRSV (Sogo and Schneider, 1982) but there is no data for or against the presence *in vivo* of circular forms of CMV sat-RNA. In addition, some properties of sat-TobRSV are different to those of sat-RNA of CMV which may argue against comparison of their replication mechanisms. The predicted secondary structure of the 357 residues of sat-TobRSV is essentially viroid and virusoid-like in being roughly linear and rod-like with 65% of its residues base-paired (Bruening, unpublished) as compared with 66 to 73% for viroids and virusoids (Sänger, 1982; Keese *et al.*, 1983). On the other hand CMV sat-RNA appears to have a more open structure with only 52% of its residues base-paired (Gordon and Symond, 1983). In addition, sat-TobRSV contains a 5'-hydroxyl and a 3'-phosphate (Bruening, unpublished), whereas CMV sat-RNA contains a m^7G cap and 2', 3'-hydroxyls(Richards *et al.*, 1978; Gordon and Symons, 1983).

C. Sequence of Sat-TobRSV Indicates a Possible Splicing Site for Virusoids

Parts of the proposed structure of sat-TobRSV show remarkable sequence and positional homology with the predicted structures of the virusoids of VTMoV and SNMV and to a lesser extent with those of SCMoV (unpublished). When most of these homologous regions are arranged as in Fig. 8, the 5'- and 3'-ends of sat-TobRSV are adjacent with the 5'-hydroxyl and 3'-phosphate suitable for ligation to give a circular monomer as required by the model of Fig. 7. It is, therefore, proposed that sat-TobRSV and virusoid RNAs are produced by cleavage of multimeric precursors at sites corresponding to between residues 357 and 1 for sat-TobRSV, between residues 48 and 49 for the virusoids of VTMoV and SNMV, and between residues 62 and 63 for the SCMoV virusoid. Implicit in this proposal is the assumption that the conserved sequences surrounding these putative sites for RNA processing are in some way functional, perhaps in determining the specific sites of cleavage. In addition, the conservation of these sequences indicates possible recognition signals for

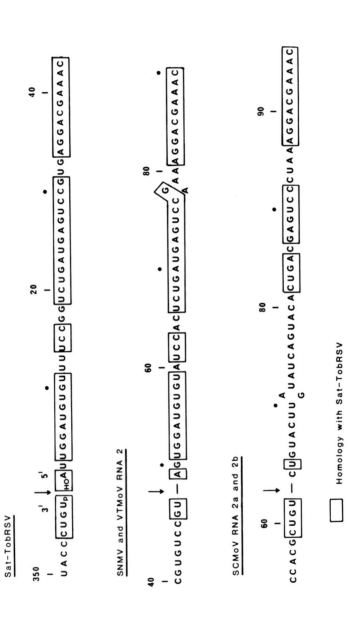

interaction with host, rather than viral, components. It may be relevant here that VTMoV and SNMV, but not SCMoV with its lesser virusoid homology, share common host plants, e.g., *Nicotiana clevelandii* (Randles *et al.*, 1981; Francki *et al.*, 1983).

Further evidence that there may be something special about the region of the proposed processing sites was obtained during the sequence determination of the virusoids of VTMoV and SNMV (Haseloff and Symons, 1981). Part of the sequencing was done by the dideoxynucleotide chain termination technique using specific primers and reverse transcriptase. With both virusoids and irrespective of whether intact circular RNAs or linear RNAs were used, there was essentially complete termination of transcription at residue 49 of both RNAs (Haseloff, unpublished). This was presumably due to the presence of sequences and/or secondary structures capable of causing reverse trancriptase to chain terminate. For example, an 8-base pair stem plus a three-base loop can be formed in VTMoV and SNMV RNA 2 at residues 40 to 58 with the proposed processing site in the single strand loop. However, a similar structure cannot be formed in the same region for SCMoV or sat-TobRSV. Hence, although there is no direct evidence to support the proposed processing sites, these sequencing results indicate potential regions of interest which may become more meaningful as our understanding of virusoid replication increases.

IV. ARE THERE ANY VIROID OR VIRUSOID-CODED POLYPEPTIDE PRODUCTS?

The small size and limited genetic information in viroids and virusoids poses the question of whether or not they code *in vivo* for polypeptide products. Although eukaryotic ribosomes do not interact with circular RNAs (Kozack, 1979), it must be considered feasible that sub-genomic linear fragments derived from either the infectious plus strand or its complement could act as mRNAs. Further, polypeptide products need not be very long to have significant biological activity in view of the dramatic effects of small polypeptides in

---

Figure 8. Proposed site for RNA processing in virusoids. Portions of the sequence of sat-TobRSV (Bruening, unpublished), RNAs 2 of SNMV and VTMoV (Haseloff and Symons, 1982) and of RNAs 2a and 2b of two isolates of SCMoV (Haseloff and Symons, unpublished) are aligned to show homologous regions (boxed). The vertical arrows indicate the 3'-end of the linear sat-TobRSV and the proposed RNA processing site of the three virusoids.

animal systems (Blundell and Wood, 1982). No viroid-specific proteins have been found in PSTV- and CEV- infected tissue (Sänger, 1982) but the methods used would not have detected small amounts of viroid-coded polypeptides. As far as we are aware, no attempts have been made to look for virusoid-coded polypeptides.

The potential viroid- and virusoid-coded polypeptides can be determined from the number of initiator AUG and GUG codons in both plus and minus strands (Table II) and their length from the position of the in-phase terminator codons. PSTV and CCCV are unique in not having any AUG codons in either their plus or minus strands (Table II). However, the other viroids and virusoids have one or more AUG codons while the GUG codons

Table II

Number of AUG and GUG Codons in Viroids and Virusoids*

RNA	Plus strand		Minus strand	
	AUG	GUG	AUG	GUG
PSTV-G	0	7	0	4
CSV-A	1	4	0	4
CEV-A	0	4	1	4
ASBV-SB1	3	4	1	3
CCCV-RNA 1	0	3	0	2
SNMV RNA 2	4	8	3	9
VTMoV RNA 2	4	6	3	7
LTSV-A RNA 2	4	3	6	6

*For references, see Table I.

occur more frequently in plus and minus strands. The lengths of potential polypeptide products vary from a few residues up to about 100.

It will be extremely difficult to determine whether or not viroid - and virusoid-coded polypeptides exist *in vivo,* especially if they are present in very small amounts. One potentially feasible approach would be to prepare antibodies to the putative polypeptides which could then be detected by immunological procedures. Given the nucleotide sequence of a viroid or virusoid, it is now possible to chemically synthesize the putative polypeptides for use as antigens for the preparation of antibodies (Sheppard, 1983; Walter and Doolittle, 1983). What makes this task much easier is the ability to detect large polypeptides using antibodies prepared against synthetic peptides which are only 10-20 residues long and, therefore, may only represent part of the total sequence (Walter and Doolittle, 1983). This approach obviously represents a major investment in time and resources but could possibly lead to unequivocal answers.

An alternative approach to investigate the synthesis of viroid – and virusoid-coded polypeptides is via *in vitro* mutagenesis. In view of the success of R.A. Owens (chapter 15 this volume) in obtaining infectious double-strand dimeric DNA clones of PSTV in the plasmid vector pBR322, it should be possible to prepare similar infectious clones of other viroids and of the virusoids. Site directed mutagenesis (Shortle *et al.*, 1981) could then be used to eliminate potential AUG or GUG initiation codons, to form termination codons, or to insert or delete a residue in order to modify the putative reading frame. The effect on infectivity of such modifications could then be tested. This approach is also technically demanding and is less direct than the immunological approach described above.

If a viroid or virusoid does code for one or more polypeptides *in vivo,* then the possession of antibodies to them should allow an investigation of their location in the cell and their possible mode of action. Such polypeptides could conceivably be responsible for one or more cytopathological effects and could play a role in the subversion of the host RNA synthesis machinery for the replication of viroids or virusoids.

V. WHAT ENZYMES ARE INVOLVED IN THE REPLICATION OF VIROIDS AND VIRUSOIDS?

So far we have mostly discussed the mechanism of the replication of viroids and virusoids with little consideration of the enzymes involved. Essentially all the work in this latter area has simply been concerned at looking for RNA polymerase systems which will copy viroids and virusoids *in vitro.* Such work is unlikely to provide any useful information of what is happening *in vivo* since replication within the cell will undoubtedly be a complex process about which we know nothing at present. Even in the case of the replication of normal plant viral RNAs, very little is known about the enzymology of the process in spite of extensive investigations over many years (Gordon *et al.*, 1982; Dorssers *et al.*, 1982).

Table III lists five groups of enzymes which can copy viroids and virusoids into RNA *in vitro.* Two of these are from *E. coli* and the other three from plant sources. Apart from the ability of the plant enzymes to partially copy viroids or virusoids, the results provide no insight into the enzyme systems involved *in vivo.*

The detailed characterization of the replication machinery of viroids and virusoids represents a very challenging problem. It will be of considerable interest to determine if

host enzymes are solely responsible for the replication of
virusoids, as is presumed to be the case at present for
viroids, or if the viral RNA of the helper virus also pro-

Table III
Enzymes which can Copy Viroids and Virusoids
into RNA In Vitro

Enzyme	Viroids or Virusoids copied	References
1. Phage RNA replicase	PSTV	Owens and Diener, 1977
2. *E. coli* DNA polymerase *E. coli* RNA polymerase	PSTV, CEV, CSV	Rohde *et al.*, 1982
3. Tomato RNA polymerase II Wheat germ RNA polymerase II	PSTV	Rackwitz *et al.*, 1981
4. Tomato RNA-dependent RNA polymerase	PSTV	Boege *et al.*, 1982
5. Cucumber mosaic virus-induced RNA polymerase	ASBV	Gordon *et al.*, 1982
	SCMoV RNA 2	Gill and Symons, unpub.

vides a functional protein(s). Perhaps the only feasible
experimental approach is to isolate a sub-cellular fraction
from infected plants which can synthesize or replicate viroids or virusoids and then to determine which proteins are
part of the replication complex and what are their functions.
This is a very demanding approach and will require all the
accumulated skills and techniques of the molecular biologist.

VI. ACKNOWLEDGMENTS

The authors thank Jenny Rosey and Sharon Freund for
assistance and the Australian Research Grants Scheme and the
Rural Credits Development Fund of the Reserve Bank of Australia for financial support.

REFERENCES

Allen, R.N., Palukaitis, P., and Symons, R.H. (1981). Purified avocado sunblotch viroid causes disease in
avocado seedlings. *Aust.Plant.Path.10M* 31-32.
Blundell, T., and Wood, S. (1982). The conformation, flexibility, and dynamics of polypeptide hormones.
Ann. Rev. Biochem. 51, 123-154.

Boege, F., Rohde, W., and Sänger, H.L. (1982). *In vitro* transcription of viroid RNA into full length copies by RNA-dependent RNA polymerase from healthy tomato leaf tissue. *Biosci. Rep.2*, 185-194.
than-unit-length viroid minus strands are present in

Branch, A.D., Robertson, H.D., and Dickson, E. (1981). Longer RNA from infected plants. *Proc.Natl.Acad.Sci. USA 78*, 6381-6385.

Branch, A.D., Robertson, H.D., Greer, C., Gegenheimer, P., Peebles, C., and Abelson, J. (1982). Cell-free circularization of viroid progeny RNA by an RNA ligase from wheat germ. *Science 217*, 1147-1149.

Brown, F., and Martin, S.J. (1965). A new model for virus ribonucleic acid replication. *Nature 208*, 861-863.

Bruening, G., Gould, A.R., Murphy, P.J., and Symons, R.H. (1982). Oligomers of avocado sunblotch viroid are found in infected avocado leaves. *FEBS Letters 148*, 71-78.

Collmer, C.W., Tousignant, M.E., and Kaper, J.M. (1983). Cucumber mosaic virus-associated RNA 5: X. The complete nucleotide sequence of a CARNA 5 incapable of inducing tomato necrosis. *Virology 127*, 230-234.

Diaz-Ruiz, J.R., and Kaper, J.M. (1978). Isolation of viral double-stranded RNAs using a LiCl fractionation procedure. *Prep.Biochem.8*, 1-17.

Dorssers, L., Zabel, P. van der Meer, J., and van Kammen, A. (1982). Purification of a host-encoded RNA-dependent RNA polymerase from cowpea mosaic virus-infected cowpea leaves. *Virology 116*, 236-249.

Fields, S., and Winter, G. (1982). Nucleotide sequences of influenza virus segments 1 and 3 reveal mosaic structure of a small viral RNA segment. *Cell 28*, 303-313.

Francki, R.I.B., Randles, J.W., Hatta, T., Davies, C., and Chu, P.W.G. (1983). Subterranean clover mottle virus from Australia with encapsidated viroid-like RNA. *Plant Pathology 32*, 47-59.

Gilbert, W., and Dressler, D. (1968). DNA replication: The rolling circle model. *Cold Spring Harbor Symp. Quant. Biol. 33*, 473-484.

Gordon, K.H.J., and Symons, R.H. (1983). Satellite RNA of cucumber mosaic virus forms a secondary structure with partial 3'-terminal homology to genomal RNAs. *Nucleic Acids Res. 11*, 947-960.

Gordon, K.H.J., Gill, D.S., and Symons, R.H. (1982). Highly purified cucumber mosaic virus-induced RNA-dependent RNA polymerase does not contain any of the full length translation products of the genomic

RNAs. *Virology,123,* 284-295.

Gould, A.R. (1981). Studies on encapsidated viroid-like RNA. II. Purification and characterization of a viroid-like RNA associated with velvet tobacco mottle virus (VTMoV). *Virology 108,* 123-133.

Gould, A.R., and Hatta T. (1981). Studies on encapsidated viroid-like RNA. III. Comparative studies on RNAs isolated from velvet tobacco mottle virus and solanum nodiflorum mottle virus. *Virology 109,* 137-147.

Gould, A.R., Palukaitis, P., Symons, R.H., and Mossop, D.W. (1978). Characterization of a satellite RNA associated with cucumber mosaic virus. *Virology 84,* 443-455.

Gross, H.J., and Riesner, D. (1980). Viroids: A class of subviral pathogens. *Angew. Chem. Int. Ed. Engl. 19,* 231-243.

Gross, H.J., Domdey, H., Lossow, C., Jank, P., Raba, M., Alberty, H., and Sänger, H.L. (1978_. Nucleotide sequence and secondary structure of potato spindle tuber viroid. *Nature 272,* 203-208.

Gross, H.J.,Liebl, U., Alberty, H., Krupp, G., Domdey, H., Ramm, K., and Sänger, H.L. (1981). A severe and a mild potato spindle tuber isolate differ in three nucleotide exchanges only. *Biosci.Rep.1,* 235-241.

Gross, H.J., Krupp, G., Domdey, H., Raba, M., Jank, P., Lossow, C.H., Alberty, H., Ramm, K., and Sänger H.L. (1982). Nucleotide sequence and secondary structure of citrus exocortis and chrysanthemum stunt viroid. *Eur. J. Biochem.121,* 249-257.

Haseloff, J., and Symons, R.H. (1981). Chrysanthemum stunt viroid: Primary sequence and secondary structure. *Nucleic Acids Res. 9,* 2741-2752.

Haseloff, J., and Symons, R.H. (1982). Comparative sequence and structure of viroid-like RNAs of two plant viruses. *Nucleic Acids Res.10,* 3681-3691.

Haseloff, J., Mohamed, N.A., and Symons, R.H. (1982). Viroid RNAs of the cadang-cadang disease of coconuts. *Nature 299,* 316-322.

Holland, J., Spindler, K., Horodyski, F., Grabau, E., Nichol, S., and Van de Pol. S. (1982). Rapid evolution of RNA genomes. *Science 215,* 1577-1585.

Imperial, J.S., Rodriguez, J.B., and Randles, J.W. (1981). Variation in the viroid-like RNA associated with cadang-cadang disease: Evidence for an increase in molecular weight with disease progress. *J. Gen. Virol. 56,* 77-85.

Jones, A.T., Mayo, M.A., and Duncan, G.H. (1983). Satellite-like properties of small circular RNA molecules in

particles of lucerne transient streak virus.
J. Gen. Virol. 64, 1167-1173.

Keese, P., Bruening, G., and Symons, R.H. (1983). Comparative sequence and structure of circular RNAs from two isolates of lucerne transient streak virus. *FEBS Lett.,* in press.

Kiefer, M.C., Daubert, S.D., Schneider, I.R., and Bruening, G. (1982). Multimeric forms of satellite of tobacco ringspot virus RNA. *Virology 121,* 262-273.

Konarska, M., Filipowicz, W., Domdey, H., and Gross, H.J. (1981). Formation of a 2'-phosphomonoester, 3', 5'-phosphodiester linkage by a novel RNA ligase in wheat germ. *Nature 293,* 112-116.

Konarska, M., Filipowicz, W., and Gross, H.J. (1982). RNA ligation via 2'-phosphomonoester, 3', 5'-phophodiester linkage: Requirement of 2', 3'-cyclic phosphate termini and involvement of a 5'-hydroxyl polynucleotide kinase. *Proc. Natl. Acad. Sci. U.S.A.79,* 1474-1478.

Kornberg, A. (1980). 'DNA replication.' Freeman, San Francisco.

Kozak, M. (1979). Inability of circular mRNA to attach to eucaryotic ribosomes. *Nature 280,* 82-85.

Laulhere, J.P., and Rozier, C. (1976). One-step extraction of plant nucleic acids. *Plant Science Letters 6,* 237-242.

Mohamed, N.A., Haseloff, J., Imperial, J.S., and Symons, R.H. (1982). Characterization of the different electrophoretic forms of the cadang-cadang viroid. *J. Gen. Virol. 63,* 181-188.

Mossop, D.W., and Francki, R.I.B. (1979). Comparative studies on two satellite RNAs of cucumber mosaic virus. *Virology 95,* 395-404.

Murant, A.F., and Mayo, M.A. (1982). Satellites of Plant viruses. *Ann. Rev. Phytopathol. 20,* 49-70.

Owens, R.A., and Diener, T.O. (1977). Synthesis of RNA complimentary to potato spindle tuber viroid using Qβ replicase. *Virology, 79,* 109-120.

Owens, R.A. and Diener, T.O. (1982). RNA intermediates in potato spindle tuber viroid replication. *Proc. Acad. Sci. USA 79,* 113-117.

Palukaitis, P., and Symons, R.H. (1980). Purification and characterization of the circular and linear forms of chrysanthemum stunt viroid. *J. Gen. Virol. 46,* 477-489.

Palukaitis, P., Rakowski, A.G., Alexander, D. McE., and Symons, R.H. (1981). Rapid indexing of the sunblotch disease of avocados using a complementary

DNA probe to avocado sunblotch viroid. *Ann. Appl. Biol. 98,* 439-449.

Rackwitz, H-R., Rohde W., and Sänger, H.L. (1981). DNA-dependent RNA polymerase II of plant origin transcribes viroid RNA into full-length copies. *Nature 291,* 297-301.

Randles, J.W., Davies, C., Hatta, T., Gould, A.R., and Francki, R.I.B. (1981). Studies on encapsidated viroid-like RNA I. Characterization of velvet tobacco mottle virus. *Virology 108,* 111-122.

Richards, K.E., Jonard, G., Jacquemond, M., and Lot, H. (1978). Nucleotide sequence of cucumber mosaic virus associated RNA 5. *Virology 89,* 395-408.

Riesner, D., Steger, G., Schumacher, J., Gross, H.J., Randles, J.W., and Sänger, H.L. (1983). Structure and function of viroids. *Biophys. Struct. Mech. 9,* 145-170.

Rohde, W., Rackwitz, H-R., Boege, F., and Sänger, H.L. (1982). Viroid RNA is accepted as a template for *in vitro* transcription by DNA-dependent DNA polymerase I and RNA polymerase from *Escherichia coli. Biosci. Rep. 2,* 929-939.

Sänger, H.L. (1982). Biology, structure, functions and possible origin of viroids. In "Nucleic Acids and Proteins in Plants" (B. Parthier and D. Boulter, eds.), pp. 368-454. Springer-Verlag, Berlin.

Schneider, I.R. (1971). Characterization of a satellite-like virus of tobacco ringspot virus. *Virology 45,* 108-122.

Schneider, I.R., and Thompson, S.M. (1977). Double-stranded nucleic acids found in tissue infected with the satellite of tobacco ringspot virus. *Virology 78,* 453-462.

Sheppard, R.C. (1983). Continuous flow methods in organic synthesis. *Chemistry in Britain,* May, 402-414.

Shortle, D., DiMaio, D., and Nathans, D. (1981). Directed mutagenesis. *Ann. Rev. Genetics 15,* 265-294.

Sogo, J.M., and Schneider, I.R. (1982). Electron microscopy of double-stranded nucleic acids found in tissue infected with the satellite of tobacco ringspot virus. *Virology 117,* 401-415.

Symons, R.H. (1981). Avocado sunblotch viroid: Primary sequence and proposed secondary structure. *Nucleic Acids Res. 9,* 6527-6537.

Visvader, J.E., and Symons, R.H. (1983). Comparative sequence and structure of different isolates of citrus exocortis viroid. *Virology 130,* 232-237.

Visvader, J.E., Gould, A.R., Bruening, G., and Symons, R.H. (1982). Citrus exocortis viroid: Nucleotide sequence and secondary structure of an Australian isolate. *FEBS Lett.* *137* 288–292.

Walter, G., and Doolittle, R.F. (1983). Antibodies against synthetic peptides. In 'Genetic Engineering: principles and Methods'. (J.K. Setlow and A. Hollaender, eds.), vol 5, pp. 61–91, Plenum, New York.

Ysebaert, M., van Emmelo, J., and Fiers, W. (1980). Total nucleotide sequence of a nearly full-size DNA copy of satellite tobacco necrosis virus RNA. *J. Mol Biol.* *143* 273–287.

Chapter 13

VIROID-LIKE RNAs INCORPORATED IN CONVENTIONAL
VIRUS CAPSIDS

R.I.B. Francki

J.W. Randles

P.W.G. Chu

J. Rohozinski

and T. Hatta

Department of Plant Pathology
Waite Agricultural Research Institute
The University of Adelaide
South Australia

I. INTRODUCTION

In recent years four new viruses have been isolated in
Australia with unusual RNA complements; they are velvet
tobacco mottle (VTMoV, Randles *et al.*, 1981), solanum nodiflorum mottle (SNMV, Greber, 1981), lucerne transient streak
(LTSV, Tien-Po *et al.*, 1981) and subterranean clover mottle
(SCMoV, Francki *et al.*, 1983b). These viruses have small
polyhedral particles with many properties in common with
viruses belonging to the sobemovirus group (Matthews, 1982).
However, in addition to a single-stranded, linear RNA similar to the RNAs of other small polyhedral viruses, they also
encapsidate small single-stranded circular and linear RNA
molecules with many properties characteristic of viroids
(Randles *et al.*, 1981; Gould, 1981; Gould and Hatta, 1981;
Haseloff and Symons, 1982). In this paper we will discuss
the properties of the four viruses, their likely modes of

SUBVIRAL PATHOGENS   265
OF PLANTS AND ANIMALS:
VIROIDS AND PRIONS

Copyright © 1985 by Academic Press, Inc.
All rights of reproduction in any form reserved.
ISBN 0-12-470230-9

replication and the possible significance of the encapsidated
viroid-like RNAs in relation to their biological function and
evolutionary origin.

II.   BIOLOGICAL PROPERTIES OF THE VIRUSES

A.)   Isolation of the viruses.

VTMoV was isolated from *Nicotiana velutina* (velvet
tobacco), a wild plant growing in the arid zone of South
Australia (Randles *et al.*, 1981). Infected plants were
stunted with a mottling and crinkling of the leaves. The
virus has not been isolated from any other species and at
present does not appear to be of any economic importance.

SNMV has been isolated from *Solanum nodiflorum*, a common weed in coastal North-Eastern Australia (Greber, 1981).
The virus has been detected in *S. nodiflorum* along the entire
Queensland coast south of Cairns. Infected plants develop
mottling of the leaves and up to 20% of plants growing in the
wild can be infected. Usually diseased plants were found to
be infected with SNMV only, but co-infection by potato virus
Y and/or tobacco streak has also been detected (Greber, 1981).

LTSV was originally isolated from *Medicago sativa*
(lucerne) in South-Eastern Australia (Victoria) by Blackstock
(1978) and was subsequently also found in New Zealand where
it appears to be widespread (Forster and Jones, 1979; R.L.
Forster, personal communication). More recently, the virus
has also been isolated in Canada (Paliwal, 1982; Y.C.Paliwal,
personal communication). Lucerne plants infected with LTSV
often develop chlorotic streaking along the lateral veins of
leaves and sometimes the leaves become distorted. However,
in some instances infected plants fail to show any discernible disease symptoms. The economic importance of LTSV to
lucerne production is not known but in one field trial, there
was shown to be an 18% loss of dry matter due to virus infection (Blackstock, 1978).

SCMoV has been isolated from *Trifolium subterraneum*
(subterranean clover) growing in several locations of South-
Western Australia (Francki *et al.* 1983b). It has also been
isolated once from *T. glomeratum* (club clover). Infected
subterranean clover plants are very stunted and develop leaf
mottling and crinkling. Such plants produce very little dry
matter. As yet, the distribution of the virus appears to be
very limited without evidence of significant spread and hence
it has not made any impact on clover pasture production.
However, should the virus spread it will undoubtedly, seriously limit pasture yield.

B.)   Experimental host ranges.

The known experimental host ranges of the four viruses

are summarized in Table 1. Those of southern bean mosaic
(SBMV, Shepherd, 1971) and sowbane mosaic (SoMV, Kado, 1971)
have also been included in Table 1 as they have many common
properties as discussed in more detail later.

Data summarized in Table 1 indicate that all the viruses
listed including two strains of LTSV can be easily distinguished from each other by their host ranges. No species
outside the Solanaceae have as yet been shown to be susceptible to SNMV. The host range of VTMoV also appears to be
confined to the Solanaceae, except that it has been shown to
infect *Gomphrena globosa* (Amaranthaceae) in which no symptoms
were produced (Randles *et al.*, 1981).

LTSV seems to have a wider host range in that although
it appears to be primarily a virus of the Leguminosae, it can
infect plants within the Solanaceae and Chenopodiaceae. Furthermore, *Zinnia elegans* (Compositae) was successfully infected with the virus. The host range of SCMoV has not been
thoroughly investigated. Further studies with all four viruses are required to provide a more precise picture of their
comparative host ranges.

SBMV, the type member of the Sobemovirus group, infects
only three of the species tested and these are listed in
Table 1. None of these appear to be hosts of VTMoV, SNMV,
LTSV or SCMoV. This is not altogether surprising because
SBMV is known to have a very narrow host range (Shepherd,
1971). SoMV is a probable member of the sobemovirus group
(Matthews,1982) and of the plants listed in Table 1 appears
to infect only members of the Chenopodiaceae. It too is
known to have a very narrow host range (Kado, 1971).

C). Vectors and mode of transmission.

Two of the viruses with viroid-like RNAs, VTMoV and
SNMV, are transmitted by insect vectors, while the mode of
natural transmissions of the other two, LTSV and SCMoV is
unknown. The two closest likely allies of the above group,
SBMV and SoMV, are both insect borne; the former by a beetle
(Walters and Henry, 1970) and the latter by a leaf miner, a
leafhopper, and a flea hopper (Kado, 1971). SoMV is also
efficiently transmitted by pollen and is seedborne.

VTMoV and SNMV appear to be distributed widely by their
known vectors. VTMoV occurs where host plants are sparsely
distributed, and the strong flight behavior of the mirid
vector, *Cyrtopeltis nicotianae* probably explains the high incidence and wide distribution of VTMoV in *N. velutina*. VTMoV
has been isolated from Cobblers Sandhill, Innamincka (Randles
et al., 1981) and Cunnamulla (G.M. Behncken, personal communication). Similarly, the long range movement of adult coccinellid beetle vectors of SNMV probably accounts for the
widespread distribution and incidence of this virus in

Table 1.
Host Ranges of the Viruses[a]

Plant Species	VTMoV	SNMV	LTSV[b]		SCMoV	SBMV	SoMV
			Aus.	N.Z.			
SOLANACEAE							
Nicotiana velutina	+[c]	+					
Solanum nodiflorum	−	+					
Nicotiana clevelandii	+[d]	+[d]	−		+[d]	−	+
Nicotiana glutinosa	+	−	−		−	−	+
Nicotiana glauca	+	−					
Nicotiana tabacum	+	+	−		+	−	+
Nicotiana rustica					+		
Datura stramonium	+	−	−			−	
Petunia hybrida	+	+			+	−	+
Physalis floridana	−	+	−				
Solanum melongena	−	+	−				−
Lycopersicon esculentum	−	+	−			−	−
Nicotiana x edwardsonii	+						
CHENOPODIACEAE							
Chenopodium amaranticolor	−	−	+		+	−	+
Chenopodium quinoa	−	−	+[d]		+[d]	−	+[d]
Beta vulgaris						−	+
Spinacia oleracea					+		+[d]
Chenopodium album			+		+		
Chenopodium trigonon							+
LEGUMINOSAE							
Trifolium stubterraneum			−	−	+[d]		
Trifolium incarnatum			+	+			
Trifolium glomerata					+		
Pisum sativum	−	+	+	+		−	−
Cicer arietinum		+					
Medicago sativa			+	+		−	
Medicago scutellata			+	+			
Medicago lupulina			+	+			
Lupinus albus			+	+		−	
Lupinus augustifolius			+	+			
Vicia faba	−	−	+		−	−	−
Glycine max	−	−	−			+	−
Phaseolus lunatus						±	
Phaseolus vulgaris	−	−	−	−		±[d]	+
Vicia sativa			+			−	
COMPOSITAE							
Zinnia elegans	−	−	+				
AMARANTHACEAE							
Gomphrena globosa	+	−					+

Table 1 continued. -
_____
a Data taken from Thornberry (1966) Teakle (1968), Blackstock
(1978), Forster and Jones (1979), Greber (1981), Randles *et
al.* (1981), Francki, et. al (1983b).
b Two isolates which can be considered as distinct have been
described; one from Australia (Aus., Blackstock, 1978) and
the other from New Zealand (N.Z., Forster and Jones, 1979).
c + indicates susceptibility, $\pm$ conflicting reports and -
immunity. Absence of a sign indicates that the appropriate
tests have not been done.
d Hosts suitable for propagating virus.
_____

S. nodiflorum (Greber, 1981). VTMoV and SNMV can be transmitted experimentally by each other's vectors (Greber, 1981)
but it seems that the respective vectors detected in the
field as described above are those which are important in
the field.

The modes of transmission of both viruses by their field
vectors show some similarities and differences. The transmission of VTMoV by *C. nicotianae* appears to be the only
confirmed report of virus transmission by a mirid bug(Randles
et al., 1981). VTMoV can be transmitted in less than 3 h
from the commencement of the acquisition feed. Acquisition
times of 10 min were the minimum observed, while longer
acquisition times of 10 min were the minimum observed, while
longer acquisition feeds increased the efficiency of transmission (J.W. Randles, unpublished).

When mirids were transferred at regular intervals,high-
est rates of transmission occurred in the first 2 days. When
a mirid inoculated 2 or more test plants, the transmission
was sometimes intermittent so that several days could elapse
between subsequent successful inoculation feeds by the same
insects. Persistence of VTMoV was for between 8 and 12 days.
In several experiments, VTMoV was transmitted through the
moult from the pre-adult larva to the adult, at a rate of
24-33% in two experiments.

Insect injection experiments have yet to be done to
resolve whether circulative transmission of VTMoV occurs in
the mirid. The available data could possible be explained by
either, a combination of stylet borne and circulative transmission, or by a semi-persistent mode of transmission in
which VTMoV is retained at a site not lost during ecdysis of
the insect.

Adults and larvae of the coccinellid beetles *Henosepu-
lachna sparsa, H. doryca australica,* and *H. guttato postulata*
transmit SNMV very efficiently, while flea beetles, *Psyl-
liodes* spp., are less efficient vectors (Greber, 1981).
Neither SNMV nor VTMoV were transmitted by *Myzus persicae.*

The acquisition period of SNMV by the coccinellids was

less than 2 h, and any latent period would have been less
than 4 h. Persistence was 2 h after 2 h acquisition, but was
at least 8 h following a 24 h acquisition (Greber, 1981).
Injected larvae did not transmit, and the ability to transmit
virus was lost during pupation. The virus-vector association
seems to be less persistent than for VTMoV, and it could be
defined as a semi-persistent association on the basis of the
available data.

III. PURIFICATION OF THE VIRUSES

All six viruses listed in Table 1 can be readily purified by a relatively simple method which has been described
in detail for the purification of red clover necrotic mosaic
virus (Gould *et al.*, 1981a). Each 100 g of leaf material was
ground in 200 ml of 0.1 M phosphate buffer, pH 7.4, containing
0.1% thioglycollic acid and was strained through cheesecloth.
The juice was clarified by centrifugation at 10,000 g for 10
min and the supernatant was emulsified with an equal volume
of a 1:1 mixture of chloroform and n-butanol and then again
centrifuged at 10,000 g for 10 min. The supernatant was
centrifuged at 78,000 g for 60 min to sediment the virus
which was then resuspended in a small volume of 20 mM phosphate buffer, pH 7.4. The differential centrifugation was
repeated twice and the virus pellets were suspended in 20 mM
phosphate buffer, pH 7.4. Such preparations were sufficiently pure for many purposes such as extraction of RNA. However,
when virus of higher purity was required, such as that for
use as immunogen, the preparations were subjected to centrifugation in 5-25% sucrose gradients (prepared in 20 mM phosphate buffer, pH 7.4). Virus was layered over the gradients
and centrifuged at 26,000 rpm for 2 h in a Spinco SW27 rotor.
The single virus band was recovered, diluted and concentrated
by centrifugation at 300,000 g for 2 h. We have found this
purification method to be very reliable for obtaining good
yields of all the six viruses listed in Table 1 in a high
degree of purity.

IV. PHYSICAL AND CHEMICAL PROPERTIES OF THE VIRUSES

A. Virus Particles
The reported particle diameters of the viruses listed in
Table 2 range from 26 to 30 nm. However, the differences are
almost certainly a reflection of the methods used for preparing specimens for electron microscopy and/or differences in
calibration of the instruments used. We have compared particles in highly purified preparations of all six viruses
after negative staining in uranyl acetate and found them to
be indistinguishable from each other (Fig. 1). When the

preparations were examined as mixtures of the viruses in
pairs, in no instance did we observe the presence of two
populations of particles which could be distinguished by
their size, shape or surface structure. Particles of all the
viruses had roughly hexagonal outlines and diameters of about
30 nm but there was never any evidence of any discernible sub-
structural detail in preparations stained with uranyl acetate.

The sedimentation properties and buoyant densities
reported for the six viruses appear very similar (Table 2).
The minor differences may well be reflections of the methods
used rather than any intrinsic differences. We conclude that
the particles of the six viruses are very similar.

B.   Coat proteins and antigenic properties.

There appears to be some variation in the sizes of the
coat protein subunits of the six viruses listed in Table 2.

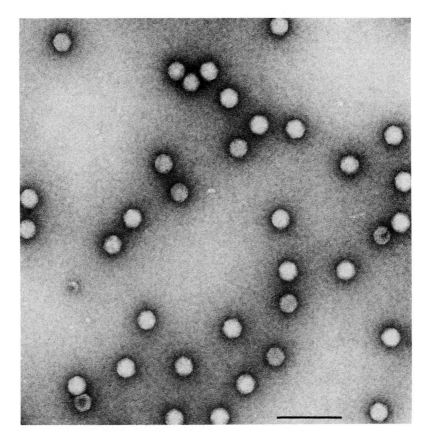

Figure 1.   Electron micrograph of a purified preparation of
LTSV particles stained with uranyl acetate. Bar represents
100 nm.

Table II.
Some Physical Properties of the Viruses

Virus	Particle diameter (nm)	s_{20w} (S)	Buoyant density in CsCl (gm $^{-3}$)	Mr coat protein polypeptide(s) ($\times 10^3$)	References
Velvet to-bacco mottle virus(VTMoV)	30	115	1.37	37 (33 + 31)[a]	Randles *et al.* (1981)
Solanum nodi-florum mottle virus (SNMV)	28-30	-[b]	-	30 (+28)	Greber (1981)
Lucerne tran-sient streak virus (LTSV)	27-28	112	1.37	32 (+29)	Forster & Jones (1980)
Subterranean clover mottle virus (SCMoV)	30	115	-	29 (+26)	Francki *et al.*, (1983b)
Southern bean mosaic virus (SBMV)	28	115	1.36	29	Shepherd (1971) Sehgal(1981)
Sowbane mosaic virus (SoMV)	26	104	1.35	31	Kado (1971), Sehgal(1981)

[a] Values in brackets are additional minor polypeptide components detected by polyacrylamide gel electrophoresis.
[b] Data unavailable

Also, the coats of some of the viruses appeared to have more
than one protein.

Antigenically, VTMoV and SNMV have been shown to be very
closely related (Randles *et al.*, 1981; Chu and Francki,
1983, and Fig. 2). The only other antigenic relationship
among the viruses listed in Table 2 is that between LTSV and
SCMoV which, however, appears to be very distant (Francki,
et al., 1983b).

The antigenic relationship between VTMoV and SNMV seemed
rather surprising when considering the apparent differences
between the chemical properties of their viral coat proteins.
Not only did they differ in the number and size of polypeptides (Fig. 3) but also in the number and size of peptides
released when the proteins were partially digested with V8
protease or papain (Chu and Francki, 1983). The proportion
of the three polypeptides detected in dissociated VTMoV
preparations after electrophoresis in polyacrylamide gels
varied considerably from experiment to experiment (Chu and
Francki, 1983). It was demonstrated that in virus preparations which were purified in the cold as quickly as possible

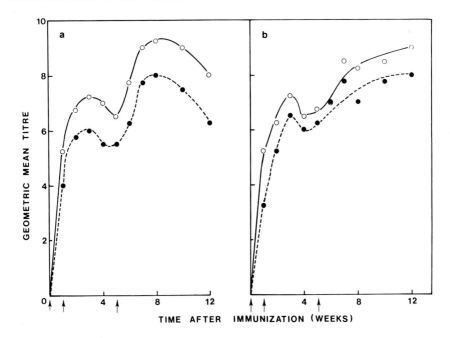

Figure 2. The immune response of rabbits to intravenous injection with VTMoV (a) and SNMV (b). Each virus (200 μg) was administered three times indicated by arrows below the abscissa. Antisera from each rabbit were assayed for homologous (o———o) and heterologous (•-----•) reactions and the results plotted as geometric means (integer 1,2,3....., corresponding to a positive reaction at antiserum dilutions of 1/2, 1/4, 1/8.......).

to minimize proteolytic activity in the plant extracts, the proportion of the largest VTMoV polypeptide (M_r 37 x 10^3)was very much higher than in preparations that had been purified over protracted times at warmer temperatures. Once the virus had been purified, the proportion of the three polypeptides remained similar over relatively long periods of storage. From these and other experiments, Chu and Francki (1983) concluded that VTMoV coat protein consists of a single poly-peptide of Mr about 37 x 10^3 which is, however, susceptible to partial degradation by proteolytic enzymes in leaf ex-tracts during virus purification.

SNMV preparations purified by the same technique as that used for VTMoV, almost invariably contained only a single polypeptide of Mr about 31 x 10^3 (Fig. 3). This size is

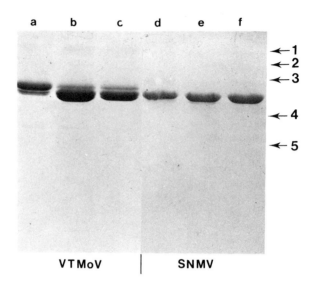

Figure 3. Polyacrylamide gel electrophoresis of VTMoV(tracks a-c) and SNMV (tracks d-f) coat protein preparations. Preparations in tracks a and d were from virus purified by the standard method; in tracks b and e from virus extracted and kept in sap for 16 hr at 4°C prior to purification; and in tracks c and f from virus extracted and kept in sap for 2 hr. at 25°C followed by 16 hr. at 4°C (after Chu and Francki, 1983). Numbers at right indicate the positions of marker proteins which included bovine serum albumin, M_r 68,000 (1); glutamate dehydrogenase M_r 53,000 (2); ovalbumin, M_r 43,000 (3); cucumber mosaic virus coat protein, M_r 24,600 (4); and tobacco mosaic virus coat protein, M_r 17,500 (5).

similar to that of the smallest polypeptide detected in VTMoV coat protein preparations. To account for the close antigenic relationship between VTMoV and SNMV, Chu and Francki (1983) suggested that after injection of VTMoV particles into animals, the proteolysis of virus particles continues until they all have their coat proteins consisting only of the partially degraded polypeptide of Mr about 31.5×10^3. They also suggested that this relatively stable form of VTMoV particles is the principal antigen to which antibodies are elicited. Such particles are much more likely to be antigenically related to those of SNMV.

It has also been suggested that VTMoV and SNMV coat proteins do not differ in size (Chu and Francki, 1983). SNMV protein may be degraded to a stable polypeptide of Mr about 31×10^3 much more rapidly than the VTMoV protein. This suggestion is supported by the results of *in vitro* translation of SNMV RNA by P. Kiberstis and D. Zimmern (personal communication). In an *in vitro* translation system programmed by SNMV RNA they detected a product which was precipitated by SNMV antiserum, but in polyacrylamide gel electrophoresis it migrated more slowly than the SNMV coat protein of Mr about 38×10^3 isolated from purified virus. Its migration corresponded to M_r about 38×10^3. It will be interesting to see if the coat protein sizes of any of the other viruses listed in Table 2 are also products of partially degraded protein rather than those which exist in particles before they are extracted from plants.

C. Virus Encapsidated RNAs.

Each of the viruses listed in Table 2 encapsidates a linear single-stranded RNA (RNA 1) of apparent M_r between 1.3 and 1.5×10^6 (Kado, 1971; Shepherd, 1971; Forster and Jones, 1980; Randles *et al.*, 1981; Gould and Hatta, 1981; Francki *et al.*, 1983b). In the case of SBMV and SNMV the presence of sub-genomic RNAs has been established (Rutgers *et al.*, 1980; P. Kiberstis and D. Zimmern, personal communication). RNAs of the other viruses also appear to contain some smaller RNAs (Fig. 4) and the RNAs 1a and 1b of VTMoV have been shown to have base sequences of RNA 1 (Gould, 1981). Four of the viruses listed in Table 2, VTMoV, SNMV, LTSV and SCMoV also encapsidate two low molecular weight RNAs (Fig. 4). One of these is circular (RNA2) whereas the other is of the same size and base sequence but is linear (RNA3). These small RNAs have many characteristics of viroids (Fig. 5) (Randles *et al.*, 1981; Gould, 1981; Gould and Hatta, 1981; Tien-Po *et al.*, 1981; Haseloff and Symons, 1982; Francki *et al.*, 1983a; Keese *et al.*, 1983) and hence we will refer to them here as viroid-like RNAs.

No isolates of either SBMV or SoMV have been obtained with encapsidated viroid-like RNAs. However, it has been demonstrated that SoMV is capable of supporting the replication of, and can encapsidate the viroid-like RNA of LTSV (Francki *et al.*, 1983a).

The viroid-like RNAs of VTMoV, SNMV, LTSV and SCMoV have no base sequence homologies with their respective long linear RNAs 1. On the other hand, their RNAs 2 and 3 are indistinguishable from each other in their base sequence (Gould, 1981; Gould and Hatta, 1981; P. Keese, personal communication; J.W. Randles, unpublished results) and thus the RNA 3 of each virus is a linear form of RNA 2. A comparison of the base sequence data of VTMoV and SNMV RNAs has revealed that their RNAs 2 have over 90% and their RNAs 1 about 20-50% sequence homology (Gould and Hatta, 1981; Haseloff and Symons, 1982). These similarities and the serological data (Fig. 2) indicate that the two viruses are closely related.

Complete base sequences of VTMoV, SNMV, LTSV(two strains),

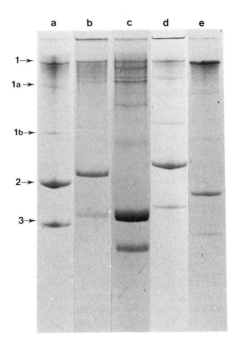

Figure 4. Polyacrylamide gel electrophoresis under denaturing conditions (in the presence of 7 M urea) of RNA preparations from VTMoV (track a), SNMV (track b), LTSV (track c),
and two distinct isolates of SCMoV (tracks d and e).

and SCMoV RNAs 2 have been determined (Haseloff and Symons,
1982; Keese *et al.*, 1983; J. Haseloff and R.H. Symons,per-
sonal communication). The salient features are that only
RNAs 2 and 3 of VTMoV and SNMV have very similar base sequences whereas the RNAs 2 and 3 of the remaining viruses, all
differ in size and sequences (Table 3). It is interesting
that two distinct species of RNAs 2 and 3 have been detected
in isolates of SCMoV and that, either or both can be present
in an isolate (Francki *et al.*, 1983b).

V. VIRUS REPLICATION

A.   The Function of Viroid-Like RNAs.
      Gould *et al.*, (1981b) reported experiments in which
infection of plants by RNA from VTMoV and SNMV could be
achieved only when both RNA 1 and RNA 2 were present in the
inoculum. Futhermore, the interaction of the two RNAs essential for infectivity appear to be highly specific because
heterologous mixtures of RNAs 1 and 2 of VTMoV and SNMV were
found to be non-infectious. This is surprising because the

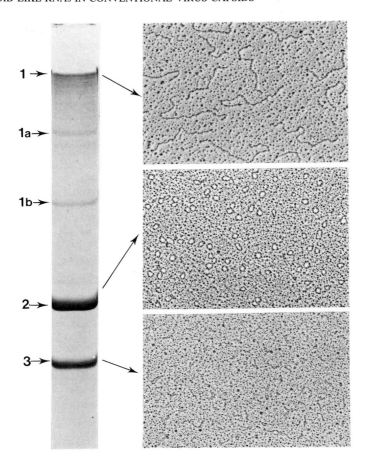

Figure 5. Polyacrylamide gel electrophoresis and electron microscopy of VTMoV RNA. RNA isolated from purified virus was electrophoresed in gels under denaturing conditions (in the presence of 7 M urea) into fractions as indicated in the electrophoretogram at the left and the fractions indicated by arrows were recovered and examined by electron microscopy as described by Randles *et al.*, (1981).

two viruses are obviously closely related, especially with respect to the high degree of base sequence homology of their RNAs 2 (Haseloff and Symons, 1982).

In contrast to VTMoV and SNMV, Jones *et al.*, (1983) have established that RNA 1 of LTSV can replicate autonomously whereas the replication of RNAs 2 and 3 is dependent on RNA 1. These workers freed an isolate of LTSV of RNAs 2 and 3 and showed that the RNA 1 alone infected *Chenopodium quinoa* inducing chlorotic local lesions. On addition of RNA 2 to the inoculum, however, necrotic lesions were induced and RNAs 2 and 3 were produced as with the original virus isolate. In the same laboratory it was also shown that RNA 2 from LTSV can

Table 3.

Size Differences of Viroid-Like RNAs from Different Viruses

Virus	No. of nucleotides per RNA2 molecule	References
Velvet tobacco mottle virus(VTMoV)	366	Haseloff & Symons (1981)
Solanum nodiflorum mottle virus (SNMV)	377	Haseloff & Symons (1982)
Lucerne transient streak virus (LTSV)	324	Keese *et al.* (1983)
Subterranean clover mottle virus (SCMoV)	327 & 388[a]	J. Haseloff & R.H.Symons (personal communication)

[a] Isolates of SCMoV have been characterized which encapsidate either one or both of these RNA sizes (Francki *et al.*, 1983b)

replicate in combination with RNA 1 from SNMV (Jones and Mayo, 1983).

In our laboratory, it has been demonstrated that RNA 2 from LTSV can replicate with SoMV, a virus which has never been isolated from the field with any low molecular weight RNA components (Francki *et al.*, 1983a). In the presence of LTSV RNA 2, SoMV produces necrotic lesions quite distinct from the chlorotic ones characteristic of normal SoMV isolates (Kado, 1971) All these observations support the conclusion that RNA 2 from LTSV behaves as a satellite RNA and with relatively little specificity.

Thus from the data available at present it appears that small circular RNA molecules present in plants can be of three types: those capable of autonomous replication like the viroids (Diener, 1981); those behaving as satellites such as the RNA 2 of LTSV which requires a helper virus for its replication (Jones *et al.*, 1983; Jones and Mayo, 1983; Francki *et al.*, 1983a); and yet others like those of VTMoV and SNMV which appear to constitute part of an RNA complex essential for virus replication (Gould *et al.*, 1981b).

B. Multiplication of Velvet Tobacco Mottle Virus.

Little experimental work has been done on the multiplication of the viruses discussed in this chapter with the exception of VTMoV. Presently available data on this virus are summarized below.

1). *In vivo* Studies.

Leaves of *N. clevelandii* inoculated with VTMoV usually develop lesions after about 4 days when the plants are maintained at 25°C; subsequently the lesions become necrotic. The virus infects the plant systemically causing symptoms in the young leaves, usually about 6 days after inoculation. The experiments described here were done on the inoculated leaves where the virus was first detected serologically between four and six days after inoculation (Fig. 6). At about 4 days after inoculation, there was a rapid increase in the RNA-dependent RNA polymerase activity of the leaf tissue (Fig. 6). However, the synthesis of RNAs 2 and 3 was detected as early as two days after inoculation (Fig. 7). Virus continued to multiply for as long as sixteen days after inoculation at which time the lesions were necrotic and the experiment was discontinued (Fig. 6).

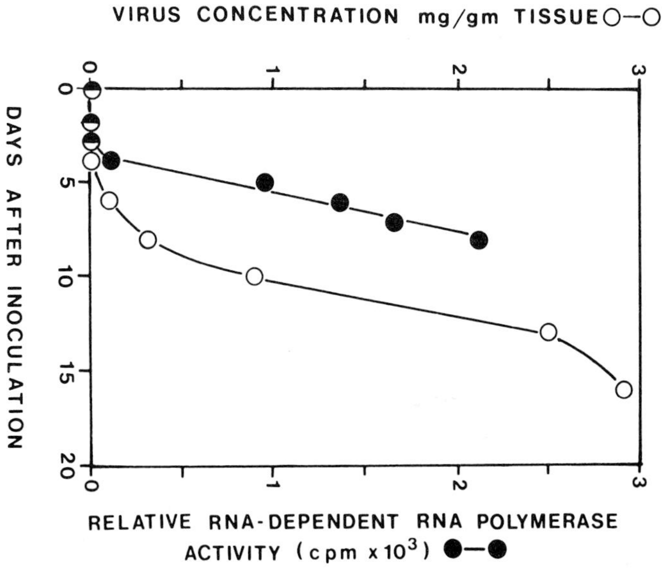

Figure 6. The time course of virus synthesis determined by enzyme-linked immuno-sorbent assay as described by Chu *et al.*, (1983) (o———o) and RNA-dependent RNA polymerase activity (•———•) of cell-free extracts from *Nicotiana cleve-landii* leaves inoculated with VTMoV. Polymerase activity was determined as described in Table 5; measurements were discontinued 8 days after inoculation because the lesions became necrotic.

DAYS AFTER INOCULATION

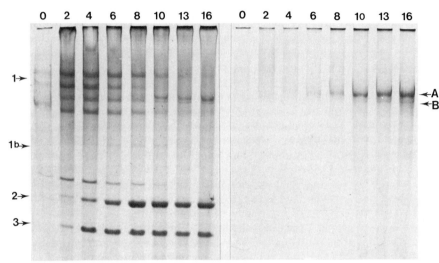

TOTAL LEAF RNA   RNase RESISTANT LEAF RNA

Figure 7. Synthesis of VTMoV–specific RNAs in inoculated leaves of *Nicotiana clevelandii* at various times after inoculation (days after inoculation are indicated by number at the top of the diagram). Preparations of total leaf RNAs were analysed in the gel shown on the left and the same preparations after incubation with 20 μg/ml of pancreatic RNase for 1 hr. at 37°C to digest all ssRNAs were analysed again in the gel shown on the right (after Chu *et al.*, 1983). Figures 1,1b, 2 and 3 indicate the electrophoretic mobilities of VTMoV RNA components (see Figures 4 and 5).

Polyacrylamide gel electrophoretic profiles of RNA preparations extracted from healthy and VTMoV–inoculated leaves revealed the presence of several virus–specific RNAs in the infected tissue (Fig. 7). Two days after inoculation small amounts of RNAs 2 and 3 were already detectable and their concentrations increased thereafter. With time after infection, the ratio of RNA 2 concentration to that of RNA 3 increased significantly suggesting that RNA 3 could be a precursor of RNA 2. Such a pathway would require the ligation of RNA 2, a reaction which has been demonstrated *in vitro* when catalysed by T4 RNA ligase (Chu *et al.*, 1983).

VTMoV RNA 1 was not detected in infected leaves by staining in gels (Fig. 7). This was not altogether surpri-

sing because RNA 1 has an electrophoretic mobility similar to
that of rRNA and probably occurs in a low concentration
relative to RNAs 2 and 3 as it does in virus particles
(Randles *et al.*, 1981; Chu *et al.*, 1983). However, a virus-specific, single stranded RNA of Mr about 0.25×10^6 was
detected between 4 and 6 days after inoculation (Fig. 7).
This RNA had the same electrophoretic mobility as RNA 1b
isolated from purified VTMoV which has been shown to have
base sequence homology with RNA 1 (Gould, 1981). The function of this virus-specific RNA is unknown but it seems
conceivable that it may be a subgenomic mRNA. Its appearance
coincides with the onset of rapid virus synthesis in inoculated leaves (Figs. 6 and 7).

Two distinct species of double-stranded RNA of M_r about
3.6 (RNA A) and 2.8×10^6 (RNA B) have been isolated from
leaves inoculated with VTMoV (Chu *et al.*, 1983). They were
not readily detected until about 8 days after inoculation
which was the time at which the rate of virus multiplication
was reaching its maximum (Fig. 5). Concentrations of these
RNAs increased thereafter, even when the rate of virus increase was declining. The concentration of RNA A was always
several-fold higher than that of RNA B. Melting and blot-
hybridization experiments indicated that RNA B is a duplex of
VTMoV RNA 1 (Chu *et al.*, 1983). Similar studies with RNA A
indicated that this molecule consists of a single strand of
RNA with base sequences complementary to VTMoV RNA 3 paired
to various lengths of RNA with base sequences of RNA 3 (Chu
et al., 1983). It would thus seem that the molecule consists
of a tandem of about 15 negative RNA 3 molecules paired to
various polymers of positive RNA 3. It has been suggested
that RNA B is a replicative form of RNA 1 and RNA A, a complex for the replication of RNAs 2 and 3 (Chu *et al.*, 1983).
It is tempting to speculate further that RNA 3 is replicated
on the long negative strand of RNA A and that some of the RNA
3 molecules are then ligated to produce RNA 2, perhaps after
being released from the template. However, it must be remem-
bered that both RNA A and RNA B accumulate in leaf tissues at
late stages of infection when the rate of virus synthesis is
declining (Chu *et al.*, 1983). This suggests that the virus-
specific double-stranded RNAs may be, at least in part, by-
products of virus synthesis.

2). RNA Replication *in vitro* .

Molecules with the electrophoretic properties of RNAs A
and B have been synthesized *in vitro* using crude RNA-dependent RNA polymerase preparations from VTMoV-infected leaves
(Fig. 8). In addition, a third double-stranded RNA (RNA C)
of Mr about 0.7×10^6 was detected as a product of the enzyme
reaction. These observations indicate that the RNA-dependent

RNA polymerase detected in extracts from infected leaves is capable of synthesizing double-stranded RNAs specific to RNAs 2 and 3 (RNA A) and also to RNA 1(RNA B). RNA C did not correspond to any of the VTMoV-specific RNA components detected in infected leaves (Chu *et al.*, 1983) and its significance remains obscure. We did consider the possibility that RNA C may be an intermediate or degradation product of RNAs A or B. However, this seems unlikely because the ratios of all the *in vitro* synthesized double-stranded RNA components were shown to be similar after incubation periods of between 5 and 30 min. The synthesis proceeded linearly for about 10 min after which the rate decreased rapidly to stop completely within 20 min of incubation.

Preliminary studies on the partial purification of the VTMoV-specific RNA-dependent RNA polymerase indicate that the enzyme is tightly bound to the template RNA. We are therefore attempting to purify the complex sufficiently so as to be able to study the *in vitro* synthesis of VTMoV-RNA in the absence of high concentrations of degradative enzymes present in crude leaf extracts used to date.

3). RNA Translation *in vitro*

Preliminary experiments with cell-free preparations of wheat germ (Chu *et al.*, 1981) have shown that a number of polypeptides are synthesized when the system is programmed by VTMoV RNA (P.W.G. Chu, unpublished data): Translation of unfractionated viral RNA as well as isolated RNA 1 yielded polypeptide products of Mr about 115, 60, 37, 30, 19, 15 and 14 x 10^3. RNAs 1a and 1b were also relatively efficient messengers, both translating polypeptides of Mr 30, 19, 15 and 14 x 10^3 and RNA 1a also translated the 37 x 10^3 polypeptide. On the other hand, VTMoV RNAs 2 and 3 had negligible messenger activity with only traces of the 15 and 14 x 10^3 Mr being detected as products.

The electrophoretic mobility of the Mr 37 x 10^3 product corresponded to that of the largest VTMoV coat protein component suggesting that it was the undergraded coat protein. However, no products corresponding to the coat protein components of Mr 33 and 31 x 10^3 were detected in any of the experiments.

A tentative conclusion from the translation studies is that VTMoV coat protein of Mr 37 x 10^3 can be translated from RNA 1 and 1a, the latter probably being the coat protein subgenomic mRNA. Furthermore, it seems likely that RNA 1 can be translated into a read-through protein of Mr about 115 x 10^3 comprising the Mr 60, 30 and 19 x 10^3 polypeptides. The 15 and 14 x 10^3 M_r proteins are probably degradation products or translation products of degraded viral RNA. It appears that RNAs 2 and 3 do not function *in vitro* as messengers.

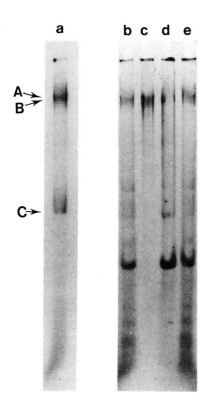

Figure 8. Polyacrylamide gel electrophoresis (in the absence of urea) of the *in vitro* products of the RNA-dependent RNA polymerase activity in the 1,000 g supernatant fraction of extracts from *Nicotiana clevelandii* leaves 7 days after inoculation with VTMoV (see Table 5 for details of preparation). Track a shows an autoradiograph of the product with two strong radioactive fractions (A and C) and a much weaker one (B) just below A. Tracks b-e show the same gel stained with Toluidine Blue and also RNA isolated from purified VTMoV (tracks b and e); a VTMoV-specific, ds-RNA preparation isolated from infected *N. clevelandii* leaves as described by Chu *et al.*, (1983) (track c); and the same track as that autoradiographed in track a (track d). Numbers at the right refer to the positions of VTMoV RNA components.

C.   Cytopathic Effects of Virus Infection

A comparison of the cytopathic effects of the six viruses studied revealed some similarities and some differences
(Table 4). Particles of all the viruses were detected in the
cytoplasm, nuclei and vacuoles of cells infected by all the
viruses (Table 4, Figs 9-14). Furthermore cells infected by
all the viruses contained in their cytoplasm, electron-dense
strands which on the basis of enzyme cytochemical tests
(Hatta and Francki, 1978) were tentatively identified as
double-stranded RNA. Some of these strands were observed to
be inside cytoplasmic vesicles in cells infected by some of
the viruses (Table 4) such as those seen in Figs. 10 and 13
but the bulk of them were seen to be in the ground cytoplasm
not associated with any organelles or membranes (Fig. 9, 13
and 14). Similar strands have been previously observed in
sections of cells infected with SoMV and SBMV (Milme, 1967;
de Zoeten and Gaard, 1969; Weintraub and Ragetli, 1970).

The number of virus particles was significantly greater
in cells infected with VTMoV, SNMV, SBMV and SMV than those
with LTSV or SCMoV (Table 4). Cells infected with SNMV
differed from those infected by all the other viruses studied
in that they contained bundles of long flexuous rods in the
cytoplasm and nuclei (Greber, 1981 and see Fig. 10). Cells
infected with SCMoV were also readily distinguished in that
their particles formed definite aggregates both in nuclei and
cytoplasm (Fig. 12) as opposed to the particles of all the
other viruses which always appeared scattered throughout the
cytoplasm and nuclei.

When VTMoV-infected leaf tissue was extracted and fractionated under conditions which would minimize the degradation of cell organelles, both the virus-specific double-
stranded RNAs and the RNA-dependent RNA polymerase were recovered almost exclusively in the soluble cytoplasmic fraction (Table 5). This suggests that viral RNA replication
takes place in the cytoplasm without the involvement of
membranes. It would seem that the membrane-free fibrils
thought to be double-stranded RNA observed in the cytoplasm
of VTMoV-infected cell sections (Fig. 9) may be the site of
RNA replication.

VI.   COMPARISON OF VIROID-LIKE RNAs to VIROIDS

The small circular RNAs encapsidated by VTMoV, SNMV,
LTSV and SCMoV are similar in many respects to viroids; hence
they have been referred to here as viroid-like RNAs but some
other workers have called them virusoids (Haseloff *et al.*,
1982). The most striking similarities of viroids and viroid-
like RNAs are their sizes, circularity, high degree of base

TABLE 4

Cytopathic Effects of the Viruses[a]

Virus	Host Species	Concentration of particles in the cytoplasm[b]	Particles in nuclei	Particles in aggregates	Strands in cytoplasm	Strands in vesicles of endoplasmic reticulum	Long flexuous rods in bundles
Velvet tobacco mottle virus (VTMoV)	*Nicotiana clevelandii*	++	+	-	+	+	-
Solanum nodiflorum mottle virus (SNMV)	*Nicotiana clevelandii* *Solanum nodiflorum*	++	+	-	+	+	+
Lucerne transient streak virus (LTSV)	*Chenopodium quinoa*[c] *Nicotiana clevelandii*[d] *Pisum sativum*	+	+	-	+	-	-
Subterranean clover mottle virus (SCMoV)	*Trifolium subterraneum* *Pisum sativum*	+	+	+	+	-	-
Southern bean mosaic virus (SBMV)	*Phaseolus vulgaris*	++	+	-	+	+	-
Sowbane mosaic virus (SoMV)	*Chenopodium quinoa*	+++	+	-	+	+	-

[a] See also Figs 9-14 for electron micrographs

[b] Relative concentrations indicated by number of plus signs

[c] Infected by the virus isolate from Australia (Blackstock, 1978)

[d] Infected by the virus isolate from New Zealand (Forster and Jones, 1979)

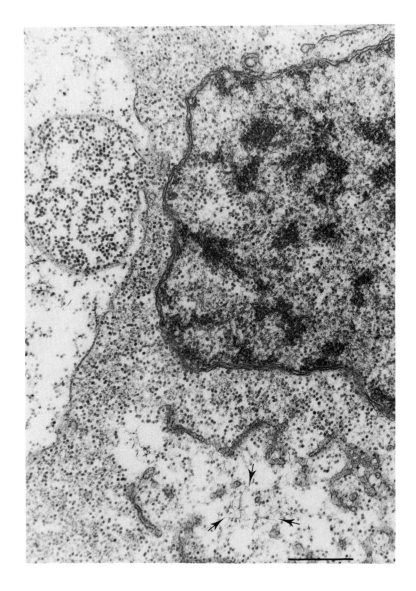

Figure 9. Thin section of a *Nicotiana clevelandii* leaf cell infected with VTMoV. All visible small isometric particles are virus particles because the tissues were treated with RNase to remove ribosomal RNA as an aid to virus particle identification (Hatta and Francki, 1981). Numerous virus particles can be seen in the nucleus, cytoplasm and vacuole. Arrows point to virus-specific strands seen in the ground cytoplasm. Bar represents 500 nm.

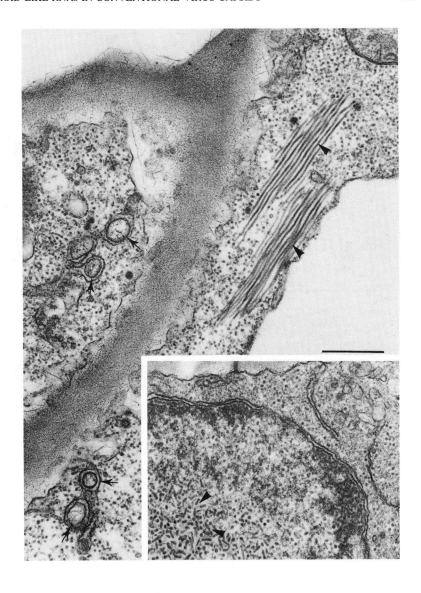

Figure 10. Thin sections of *Nicotiana clevelandii* leaf cells infected with SNMV (RNase treatment of tissue as described in Fig. 9). Virus particles can be seen in both cytoplasm and nucleus as can virus-specific bundles of rods (arrow heads). Vesicles with virus-specific strands in the ground cytoplasm can also be seen (arrows). Bar represents 500 nm.

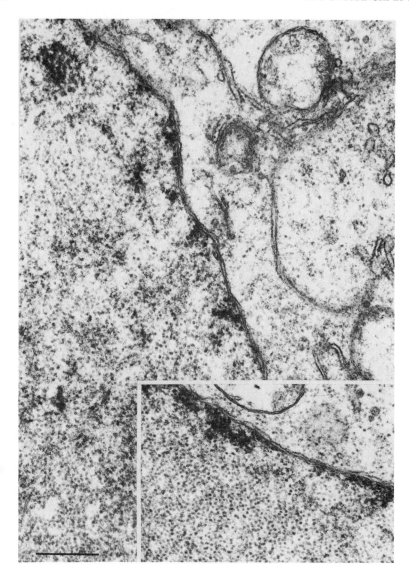

Figure 11.   Thin sections of *Chenopodium quinoa* leaf cells infected with LTSV (RNase treatment of tissue as described in Fig. 9). Fewer virus particles can be seen in the cytoplasm than in the nuclei. Bar represents 500 nm.

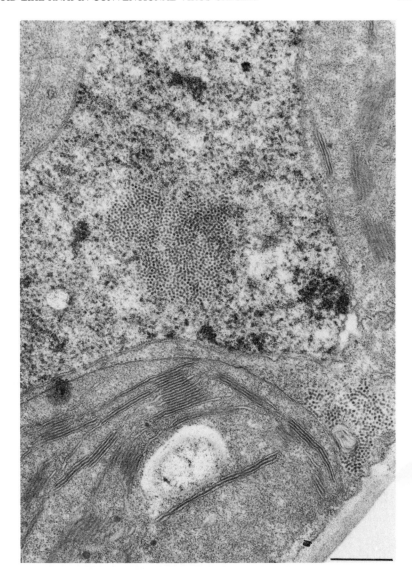

Figure 12. Thin section of a *Trifolium subterraneum* leaf cell infected with SCMoV (RNase treatment of tissue as described in Fig. 9). Virus particles in characteristic aggregates can be seen in both nucleus and cytoplasm. Bar represents 500 nm.

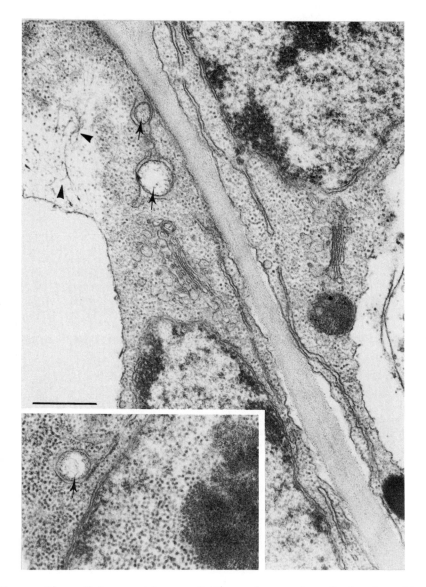

Figure 13. Thin sections of *Phaseolus vulgaris* leaf cells infected with SBMV (RNase treatment of tissue as described in Fig. 9). Virus particles can be seen in both nucleus and cytoplasm. Virus-specific strands can be seen in the ground cytoplasm (arrowheads) and in cytoplasmic vesicles (arrows). Bar represents 500 nm.

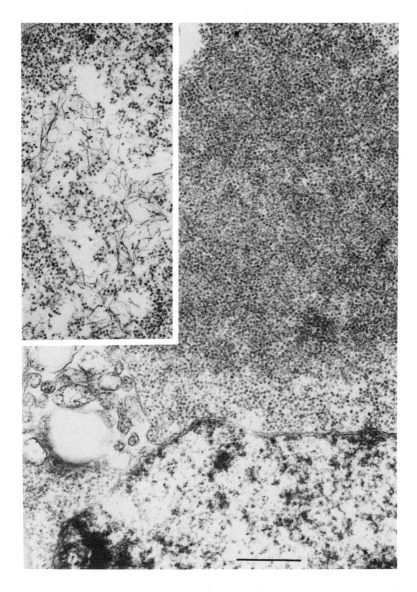

Figure 14. Thin sections of *Chenopodium quinoa* leaf cells infected with SoMV (RNase treatment of tissue as described in Fig. 9). Masses of particles can be seen in the cytoplasm but particles were also seen in the nuclei of many cells. Virus-specific strands were also often seen in the ground cytoplasm (inset). Bar represents 500 nm.

Table 5.

Dection of Virus-specific Double-stranded RNAs and
RNA-dependent RNA Polymerase Activity in Cellular Fractions
from VTMoV-infected Cell Fractions.

Cellular Fraction[a]	Relative concentration of double-stranded RNA[b]	DNA-dependent polymerase activity[c]	
		CPM	%
Total leaf extract (not fractionated)	+++	2,791	100
1,000g pellet (nuclei and chloroplasts)	±	356	13
1,000g supernatant	+++	1,927	69
17,000g pellet (mitochondria and endoplasmic reticulum)	−	268	10
17,000g supernatant (soluble cytoplasm)	+++	1,697	60

a *Nicotiana clevelandii leaves,* harvested 7 days after inoculation with VTMoV were chopped by hand with a razor-
   blade (Spencer and Wildman, 1964) in 50 mM Tris-HCl, 0.1M
   NH_4Cl, 90 mM 2-mercaptoethanol and 0.4 M sucrose, pH 8.5
   (2 ml/1 g tissue). The extract was strained through
   miracloth and subjected to fractionation by centrifugation for 10 min. at forces indicated.
b Nucleic acids were extracted from each fraction and
   analysed by polyacrylamide gel electrophoresis (Chu *et
   al.*, 1983). Number of plus signs indicates relative
   concentration of virus-specific double-stranded RNA.
c RNA-dependent RNA polymerase was estimated by the incorporation of α-^{32}P guanosine triphosphate into a trichlor-
   acetic acid precipitate after incubation for 20 min. at
   20°C. Reaction mixtures contained 100 μl of cell fractions and 250 μl of assay medium (47 mM Tris-HCl pH 8.5,
   40 mM NH_4Cl, 36mM 2-mercaptoethanol, 6 mM $MgSO_4$, 20 mM
   KCl, 8 mM EGTA, 2 mg/ml bovine serum albumin, 10 μg/ml
   actinomycin D, 20 μg/ml each of ATP, UTP and CTP, 0.01
   μg/ml GTP containing 8 x 10^5 cpm of ^{32}P labelled GTP).

pairing and apparent lack of messenger activity. On the
other hand, there are some significant differences between
the two types of RNAs. The most striking is that viroids are
capable of autonomous replication but occur only in low
concentrations in infected plants. Viroid-like RNAs on the
other hand are dependent for their replication on the long
linear RNAs which are also encapsidated. Both RNA 2 and RNA
3 reach high concentrations in infected cells. In the case
of VTMoV, these RNAs can account for 36-50% of the total RNA

in the leaves (Randles *et al.*, 1981). It seems that whereas viroids replicate in the nuclei (Diener, 1979), the replication of the viroid-like RNA of at least VTMoV takes place in the cytoplasm (Table 5).

A comparison of the physical properties of the viroid-like RNAs of VTMoV and SNMV with those of viroids has shown that the viroid-like RNAs are thermally less stable and melt with less cooperativity (Randles *et al.*, 1982). Hydrodynamically, the native viroid-like RNAs are more flexible than viroids (Riesner *et al.*, 1982). The significance of these physical differences to the replication and pathogenicity of the two types of RNAs remains to be determined.

VII. THE TAXONOMIC POSITION OF VIRUSES WITH ENCAPSIDATED VIROID-LIKE RNAs

The striking similarity of VTMoV, SNMV, LTSV, and SCMoV to viruses of the sobemovirus group has been stressed in this paper and in earlier publications (Forster and Jones, 1980; Randles *et al.*, 1981; Gould *et al.*, 1981b; Francki *et al.*, 1983b). It was suggested that the encapsidation of viroid-like RNAs by these viruses and their requirement for infectivity set them apart sufficiently so as to preclude their inclusion in the sobemovirus group (Tien-Po *et al.*, 1981). However, it is probably premature at present to establish a new group for these unusual viruses; especially as it appears that viroid-like RNAs can be either satellites such as that in LTSV (Jones *et al.*, 1983; Francki *et al.*, 1983a) or structures essential for infectivity as reported for VTMoV and SNMV (Gould *et al.*, 1981b).

VIII. SPECULATION ON THE ORIGIN AND EVOLUTION OF VIROID-LIKE RNAs

The origin and evolution of small circular RNAs in plants is of considerable interest; especially the possibility that it may be connected with that of conventional viruses. Although it is probably far too early to discuss this question in a meaningful way because of the limited data available, we find some speculative ideas attractive. Like Diener (1981), we consider the viroids unlikely to be either primitive or degenerate viruses. Their unique molecular structure and apparent lack of messenger activity provide the most persuasive arguments in favor of this conclusion.

If viruses and viroids did indeed originate independently, it is attractive to consider the possibility that the viroid-like RNAs associated with viruses originated from the coinfection of plants with viruses and viroids. Initially, such associations would have consisted of virus and viroid replicating in the plant autonomously but simultaneously, with the viroid being encapsidated by the virus. The association may then have evolved into one in which the viroid lost its ability to replicate autonomously and was forced to use some essential function of the viral RNA; becoming a satellite RNA like the RNA 2 of LTSV (Jones *et al.*, 1983; Jones and Mayo, 1983; Francki *et al.*, 1983a). In turn, this evolutionary step may have been followed by the virus component losing some essential function which, however, could be provided by the satellite viroid-like RNA. Viruses such as VTMoV and SNMV may be the end products of these evolutionary steps where both RNA 1 and RNA 2 appear to be essential for their mutual replication (Gould *et al.*, 1981b).

The evolutionary sequence suggested above, would be supported by a demonstration that a viroid could be encapsidated by a virus. Attempts to achieve this experimentally were made by Gould *et al.*, (1981b) who inoculated plants with mixtures of several virus-viroid combinations but failed to detect any viroid encapsidation. However, only a limited number of combinations were tested and it will be interesting to test others, especially ones where both viroid and virus are known to infect the same plant species. The most likely virus candidates for success in this type of experiment are members of the sobemovirus group. Unfortunately such viruses have very restricted host ranges. If a system where encapsidation of a viroid by the coat protein of a coinfecting virus can be found, it will be interesting to determine if dependence of one component on the other develops after prolonged passaging of the two in plants. The time taken for the establishment of such changes may not be very long because the rate of RNA mutation is thought to be high due to the lack of error suppressing and proofreading mechanisms such as those associated with DNA replication (Reanney, 1982).

REFERENCES

Blackstock, J. McK. (1978) Lucerne transient streak and lucerne latent, two new viruses of lucerne, *Aust. J. Agric. Res. 29*, 291-304.

Chu, P.W.G., Boccardo, G., and Francki, R.I.B. (1981). Requirement of a genome-associated protein of tobacco ringspot virus for infectivity but not for *in vitro* translation. *Virology 109*, 428-430.

Chu, P.W.G., and Francki, R.I.B. (1983). Chemical and serological comparison of the coat proteins of velvet tobacco mottle and Solanum nodiflorum mottle viruses. *Virology 129*, 350-356.

Chu, P.W.G.,Francki, R.I.B. and Randles, J.W. (1983). Detection, isolation, and characterization of high molecular weight double-stranded RNAs in plants infected with velvet tobacco mottle virus. *Virology 126*, 480-492.

de Zoeten, G.A., and Gaard, G. (1969). Possibilities for inter- and intra-cellular translocation of some icosahedral plant viruses. *J. Cell.Biol. 40*, 814-823.

Diener, T.O. (1979). "Viroids and Viroid Diseases" Wiley Interscience, New York.

Diener, T.O. (1981). Viroids: abnormal products of plant metabolism. *Ann. Rev. Plant Physiol. 32*, 313-325.

Forster, R.L.S. and Jones,A.T.(1979). Properties of lucerne transient streak virus and evidence of the affinity to southern bean mosaic virus. *Ann. Appl. Biol.93*, 181-189.

Forster, R.L.S. and Jones, A.T. (1980). Lucerne transient streak *Commonwealth Mycological Institute/Association of Applied Biologists. Descriptions of Plant Viruses.* No. 224.

Francki, R.I.B., Chu, P.W.G., and Keese, P.K.(1983a). The satellite nature of viroid-like RNA from lucerne transient streak virus. In *Plant Infectious Agents: Viruses, Viroids, Virusoids and Satellites* (eds. H.D. Robertson, S.H. Howell, M. Zaitlin and R.L. Malmberg), *Current Communications in Molecular Biology* Cold Spring Harbor Laboratory 175-180.

Francki, R.I.B.,, Randles, J.W., Hatta, T., Davies, C. and Chu, P.W.G. (1983b). Subterranean clover mottle virus: another virus from Australia with encapsidated viroid-like RNA. *Plant Pathology 32*, 47-59.

Gould, A.R. (1981). Studies on encapsidated viroid-like RNA. II. Purification and characterization of a viroid-like RNA associated with velvet tobacco mottle virus (VTMoV). *Virology 108*, 123-133.

Gould, A.R., Francki, R.I.B., Hatta, T., and Hollings, M. (1981a). The bipartite genome of red clover necrotic mosaic virus. *Virology 108*, 499-506.

Gould, A.R., Francki, R.I.B., and Randles, J.W. (1981b). Studies on encapsidated viroid-like RNA. IV. Requirement for infectivity and specificity of two RNA components from velvet tobacco mottle virus. *Virology 110*, 420-426.

Gould, A.R., and Hatta, T. (1981). Studies on encapsidated viroid-like RNA. III. Comparative studies on RNAs isolated from velvet tobacco mottle virus and Solanum nodiflorum mottle virus. *Virology 109*, 137-147.

Greber, R.S. (1981). Some characteristics of Solanum nodi-
    florum mottle virus – a beetle-transmitted isometric
    virus from Australia. *Aust. J. Biol. Sci. 34,* 369-
    378.
Haseloff, J., Mohamed, N.A., and Symons, R.H. (1982). Viroid
    RNAs of cadang-cadang disease of coconuts. *Nature*
    (London) *299,* 316-321.
Haseloff, J., and Symons, R.H. (1982). Comparative sequence
    and structure of viroid-like RNAs of two plant
    viruses. *Nucleic Acids Res.10,* 3681-3691.
Hatta, T., and Francki, R.I.B. (1981). The identification of
    small polyhedral virus particles in thin sections
    of plant cells by an enzyme cytochemical technique.
    J. Ultrastructure Res. 74, 116-129.
Hatta, T., and Francki, R.I.B. (1978). Enzyme cytochemical
    indentification of single-stranded and double-
    stranded RNAs in virus infected plant and insect
    cells. *Virology 88,* 105-117.
Jones, A.T., and Mayo, M.A. (1983). Interaction of lucerne
    transient streak virus and the viroid-like RNA-2 of
    Solanum nodiflorum mottle virus. *J. Gen. Virol.
    64,* 1771-1774.
Jones, A.T., Mayo, M.A., and Duncan, G.H. (1983). Satellite-
    like properties of small circular RNA molecules in
    particles of lucerne transient streak virus.   *J.
    Gen. Virol. 64,* 1167-1173.
Kado, C.I. (1971). Sowbane mosaic virus. *Commonwealth
    Mycological Institute/Association of Applied
    Biologists. Descriptions of Plant Viruses No.64.*
Keese, P., Bruening, G., and Symons, R.H. (1983). Compara-
    tive sequence and structure of circular RNAs from
    two isolates of lucerne transient streak virus.
    FEBS Letters 159, 185-190.
Matthews, R.E.F. (1982). Classification and nomenclature of
    viruses. Fourth report of the International Commit-
    tee on Taxonomy of Viruses. *Intervirology 17.* 1-199.
Milne, R.G. (1967). Electron microscopy of leaves infected
    with sowbane mosaic virus and other small polyhe-
    dral viruses. *Virology 32,* 589-600.
Paliwal, Y.C. (1982). Lucerne transient streak – a virus of
    alfalfa newly recognized in North America. *Phyto-
    pathology 72,* 989 (Abstract).
Randles, J.W., Davies, C. Hatta,T., Gould, A.R., and Francki,
    R.I.B. (1981). Studies on encapsidated viroid-like
    RNA. I. Characterization of velvet tobacco mottle
    virus. *Virology 108,* 111-122.
Randles, J.W., Steger, G., and Riesner, D. (1982). Structur-
    al transitions in viroid-like RNAs associated with

cadang-cadang disease, velvet tobacco mottle virus and Solanum nodiflorum mottle virus. *Nucleic Acids Res. 10,* 5569-5586.

Reanney, D.C. (1982). The evolution of RNA viruses. *Ann.Rev. Microbiol. 36,* 47-73.

Riesner, D., Kaper, J.M., and Randles, J.W.(1982). Stiffness of viroids and viroid-like RNA in solution. *Nucleic Acids. Res. 10,* 5587-5598.

Rutgers, T., Salerno-Rife, T., and Kaesberg, P. (1980). Messenger RNA for the coat protein of southern bean mosaic virus. *Virology 104,* 506-509.

Sehgal, O.P. (1981). Southern bean mosaic virus group. In "Handbook of Plant Virus Infections - Comparative Diagnosis" (E. Kurstak, ed.) pp. 91-121 Elsevier/ North-Holland, Amsterdam.

Shepherd, R.J. (1971). Southern bean mosaic virus. *Commonwealth Mycological Institute/Association of Applied Biologists Descriptions of Plant Viruses No. 57.*

Spencer, D., and Wildman, S.G. (1964). The incorporation of amino acids into protein by cell-free extracts from tobacco leaves. *Bochemistry 3,* 954-959.

Teakle, D.S. (1968). Sowbane mosaic virus infecting *Chenopodium trigonon* in Queensland. *Aust. J. Biol.Sci. 21,* 649-653.

Tien-Po, Davies, C., Hatta, T., and Francki, R.I.B. (1981). Viroid-like RNA encapsidated in lucerne transient streak virus. *FEBS Letters 132,* 353-356.

Thornberry, H.H. (1966). Index of Plant Virus Diseases, Agric. Handbook No. 307, U.S. Dept. Agric.

Walters, H.J., and Henry, D.G.(1970). Bean leaf beetle as a vector of the cowpea strain of southern bean mosaic virus. *Phytopathology 60,* 177-178.

Weintraub, M., and Ragetli, H.W.J. (1970). Electron microscopy of the bean and cowpea strains of southern bean mosaic virus within leaf cells. *J. Utrastructure Res. 32,* 167-189.

Chapter 14

PM-ANTIGEN: A DISEASE-ASSOCIATED HOST PROTEIN
IN VIROID-INFECTED TOMATO

T. O. Diener, D. R. Smith

Plant Virology Laboratory
Plant Protection Institute
Agricultural Research Service
Beltsville, Maryland

J. Galindo A.

Centro de Fitopatologia
Colegio de Postgraduados
Chapingo Mex., Mexico

I.   INTRODUCTION

Ever since viroids were recognized as pathogenic, low molecular weight RNAs (Diener, 1971), the question arose as to whether the detrimental consequences of viroid infection in some host plants are mediated via polypeptides translated from the RNAs (Diener, 1982). Because known viroids are composed of only 246 (coconut cadang-cadang RNA 1) to 371 (citrus exocortis viroid)nucleotides (Haseloff *et al.*, 1982), such polypeptides could contain no more than 123 amino acid residues.

Early testing for *in vitro* messenger activity of the potato spindle tuber viroid (PSTV) and the citrus exocortis viroid (CEV) in a variety of cell-free protein-synthesizing systems indicated that neither viroid functions in this capacity (Davies *et al.*, 1974; Hall *et al.*, 1974). Also, CEV is not translated in *Xenopus laevis* oocytes, even after polyadenylylation *in vitro,* and does not interfere with the translation of endogenous messenger RNAs (Semancik *et al.*, 1977). With PSTV, lack of mRNA activity is not surprising,

SUBVIRAL PATHOGENS
OF PLANTS AND ANIMALS:
VIROIDS AND PRIONS

299

Copyright © 1985 by Academic Press, Inc.
All rights of reproduction in any form reserved.
ISBN 0-12-470230-9

because no AUG initiation codons are present in its nucleotide sequence or in that of its complement (Matthews, 1978).

Comparisons of protein species in healthy and PSTV-
infected tomato (Zaitlin and Hariharasubramanian, 1972) or
healthy and CEV-infected *Gynura aurantiaca* (Conejero and Semancik, 1977) did not reveal qualitative differences but
showed that in each case the amounts of at least two proteins
are enhanced in infected as compared with healthy plants.
With CEV, the two enhanced proteins are of low molecular
weight (1.5×10^4 and 1.8×10^4). More recent studies have
indicated that these two proteins are host-specific and not
viroid-coded proteins (Flores *et al.* 1978; Conejero *et al.*,
1979).

On the other hand, two investigators have reported the
production of PSTV-specific antisera (Hunter, 1964; Bagnall,
1967). Because these studies were performed at a time when
the "V" in PSTV still stood for "virus", the antisera were
believed to be specific for the presumed virus or its protein
subunits.

The present investigation developed from a study of the
tomato planta macho disease which, at the time was also
believed to be caused by a virus (Belalcazar and Galindo,
1974). Density-gradient centrifugation of expressed sap from
infected plants resulted in formation of a light-scattering
band with which infectivity was associated; and injection of
this material into rabbits led to the production of an antiserum that reacted, after absorption with sap from healthy
plants, specifically with extracts from infected plants
(Belalcazar and Galindo, 1974). After recognition of the
fact that the disease is caused by a viroid, the tomato
planta macho viroid (TPMV) (Galindo *et al.*, 1982), the question arose as to whether the disease-specific serological
reaction observed earlier had been due to a viroid-specified
antigen or to a host constituent the concentration of which
was greatly enhanced as a consequence of viroid infection.

We report here that the latter alternative is correct,
and that the antigen is a host protein of M_r 70,000. We also
report the results of experiments suggesting that accumulation of the antigen is connected with symptom formation in
infected plants rather than viroid replication *per se*. .

II.   RECOGNITION OF SPECIFIC ANTIGEN

Viroids were maintained and propagated in tomato
Lycopersicon esculentum, cv Rutgers) [TPMV, PSTV, and tomato
apical stunt viroid (TASV)], in *Chrysanthemum morifolium,*
cv. Mistletoe [chrysanthemum stunt viroid (CSV)], or in
Columnea erythrophae [Columnea Viroid (CV)]. Rutgers tomato
plants were inoculated mechanically with TPMV at the cotyle-

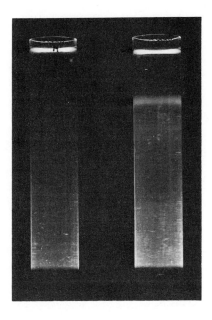

Figure 1. Density gradient centrifugation of sap expressed from healthy (left) and TPMV-infected tomato plants. See text for details. Arrow head points to light-scattering band visible only with sap from infected plants.

donary stage and kept in a greenhouse at about 28°C until symptoms were well developed (15-21 days p.i.). Leaves were extracted fresh or after frozen storage at -20°C.

Sap expressed from fresh or frozen leaves of TPMV-infected plants was clarified by centrifugation at 9000 rpm for 20 min (Sorvall[+] SS 34 rotor). Clarified sap was layered onto linear 0.5-33% (w/v) aqueous sucrose gradients and centrifuged for 3 hrs at 36,000 rpm (Spinco model L3-50,SW 41 rotor). As shown in Fig. 1, in gradients containing sap from infected plants, a prominent light-scattering band developed, whereas in tubes in which identically prepared sap from healthy plants was centrifuged, no such band was recognizable. Material in the light-scattering band was removed, emulsified with an equal volume of Freund's complete adjuvant, and used for

---

+Mention of a commercial company or specific equipment does not constitute its endorsement by the U.S. Department of Agriculture over similar equipment or companies not named.

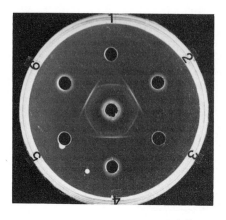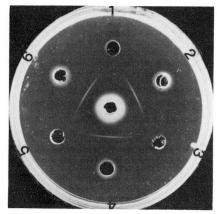

Figure 2. Double diffusion tests between antiserum (center wells) and sap from healthy (wells No. 1, 3, and 5) or TPMV-infected (wells No. 2, 4, and 6) tomato plants. A, reaction with nonabsorbed antiserum. B, reaction with antiserum after intragel absorption with sap from healthy plants.

the immunization of rabbits. Five subcutaneous injections of 1 ml each of the antigen-adjuvant emulsion were spaced over 2.5 weeks, followed 4 days later by subcutaneous injection of 1 ml of adjuvant-free antigen. The rabbits were bled and serum prepared 5 days later.

The resulting antisera were examined in double diffusion tests against sap from healthy or TPMV-infected tomato plants. As shown in Fig. 2A, two types of precipitin lines developed. One reaction, consisting of a well defined line and one or two diffuse ones slightly closer to the antiserum well, developed opposite antigen wells containing sap from either healthy or infected plants. A second reaction, consisting of a sharp precipitin line closer to the antigen wells, developed only opposite wells containing sap from infected plants.

Evidently, the light-scattering band used to produce the antiserum contained several antigens common to both healthy and infected plants as well as one antigen apparently present only in extracts from infected plants. To remove the common antigenic determinants, antisera were absorbed with extracts from healthy plants. Four volumes of antiserum were mixed with 1 volume of sap, the mixtures incubated for 24 hrs at 35°C, centrifuged for 30 mins at 3000 rpm, and the supernatant collected. As shown in Fig. 2B, after absorption with

clarified sap from healthy plants, the antiserum indeed reacted specifically with extracts from infected plants. For
simplicity, the antigen that is apparently present only in
TPMV-infected plants will be referred to as the planta macho
(PM) antigen.

III.   OCCURRENCE OF PM ANTIGEN

To determine the appearance of PM antigen during the
infection process, its subcellular distribution and distribution within infected plants, fresh or frozen infected tissue
was ground with mortar and pestle in 0.1 M sodium phosphate
(pH 7), 0.05 M Na_2SO_3, 0.05% (w/v) sodium diethyldithiocarba-
mate, and 0.25% (w/v) polyvinylpyrrolidone (3 ml/g tissue).
The extracts were filtered through one layer of Miracloth and
were clarified by centrifugation for 20 mins at 10,500 g.
The resulting preparations were then examined for the presence of PM antigen in double diffusion tests.

1.Kinetics of Apearance of PM Antigen in Infected Plants.
Extracts were prepared from TPMV or PSTV-infected plants
10, 13, 17, 21, 25, 27, and 32 days p.i. and were tested for
the presence of PM antigen. The PM antigen could first be
detected in plants infected with either viroid 17 days p.i.
At later sampling days, its concentration became progressively greater. Symptoms of viroid infection became noticeable
12 and 15 days p.i. with TPMV and PSTV, respectively. The
appearance of PM antigen, therefore, was correlated with the
appearance of symptoms.

In these double-diffusion tests, precipitin lines were
visible when either the antigen-containing extract (from
plants with good symptoms) or the antiserum were diluted as
much as eight-fold, but in microprecipitin tests a dilution
endpoint of 1/64 has been determined (Belalcazar and Galindo,
1974).

2. Distribution of PM Antigen within Infected Plants.
Extracts from leaves occupying various positions on
infected plants were also examined in double diffusion tests
for the presence of PM antigen. As indicated in Table I,
precipitin lines developed in all reactions, but the distance
of the lines from the antigen wells progressively increased
in reactions with leaves from the base towards the top of the
plants. Thus, the PM antigen appears to be present in higher
concentration in leaves on upper parts as compared with
leaves on lower parts of infected plants. The distribution of
the PM antigen therefore correlates with the severity of leaf
symptoms -- the latter being more pronounced in upper leaves
than in lower leaves.

Table I.

Relative Concentration of the PM Antigen in Leaves
of Infected Tomato Plants.

Leaf position from base of plant	Leaf symptom[a/]	Distance from precipitin line to sample well[b/]			
		Plant 1	Plant 2	Plant 3	Average
2nd	−	25	30	30	28.3
3rd	−	34	37	40	37.0
4th	+	50	49	50	49.6
5th	++	50	50	50	50.6
6th	+++	57	60	55	57.3

[a/]−, no symptoms; ±, slight symptoms; +++, severe symptoms.

[b/]Longer distance indicates higher concentration.

3. Subcellular Location of PM Antigen.

TPMV-infected tissue was ground in 0.02 M Tris-HCl (pH 7.5), 0.4 M sucrose, 0.02 M KCl, 0.002 M $MgCl_2$, and 0.04 M 2-mercaptoethanol. The extract was filtered through one layer of Miracloth and fractionated by sequential centrifugation for 10 mins each at 240 g, 10^3 g, and 10^4 g, for 30 mins at 8 x 10^4 g, and finally for 2 hrs at 10^5 g. Successive pellets yielded nuclei-, chloroplast-, mitochondria-, membrane-, and ribosome-rich fractions, respectively. Each pellet was resuspended in 1 ml of 0.02 M sodium phosphate, pH 7.0. Each preparation, as well as the postribosomal supernatant, was assayed serologically for PM antigen and by bioassay on tomato (Raymer and Diener, 1969) for TPMV. Results showed that only the postribosomal supernatant contained PM antigen. In fractions enriched with nuclei, chloroplasts, mitochondria, or ribosomes, the PM antigen could not be detected.

4. Specificity of PM Antigen Occurrence.

To determine whether the PM antigen accumulates only in TPMV-infected plants or also in plants infected with other viroids or with viruses, double diffusion tests were made between absorbed antiserum and extracts from tomato plants infected with other pathogens.

Fig. 3 shows that precipitin lines developed between antiserum wells and wells containing sap from tomato plants infected with PSTV or cucumber mosaic virus with CARNA 5 (Kaper and Waterworth, 1977), but not with sap from healthy

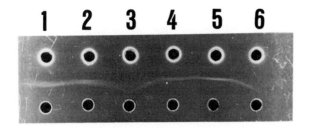

Figure 3. Double diffusion test between antiserum (after intragel absorption with sap from healthy plants) (upper wells) and saps(lower wells) from healthy and infected tomato plants. All saps were collected and tested 25 days p.i., except that from cucumber mosaic virus (CMV) + CARNA 5- infected plants(21 days p.i.). 1, TPMV-infected, diluted 1:8; 2, PSTV-infected, undiluted; 3, healthy; 4, TPMV-infected, undiluted; 5, CMV + CARNA 5-infected; and 6, CMV-infected.

Table II.

Presence or Absence of Symptoms and PM Antigen in Various Pathogen-Host Plant Combinations.

Pathogen	Host plant	Symptoms	PM antigen[a]
–	Tomato (cv.Rutgers)	–	–
TPMV	"	+	+
PSTV	"	+	+
TASV	"	+	+
CV	"	+	+
CSV	"	–	–
PSTV	Potato	+	–
PSTV	*Gynura aurantiaca*	+	–
CSV	Chrysanthemum (cv.Mistletoe)	+	–
CV	*Columnea erythrophae*	–	–
Tobacco mosaic virus	Tomato(cv.Rutgers)	+	–
Cucumber mosaic virus (CMV)	"	"	+	–
CMV + CARNA 5	"	"	+	+

[a] Determined serologically.

plants or plants infected with cucumber mosaic virus in the absence of CARNA 5. All precipitin lines joined together and also with lines produced by sap from TPMV-infected plants, indicating identity of the reacting antigens in the various extracts.

In other experiments (Table II). precipitin lines joining with those obtained with TPMV-infected tissue were

observed with extracts from tomato plants infected with any
one of several viroids, but not with extracts from other
plant species infected with some of these same viroids. The
only exception was the chrysanthemum stunt viroid, with which
no precipitin lines were obtained, regardless of whether
extracts from infected tomato or chrysanthemum plants were
tested. Infection of tomato plants with conventional viruses,
either tobacco mosaic virus or cucumber mosaic virus, did not
result in the appearance of detectable amounts of PM antigen
(Table II).

IV.   PURIFICATION OF PM ANTIGEN

To determine the identity of PM antigen, extracts from
TPMV-infected tomato plants were fractionated as follows.
Clarified antigen extracts (see above) from TPMV-infected and healthy Rutgers tomato plants were fractionated by
ammonium sulfate precipitation. Material remaining in solution at 50% (w/w) saturation but precipitating at 60% saturation was resuspended in 0.02 M sodium phosphate (pH 7.0),
0.025% sodium azide and subjected to gel filtration in a
Sephadex G 100 column. The eluate was monitored at 280 nm
and each fraction (4ml) assayed serologically for PM antigen.
PM antigen-containing fractions were electrophoresed in
cylindrical 5 percent polyacrylamide gels, the position in
one gel of the PM antigen determined by staining with Coomas-
sie blue, and equivalent gel portions excised from all other
gels. Gel slices were ground in water, filtered through
glass wool, and the solution clarified by low-speed centrifugation. Purity of PM antigen preparations was evaluated by
electrophoresis in polyacrylamide slab gels. Proteins to be
analyzed were dissolved in 0.0625 M Tris-HCl (pH 6.8), 20
mg/ml sodium dodecylsulfate, 10% glycerol, and 0.1 M dithiothreitol, heated for 5 mins at 100°C, and subjected to discontinuous PAGE, essentially as described by Laemmli (1970).
Ammonium sulfate fractionation of extracts led to substantial enrichment of the PM antigen, because most of it
remained in solution at 50 percent saturation, but was precipitated at 60 percent saturation, whereas most ammonium
sulfate-precipitable components precipitated at or below 50
percent saturation (Table III).
Further purification of the PM antigen was obtained by
gel filtration of 50-60 percent ammonium sulfate saturation
fractions from TPMV-infected plants. Equivalent fractions
from healthy plants were processed as controls. Elution of
the PM antigen was monitored by double diffusion tests with
absorbed antiserum. Figure 4 illustrates typical UV absorption profiles of eluates from Sephadex columns. Comparison

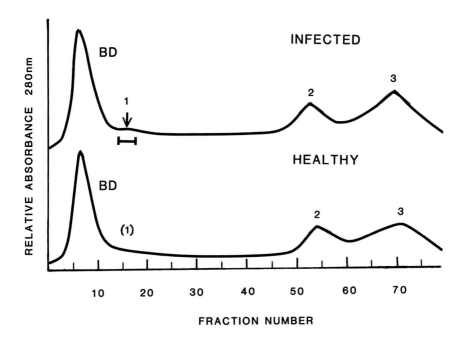

Figure 4. Ultraviolet light (280 nm) absorption profiles of gel filtration eluates of preparations from TPMV-infected (upper panel) and healthy (lower panel) tomato plants. See text for details. BD, Blue Dextran; 1, 2, 3, successive UV-absorption peaks; bar, position of PM antigen (determined immunologically).

Table III
Ammonium Sulfate Fractionation of Extracts from
TPMV-Infected Tomato Plants.

$(NH_4)_2SO_4$ saturation interval	Relative amount of	
	Precipitate	PM antigen[a]
0-20%	++++	−
20-30	++++	−
30-40	+++	−
40-50	++	+
50-60	+	+++
60-70	+	−
70-80	+	−

[a]Determined serologically.

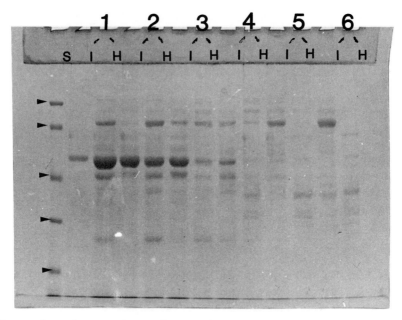

Figure 5. Separation of proteins present in gel filtration eluates in an 8% polyacrylamide slab gel. S, molecular weight markers (identified by arrowheads from top to bottom: phosphorylase B, M_r 92,500; bovine serum albumin, M_r 66,200; ovalbumin, M_r 45,000; carbonic anhydrase, M_r 31,000; and soybean trypsin inhibitor, M_r 21,500). I, infected; H, healthy; 1-6, consecutive gel eluate fractions.

with marker proteins of known molecular weight indicated that the PM antigen had an apparent molecular weight of about 70,000 (bar in Fig. 4, upper panel).

Ĩ The composition of gel eluate fractions from the void volume of the column to beyond the front-running peak and of equivalent fractions from healthy plants was determined by gel electrophoresis.

Ĩ Figure 5 shows that in those fractions that, according to serological evidence, contained most of the PM antigen (Nos. 5 and 6) a component with an electrophoretic mobility corresponding to a molecular weight of 70,000 was present in fractions from infected plants, but not in equivalent fractions from healthy plants. Figure 5 shows that a component with identical mobility was present in extracts from healthy

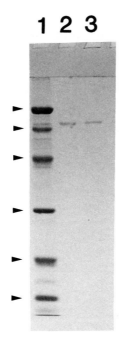

Figure 6. PAGE of purified PM antigen (lanes 2 and 3) and
molecular weight markers (lane 1) (identified by arrow heads,
same as in Fig. 5, except lowest band, which is lysozyme, M_r
14,400).

plants, but that this component eluted earlier from the column (fraction Nos. 1 - 3) than did the M_r 70,000 component
from infected plants. No precipitin line developed when
fractions containing the M_r 70,000 component from healthy
plants was tested with absorbed antiserum.

Final purification was achieved by electrophoresis of PM
antigen-containing gel filtration eluates in cylindrical
polyacrylamide gels, followed by cutting out of appropriate
gel slices, and elution of the antigen from the gel. Such
preparations contained the M_r 70,000 component and were free
of detectable contaminants (Figure 6). In double diffusion
tests between purified preparations and absorbed antiserum, a
single precipitin line developed. Comparison with the precipitin line of sap from TPMV-infected plants indicated
identity of the antigens in the two preparations.

To determine chemical identity of the PM antigen, purified preparations were incubated with proteinase K (50 µg/ml,
5 hrs at 37°C) and the reaction mixture analyzed. No intact
PM antigen remained, indicating that the antigen is a protein. Incubation with glycosidases (*T. cornutus*, or *C.
lampas*, 50 µ g/ml each,2 hrs at 25°C), with β -glucosidase

(100 μg/ml, 2 hrs at 37°C), or with β-glucuronidase (100
μg/ml, 2 hrs at 37°C) had no effect on the electrophoretic
mobility of the protein, indicating that the antigen probably
is not a glycoprotein.

V.   DOES PM ANTIGEN OCCUR IN HEALTHY PLANTS?

To determine whether the PM antigen is present in small
amounts in healthy plants or whether its synthesis is induced
only in viroid-infected plants, gel eluate fractions from
healthy plants equivalent to those from infected plants that
contain the PM antigen (fractions 5 and 6, Fig. 5) were
concentrated by ultrafiltration through Amicon YM 30 Diaflow
ultrafilters. After passage of the solutions filters were
washed with 0.02 M phosphate (pH 7.0), 0.025% sodium azide,
and material remaining on the filter taken up in the same
buffer. As compared with the gel filtration eluate, final
preparations were 15- to 30-fold concentrated. Figure 7

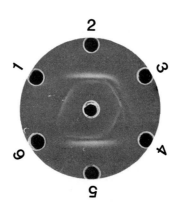

Figure 7. Double diffusion test between nonabsorbed antiserum
(center well) and sap from healthy plants (wells 1 and 4),
sap from TPMV-infected plants(wells 2 and 5),and concentrates
from healthy plants, as follows. Well 3, fraction corresponding to the one from infected plants that contains the PM
antigen (fractions 5 and 6, Fig. 5); well 6, fraction containing the M_r 70,000 protein (fractions 1 and 2, Fig. 5).

shows that a precipitin line joining that obtained with sap
from infected plants was recognizable with the concentrate
from healthy plants. To preclude possible confusion with the
reaction common to healthy and infected plants (see Fig. 2A),
these tests were made with nonabsorbed antiserum. Thus, the
common reaction is present in Fig. 7 with all samples, except
for a concentrate of a gel filtration eluate from healthy

plants (well No. 6) that contained neither the common antigen nor the PM antigen. This concentrate originated from a gel filtration eluate containing the M_r 70,000 protein found in healthy plants (fractions 1-3, Fig. 5). Fig.7 demonstrates, in addition, the presence in the concentrate tested in well No. 3 of an antigen that is neither detectable with unconcentrated sap from healthy or infected plants. Its identity is unknown.

VI.   DISCUSSION

Our results demonstrate that injection into rabbits of sap from TPMV-infected tomato plants results in formation of an antiserum that reacts, after absorption with sap from healthy plants, specifically with sap from TPMV-infected plants. We show that the antigen responsible for this reaction (PM antigen) is a protein with a molecular weight of about 70,000. Aside from the fact that the viroid does not contain sufficient coding capacity to specify a protein of this size, other evidence clearly indicates that PM antigen is a host-specific, not viroid-coded protein. When extracts from healthy plants were processed by the methods developed for the purification of PM antigen and equivalent fractions substantially concentrated, double diffusion tests revealed the presence of small amounts of PM antigen in the preparations from uninfected plants. Thus, infection of tomato plants with TPMV leads to a dramatic increase in the concentration of a host protein that normally occurs only in trace amounts, but not, as appears to be the case on first sight, to the induction of a novel protein. That PM antigen is a host-specific protein is also indicated by the fact that it accumulates in tomato plants infected with viroids other than TPMV, namely PSTV, tomato apical stunt viroid (TASV), and columnea viroid (CV), as well as in plants infected with CARNA 5 (in the presence of cucumber mosaic virus). Furthermore, the lack of reaction between the antiserum and sap from host species other than tomato infected (and showing symptoms of infection) with two of the same viroids (PSTV in potato and chrysanthemum stunt viroid in chrysanthemum) similarly indicates that the protein is specified by the host, and not by the viroid.

Our results indicate that the protein is associated with disease processes in infected plants and not with viroid replication *per se*. Thus, the protein is not detectable in symptomless infections (Chrysanthemum stunt viroid in tomato) and it appears in leaves mostly after symptom appearance, not before. Also, its concentration seems to correlate with symptom severity, whereas its subcellular distribution (in the postribosomal supernatant) is unlike that of the viroid (which is present mostly in cell nuclei).

On the other hand, accumulation of PM antigen does not appear to be a general stress reaction of tomato plants. Thus, it could not be detected in plants infected with conventional viruses (tobacco and cucumber mosaic) although symptoms were expressed in both cases. Accumulation of PM antigen, however, occurs not only in viroid-infected, symptom-bearing tomato plants, but is also associated with infection by a satellite RNA, CARNA 5, possibly indicating similarity of pathogenic mechanisms.

The biological significance of PM antigen remains to be determined. In particular, it is not clear whether accumulation of the protein is a product of metabolic aberrations occurring in diseased tissue or whether, on the contrary, its accumulation causes such aberrations.

Whether or not PM antigen is identical with the antigen(s) described by Hunter (1964) or Bagnall (1967) from PSTV-infected plants also remains to be determined.

REFERENCES

Bagnall, R.H. (1967). Serology of the potato spindle tuber virus. *Phytopathology 57*, 533-534.
Belalcazar, C.S. & Galindo A., J. (1974). Estudio sobre el virus de la "Planta Macho" del jitomate *(Lycopersicon esculentum* Mill). *Agrociencia 18*, 79-88.
Conejero, V. & Semancik, J.S. (1977). Exocortis viroid: Alteration in the proteins of *Gynura aurantiaca* accompanying viroid infection. *Virology 77*, 221-232.
Conejero, V., Picazo, I. & Segado, P. (1979). Citrus excortis viroid (CEV): Protein alterations in different hosts following viroid infection. *Virology 97*, 454-456.
Davies, J. W., Kaesberg, P. & Diener, T.O. (1974). Potato spindle tuber viroid XII. An investigation of viroid RNA as messenger for protein synthesis. *Virology 61*, 281-286.
Diener, T.O. (1971). Potato spindle tuber "virus". IV. A replicating, low molecular weight RNA. *Virology 45*, 411-428.
Diener, T.O. (1982). Viroids and their interactions with host cells. *Annu. Rev. Microbiol. 36*, 239-258.
Flores, R., Chroboczek, J. & Semancik, J.S. (1978). Some properties of the CEV-P$_1$ protein from citrus exocortis viroid-infected *Gynura aurantiaca* DC. *Physiol. Plant Pathol. 13*, 193-201.

Galindo A., J, Smith, D.R. & Diener, T.O. (1982). Etiology of Planta Macho, a viroid disease of tomato. *Phytopathology 72*, 49-54.

Hall, T.C., Wepprich, R.K., Davies, J.W., Weathers, L.G. & Semancik, J.S. (1974). Functional distinctions between the ribonucleic acids from citrus exocortis viroid and plant viruses: Cell-free translation and aminoacylation. *Virology 61*, 486-492.

Haseloff, J., Mohamed, N.A. & Symons, R.H. (1982). Viroid RNAs of cadang-cadang disease of coconuts. *Nature (London) 299*, 316-321.

Hunter, J.E. (1964). Studies on potato spindle tuber virus. Ph. D. dissertation, Univ. New Hampshire, 97 pp.

Kaper, J.M. & Waterworth, H.E. (1977). Cucumber mosaic virus associated RNA 5: Causal agent for tomato necrosis. *Science 196*, 429-431.

Laemmli, U.K. (1970). Cleavage of structural proteins during the assembly of the head of bacteriophage T4. *Nature (London) 227*, 680-685.

Matthews, R.E.F. (1978). Are viroids negative-strand viruses? *Nature (London) 276*, 850.

Raymer, W.B. & Diener, T.O. (1969). Potato spindle tuber virus: A plant virus with properties of a free nucleic acid. I. Assay, extraction, and concentration *Virology 37*, 343-350.

Semancik, J.S., Conejero, V. & Gerhart, J. (1977). Citrus exocortis viroid: Survey of protein synthesis in *Xenopus laevis* oocytes following addition of viroid RNA. *Virology 80*, 218-221.

Semancik, J.S., Tsuruda, D., Zaner, L., Geelen, J.W.M.C. & Weathers, L.G. (1976). Exocortis disease: Subcellular distribution of pathogenic (viroid) RNA. *Virology 69*, 669-676.

Zaitlin, M. & Hariharasubramanian, V. (1972). A gel electrophoretic analysis of proteins from plants infected with tobacco mosaic and potato spindle tuber viruses. *Virology 47*, 296-305.

Chapter 15

CONSTRUCTION OF INFECTIOUS POTATO SPINDLE TUBER VIROID cDNA CLONES: IMPLICATION FOR INVESTIGATIONS OF VIROID STRUCTURE-FUNCTION RELATIONSHIPS

Robert A. Owens
Plant Virology Laboratory
Beltsville, MD USA 20705

Michael C. Kiefer
Department of Botany, University of Maryland,
College Park, MD USA 20742

Dean E. Cress
Tissue Culture and Molecular Genetics Laboratory
Beltsville, MD USA 20705

INTRODUCTION

The phrase "molecular biology of plant viroids" encompasses several interrelated topics such as the mechanisms of viroid structure formation, replication, and symptom induction. Progress in these individual areas has been uneven, with the result that we now know much more about the physical-chemical aspects of viroid structure than how viroids function biologically. The rapid accumulation of nucleotide sequence and other structural data has stimulated several groups to propose working hypotheses that attempt to explain the relationship between viroid structure and function. What has been lacking is an experimental system to rigorously test and refine these working hypotheses.

In this chapter we will describe such a system and indicate several ways it can be used to probe the relationship between viroid structure and function. We have shown that

Copyright © 1985 by Academic Press, Inc.
All rights of reproduction in any form reserved.
ISBN 0-12-470230-9

inoculation of plants with recombinant plasmid DNAs containing tandem dimers of full-length potato spindle tuber viroid
(PSTV) cDNA results in the appearance of viroid RNA progeny
and the characteristic disease symptoms. *In vitro* modification of specific sequences present in the cloned genome followed by bioassay to detect phenotypic variation, an approach
often termed "reverse genetics", can now be used to investigate viroid structure-function relationships.

I.   PLANT VIROIDS FROM A MOLECULAR PERSPECTIVE

Determination of the complete nucleotide sequences of
several viroids (PSTV, Gross *et al.*, 1978; CSV and CEV,
Haseloff and Symons 1981, Gross *et al.* 1982; Visvader *et
al.*, 1982; ASBV, Symons 1981; CCCV, Haseloff *et al.*, 1982;
TPMV and TASV, Kiefer *et al.*, 1983) and detailed investigations of their physical-chemical properties (Riesner *et
al.*, 1979; Randles *et al.*, 1982) have provided a detailed
model of viroid structure. Comparative sequence analyses
divide known viroids into 3 groups: PSTV, CEV, CSV, TASV,
and TPMV share 60-70% sequence homology and constitute the
"PSTV group"; CCCV is more distantly related and shares a
central conserved region with the "PSTV group"; ASBV is
further removed, sharing only limited and scattered regions
of homology with members of the "PSTV group".
These small, covalently closed circular RNA molecules
have a highly base-paired, rather stiff rod-like native conformation. PSTV contains a serial arrangement of 26 double-
stranded segments interrupted by bulge loops of varying sizes; these single-stranded loops do not interact to fold the
extended secondary structure into a more globular tertiary
conformation. The native structure of viroids is a unique
combination of stability and flexibility; thermal denaturation converts the native rod-like structure to a hairpin-con-
taining circle in a highly cooperative fashion yet at a low
temperature (Henco *et al.*, 1979).
The left side of the viroid hairpin is intrinsically less
stable than the right side, but the formation of 2-3 short,
more stable "secondary" hairpins destabilizes the corresponding double-stranded domain on the right and allows denaturation to occur in a single, cooperative step. Although the
functional implications of this unique structure are not yet
clear, strict conservation of secondary hairpin I and the
stem of hairpin II suggests that they have vital functions
for members of the "PSTV group" *in vivo* (reviewed by Sänger,
1982). Sequence homologies among members of the "PSTV group"
are concentrated in the longer, less stable domain on the
left-side of the native structure as compared to the shorter

and more stable domain on the right (Gross *et al.*, 1982).

Knowledge of the mechanisms of viroid replication and symptom induction has accumulated more slowly than knowledge of their structure. Grill and Semancik (1978) provided the first evidence that viroid replication involves RNA-directed RNA synthesis by their demonstration that infected tissue contains RNA molecules complementary to the infecting viroid. Owens and Cress(1980)and Zelcer *et al.*, (1982)have shown that this RNA is complementary to the entire viroid, a prerequisite for its possible involvement in viroid replication. Further characterization of double-stranded viroid RNAs isolated from infected tissues and presumed to be replication intermediates have led several groups to propose a "rolling circle" mechanism for viroid replication (Branch *et al.*, 1981; Owens and Diener 1982; Symons *et al.*, 1982). Multimeric forms of both the complementary RNA (Branch *et al.* 1981; Rohde and Sänger 1981; Owens and Diener 1982) and the viroid (Semancik and Desjardins 1980; Bruening *et al.*, 1982; Branch and Robertson 1983) have been detected. Neither viroid-infected nor healthy tomato tissue contain DNA sequences complementary to PSTV (Zaitlin *et al.*, 1980; Branch and Dickson 1980; Hadidi *et al.*, 1981).

The enzymes involved in viroid replication *in vivo* have not been identified. Inhibition of viroid replication in tomato protoplasts inoculated with CPFV *in vitro* (Mühlbach and Sänger, 1979) and in nuclei isolated from CEV-infected *Gynura* leaves (Flores and Semancik 1982) by low levels of α-amanitin suggests that DNA-dependent RNA polymerase II is involved in viroid replication. Although Rackwitz *et al.* (1981) have shown that plant DNA-dependent RNA polymerase II can synthesize full-length linear complementary RNA from a PSTV template *in vitro,* a number of other DNA-dependent and RNA-dependent polymerases will also accept PSTV as template. These enzymes include *E. coli* DNA polymerase I (Rohde *et al.*, 1982), tomato RNA-dependent RNA polymerase (Boege *et al.*, 1982), and bacteriophage Qβ replicase (Owens and Diener 1977). A judicious combination of *in vivo* and *in vitro* approaches will be required to identify the enzyme(s) actually responsible for viroid replication.

Conversion of multimeric viroid RNAs to the monomeric circular form that is the most abundant viroid-related RNA in an infected cell must involve both cleavage and ligation reactions. RNA ligase purified from wheat germ can circularize naturally occurring linear PSTV molecules that contain 2',3'-cyclic phosphate termini (Branch *et al.*, 1982; Kikuchi *et al.* 1982). Endonucleolytic cleavage of a multimeric viroid RNA could generate the 2',3'-cyclic phosphate termini required by this RNA ligase. Kikuchi *et al.*, (1982) and

Palukaitis and Zaitlin (1983) have reported that naturally
occurring linear PSTV molecules contain a nick with a 5'
hydroxyl terminus in either the right-hairpin loop (nucleotides 177-181) or between nucleotides 348 and 349. These
results make an enzymatic mechanism for cleavage and ligation
reactions plausible, but an autocatalytic cleavage/ligation
mechanism similar to that reported for the ribosomal RNA
intron of *Tetrahymena* (Kruger *et al.*, 1982) could also convert multimeric viroid RNA to circular monomers *in vivo*.

The stunting and epinasty which often accompany viroid
infection suggest that these pathogens induce hormonal im-
balances and altered cell development in their hosts. The
mechanism of symptom induction is presently unknown. Evidence that viroids do not code for proteins suggests that
their biological properties are a consequence of direct
viroid-host molecular interaction (reviewed by Diener 1979;
Zaitlin 1979; and Sänger 1982). Synthesis of certain host
proteins increases dramatically as part of a general physiological response to infection, but other pathogens (i.e.
conventional viruses and fungi) or even senescence induce
similar alterations in the host protein profile (Conejero *et
al.*, 1979; Camacho Henriquez and Sänger, 1982a, 1982b). In
another sense viroid-host interaction must be quite specific because strains of PSTV that induce mild, intermediate,
and severe symptoms contain only minor sequence differences
(Dickson *et al.*, 1979; Gross *et al.*, 1981; Sänger 1982) and
PSTV infection in many tomato cultivars is essentially symptomless.

Figure 1. Construction of full-length double-stranded PSTV
cDNAs. (a). Ligation of specific fragments from overlapping,
partial length cDNAs followed by addition of synthetic oligonucleotide linkers yields a full-length cDNA whose termini
are derived from the unique HaeIII cleavage site (PSTV nucleotides 145-148). The inner circle represents the 359 nucleotide sequence of PSTV (Gross *et al.*, 1978); positions of 5
unique restriction sites in double-stranded PSTV cDNA are
shown. The concentric curves indicate the portions of the
complete PSTV cDNA sequence present in partial-length clones
pDC-29 and pDC-22. Heavy portions of these curves indicate
the contiguous AvaII-HaeIII fragments used for ligation. (b).
Schematic representations of recombinant plasmids depict the
orientation of the PSTV cDNA inserts with respect to the
adjacent plasmid promoters. PSTV cDNA sequences are shown as
heavy solid lines with the vertical marks indicating their
HaeIII termini (left) or BamHI termini (right); the arrows
indicate the orientation of the PSTV DNA sequences. Plasmid
DNA sequences are shown as broken lines.

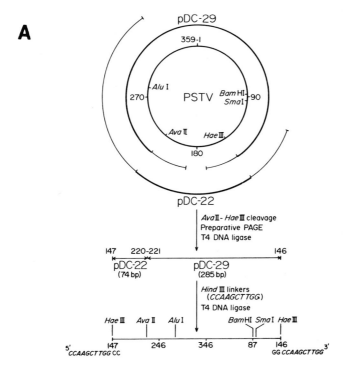

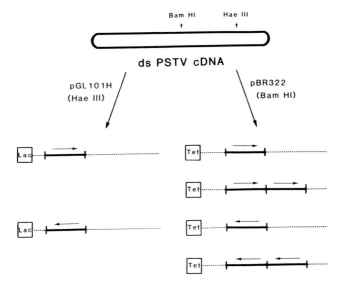

Figure 1.

Several speculative mechanisms for viroid pathogenesis
have been proposed: interference with the processing (splicing) of host mRNA (Diener 1981; Dickson 1981; Gross *et*
al., 1982; Kiss and Solymosy 1982; Zimmern 1982) and competition with genomic DNA templates for DNA-dependent RNA
polymerase II (Rackwitz *et al.*, 1981) are two examples. It
is perhaps safe to assume that the actual mechanism of viroid
pathogenesis is much more complex than any of these working
hypotheses.

II.   DEMONSTRATION THAT CERTAIN VIROID cDNA
CLONES ARE INFECTIOUS

A.   Construction of Recombinant Plasmids.

Owens and Cress (1980) have reported the construction of
recombinant pBR322 plasmids containing DNA inserts complementary to portions of the PSTV genome. Figure 1A depicts the
construction of plasmids containing full-length PSTV cDNAs
from two overlapping, partial-length cDNAs. Nucleotide sequence analysis of these partial-length cDNAs had shown
that the resulting full-length PSTV cDNA clones would have a
DNA sequence that corresponds to the intermediate strain of
PSTV (Gross *et al.*, 1978).

Equimolar amounts of the contiguous AvaII-HaeIII restriction fragments from clones pDC-29 and pDC-22 were incubated
at 16°C with a low concentration of T4 DNA ligase to promote
ligation at the AvaII cohesive ends and then were digested
with HaeIII. The 359 bp double-stranded PSTV cDNA that
resulted was purified by polyacrylamide gel electrophoresis
and ligated to [5' - ^{32}P] labelled synthetic decanucleotide
linkers encoding the HindIII recognition site. Following
digestion with HindIII, the desired 365 bp fragment was
purified by polyacrylamide gel electrophoresis and eluted.

The full-length double-stranded PSTV cDNA was inserted
into the HindIII site of plasmid pBR322, and the recombinant
molecules were transformed into *E. coli* C600(r_k^- m^+).Clones
carrying the PSTV cDNA insertion were selected on the basis
of their ampicillin-resistant, tetracycline-sensitive pheno-
type. Restriction digestions with HindIII, HaeIII, and BamHI
were used to identify the structure of the inserts and their
orientation within the plasmid vector. Use of this particular HindIII decanucleotide linker reconstructed the terminal
HaeIII sites of the PSTV cDNA insert. HaeIII digestion of
these recombinant plasmids releases a 359 bp full-length
double-stranded PSTV cDNA.

The 365 bp HindIII fragment was subsequently inserted
into plasmid pGL101H, a vector derived from pBR322 by addition of a 95 bp fragment containing the *lac*UV5 promoter

(Gail Lauer, personal communication). Such a construction theoretically permits transcription of the PSTV cDNA sequences under the control of an efficient plasmid promoter.

Dimeric PSTV cDNA inserts were of particular interest in light of the evidence for multimeric viroid replicative intermediates (summarized in Section I.) To facilitate construction of cDNA dimers, it was desirable to obtain PSTV cDNA with cohesive termini. Therefore, a permuted form of the full-length PSTV cDNA insert having BamHI termini was constructed by incubating the 359 bp PSTV cDNA having HaeIII termini with T4 DNA ligase and subsequent digestion with BamHI. The resulting 359 bp fragment was purified by polyacrylamide gel electrophoresis, inserted into the BamHI site pBR322, and transformed in *E. coli* C600. Recombinants were identified as ampicillin-resistant, tetracycline-sensitive colonies. The presence of monomeric or head-to-tail dimeric PSTV cDNA inserts in both orientations was determined by digestions with BamHI and SmaI. Figure 1B is a schematic representation of the various recombinant plasmids showing the orientation of their PSTV cDNA inserts with respect to the adjacent plasmid promoters.

    B. Viroid-related Transcripts in *E. coli* .

Because the PSTV cDNA sequences in our recombinant plasmids were inserted downstream from either the *tet* (pBR 322)or *lac* UV5 (pGL101H) promoter (Figure 1B), it was possible that stable PSTV-related RNAs could be produced in the *E. coli* strains harboring the various recombinant plasmids described above. The polarity of such transcripts can be established by hybridization of RNAs extracted from exponentially growing *E. coli* cultures with strand-specific probes.
Figure 2 presents the results of such an analysis of glyoxal-denatured *E.coli* RNA after fractionation by agarose gel electrophoresis and transfer to nitrocellulose.

Each *E.coli* clone tested contained PSTV-related transcripts that were heterogeneous in size but of only one polarity. Susceptibility to pancreatic RNase digestion (compare lanes f and g) proved that the hybridizing material was RNA. Apparent discrete transcripts between 359 and 718 nucleotides in length are visible in all four RNA preparations analyzed, and the transcripts from the dimeric pVB-6 cDNA were noticeably longer than those from the monomeric pGL101H-2 cDNA (compare lanes d and f). Transcripts having the polarity of PSTV (lanes d and f) were more abundant than transcripts of the opposite polarity (cPSTV, lanes e' and h'). *E. coli* clones harboring the pGL101H plasmids contained a higher concentration of PSTV-related RNA than the pBR322 recombinants (compare lanes d and f or lanes e and h), possibly indicating greater activity of the *lacUV5* promoter.

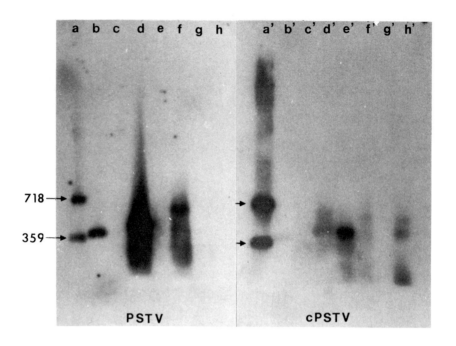

Figure 2. Analysis of 1M glyoxal-denatured, PSTV-related
RNAs isolated from *E. coli* C600 cells harboring recombinant
plasmids. (a & a') DNA size standards prepared by BamHI
digestion of pVB-6 DNA and a pVB-6 derivative whose central
BamHI site has been removed by bisulfite mutagenesis.(b & b')
0.25 µg total cellular RNA isolated from PSTV-infected tomato
leaf tissue. (c-h & c' -h')25 µg 2M LiCl-soluble RNA isolated
from *E. coli* clones harboring pBR322 (c & c'), pGL101H-2 (d
& d'), pGl01H-3 (e & e'), pVB-6 (f & f' and g & g'), and
pVB-8 (h & h'). RNAs in lanes g & g' were incubated with
40 µg/ml pancreatic RNase before denaturation and electrophoresis. Glyoxal-denatured RNAs were fractionated on 1.5%
agarose gels (Carmichael and McMaster 1980) and transferred
to nitrocellulose before hybridization analysis of PSTV-
related RNAs (Owens and Diener 1982). Strand-specific hybridization probes were complementary to nucleotides 105-146 of
PSTV or nucleotides 147-183 of cPSTV.

C. Infectivity Analyses

After constructing a series of recombinant plasmids
containing full-length monomeric and dimeric PSTV cDNA inserts and demonstrating that they are transcribed in *E.coli*
we asked the following question: Are the double-stranded
plasmid DNAs or their stable RNA transcripts which we can
extract from *E. coli* infectious when inoculated onto tomato

seedlings? Infectivity was assayed by the appearance of the characteristic disease symptoms (stunting and epinasty) and by nucleic acid spot hybridization analysis of leaf sap prepared from the bioassay plants (Owens and Diener 1981).

Table 1.
Infectivities of Cloned PSTV cDNAs

Clones	Length	Vector	Transcript Polarities	Infectivity DNA	RNA
pDC-29	336 nuc.	pBR322	both (unstable)	not done	0/1
pGL101H-3	359 nuc. monomer	pGL101H	cPSTV	0/1	not done
pGL101H-2	"	"	PSTV	0/2	1/2 [1/5]
pVB-1	"	pBR322	cPSTV	0/4	0/1
pVB-2	"	"	PSTV	0/4	0/2
pVB-8	718 nuc. dimer	"	cPSTV	2/2 [5/10-6/12]	0/2
pVB-6	"	"	PSTV	8/10 [1/5-9/10]	6/7 [1/6-9/10]

Infectivity values: Trials where infectivity was detected/ total trials. [ ] = Plants testing positive by hybridization/inoculated plants.
Inoculum concentrations: 200-1000 µg/ml plasmid DNA or 600-3000 µg/ml *E. coli* 2M LiCl-soluble RNA.

Table 1 summarizes the results obtained with five different PSTV cDNA clones and their corresponding RNA preparations. Infectivity of intact plasmid DNA was consistently observed for the dimeric cDNA clones pVB-6 and pVB-8, while no evidence was obtained for infectivity of any of the monomeric cDNA clones. Disease symptoms were almost always observed when positive hybridization results were obtained, indicating that the infection usually produced high titers of viroid progeny. PSTV could not be detected in the buffer-inoculated control plants included in each experiment.

Infectivity from the *E. coli* RNA preparations was observed for pVB-6, which produces transcripts with the polarity of PSTV, but not for pVB-8 which produces transcripts of the opposite polarity. Incubation [30 minutes at 37°C in the presence of 10 mM Tris-HCl(pH 7.5)-2 mM MgCl] with 40 µg/ml pancreatic RNase destroyed the infectivity of RNA prepared from *E. coli* cells containing plasmid pVB-6, but incubation with 50 µ g/ml pancreatic DNase had no effect. The only instance where RNA transcribed from a monomeric cDNA clone appeared to be infectious was pGL101H-2, a clone whose transcripts also have the polarity of PSTV. In this case only 1 of 5 inoculated plants in a single experiment contained PSTV progeny. The potential significance of this low level of infectivity will be discussed below.

Because the procedure used to isolate supercoiled plasmid DNAs from *E. coli* does not remove all traces of RNA contamination (data not shown), it was necessary to determine whether the infectivity observed with plasmid DNA could be due to the presence of low levels of a highly infectious RNA species. To test this possibility pVB-6 was digested with EcoRI plus SalI, enzymes which cleave the plasmid vector sequences outside the PSTV cDNA insert. A portion of this digest was incubated with 0.3N NaOH under conditions that would degrade any contaminating RNA and then renatured to recover the double-stranded EcoRI-SalI fragment containing the dimeric PSTV cDNA. The data presented in Table 2 show that the infectivity was not significantly affected by alkaline hydrolysis, indicating that the double-stranded DNA itself is infectious. This conclusion is further supported by experiments in which incubation with pancreatic RNAase had no effect on infectivity of intact plasmid DNA. Digestion with BamHI plus HaeIII leaves no intact PSTV cDNA and completely destroyed the infectivity of pVB-6 and pVB-8 DNAs.

Table 2.
Inactivation of infectious PSTV cDNAs.

DNA		Transcript Polarities	Infectivity	
None			0/6	
pVB-6:	EcoRI + SalI	PSTV	5/6	4/6
	EcoRI + SalI alkaline hydrolysis renaturation		2/6	3/6
pVB-6:	Untreated	PSTV	4/6	
	Pancreatic + T1 RNase		4/6	
	BamHI + HaeIII		0/6	
pVB-8:	Untreated	cPSTV	3/6	
	Pancreatic + T1 RNase		3/6	
	BamHI + HaeIII		0/6	

Infectivity values: Plants testing positive by hybridization/ inoculated plants.

Inoculum concentration: 1000 µg/ml plasmid DNA.

Pancreatic RNase digestion: 2 hours at 37°C in presence of 10 mM Tris-HC1, 1 mM EDTA (pH 8.0) containing 10 µg pancreatic RNase and 250 units/ml T1 RNase.

Restriction digestion: 2 hours at 37°C in presence of 35 mM Tris-acetate, 66 mM potassium acetate, 10 mM magnesium acetate, 0.5 mM DDT, and 100 µg/ml BSA (pH 7.9) containing

Table 2. continued

600 units/ml placental RNase inhibitor and 0.5-1.0 unit restriction enzymes/ μgDNA.
Alkaline hydrolysis: 14-16 hours at 37°C in presence of 0.3N NaOH.

D. Sequence Analysis of Viroid Progeny.

The infectivity of the recombinant DNAs was confirmed by direct RNA sequence analysis of viroid progeny extracted from the bioassay plants. Because the RNA sequence of the PSTV strain used as template for cDNA cloning has been shown to differ from that of the severe strain of PSTV which we now routinely propagate (Sänger 1982; J. Odell, personal communication), sequence analysis can be used to determine whether or not PSTV progeny are derived from the recombinant DNA inoculum.

Two methods were used to determine the nucleotide sequence of PSTV prepared from the bioassay plants. The sequence of selected regions was determined by partial enzymatic cleavage after preliminary fragmentation of purified PSTV with RNase U2 and 5' -terminal labelling by incubation with T4 polynucleotide kinase and [γ-^{32}P]ATP (Haseloff and Symons 1981). Complete RNA sequences were determined by base-specific modification and cleavage of PSTV cDNAs transcribed from 2 M LiCl-soluble RNA (Ghosh et al., 1980). Restriction fragments labelled at their 5' terminus and complementary to PSTV nucleotides 105-146 and 266-288 were used as primers for cDNA synthesis.

Fragment patterns in partial RNase U2 digests of severe strain PSTV and PSTV purified from tomatoes inoculated with pVB-6 DNA were consistent with the expected sequence differences, and fragments containing the region of interest were sequenced by base-specific partial enzymatic cleavage. PSTV isolated from plants inoculated with pVB-6 DNA contained the GAGCAGAAAG sequence (PSTV nucleotides 42-51) found in the cloned cDNA rather than the GACAAGAAAG sequence found in the PSTV severe strain which we now propagate.

The complete nucleotide sequence of the PSTV progeny, determined by base-specific chemical modification and cleavage of [5' -^{32}P] labelled cDNAs, was identical to the sequence of the cloned PSTV DNA. Particular attention in sequence analysis was devoted to PSTV sequences between nucleotides 43-53, 116-124, and 305-317, regions previously shown to vary in different naturally-occurring PSTV strains (reviewed by Sänger 1982)

III.   IMPLICATION FOR FUTURE RESEARCH

We have shown that inoculation of tomato seedlings with recombinant DNAs containing head-to-tail PSTV cDNA dimers results in the appearance of PSTV progeny with the RNA sequence predicted by the sequence of the cloned PSTV cDNA. *E. coli* cells harboring certain recombinant plasmids also contain infectious viroid RNA transcripts.   Plant viroids, therefore, join two single-stranded RNA viruses, bacteriophage Qβ (Taniguchi *et al.*, 1978) and poliovirus (Rancaniello and Baltimore 1981), as the third example where a cloned cDNA copy of an RNA genome is able to generate infectious RNA progeny after transfection into a host cell.   It is not known in detail how these cDNAs initiate the infection process, but there appear to be significant differences among the three systems.   Explanations for these differences may be important to future efforts to use infectious viroid cDNAs to study viroid structure-function relationships.

Although intact recombinant DNAs containing monomeric Qβ or polio-virus cDNA inserts are infectious, only DNAs containing a head-to-tail PSTV cDNA dimer were infectious in our studies.   The infectivity of head-to-tail dimers of PSTV could not be tested because plasmids containing long perfect palindromic sequences are not viable (Betz and Sandler 1981). Primary transcription of the Qβ or polio-virus cDNAs by host DNA-dependent RNA polymerase could initiate within either plasmid sequences or the adjacent homopolymeric "tails", but our full-length PSTV cDNA clones do not contain homopolymeric "tails".   Neither Qβ phage production (Taniguchi *et al.*, 1978) nor PSTV replication (Tables 1 and 2) depends upon orientation of the cDNA insert, arguing against the use of a promoter in the plasmid vector.   These two observations, an apparent requirement that the PSTV cDNA be present as a dimer and infectivity that is independent of insert orientation, suggest that either the DNA template for PSTV replication is generated by DNA recombination *in vivo* or that a longer than unit-length PSTV transcript is required to initiate the infection process.

At the present time, the first possibility seems more plausible for the recombinant DNAs of DNA plant viruses than for those of viroids.   While intact recombinant DNAs containing monomeric polyoma (Chan *et al.* 1979; Fried *et al.*, 1979), SV40 (Schaffner 1980), or cauliflower mosaic virus (CaMV) (Howell *et al.*, 1981;   Lebeurier *et al.*, 1982) DNA inserts were non-infectious, DNAs containing head-to-tail multimers (or partial multimers) were infectious.   Excision of monomeric circular viral DNAs from these multimers would allow replication to proceed by exactly the same mechanism used by conventional viral DNA.   However, neither healthy nor PSTV-infected tomato tissue contains DNA sequences complementary to PSTV (Branch and Dickson 1980;   Zaitlin *et al.*, 1980;

Hadidi *et al.*, 1981). Viroid replication involves RNA-RNA replicative intermediates (Grill and Semancik 1978), and it is
not immediately apparent why possible excision of a circular
double-stranded PSTV cDNA template should facilitate infectivity.
    The second potential explanation, a requirement for a
longer than unit-length PSTV transcript that undergoes cleavage and ligation to circular PSTV monomers in the tomato host
cell, seems more likely at this time. Head-to-tail dimers of
PSTV cDNA provide a potential template for synthesis of mul-
ltimeric PSTV transcripts; subsequent cleavage and ligation
would convert these transcripts to circular PSTV RNA within
the inoculated plant cells. Thereafter PSTV replication could
proceed by the normal RNA-directed RNA synthesis mechanism.
Available data concerning the infectivity of PSTVrelated RNAs
isolated from *E. coli* cells (Table 1) supports this conclusion
and, furthermore, indicates that the initial cDNA transcript
must contain the sequence of PSTV to initiate infection. RNA
prepared from clone pVB-8 contains only molecules complementary to PSTV and was not infectious.
    Two major questions must be answered before we can bring
the full power of "reverse genetics" to bear on the problem
of viroid structure-function relationships. First, we need
to unequivocally determine whether or not monomeric PSTV cDNA
is infectious.The apparent low level of infectivity observed
with` *E. coli* transcripts from the monomeric cDNA clone pGL101
H-2 (Table 1) suggests that DNAs containing non-duplicated
PSTV sequences might also be infectious.Experiments now in
progress to compare the infectivities of a series of purified
restriction fragments containing either monomeric or dimeric
PSTV cDNAs should answer this question.For obvious reasons,
site-specific *in vitro* mutagenesis of cloned PSTV cDNA monomers would be much simpler than mutagenesis of cDNA dimers.
    Second, we are examining the fate of the recombinant DNA
molecules used to inoculate the tomato plants. We have no
reason to expect that either the recombinant plasmid from
E. coli or a hypothetical monomeric circular PSTV cDNA generated by DNA recombination in the infected cell should replicate in tomato, but experimental evidence is required.
    An obvious goal in further studies with infectious PSTV
cDNAs will be to determine the effect of changes in specific
regions of the PSTV sequence upon viroid replication and/or
pathogenesis. We are using two different approaches to help
identify the relationship between viroid structure and function - traditional *in vitro* mutagenesis techniques for changing individual nucleotides in a given viroid as well as
replacement of entire regions of one viroid with corresponding regions from a second viroid. These approaches are

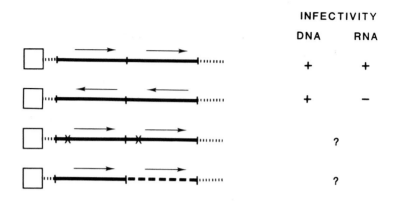

Figure 3. Alternative aproaches to *in vitro* mutagenesis of cloned viroid cDNA dimers. Double-stranded viroid cDNAs are shown as heavy solid or dashed lines with vertical marks indicating their BamHI termini; the arrows indicate the orientation of viroid DNA sequence with respect to the adjacent plasmid promoter (empty boxes). The head-to-tail viroid cDNA dimers shown in the first two lines correspond to PSTV cDNA clones pVB-6 and pVB-8. Sites where individual nucleotides in viroid cDNA dimer have been changed by *in vitro* mutagenesis are indicated by an"X"in the third line. The fourth line depicts the construction of mixed viroid cDNA dimers.

logical extensions of the work we have just described and complement comparative sequence analyses of naturally occuring viroids and viroid strains (reviewed by Sänger 1982). Sequence comparisons of PSTV strains which differ dramatically in symptom severity (reviewed by Sänger 1982) suggest that nucleotides near positions 45, 120, and 315 are involved in regulating symptom expression. Two other sequences (PSTV nucleotides 85-104 and 254-277) form the "central conserved region" found in all members of the PSTV viroid group as well as in CCCV. Sänger (1982) has proposed that this region could play an important role in replication, and at least two investigators (Diener 1981; Gross *et al.* 1982) have noted the extensive sequence homology between PSTV nucleotides 258-282 and the 5'-end of eukaryotic U1 RNA. Site-specific mutagenesis with sodium bisulfite (Shortle and Botstein 1983) or synthetic oligonucleotides (Zoller and Smith 1983) can be used to systematically investigate the relationship between individual nucleotides in these (or any other) regions of the viroid genome and viroid function.

A second type of *in vitro* genetic manipulation, replacement of entire regions of one viroid with the corresponding regions from a second viroid, is also possible. If

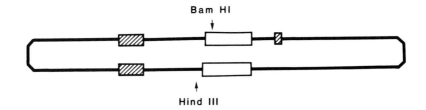

Bam HI

Hind III

Figure 4.   Schematic representation of the structure of a
PSTV group viroid.   A full-length viroid cDNA (solid line)
has been arranged in the same conformaton as the native viroid RNA.   The open boxes represent the sequences composing
the central conserved region, and the shaded boxes represent
portions of the PSTV sequence found to vary among different
strains.   All members of the PSTV group contain the GGAUCC
sequence necessary to form a BamHI recognition/cleavage site
in their cloned cDNAs and at least 5 of the 6 nucleotides
(AAGCUU) necessary to form a HindIII site.

a longer than unit-length viroid transcript is required to
initiate the infection process, inoculation of plants with a
mixed viroid cDNA dimer (Figure 3, bottom) may result in the
appearance of chimeric viroid progeny.   If certain viroid
cDNA monomers should prove infectious (see above), it is also
possible to construct chimeric cDNA monomers.
        Figure 4 shows that digestion of cloned viroid cDNAs
with BamHI and HindIII could be used to separate the less
stable but more homologous left halves of PSTV group members
from their more stable but more divergent right halves.   We
are currently constructing chimeric viroid cDNA monomers from
Bam-HindIII fragments of clones PSTV and TASV cDNAs.   Head-to
tail dimers of the chimeric cDNA monomers will also be
constructed.   If any of these chimeric cDNA prove infectious,
nucleotide sequence and physical-chemical analyses of the
progeny RNA will identify the relative contributions of
different viroid regions to such biological functions as
symptom expression and host range.

REFERENCES

Betz, J.L., and Sadler, J.R. (1981).   Variants of a cloned
        synthetic lactose operator.   I.A. Palindromic
        lactose operator derived from one strand of the
        cloned 40-base pair operator.   Gene *13*, 1-12.
Boege F., Rohde W., and Sänger, H.L. (1982).   *In vitro*
        transcription of viroid RNA into full length copies
        by RNA-dependent RNA polymerase from healthy tomato
        leaf tissue.   *Biosci. Rep. 2*, 185-194.

Branch, A.D., and Dickson, E. (1980). Tomato DNA contains no
    detectable regions complementary to potato spindle
    tuber viroid as assayed by southern hybridization.
    Virology 104, 10–26.
Branch, A.D., and Robertson, H.D. (1983). A model for the
    replication of small pathogenic RNA molecules
    in plant cells. In "Plant Infectious Agents––
    Viruses, Viroids. Virusoids, and Satellites" (H.D.
    Robertson, S.H.Howell, M.Zaitlin, and R.L.Malmberg,
    eds.),pp. 141–148. Cold Spring Harbor Laboratory,
    New York.
Branch, A.D., Robertson, H.D., and Dickson, E. (1981).
    Longer–than–unit–length viroid minus strands are
    present in RNA from infected plants. *Proc. Natl.
    Acad. Sci. U.S.A. 78*, 6381–6385.
Branch, A.D., Robertson, H.D., Greer, C., Gegenheimer, P.,
    Peebles, C., and Abelson, J.(1982). Cell–free
    circularization of viroid progeny RNA by an RNA
    ligase from wheat germ. *Science 217*, 1147–1149.
Camacho Henriquez, A., and Sänger,H.L. (1982a). Analysis
    of acid–extractable tomato leaf proteins after
    infection with a viroid, two viruses and a fungus
    and partial purification of the "pathogenesis-
    related" protein p 14. *Arch. Virol. 74*, 167–180.
Camacho Henriques, A., and Sänger, H.L. (1982b). Gel electro-
    phoretic analysis of phenol–extractable leaf pro-
    teins from different viroid/host combinations.
    Arch. Virol. 74, 181–196.
Chan, H.W., Israel, M.A., Garon, C.E., Rowe, W.P., and
    Martin, M.A. (1979). Molecular cloning of polyoma
    virus DNA in *Escherichia coli:* Lambda phage vector
    system. *Science 203*, 887–891.
Conejero, V., Picazo, I., and Segado, P. (1979). Citrus exo-
    cortis viroid (CEV): Protein alterations in dif-
    ferent hosts following viroid infection.
    Virology 97, 454–456.
Dickson, E. (1981). A model for the involvement of viroids
    in RNA splicing. *Virology 115*, 216–221.
Dickson, E., Robertson, H.D., Niblett, C.L., Horst, R.K.,
    and Zaitlin, M. (1979). Minor differences between
    nucleotide sequences of mild and severe strains of
    potato spindle tuber viroid. *Nature 277*, 60–62.
Diener, T.O. (1979a). Viroids: Structure and function.
    Science 205, 859–866.
Diener, T.O. (1979b). Viroids and viroid diseases. Wiley
    and Sons, New York.
Diener, T.O. (1981a). Are viroids escaped introns? *Proc.
    Natl. Acad. Sci. U.S.A. 78*, 5014–5015.
Flores, R. and Semancik, J.S. (1982). Properties of a cell-
    free system for synthesis of citrus exocortis vi-
    roid. *Proc. Natl. Acad. Sci. U.S.A. 79*, 6285–6288.

Fried, M., Klein, B., Murray, K., Greenaway, P., Tooze, J.,
    Boll, W., and Weissmann, C. (1979). Infectivity in
    mouse fibroblasts of polyoma DNA integrated into
    plasmid pBR322 or lambdoid phage DNA. *Nature 279,
    London* 811-816.
Ghosh, P.K., Reddy, V.B., Piatak, M., Lebowitz, P. and
    Weissman, S.M. (1980). Determination of RNA
    sequences by primer directed synthesis and sequenc-
    ing of their cDNA transcripts. In "Methods in
    Enzymology" (L. Grossman and K. Moldave, eds.) Vol.
    65, pp. 580-595. Academic Press, New York.
Grill,L.K. and Semancik, J.S. (1978). RNA sequences com-
    plementary to citrus exocortis viroid in nucleic
    acid preparations from infected *Gynura aurantiaca*.
    Proc. Natl. Acad. Sci. U.S.A. 75, 896-900.
Grill, L.K., Negruk, V.I., and Semancik, J.S. (1980). Proper-
    ties of the complementary RNA sequences associated
    with infection by the citrus exocortis viroid.
    Virology 107, 25-33.
Gross, H.J., Domdey, H., Lossow, C., Jank, P., Raba, M.,
    Albert, H., and Sänger, H.L.(1978). Nucleotide
    sequence and secondary structure of potato spindle
    tuber viroid. *Nature (London) 273*, 203-208.
Gross, H.J., Liebl, U., Alberty, H., Krupp, G., Domdey, H.,
    Ramm, K., and Sänger, H.L.(1981). A severe and a
    mild potato spindle tuber viroid isolate differ in
    3 nucleotide exchanges only. *Biosci. Rep. 1*, 235-
    241.
Gross, H.J., Krupp, G., Domdey, H., Raba, M., Alberty, H.,
    Lossow, C.H., Ramm, K. and Sänger, H.L. (1982).
    Nucleotide sequence and secondary structure of cit-
    rus exocortis and chrysanthemum stunt viroid.
    Eur. J. Biochem. 121, 249-257.
Hadidi, A., Cress,D.E., and Diener, T.O. (1981). Nuclear
    DNA from uninfected or potato spindle tuber viroid-
    infected tomato plants contains no detectable se-
    quences complementary to cloned double-stranded vi-
    roid cDNA. *Proc.Nat.Acad.Sci. U.S.A. 78*, 6932-6935.
Haseloff, J. and Symons, R.H. (1981). Chrysanthemum stunt
    viroid-primary sequence and secondary structure.
    Nucl. Acids Res. 9, 2741-2752.
Haseloff, J., Mohamed, N.A., and Symons, R.H. (1982).
    Viroid RNAs of the cadang-cadang disease of coco-
    nuts. *Nature (London) 299*, 316-322.
Henco, K., Sänger, H.L., and Riesner, D. (1979). Fine struc-
    ture melting of viroids as studied by kinetic meth-
    ods. *Nucl. Acids Res. 6*, 3041-3059.
Howell, S.H., Walker,L.L., and Walden, R.M. (1981). Rescue

of *in vitro* generated mutants of cloned cauliflower mosaic virus genome in infected plants. *Nature (London) 293,* 483-486.

Kiefer, M.C., Owens, R.A., and Diener, T.O. (1983). Structural similarities between viroids and transposable genetic elements. *Proc. Natl. Acad. Sci.U.S.A. 80,* 6234-6238.

Kikuchi, Y., Tyc, K.,Filipowicz, W., Sänger, H.L. and Gross, H.J. (1982). Circularization of linear viroid RNA via 2'-phosphomonoester, 3',5'-phosphodiester bonds by a novel type of RNA ligase from wheat germ and *Chlamydomonas. Nucl.Acids Res. 10,* 7521-7529.

Kiss, T. and Solymosy F.(1982).Sequence homologies between a viroid and a small nuclear RNA (snRNA) species of mammalian origin. *FEBS Lett. 144,* 318-320.

Kruger, K., Grabowski,P. J., Zaug, A. J., Sands, J.,Gottschling, D. E., and Cech, T. R. (1982). Self-splicing RNA: Autoexcision and autocyclization of the ribosomal RNA intervening sequences of *Tetrahymena. Cell 31,* 147-157.

Lebeurier, G., Hirth, L, Hahn, B., and Hohn, T. (1982). *In vivo* recombination of cauliflower mosaic virus DNA. *Proc. Natl. Acad. Sci. U.S.A. 79,* 2932-29 36.

Mühlbach, H-P., and Sänger, H.L.(1979). Viroid replication is inhibited by α-amanitin. *Nature (London) 278,* 185-188.

Owens, R. A. and Cress, D.E. (1980). Molecular cloning and characterization of potato spindle tuber viroid cDNA sequences. *Proc. Natl. Acad. Sci. U.S.A. 77,* 5302-5306.

Owens, R.A. and Diener, T.O. (1977). Synthesis of RNA complementary to potato spindle tuber viroid using Qβ replicase. *Virology 79,* 109-120.

Owens, R.A. and Diener, T.O. (1981). Sensitive and rapid diagnosis of potato spindle tuber viroid disease by nucleic acid hybridization. *Science, 213,* 670-672.

Owens, R.A. and Diener, T.O. (1982). RNA intermediates in potato spindle tuber viroid replication. *Proc. Natl. Acad. Sci. U.S.A. 79,* 113-117.

Palukaitis, P. and Zaitlin, M. (1983). The nature and biological significance of linear potato spindle tuber viroid molecules. In "Plant Infectious Agents--Viruses, Viroids, Virusoids, and Satellites" (H. D. Robertson, S. H. Howell, M. Zaitlin, and R. L. Malmberg, eds.) pp. 136-140. Cold Spring Harbor Laboratory, New York.

Racaniello, V.R. and Baltimore, D. (1981). Cloned poliovirus complementary DNA is infectious in mammalian
cells. *Science 214*, 916-919.

Rackwitz, H. R., Rohde, W. and Sänger, H.L. (1981). DNA-
dependent RNA polymerase II of plant origin transcribes viroid RNA into full-length copies. *Nature
(London) 291*, 136-144.

Randles, J.W., Steger, G. and Riesner, D. (1982). Structural transitions in viroid-like RNAs associated
with cadang-cadang disease, velvet tobacco mottle
virus, and *Solanum nodiflorum* mottle virus. *Nuc.
Acids Res. 10*, 5569-5586.

Riesner, D. Henco, K., Rokohl, U., Klotz, G., Kleinschmidt,
A.K., Gross, H. J., Domdey, H., and Sänger,H.L.
(1979). Structure and structure formation of
viroids. *J. Mol. Biol. 133*, 85-115.

Rohde, W. and Sänger, H.L. (1981). Detection of complementary RNA intermediates of viroid replication by
northern blot hybridization. *Biosci. Rep. 1*,
327-336.

Rohde, W., Rackwitz, H-R., Boege, F., and Sänger, H.L.
(1982). Viroid RNA is accepted as a template for
in vitro transcription by DNA-dependent DNA polymerase I and RNA polymerase from *Escherichia coli*.
Biosci. Rep. 2, 929-939.

Sänger, H.L. (1982). Biology, structure, functions, and
possible origin of viroids. In "Encyclopedia of
Plant Physiology New Series" (B. Parthier and
D. Boulter, eds.) volume 14B, pp. 368-454.
Springer-Verlag, Berlin.

Schaffner, W. (1980). Direct transfer of cloned genes from
bacteria to mammalian cells. *Proc. Natl. Acad.
U.S.A. 77*, 2163-2167.

Semancik, J.S. and Desjardins, P.R. (1980). Multiple small
RNA species and the viroid hypothesis for the sunblotch disease of avocado. *Virology 104*, 117-121.

Shortle, D. and Botstein, D. (1983). Directed mutagenesis
with sodium bisulfite. In "Methods in Enzymology"
(R. Wu, L. Grossman, and K. Moldave, eds.) Vol.
100, pp. 457-468. Academic Press, New York.

Symons, R.H. (1981). Avocado sunblotch viroid - primary sequence and proposed secondary structure. *Nucl.
Acids Res. 9*, 6527-6537.

Taniguchi, R., Palmieri, M., and Weissmann, C. (1978).
DNA-containing hybrid plasmids giving rise to Qβ
phage formation in the bacterial host. *Nature
(London) 274*, 223-228.

Visvader, J. E., Gould, A.R., Bruening, G. E., and Symons, R.H. (1982). Citrus exocortis viroid-nucleotide-sequence and socondary structure of an Australian isolate. *FEBS Lett. 137,* 288-292.

Zaitlin, M. (1979). How viruses and viroids induce disease. In "Plant Disease, An Advanced Treatise" (J.G. Horsfall and E.B. Cowling, eds.) Vol IV, pp. 257-271. Academic Press, New York.

Zaitlin, M., Niblett, C.L., Dickson, E., and Goldberg, R.B. (1980). Tomato DNA contains no detectable regions complementary to potato spindle tuber viroid as assayed by solution and filter hybridization. *Virology 104,* 1-9.

Zimmern, D. (1982). Do viroids and RNA viruses derive from a system that exchange genetic information between eukaryotic cells. *Trends Biochem. Sci.7,* 205-207.

Zoller, M. J. and Smith, M. (1983). Oligonucleotide-directed mutagenesis of DNA fragments cloned into M13 vectors. In "Methods in Enzymology" (R. Wu, L. Grossman, and K. Moldave, eds.) Vol. *100,* pp. 468-500. Academic Press, New York.

PART IV
Subviral Pathogens of Animals

Chapter 16

PRIONS--STRUCTURE, BIOLOGY, AND DISEASES

Stanley B. Prusiner, Darlene F. Groth,
David C. Bolton, Karen A. Bowman,
S. Patricia Cochran, Paul E. Bendheim,
and Michael P. McKinley

Departments of Neurology
and Biochemistry and Biophysics
University of California
San Francisco, California

INTRODUCTION

Most of our knowledge about the molecular structure of prions has been derived from experimental studies on the scrapie agent. The unusual biological properties of the scrapie agent were evident even before there was an interest in its chemical and physical structure; the infectious agent caused a devastating degeneration of the central nervous system (CNS) in the absence of an inflammatory response (Beck *et al.*, 1964; Kasper *et al.*, 1981; Zlotnik, 1962). Although the immune system appeared to remain intact, its surveillance mechanisms were unaware of a raging infection. Early studies showed that the scrapie agent was resistant to formalin and heat(Gordon, 1946). The agent achieved status as a scientific curiosity when its extreme resistance to ionizing and ultraviolet (UV) irradiation was discovered (Alper *et al.*, 1966, 1967).

Portions of this chapter are taken from an article entitled "Prions – Novel Infectious Pathogens" by Stanley B. Prusiner to be published in *Advances in Virus Research*.

Copyright © 1985 by Academic Press, Inc.
All rights of reproduction in any form reserved.
ISBN 0-12-470230-9

The use of sheep and goats to bioassay samples containing the scrapie agent greatly hampered early attempts to
separate or purify the agent away from tissue elements (Pattison and Millson, 1960). A whole herd of animals was needed
to determine the titer of a single sample. In addition,
highly susceptible breeds of sheep gave inconsistant data.
Goats were much better hosts for scrapie infection since they
exhibited much more uniform susceptibility. A more promising
bioassay was developed in 1961 based on the observation that
scrapie could be transmitted to mice (Chandler, 1961). For
nearly two decades, the accepted bioassay for a single sample
containing the scrapie agent required that 50 to 60 inoculated mice be held for as long as 12 months prior to final
scoring of an endpoint titration. As early as 1963, an
alternative bioassay using incubation period measurements was
suggested (Eklund *et al.*, , 1963; Hunter *et al.*, 1963).
Although several investigators reported such measurements,
the method remained unexploited for many years.

Five years ago, we developed a bioassay for the scrapie
agent employing incubation period measurements (Prusiner *et
al.*, 1980d, 1982b). The hamster was used because it had
been reported that these animals developed scrapie twice as
fast as mice and the titers of the agent in their brains were
10- to 100-fold higher (Marsh and Kimberlin, 1975). An
objective, manageable bioassay was devised by measuring both
the time intervals from inoculation to onset of illness and
from inoculation to death. Although still cumbersome, extremely costly and quite slow, the incubation time interval
assay represents a significant improvement over the older
methods. It has permitted substantial progress to be made in
the last five years.

At present, we know that the scrapie agent contains a
protein which is required for its infectivity (Prusiner *et
al.*, 1981b). Hydrolytic degradation of protein catalyzed by proteases, reversible chemical modification by diethylpyrocarbonate (DEP) and denaturation by four different
types of reagents all led to a diminution of scrapie infectivity (McKinley *et al.*, 1981;Prusiner,1982;Prusiner *et al.*,
1981b). Recently, a protein has been identified by radioiodination and electrophoresis through sodium dodecyl sulfate
(SDS) polyacrylamide gels (Bolton *et al.*, 1982; Prusiner *et
al.*, 1982a). It is an unusual protein, designated PrP, in
that it exhibits size microheterogeneity and is resistant to
digestion by proteases.The resistance to hydrolysis catalyzed
by proteases disappears when the native protein is denatured.

Attempts to demonstrate a nucleic acid within the scrapie agent have been unsuccessful (Prusiner, 1982). In addition, size estimates of the infectious agent suggest that it
is probably too small to contain even a single gene. Even

though the possibility of a small nucleic acid within the core of the scrapie agent cannot be excluded at present, the unusual properties of the agent seem to distinguish it from both viruses and viroids. These unusual properties and the discovery of a protein within the infectious scrapie agent prompted us to introduce a new term for this class of infectious pathogens. They are called "prions".

Earlier studies by other investigators showed that humans develop two scrapie-like diseases: kuru and Creutzfeldt-Jakob disease (CJD) (Gajdusek, 1977). In this review, we discuss the properties of the scrapie prion and its relationship to the infectious agents causing other apparently similar diseases.

II.   TERMINOLOGY

More than two score years ago, Greig called attention to the unusual and elusive aspects of scrapie when writing about the various names that had been used to describe this disorder (Greig, 1940). He wrote:

"The nature of the disease to which the name 'scrapie' is usually applied has long remained obscure. It is perhaps for this reason that the names by which the disease is known are colloquial in character and refer to certain of its more outstanding symptoms, particularly the persistent itch and the disturbances in gait; thus, in England it was known as rubbers, the goggles; in Scotland as scrapie, cuddy trot, and yeuky pine; in France it is named la tremblante (the trembles); and in Germany it is referred to as Gnubber Krankheit (itching disease) and Traber Krankheit (trotting disease)".

Studies over the last 20 years have shown that the molecular properties of the infectious agent causing scrapie are different from those of both viruses and viroids (Prusiner, 1982). Because of these differences, the term "prion" was introduced to denote this novel class of infectious pathogens. The word, prion, was derived from *prot*einaceous and *inf*ectious because the first macromolecule to be identified within the scrapie agent was a protein (Prusiner, 1982). The definition of a prion must remain operational until its entire structure is known: "prions are small proteinaceous infectious particles which are resistant to inactivation by most procedures that modify nucleic acids" (Prusiner, 1982). At present, we still do not know if the prion contains a nucleic acid. It is unlikely that prions contain genes coding for their proteins; however, the presence of a small nucleic acid or oligonucleotide within the interior of the prion has not been excluded. Certainly if prions are comprised of protein alone or a nucleoprotein complex with a polynucleotide too small to code for the prion protein, these features will distinguish them from viruses (Prusiner, 1982).

A protein of M_r 27,000-30,000 is a structural macromolecule within the prion and is denoted by the symbol, PrP, from *prion protein* (McKinley *et al.*, 1983). This terminology is analogous to that used for structural *viral proteins* denoted VP.

Genetic loci controlling the incubation periods in sheep and mice have been found. In sheep the alleles of this locus have been termed SIP from *short incubation period* and LIP from *long incubation period* (Dickinson, 1976). Two and perhaps three loci in mice have been discovered. The first was called SINC from *scrapie incubation* (Dickinson and Meikle, 1969). The second locus to be described has been found for both scrappie and CJD in mice; it is called PID-1 from *prion incubation determinant* (Kingsbury *et al.*, 1983). At present, it is unclear whether or not a third locus exists which is sex-linked.

An additional note concerns the term "incubation time interval assay" (Prusiner *et al.*, 1982b). Although the use of incubation period measurements for determining viral or prion titers is not new, the methodology that we have employed to determine the titer of the infectious agent was sufficiently different to require a new terminology.

III. PRION DISEASES

Six diseases, three of animals and three of humans, are probably caused by prions. The slow infectious agents causing transmissible mink encephalopathy (TME), chronic wasting disease (CWD), kuru, CJD, and Gerstmann-Sträussler syndrome (GSS) are not well characterized; thus, further knowledge about the properties of these infectious agents must be obtained before they can be firmly classified as prions (Gajdusek, 1977: Hartsough and Burger, 1965; Masters *et al.*, 1981; Williams and Young, 1980).

All of these transmissible diseases share many features and are confined to the CNS. Prolonged incubation periods ranging from two months to more than two decades have been observed (Sigurdsson 1954). The clinical course in prion diseases is usually rather stereotyped and progresses to death. The clinical phase of prion illnesses may last for periods ranging from a few weeks to a few years. A reactive astrocytosis is found throughout the CNS in all these diseases (Beck *et al.*, 1964; Zlotnik, 1962). Neuronal vacuolation is also found, but it is not a constant or obligatory feature. The infectious agents or prions causing these diseases possess unusual molecular properties that distinguish them from both viruses and viroids (Prusiner, 1982).

IV. ASSAYS FOR SCRAPIE PRIONS

At present, the only methods for measuring scrapie prion infectivity remain the incubation time interval assay and the endpoint titration. Both methods are extremely slow because they require waiting for the onset of clinical neurological dysfunction following a prolonged incubation period.

The length of the incubation period varies greatly with the animal species, route of inoculation and dose of prions. Clearly, the hamster inoculated intracerebrally with a high doses (10^7 ID_{50} units) has the shortest incubation period. Thus, it is the preferred animal for scrapie research.

A.   Endpoint Titration

An endpoint titration for the scrapie prion is performed by serially diluting a sample at 10-fold increments (Prusiner *et al.*, 1978a). Each dilution is typically inoculated intracerebrally into six mice and the waiting process ensues. Since the highest dilutions at which scrapie develops are the only observations of interest, frequently 12 months passed before the titration was scored. From the score at the highest positive dilutions, a titer or concentration of infectious agent in the original sample can be calculated. Not only are the resources great with respect to animals and time, but pipetting 10 serial 10-fold dilutions can create additional problems with the accuracy of the measurements. Because of the increased cost, only limited numbers of endpoint titrations have been performed in hamsters. Five to six months passed before the titration in hamsters was scored.

B.   Incubation Time Interval Assay

The incubation time interval assay reduces the number of animals, the time required for bioassay and potential pipetting errors compared to the endpoint titration (Prusiner *et al.*, 1980d, 1982b). With hamsters, studies on the scrapie agent have been dramatically accelerated by development of a bioassay based on measurements of incubation time (Prusiner *et al.*, 1980d, 1982b). It is now possible to assay samples with the use of four animals in 60 to 70 days if the titers of the scrapie agent in the sample are high. As shown in Fig. 1, the interval from inoculation to onset of illness (y) was inversely proportional to the dose injected intracerebrally into random bred weanling Syrian hamsters. The logarithm of the mean interval ($\bar{y}$) in days minus a time factor of 40 is a linear function of the logarithm of the dose over a wide range; the time factor was determined by maximizing the linear relation between the time interval and dose. With a factor of 40, the regression coefficient of the line is 0.87. A similar analysis was performed for the time interval from inoculation to death (z). With a time factor of 61, the regression coefficient of the line is 0.86 (Fig. 1A).

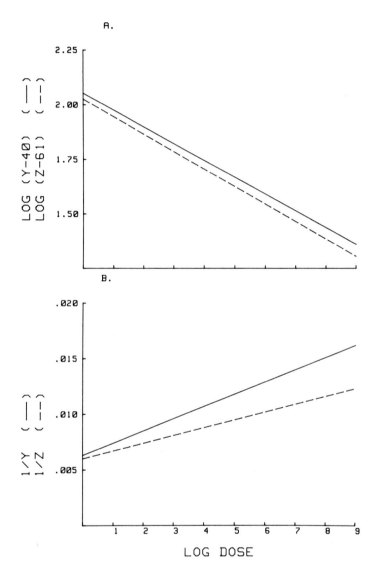

Fig. 1. Bioassay of the scrapie prion by incubation time interval measurements. Linear relationships were obtained by plotting (A) logarithm of time intervals minus a time factor as function of logarithm of dose and (B) reciprocal of time intervals as a function of logarithm of dose. The time interval for inoculation to onset of illness is denoted by Y and from inoculation to death by Z.

Equations were written to describe these linear functions which relate the titer of the inoculum to the time intervals both from inoculation to onset of illness (Eq. 1) and from inoculation to death (Eq. 2):

$$\text{Log } T_y = 26.66 - (12.99) \log (y - 40) - \log D \quad (1)$$
$$\text{Log } T_y = 25.33 - (12.47) \log (z - 61) - \log D \quad (2)$$

where T is the titer expressed in ID_{50} units per milliliter, D is the dilution defined as the fractional concentration of the diluted sample, y is the mean interval from inoculation to onset of clinical illness in days, and z is the mean interval from inoculation to death in days. The most precise estimate of titer is obtained by calculating a weighted average for T_y and T_z.

Linear relationships were also obtained when the reciprocals of the time intervals were plotted as a function of the logarithm of the dose (Fig. 1B).

A comparison of the endpoint titration and incubation time interval assay is shown in Table I. The economics of

Table I
Comparison of Bioassays for the Scrapie Prion

	Endpoint Titration	Incubation Time Interval
Rodent species	Mice	Hamsters
Time (days)	360	60–70
Animals (no.)	60	4
Sample dilution	10^{-1} to 10^{-10}	10^{-1}

both time and resources afforded by the incubation time interval assay are highly significant. We estimate that our research has been accelerated more than 100-fold by the incubation time interval assay. It is doubtful that the purification and characterization studies described below could have been performed using the endpoint titration method to assay the samples.

C.   Radiolabelling of Scrapie PrP

While the incubation time interval assay has been the cornerstone of our work to date, we are beginning to use radiolabelling of PrP as an indicator for the presence of the scrapie agent. As described in Section X.D., evidence that PrP is part of the scrapie prion is now compelling. A simple procedure for determining the presence and amount of PrP involves: radiolabelling the purified native protein (PrP) with [^{125}I]–Bolton–Hunter reagent, digesting it with protein-ase K for 30 to 60 mins. at 37°C, and then denaturing it pri-or to electrophoresis on a 15% polyacrylamide gel. The amount of. PrP can be quantitated by densitometric scanning of autoradiograms produced from the polyacrylamide gels. Pre-sumably, the production of antibodies to PrP in the future will allow the development of a rapid immunoassay which will replace measurements of PrP using gel electrophoresis.

V.   PATHOGENESIS

The pathogenesis of scrapie in mice, goats and sheep has been studied extensively. In general, the highest titers of the scrapie prion early during the course of infection are found in lymphoid tissue (Eklund *et al.* , 1967;   Hadlow *et al.* 1974, 1980). The concentration of the prion in lymphoid tissues such as spleen and lymph nodes plateaus relatively early at a level 10- to 100-fold below that eventually reach-ed in the brain. Hadlow and his colleagues suggest that ini-tial infection occurs through the lymphoid system with subse-quent spread to the CNS when a peripheral route of inocula-tion is used. While all of the data obtained by animal bioassays is consistent with this view,further technological developments in the assay of prions are required before firm knowledge about the spread of scrapie can be ascertained. We do not know if replication of prions actually occurs in lymphoid tissue or they simply accumulate there after export from another tissue. We have virtually no information about which lymphoid cell type(s) contain prions.

Several investigators have tried to study the spread of the scrapie and CJD agents in experimental rodent models. Evidence for spread of scrapie prions along peripheral nerves and CNS fiber tracts has been reported (Fraser, 1982; Kimberlin and Walker, 1979, 1980;   Kimberlin *et al.*, 1983). However, the lack of sensitive histological techniques for detecting prions makes the interpretation of these data difficult. After intravenous inoculation of mice with the scrapie agent ($10^{6.3}$ ID$_{50}$ units), the prion concentration decreased rapidly with a $t_{1/2}$ of 5.2 mins (Hotchin *et al.*, 1983). The CJD agent has been detected in the buffy coat of guinea pigs indicating a blood-borne route for the spread of the agent (Manuelidis *et al.*,1978).

The brain, spinal cord and eye are the only tissues in which high titers of the prion are found and pathological changes are observed (Baringer *et al.*, 1981). Both scrapie and CJD are pure neurological disorders - no symptoms referrable to organs outside the CNS are observed. Thus, the clinical presentation of these illnesses is consistent with their pathologies. Why the scrapie and CJD agents accumulate most extensively in the CNS is unknown. How prions cause vacuolation of neurons and stimulate astrocytic proliferation is also unknown. We do not even know in which cells of the CNS prions multiply.

Recent studies on the pathogenesis of scrapie in hamsters show that after intracerebral inoculation with 10 ID_{50} units, the animals are free of symptoms for more than 50 days (Baringer *et al.*, 1981). However, by 48 days, the titers of the scrapie prion in all regions of brain and spinal cord are maximal. At this time, virtually no pathological changes are evident. By 60 days after inoculation, the animals showed clear signs of neurological dysfunction. During the ensuing 10 to 15 days, the animals demonstrated a progression of their neurological symptoms followed by death. Animals sacrificed at 71 days showed extensive pathological changes, but titers of the prion remained the same as those found at 48 days. From these results, we are forced to conclude that prion replication precedes the pathologic process since the prion titer reaches a maximum before clinical signs and pathologic changes become evident. Thus, the trigger for development of neuronal dysfunction is unknown.

Recently, the $[^{14}C]$-2-deoxyglycose (2-DG) autoradiographic technique for measuring regional cerebral metabolism (Sokoloff *et al.*, 1977) has been applied to studies on the pathogenesis of scrapie. Hamsters were inoculated in the striatum or substantia nigra with 10^4 ID_{50} units using a stereotactic apparatus. Fifty to sixty days after inoculation and 3 to 4 weeks prior to the onset of clinical signs, autoradiographs showed diminished glucose metabolism in the thalamus, medial geniculate bodies and inferior colliculi (Gregoire *et al.*, 1983a, 1983b). The authors suggest that temporal changes in 2-DG metabolism reflect the spread of the scrapie agent within the brain; however, they present no infectivity data to support this hypothesis.

A. Lack of Immune Response

One of the fascinating aspects of scrapie and CJD pathogenesis is the lack of an immune response throughout the courses of these illnesses. The infectious scrapie prion apparently replicates in both the lymphoid system and the CNS without any host inflammatory response. The infection is so devastating that it causes widespread destruction of the CNS and kills the animal. Why there is no inflammatory response is unknown. Numerous attempts to demonstrate anti-scrapie antibodies have all been unsuccessful, to date (Table II). The lack of an immune response is all the more puzzling since

Table II
Attempts to Demonstrate Anti-Scrapie Antibodies

Serological Technique	Antigen Preparation	Reference
Neutraliz- ation	Brain suspension	Pattison *et al.*, 1964; Clarke and Haig,1966; Gibbs *et al.*, 1965; Gibbs, 1967; Gardash'yan *et al.* 1971
	Freon-clarified brain	Porter *et al.*, 1973
Precipitation	Brain cerebrospinal fluid	Chandler, 1959
	Cerebrospinal fluid	Moulton and Palmer,1959
	Spleen homogenate	Gardiner, 1965
	Brain suspension	Gibbs *et al.*, 1965
Complement- fixation	Spleen extract	Chandler, 1959
	Brain extract	Chandler, 1959
	Brain suspension	Gibbs *et al.*, 1965;
Gardash'yan	1971	*et al.*,
Immunofluor- escence	Brain section	Moulton and Palmer, 1959
	Brain suspension	Gibbs *et al.*, 1965
	Monolayer from brain explant cultures	Porter *et al.*, 1973
Anti-nuclear body	DNA *(E. coli)* RNA (virus)	Cunnington *et al.*, 1976
Passive hemmag- glutination	Cerebrospinal fluid Brain extract	Chandler, 1959
Passive hemolysis	Brain extract	Chandler, 1959
Passive anaphylaxis	Cerebrospinal Fluid	Chandler, 1959
Immuno- conglutinin	Brain or spleen extracts	Chandler, 1959
Anti- cardiolipin	Cardiolipin	Chandler, 1959
ELISA	Fraction E_6	Kasper *et al.*, 1981,1982

the prion is known to contain an M_r 27,000 − 30,000 protein (PrP). Perhaps PrP is an extremely poor antigen, presumably due to its hydrophobicity and binding of phospholipids. Alternatively, PrP may share a sufficient number of antigenic determinants with normal cellular proteins rendering the host tolerant to it. Or perhaps, the prion selectively shuts off a group of lymphoid cells that could potentially respond to its presence. Only future studies will distinguish between these possibilities.

Multiple attempts to produce antibodies to PrP in mice have failed (Bendheim *et al.*, unpublished observations).

Denatured preparations of PrP alone or coupled to either azobenzenearsonate or keyhole limpet hemocyanin have failed to elicit the production of antibodies. Thus, PrP and the prion display a similar lack of immunogenicity.

In many but not all sheep with scrapie, an IgG2 fraction has been reported to be elevated in both sera and cerebrospinal fluid (DSF) (Collis and Kimberlin, 1983). Since not all the animals with scrapie showed this elevation of IgG2, either it is not an obligatory change or the rise in IgG2 was too brief to be detected in all cases. The elevated IgG2 values in the CSF appear to arise by passive filtration of the molecules from blood rather than IgG2 synthesis within the CNS.

Recent observations show that a gene within the major histocompatibility comples (HMC) of the mouse controls the length of incubation period in experimental CJD and probably in scrapie (Kingsbury *et al.*, 1983) (Section VI.C.). Modulation of prion diseases by a gene in the MHC was unexpected since prions replicate and cause disease in the absence of any detectable immune response. It is well documented that the courses of many viral illnesses are modified by the MHC (Klein, 1975).

B. Amyloid Plaques

There continues to be considerable interest about the amyloid plaques found in prion diseases. The CNS of animals with scrapie, CWD and experimental CJD, as well as humans with kuru, CJD and GSS, have been observed to contain collections of amyloid (Bahmanjar *et al.*, personal communication; Beck and Daniel, 1979; Beck *et al.*, 1964; Bruce and Fraser, 1975, 1982; Field *et al.*, 1967a; Fraser and Bruce, 1973; Moretz *et al.*, 1983, Wisniewski *et al.*, 1975, 1981). These amyloid plaques stain with Congo red or trichrome. Presumably, the amyloid is composed of immunoglobulin light chains, but there is no direct experimental evidence supporting this hypothesis.

Isolates of the scrapie agent (87A and 87V) injected in VM mice have been reported to produce large numbers of amyloid plaques (Bruce and Fraser, 1982). Such plaques have been reported in the brains of sheep and goats with scrapie as well as in the brains of NIH-Swiss Webster mice after primary transmission of scrapie from sheep (Fukatsu *et al.*, 1983). Recent studies show that the majority of cases with CWD exhibit significant numbers of amyloid plaques (Bahmanjar *et al.*, personal communication). Mice with experimental CJD exhibit amyloid plaques, but the plaques disappear upon second passage of the agent in mice (Tateishi, in press).

The majority of cases of kuru show plaques which are presumably comprised of amyloid within their cores (Beck and Daniel, 1979). The kuru plaques differ from senile plaques in that senile plaques have a collection of amorphous material, presumably degenerating dendrites, around their amyloid core. The kuru plaques do not possess such a large halo. Both kuru and senile plaques have been reported in CJD, but they are not a constant feature of the disease (Chou and Martin, 1971; Yagishita, 1981). Kuru plaques do seem to be a constant feature of GSS (Masters *et al.*, 1981; Seitelberger, 1981).

The senile plaques seen in CJD are similar to those found in aged animals and humans, as well as in patients with the presenile and senile forms of Alzheimer's disease (Divry, 1934; Terry and Wisniewski, 1970; Wilcock and Esiri, 1982; Wisniewski *et al.*, 1983). The role of senile plaques in the pathogenesis of Alzheimer's disease remains to be established. Obvious amyloid plaques are a variable and nonobligatory feature of prion diseases. Whether or not studies on the cause and pathogenesis of CJD will lead to a better understanding of Alzheimer's disease remains to be established.

VI.   HOST GENES CONTROLLING INCUBATION TIMES

A.   SIP/LIP

In early studies on scrapie in sheep, the influence of host background was appreciated. Certain breeds of sheep were found to be much more susceptible to scrapie infection than others (Gordon, 1966) (Table III). The alleles of a gene labelled SIP and LIP have been suggested to control the length of the incubation period in sheep (Dickinson, 1976). Studies on sheep were difficult because even susceptible breeds lacked uniform response to the scrapie agent. Subsequent studies with goats showed that these animals are more uniformly susceptible to scrapie (Pattison and Millson, 1960).

B.   SINC

The lack of highly inbred strains of sheep and goats as well as their long scrapie incubation periods made them far less useful than mice in the study of host genetic influence on the development of scrapie. Early studies on scrapie in mice reported the existence of a SINC gene which controls the length of the incubation period. Two alleles have been defined by Dickinson and his colleagues who reported that most mice exhibited short incubation periods when inoculated with the ME-7 agent isolate (S7,S7) (Dickinson and Meikle, 1971; Outram, 1976). In contrast, the VM mouse showed a prolonged incubation period (P7, P7). The F_1 generation of crosses between VM and other mice exhibited three different responses: 1) partial dominance with incubation periods falling between those of the parents, 2) overdominance with in-

Table III
Comparative Susceptibility of Different Breeds
of Sheep to Scrapie[1]

Breed[2]	No.[3]	Percent[4]	Breed[2]	No.[3]	Percent[4]
Herdwick	28/36	78	Dorset Horn	6/45	13
Dalesbred	31/43	72	Suffolk	6/51	12
Swaledale	25/46	54	Leicester	5/42	12
S.S.Cheviot	16/45	36	Welsh Mountain	4/42	10
Derby.Girtstone	16/46	35	Hampshire Down	3/30	10
Exmoor Horn	14/41	34	N.S. Cheviot	4/45	9
Border Leicester	11/42	26	Southdown	3/38	8
Scot.Blackface	8/44	18	Wiltshire Horn	4/57	7
South Devon	6/35	17	Shropshire	2/41	5
Romney Marsh	7/43	16	Kerry Hill	1/41	2
Welsh Cheviot	6/40	15	Clun Forest	1/52	2
Ryeland	5/34	15	Dorset Down	0/48	0

[1]Data from Gordon (1966); incubation periods ranged from 3.5 to 24 months.
[2]Sheep inoculated subcutaneously with 5 ml of 10% suspension of scrapie-infected brain tissue in saline.
[3]Number with scrapie after two years of observation over the number tested.
[4]Percent developing scrapie.

cubation periods longer than either parent, and 3) dominance. Different agent isolates have been reported to alter the response of the mice.

C.   PID

Recent studies indicate that amongst mice classified as S7,S7 by Dickinson, one and possibly two genes are operative in controlling the scrapie and CJD incubation periods (Kingsbury *et al.*, 1983). Alleles of one of the genes coding for longer incubation times appear to be autosomal dominant. Using congenic mice inoculated with the CJD agent, the PID-1 gene was found to be located in the D-subregion of the major histocompatibility complex (H-2) on chromosome 17. The q allele codes for short incubation times while the d allele codes for longer ones. The p, s, b and k alleles code for intermediate times. The sex of the animal was also observed to have a profound effect on the length of the incubation time in some strains of mice. Whether or not this phenomenon is sex-linked remains to be established.

A comparison of the SINC and PID-1 genes is given in Table IV.

Table IV
Comparison of PID and SINC Genes
Controlling Prion Incubation Times

	PID	SINC
Control of incubation times	CJD, scrapie	Scrapie
Location	Chromosome 17	Unknown
Fine structure	D subregion of H-2 complex	
Alleles coding for longer incubation times	Autosomal dominant	Partial or overdominant

VII.   TRANSMISSION OF PRIONS

The mechanisms whereby prions are transmitted in nature are largely unknown. Oral transmission of scrapie to sheep and goats has been shown experimentally, but no information is available about the natural means of spread (Pattison and Millson, 1976). TME is presumed to occur after mink ingest scrapie-infected meat, but there is no firm evidence to support this hypothesis. The means by which CJD spreads is unknown, but the transmission of kuru by ritualistic cannibalism seems well documented.

Experimental transmission of prion diseases to laboatory animals has been extensively studied over the past three decades. Variation amongst animal species in their susceptibility to prion diseases implies that prions possess diverse molecular structures. Differences in incubation periods for various isolates or "strains" also suggest multiple structures for prions (Dickinson and Fraser, 1977; Prusiner, 1982). These observations on the apparent diversity of prions as well as the ability of prions to adapt upon repeated passage in a given host are of importance in understanding how prions replicate (Prusiner, 1982). However, such findings cannot substitute for biophysical and biochemical studies in determining the molecular structure of prions.

A.   Isolates or Strains of Prions

Dickinson and co-workers have isolated numerous"strains" of the scrapie agent by passage in mice at limiting dilution (Dickinson and Fraser, 1977). These strains appear to be quite stable once isolated. There is no evidence for the mutation of one strain into another. The various prion strains have been characterized by their incubation periods and neuropathological profiles. The purity of these isolates is unknown since plaque purification methods are unavailable; the scrapie agent does not replicate well in cell culture. Kimberlin and Walker (1978) appear to have separated prions causing scrapie in mice from those causing scrapie in hamsters. Again, the purity of these isolates is unknown.

If a large number of strains of the scrapie agent exist as suggested from the foregoing summary, the most plausible model for the prion would seem to require a nucleic acid. As discussed in Section VIII. B., there is no evidence to date for such a structure. Whether prions contain a small polynucleotide within their core remains to be established (Prusiner, 1982).

B. Adaptation of Prions upon Passage

Adaptation of prions has been observed upon repeated passage in the same host species as evidenced by reduction in the lengths of incubation periods (Gibbs *et al.*, 1979; Kimberlin and Walker, 1977; Kingsbury *et al.*. 1982; Manuelidis and Manuelidis, 1979; Prusiner *et al.*, 1980a; Tateishi *et al.*, 1979). This adaptation process has been widely observed in both experimental scrapie and CJD. Frequently, a reduction of the incubation period by as much as 50% is seen by repeated passage in a given species. As discussed above, the genetic background of the host may also be of importance in determining the length of the incubation period.

Hadlow observed that the scrapie agent when passaged in mink retained its ability to infect goats, but lost its ability to infect mice (Hadlow, unpublished observations). Interestingly, the infectious agent causing mink encephalopathy has a similar host range (Marsh and Kimberlin, 1975). The TME agent can be passaged in goats but not mice. The nature of the molecular changes that distinquish the scrapie agent propagated in mink from that found in goats and mice will be important.

VIII. BIOPHYSICAL AND BIOCHEMICAL PROPERTIES OF SCRAPIE PRIONS

A. Purification and Hydrophobicity of Prions

Purification of the scrapie agent has been crucial for studies defining the properties of the infectious particle. The need to purify the agent away from cellular molecules prior to meaningful characterization studies is no different from investigations on many other biological macromolecules. Several investigators have mounted major efforts to purify and characterize the scrapie agent over the past two decades (Hunter, 1979; Kimberlin, 1976; Millson *et al.*, 1976; Prusiner *et al.*, 1979). Early studies suggested that the scrapie agent was distributed throughout virtually all subcellular fractions (Hunter, 1979; Kimberlin, 1976). The interpretation of those observations was complicated by the imprecision of the endpoint titrations of the agent. Nevertheless,

the scrapie agent was reported to be intimately associated
with cellular membranes, and from this association the "membrane hypothesis" evolved (Gibbons and Hunter, 1967; Hunter
et al., 1968). When various extraction procedures failed to
release the agent from membrane fractions, it was concluded
that the agent is a replicating membrane fragment that cannot
be separated from cellular membranes.

Several different purification procedures have been reported. One involved copurification of the scrapie agent and
microsomes (Semancik *et al.*, 1976). Another involved isolation of a "membrane-free" fraction after prolonged ultracentrifugation (Malone *et al.*, 1978). This fraction contained 1%
to 10% of the scrapie agent and was precipitated with ammonium sulfate prior to SDS gel electrophoresis. After electrophoresis, the agent was eluted from the gel in order to
obtain a further purification (Malone *et al.*, 1979). Although
the results of these studies seemed encouraging initially,
subsequent work has been disappointing (Prusiner   *et al.*,
1980c).

Using equilibrium sucrose and sodium chloride density
gradients, Siakotos and co-workers (1976) attempted to purify
the scrapie agent from murine brain. They suggested that
there was a peak of infectivity at a sucrose density of 1.19
g/cm^3. However, multiple peaks of infectivity were found
throughout the gradients, indicating considerable heterogeneity of the agent with respect to density. These results show
that density gradient centrifugation when applied to crude
suspensions of membranous material from brain is probably not
useful in isolating the scrapie agent. Other studies from
the laboratory of Gajdusek demonstrated considerable heterogeneity of the agent in metrizamide and cesium chloride
density gradients. (Brown *et al.*, 1978).

Since the initial purification of many biological
macromolecules involves a series of differential centrifuga-
tions (Prusiner, 1978), we began our studies on the scrapie
agent by defining its sedimentation properties in fixed-angle
rotors in order to develop a preparative protocol. These
studies showed that the agent from both murine spleen and
brain sedimented over a range of particle sizes from 60 S to
1,000 S (Prusiner *et al.*, 1978a).

On the basis of the information derived from these sedimentation profiles, a partial purification scheme for the
murine scrapie agent from spleen was derived (Prusiner *et
al.*, 1978b). The preparation was devoid of cellular membranes and enriched for the scrapie agent 20- to 30-fold with
respect to protein and DNA. Studies on the agent by rate-
zonal sucrose gradient centrifugation gave sedimentation coefficients for the agent ranging from 40 S to >500 S. Su-

crose density gradient centrifugation revealed a particle density ranging from 1.08 to more than 1.30 g/cm^3, an indication that some forms of the agent might be associated with lipids. Further sedimentation studies showed that the agent aggregated with cellular elements upon heating the agent in a partially purified fraction (Prusiner *et al.*, 1980b). The agent was stable in nonionic and nondenaturing anionic detergents, but was inactivated by SDS. Free-flow electrophoresis showed that most of the agent has a net negative charge, but significant charge heterogeneity was found (Prusiner *et al.*, 1980b).

Heterogeneity of the scrapie agent with respect to size, density, and charge suggested that hydrophobic domains on its surface might be responsible for these phenomena (Prusiner *et al.*, 1980e).Such domains are usually formed by the juxtaposition of nonpolar side chains of amino acids within a protein.

These initial studies on the murine agent from spleen revealed the complexities of scrapie agent purification. We then developed an improved assay based on measurements of the incubation time (Prusiner *et al.*, 1982b). With this new bioassay, we created a purification scheme for the agent from hamster brain, where the titers are highest (Kimberlin and Walker, 1977). The initial steps of the purification were similar to those for the murine agent (Prusiner *et al.*, 1978b). Deoxycholate extracts (P_4) were digested sequentially with micrococcal nuclease and proteinase K. The digestions were performed at 4°C to prevent aggregation of the agent, which is observed at elevated temperatures (Prusiner *et al.*, 1978b, 1980e). The digested preparations were then subjected to cholate-sodium dodecyl sarcosinate (Sarkosyl) extraction followed by ammonium sulfate precipitation (P_5). Most of the remaining digested proteins and nucleic acids were separated from the scrapie agent by Sarkosyl agarose gel electrophoresis at 4°C (Prusiner *et al.*, 1981b). Such preparations of the eluted scrapie agent (E_6) were approximately 100-fold purified with respect to cellular protein (Prusiner *et al.*, 1981b). With these enriched preparations we demonstrated that a protein within the agent is required for infectivity (McKinley *et al.*, 1981; Prusiner *et al.*, 1981b Fraction E_6 contained $10^{6.5}$ to $10^{8.5}$ ID $_{50}$ units of agent, 20 to 50 g/ml of protein, <1 g/ml of DNA, and <10 g/ml of RNA.

More recently we have developed an improved purification protocol for the scrapie agent (Prusiner *et al.* 1982a). This protocol has several advantages over the earlier ones noted above. In the earlier protocols, the sedimentation of the agent in a microsomal membrane fraction required prolonged ultra-centrifugation and thus severely limited the size of the preparations. In addition, the preparative Sarkosyl electrophoresis of the agent was slow, tedious and of limited capacity. In our new purification protocol, differential ultracentrifugation was supplanted by polyethylene glycol 8000 (PEG-8000) precipitation, and preparative gel electrophoresis was replaced by rate-zonal gradient centrifugation. This new protocol has allowed us to purify the agent from 100- to 1,000-fold with respect to protein. The protocol includes Triton X-100/ sodium deoxycholate extraction and PEG-8000 precipitation, nuclease and protease digestion, cholate and Sarkosyl extraction, ammonium sulfate precipitation, Triton X1000/SDS extraction and rate-zonal sedimentation through a discontinuous sucrose gradient (Fig. 2).

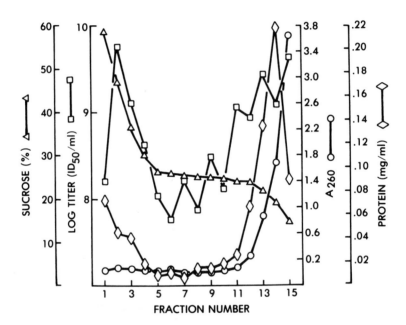

Figure 2. Rate-Zonal discontinuous sucrose gradient centrifugation for purification of the scrapie prion. Fraction P_4 (4mL) suspended in 2% (v/v) Triton X-100/0.8% (w/v) SDS was layered onto a sucrose step gradient containing 4mL of 60% (w/v) sucrose at the bottom and 32 mL of 25% sucrose. The sucrose solutions contained 20 mM Tris-OAc, pH 8.3, 1mM EDTA, and no detergent. The gradients were centrifuged at 50,000 rpm for 120 min in a vertical VTi50 rotor at 4°C and fractionated from the bottom. Fractions were stored at -70°C prior to assay for the scrapie agent (- -), sucrose (- - protein (- -), and A_{260} (-0-).

Highest degree of purification was found in a fraction from the 25%/60% sucrose interface near the bottom of the gradient (fraction 2). Typically, the titer in fraction 2 was $10^{9.5}$ ID_{50} units/ml and the protein concentration was 40 µg/ml. When Triton X-100 or octylglucoside extractions were used in place of the Triton X-100/SDS extraction, the distribution of the scrapie agent in the discontinous sucrose gradients was altered and no substantial purification was obtained.

The hydrophobicity of the scrapie agent has complicated purification as described above. Further evidence for the hydrophobicity of the scrapie agent comes from its binding to phenyl-Sepharose (Prusiner *et al.*, 1981b). The agent could not be eluted in 8.5 M ethylene glycol; however, inclusion of 4% Nonidet P-40 and 2% Sarkosyl in the ethylene glycol eluate resulted in the almost quantitative recovery of the agent from phenyl-Sepharose. In addition, the hydrophobicity was reflected by diminished titers when detergent was removed from fraction E_6 (Prusiner *et al.*, 1981b). Presumably this decrease in infectivity was due to aggregation.

Table V
Resistance of the Scrapie Prion
to Procedures that Attack Nucleic Acids

Procedure	Reagent	Possible Explanations
Nucleases	RNases DNases	Enzymes unable to penetrate protein shell
UV irradiation	254 nm	Shielded by protein shell or no critical nucleotide dimers formed
Divalent cation hydrolysis	Zn^{2+}	Ions unable to penetrate protein shell
Psoralen photoreaction	AMT,HEP, HMT,MMT,TMP	Monoadducts of single-stranded genome do not inactive or psoralens unable to penetrate protein shell
Chemical modification	Hydroxylamine	Nucleophiles react only with surface protein and are unable to penetrate the shell or react minimally with double-stranded genome

Abbreviations: AMT, 4' aminomethyl-4, 5',8-trimethylpsoralen; HEP, 1- - 4 'hydroxyethylpsoralen; HMT, 4'hydroxymethyl 4,5', 8-trimethylpsoralen; MMT, 4'-methoxymethyl-4,5',8-trimethyl-psoralen.

B.   Search for Nucleic Acid in the Prion

Multiple studies have shown that the scrapie agent in crude preparations was resistant to nuclease digestion (Hunter, 1979; Millson *et al.* 1976; Prusiner *et al.*, 1980e) and to UV irradiation at 254 nm (Alper *et al.*, 1967; Latarjet, 1979). The objection to these studies was that a protective coat prevented nucleases from penetrating the agent, as well as shielding it from radiation (Table V).

At several different stages of purification we have searched for susceptibility of the agent to nuclease digestion. No decrease in scrapie infectivity has been observed following digestion with micrococcal nuclease, nuclease P, deoxyribonucleases I and II, ribonucleases A and T_1, and phosphodiesterases I and II at 10, 100 and 500 µg/ml for 3 to 30 hours at 37°C. Ribonucleases III and H at 1 and 10 units/ml also showed no effect upon scrapie prion titer. Although nuclease sensitivity has been described for the scrapie agent (Marsh *et al.*, 1978), we have been unable to confirm this observation (Prusiner *et al.*, 1980c).

The complete lack of scrapie agent sensitivity to nucleases in view of inactivation by proteases is of interest. Numerous viruses are resistant to nucleases; presumably, these enzymes do not penetrate the viral protein coats (Rose, 1974; Schaffer and Schwerdt, 1959). Addition of ribonucleases A at 0.1 µg/ml to a crude nucleic acid extract containing potato spindle tuber viroid (PSTV) decreased the PSTV titer by a factor of $>10^6$ in 1 hour at 25°C (Diener and Raymer, 1969). Hydrolysis of a single phosphodiester bond within a viroid probably inactivates it (Diener, 1979; Sänger *et al.*, 1979). In contrast, there are many examples of proteins that retain their biological activities after limited proteolysis (Mihalyi, 1978). We do not know in the case of the scrapie agent how many peptide bonds must be cleaved to cause inactivation.

Studies with the optically clear fraction E_6 as well as sucrose gradient fraction 2 have confirmed the resistance of the scrapie agent to UV inactivation (Alper *et al.*, 1967; Latarjet, 1979). Fractions S_2, P_5 and E_6 as well as gradient fraction 2 were irradiated at 254 nm with increasing doses. Although no inactivation of the agent in fraction S_2 was observed, a minimal but probably significant decrease was found in fractions P_5 and E_6 as well as gradient fraction 2 (Prusiner *et al.*, unpublished observations). The kinetics of inactivation by irradiation at 254 nm suggest a single-hit process. The resistance of the scrapie agent to inactivation by irradiation at 254 nm is much greater than that observed for viruses and viroids (Prusiner, 1982). Clearly, the inactivation of the scrapie agent at extreme energy levels indicates a photochemistry of a far different nature from that observed for virus and viroid inactivation through the formation of thymine or uracil dimers. Proteins are relatively resistant to irradiation at 254 nm (McLaren and Shugar, 1964) and are probably the target within the scrapie agent in these irradiation studies.

Observations on the resistance of the scrapie agent to procedures attaching nucleic acids have been extended by means of three other techniques (Table V). The agent has been incubated at pH 7 in the presence of 2 mM $Zn(NO_3)_2$ at 65°C for periods as long as 24 hours without loss of infectivity (Table VI).

Table VI
Resistance of the Scrapie Prion to
Zn^{++} Catalyzed Hydrolysis at 65°

Time (h)	Zn $(NO_3)_2$ Concentration		
	0	0.2 mM	2 mM
	(log titer [ID_{50} units/ml])		
–	7.3 + .03		
2	8.0 + .26	7.6 + .35	7.0 + .16
4	7.3 + .37	7.2 + .16	7.1 + .16
8	7.1 + .16	7.5 + .20	7.5 + .26
24	7.1 + .23	7.0 + .07	7.1 + .13

Fraction E_6 was dialyzed for 24 h at 4° C against 10mM $NaNO_3$, pH 7.4, containing 0.2% (w/v) Sarkosyl (DG 232).

Under these conditions polymers of RNA are completely reduced to mononucleotides, and polymers of DNA undergo considerable hydrolysis (Butzow and Eichhorn, 1965, 1975). Photochemical inactivation of the scrapie agent with psoralens was attempted with samples at several levels of purification, both from murine spleen and hamster brain. Five different psoralens of varying degrees of hydrophobicity were used (Isaacs et al., 1977). It was expected that the most hydrophobic psoralens would readily partition into the scrapie agent. No inactivation of the scrapie agent was observed with any of these psoralens over a wide range of dosages (McKinley et al., 1983a). Psoralens may form diadducts upon photoactivation within base-paired regions of nucleic acids and mono-adducts within single-stranded regions (Hanson et al., 1978; Hearst and Thiry, 1977). Psoralens have several advantages in searching for a nucleic acid genome: 1) low reactivity with proteins, 2) penetration of viral protein and lipid coats, and 3) formation of stable covalent linkages on photoactivation. Psoralens have been found to inactivate numerous viruses, but not, for example, picornaviruses (Hanson, personal communication). Psoralens, like acridine orange and neutral red dyes (Crowther and Melnick, 1961), do not penetrate the protein coat of poliovirus. Photoadducts with viral RNA were formed when psoralens or the above tricyclic dyes were added to cultured cells replicating the poliovirus.

In contrast to psoralens, hydroxylamine readily inactivates poliovirus at neutral pH(Bogert *et al.*, 1971). Hydroxylamine does not generally react with proteins at neutral pH, but it does decarbethoxylate modified proteins and it does modify cytosine bases (Bornstein and Balian, 1970). At concentrations up to 0.5 M at neutral pH hydroxylamine failed to alter scrapie agent infectivity(McKinley *et al.*, 1981). Under these conditions, most animal and plant viruses as well as bacteriophage are inactivated by hydroxylamine except for the paramyxoviruses which are resistant(Franklin and Wecker,1959; Freese *et al.* 1961; Phillips and Brown, 1967; Schuster and Wittman, 1963; Tessman, 1968). In contrast, inactivation of the scrapie agent by carbethoxylation upon treatment with DEP was found to be reversible with NH_2OH (McKinley *et al.*, 1981).

The extreme resistance of the scrapie agent to inactivation by procedures that modify nucleic acids suggests that its structure is different from that of both viruses and viroids. While there are examples of viruses that are resistant to inactivation by two or even three of the five procedures in Table VII, we are unaware of any viruses which, like

Table VII

Evidence that Scrapie Prion Infectivity Depends on Protein		
Procedure	Stable	Labile
Protease digestion		Proteinase K,
Chemical modification	Hydroxyphenyl-propionamide	trypsin DEP, butanedione, PMSF
Denaturing reagents		
Detergents	TX100,NP40,OGS, SB-314,ET-12H,CHAPS, cholate, Sarkosyl,	SDS, LDS, SDeS
Salts	Na^+,K^+,Cl^-,SO_4^{-2}, PO_4^{-3},EDTA	Gdn^+, TCA^-,SCN^-
Organic solvents	Methanol,ethanol, propanol	Phenol,2-chloro-ethanol Urea

Abbreviations: DEP, diethylpyrocarbonate; PMSF, phenylmethylsulfonylfluoride; TX-100, Triton X-100; NP40, Nonidet P-40; OGS, octylglucoside; SB 3-14, sulfobetaine 3-14; ET-12H, 1-dodecyl propanediol-3-phosphorylcholine; CHAPS,3-[(3-cholamidopropyl) dimethylammonio]-1-propanesulfonate; Sarkosyl, sodium dodecyl sarcosinate; SDS, sodium dodecyl sulfate; LDS, lithium dodecyl sulfate; SDeS, sodium decyl sulfate; EDTA, ethylenediaminetetraacetic acid; Gdn, guanidinium; TCA, trichoroacetic acid; SCN, thiocyanate.

the scrapie agent, are resistant by all of these procedures. However, the possibility must be considered that the putative genome of the scrapie agent is buried within a tightly packed protein shell which excludes nucleases. UV irradiation, Zn^{2+}, psoralens, and NH_2OH. Also, we cannot exclude an unusual nucleic acid with a different base structure or polymer packing that might exhibit the resistant characteristic described for the scrapie agent.

In a comparative study of the scrapie agent and PSTV, we found that the two pathogens had virtually opposite properties. The viroid resisted inactivation by procedures that modify or hydrolyze proteins while the prion was inactivated by these methods. In contrast, the prion resisted inactivation by procedures that modify or hydrolyze nucleic acids while the viroid was inactivated by these methods. From these observations we concluded that except for the small size of these infectious pathogens, viroids and prions seem to be antithetical.

Of interest are studies showing a large oxygen effect upon exposure of the scrapie agent to ionizing radiation (Alper *et al.*, 1978). Viruses and nucleic acids characteristically show a small oxygen effect. Biological membranes and probably lipoproteins show large oxygen effect. The increased sensitivity of the scrapie agent to ionizing radiation in the presence of oxygen presumably reflects the hydrophobic protein with bound lipids that is required for infectivity (Prusiner *et al.*, 1981b). These data do not eliminate the possibility that the agent also contains a nucleic acid.

C. Molecular Size of the Prion

One explanation for the extreme resistance of the scrapie agent to inactivation by irradiation at 254 nm is that the putative nucleic acid within the agent is quite small (Alper *et al.*, 1966, 1967; Latarjet, 1979; Prusiner, 1982). The resistance of the agent to inactivation by irradiation at 254 nm by pyrimidine dimer formation could be explained by a putative nucleic acid of 50 bases or less (Prusiner *et al.* , unpublished observations). This estimate assumes that the pyrimidines are randomly distributed within the nucleic acid and that one dimer is sufficient to inactivate the agent. Alternatively, the protein(s) of the scrapie agent might be modified by irradiation at 254 nm. Interestingly, a similar size for the putative nucleic acid of the scrapie agent can be calculated from the psoralen experiments. Assuming that the psoralen was able to freely penetrate the protein exterior of the agent, then only a scrapie nucleic acid of 40 bases or less could have eluded psoralen photoadduct formation under the conditions of our experiments (McKinley *et al.*, 1983a). These data are consistent with other lines of evidence indicating that the scrapie particle is quite small, as described below. The extreme resistance of the scrapie agent to inactivation by ionizing radiation raised the possibility that the agent is quite small (Alper *et al.*, 1966). Target calculations have given minimum M_r ranging from 64,000 to 150,000 (Alper *et al.*, 1966; Latarjet, 1979). However, two important factors could not be taken into account in these calculations. The first is the possibility that multiple copies of the agent might exist within a single infectious particle as would occur with aggregation. We have good evidence that the agent readily associates with cellular elements and probably aggregates with itself in purified preparation (Prusiner *et al.*, 1978b, 1979, 1980b). The second is the efficiency of the cellular repair processes. For example, polyoma virus dsDNA (3×10^6 daltons) has been found to be almost as resistant to ionizing radiation as either viroids or the scrapie agent (Latarjet *et al.*, ,1967; Semancik *et al.*, 1973). The extreme efficiency of the cellular repair processes for the polyoma virus dsDNA genome accounts for its apparent resistance to damage by ionizing radiation (Latarjet, 1979).

Studies on the scrapie agent in murine spleen have shown a continuum of sizes ranging from 40 S or less to more than 500 S by rate-zonal sucrose gradients (Prusiner *et al.*, 1978 b, 1979). Parvoviruses are among the smallest viruses identified and they have sedimentation coefficients of 100 S to 110 S (Rose, 1974; Schaffer and Schwerdt, 1959). In heated preparations extracted with sodium deoxycholate, the scrapie agent associated with cellular elements to form large infectious particles of >10,000 S(Prusiner *et al.*, 1979, 1980b). Such particles are the size of mitochondria. Sedimentation studies of CJD agents adapted to both guinea pigs and mice suggest that the sizes of these agents are similar to that observed for the scrapie agent (Kingsbury, in preparation).

Gel electrophoresis has shown that the scrapie agent exists as a succession of particles of varying size (Prusiner *et al.*, 1980c, 1980e). Sarkosyl agarose gel electrophoresis of partially purified fractions showed that some forms migrated more slowly than DNA restriction endonuclease fragments of 15×10^6 dalton DNA fragments. Digestion of crude preparations with nucleases and proteases facilitated the entry of the agent into these gels. One report showed that most of the scrapie agent migrated with 5 S RNA molecules in the presence of SDS (Malone *et al.*, 1979). We were unable to confirm these findings since SDS inactivated the agent (Prusiner *et al.*, 1980c, 1980d).

Gel filtration studies with anionic detergents and chaotropic ions have given results similar to those described for early rate-zonal sucrose gradients and gel electrophoresis. Typically most of the agent eluted in the void volume followed by a continuum of particles apparently of decreasing size (Prusiner *et al.*, 1980e, 1981a). In contrast, incubation of the scrapie agent overnight with 10% (weight to volume) sulfobetaine 3-14, a zwitterionic detergent, appears to have dissociated the agent (Prusiner and Groth, unpublished observations). Under these conditions the scrapie agent eluted as a peak behind bovine serum albumin (BSA), but slightly ahead of ovalbumin. If the agent has a globular shape in sulfobetaine 3-14, then it may have a M_r of 50,000 or less. How much detergent is bound to the agent and how the detergent influences the apparent M_r of the agent remains to be determined (Reynolds, 1981). Similar observations have been recorded with another detergent, 1-dodecyl propanediol-3-phosphorylcholine, which is a synthetic derivative of lysolecithin. Confirmation of these findings by other techniques is mandatory since anomalous behavior of proteins during gel filtration is well known (Andrews, 1971; Nozaki *et al.*, 1976).

Rate-zonal gradient centrifugation studies have indicated that the scrapie agent may have an observed sedimentation coefficient as low as ~ 2 S. Since we do not know the density of the scrapie agent in detergent solutions, it is possible that the agent was floating in these rate-zonal gradients and that this value is artifactually low. We have also found that the scrapie agent, after disaggregation in zwitterionic detergents, passes through nucleopore filters with 15 nm pores (Prusiner and Groth, unpublished observations). There are no viruses that pass through pores of this size; in fact, ferritin molecules which are 14 nm in diameter barely pass through such pores.

If the scrapie agent does have an M_r of 50,000 or less, then a nucleic acid within such a globular structure will be too small to code for a protein. A spherical scrapie agent of M_r 50,000 would have a diameter of 4 to 6nm (North and Rich, 1961; Tanford, 1961). Let us assume that the agent has a protective protein which is 1 nm (10 Å) thick. The volume of the core will be 14.1 nm^3. From measurements of DNA packing in crystals and bacteriophage (Earnshaw and Casjens, 1980; Giannoni *et al.*, 1969; Langridge *et al.*, 1960). there is space for a 12-nucleotide polymer consisting of six base pairs. Dehydration of the polymer would permit 32 nucleotides to be encapsidated. Indeed, if such oligonucleotides exist within the agent, they must have a function other than that of a template directing the synthesis of scrapie coat proteins.

D.   Scrapie Prion Contains a Protein (PrP)

Convincing evidence that scrapie agent infectivity depends upon a protein(s) was provided by experiments reported

in 1981 (Prusiner *et al.*, 1981b). Those studies depended
upon the development of a purification scheme for the agent
from hamster brain using Sarkosyl gel electrophoresis. The
infectivity of the scrapie agent was shown to be susceptible
to degradation by proteinase K. Diminution of infectivity was
shown to be dependent upon the time of digestion, the concentration of proteinase K and the activity of the enzyme.
Similar results were also obtained with trypsin (Prisiner,
1982). As shown in Figure 3, the titer of the scrapie agent

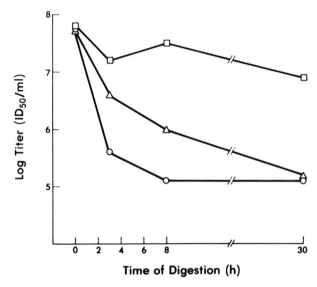

Figure 3. Inactivation of the scrapie prion by digestion
with Trypsin. Fraction E_6 was digested with trypsin,0   g/ml
(- ▫ -),100   g/ml (- Δ -) or 500 g/ml (-0-) for increasing
periods of time up to 30 h. Aliquots were taken for bioassay
in animals after the digestion was terminated with 10 mM
phenylmethylsulfonylfluoride (PMSF) and freezing with dry ice
followed by storage at - 70°.

progressively declined as the time of trypsin digestion increased. The kinetics of scrapie agent degradation were
altered by increasing the amount of trypsin. Higher concentrations of trypsin accelerated the decline in scrapie
agent titer. A recent report has confirmed our findings in
partially purified fractions from murine brain (Lax *et al.*,
1983). Proteinase K was found to consistently reduce the
titer of these fractions. Although earlier studies with
proteases showed occasional reductions of scrapie infectivity
(Cho, 1980; Hunter and Millson, 1967; Hunter *et al.*, 1969),

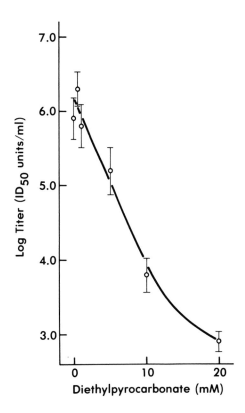

Figure 4. Dose-dependent inactivation of the scrapie prion with increasing concentrations of DEP. Standard errors of titers are denoted by bars. Fraction E_6 containing the scrapie agent and 75 g/ml of protein was dialyzed overnight at 4°C against 20 mM Tris-HCl, pH 7.4, containing 1 mM EDTA and 0.2% Sarkosyl. Freshly prepared aqueous DEP was added to give the desired final concentration of DEP in a 0.1-ml incubation mixture. All samples were mixed well and allowed to incubate at room temperature for 30 min. Reactions were terminated by plunging the vials into a dry ice-ethanol bath. Vials were then store at-20°C for 3 to 4 weeks prior to bioassay.

the inconsistency and paucity of the experimental data left considerable doubt about the proper interpretation of the results.

In addition to the protease studies, we showed that the scrapie agent could be inactivated by chemical modification with DEP (McKinley *et al.*, 1981) (Figure 4). The chemical modification was found to be reversible using hydroxylamine and was accompanied by a restoration of scrapie agent infectivity. The specificity of reversible chemical modification by DEP provided another important line of evidence showing a protein(s) was required for infectivity.

Once convincing studies showed the presence of a protein(s) within the scrapie agent, the results of earlier studies with denaturation reagents could be accurately interpreted. SDS, urea, guanidinium thiocyanate and phenol had all been found to inactivate the scrapie agent, but the actions of these reagents were not sufficiently specific to establish that a protein(s) was required for infectivity. For example, Hunter and co-workers (1969) showed that exposure of the scrapie agent to 6.0 M urea decreased the titer by a factor of 100. This high concentration of urea could have denatured protein or nucleic acid. We have found that exposure of the scrapie agent in partially purified fractions to 3 M urea at 4°C decreases the titer by a factor of 50 (Figure 5). Removal of the urea after 2 hours was accompanied by a return of infectivity. This observation is similar to our findings with KSCN where removal of the KSCN was accompanied by an apparent return of infectivity(Prusiner *et al.*, 1981a). Whether urea or cyanate ions (Start *et al.*, 1960) are responsible for the loss of scrapie infectivity in these experiments is not known. From our data the most likely target with -in the scrapie agent for denaturation by urea is a protein.

Evidence that scrapie infectivity depends upon a protein(s) is summarized in Table VIII. Both proteinase K and

Table VIII
Scrapie Protein and Prion -
Evidence that PrP is a Structural Component of the Prion

1. PrP is found only in animals infected with the prion.
2. Scrapie prion and PrP copurify by two different procedures.
3. Concentration of PrP is directly related to the titer of prions.
4. Several properties of PrP are similar to those of the prion (poor immunogenicity, resistance to proteases, chemical modification by DEP).
5. Changing the properties of PrP results in a corresponding alteration in the prion.

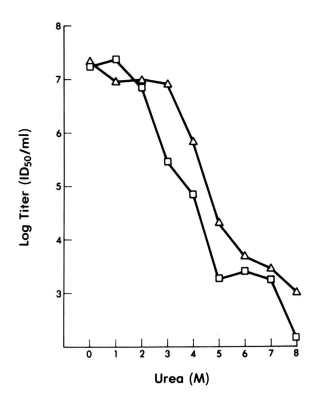

Figure 5. Inactivation of the scrapie prion by urea. Fraction P5 was dispersed in 2.0% (v/v) Triton X-100 for 16 h at 4° and then exposed to urea concentrations up to 8 M for 2 h an aliquot was frozen at -70° (-☐-) and another was dialyzed (-Δ-) at 4° against 20 mM Tris-OAc, pH 8.3,1.0 mM EDTA and 2.0% Triton X-100. Spectropore dialysis tubing with pores retaining molecules of M_r >12-14 K was used. Typically 0.4 ml of sample was dialyzed against 400 ml of buffer for 1-2 h. Three changes of dialysate were made. Upon completing the dialysis, samples were stored at - 70° prior to biossay. Enzyme grade urea purchased from Schwartz Mann was freshly prepared immediately prior to the experiment in order to minimize the concentration of cyanate.

trypsin, which catalyze the hydrolysis of peptide bonds, destroy scrapie infectivity in fractions prepared by Sarkosyl gel electrophoresis. As noted above, nucleases and phosphodiesterases do not alter the infectivity of the scrapie

agent. Chemical modification of free amino groups by iodinated 3-(4-hydroxyphenyl) propionic acid *N*-hydroxylsuccinimide
ester (Bolton-Hunter reagent) has no effect on scrapie infectivity in contrast to modification by DEP which reversibly
inactivates the agent (McKinley, *et al.*, 1983). These results suggest that PrP has an active site which is required
for maintenance of agent infectivity. The catalytic activities of numerous enzymes have been shown to be reduced after
chemical modification of histidine residues with DEP and to
be restored upon treatment with hydroxylamine (Miles, 1977).

Inactivation of the scrapie agent or prion was found
after exposure to denaturing detergents, strong chaotropic
salts, harsh organic solvents and denaturants like urea.
Nondenaturing detergents, salts and solvents were found not
to alter prion infectivity.

When the cumulative evidence for a protein within the
scrapie agent became compelling, we began to search for
scrapie specific proteins. In our initial studies, we radioiodinated fractions purified by the Sarkosyl gel electrophoresis procedure. The radioiodinated proteins were then separated by SDS polyacrylamide gel electrophoresis; scrapie and
control samples were compared by this method in search of a
polypeptide which was unique to fractions from scrapie-infected brain. Although we observed a polypeptide of M_r 29000
that was present in some scrapie preparations and absent in
controls, our results were inconsistent. This inconsistency
may have been due to insufficient amounts of scrapie protein
in many of our purified preparations. With the development
of an improved purification scheme, the scrapie protein could
be found in every preparation.

Subsequent studies showed that this protein could be
readily iodinated (Bolton *et al.* 1982) with [^{125}I] 3-(4hy-
droxyphenol) propionic acid *N*-hydroxysuccinimide ester which
reacts with free amino groups of proteins (Bolton and Hunter,
1973). The unreacted ester was removed by reacting it with
glycine and separating the proteins from the iodinated glycine by precipitation with quinine hemisulfate. The radioiodinated proteins were then separated from each other by SDS
polyacrylamide gel electrophoresis shown in Figure 6. The
radioiodinated polypeptide migrating with an apparent M_r of
27,000-30,000 is the scrapie prion protein (PrP). The cause
of its microheterogeneity is unknown.

PrP can be distinguished from normal brain proteins by:
1) its micro-heterogeneity (M_r 27,000-30,000) observed during
SDS polyacrylamide gel electrophoresis and 2) its resistance
to protease digestion in the native or nondenatured state.
Fig. 6 illustrates a comparison between purified scrapie and
normal brain fractions from Triton X-100/SDS discontinuous

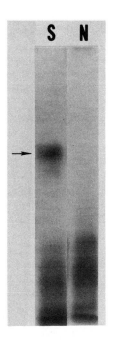

Figure 6. Scrapie prion protein (PrP) radioiodinated and separated by SDS polyacrylamide gel electrophoresis. Fraction 2 from a Triton X-100/SDS discontinuous sucrose gradient containing the scrapie agent (S), or an analogous fraction purified from normal hamster brain (N), was concentrated by precipitation with SDS and quinine hemisulfate. The proteins were radio-iodinated with N-succinimidyl 3-(4-hydroxy-5-[^{125}I]-iodophenyl)propionate and then reprecipitated as above The pellets were suspended in 10mM Tris buffer, pH 7.4, containing 0.2% Sarkosyl and proteinase K (100 g/ml). The samples were incubated at 37°C for 30 min and the digestions stopped by boiling in electrophoresis buffer containing 2% SDS and 5% mercaptoethanol. The digested proteins were analyzed by electrophoresis in a 15% polyacrylamide gel. An autoradiogram of the gel is shown.

sucrose gradients after treatment with proteinase K. Though both samples originally contained similar amounts of protein, protease digestion under nondenaturing conditions hydrolyzed all proteins in the normal brain fraction, but left PrP intact in the scrapie fraction.

Having found a protein which was present only in fractions purified from scrapie-infected brains, we asked if 1) this protein is a structural component of the prion or 2) it arises as a pathologic by-product during infection. To answer this question, multiple experimental approaches were employed. The very diversity to the methods used coupled with the sameness and consistency of the answer indicates that this scrapie protein (PrP) must be a structural component of the prion (Table VIII).

Samples purified from age-matched hamsters either uninoculated or inoculated with normal brain have failed to show evidence of PrP (Bolton *et al.*, 1982). If PrP is found in normals, then it is present at levels <0.1% of that found in scrapie-infected brains (Bolton *et al.*, in preparation).

PrP has been found using two different purification schemes: one employing Sarkosyl gel electrophoresis and the other with sedimentation through a discontinuous sucrose gradient (Bolton *et al.*, in preparation). In both purification schemes the scrapie prion and PrP have been found to copurify. This copurification indicates that the molecular properties of both the infectious prion and PrP must be similar.

Further evidence that PrP is a structural component of the scrapie prion comes from studies showing that the amount of this protein correlates with the number of infectious particles. A relationship between PrP concentration and the scrapie agent titer was observed. The kinetics for degradation of both the infectious prion and native PrP by proteinase K were similar (McKinley *et al.*, 1983). More than 2 hours of digestion at 37° with 100 mg/ml of proteinase K were required to demonstrate a decrease in prion titer or PrP concentration. One possible explanation for these results lies in the specificity of these proteases. Proteinase K is a nonspecific protease while trypsin and SV-8 protease are both amino acid specific. Presumably, no surface lys or arg within the prion are accessible for trypsin catalyzed cleavage; similarly, no surface glu are acessible for SV-8 protease cleavage. The correlation between the infectious prion and native PrP provides additional support for the hypothesis that the protein is a component of the scrapie agent.

It is noteworthy that trypsin catalyzed the hydrolysis of peptide bonds within prions in fraction E_6 prepared by Sarkosyl gel electrophoresis, while trypsin did not alter the infectivity of prions in fraction 2 prepared by discontinous sucrose gradients. One possible explanation for this differential sensitivity to proteases is the difference in detergents used in purification of the two fractions. E_6 was prepared using only anionic detergents throughout the entire procedure (Prusiner *et al.* 1980c), while F_2 was purified using combinations of anionic and nonionic detergents(Prusiner *et al.*, 1982a). Further studies are clearly required to elucidate the mechanism responsible for this difference in sensitivity of prions to digestion by trypsin.

In addition to the parallel resistances of the infectious prion and native PrP to digestion by proteases, other properties of the prion and PrP have also been found to be similar. PrP can be radiolabelled with [^{14}C]-DEP and DEP reversibly inactivates the prion by chemical modification (Bolton *et al.*, 1982; McKinley *et al.*, 1981). Both PrP and the prion appear to be poor immunogens, as discussed in Section V.A.

Denaturation of prions by boiling for 2 min in the presence of SDS caused a reduction of infectivity by a factor of 10,000 and significant enhancement in proteolytic degradation of PrP (Bolton *et al.*, in preparation). While degradation of native PrP by proteinase K required >2 h at 37°C, cleavage of denatured PrP was accomplished in <0.5 h at 25°C. Denaturation also rendered PrP suseptible to proteolytic cleavage by SV-8 protease; whereas, native PrP is completely resistant to SV-8 catalyzed hydrolysis.

The resistance of native PrP to degradation by proteases resembles that reported for some other proteins including: avidin (Green 1975), DNA binding protein (Krauth and Werner, 1979), laminin (Ott *et al.*, 1982), RNA 3'-terminal phosphate cyclase (Filipowicz *et al.*, 1983), A lens crystallin (Bloemendal *et al.* 1982), amyloid (Cohen and Calkins, 1964; Emeson *et al.*, 1966; Kim *et al.*, 1969; Pras *et al.*, 1969; Ruinen *et al.*, 1968; Sorenson and Binington, 1964), hemoglobin (Kimura *et al.*, 1978), transformation-sensitive membrane glycoprotein (Carter and Hakomori 1978), peptidyltransferase (Cox and Kotecha, 1980), acetylcholinesterase (Vigny *et al.*, 1979) and chloroplast pigment protein (Süss *et al.*, 1976). The mechanisms of protease resistance appear to include: 1) conformation of the protein, 2) aggregation of the protein and 3) binding of lipids as well as oligosaccharides to the protein (Mihalyi, 1978; Rupley, 1967). In the case of PrP, all three of these mechanisms may be of importance in maintaining PrP in a protease resistant state.

The discovery of PrP is already having a profound effect upon scrapie research. The protein can be detected and quantitated within one day after radioisotopic labelling. This represents a substantial decrease in the time required to gain information about the structure of the prion. With a handle on one component of the prion, the discovery of any other components will hopefully follow in the not too distant future.

E. Electron Microscopy

Numerous attempts have been made to identify the scrapie agent using electron microscopy. To date, no definitive morphological identification of the agent has been made.

Curious arrays of spherical particles about 25nm in diameter have been found within postsynaptic evaginations in the brains of scrapie-infected mice (Baringer *et al.* 1979; Bignami and Parry, 1971, 1972; David-Ferreira *et al.*, 1968; Lamar *et al.*, 1974; Lampert *et al.*, 1971). Similar structures in brains of scrapie-infected sheep and of humans with CJD have raised the possibility that the scrapie and CJD agents are composed of such particles. The conspicuous absence of these spherical particles from hamster brains, which have the highest known titers of the prion, make such particles unlikely candidates for the prion (Baringer and Prusiner, 1978).

Spiroplasma-like structures have been found in the brains of patients dying of CJD and some investigators have suggested that the CJD agent is a spiroplasma (Bastian, 1979; Bastian *et al.*, 1981). A recent study reports that no spiroplasma or other mycoplasma were cultivated from brain tissue of 18 CJD cases and no antibodies to several spiroplasmas were detected in sera from 15 patients (Leach *et al.*,1983). Attempts to detect spiroplasma DNA from CJD and scrapie brain tissue using radiolabelled cDNA probes have been negative (Gibbs, personal communication). Furthermore, the unusual molecular properties of the scrapie agent make it much different from spiroplasma.

Several early studies reported abnormal tubular-like structures in scrapie-infected rodent brain (Field *et al.* 1967b; Field and Narang, 1972; Narang, 1974a, 1974b, 1974c; Raine and Field, 1967). The studies were inconclusive because scrapie agent infectivity was never correlated with these ultrastructural findings. More recently, one report has called attention to filamentous structures measuring 4-6 nm in diameter which could be distinguished from amyloid fibrils (Merz *et al.*, 1981). Two or four filaments form helical fibrils which were found in preparation from brains of rodents with scrapie and brains of humans dying of CJD (Merz *et al.*, 1981, 1983). The fibrils have also been found in preparations from scrapie-infected mouse spleen (Merz *et al.*, *al.* 1983a). The relationship, if any, of these fibrils to the scrapie agent is unclear.

Rod-like structures have been found in purified fractions of the scrapie agent prepared from infected hamster brain using both the Sarkosyl gel electrophoresis procedure (Prusiner *et al.*, 1981 b) and the discontinous sucrose

gradient method (Prusiner *et al.*, 1982a). These rods measure
25 nm in diameter by 100 to 300 nm in length as seen in
rotary shadowed specimens. After negative staining with
uranyl formate, the rods have a diameter varying between 12
and 18 nm (McKinley *et al.*, 1983b). The relationship of
the rods to the infectious prion and PrP is unclear. The
ability of the rods to aggregate gives them an appearance
similar to that of purified amyloid (Cohen *et al.*, 1982)
(Fig. 7). As discussed above, amyloid deposits are frequently found with plaques in the brains of animals and humans
infected with the scrapie, CJD and kuru agents.

IX. MOLECULAR MODELS FOR THE PRION

A. Hypothetical Structures for the Prion

Investigators have been aware of the unusual properties
of the scrapie agent for many years. Hypotheses on the chemical structure of the scrapie agent have included: Sarcosporidia parasite (M'Fadyean, 1918; M'Gowan, 1914), "filterable"
virus (Cho, 1976; Cuille and Chelle, 1939; Eklund *et al.*,
1963; Wilson *et al.*, 1950), small DNA virus (Kimberlin and
Hunter, 1967), replicating protein (Griffith, 1967; Lewin,
1972, 1981; Pattison and Jones, 1967), replicating abnormal
polysaccharide within membranes (Gibbons and Hunter, 1967;
Hunter *et al.*, 1968), DNA subvirus controlled by a transmissible linkage substance (Adams and Field,1968), provirus consisting of recessive genes generating RNA particles (Darlington, 1969; Parry, 1962, 1969), naked nucleic acid similar to
plant viroids (Diener, 1972, 1973), unconventional virus
(Adams 1973; Gajdusek, 1977, 1978; Gajdusek and Gibbs, 1978;
Hunter 1972; Pattison, 1965; Stamp,1967), aggregated conventional virus with unusual properties (Rohwer and Gajdusek,
1980), replicating polysaccharide (Field,1966, 1967), nucleoprotein complex(Latarjet *et al.*, 1970),nucleic acid surrounded by a polysaccharide coat (Adams and Caspary, 1967; Narang,
1974b; Siakotos *et al.*, 1979), spiroplasma like organism
(Bastian, 1979; Bastian *et al.*, 1981; Gray, *et al.*, 1980),
multicomponent system with one component quite small(Hunter
et al., 1973; Somerville *et al.*, 1976), membranebound DNA
(Hunter *et al.*, 1973; Marsh *et al.*, 1978 Somerville *et
al.*, 1976), and a viroid-like nucleic acid surrounded by
cellular proteins (Kimberlin, 1982a, 1982b).

The unusual properties of the scrapie agent coupled with
the slow, tedious and imprecise bioassays have served to
stimulate this enlarging array of hypotheses. Only purific −
ation of the scrapie agent to homogeneity and determination
of its macromolecular structure will determine which of these
hypotheses, if any, are correct.

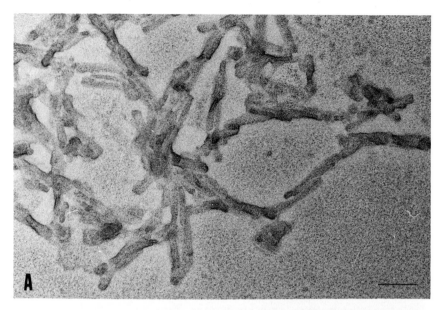

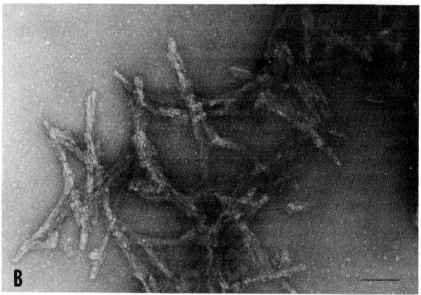

Figure 7.   Electron   micrographs   of rod-like   structures in
purified fractions containing the scrapie prion.   Fraction 2
from a Triton   X-100/SDS   discontinuous   sucrose gradient was
applied to formvar coated grids which had been freshly carbon
shadowed, glow discharged   and   treated with 1   g/ml poly-L-
lysine.   Solid bars are 100 nm.   (A) Sample was rotary shadow-

B. Current Models of the Prion Cannot Exclude a Nucleic Acid

Experimental data indicates that the molecular properties of the scrapie prion distinguish it from viruses, viroids and plasmids. The prion contains a single major protein (PrP) of apparent M_r 27,000 to 30,000. Whether or not the prion contains minor protein components as well as a nucleic acid core remains to be established (Table IX). PrP

Table IX
Current Molecular Models for the Prion

1. Prions contain undetected nucleic acids
   A. Genome codes for prion protein(s)
   B. Oligonucleotide
2. Prions are devoid of nucleic acids

is required for infectivity. Denaturation, chemical modification or hydrolysis of PrP was accompanied by a diminution in the infectivity of the prion. The resistance of the prion to procedures that modify or hydrolyze nucleic acids and its apparent small size suggest that the prion is a novel infectious pathogen.

While the possibility that the prion contains a nucleic acid core surrounded by a tightly packed protein coat seems the most plausible, there is no experimental evidence for polynucleotide within the prion. The second possibility is that the prion contains only protein and is devoid of nucleic acid. The latter model is consistent with the experimental data, but is clearly heretical. Skepticism of the second model is certainly justified. Only purification of the scrapie agent to homogeneity and determination of its chemical structure will allow a rigorous conclusion as to which of these two models is correct.

If a currently undetected nucleic acid is found within the prion, its size and function will be of great interest.

---

ed with tungsten at an angle of incidence of 8°. Dimensions of indiividual rods vary from 100 to 200 nm in length and have a diameter of 25 nm. (B) Sample was negatively stained with freshly prepared 1% uranyl formate. Dimensions of individual rods vary from 150 to 200 nm in length and have a diameter of 10 to 20 nm. All micrographs were taken using a JEOL 100B electron microscope at 60 Kev.

The results of many studies on the scrapie agent make it unlikely that the prion contains a nucleic acid of sufficient size to code for PrP. On the other hand, we cannot exclude the possibility that the prion contains an oligonucleotide. Should that prove to be the case, this would be a major feature distinquishing prions from viruses.

There seems to be little advantage in championing one model over another; however, several previously postulated structures for the scrapie agent can now be discarded. The requirement of a protein for infectivity eliminates the possibilities that the scrapie agent is composed entirely of polysaccharide or nucleic acid. Thus, the replicating polysaccharide and naked nucleic acid-viroid hypotheses are not longer viable. The hypothetical nucleic acid surrounded by a polysaccharide coat can also be elimanated. The recent identification of a structural protein (PrP) within the prion and its absence in preparations from uninfected controls allows us to discard hypotheses suggesting that the putative scrapie nucleic acid is surrounded by nonspecific cellular proteins. Studies demonstrating the small size of the scrapie agent distinguish it from conventional viruses, spiroplasmalike organisms, and parasites such as Sarcosporidia.

Rigid categorization of the scrapie agent at this time remains premature. Determination of its entire molecular structure will be required prior to deciding whether prions represent a distinct subgroup of extraordinarily small and unusual viruses or a pathogen which is clearly distinguishable from viruses.

X. CONCLUDING REMARKS

Although further studies are required, a considerable body of evidence suggests that prions are subviral pathogens. Recent investigations have clearly shown that the molecular properties of prions are antithetical to those of viroids (Diener *et al.*, 1982).

It is of interest to ask whether additional subviral pathogens with structures fundamentally different from those of prions and viroids will be found. The unprecedented nature of both viroids and prions suggests that other subviral pathogens, if found, will present equally perplexing stories as their molecular structures become unraveled.

Since the causes of many devastating diseases remain unknown, it is important to ask whether any of these disorders are caused by viroids or prions. Alternatively, one or more of these diseases might offer the necessary inroad to detecting a new subviral pathogen different from either viroids or prions.

ACKNOWLEDGEMENT

Authors thank Mss. F. Elvin, L. Gallagher and R. Mead for their administrative and editorial help.
Support for this work was provided by research grants from the National Institutes of Health (NS14069 and AG02132) as well as by gifts from R. J. Reynolds Industries, Inc., Sherman Fairchild Foundation and W. M. Keck Foundation.

REFERENCES

Adams, D.H. (1970). The nature of the scrapie agent: a review of recent progress. *Pathol. Biol. 18*, 559--577.
Adams, D.H. (1973). Nucleic acids and slow virus infections. *Biochem. Soc. Trans.18*, 1061-1064.
Adams, D.H., and Caspary, E.A. (1967). Nature of the scrapie virus. *Br.Med. J. 3*, 173.
Adams, D.H., and Field, E. J. (1968). The infective process in scrapie. *Lancet 2*, 714-716.
Alper, T., Haig, D.A., and Clarke, M.C. (1966). The exceptionally small size of the scrapie agent. *Biochem. Biophys. Res. Commun. 22*, 278-284.
Alper, T., Cramp, W. A., Haig, D.A.,and Clarke, M.C. (1967). Does the agent of scrapie replicate without nucleic acid? *Nature 214*, 764-766.
Alper, T., Haig, D.A. and Clarke, M.C. (1978). The scrapie agent: evidence against its dependence for replication on intrinsic nucleic acid. *J. Gen. Virol. 41*, 503-516.
Andrews, P. (1917). Estimation of molecular size and molecular weights of biological compounds by gel filtration. *Methods Biochem. Anal.18*, 1-53.
Bahmanjar, S., Williams, E.S., Johnson, F., Young, S., and Gajdusek, D.C. (personal communication).
Baringer, J. R., and Prusiner, S. B. (1978). Experimental scrapie in mice - ultrastructural observations. *Ann. Neurol.4*, 205-211.
Baringer, J. R., Wong, J., Klassen, T., and Prusiner, S.B. (1979). Further observations on the neuropathology of experimental scrapie in mouse and hamster. *In* "Slow Transmissible Diseases of the Nervous System" (S. B. Prusiner and W. J. Hadlow, eds.), Vol. II, pp. 111-121. Academic Press, New York.
Baringer, J. R., Bowman, K. A., and Prusiner, S. B. (1981). Regional neuropathology and titers in hamster scrapie. *J. Neuropathol. Exp. Neurol. 40* 329.

Bastian, F.O. (1979). Spiroplasma-like inclusions in Creutz-
     feldt-Jakob disease. *Arch. Pathol. Lab. Med.*
     103, 665-669.
Bastian, F.O., Hart, M.N., and Cancilla, P.A. (1981). Ad-
     ditional evidence of spiroplasma in Creutzfeldt-
     Jakob disease. *Lancet 1*, 660.
Beck, E., and Daniel, P.M. (1979). Kuru and Creutzfeldt-
     Jakob disease: neuropathological lesions and their
     significance. *In* "Slow Transmissible Diseases of
     the Nervous System" (S.B. Prusiner and W. J. Hadlow,
     eds.), Vol. I. pp. 253-270. Academic Press,N.Y.
Beck, E., Daniel, P.M., and Parry, H. B. (1964). Degeneration
     of the cerebellar and hypothalamo-neuropypophyseal
     systems in sheep with scrapie; and its relationship
     to human system degenerations. *Brain 87*, 153-176.
Bendheim, P.E., Groth, D.F., and Prusiner, S.B. (unpublished
     observations.).
Bignami, A., and Parry, H. B. (1971). Aggregations of 35-
     nanometer particles associated with neuronal cyto-
     pathic changes in natural scrapie. *Science 171*,
     389-390.
Bignami, A., and Parry, H. B. (1972). Electron microscopic
     studies of the brain of sheep with natural scrapie.
     I. The fine structure of neuronal vacuolation.
     Brain 95, 319-326.
Bioemendal, H., Hermsen, T., Dunia, I., and Benedetti, E.L.
     (1982). Association of crystallins with plasma
     membranes. *Exp. Eye Res. 35*, 61-67.
Bolton, A.E., and Hunter, W. M. (1973). The labelling of
     proteins to high specific radioactivities by
     conjugation to a ^{125}I-containing acylating agent.
     Biochem. J. 133, 529-539.
Bolton, D.C., McKinley, M.P. and Prusiner, S.B. (1982).
     Identification of a protein that purifies with
     the scrapie prion. *Science 218*, 1309-1311.
Bolton, D.C., McKinley, M.P., and Prusiner, S.B. (in prepara-
     tion).
Borgert, K., Koschel, K., Täuber, H., and Wecker, E. (1971).
     Effect of inactivation by hydroxylamine on early
     functions of poliovirus. *J. Virol. 8*, 1-6.
Bornstein, P., and Balian, G. (1970). The specific non-
     enzymatic cleavage of bovine ribonuclease with
     hydroxylamine. *J. Biol. Chem. 245*, 4854-4856.
Brown, P., Green, E.M., and Gajdusek, D.C. (1978). Effect of
     different gradient solutions on the buoyant density
     of scrapie infectivity. *Proc. Soc. Exp. Biol.*
     Med. 158, 513-516.

Bruce, M.E., and Fraser, H. (1975). Amyloid plaques in the brains of mice infected with scrapie: morphological variation and staining properties. *Neuropathol. Appl. Neurobiol.1*, 189-202.

Bruce, M.E., and Fraser, H. (1982). Effects of age on cerebral amyloid plaques in murine scrapie. *Neuropathol. Appl. Neurobiol.8*, 71-74.

Butzow, J.J., and Eichhorn, G.L. (1965). Interactions of metal ions with polynucleotides and related compounds. IV. Degradation of polynucleotides by zinc and other divalent metal ions. *Biopolymers 3*, 95-107.

Butzow, J. J. and Eichhorn, G.L. (1975). Different susceptibility of DNA and RNA to cleavage by metal ions. *Nature 254*, 358-359.

Carter, W.G., and Hakomori, S. (1978). A protease-resistant, transformation-sensitive membrane glycoprotein and an intermediate filament-forming protein of hamster embryo fibroblasts. *J. Biol. Chem. 253*, 2867-2874.

Chandler, R.L.,(1959). Attempts to demonstrate antibodies in scrapie diseases. *Vet. Rec. 71*, 58-59.

Chandler, R.L. (1961). Encephalopathy in mice produced by inocualtion with scrapie brain material. *Lancet 1.* 1378-1379.

Cho, H.J. (1976). Is the scrapie agent a virus? *Nature 262*, 411-412.

Cho, H.J. (1980) Requirement of a protein component for scrapie infectivity. *Intervirology 14*, 213-216.

Chou, S.M., and Martin, J.D. (1971). Kuru-plaques in a case of Creutzfeldt-Jakob disease. *Acta Neuropathol. (Berl.)17*, 150-155.

Clarke, M.C., and Haig, D.A. (1966). Attempts to demonstrate neutralizing antibodies in the sera of scrapie-affected animals. *Vet. Rec. 78*, 647-649.

Cohen, A. S. and Calkins, E. (1964). The isolation of amyloid fibrils and a study of the effect of collagenase and hyaluronidase, *J.Cell Biol. 21*, 481-486.

Cohen, A.S., Shirahama, T., and Skinner, M. (1982). Electron microscopy of amyloid. *In* "Electron Microscopy of Proteins" (J. R. Harris, ed.), Vol. III, pp. 165-206. Academic Press, New York.

Collis, S.C., and Kimberlin, R.H. (1983). Further studies on changes in immunoglobulin G in the sera and CSF of Herdwick sheep with natural and experimental scrapie. *J. Comp. Pathol.93*, 331-338.

Cox, R.A. and Kotecha, S. (1980). Resistance of the peptidyltransferase centre of rabbit ribosomes to attack by nucleases and proteinases. *Biochem. J. 190*, 199-214.

Crowther, D., and Melnick, J.L. (1961). The incorporation of neutral red and acridine orange into developing poliovirus particles making them photosensitive. *Virology 14*, 11-21.

Cuille, J., and Chelle, P.L. (1939). Experimental transmission of trembling to the goat. *C. R. Seances Acad. Sci. 208*, 1058-1060.

Cunnington, P.G., Kimberlin, R.H., Hunter, G.D.,and Newsome, P.M. (1976). Absence of antibodies to double-stranded RNA and DNA in the sera of scrapie-infected sheep and mice. IRCS Medical Science: Biochemistry; Cell and Membrane Biology; Immunology and Allergy; Microbiology, Parasitology and Infectious Diseases *4*, 250.

Darlington, C.D. (1969). Virus and provirus in the evolution of disease. *In* "Virus Diseases and the Nervous System" (C. W. M. Whitty, J.T. Hughes and F.O. McCallum, eds.), pp. 133-138. Blackwell, Oxford.

David-Ferreira, J.R., David-Ferreira, K.L., Gibbs, C.J., Jr., and Morris, J.A. (1968). Scrapie in mice: ultrastructural observations in the cerebral cortex. *Proc. Soc. Exp. Biol. Med.127*, 313-320.

Dickinson, A.G. (1976). Scrapie in sheep and goats. *In* "Slow Virus Diseases of Animals and Man" (R. H. Kimberlin, ed.), pp. 209-241. North-Holland, Amsterdam.

Dickinson, A.G., and Fraser, H. (1977). Scrapie: pathogenesis in inbred mice: an assessment of host control and response involving many strains of agent. *In* "Slow Virus Infections of the Central Nervous System" (V. ter Meulen and M. Katz, eds.), pp. 3-14. Springer Verlag, New York.

Dickinson, A.G., and Meikle, V.M. (1969). A comparison of some biological characteristics of the mouse passaged scrapie agents, 22A and ME7. *Genet. Res. 13*, 213-225.

Dickinson, A.G., and Meikle, V.M. (1971). Host-genotype and agent effects in scrapie incubation: change in allelic interaction with different strains of agent. *Mol. Gen. Genet.112*, 73-79.

Diener, T.O. (1972). Is the scrapie agent a viroid? *Nature 235*, 218-219.

Diener, T.O. (1973). Similarities between the scrapie agent and the agent of the potato spindle tuber disease. *Ann. Clin. Res.5*, 268-278.

Diener, T.O. (1979). "Viroids and Viroid Diseases," pp. 1-252. John Wiley, New York.

Diener, T.O., and Raymer, W. B. (1969). Potato spindle tuber virus: a plant virus with properties of a free nucleic acid. II. Characterization and partial purification. *Virology 37*, 351-366.

Diener, T.O., McKinley, M.P., and Prusiner, S.B. (1982). Viroids and prions. *Proc. Natl. Acad. Sci. U.S.A. 79*, 5220-5224.

Divry, P. (1927). Etude histochimique des plaques séniles. *A. Belg. Neurol. Psychiat.27*, 643-654.

Earnshaw, W. C., and Casjens, S.R. (1980). DNA packaging by the double-stranded DNA bacteriophages. *Cell 21*, 319-331.

Eklund, C. M. Hadlow, W. J., and Kennedy, R.C. (1963). Some properties of the scrapie agent and its behavior in mice. *Proc. Soc. Exp. Biol. Med.112.* 974-979.

Eklund, C.M. Kennedy, R.C., and Hadlow, W.JH. (1967). Pathogenesis of scrapie vrrus infection in the mouse. *J. Infect. Dis. 117*, 15-22.

Emeson, E.E., Kikkawa, Y., and Gueft, B. (1966). New features of amyloid found after digestion with trypsin. *J. Cell Biol. 28*, 570-577

Field, E.J. (1966). Transmission experiments with multiple sclerosis: an interim report. *Br. Med. J. 2*, 564-565.

Field, E. J. (1967). The significance of astroglial in scrapie, kuru, multiple sclerosis and old age together with a note on the possible nature of the scrapie agent. *Dtsch. Z. Nervenheilkd. 1972*, *265-274.*

Field, E.J., and Narang, H.K. (1972). An electron microscope study of scrapie in the rat: further observations on "inclusion bodies" and virus-like particles. *J. Neurol. Sci. 17*, 347-364.

Field, E. J., Raine, C.S., and Joyce, G. (1967a). Scrapie in the rat: an electron-microscope study. I. Amyloid bodies and deposits. *Acta Neuropathol. (Berl.)8*, 47-56.

Field, E. J., Raine, C.S., and Joyce, G. (1967b). Scrapie in the rat: an electron-microscope study. II. Glial inclusions. *Acta Neuropathol.(Berl.9,)* 305- -315.

Filipowicz, W., Konarska, M., Gross, H. J., and Shatkin, A. J. (1983). RNA 3'-terminal phosphate cyclase activity and RNA ligation in hela cell extract. *Nucleic Acids Res.11*, 1405-1418.

Franklin, R.M., and Wecker, E. (1959). Inactivation of some animal viruses by hydroxylamine and the structure of ribonucleic acid. *Nature 184*, 343-345.

Fraser, H. (1982). Neuronal spread of scrapie agent and targeting of lesions within the retino-tectal pathway. *Nature 295*, 149–150.

Fraser, H., and Bruce, M.E. (1973). Argyrophilic plaques in mice inoculated with scrapie from particular sources. *Lancet 1*, 617.

Freese, E., Bautz-Freese, E., and Bautz, E. (1961). Hydroxylamine as a mutagenic and inactivating agent. *J. Mol. Biol. 3*, 133–143.

Fakatsu, R., Amyx, H.L., Gibbs, C. J., Jr., and Gajdusek, D.C. (1983). Development of cerebral amyloid plaques in experimental murine scrapie. *J. Neuropathol. Exp. Neurol. 42*, 348.

Gajdusek, D.C. (1977). Unconventional viruses and the origin and disappearance of kuru. *Science 197*, 943–960.

Gajdusek, D. C. (1978). Unconventional viruses. *In* "Human Diseases Caused by Viruses" (H. Rothschild, F., Allison, Jr. and C. Howe, eds.) pp. 231–258. Oxford University Press, New York.

Gajdusek, C.C., and Gibbs, C.J., Jr. (1978). Unconventional viruses causing the spongiform virus encephalopathies. A fruitless search for the coat and core. *In* "Viruses and Environment" (E. Kurstak and K. Maramorosch, eds.), pp. 79–98. Academic Press, New York.

Gardash'yan, A.M., Nartisissov, N.V., and Bobkova, O.V.(1971) Study of the serologic reactions in mice with scrapie. *Bull. Exp. Biol. Med. 6*, 67–69.

Gardiner, A.C. (1965). Gel diffusion reactions of tissues and sera from scrapie-affected animals. *Res. Vet. Sci. 7*, 190–195.

Giannoni, G., Padden, F. J., Jr., and Keith, H. D. (1969). Crystallization of DNA from dilute solution. *Proc. Natl. Acad. Sci. U.S.A. 62*, 964–971.

Gibbons, R. A., and Hunter, G. D. (1967). Nature of the scrapie agent. *Nature 215*, 1041–1043.

Gibbs, C.J., Jr. (1967). Search for infectious etiology in chronic and subacute degenerative diseases of the central nervous system. *Curr. Top. Microbiol. Immunol. 40*, 44–58.

Gibs, C. Jr., Jr. (personal communication).

Gibbs, C. J., Jr., Gajdusek, D.C. and Morris, J.A. (1965). Viral characteristics of the scrapie agent in mice. *In* "Slow, Latent and temperate Virus Infections" (D. C. Gajdusek, C.J. Gibbs, Jr. and M. Alpers, eds.). Publication No. 1378, pp. 195–202. National Institutes of Health, Bethesda.

Gibbs, C. J.,Jr., Gajdusek, D.C., and Amyx, H.(1979). Strain variation in the viruses of Creutzfeldt-Jakob disease and kuru. *In* "Slow Transmissible Diseases of the Nervous System" (S. B. Prusiner and W. J.Hadlow, eds.), Vol. II, pp. 87-110. Academic Press, New York.

Gordon, W. S. (1946). Advances in veterinary research. *Vet. Rec. 58*, 516-520.

Gordon. W.S (1966) Review of work on scrapie at Compton, England, 1952-1964. *In* "Report of Scrapie Seminar," ARS 91-53, pp. 19-36. U.S. Dept. of Agriculture, Washington, D.C.

Gray, A., Francis, R.T., and Scholtz, C.L. (1980). Spiroplasma and Creutzfeldt-Jakob disease. *Lancet 2*, 152.

Green, N.M. (1975). Avidin. *Adv. Protein Chem. 29*, 850 133.

Gregoire, N., Gorde, J. -M., Nezri, C., Salamon, G., and Bert, J. (1983a). Mapping of the cerebral metabolims's changes in an experimental model of slow virus diseases. *J. Cerebral Blood Flow Metabolism [Suppl.1] 3*, S500-S501.

Gregoire, N., Gorde-Durand, J.M., Bouras, C., Salamon, G., and Bert, J. (1983b). Cerebral glucose utilization: local changes after microinoculation of scrapie agent in hamster. *Neurosci. Lett. 36*, 181-187.

Grieg, J.R. (1940). Scrapie. *Trans. Highlands Agricultural Soc. 52*, 71-90.

Griffith, J. S. (1967). Self-replication and scrapie. *Nature 215*, 1043-1044.

Hadlow, W. J. (unpublished observations).

Hadlow, W. J., Eklund, C.M., Kennedy, R.C., Jackson, T.A., Whitford, H.W., and Boyle, C.C. (1974). Course of experimental scrapie virus infection in the goat. *J. Infect. Dis. 129*, 559-567.

Hadlow, W.J., Kennedy, R.C., Race, R.E., and Eklund, C.M. (1980). Virologic and neurohistologic findings in dairy goats affected with natural scrapie. *Vet. Pathol. 17*, 187-199.

Hanson, C.V.(personal communication).

Hanson, C.V., Riggs, J.L., and Lennette, E. H. (1978). Photochemical inactivation of DNA and RNA viruses by psoralen derivatives. *J. Gen.Virol. 40*, 345-358.

Hartsough, G. R., and Burger, D. (1965). Encephalopathy of mink. I. Epizootiologic and clinical observations. *J. Infect. Dis. 115*, 387-392.

Hearst, J.E., and Thiry, L. (1977). The photoinactivation of an RNA animal virus, vesicular stomatitis virus, with the aid of newly synthesized psoralen derivatives. *Nucleic Acids Res. 4,* 1339-1348.

Hotchin, J., Sikora, E., and Baker, F. (1983). Disappearance of scrapie virus from tissues of the mouse. *Intervirology 19,* 205-212.

Hunter, G. D. (1972). Scrapie: a prototype slow infection. *J. Infect. Dis.125,* 427-440.

Hunter, G. D. (1979). The enigma of the scrapie agent: biochemical approaches and the involvement of membranes and nucleic acids. *In* "Slow Transmissible Diseases of the Nervous System" (S. B. Prusiner and W.J. Hadlow, eds.), Vol.II, pp. 365-385. Academic Press, New York.

Hunter, G. D., and Millson, G.C. (1967). Attempst to release the scrapie agent from tissue debris. *J. Comp. Pathol. 77,* 301-307.

Hunter, G. D., Millson, G. C., and Chandler, R.L. (1963). Observations on the comparative infectivity of cellular fractions derived from homogenates of mouse-scrapie brain. Res. *Vet. Sci. 4,* 543-549.

Hunter, G. D., Kimberlin, R.H., and Gibbons, R. A. (1968). Scrapie: a modified membrane hypothesis. *J. Theor. Biol. 20,* 355-357.

Hunter, G. D. Gibbons, R.A. Kimberlin, R.H., and Millson, G. C. (1969). Further studies of the infectivity and stability of extracts and homogenates derived from scrapie affected mouse brains. *J. Comp. Pathol. 79,* 101-108.

Hunter, G. D., Kimberlin, R. H., Collis, S., and Millson, G. C. (1973). Viral and non-viral properties of the scrapie agent. *Ann. Clin. Res. 5,* 262-267.

Isaacs, S. T., Shen, C.J., Hearst, J.E., and Rapoport, H. (1977). Synthesis and characterization of new psoralen derivatives with superior photoreactivity with DNA and RNA. *Biochemistry 16,* 1058-1064.

Kasper, K. C., Bowman, K., Stites, D.P., and Prusiner, S.B. (1981). Toward development of assays for scrapie-specific antibodies. *In* "Hamster Immune Responses in Infectious and Oncologic Diseases"(J.W.Streilein, D.A. Hart, J. Stein-Streilein, W.R. Duncan and R.E. Billingham, eds.), pp. 401-413. Plenum Press, New York.

Kasper, K.C.,Stites, D.P., Bowman, K.A., Panitch, H., and Prusiner, S.B. (1982). Immunological studies of scrapie infection. *J. Neuroimmunol.3,* 187-201.

Kim, I. C., Franzblan, C., Shirahama, T., and Cohen, A.S. (1969). The effect of papain, pronase, nagarase and trypsin on isolated amyloid fibrils. *Biochim. Biophys. Acta 181*, 465-467.

Kimberlin, R. H. (1976). "Scrapie in the Mouse," pp. 1-77. Meadowfield Press, Durham.

Kimberlin, R.H. (1982a). Reflections on the nature of the scrapie agent. *TIBS 7*, 392-394.

Kimberlin, R.H. (1982b). Scrapie agent: prions or virinos? *Nature 297*, 107-108.

Kimberlin, R. H., and Hunter, G.D. (1967). DNA synthesis in scrapie-affected mouse brain. *J. Gen. Virol.1*, 115-124.

Kimberlin, R.H., and Walker, C.A. (1977). Characteristics of a short incubation model of scrapie in the Golden hamster. *J. Gen. Virol. 34*, 295-304.

Kimberlin, R. H., and Walker, C.A. (1978). Evidence that the transmission of one source of scrapie agent to hamsters involves separation of agent strains from a mixture. *J. Gen. Virol. 39*, 487-496.

Kimberlin, R. H., and Walker, C.A. (1979). Pathogenesis of mouse scrapie: dynamics of agent replication in spleen, spinal cord and brain after infection by different routes. *J. Comp. Pathol. 89*. 551-562.

Kimberlin, R. H., and Walker, C. A. (1980). Pathogenesis of mouse scrapie; evidence for neural spread of infection to the DNA. *J. Gen. Virol. 51*, 183-187.

Kimberlin, R. H., Field, H.J., and Walker, C. A. (1983). Pathogenesis of mouse scrapie: evidence for spread of infection from central to peripheral nervous system. *J. Gen. Virol. 64*, 713-716.

Kimura, H. Yamato, S., and Murachi, T. (1978). Increase in susceptibility of hemoglobin to proteases upon treatment with *r*-Mercuribenzoate. *J. Biochem. 84*, 205-211.

Kingsbury, D. T. (in preparation)

Kingsbury, D. T., Smeltzer, D. A., Amyx, H.L., Gibbs, C.J. Jr., and Gajdusek, D. C. (1982). Evidence for an unconventional virus in mouse-adapted Creutzfeldt-Jakob disease. *Infect. Immun.37*, 1050-1053.

Kingsbury, D. T., Kasper, K. C., Stites, D. P., Watson, J.D. Hogan, R.N., and Prusiner, S.B. (1983). Genetic control of scrapie and Creutzfeldt-Jakob disease in mice. *J. Immunol. 131*. 491-496.

Klein, J. (1975). "Biology of the mouse Histocompatibility H-2 Complex", pp. 1-620. Springer Verlag, New York.

Krauth, W., and Werner, D. (1979). Analysis of the most tightly bound proteins in eukaryotic DNA. *Biochim. Biophys. Acta 564,* 390-401.

Lamar, C. H., Gustafson, D.P., Krasovich, M., and Hinsman, E.J. (1974). Ultrastructural studies of spleens, brains, and brain cell cultures of mice with scrapie. *Vet. Pathol. 11,* 13-19.

Lampert, P., Hooks,J., Gibbs, C. J., Jr., and Gajdusek, D.C. (1971). Altered plasma membranes in experimental scrapie. *Acta Neuropathol. (Berl.) 19,* 81-93.

Langridge, R., Wilson, H. R., Hooper, C. W., Wilkins, M.H.F. and Hamilton, L.D. (1960). The molecular configuration of deoxyribonucleic acid. I. X-ray diffraction study of a crystalline form of the lithium salt. *J. Mol. Biol. 2,* 19-37.

Latarjet, R. (1979). Inactivation of the agents of scrapie, Creutzfeldt-Jakob disease, and Kuru by radiations. *In* "Slow Transmissible Diseases of the Nervous System" (S. B. Prusiner and W. J. Hadlow, eds.), Vol. II, pp. 387-408. Academic Press, New York.

Latarjet, R., Cramer, R., and Montagnier, L. (1967). Inactivation by UV-,X-, and λ-radiations, of the infecting and transforming capacities of polyoma virus. *Virology 33,* 104-111.

Latarjet, R., Muel, B., Haig, D.A., Clarke, M. C., and Alper, T. (1970). Inactivation of the scrapie agent by near monochromatic ultraviolet light. *Nature 227,* 1341-1343.

Lax, A. J., Millson, G. C., and Manning, E. J. (1983). Involvement of protein in scrapie agent infectivity. *Res. Vet. Sci. 34,* 155-158.

Leach, R. H., Matthews, W. B., and Will, R. (1983). Creutzfeldt-Jakob disease: failure to detect spiroplasmas by cultivation and serological tests. *J. Neurol. Sci. 59,* 349-353.

Lewin, P. (1972). Scrapie: an infective peptide? *Lancet 1,* 748.

Lewin, P. (1981). Infectious peptides in slow virus infections: a hypothesis. *Can. Med. Assoc. J. 124,* 1436-1437.

Malone, T. G., Marsh, R.F., Hanson, R.P., and Semancik, J.S. (1978). Membrane-free scrapie activity. *J. Virol. 25,* 933-935.

Malone, T. G. Marsh, R.F., Hanson, R.P. and Semancik, J.S. (1979). Evidence for the low molecular weight nature of the scrapie agent. *Nature 278,* 575-576.

Manuelidis, E.E., and Manuelidis, L. (1979). Observations on Creutzfeldt-Jakob disease propagated in small rodents. *In* "Slow Tranmissible Diseases of the Nervous System" (S. B. Prusiner, and W. J. Hadlow, eds.), Vol. II. pp. 147-173. Academic Press, New York.

Manuelidis, E.E. Gorgacz, E. J., and Manuelidis, L. (1978). Viremia in experimental Creutzfeldt-Jakob disease. *Science 200*, 1069-1071.

Marsh, R. F., and Kimberlin, R. H. (1975). Comparison of scrapie and transmissible mink encephalopathy in hamsters. II. Clinical signs, pathology and pathogenesis. *J. Infect. Dis.131*, 104-110.

Marsh, R. F., Malone, T. G., Semancik, J. S.,Lancaster, W.D., and Hanson, R. P. (1978). Evidence for an esential DNA component in the scrapie agent. *Nature 275*, 146147.

Masters, C. L., Gajdusek, D. C., and Gibbs, C. J., Jr. (1981). Creutzfeldt-Jakob disease virus isolations from the Gerstmann-Sträussler syndrome. *Brain 104*, 559-588.

McKinley, M.P., Masiarz, F. R., and Prusiner, S.B. (1981). Reversible chemical modification of the scrapie agent. *Science 214*, 1259-1261.

McKinley, M. P., Masiarz, F. R., Isaacs, S. T., Hearst, J.E., and Prusiner, S.B. (1983a). Resistance of the scrapie agent to inactivation by psoralens. *Photochem. Photobiol.37*, 539-545.

McKinley, M.P., Bolton, D.C., and Prusiner, S.B. (1983). Fibril-like structures in preparations of scrapie prions purified from hamster brain. *Proc. Electr. Microsc. Soc. Am. 41*, 802-803.

McKinley, M. P., Bolton, D.C., and Prusiner, S.B. (in press). A protease-resistant protein is a structural component of the scrapie prion. *Cell.*

McLaren, A.D., and Shugar, D. (1964). "Photochemistry of Proteins and Nucleic Acids." Pergamon Press, New York.

Merz, P. A., Somerville, R.A., Wisniewski, H. M.., and Iqbal, K. (1981). Abnormal fibrils from scrapie-infected brain. *Acta Neuropathol.(Berl.) 54*, 63-74.

Merz, P. A., Carp, R.I., Kascsak, R., Somerville, R.A., and Wisniewski, H. M. (1983a). Scrapie associated fibrils in spleens of preclinical and clinical scrapie infected mice. Am. Soc. Virol. Ann. Meet., Abstract No. 246.

Merz, P. A. Rohwer, R.,Somerville, R., Wisniewski, H.M., Gibbs, C.J.,Jr. and Gajdusek, D.C. (1983b). Scrapie associated fibrils in human Creutzfeldt-Jakob disease. *J. Neuropathol. Exp. Neurol. 42*, 327.

M'Fadyean, J. (1918). Scrapie. *J. Comp. Pathol. 31*, 102-131.
M'Gowan, J. P. (1914). "Investigation into the Disease of Sheep called 'Scrapie',"pp. 1-114. Blackwood, Edinburgh.
Mihalyi, E. (1978). Conformation and proteolysis. "Application of Proteolytic Enzymes to Protein Structure Studies", Vol. I, 2nd Edition, pp. 152-193. CRC Press, Cleveland.
Miles, E.W. (1977). Modification of histidyl residues in proteins by diethylpyrocarbonate. *In* "Methods in Enzymology" (C. H. W. Hirs and S.N. Timasheff, eds.), Vol. XLVII, pp. 431-442. Academic Press New York.
Millson, G.C., Hunter, G. D., and Kimberlin, R.H. (1976). The physico-chemical nature of the scrapie agent. *In* "Slow Virus Diseases of Animals and Man" (R.H. Kimberlin, ed.), pp. 243-266. American Elsevier, New York.
Moretz, R. C., Wisniewski, H.M., and Lossinsky, A.S. (1983). Pathogenesis of neuritic and amyloid plaques in scrapie – ultrastructural study of early changes in the cortical neuropil. *In* "Aging of the Brain" (D. Samuel, ed.), pp. 61-79. Raven Press, New York.
Moulton, J.E., and Palmer, A.C. (1959). Attempts to demonstrate transmissible agent of scrapie in experimentally infected goats by means of fluorescent antibody. *Cornell Vet.49*, 349-359.
Narang, H. K. (1974a) An electron microscopic study of natural scrapie sheep brain: further observations on virus-like particles and paramyxovirus-like tubules. *Acta Neuropathol. (Berl.)28*, 317-329.
Narang, H. K. (1974b) Ruthenium red and lanthanum nitrate-a possible tracer and negative stain for scrapie "particles"? *Acta Neuropathol. (Berl.)29*, 37-43.
Narang, H. K. (1974c). An electron microscopic study of the scrapie mouse and rat: further observations on virus-like particles with ruthenium red and lanthanum nitrate as a possible trace and negative stain. *Neurobiology 4*, 349-363.
Nozaki, Y., Schechter, N.M., Reynolds, J.A., and Tanford, C. (1976). Use of gel chromatography for the determination of the Stokes radii of proteins in the presence and absence of detergents. A re-examination. *Biochemistry 15*, 3884-3890.
Nozth, A.C.T., and Rich, A. (1961). X-ray diffraction studies of bacterial viruses. *Nature 191*, 1242-1245.
Ott, U., Odermatt, E., Engel, J., Furthmayr, H., and Timpl, R. (1982). Protease resistance and conformation of laminin. *Eur. J. Biochem. 123*, 63-72.

Outram, G. W. (1976). The pathogenesis of scrapie in mice. *In* "Slow Virus Diseases of Animals and Man" (R.H. Kimberlin, ed.),pp. 325-357. North-Holland, Amsterdam.

Parry, H. B. (1962). Scrapie: a transmissible and hereditary disease of sheep. *Heredity 17*, 75-105.

Parry, H.B. (196). Scrapie – natural and experimental. *In* "Virus Diseases and the Nervous System" (C. W.M. Whitt, J.T. Hughes and F.O. McCallum, eds.), pp. 99-105. Blackwell, Oxford.

Pattison, I.H. (1965). Resistance of the scrapie agent to formalin. *J. Comp. Pathol. 75*, 159-164.

Pattison, I. H., and Jones, K.M. (1967). The possible nature of the transmissible agent of scrapie. *Vet. Rec. 80*, 1-8.

Pattison, I. H., and Millson, G.C. (1960). Further observations on the excperimental production of scrapie in goats and sheep. *J. Comp. Pathol.70*, 182-193.

Pattison, I. H., and Millson, G. C. (1961). Experimental transmission of scrapie to goats and sheep by the oral route. *J. Comp. Pathol.71*, 171-176.

Pattison, I.H., Millson, G.C. and Smith, K. (1964). An examination of the action of whole blood, blood cells or serum on the goat scrapie agent. *Res. Vet. Sci. 5*, 116-121.

Phillips, J. H., and Brown, D.M. (1967). The mutagenic action of hydroxylamine. *Prog. Nucleic Acid Res. Mol. Biol. 7*, 349-368.

Porter, D.D. , Porter, H.G., and Cox, N.A. (1973). Failure to demonstrate a humoral immune response to scrapie infection in mice. *J. Immunol. 111*, 1407-1410.

Pras, M., Zucker-Franklin, D., Rimon, A., and Franklin, E.C. (1969). Physical, chemical and ultrastructural studies of water-soluble human amyloid fibrils. *J. Exp. Med. 130*, 777-791.

Prusiner, S. B. (1978). An approach to the isolation of biological particles using sedimentation analysis. *J. Biol. Chem. 253*, 916-921.

Prusiner, S. B. (1982). Novel proteinaceous infectious particles cause scrapie. *Science 216*, 136-144.

Prusiner, S. B. (unpublished observations).

Prusiner, S. B., and Groth, D.F. (unpublished observations.)

Prusiner, S. B., Hadlow, W. J., Eklund, C. M., Race, R.E., and Cochran, S.P. (1978a). Sedimentation characteristics of the scrapie agent from murine spleen and brain. *Biochemistry 17*, 4987-4992.

Prusiner, S.B., Hadlow, W.J., Garfin, D.E., Cochran, S.P., Baringer, J. R., Race, R. E., and Eklund, C.M. (1978b). Partial purification and evidence for multiple molecular forms of the scrapie agent. *Biochemistry 17*, 4993-4999.

Prusiner, S. B., Garfin, D.E., Baringer, J.R., Cochran, S.P., Hadlow, W.J., Race, R.E., Eklund, C.M. (1979). On the partial purification and apparent hydrophobicity of the scrapie agent. *In* "Slow Transmissible Diseases of the Nervous System"(S.B. Prusiner and W. J. Hadlow, eds.), Vol, II, pp. 425-464. Academic Press, New York.

Prusiner, S.B., Cochran, S.P., Groth, D.F., Hadley, D., Martinez, H.M., and Hadlow, W.J. (1980a). Aging of the nervous system and prolonged incubation periods of the spongiform encephalopathies. *In* "Aging of the Brain and Dementia" (L. Amaducci, A.N. Davison and P. Antuono, eds.), pp. 205-216. Raven Press, New York.

Prusiner, S. B., Garfin, D.E., Cochran, S.P., McKinley, M.P., and Groth, D. F. (1980b). Experimental scrapie in the mouse: electrophoretic and sedimentation properties of the partially purifed agent. *J. Neurochem. 35*, 574-582.

Prusiner, S. B., Groth, D. F., Bildstein, C., Masiarz, F.R., McKinley, M.P., and Cochran, S.P. (1980c). Electrophoretic properties of the scrapie agent in agarose gels. *Proc. Natl. Acad. Sci. USA 77*, 2984-2988.

Prusiner, S.B., Groth, D.F., Cochran, S.P., Masiarz, F.R., McKinley, M. P., and Martinez, H.M. (1980d). Molecular properties, partial purification and assay by incubation period measurements of the hamster scrapie agent. *Biochemistry 19*, 4883-4891.

Prusiner, S. B., Groth, D.F., Cochran, S.P., Mc Kinley, M.P., and Masiarz, F.R. (1980e). Gel electrophoresis and glass permeation chromatography of the hamster scrapie agent after enzymic digestion and detergent extraction. *Biochemistry 19*, 4892-4898.

Prusiner, S. B., Groth, D.F., McKinley, M.P., Cochran, S.P., Bowman, K.A., and Kasper, K. C. (1981a). Thiocyanate and hydroxyl ions inactivate the scrapie agent *Proc. Natl. Acad. Sci. USA 78*, 4606-4610.

Prusiner, S. B., McKinley, M.P., Groth, D. F., Bowman,K.A., Mock, N.I., Cochran, S.P., and Masiarz,F.R.(1981b). Scrapie agent contains a hydrophobic protein. *Proc. Natl. Acad. Sci. USA 78*, 6675-6679.

Prusiner, S. B., Bolton, D.C., Groth, D.F., Bowman, K.A., Cochran, S.P., and McKinley, M.P. (1982a). Further purification and characterization of scrapie prions. *Biochemistry 21*, 6942-6950.

Prusiner, S. B., Cochran, S.P., Groth, D.F., Downey, D.E., Bowman, K.A., and Martinez, H. M.(1982b). Measurement of the scrapie agent using an incubation time interval assay. *Ann. Neurol.* *11,* 353-358.

Raine, C. S., and Field, E. J. (1967). Orientated tubules in axoplasm of cerebellar myelinated nerve fibres in the rat. A study of normal and scrapie animals. *Acta Neuropathol. (Berl.) 9,* 298-304.

Reynolds, J. A. (1981). Solubilization and characterization of membrane proteins. *In* "Membrane Receptors" (S. Jacobs and P. Cuatrecasas, eds.). Ser. B., Vol. XI, pp. 33-60. Chapman and Hall, London.

Rohwer, R.G., and Gajdusek, D.C. (1980). Scrapie - virus or viroid, the case for a virus. *In* "Search for the cause of Multiple Sclerosis and Other Chronic Diseases of the Central Nervous System" (A. Boese, ed.), pp. 333-355. Chemie, Weinheim.

Rose, J. A. (1974). Parvovirus reproduction. *In* "Comprehensive Virology" (H. Fraenkel-Conrat and R.R. Wagner, eds.), Vol, III, pp. 1-61. Plenum Press, New York

Ruinen, L., Van Bruggen, E.F. J., Scholten, J. H., Gruber, M., and Mandema, E. (1968). Comparison of the structures observed in the human splenic amyloid fractions by electron microscopy. *In* "Amyloidosis" (E. Mandema, L. Ruinen, J. H. Scholten and A.S. Cohen, eds.), pp. 194-205. Excerpta Medica, Amsterdam.

Sänger,H.L., Ramm, K., Domdey, H., Gross, H. J., Henco, K. and Riesner, D. (1979). Conversion of circular viroid molecules to linear strands. *FEBS Lett. 88,* 117-122.

Schaffer, F. L., and Schwerdt, C.E. (1959). Purification and properties of poliovirus. *Adv. Virus Res.,6,* 159-204.

Schuster, H.J., and Wittman, H.-G (1963). The inactivating and mutagenic action of hydroxylamine on tobacco mosaic virus ribonucleic acid. *Virology 19,* 421-430.

Seitelberger, F. (1981). Straübler's disease. *Acta Neuropathol. (Berl.) [Suppl.] 7,* 341-343.

Semancik, J.S., Morris, T.J., and Weathers, L. G. (1973). Structure and conformation of low molecular weight pathogenic RNA from exocortis disease. *Virology 53,* 448-456.

Semancik, J. S., Marsh, R. F., Geelen, J.L. and Hanson, R.P. (1976). Properties of the scrapie agent-endomembrane complex from hamster brain. *J. Virol. 18,* 693-700.

Siakotos, A.N., Gajdusek, D.C., Gibbs, C.J., Jr., Traub, R.D. and Bucana, C. (1976). Partial purification of the scrapie agent from mouse brain by pressure disruption and zonal centrifugation in sucrose-sodium chloride gradients. *Virology 70*, 230-237.

Siakotos, A.N., Raveed, D., and Longa, G. (1979). The discovery of a particle unique to brain and spleen subcellular fractions from scrapie-infected mice. *J. Gen. Virol. 43*, 417-422.

Sigurdsson, B. (1954). Rida, a chronic encephalitis of sheep with general remarks on infections which develop slowly and some of their special characteristics. *Br. Vet. J. 110*, 341-354.

Sokoloff, L., Reivich, M., Kenndey, C., Des Rosiers, M.H., Patlak, C.S., Pettigren, K. D., Sakurada, O., and Shinohara, M. (1977). The [^{14}C] deoxyglucose method for the measurement of local cerebral glucose utilization: theory, procedure, and normal values in the conscious and anesthetized albino rat. *J. Neurochem.* 28. 897-916.

Somerville, R.A., Millson, G. C., and Hunter, G.D. (1976). Changes in a protein-nucleic acid complex from synaptic plasma membrane of scrapie-infected mouse brain. *Biochem. Soc. Trans. 4*, 1112-1114.

Sorenson, G. D., and Binington, H. B,. (1964). Resistance of murine amyloid fibrils to proteolytic enzymes. *Fed. Proc. 23*, 550.

Stamp, J.T.(1967). Scrapie and its wider implications. *Br. Med. Bull. 23*, 133-137.

Stark, G. R., Stein, W.H., and Moore, S. (1960). Reactions of the cyanate present in aqueous urea with amino acids and proteins. *J. Biol. Chem. 235*, 3177-3181.

Tanford, C. (1961). "Physical Chemistry of Macromolecules," pp. 317-456. John Wiley, New York.

Tateishi, J., Ohta, M., Koga, M., Sato, Y., and Kuroiwa, Y. (1979). Transmission of chronic spongiform encephalopathy with kuru plaques from humans to small rodents. *Ann. Neurol. 5*, 581-584.

Tateishi, J., Niagara, H., Hikita, K., and Sato, Y. (in press). Amyloid plaques in the brains of mice with Creutzfeldt-Jakob disease. *Ann. Neurol.*

Terry, R. D., and Wisniewski, H. (1970). The ultrastructure of the neurofibrillary tangle and the senile plaque. *In* "CIBA Foundation Symposium on Alzheimer's Disease and related Disorders" (G.E.W. Wollstenholme and M. O'Connor, eds.), pp. 145-168. Churchill Livingston, London.

Tessman, I. (1968). Mutagenic treatment of double and single-stranded DNA phages T4 and S13 with hydroxylamine. *Virology 35*, 330-333.

Wilcock, G. K., and Esiri, M.M. (1982). Plaques, tangles and dementia. *J. Neurol. Sci. 56*, 343-356.

Williams, E. S., and Young, S. (1980). Chronic wasting disease of captive mule deer: a spongiform encephalopathy. *J. Wildl. Dis. 16*, 89-98.

Wilson, D.R., Anderson, R.D., and Smith, W. (1950). Studies in scrapie. *J. Comp. Pathol. 60*, 267-282.

Wisniewski, H. M. Bruce, M.E., and Fraser, H. (1975). Infectious etiology of neuritic (senile) plaques in mice. *Science 190*, 1108-1110.

Wisniewski, H.M., Mortez, R.C., and Lossinsky, A.S. (1981). Evidence for induction of localized amyloid deposits and neuritic plaques by an infectious agent. *Ann. Neurol. 10*, 517-522.

Wisniewski, H.M., Merz, G.S., Merz, P.A., Wen, G.Y., and Iqbal, K. (1983). Morphology and biochemistry of neuronal paired helical filaments and amyloid fibers in humans and animals. *In* "Progress in Neuropathology" (H. M. Zimmerman, ed.), Vol. V, pp. 139-150. Raven Press, New York.

Yagishita, S. (1981). Creutzfeldt-Jakob disease with kuru-like plaques in Japan. *Acta Pathol. (Jpn)31*, 923--942.

Zlotnik, I. (1962). The pathology of scrapie: a comparative study of lesions in the brain of sheep and goats. *Acta Neuropathol. (Berl.) [Suppl.] 1*, 61-70.

Chapter 17

THE ENIGMA OF DNA IN THE ETIOLOGY OF SCRAPIE

*D. H. Adams

* External Staff, Medical Research Council

Department of Virology Annexe
1-4 Claremont Terrace
Newcastle upon Tyne
NE 2 4AE   United Kingdom

I.   SCRAPIE

Since virtually everyone who has ever worked with scrapie has written a literature review as part of the process of setting out their own ideas, in some ways there is little new to be said. Consequently the following comments will be restricted to those developments which historically seem to have been the most significant in forming the view of the scrapie virus as a most unusual agent.

Athough scrapie has been known for about three hundred years as a disease of sheep central nervous system, the first real indication of its nature was the successful transmission from affected to normal sheep, followed by passages from sheep to goat and goat to goat, by Cuille and Chelle nearly 50 years ago. At the end of their experiments, Cuille and Chelle (1938, 1939) appeared to have little doubt that scrapie was a disease resulting from infection with a transmissible (filterable) virus. The main caveat was the length of the period between infection and disease − in some cases

SUBVIRAL PATHOGENS
OF PLANTS AND ANIMALS:
VIROIDS AND PRIONS

Copyright © 1985 by Academic Press, Inc.
All rights of reproduction in any form reserved.
ISBN 0-12-470230-9

as long as four years, but never less than about four months,
which at the time was quite unheard of in terms of virus
diseases. Wilson *et al.* (1950) and unpublished (quoted by
Stamp *et al.*, 1959) confirmed these findings and extended
scrapie transmission to nine passages showing without doubt
that a replicating agent was involved. They also concluded
that the disease was due to a virus infection of the central
nervous system. However, by this time, an unscheduled experiment had been carried out which was considered highly
significant. Of a very large group of sheep which had been
inoculated with formalin 'inactivated' louping-ill virus vaccine, a high proportion subsequently developed scrapie,(Gordon, 1946). The reasonable explanation has always been that
the vaccine was accidentally prepared from scrapie infected
sheep, and that the scrapie virus was not inactivated by the
formalin used.

Under the considerable difficulties involved in the use
of sheep as the experimental animal – not the least being
that a substantial proportion of those inoculated with infective material were resistant and never developed a recognisa-
ble disease which was the only assay available at the time.
Stamp *et al.* (1959) attempted to measure the *in vitro* inactivation of the virus by a number of then conventional procedures. The experimental results confirmed and extended previous studies in suggesting that homogenates of scrapie infected tissues were not inactivated by boiling for up to 8
hours, by freezing and thawing, by storage for very long
periods or by treatment with the nitrogen mustard acetyle-
thyleneimine. On the basis of these results, the authors
concluded that 'it seems most unlikely that the factor could
be nucleo protein in nature'.

However, in a contemporary review of viral inactivation and chemotherapy procedures, Hurst (1957) laid great
stress on the very wide variability shown either between viruses or by the same virus under different conditions. For
example, the use of formalin to inactivate viruses in the
course of vaccine production involved very close control. Too
little might not destroy all the virus: too much could affect the antigenicity of the viral protein. The literature
in fact contains many examples of 'inactivated' vaccines
still containing the original virus or contaminating viruses
(e.g. SV40 from monkey kidney cells) in active forms.
While many such incidents have been caused by poor technique,
it is by no means clear that this is true in all cases. The
suggestion has often been made of the existence of relatively
small proportions of at least some viruses which appear more
resistant to inactivation procedures.

The louping-ill incident showed that an exposure to
formalin which inactivates the virus does not, or does not

completely, inactivate scrapie but little else. Further, although the procedures applied by Stamp *et al.* (1959)undoubtedly left active scrapie virus in the preparations, it is impossible to say what proportion of that originally present was involved, since standard titration methods could not be used under the circumstances. Even later work on the formalin inactivation of scrapie (Pattison, 1965) has similar problems of interpretation. Pattison certainly showed that active scrapie virus remained after even quite drastic formalin inactivation procedures (applied to unpurified brain homogenates). These included exposure to up to 20% formalin for 18h at 37°C or pickling in up to 12% buffered formal saline at room temperature for as long as 28 months. However, most of the work was done using goats (3 controls and experimental groups as small as 1) which make it statistically impossible to justify Pattison's claim that the length of incubation period was not reduced: to have been able to show this would be a *prima facie* indication that the titer had been little changed. Some experiments were done in mice, all of which developed scrapie after inoculation with formalin treated material. In this case, however, non-formalised scrapie does not appear to have been included for comparison of the incubation period. Thus, although the resistance of at least some fraction of scrapie to formalin is clearly high and possibly very high, the results as they stand cannot be said to show that scrapie differs fundamentally from other viruses - particularly if the possibility of a relatively small resistant fraction is taken into account. In reviewing the effects of formalin, Millson *et al.* (1976) commented that 'the inactivation of scrapie was probably substantial in some experiments'. Bell *et al.* (1972) also showed that scrapie is by no means immune to inactivation. Treatment with iodine-alcohol which destroyed infectivity in a group of control viruses also reduced scrapie titer to below 0.1%.

As Adams (1970) pointed out, a similar caveat must be added in respect of the resistance to heat inactivation. Studies made after Stamp *et al.* (1959)(summarized in Table 1 of Adams, 1970) showed clearly this very phenomenon in that only a relatively small proportion of scrapie virus survived heat traeatment even when this was not unduly severe. Further, as also stressed by Eklund *et al.* (1963) that the remaining titer depended considerably on the conditions used for the preparation of the samples, including the obvious problem in reconstituting coagulated debris resulting from heat treatment. Eklund *et al.* (1963) also commented that their findings 'suggest that the scrapie agent is not a member of a unique group of pathogens but is a medium sized virus whose resistance to heat is analogous to that of hepatitis virus'. Interestingly enough, Hunter and Millson (1964)

found that heat inactivation of scrapie began at a temperature close to the melting point of DNA. These demonstrations
of a heat/formalin resistant fraction of scrapie infectivity
- and it must be stressed that this was a very small proportion - immediately raise an important question. Is the assumption to be made that the resistance of the scrapie virus
is typified by the 99.9% of the more sensitive or the 0.1% of
the more resistant fraction? The possibility certainly
arises that there may be a greater difference between the
sensitive and resistant scrapie fractions than between the
'sensitive' scrapie fraction and other viruses.

The most likely explanation of greater or lesser amounts
of residual surviving virus after any inactivation procedure
is that some fraction is associated with or sequestered by
cellular components forming a protective microenvironment.
Scrapie shows this property to a much greater extent than
other viruses, and one of the greatest practical difficulties
encountered with scrapie, which has caused intense frustra-
tion in scrapie workers over the years, is its almost indissoluble association with tissue components(Hunter and Millson,
1967) Millson *et al.*, 1971). Indeed, from what has already
been said and as will be seen subsequently, this has almost
certainly been a primary root cause of the controversy over
its nature. It is perhaps unfortunate that the extent to
which such interaction with other structures can protect an
infective agent has only recently been fully appreciated in
practise. Nevertheless, the combination of the observations
of an unexpected resistance to inactivation with an unexpectedly long incubation period, laid the foundations for the
'unconventionality' of the scrapie virus. If it is accepted
that this represents a problem, there are clearly two basic
possibilities for its solution. Either that the properties
of the scrapie agent really are such as to set it aside from
other viruses, or a recognition that the observations leading to this conclusion may have been made on too small a
virus group which was not representative of the whole spectrum. Such decisions have to be made continually during
scientific enquiry, but it is a matter of history that even
when wide or apparently unbridgeable gaps appear, there is a
high probability of these narrowing or even closing as knowledge expands. However, and for no obviously valid reason,
investigators at the time opted for the former alternative as
examplified by the 'no nucleo protein' conclusion of Stamp
et al. (1959).

In practical terms, the almost indissoluble association
of the scrapie virus with cellular material has also meant
that all experiments on the nature and properties of scrapie
have used preparations containing vanishingly small proportions of infective agent. This has not only accentuated the

problems involved in assessing stability but has made it particularly difficult for different groups of workers to obtain
the same results under apparently similar circumstances even
when the experiments involved   appear   simple   and   straight
forward.   To give just one example, Hunter *et al.*   (1969)
claimed that periodate was a specific inhibitor of scrapie
infectivity and used this result as supporting evidence for
their 'replicating membrane' theory of scrapie.   However,
Adams *et al.* (1972) were quite unable to confirm these results, finding only a very slight inactivation by the same
compound under at least reasonably similar circumstances.
Despite some discussion between the two groups, the reasons
for the almost total disagreement were never elucidated.
     Despite the really very shaky nature of the evidence and
some dissenting voices, by the mid 1960's the generally
accepted view was that the scrapie virus was highly unusual,
possibly not a virus at all, and the term 'agent' came into
general use presumably as a means of underlining these doubts.
In retrospect, it is puzzling to realize how ready investigators were at this time to reject the simplest interpretation —
even of their own data — when the results appeared to conflict with orthodox principles which were believed to have
been established.   Alper *et al.* (1966) bombarded scrapie
preparations with ionizing radiation and found what appeared
to be an exceptionally high resistance to inactivation,
compared with that expected from experiments with a number of
conventional virus and nucleic acid targets reported in the
literature.   From the pre-existing data, a relationship between radiation dose and target size for a standard percentage inactivation had already been established.   Fitting the
scrapie results to the curve, gave an indicated size in the
region of 10^5 daltons.   Since at that time, the size of the
smallest known viral core was at least an order of magnitude
greater, the indicated figures were rejected as 'implausibly
small' for a conventional virus core in favor of the conclusion that the scrapie agent must be of an unusual composition.   In a continuation of these experiments using ultraviolet radiation against suspensions of infected mouse brain
extracts, Alper *et al.* (1967) found what seemed to be an
even more remarkable resistance to inactivation and concluded
that the results 'confirmed that the agent responsible does
not depend on nucleic acid for its ability to replicate'.
This view was strengthened by further studies showing that
the resistance of the scrapie agent was similar to that of a
number of proteins of approximately the molecular size suggested by the previous ionizing radiation data (Latarjet *et
al.*, 1970).   In coming to these conclusions, the authors
never seem to have seriously considered the possibility that
coat or other microenvironmental protection in unpurified

preparations or even the indicated small size of the putative nucleic acid core could have been responsible for the observed results.

This work in particular, coupled with that which had gone before, led at about this time to an intense bout of speculation in the scientific and popular press that the scrapie agent was a completely new and unknown form of self-replicating disease producing entity. And many perhaps somewhat unlikely solutions were put forward, including a replicating protein (Pattison and Jones, 1967), replicating polysaccharide (Field, 1966) and a replicating membrane structure (Hunter *et al.*, 1968). Although *prima facie* these suggestions might seem to fit more easily with the observed properties of scrapie, they merely shift the problem from one place to another and at the same time raise other and more fundamental difficulties. In particular, no really acceptable mechanism by which such molecules self-replicate has ever been suggested and indeed the problems involved are again highlighted by recent attempts (Lewin, 1982). It is also difficult to accept that scrapie should be such a unique exception – at least until all other explanations have been negated.

The caveats about the basic data and its interpretation have already been stressed in this chapter. However, it may also be opportune at this point to add the reminder that despite everything which has been said about the abnormal properties of the scrapie agent there are very few investigations in which its properties have been directly compared under the same conditions with those of other viruses, and particularly with a wide range of other viruses. Also, probably because of its supposedly abnormal properties, attempts to inactivate scrapie infectivity have been made on a scale unusual in the study of any viral agent and so comparative data for other viruses may not even exist (see e.g. Millson *et al.*, 1976). There have also been few, if any, attempts to compare scrapie in depth with other viruses which are accepted as such but whose behavior may be unusual. For example, with hepatitis A or B (the latter reported by Eklund *et al.*, (1963) to have a resistance to heat similar to scrapie) or the U1 and U2 strains of tobacco mosaic virus which showed considerable coat-associated difference in their responses to UV irradiation. The assumption seems to have been made at all stages that the properties of a relatively small group of purified or semipurified, and probably relatively sensitive, viruses are not only representative of viruses as a whole, but are capable of meaningful comparison with a virus cell associated to the extend that scrapie is. Referring to the nature of the scrapie agent Adams (1970) commented that 'by no means the least difficulty in formulating hypotheses to fit the

facts is to determine what the facts actually are'. Looking
at the mass of assorted, and ofteu difficult to interpret,
data which has appeared subsequently, the rider might now be
added 'to determine how much of the accumulated data is really
relevant to the problem.' It might well be said that the main
conclusion to be drawn is that inactivation procedures give
very inclusive and uninterpretable indications of basic structure. Added to this it seems clear that the view taken of
scrapie by successive investigators has depended greatly on
whether priority has been given to the similarities or the
differences between scrapie and other viruses. Again with
the proviso that the differences themselves may be relatively
interminate and difficult to interpret.

And indeed there has been a very recent salutory warning
of the potential fallibility of restrictive assumptions concerning stability in the report by Baross and Deming(1983)
on the replication of 'black smoker' bacteria at 250°. Independent confirmation must clearly be awaited but it would
not be surprising if a radical change has to be made in present concepts of the stability limits of biological systems.
A first reaction might be that the necessarily associated
high pressure is a key factor in stabilizing macromolecules −
perhaps, for example, pressurization will increase the melting
temperature of DNA. Much of what has been said so far in this
chapter has been related to protection of macromolecular
function by the appropriate shielding or chemical bonding, and
it may well be that high pressure either on its own, or particularly in conjunction with a specialized type of bonding is
a powerful stabilizing influence. It would be fascinating to
see, for example, whether either or both the heat sensitive
and heat resistant fractions of the scrapie virus would
withstand higher temperatures if first pressurized − or, come
to that, other viruses too.

To summarize at this stage, the scrapie problem seems to
depend crucially on the ability of a nucleic acid − or even
perhaps a small proportion of it − to find or to self organ-
ize, which may be more to the point, a protective cellular
microenvironment. This may be unusual but it does not auto-
matically set scrapie aside from other viruses.

If it is possible for nucleic acid to operate in this way
− and further comment on this will be made later − such a
view may well become more and more acceptable as the properties of other 'unconventional' viruses become better understood. There then seems no reason why scrapie should be
other than a nucleic acid based virus and it must be stressed
(a) that this is still by far the simplest and most acceptable hypothesis and (b) that no decisive evidence against it
has yet been tabled despite all the efforts. Certainly the
small size of the scrapie core which seemed to Alper

et al. (1966) such a stumbling block, finally disappeared
as a result of Diener's extensive and elegant studies on the
small RNA comprising the potato spindle tuber viroid. The
results given in other chapters of this book show that the
other known plant viroids are also similar in size to PSTV -
within the range of approximately 1.5-2 x 10^5 daltons.
Diener also demonstrated experimentally that virus nucleic
acid cores of this size have considerable resistance to UV
radiation - as might well have been expected in fact, and
that protection by cell constituents can also be a major
factor in UV resistance (see Diener, 1973, 1979).

II. TRANSFECTION

A perhaps deceptively straightforward way of showing the
nucleic acid basis of a replicating entity in tissue is of
course to extract tisue nucleic acid and demonstrate that
this will either cause disease, infect cells with the production of intact virus, or at least contain a fraction not
normally associated with the tissue. Several attempts at all
aspects have been made using scrapie infected tissues and an
up to date list has been given by Prusiner (1982). However,
as with so many other investigations bearing on the scrapie
problem, unequivocal and repeatable results have been very
elusive, although in the circumstances this might not be unexpected. Firstly, it is very difficult to replicate scrapie
under culture conditions. Secondly, transfection by purified
nucleic acid (mostly with DNA) has never been simple to
demonstrate because of its very low infectivity. The best
results have usually been obtained when relatively uncontami-
nated viral DNA has been isolated in some quantity, and then
coupling a relatively large inoculum with supplementary procedures designed to improve the efficiency of infection. The
presence of other (e.g. cellular) nucleic acid in such preparations normally reduces infectivity - in some cases substantially. From these considerations, scrapie nucleic acid
would be expected to be a poor starter. It can only be present - as has already been said - in vanishingly small amounts
in infected tissue and consequently scrapie nucleic acid
could in any event only be prepared as a small fraction of
associated tissue nucleic acid. This makes it not only difficult to detect (see e.g. Adams, 1972) but probably also
almost impossible to reproducibly demonstrate transfection.
In the latter connection, no in depth study of the various
supplementary procedures appears to have been made using
scrapie preparations, although they are known to give variable results with other viruses. However, there have been
enough successful indications of the presence of an abnormal
nucleic acid in scrapie tissue to make the probability very
high.

Nevertheless, the earlier doubts on the nature of the scrapie virus appear to have been revived recently by Prusiner's group in particular, with the description of scrapie as a 'novel proteinaceous infectious particle' (prion) and these views have recently been summarized in a review article, (Prusiner, 1982). However, from what is said it is not altogether clear whether Prusiner believes scrapie to be a nucleic acid based agent or not. It is also difficult to understand the emphasis, reiterated throughout the article, on the observations that the infectivity of scrapie is associated with or related to protein, since all viruses usually described as conventional are associated with protein on which, to a greater or lesser extent, their infectivity depends. Such dependence may be total when virus associated protein has a specific and essential function e.g. as a polymerase for viral nucleic acid replication. Alternatively, dependence may be partial where, for example, virus associated protein facilitates entry of the nucleic acid into the host cell and in so doing enhances infectivity by up to several orders of magnitude.

However, despite some difficulty in interpretation already mentioned the 'prion' concept of Prusiner seems to envisage something more - even to be orientated towards the earlier view of a presumably self replicating-protein as a virus core. Nevertheless (Prusiner, 1982) there still appears to be a loophole allowing for the presence of nucleic acid; particularly if the size is much less than the 10^5 daltons suggested by the ionizing radiation data which, with all the caveats, is still the most reliable estimate. Prusiner's latest work (summarized in his Chapter) concerns the isolation and characterization of a 30,000 dalton protein which is associated with scrapie infectivity. So far there is no satisfactory explanation of its origin, function, or relationship, if any, to scrapie disease. The crunch, presumably, is whether it can be shown unequivocally (a) to be associated with no nucleic acid - not even an oligonucleotide; (b) that it is infectious. It must be said that the most probable explanation of the presence of such a normally undetected protein is that it is associated with pathological changes resulting from virus infection, i.e. that it is host-specified. Unless it is of an unusual composition with extensive amino acid sequence repetition, it is too large to be scrapie nucleic acid specified even if this is as large as 10^5 daltons, and if a smaller size is assumed, the problem is even more complicated.

Further, in Table 2 of Prusiner (1982), six procedures attacking nucleic acid and to which the scrapie agent is resistant are listed. The possible explanation given for at least five of these involves an inability of the procedure to

penetrate, or break or affect what is called a surrounding
protein 'shell'. Beginning again from the standpoint that
virtually all – if not all – viruses have protein surrounding
the nucleic acid core, it is again not easy to see what the
significance is. However, the term 'shell' would appear to
be descriptive of some type of unusual association – presumably between protein and nucleic acid – which is highly impene-
trable and thereby protective although no detailed description of the possible structure involved is given. Prusiner
also comments that 'while there are some viruses which may be
resistant to two or possibly three of the six procedures
listed, there are none known which are resistant to all'.
However, this argument does seem to have a logical flaw in
that if, as suggested, a special shell is the reason for resistance to five and possibly all the procedures, it cannot
be said either that they are independent or that the scrapie
virus is necessarily that unusual. Further, if it is accepted that a fraction of some viruses (including scrapie) has a
greater resistance to inactivation than the whole, the surrounding 'shell' structure may be variable in extent, composition or penetrability, or some equilibrium may exist between 'protected' and 'unprotected' fractions. Nevertheless,
the argument seems once again to have come to the point made
previously in the present chapter that the essential difference in scrapie is not an absence of nucleic acid, but that
at least a proportion of its nucleic acid is contained in an
unusually protective microenvironment. What is difficult to
picture, is how protein would be able, particularly on its
own, to form the shell-like structure which Prusiner quite
rightly envisages. While protein may associate very closely
with nucleic acid, as for example in histone-DNA interaction,
and even form covalent bonds on a limited scale, the resulting structures are difficult to visualise in terms of a
sufficiently stable and protective shell. There has also
been a recent report of different core binding affinities
with viral proteins, in that a genome (ds RNA) linked protein
in infectious pancreatic necrosis virus remains attached to
RNA during extraction procedures so long as proteinase is not
used (Persson and MacDonald, 1982). Again, however, this
would not seem to be the type of structure which would be
involved in scrapie protection. Carbohydrate is not only
very radiation resistant, but readily able to form covalent
bonds to nucleic acid, particularly if hydroxylated bases are
present. On the grounds that this would greatly facilitate
the syphoning off of energy absorbed during UV irradiation or
heat treatment of the latter,Adams and Caspary (1967)suggest-
ed carbohydrate as a major component of a scrapie nucleic
acid coat. The proposal was dismissed rather summarily by
Prusiner (1982) on the evidence of the essential association

of protein with scrapie infectivity. However, there was neither intention or suggestion by Adams and Caspary to exclude protein, and indeed, our proposal included mucopolysaccharide as an alternative. Our principal aim at the time was to concentrate on the material in immediate proximity to the nucleic acid. Even if this was entirely composed of polysaccharide, there would be nothing inconsistent with the putative nucleic acid polysaccharide structure being attached to or covered with protein or lipoprotein involved with infectivity. *Prima facie* such a structure would seem to fit much more readily with Prusiner's concept of a 'shell', but once again, would not fundamentally set scrapie aside from other viruses.

However, if it is acepted that, although possibly on the fringe, the scrapie agent is a recognizable virus within the criteria which differentiate viruses from non-viruses, it must be agreed that scrapie has provided more than its fair share of difficulties. To begin with, it is reasonable to suggest (Adams and Bell, 1976) that DNA rather than RNA would be the likely constituent of the scrapie agent core if only because of the greater stability of the former. Beginning from the standpoint, therefore, that scrapie is a 10^5 dalton (or even smaller, Prusiner, 1982) DNA core virus, it may be suggested that apart from the difficulties in data interpretation already discussed,the problem of the classification of scrapie has also been compounded because the wrong questions are being asked. Much less is known than tends to be assumed either about the extent to which the basic stability of DNA can be influenced by its microenvironment or the extent to which DNA may be able to program and regulate intra and inter cellular processes or the mechanisms involved. Perhaps, therefore, in attempting to understand how scrapie relates to other biological systems, the basic question which should be asked is 'what do the properties of scrapie tell us about the potentialities of DNA itself' instead of making a number of relatively unsubstantiated assumptions about the properties of DNA and then being surprised at the difficulties of matching these with the observed properties of scrapie.

This aspect will now be considered in some detail in the context of normal cellular organization and its reprogramming by viral nucleic acid.

III. PROBLEMS ASSOCIATED WITH DNA

Like that of scrapie, the history of DNA has also been paved with problems arising from the assumption of entrenched views based on little, if any, hard evidence which have been relinquished or modified only after a protracted rearguard action. Taking just two examples, to maintain only something

like 30 years ago that cellular DNA existed outside the con-
fines of the nucleus was tantamount to committing scientific
suicide. Although the presence of DNA in mitochondria is
now completely accepted, the extent to which early and per-
fectly viable results showing this were discounted and ig-
nored, seems now difficult to understand. Until just over
ten years ago, few were prepared to accept reverse transcription of RNA to DNA as a mechanism of virus replication,
until Temin demonstrated this so unequivocally. Undoubtedly
there are more such problems just below the surface.

IV. CELLULAR ORGANIZATION

After virus infection, the cellular machinery is to a
greater or lesser extent taken over and reorganized in the
interests of the virus rather than the cell, or put in a
slightly different way, a general property of viruses is to
reprogram cellular organization. Since the concept of reprogramming implies an underlying program, this aspect will now
be considered, firstly in relation to normal cellular organization. While there is a vast literature on factors controlling and regulating individual cellular reactions or
small groups of reactions, little attention seems to have
been paid to the very fundamental problem of the integration
of the various controlling factors with one another. It
would seem a *reductio ad absurdum* to consider that all such
localized reactions could proceed independently and on a self
selection basis, and at rates which are not closely integrated with the needs of the whole cell or tissue. The result
could only be anarchy and totally inappropriate to the elegant, minutely organized and integrated system of the living
organism which not only maintains itself in a viable state
but is capable of responding to and counteracting the effects
of a considerable degree of perturbation. In fact, such a
degree of correlation almost seems to demand the equivalent
of a cellular microprocessor or group of microprocessors
capable of programming cellular activity and exerting overall
control. If such exist chemically, it seems difficult to
consider them in terms other than DNA, with RNA possibly in
a subsidiary role.

However, such a concept raises immediately a number of
problems. Particularly since the discovery of the triplet
code, the term 'informational' in respect of DNA seems to
have been equated almost exclusively with an ability to direct the synthesis of specific proteins via a preliminary
transcription to RNA. This view has recently been summarized
by Singh (1982), who commented that 'the role of DNA as a
carrier of information can only be defined in reference to a
formal description of a code for amino acids embodied in the

sequence of nucleotides'. Further, any subsequent changes which may occur in cellular function are ascribed exclusively to the encoded protein. The extent to which this view has become scientific orthodoxy may be illustrated by reference to two recent papers, on the mechanism of oncogene activation (Tabin *et al.*, 1982) and on the acquisition of transforming properties by the T24 oncogene (Reddy *et al.*, 1982). Both groups concluded after a series of thorough and elegant experiments, that in each case a point mutation is responsible and interpret this in terms of a single amino acid substitution (gly for val) in the respective encoded proteins. However, as shown by the discussions, this conclusion has brought considerable difficulties in explaining how such a simple substitution in a protein could account for the resulting and very fundamental change in cellular organization. *A priori* this suggests that it might be simpler to consider such changes to result directly from alterations in nucleic acid structure and that the associated changes in protein amino acid sequence may be irrelevant.

It could not of course be disputed that a primary and major function of DNA is to direct the encoding of proteins which themselves have specific functions in the cellular enviromment. Indeed, the original reaction by Alper *et al.* (1966) to the indicated small size of the scrapie virus, suggested by the ionizing radiation data, was that this would be too small to encode for a sufficient amount of virus associated protein. If, however, the assumption is made that at least some fraction of DNA and perhaps to a somewhat lesser extent, RNA, is a carrier of programmable information, which is expressed independently of transcription/translation, many of these problems present themselves in a new light. So far as viruses are concerned, the relationship of the associated structural and nonstructural proteins to the ability of the virus to reprogram the metabolic activity of its host cell has never been satisfactorily explained, although the implicit assumption always seems to have been made that they are in some way essential. It may perhaps be stressed at this point that 'reprogramming capability' is not synonymous with 'infectivity'. The number of virus associated proteins appears to account for all (and in some cases actually exceeds) the triplet coding capacity. This clearly simplifies the problem in that if there is no spare coding capacity, then all the proteins which can be associated with the virus are on view as core, capsid, coat, or early nonstructural components. It has also been clear for some years that viruses vary widely in the type, number and function of their associated proteins. A number of (mostly RNA) viruses carry a specific polymerase within the virion. In some cases, external virion proteins also have other specific functions which are essential for

virus multiplication. Fields and Green (1982) have stressed
a number of these in a very recent review. For example, that
the three outer capsid proteins of reoviruses respectively
bind to the cell surface receptors, determine the capacity
for viral growth at mucosal surfaces: and inhibit cell macromolecular syntheses. However, great care must be exercised in
the interpretation of such data. While it shows that viral
proteins may have specific and indeed essential functions,
the pattern differs from one virus to another. The smaller
animal viruses, such as the picorna and parvoviruses, code
for as few as three proteins, of which one has the restricted
function of a polymerase for the viral RNA, leaving only two
available for anything else. Some plant viruses (e.g. velvet
tobacco mottle, Francki et al. Chapter) code for only a single
protein, yet such nucleic acid entities with minimal associated protein are clearly complete viruses.

In summary, therefore,no virion protein related-function
appears to be universally necesary for virus activity.

It is difficult to conclude otherwise than that the
overall control/regulation of viral activity remains firmly
under the direction of the viral nucleic acid - or in other
words the encoded proteins are simply messengers carrying out
instructions. This interpretation is heavily underlined by
Diener's discovery that PSTV RNA is not translated and this
now appears to be a universal property of viroids as a group.
Consequently, although nucleic acid may operate through virus
specified protein, such delegation is not essential for cellular reprogramming by viral nucleic acid or for disease production.

For a long period, scrapie workers have been puzzled by
their inability to demonstrate any antigenicity associated
with scrapie infection. After Diener, the most logical explanation has seemed to be that scrapie DNA similarly is
not transcribed/translated and recently Kimberlin (1982) suggested this among a number of alternatives as an explanation
of the properties of the scrapie virus. Prusiner's evidence
that associated protein is necessary for scrapie infectivity
would not exclude its being cell specified and this may well
be true of the 3×10^4 dalton protein he describes in another
chapter of this volume. On this assumption, the scrapie virus
reinforces the suggestion that protein encoding of viral nucleic acid is not essential either for expression of information or for disease production.

Added to the above, there is now evidence that fragments
of viral nucleic acid may themselves be able to enter host
cells and exert a profound influence on their metabolism.
This is suggested by the report that an SV 40 fragment of
molecular weight probably no more than 17,000 daltons can
immortalize rat embryo cells (Colby and Shenk, 1982).

Prima facie this would appear to involve a major reorganization of cellular function by this small fragment, which even if translated — which seems unlikely — would code only for a small polypeptide. Whether even smaller fragments could retain such activity is not clear although there is no obvious reason why oligonucleotides could not function similarly.

It seems also that the whole process of cellular reprogramming by viral nucleic acid is one of remarkable precision even where this extends over a long time period, and scrapie provides a very clear example. Pure line mice inoculated intracerebrally with a given amount of single strain of scrapie agent such as ME7 (Dickinson and Fraser, 1968) all die within a few days of each other, about six months later. So reproducable is this process that it is possible at the time of inoculation to predict almost to the day the mean death point. The time period involved differs with the agent strain and the strain of mice. Dickinson *et al.* (1972) showed also that when both long and short incubation period strains of scrapie were injected into the same animal, there was competition between them in determining the resultant length of the incubation period. These effects were explained in terms of a complex network of allele interactions (Dickinson and Meikle, 1971 ; Dickinson *et al.*, 1972). However, if these results are reinterpreted along the lines described above, they suggest that a 10^5 dalton DNA is not only able to program with great precision what must be a very complex sequence of integrated reactions, but that the time sequences also depend on a scrapie DNA-host DNA interaction.

The conclusions so far in relation to the nature and classification of viruses might be summarized as follows:

1. Although there may be considerable and wide ranging variation in detail, all virus entities belong to one taxonomic grouping (see Matthews, 1982) and are capable of initiating their own self replication. They are also carriers of 'information' which is used to reprogram the metabolism of their host cells, so that the host cell virus complex is to a greater or lesser extend orientated towards the requirements of the virus rather than the cell.

2. The essential replicatable material in all cases is a nucleic acid which may vary in size from 10^5 or less to over two hundred million daltons.

3. Viruses as a group exhibit a very wide range of sensitivity to inactivation by a wide range of procedures. Some, e.g. herpes, are extremely sensitive, others, e.g. scrapie, are extremely resistant. These variations probably depend to a large extent on the ability of the viral nucleic acid or at least a proportion of it, to organise a protective microenvironment.

4. Viruses as a group also have a wide range of incubation periods or times to peak titer, varying from a few hours to many years. However, since the scrapie virus is now clearly capable of reaching peak titer within a very few weeks in the right circumstances, there are now no gaps within the animal spectrum (see Adams and Bell, 1976). Some plant viroids - e.g. cadang - cadang also have incubation periods of as long as two years (see Randles Chapter).

5. The nucleic acid is associated in the virion with a number of virus specified proteins varying from none in the case of viroids and probably scrapie, to as many as thirty in the case of pox viruses. Although many of these may have a specific, usually very circumscribed function, in certain virus families they are not otherwise essential in the sense that viral nucleic acid is clearly capable of re-programming host cell organization and of causing disease without the intervention of virus encoded protein.

6. Taken together, points 1 through 5 above suggest that the introduction of sub-groups such as 'viroids' or 'prions' seems more likely to obscure the essential unity among different viral groups and families than to serve any useful purpose. The conclusion summarized in (5) above that virus encoded or specified protein is not essential for host cell reprogramming and disease production clearly raises the nature of the mechanism by which viral nucleic acid operates within its host cell. Brief mention has already been made of the possibility of a 'microprocessor' function for nucleic acid, and this aspect will now be considered further.

V.   NUCLEIC ACID AS 'MICROPROCESSOR'

Early views on the relationship of DNA to the rest of the cell were summarized by Simon (1962) in the comment 'DNA carries a series of instructions for the construction and maintenance of the organism from nutrient materials'. In the same article, Simon compared the organization involved to 'a recipe' or alternatively to 'a computer program which is also a sequence of instructions governing the construction of symbolic structures'. As already indicated, the progression of such ideas appears to have followed the line that 'information' in relation to DNA is synonymous with the triplet code and the expression of that capability. More recently, this general view has been consolidated during the course of a literature explosion covering a wide range of DNA-related activities such as the mechanisms controlling gene expression, the relationship between DNA function and sequence and the changes in encoding ability resulting from recombinant technology. Even the areas of investigation are difficult to list briefly - the details virtually impossible. An enormous amount of work has also been done – as indicated earlier – on mechanisms concerned with initiation, termination, rate control and other aspects of individual reactions and groups of reactions, and the major role of enzymic and feed-back processes, extending throughout the whole range of cellular organization.

However, following what has already been said, it is suggested that buried under this vast literature edifice, and possibly hidden by the trees, is the fundamental problem of how this very wide range of instructions specified by different parts of chromosomal DNA is correlated and integrated into a unified whole.

Much has also been written on hierarchical structures as models of cells. For example, Adams and Bell (1976) suggested the analogy between the organization of an individual cell and that of a complex industrial corporation, with an executive board of several directors (DNA) formulating all major policy decisions and handing these down for action at lower levels. Clearly such a process involves feed back but even in an industrial organization this would not be sufficiently all encompassing in itself to maintain an integrated system, without person to person communication between the individual directors themselves and between individual directors and the board as a whole. Thus the integration of the system involves the two separate but complementary processes of vertical and horizontal transmission of information. The organization of a living cell and the integration of the activity of individual cells within tissues or groups of tissues within a living animal is considerably, if not immeasurably, more complex. If cellular organization is depicted in similar terms, with DNA at the top level, then the triplet coding system is primarily concerned with the vertical transmission of information from DNA to non DNA molecules and systems. However, in order to achieve the necessary wide ranging correlation/integration there similarly seems little alternative but to suggest an additional horizontal information transfer mechanism and that this must involve direct DNA-DNA intercommunication at the top level of the hierarchy.

Perhaps a more practical approximation to such a cellular hierarchy might be a flat topped pyramid with intercommunicating DNA occupying the top levels. Whether all DNA would be equivalent in this respect, i.e. at the same level or whether top level DNA is superimposed on subsystems of DNA fractions at lower levels is an open question. However, there would seem no barrier in principle to direct DNA-DNA interaction if molecules or groups of molecules posess the equivalent of a 'microprocessor' capability. In that case the top level of the cellular hierarchy could be seen as an interlinked microprocessor network linked again to similar networks in other cells and extending to the whole body. *Prima facie* the most appropriate analogy would seem to be a computer system with variable arrangements of individual unit connections into e.g. linear, star or linear-loop combinations. While in a standard computer such intercommunication would involve electrical circuitry, there is no reason why the necessary switching comprising the essence of the system could not be operated by purely chemical changes – indeed chemically switched computers have been known for some time and are still being developed.

VI.   VIRAL NUCLEIC ACID

Some indications of the basic parameters involved in the above concept may be gained from further consideration of the interaction betwen viruses and their host cells. If, in addition to any triplet code mediated function, viral nucleic acid is seen in the role of a new microprocessor unit entering an existing network, four conclusions follow. Firstly, initiation of cellular reprogramming after virus infection probably requires the insertion into the individual cell system of very few viral nucleic acid molecules – possibly only one initially, although some replication into multiple units may be necessary to establish the process to the point of no return. Basically, however, this suggests a relationship of the order of one nucleic acid molecule = one microprocessor unit.

Secondly, such is the efficiency of cellular reprogramming by viral nucleic acid, that it seems reasonable to suppose that information transfer between cells would be carried out most efficiently by exchange of cellular nucleic acid, and that a single nucleic acid molecule could transmit significant information/instruction.

Thirdly, that since viral RNA appears to be equal in efficiency to viral DNA in cellular reprogramming, 'microprocessor' capability cannot be the exclusive property of DNA. Whether this extends, or may under special circumstances extend to some fraction of cellular RNA is not clear. However, the possibility of any other macromolecules such as protein or carbohydrate being able to act in this way seems remote. Added to the problem of self replication already discussed, the conclusion would be that there is no alternative to nucleic acid as viral core material.

Fourthly, depending on the switching mechanism involved, it would not be necessary for viral nucleic acid to undergo a triplet coded translation in order to communicate its new information/instructions to the proposed cellular microprocessor network.

VII.   MECHANISM OF DNA CONTROL

Two fundamentally different mechanisms are thus envisaged in the cellular hierarchy. Firstly, a 'horizontal' exchange of information possibly transmitted by movements of specialized DNA or DNA fractions between top level DNA which has the primary purpose of correlating and integrating the activities of such DNA into a unified system for the overall direction of the activity of whole cells and groups of cells. Secondly, the triplet code-based mechanism which primarily involves the expression of individual pieces of DNA by vertical (downwards) transmission, as has already been said to non DNA molecules. Triplet code implementation occurs by transmission of such information to sucessively lower levels and in the process, its diversification into quanta, each of which activates a specialized system. The end part at the bottom of the hierarchy involves the bringing into play of small purpose-built messenger molecules such as hormones, which would be e.g. released to carry out the special function which is their only capability, at rates programmed into the system by instructions from higher levels. Such processes must also of course be regulated by feed back mechanisms a simple example being rate of insulin secretion which is at least partly determined by circulating blood glucose levels. To that relatively limited extent, such sub-systems may be self-regulating and self-adjusting. The activity of proteins as enzymes seems principally under the control of local or locally acting factors. Just as in any other complex organization, such control and regulation can take place (within limits) at lower levels, with only minimal intervention from the top. While in many instances, the local regulating factors are known and their mechanisms have been elucidated, the problem of the nature of the control exercised at top level remains. As has been indicated, such evidence as there is suggests that at least a piece of nucleic acid has to enter a cell in order to redirect its activity and a similar mechanism involving nucleic acid translocation may occur within cells. Alternatively, the evidence from the oncogene studies (referred to earlier) suggests that something similar can occur without external intervention after no more than a single point mutation in the relevant nucleic acid.

VIII.   THE ROLE OF CELLULAR NUCLEIC ACID IN THE PROGRAMMING OF NORMAL CELLULAR ACTIVITY

Virus-host cell interactions are complex but in scrapie, at least, the process is spread out over a time period long enough to be able to show interaction between strains of scrapie themselves and with their host and to indicate that

reprogramming by viral DNA involves a conflict with the host
organizational structure which can be opposed by the latter.
In principle, therefore, scrapie infection of the host cell
might seem to be a possible way of investigating the whole
problem of the programming ability of DNA. However, in
practice this would probably be very difficult - not only are
there problems over growing scrapie virus in tissue culture,
but as has been seen, the history so far of scrapie investigation shows how intractable the problems of working with the
virus can be.

There is, however, another avenue of investigating this
problem which *prima facie* may be more promising. As has been
pointed out, biological organization must involve not only
the integration of control mechanisms within cells, but communication of information between one cell and another for
the same purpose. If DNA is to be the key structure involved
in this process, there is little alternative to the conclusion that cellular DNA and/or RNA must be able to move between cells, and indeed through the general circulation as
virus associated nucleic acid does. In fact, it has been
known for many years that such processes do occur, although
movements between cells have so far involved mostly prokaryotes. In a study of the blood borne plasma lactate dehydrogenase elevating virus, Adams and Bowman (1964) found not
only that RNA was present in high titer infected mouse plasma,
but that almost half the total RNA was still present in the
plasma of uninfected and apparently completely normal mice
(with of course normal PLDH levels). Further, that this
RNA was complexed in some way and protected against RNAse.
There are also many reports that DNA and RNA are extruded by
cultured eukaryotic cells into their surrounding media (reviewed by Stroun *et al.* 1977), but no satisfactory explanation has ever been given of the function or purpose either of
such nucleic acid extrusion, or nucleic acid in circulation.
Echoing the comments already made concerning the history of
DNA, there is a strongly entrenched opinion that nucleic acid
extrusion from cells in culture is the result of cell death
or damage and therefore artefactual. While it cannot be
denied that some nucleic acid present in cell culture supernatants may have arisen from such causes, the evidence clearly shows that this cannot be the whole explanation, (see e.g.
Stroun *et al.*, 1977; Reid and Charlson, 1979; Adams and
Gahan, 1982).

Work has in fact begun in these laboratories in an
attempt to investigate the possibility that some of the
DNA/RNA which is extruded by cultured cells is connected with
cell-cell transfer of 'information'. However, although these
studies are as yet in a preliminary stage, this possibility
has been supported by a report (Anker *et al.*, 1979) that

lymphocyte T-B cell interaction involves DNA extruded by the former.

No attempt will be made to present the details of these preliminary experiments in the present article - they will be published elsewhere. However, a brief summary of some of the findings which appear relevant will be given. Firstly, there is now evidence that the DNA extruded from both cultured rat spleen cells and chick embryo fibroblasts (CEF) is of cytosol origin. Fig. 1 shows the pattern of [^{3}H] thymidine labelled material extruded by CEF cells into their surrounding medium after chromatography on an agarose column (exclusion 1.5 x 10^7 daltons), in comparison with [^{3}H] thymidine labelled material found in the cell cytosol fraction. The cell supernatant shows a band of molecular sizes with a peak in the region of 6 x 10^5 daltons: the cell cytosol pattern is similar but contains more higher molecular weight material. However, in both instances at least a proportion of the 6 x 10^5 dalton DNA appears to be complexed with protein. Rat spleen cell cultures (not shown) give similar results but with both the media supernatant and cytosol peaks at the higher molecular weight of about 3 x 10^6 daltons. Comparison of media supernatants and cytosols after labelling with other precursors such as [^{3}H] lysine, [^{3}H] uridine or [^{3}H] ethanolamine show that labelled macromolecules are extruded in all cases. However, while there are differences in the patterns shown by different precursors, the supernatant/cytosol patterns for each precursor are similar to one another. There are also differences in the cytosol/supernatant media labeling ratios between precursors, showing that the cell derived macromolecules in the supernatant are not all released at the same rate. Consequently the results are not consistent with cellular death; neither does the cell death rate correlate with the proportion released. Rat spleen cells are also able to extrude into their supernatant medium a low density complex containing DNA and lipid (Adams and Gahan, 1982). Fig. 2 shows the effect of upward sucrose density gradient centrifugation of supernatant media from rat spleen cells labelled with [^{3}H] thymidine and the presence of a peak at an indicated density of 1.03g/ml coincident with a small peak of absorption at 260nm. However, not all groups of rats have shown this phenomenon. Despite careful investigation the reasons are not clear: it appears likely that its presence depends on the antigenic status of the donor animals. Nevertheless, some of the basic properties of this low density complex have been established (Adams and Gahan, 1983). As well as DNA and lipid it contains protein, but no RNA: it is destroyed by freezing and thawing, exposure to detergents or standing at 4° for a few days. It is not found in rat spleen or CEF cell cytosols or in CEF cell supernatant media. The

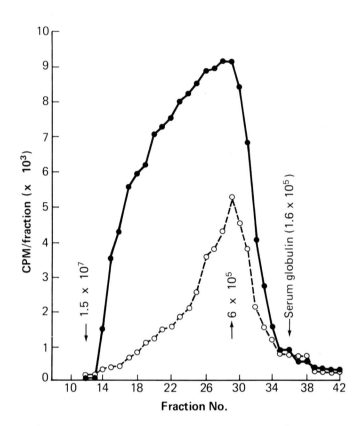

Figure 1.   Chick embryo fibroblasts incubated with [^{3}H]
thymidine 18h. Centrifuged, washed and reincubated with fresh
(unlabelled) medium 2h.   Supernatant   media   separated   and
centrifuged at 50Kg for 1h to remove debris.   Cell pellet
resuspended and gently homogenized in fresh medium and nuclei,
mitochondria and other debris removed by centrifugation at
50Kg for 1h.   Both preparations were then chromatographed on
agarose gel columns (eluant 0.02M sodium phosphate pH6.8) and
fractions collected and counted.   Gel exclusion limit 1.5x10^7
daltons (void volume at fraction 12).

●————————● cytosol

o————————o media supernatant

results   suggest   that it   is formed   in the   lymphocyte by a
fraction of cytosol DNA which associates with additional
lipid in its passage through the cellular plasma membrane
system. To account for its low density of 1.03 the proportion of lipid must be very high – of the order of 70% – which

is suggestive of DNA entrapped in a natural liposome. This would clearly facilitate its entry into other cells.

Non-organelle-related cytoplasmic DNA has in fact received very little attention although the subject has been reviewed by Reid and Charlson (1979). They concluded that in eukaryotic cells cytoplasmic DNA exists, other than that present in mitochondria, which is disseminated throughout the membrane system of the cytoplasma, the cell wall and into the mucoid coat. Further, that this represents a specific fraction and does not result from nuclear or mitochondrial contamination. The function of this DNA is unknown, and there appears to be no evidence concerning its possible transcription/translation. It is also of interest that Smith and Vinograd (1972) reported the presence of small polydisperse circular DNA which was not of mitochondrial origin, in the cytoplasm of Hela cells. Recently a small cytoplasmic RNA has also been described which differs from ribosomal RNA and which appears to be concerned with protein secretion (Walter and Blobel 1982). However, it is not yet known whether this is part of the RNA which we have found extruded into cell supernatant media, or whether it has any relationship to cytosol DNA.

Presumably, however, cytosol DNA is sythesized in the nucleus and then moves to the cytosol. If, as suggested by the data, it may then move out of the cell, it, or some fraction of it, would seem *prima facie* a candidate for the role of information carrier at least between if not within cells. Thinking along these lines there are, however, puzzling features about the macromolecular extrusion which has been described from cultured primary cells. For example, the clear similarity between the macromolecular composition of the cytosol and media supernatant indicates a lack of selectivity in the composition of the extruded material which would seem surprising if it is to have a specific function. We have made many attempts to obtain evidence of processing during extrusion but as already indicated this is so far confined to the lymphocyte low density DNA complex, which appears to be a special case, and the observation of different cytosol/cell supernatant ratios with e.g.DNA vs protein.

A further complication is that the rate of protein loss, in particular from CEF cells, would seem to be such as to place a very heavy load on the synthetic machinery. However, these observations using cultured cells could be explained if, in their original environment as a discrete tissue, there is a relatively unobstructed trans-plasma membrane interchange of cytosol macromolecules between one cell and another. Effectively, therefore, that the constituent cell nuclei of a tissue exist in a continuous cytosol. This could provide the basis of a networking system for information

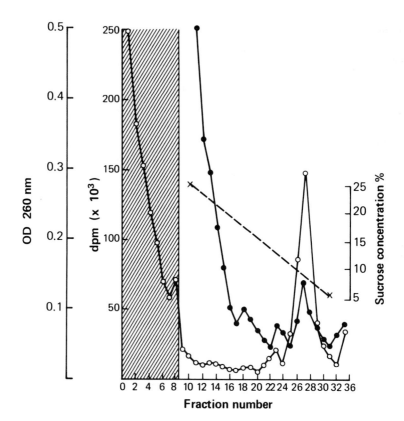

Figure 2. Rat spleen cells were isolated and incubated 18h with [³H] thymidine, then separated, resuspended in fresh unlabelled medium and incubated a further 2h. After separating the cells the resulting supernatant medium was centrifuged at 50Kg for 1h. A sample (2.3ml) was made up to 30% with respect to sucrose and layered under a continuous 5–25% sucrose gradient and centrifuged 2h at 3 x 10⁵g max in a Ti 40 swing out rotor (Beckman). Fractions (0.33ml) were collected from the bottom of the tubes using a long needle passed through the solution, OD260 measured and counted. The first 8–9 samples comprised the original sample.

Ordinates	OD 260 nm
(left)	dpm x 10³
right	% sucrose
Abscissa	Fraction No.
V ---- V	OD 260 nm
o ---- o	dpm
x ---- x	Sucrose concentration in gradient

exchange by cell-specified carrier macromolecules and also facilitate the cell-cell spread of viruses.

To deliver a message to another cell it would probably be necessary for viral, or mobile carrier cellular nucleic acid to come into relatively close contact with recipient chromosomal DNA (or in some cases cellular RNA). If the former are microprocessor network components it would also seem likely that normal intracellular distribution would operate by a similar but internal relocation mechanism. Each participating section of chromosomal DNA must then necessarily act as both information transmitter and receiver according to the prevailing circumstances. However, even if the carrier is a small DNA molecule it does not follow necessarily that all segments of it are primarily involved in information transfer. As indicated earlier, there are an increasing number of reports concerning the ability of comparatively small DNA fragments to fundamentally reorganize cellular activity. Possibly, for less dramatic changes, such as would seem likely to be involved in day-to-day organizational control, the necessary instructions could be mediated by fragments no larger than oligonucleotides – either transported on larger molecules or as short segments strategically positioned in a larger piece of DNA.

The essence of the proposal is that information carrying DNA (probably synthesized to order – perhaps in some of the chromosomal DNA regions whose function is obscure), moves within, or out of, the cell in order to transmit its information to recipient DNA. There are at least two general mechanisms by which such transfer might occur.

1.   Carrier DNA or segments of it integrate with the recipient DNA. However, although this might occur in special circumstances, it appears less likely as a general mechanism because of the necessity to build into all message transfer systems a limitation in message duration to enable the system to be cleared. Such a limitation may not however apply to viral nucleic acid.

2.   Carrier DNA (or segments) associates with recipient DNA- and possibly RNA also – at strategic sites on a transient basis by e.g. hydrogen bonding, thereby regulating triplet code expression by the recipient both qualitatively and quantitatively. Alternately that interaction might occur indirectly, without formal bonding, if positioning a new piece of DNA in close proximity is capable of causing a conformational change in recipient DNA. This could occur through localized and possibly quite elementary microenvironmental changes such as an alteration in hydrogen ion or salt concentration. If such a process can occur it would also seem possible for transmitting DNA to induce a conformational change in the carrier which is then passed on to the recipient. Such a mechanism would not only economize on carrier DNA by permitting its reuse but would also seem to have some analogy

with switching mechanisms involved in chemically switched
computers.

Further, if what has been suggested is correct, the
triplet code mechanism would play no part in the primary
interactions although it would in general be involved subsequently to put the new instructions into effect.

There is now a considerable literature describing DNA
movements within cells, the function, purpose and control of
which is often uncertain, and which may be relevant. DNA
transposition is well established in prokaryotic cells, i.e.
the appearance of a new defined length of DNA (the transposable element) in the middle of another DNA sequence. Transposable elements may also fuse unrelated DNA molecules and contain transcriptional stop/start sequences. Although most
such DNA transposition appear to involve the insertion of DNA
sequences of up to several thousand base pairs shorter sequences down to about 200bp of unknown function also appear to be
involved (see review by Calos and Miller, 1980). The phenomenon of mobile extra-chromosomal DNA in eukaryotic cells has
been discussed by Calabretta *et al.* (1982) who detected DNA
rearrangements involving restriction fragment length polymor-
phism and variation in the copy number in human tissue genomes by blot hybridization with a clones segment of human
DNA initially present in a cluster of Alu repeat sequences.
They concluded that these rearrangements, which involve both
extra-chromosomal ciruclar duplex DNA and integrated sequences indicate the presence of transposable elements.
Reid (1983) has considered the possibility that migrating
mitochondrial DNA may activate oncogenes.

However, among present concepts that which is possibly
the most relevant concerns the 'hit and run' mechanism, suggested to occur, for example, in oncogene activation by fragments of herpes simplex viruses (Galloway and McDougall,
1983). The description originates because although viral
gene fragments appear capable of initiating and maintaining
transformation, no set of viral genes seems to be consistently
or necessarily retained or expressed in the transformed cells.

IX   CONCLUSION

The views which have been expressed began from two
basic considerations. Firstly that all virus entities, including scrapie, are nucleic acid cored, and that information
residing in the nucleic acid core is used to take over and
reprogram the host cell. Secondly, that within the virus
spectrum viroid nucleic acid at least is not translated and
that the same is probably true of scrapie. If, therefore,
protein encoding by the viral core is not essential in certain cases for the establishment of virus infection it is a

short logical step to the conclusion that virus specified proteins in general are not essential for host cell reprogramming and disease production, although in many cases they may be essential for viral replication. At this point it is difficult to conclude other than that the triplet coding mechanism is insufficient to account for the total information transfer process. A possible solution has been suggested in terms of a microprocessor type of direct DNA=DNA intercommunication applying both to intra and intercellular organization and the effects following entry of viral nucleic acid into cells-the latter, in the case of RNA viruses, involving a similar viral RNA-host DNA interaction.

Whether the suggested mechanism is valid or not has yet to be determined. However, if it is rejected, the question must still be asked 'how does viroid RNA operate as an apparently complete and functional virus if it is not translated and what are the wider implications for virus-host cell relationships?'

Not only do these proposals provide the basis of a solution to this and other problems but, for example, they also offer a ready explanation of the evidence presented in other chapters of this book that small changes in viroid RNA sequence may markedly affect the severity of the induced disease. Further, removing the necessity for function dependence on protein encoding reduces considerably any limitation on the minimum size of viral cores, and would allow the conclusion that even comparatively small oligonucleotides are potentially infective. Prusiner (1982) appears to believe that if a nucleic acid core exists in scrapie it could be as small as 12-32 nucleotides or up to 10^4 daltons, and comments that this must have a function other than a scrapie coat protein template. Within the context of the proposals made in this chapter such a conclusion would present no problem. This may well turn out to be at least part of the 'enigma' of DNA.

X. SUMMARY

It is suggested: Firstly that the problems associated with the scrapie agent have arisen primarily because of inappropriate interpretation of the data coupled, at successive stages, with a failure to recognise the rigidity and inflexibility of conventionally accepted thinking. Secondly, that so-called 'conventional' viruses of plants and animals, including scrapie and viroids, are part of a single nucleic acid based group holding in common the ability not only to self replicate but to reprogram cellular organization. Further, that this latter ability of viruses is part of a much wider system of both inter and intracellular dissemination

and integration of 'information'. Thirdly, that such integration, based on the ability of both cellular and viral DNA and
viral RNA to program/reprogram cellular organization, operates through a mechanism complementary to but distinct from
triplet code directed transcription/translation, resembling a
chemically switched microprocessor network with individual
units perhaps no larger than a single nucleic acid molecule.
Fourthly, that if these views are correct, any substitute for
nucleic acid as a virus core must not only be capable of self
replication, but show a similar 'microprocessor' capacity.
It would seem most unlikely that any known macromolecule
other than nucleic acid could fill both criteria. Fifthly,
the possibility is suggested that non-organelle related cytosol DNA may function as an information carrier at least
between cells and possibly within cells also. Finally it is
suggested that protein specified by viral nucleic acid is
neither essential for reprogramming of the host cell, nor
universally essential for viral replication and disease production. This removes many limitations on the minimum size
for viral cores and potentially would permit even oligonucleotides to function as such. In particular, recent literature
conclusions that scrapie DNA may be of the order of 10^4
daltons may be explained in these terms.

ACKNOWLEDGEMENTS

        I am most indebted to the following colleagues
for reading, and making helpful comments on, the manuscript
- Dr. Tom Bell, Professor Peter Gahan, Dr. Louis Lim, Alison
McIntosh and Professor Richard Madeley. Further to Dr. A.M.
Lamont and Professor B. Randell of the Computing Laboratory,
Newcastle upon Tyne for helpful discussion. I am also very
grateful to Marjorie Caine for coping so ably with the secre-
tarial problems.
        I wish to thank Springer-Verlag for their permission to
reproduce Figure 2.

REFERENCES

Adams, D.H. (1970). The nature of the scrapie agent. A
        review of recent progress. Path.Biol. 18.,559-577.
Adams, D.H. (1972), Studies on DNA from normal and scrapie
        affected mouse brain. J. Neurochem. 19, 1869-1882.
Adams, D.H. and Bell, T.M. (1976). Slow viruses. (Addison
        Wesley Publishing Company Inc., Reading, Mass.).
Adams, D.H. and Bowman, B.M. (1964). Studies of plasma
        lactate dehydrogenase elevating factors.
        Biochem. J.,90, 477-483.

Adams, D.H. and Caspary, E.A. (1967). Nature of the scrapie virus. *Brit. Med. J. iii*, 173.

Adams, D.H.,Field, E.J. and Joyce, G. (1972). Periodate – an inhibitor of the scrapie agent? *Res. Vet. Sci., 13*, 195–198.

Adams, D.H. and Gahan, P.B. (1982). Stimulated and non-stimulated rat spleen cells release different DNA-complexes. *Differentiation,22*, 47–52.

Adams,D.H. and Gahan, P.B.(1983). The DNA extruded by rat spleen cells in culture. *Int. J. Biochem. 15*, 547–552.

Alper, T., Cramp, W.A., Haig, D.A. and Clarke, M.C. (1967). Does the scrapie agent replicate without nucleic acid? *Nature (London),214*, 764–766.

Alper, T. Haig, D.A. and Clarke, M.C. (1966). The exceptionally small size of the scrapie agent. *Biochem. Biophys. Res. Comm.,22*, 278–284.

Anker, P., Jachertz, D., Stroun, M. Brogger, R., Lederrey, C., Henri, J. and Maurice, P.A. (1980). The role of extracellular DNA in the transfer of information from T to B human lymphocytes in the course of an immune response. *J. Immun. Genet., 7*, 475–481.

Baross, J.A. and Deming, J.W. (1983). Growth of 'black smoker' bacteria at temperatures of at least 250°C. *Natur@ (London) 303*, 423–426.

Bell, T.M., Field, E.J. and Joyce, G. (1972). Action of an alcoholic solution of iodine on the scrapie agent. *Res. Vet. Sci.,13*, 198–199.

Calabretta, B., Robberson, D. L., Barrera-Saldana, H. A., Lambron, T.P. and Saunders, G.F. (1982). Genome instability in a region of human DNA enriched in Alu repeat sequences. *Nature (London) 296.* 219–225.

Calos, M.P. and Miller, J. H. (1980). Transposable elements. *Cell 20*, 579–595.

Colby, W.W. and Shenk, T. (1982). Fragments of the simian virus 40 transforming gene facilitate transformation of rat embryo cells. *Proc. Nat. Acad. Sci., U.S.A., 79c* 5189–5193.

Cuille, J. and Chelle, P.L. (1938). La tremblante du mouton – est elle determinee par un virus filterable? *C.R. Acad. Sci., (Paris)*, 206, 1087–1088.

Cuille, J. and Chelle, P.L. (1939). Transmission experimentale de la tremblante a la chevre. *C. R. Acad. Sci., (Paris), 208*, 1058–1060.

Dickinson, A.G., Fraser, H., Meikle, V.M.H. and Outram, G.W. (1972). Competition between different scrapie agents in mice. *Nature New Biol., 237*, 244–245.

Dickinson, A.G. and Meikle, V.H.H. (1971). Host-genotype and agent effects in scrapie incubation: change in allele-interaction with different strains of agent. *Molec. Gen. Genet. 112*, 73-79.

Diener, T.O. (1973). Similarities between the scrapie agent and the agent of the potato spindle tuber disease. *Annals. Clin. Res. 5*, 268-278.

Diener, T.O. (1979). Viroids and viroid disease. (Wiley, New York).

Eklund, C.M., Hadlow, W.J. and Kennedy, R.C. (1963). Some properties of the scrapie agent and its behavior in mice. *Proc. Soc. Exper. Biol. Med., 112*, 974-979.

Field, E. J. (1966). Transmission experiments with multiple sclerosis: an interim report. *Brit. Med. J.,ii*, 564-565.

Galloway, D.A. and McDougall, J.K. (1983). The oncogenic potential of Herpes simplex viruses: evidence for a 'hit and run' mechanism. *Nature (London)302*, 21-24.

Gordon, W.S. (1946). Louping-ill, Tick-borne fever and Scrapie. *Vet. Rec., 58*, 516-520.

Hunter, G.D., Gibbons, R.A., Kimberlin, R.H. and Millson, G.C. (1969). Further studies of the infectivity and stability of extracts and homogenates derived from scrapie-affected mouse brain. *J. Comp. Path.,79*, 101-108.

Hunter, G.D., Kimberlin, R.,H. and Gibbons, R.A. (1968). Scrapie: a modified membrane hypothesis. *J. Theoret. Biol., 20* 355-357.

Hunter, G.D. and Millson, G.C. (1964). Studies on the heat stability and chromatographic behavior of the scrapie agent. *J. gen. Microbiol. 37*, 251-258.

Hunter, G.D. and Millson, G.C. (1967). Release of scrapie agent. *J. Comp. Path.,77*, 301-307.

Hurst, E.W. (1957). Approaches to the chemotherapy of virus diseases. *J. Pharm.,9*, 273-292.

Kimberlin, R.H. (1982). Scrapie agent: prions or virions. *Nature, (London),297*, 107-108.

Laterjet, B., Muel, B., Haig, D.A., Clarke, M.C. and Alper,T. (1970). Inactivation of the scrapie agent by near monochromatic ultraviolet light. *Nature (London) 227*, 1341-1346.

Lewin, P.K., (1982). Infectious peptides: postulated mechanisms of protovirus replication in scrapie. *Can. Med. Assoc. Journ. 127*, 471-472.

Matthews, R.E.F. (1982). Classification and nomenclature of viruses. *Intervirology, 17*, 1-199.

Millson, G.C., Hunter, G.D. and Kimberlin, R.H. (1971). An examination of the scrapie agent in cell membrane mixtures. *J. Comp. Path.*, *81* 255-265.

Millson, G.C. Hunter, G.D. and Kimberline, R.H. (1976). The physio chemical nature of the scrapie agent. *F&* "Slow virus diseases of animals and man", (R.H. Kimberlin, ed.), pp. 243-265, North Holland Publishing Co.

Pattison, I.H. (1965). Resistance of the scrapie agent to formalin. *J. Comp. Path.* *75*, 159-164.

Persson, R. H. and MacDonald, R.D. (1982). Evidence that the infectious pancreatic necrosis virus has a genome-linked protein. *J. Virol.* 44 437-443.

Prusiner, S. B. (1982). Novel proteinaceous infectious particles cause scrapie. *Science*, *216*, 136-144.

Reddy, E.P., Reynolds, R.K., Santos, E. and Barbacid, M. (1982). A point mutation is responsible for the acquisition of transforming properties by the T24 human bladder carcinoma oncogene! *Nature (London)* *300n* 349-352.

Reid, B.L. and Charlson A.J. (1979). Cytoplasmic and cell surface deoxyribonucleic acids with consideration of their origin. *Interm. Rev. Cytol.,* 27-52.

Reid, R.A. (1983). Can migratory mitochondrial DNA activate oncogenes? *T.I.B.S.*, *8* 190-191.

Simon, H.A. (1962). The architecture of complexity. *Proc. Amer. Phil. Soc.*, *106* 467-482.

Singh, U.N. (1982). On the origin of a self-organizing system: structural versus functional organization. *J. Theoret. Biol.99*, 15-20.

Smith, C.A. and Vinograd, J. (1972). Small polydisperse circular DNA of Hela cells. *J. Mol. Biol.*, *69* 163-178.

Stamp, J.T. Brotherston, J.G., Zlotnik, L., Mackay, J.M.K. and Smith, W. (1959). Further studies on scrapie. *J. Comp. Path.*, *69* 268-280.

Stroun, M., Anker, P., Maurice, P. and Gahan, P.B.(1977). Circulating DNA in higher organisms. *Interm. Rev. Cytol.*, *51* 1-47.

Tabin, C.J., Bradley, S.M., Bargmann, G.L., Wenberg, R.A. and: Papageorge, A.G., Scolnick, E.M. and: Dhar, R. Lowy, D.R., Chang, E.H. (1982). Mechanism of activation of a human oncogene. *Nature,(London)300*, 143-149.

Walter, P. and Blobel, G. (1982). Small cytoplasmic RNA is an integral component of the signal recognition particle. *Nature (London)* *299*, 691-693.

Wilson, D.R., Anderson, R.D. and Smith, W. (1950). Studies in scrapie. *J. Comp. Path.,60,* 267-282.

Chapter 18

BIOLOGICAL PROPERTIES OF SCRAPIE:
AN UNCONVENTIONAL SLOW VIRUS

Richard I. Carp, Patricia A. Merz, Roger C. Moretz,
Robert A. Somerville, Sharon M. Callahan and
Henryk M. Wisniewski

Institute for Basic Research in
Developmental Disabilities
1050 Forest Hill Road, Staten Island, NY 10314

I.   INTRODUCTION

The view of scrapie research from those on the outside is filled with awe and mystery. The unconventional characteristics of the infectious material and of the disease process appear to offer few of the conceptual or experimental "handles" provided by conventional viruses. If one searches pointedly for properties shared with well characterized animal, plant and bacterial viruses commonality can be found on almost every characteristic, however, no single conventional virus exhibits a combination of properties similar to that of scrapie and its related unconventional agents. Because of the lack of conventional handles such as immunological reactions, a specific biochemical change, purified agent, a cytopathic effect in tissue culture, a visualized particle associated with infectivity, progress seems slow and apparent advances often lead to subsequent despair as results are

SUBVIRAL PATHOGENS
OF PLANTS AND ANIMALS:
VIROIDS AND PRIONS

Copyright © 1985 by Academic Press, Inc.
All rights of reproduction in any form reserved.
ISBN 0-12-470230-9

confronted by the hard realities of previously unrecognized
scrapie strictures. The feeling, therefore, is often akin to
that of Sysyphus forced by the Gods to push a gigantic boulder
to the top of a hill only to find it again at the bottom
after seeming so close to his goal. However, there have
been real accomplishments and in some areas the mystery has
been reduced. These advances have accrued primarily to those
who have been willing to accept the constraints imposed by
scrapie. In the ensuing pages we will discuss aspects of
scrapie which prove that it is an infectious disease; we will
detail the characteristics of slow infections and review the
characteristics of scrapie which establish it as the archetype
of unconventional slow virus diseases; we will note several
established parameters of transmission and pathogenesis; we
will describe in detail the genetic findings with scrapie;
we will describe changes in the blood-brain barrier in scrapie
mice; we will report on a fibrous particle seen consistently
in scrapie preparations but not controls; we will outline
difficulties in correlating results of infectivity assays with
effects on scrapie agent; and finally we will relate some of
these findings to the title of this book.

We will not discuss in detail the unusual physical –
chemical characteristics of the scrapie agent that have been
described (Hunter, 1972; Millson *et al.*, 1976; Gajdusek,
1977; Prusiner, 1982). However, the topics discussed and
their treatment have been dictated, in part, by these characteristics. The inability to isolate scrapie agent and to
determine its nature has led to many questions. For example,
the properties of the agent that have been reported have led
researchers in "non-scrapie" disciplines to ask: "Is there an
infectious agent in the disease?" Hence the brief discussion
of evidence for infectivity and for a replicating agent. In
addition, conjecture on the nature of the agent based upon
its currently understood biochemical characteristics must be
viewed in the context of the well established genetic components seen in scrapie-host interactions, findings which we
have confirmed and expanded.

Any general overview of scrapie must perforce begin with
a description of the disease and the "agent" with emphasis
on unusual characteristics. Scrapie is a disease occurring
naturally in sheep and goats. The disease has been transmitted experimentally to mice, hamsters and other laboratory
animals (Chandler, 1963; Carp and Thormar, 1975). Symptoms
differ depending on a variety of parameters including host
species (e.g. the scratching which gave the disease its name
is often seen in sheep but not in mice) but almost invariably
include incoordination which ends in wasting as the animals
lose the capability to eat and drink. The disease invariably

ends in death. The histopathological changes are limited to
the central nervous system and are characterized by vacuolation, astrocytosis and gliosis. Inflammatory reactions are
not seen. In some cases, depending on the genetic characteristics of host and agent, neuritic and amyloid plaques develop. The agent does not cause cytopathic effects in tissue
culture. The agent has not been purified or visualized by the
electron microscope. There are no immunological manifestations of the disease: no changes in cellular immunity; no
antibody response to the causative agent; interferon is not
produced and the disease is not altered by the addition of
interferon or interferon inducers. In fact, once the strain
of scrapie, genotype of host, dose and route of infection
have been established, the details of the outcome of the
disease process are determined. The only way to modify the
process is by administration of compounds which affect the
lymphoreticular system shortly before or a few hours after
peripheral (non-CNS) injection of scrapie agent (Outram *et
al.*, 1974; Dickinson *et al.*, 1978; Kimberlin and Cunnington,
1978; Carp and Warner, 1980). The physical-chemical characterization of scrapie agent shows the following features: (1)
There is close association of infectivity with cellular
material; (2) Infectivity is resistant to 10% formalin, heat,
UV, X-ray, β propiolactone, nucleases, lipases; (3) Infectivity is reduced but not eliminated by exposure to lipid solvents. Proteases are especially effective in reducing infectivity after detergent or lipid solvent treatments; (4)Infect-
ivity is reduced by phenol, chlorox, potassium permanganate
and high molar solutions of lithium chloride and guanididium
hydrogen bromide. Detailed descriptions of the characteristics of scrapie infectivity and of the disease have been the
subject of a number of recent reviews and commentaries (Dickinson, 1976; Millson *et al.*, 1976; Gajdusek, 1977; Dickinson
and Fraser, 1979; Prusiner, 1982; Kimberlin, 1982a,b; Dickinson and Outram, 1983).

II. SCRAPIE: AN INFECTIOUS DISEASE

A.   Proof of Agent Infectivity and Replication
There appears to be no question concerning the infectivity of scrapie to those of us who work with the disease.
Brain or spleen homogenates prepared from sick animals can be
diluted a million fold or more and still cause disease,
various routes of injection can be utilized, and there is
ample data supporting genetic control not only by the host
but also the material injected. In Sigurdsson's (Sigurdsson,
1954) paper which defined parameters for slow infection
processes he notes that the Icelandic farmers whose flocks

were affected all agreed that the disease was transmitted
from diseased to healthy animals. The insight of the Icelandic farmers and the "act of faith" employed by many scrapie
workers have been confirmed by direct evidence for both the
natural hosts, sheep and goats, and experimental hosts, mice
and hamsters.

       1. Natural infection of scrapie in sheep and goats

      In early work (Brotherston *et al.*, 1968), 10 of 17 goats
developed the disease after having been placed in pens with
sheep which had been infected with scrapie naturally.
Similarly, 3 of 7 Scottish Blackface sheep became sick after
close contact (in pens) with naturally affected sheep for
periods of 3 years 9 months to 4 years 4 months. The flocks
which supplied the "sentinal" animals did not develop scrapie.
In a more extensive study using natural field conditions,
Dickinson *et al.*, (1974) showed that 28% of 75 Scottish
Blackface sheep developed scrapie after having been placed in
field condition "contact" with Suffolk sheep in which scrapie
was endemic. The Scottish Blackface source flock for the
"sentinal" sheep in this experiment had been observed for 12
years without incidence of scrapie in >18,000 animals. Similar results were obtained by Hourrigan *et al.*, (1979) with a
number of sheep and goat breeds following exposure to scrapie
sheep.

      One experience in Iceland described by Palsson (1979) is
remarkable. Farms left vacant for up to three years after
destruction of scrapie positive flocks were repopulated with
sheep from herds with no history of scrapie. Over the ensuing
years sheep on a number of these farms developed scrapie even
though the source flocks remained scrapie - free.

      2. Replication of scrapie in Mice and Hamsters

      In the process of producing what are termed "cloned"
populations of scrapie agent several laboratories have used
protocols similar to that shown in Figure 1 (Dickinson and
Outram, 1983; Kimberlin, personal communication). Scrapie
positive mice or hamsters injected with a limiting dilution
of a scrapie brain homogenate were harvested and brain homogenates prepared. Those homogenates prepared from animals
injected with the minimal amounts of infectivity, were shown
by titration to contain $>10^6$ infectious units. Again, animals at the end point of the titration were harvested and the
amount of infectivity quantitated. By repeating this at
least three times, material in the original homogenate was
diluted more than 10^{18} fold. The values obtained ($>10^{18}$)
approach and in some cases surpass Avogadro's number which
proves scrapie agent replicated.

CLONING SCRAPIE AGENTS

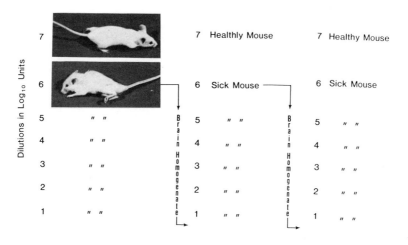

Figure 1. Cloning scrapie agents by 3 serial titrations to an end point. Positive mice at the end point of each titration were used as the source for brain homogenates that were diluted in the subsequent titration.

III.   SCRAPIE: AN UNCONVENTIONAL SLOW INFECTION
    Almost 30 years ago Bjorn Sigurdsson, an Icelandic medical virologist, who was studying a group of diseases in Icelandic sheep proposed the concept of slow infections in a series of 3 lectures given at the University of London. The criteria he established were aimed at distinguishing that group of diseases from acute and chronic infections. One of the diseases he described was Rida, the Icelandic term for scrapie (Sigurdsson 1954).
    A.   The ciriteria defining slow infections
    Sigurdsson established the following 3 criteria: (1) A very long initial period of latency lasting from several months to several years. (2) A rather regular protracted course after clinical signs have appeared, usually ending in

serious disease or death. (3) Limitation of the infection to a single host species and anatomical lesions in only a single organ or tissue system.

Sigurdsson correctly predicted that the third point might have to be modified by further findings. For example, scrapie and those diseases caused by similar agents (Kuru, Creutzfeld-Jakob Disease and Transmissable Mink Encephalopathy) can be transmitted experimentally to a wide variety of species (Gibbs and Gajdusek, 1973; Gajdusek, 1977; Marsh and Hanson, 1979).

B. Scrapie and the Criteria for Unconventional Slow Infections

Scrapie fits exactly those criteria of Sigurdsson that have stood the test of time. It has a long incubation period lasting several months or years. The shortest experimental agent-host combination is with a particular strain of scrapie agent in hamsters in which the incubation period is approximately 60 days (Kimberline and Walker, 1977). There are scrapie agent-mouse strain combinations in which the incubation period is 120-130 days and others in which it is 500-700 days (Dickinson and Meikle, 1971; Dickinson and Fraser, 1979; Dickinson *et al.*, 1983). In sheep, incubation periods of several years can occur even after injection of high titer material. For the second criterion, the course of clinical disease usually lasts several weeks in mice and can continue for several months in sheep. Animals become progressively sicker and the disease invariably ends in death.

The term unconventional is appropriate for scrapie and the related diseases in that it denotes the unusual properties of these agents and diseases and distinguishes this group from the slow infections caused by conventional viruses, e.g. Visna (Carp and Thormar, 1975; Gajdusek, 1977).

Sigurdsson compared the characteristics of acute, chronic and slow infections. The characteristic that distinguished slow from acute infections was simply the length of the incubation period. For comparison of chronic and slow infections he stressed for the latter, the precise course, with a predictable incubation period, a specific symptomatology and a uniform progression to death. Although at the time Sigurdsson had comparatively little information to form the basis for his view of these diseases, he was amazingly prescient in his comments about the various aspects of slow infections, particularly as they relate to scrapie: "They are chronic mainly in the sense that they are slow. On the other hand, these diseases follow a course which is just as regular as the course of the acute infections only the time factor is different. In the first place the so-called incubation period, although extremely long, apparently does not vary within very wide limits. The appearance and the progression of the clinical signs follow a set pattern. Once these diseases have reached a recognizable stage their course is determined, they progress continuously and they always kill. Moreover, death ensues after a certain sequence of pathological events has been accomplished. The progression of these diseases indicates a process that follows its own course without much outside interference. If the host tries to defend itself at all, it would appear that such attempts prove rather ineffectual."

In the years since this statement, work on scrapie has confirmed the points: The precision of events during the course of scrapie has been documented in great detail by the work of Dickinson and colleagues (Dickinson and Meikle, 1969; Fraser and Dickinson, 1973; Outram, 1976; Dickinson, and Fraser, 1979; Fraser, 1979), who concluded that those events seem to follow a "clock-work" predictability. Further, as stated previously, attempts to influence the course of the disease have been unsuccessful except at the very earliest stages of host interaction with peripherally injected agent (Outram *et al.*, 1974, Kimberlin and Cunnington, 1978; Dickinson *et al.*, 1978; Carp and Warner, 1980). Finally, we do not know of any mechanisms employed by the host to defend against the agent or to ameliorate the disease process. If there are such mechanisms they may slow but do not prevent the inevitable outcome.

IV. TRANSMISSION OF SCRAPIE

As an infectious disease scrapie is transmitted both naturally and experimentally.

A. Natural Transmission

We have already noted that transmission can occur in sheep and goats during close contact in pens (Brotherson *et al.*, 1968) and in field conditions(Dickinson *et al.*, 1974). Maternal transmission can play a role in natural transmission as shown by: (1) Lambs removed from ewes at birth and reared in an area away from possible postnatal contact with agent developed disease (Dickinson *et al.*, 1974) and (2) Reciprocal crosses between a high incidence breed of sheep (Suffolk) and a low incidence breed (Scottish Blackface) showed that lambs derived from scrapie positive ewes were more likely to develop scrapie than those from scrapie positive rams(Dickinson *et al.*, 1974; Dickinson, 1976). The precise mechanisms of maternal and non-maternal transmission are not known. In non-maternal transmission certain facts would suggest an oral route is likely: It is known that the oral route is an effective means of experimental transmission of scrapie (Pattison and Millson, 1961; Pattison *et al.*, 1974; Gibbs *et al.*, 1980; Carp, 1981). Further, scrapie infectivity was found in the placenta and sheep often eat this material (Pattison *et al.*, 1974). Certainly this process cannot be the only non-maternal mechanism of transmission since, as stated previously, some scrapie-free sheep introduced into empty fields that had contained scrapie positive sheep 1-3 years previously developed scrapie (Palsson, 1979).

Scrapie does not occur naturally in mice but after experimental introduction it can spread within a cage. Some results have suggested that fighting was necessary for transmission (Pattison, 1964) whereas other studies have shown transmission in the absence of fighting (Dickinson *et al.*, 1964; Zlotnik, 1968). Maternal transmission has not been demonstrated in mice (Clarke and Haig, 1971a).

B. Experimental Transmission

A wide variety of species and routes of introduction have been used sucessfully in experimental transmission of scrapie (Table 1). The shortest incubation periods have been observed in hamsters (60 days with one scrapie strain passaged in this species) (Kimberlin and Walker, 1977) and voles (Chandler and Turfrey, 1972).

In the mouse the intracerebral (IC) route was the most efficient followed by intravenous, intraperitoneal, and subcutaneous in that order (Kimberlin and Walker, 1978a). The relationship between incubation period and dose yielded similar curves (after correction for differences in efficiency) for the 3 peripheral routes. The dose-response curve for IC

Table I
Scrapie in Various Species, and Routes
Used for Experimental Transmission

Hosts		Routes Used For
Natural	Experimental	Experimental Transmission[a]
sheep	sheep	intracerebral (IC)
goats	goats	intravenous (IV)
	mice	intraperitoneal (IP)
	rats	subcutaneous (SC)
	hamsters	oral
	Syrian and	intraocular
	Chinese	intraspinal
	voles	intrasciatic
	mink	intratongue
	monkeys	via ear punch
	Cynamolgus	

[a] All of these routes have been used only with the mouse system. For other hosts just one or a few of the routes have been used.

route was similar at low doses but differed from peripherally
injected agent at high doses. Regardless of route or dose,the
final levels of infectivity in mice sick with scrapie were
similar. The conclusion of the authors is that differences
in pathogenesis with different routes is based on events that
occur early in agent-host interactions which determine the
efficiency of infection.

V. PATHOGENESIS

It appears that an understanding of the pathogenesis of
scrapie must begin with an analysis of the interaction between
scrapie and cells of the lymphoreticular system (LRS). An
early finding with scrapie was the fact that shortly after
peripheral injection scrapie infectivity was found in lymphoid
organs, such as spleen and lymph nodes, and these titers
increased with time (Eklund *et al.*, 1967). Following subcutaneous injection, agent was present at high titers in these
organs for 2-3 months prior to appearance of agent in the
CNS. Furthermore, modification of the LRS just prior to
peripheral injection influences the progression of scrapie
disease. There are a number of examples of this: Immunostim-
ulative agents such as phytohemagglutinin (Dickinson *et al.*,
1978), methanol extraction residue of BCG (Kimberlin and
Cunnington, 1978) and human lymphokines (Carp and Warner,
1980) shorten incubation periods when given within 4 hours
prior to infection of scrapie. In contrast, immunosuppressive agents such as prednisone (Outram *et al.*, 1974) lengthen
incubation periods. It is remarkable that a disease with
incubation periods of 6 months and more can be influenced
profoundly by manipulation of the host LRS system at or within hours of the time of injection. Incubation periods in
mice which do not have a spleen, either because of surgical
intervention (Fraser and Dickinson, 1970; Clarke and Haig,
1971b) or because of a genetic defect (Dickinson and Fraser,
1972) are longer than in comparable mice with spleens. In
contrast thymectomy has no effect on incubation period
(McFarlin *et al.*, 1971). These results have prompted Outram
et al., 1975) to propose the Trojan Horse concept. In this
concept, those cells that ordinarily aid the body in warding
off disease are used by the scrapie agent either for replication or for an important processing step required for spread
and/or replication of the agent.

Another possible example of the importance of the LRS is
the result obtained with neonatal mice. Injection of mice
with a dose that is lethal for weanling mice within the first
few days of life leads to an extended incubation period or in
some instances survival (Outram *et al.*, 1973; Hotchin and
Buckley, 1977). The suggestion made by these investigators

is that the pathogenesis of scrapie requires the development
or maturation of a cell type, probably of the LRS system,
which does not occur until 4-6 days after birth.

One method for analyzing the interaction between scrapie
and LRS cells is to isolate specific LRS cell types from
normal animals, expose these cells to agent in vitro and

Table II
Attachment of Scrapie (ME7) to Peritoneal
Macrophages and Kidney Cells

Exp. No.	ME7 Incubated with	Temp.°C	Mice In- jected with	Number	Incub. Per. in Days Mean ± S.E.
1	no cells	37	ME7 alone	6	173$\pm$2
	macrophages	37	cells	6	188$\pm$4
	macrophages	37	supernatant	6	167$\pm$3
	no cells	4	ME7 alone	6	174$\pm$2
	macrophages	4	cells	6	205$\pm$3
	macrophages	4	supernatant	6	173$\pm$3
2	no cells	37	ME7 alone	5	170$\pm$4
	kidney cells	37	cells	5	242$\pm$11
	kidney cells	37	supernatant	5	173$\pm$3
	kidney cells	37	cell-agent mixture	6	173$\pm$3

Table III
Changes in Scrapie Incubation Period for Washed ME7-infected
Macrophages During *in Vitro* Incubation at 37°C for 4-5 days

Exp. No.	Inoculum	Dilution of Scrapie Homogenate	*In Vitro* Incu- bation Period 2H	4-5 Days	P of no Diff. from Inc. Period of 2H Sample
1	ME7		165$\pm$1[a]	168$\pm$1	>0.1
	Cells		170$\pm$3	183$\pm$3	<0.05
2	ME7		157$\pm$4	155$\pm$3	>0.5
	Cells		165$\pm$4	201$\pm$7	<0.01
3	ME7		166$\pm$2	163$\pm$0	>0.2
	Cells		191$\pm$5	204$\pm$7	>0.1
4	ME7	-2	166$\pm$1	169$\pm$1	>0.1
	ME7	-3	172$\pm$7	177$\pm$2	>0.5
	Cells(C57BL)	-2	171$\pm$3	184$\pm$3	<0.02
	Cells(C57BL)	-3	185$\pm$4	233$\pm$14	<0.05
	Cells(Hamster)	-2	166$\pm$4	181$\pm$5	<0.05
	Cells(Hamster)	-3	182$\pm$3	218$\pm$11	<0.02

[a] Scrapie Incubation Period in Days (Mean $\pm$ S.E.).

determine what happens to scrapie infectivity with extended
time in culture. In initial studies we showed that scrapie

attaches to peritoneal exudate cells, that this attachment occurs to a greater extent at 37°C than at 4°C and that infectivity attaches to peritoneal exudate cells more effectively than to kidney cells (Table II) (Carp and Callahan, 1981). With continued *in vitro* incubation, scrapie infectivity decreased and the drop was greater in cell-agent mixtures than in agent incubated in the absence of cells (Table III) (Carp and Callahan, 1982). Scrapie interactions with other cell types following *in vitro* exposure to agent are currently being investigated. For *in vivo* experiments, the recent development of effective means of purifying various LRS cell types should allow us to determine which of these cell types harbor scrapie at various times during the incubation period and these experiments are currently in progress.

In studies using intraocular injection Fraser (1981) has shown that lesions developed first in the contralateral superior colliculi and that infectivity was also higher in the contralateral than in the ipsilateral superior colliculi. This suggests that agent follows the optic nerve, possibly by orthograde axonal spread. Spread via nerves is also suggested by studies of Kimberlin and Walker (1980, 1982) who showed that after IP injection scrapie infectivity appeared first in the spinal cord at the level of the thoracic vertebrae 4-9 and then spread anteriorly and posteriorly. In the mouse, the splenic nerve probably enters the spinal cord at the level of thoracic vertebrae 4-9 and it is thought that agent spreads from the spleen to the cord via this nerve. Interestingly, these same authors have shown that the incubation period for intraspinally injected scrapie is shorter than for similar doses given IC (Kimberlin and Walker, 1983) and we have confirmed this finding.

VI.   GENETICS

A genetic component in scrapie-host interactions was suspected some time ago because breeds of sheep differed in their incidence of infection with natural scrapie. Credit for clear demonstration of the importance of genetic control of scrapie both in the natural and experimental diseases belongs to Dr. Alan G. Dickinson and his colleagues in Edinburgh. In a sophisticated series of studies in inbred mice they described genetically controlled differences in 3 parameters: (1) Incubation period; (2) The intensity of vacuolation in 9 specified areas of gray matter and 3 white matter areas; these were termed lesion profiles and (3) The incidence of amyloid plaques formation. Using the scrapie agents and the appropriate mouse strains which had been developed and/or characterized by the Edinburgh group we tested several of the key findings they had reported. Our results have confirmed their findings in every respect.

A. Incubation Period

The mouse gene Sinc (an acronym for scrapie incubation) was defined originally by the fact that mouse strains differ in their incubation period for a specific scrapie strain, ME7 (Dickinson and Meikle, 1969). Those mouse strains with a short incubation period for ME7 have a genotype termed s7s7, whereas those with a long incubation are p7p7. Three mouse strains with the p7p7 genotype, VM, IM and MB have been developed. The VM strain was derived from mice that were segregating with diferent incubation periods for ME7. The IM and MB strains were subsequently derived from VM mice (Dickinson, personal communication). All other mouse strains that have been tested are s7s7. The incubation periods for many scrapie agents are similar to those obtained for ME7 in the two mouse genotypes, however, there are a number of strains, 22A and 87V for example, which have a longer incubation period in s7s7 mice than in p7p7 strains (Dickinson and Meikle, 1969; Dickinson and Fraser, 1979). Our results with these 3 scrapie agents in p7p7 and s7s7 strains are shown in Table IV. These data are virtually the same as those already reported (Dickinson and Fraser, 1979; Dickinson *et al.* 1983). In addition we have examined a number of other mouse strains which are listed in Table V. All of the strains were s7s7. Among this group the SJL strain is interesting in that it had an extremely short incubation period for ME7. The incubation periods for two other agents, 139A and 22L, were also short in SJL mice (Table VI). In contrast, for NZW mice

Table IV
Incubation Periods in Days and Presence of Plaques for 3 Standard Scrapie Strains in C57BL and VM Mice[a]

| | Mouse | Strain | | |
| | C57BL (s7s7) | | VM(p7p7) | |
Scrapie strain	Days+SE	Plaques	Days+SE	Plaques
ME7	153+1	No	300+3	Yes
22A	381+5	Yes	180+2	No
87V	467+21[b]	Yes[b]	311+5	Yes

[a] Injected IC with a 1% brain homogenate. Brains were obtained from mice showing clinical signs of scrapie.
[b] Data from Bruce *et al.*, 1976.

Table V
Incubation Periods in Days and Plaque Formation
for ME7 and 22A in Various Mouse Strains[a]

Mouse Strain		No.	ME7 Mean + SE	No.	22A Mean + SE	Plaques ME7	22A
NZW	♂	15	158 + 2	15	422 + 5	–	–
	♀	6	164 + 3	4	396 + 15	–	–
NZB	♂	8	167 + 4	8	458 + 31	–	–
F$_1$,NZB	♂	21	163 + 2	25	369 + 17	–	ND[c]
X NZW	♀	14	160 + 2	14	–[b]	–	ND
C58	♀	4	156 + 1	4	348 + 34	–	ND
DBA-2	♀	5	143 + 2	–	ND	ND	ND
CBA/J	♀	12	167 + 3	6	384 + 9	+[d]	+[d]
SJL/J	♀	10	123 + 2	5	379 + 14	ND	ND

[a] Mice were injected IC with 0.03 ml of a 1% brain homogenate
[b] Scrapie incubation period could not be determined because female NZB x NZW F$_1$ mice die of an autoimmune disease prior to clinical scrapie.
[c] ND = not done.
[d] For CBA/J mice, 25% showed plaques with ME7; 100% with 22A

the incubation period was comparatively long for ME7 (158 + 2 days) but short for 139A (121 + 3 days). For another s7s7 strain, C57BL, the incubation period for 22L was 14-15 days shorter than for 139A and ME7. It appears that within the s7s7 group of mouse strains there are additional genetic controls which influence incubation period. Another laboratory has reached similar conclusions(Kingsbury *et al.*, 1983).

B. Distribution and Intensity of Vacuolation

The intensity of vacuolation in various regions of the brain is also under genetic control of both agent and host (Fraser and Dickinson, 1973; Fraser, 1979). Often the topography and intensity are sufficiently distinctive that they

Table VI
Differences in Incubation Period for Several Scrapie
Agents Among s7s7 Strains of Mice

Scrapie Agent	Mouse Strain		
	C57BL	SJL	NZW
ME7	153 + 1[a]	123 + 2	158 + 2
139A	152 + 3	113 + 2	121 + 3
22L	138 + 1	128 + 2	ND

Incubation Period in Days (Mean Standard Error).

can serve as a "signature" for specific scrapie agent mouse strain combinations. When examined by a pathologist experienced in these analyses, the agent-strain combination can often be identified. The distribution and extent of vacuola-

tion that we have determined for several agent-strain combi-
nations(e.g. ME7 and 139A in C57BL) are similar to those
reported for these combinations by the Edinburgh group
(Fraser, 1979; Dickinson, personal communications).

C. Amyloid and Neuritic (Senile) Plaques

The development of amyloid plaques in certain agent-
mouse strain combinations was first described by Fraser and
Bruce (1973). Later the presence of a neuritic component in
some of the scrapie plaques was described and the similarity
of these plaques to those observed in Alzheimer's Disease was
noted (Wisniewski *et al.* 1975). Parenthetically, these and
other similarities between Alzheimer's and the diseases caused by unconventional slow viruses have been discussed in
detail in two recent reviews (Brown *et al.* 1982; Carp *et
al.*, 1984a). Plaques were also seen in some sheep sick with
scrapie, however because of the large size of sheep brain
further work has been limited (Beck and Daniel, 1965).Addi-
tional work in the mouse system established that the incidence of amyloid and neuritic plaque formation depended on
both scrapie agent and mouse strain, with some combinations
showing many plaques, other combinations a few and still
others none (Fraser and Bruce, 1973; Bruce *et al.*, 1976;
Fraser, 1979). Results obtained by two approaches have suggested that plaque development is at least in part directly
related to the local concentration of agent(Bruce and Fraser,
1981; Wisniewski *et al.*,1981).

We have confirmed the Edinburgh group's finding that
plaque formation depends on both scrapie agent and mouse
strain. For example we have found amyloid plaques in those
agent strain combinations previously reported to be positive
(e.g. 87V and ME7 in VM and 22A in C57BL) (See Table IV).
Typical plaques (brain section from the 87V-VM combination)
are shown in thick sections stained with Bodian – PAS (Figure
2a) and toluidine blue (Figure 2b). In Figure 3, an electron
micrograph of a typical plaque is shown.

In addition to the agent-strain combinations previously
examined, plaques have been found in 25% of CBA mice injected with ME7 (Table V). The incubation period in this combination is 163 ± 3 days. In our experience, this is the shortest incubation period combination in which plaques occur at a
frequency as high as 25%.

D. Weight Changes During the Preclinical Phase of
Disease

We have been analyzing total body weights in various
agent-strain combinations throughout the incubation period.
During clinical disease total body weight decreased in all
combinations, a common finding with most scrapie agent-mouse
strain combinations (Kimberlin and Millson, 1967). However,
during the preclinical phase there were increases in total

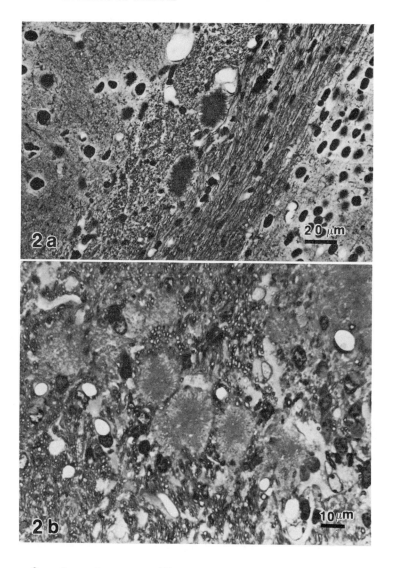

Figure 2. Scrapie agent 87V was injected IC (0.03 ml of a 1% homogenate) into VM mice. Brain sections were prepared from mice showing clinical disease, approximately 300 days post injection. Sections were stained with Bodian-PAS in (a) and toluidine blue in (b).

body weight (compared to mice injected with normal mouse brain) in some agent-strain combinations but not in others (Carp *et al.*, 1984b). There was a contribution from both agent and mouse strain. Increases in weight were seen in ME7

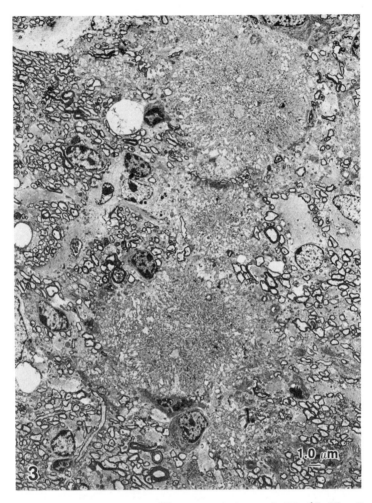

Figure 3. Scrapie agent 87V was injected IC (0.03 ml of a 1% momogenate) into VM mice. Thin sections of brain were prepared from mice showing clinical disease, approximately 300 days post infection. This section is at a magnification of 4000X.

and 22L-injected SJL mice but not 139A-injected SJL's. ME7 caused an increase in weight in CBA mice, but 22L and 139A did not. CBA mice injected with either ME-ME7 or normal mouse brain are pictured in Figure 4. The genetic contribution of mouse strains is shown by the fact that 22L caused an increase in SJL mice but not CBA or C57BL mice. Clearly, this parameter is not controlled by the Sinc gene since these three strains have the same genotype, s7s7. In Table VII

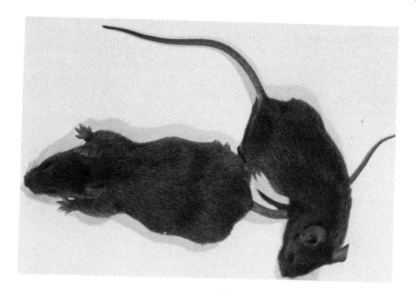

Figure 4. CBA/J mice injected IC with 0.03 ml of a 1% brain homogenate. Mouse on right received normal mouse brain; mouse on left received ME7. Picture was taken 115 days post injection, 3-4 weeks prior to the onset of clinical disease in ME7 injected mice.

Table VII
Effects of Various Scrapie Agents on Total Body
Weight of Several Mouse Strains[a]

Scrapie Agent	Mouse Strains			
	SJL/J	CBA/J	C57BL	VM
ME7	+[b]	+	ND[d]	–
139A	–	–	–	ND
22L	+	–	–	ND
22A	–?[c]	–	ND	–

[a] Effects were seen in the preclinical phase of disease.
[b] + = increase in weight; – = no increase in weight.
[c] SJL/J mice develop reticulum cell sarcomas which prevent a proper asessment of their weight changes during the latter part of the preclinical phase of disease.
[d] ND = not done.

data for these and several other agent-strain combinations are summarized.

In those positive combinations the increase in weight was seen first after the completion of approximately 60-80%

of the preclinical phase of disease. The increasing weight
reached a peak just prior to or just after the start of the
clinical phase of disease. The difference in weight between
normal and scrapie mice was equivalent to as much as 20% of
the weight of the mice injected with normal mouse brain.
This increase in weight was caused by an accumulation of fat
rather than a generalized increase in body size. This is
shown clearly in Figure 5 in which the peritoneal cavities

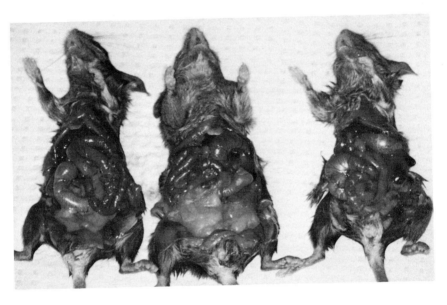

Figure 5.   CBA/J mice injected IC with 0.03 ml of a 1% brain
homogenate. Mouse on right received 139A, mouse in center
ME7 and mouse on left normal mouse brain. Picture was taken
122 days post injection, 2-3 weeks prior to the expected
onset of clinical disease in ME7 injected mice and within
1-2 weeks of the onset of clinical disease in 139A injected
mice.

of CBA mice injected IC With ME7, 139A or normal mouse brain
are compared. The ME7 infected mouse shows large accumula-
tions of fat, whereas the others do not. Further evidence on
this point was provided by the fact that during the early
clinical phase of the disease in combinations which showed a
weight increase, the weight of visceral organs was less than
in normal brain injected mice despite the fact that total
body weight was more in the scrapie mice. Mice in all of
these agent-strain combinations showed a decrease in weight
as clinical disease progressed.

E. Other Aspects of Genetic Control

In addition to the above markers, differences in the rates of heat inactivation between different strains (Dickinson and Taylor, 1978) and variation in the ratio of 1P to 1C infectivity (Dickinson and Outram, 1983) have been reported. There have been a number of studies describing behavioral changes in the preclinical and clinical phases of scrapie and in several instances these were shown to differ in various agent-strain combinations (Outram, 1972; McFarland *et al.*, 1980).

The genetic control of scrapie even extends to species specificity in that there are strains of scrapie which cause disease in some species but not others. Brain homogenates prepared from some sheep (approximately 20% of those tested) fail to cause disease in mice (Fraser, 1983). Even more remarkable the hamster passaged scrapie strain, 263K, failed to cause disease in mice (Kimberlin and Walker, 1978b). Extremely high infectivity titers for hamsters are found in the brains of hamsters sick with 263K, but mice injected with hamster brain homogenate remained normal after 1 year. In our own study, combined 1P and 1C injection of C57BL mice with high doses of 263K failed to produce typical clinical scrapie after 630 days. However, brains of these mice had low levels of vacuolar changes typical of scrapie and contained low amounts of agent as determined by hamster injection (Carp, unpublished). A list of parameters in scrapie that are currently known to be under genetic control is shown in Table VIII.

Table VIII
Scrapie Parameters under Genetic Control

Parameters	References
Incubation Period	Dickinson and Meikle (1971)
Lesion Profile	Fraser and Dickinson (1973)
Induction of Amyloid Plaques	Bruce *et al.* (1976)
Sensitivity to Heat	Dickinson and Taylor (1978)
Behavioral Changes	Outram (1972),McFarland *et al.* (1980)
Species Specificity	Kimberlin and Walker (1977, 1978b)
Preclinical Weight Gain	Carp *et al.* (1984b)

There are other characteristics of scrapie which show that it displays genetic variation and that key elements of its replication are under control. For some scrapie isolates genetically controlled characteristics remain constant, whereas other strains have been reported to undergo mutation (Bruce and Dickinson, 1979). The situation in which characteristics do not change has been referred to as Class I stability, whereas the strains which show descrete mutational

change are said to show Class III stability. In another type
of stability, Class II, agents gradually change in a predictable manner during serial passages in mice of one Sinc genotype, whereas they remain completely stable during passage
in the other Sinc genotype. For example the characteristics
of the 22A agent remain constant during passages in VM mice,
however, serial passages of 22A in an s7s7 strain, C57BL,
lead to a gradual shortening of incubation periods in C57BL
mice and gradual lengthening in VM mice. The characteristics
stabilize after 5 serial C57BL-passages. This experiment has
been done 16 times and in every instance the results were
similar (Bruce and Dickinson, 1979).

In summary, we have confirmed the basic findings of the
Edinburgh group regarding genetic control of scrapie-host
interactions. These include their findings on incubation
periods, distribution and intensity of vacuolation and the
presence or absence of amyloid plaques. In addition, we have
examined a number of mouse strains not previously tested for
these parameters. Also, we have described a new potential
genetic marker: the presence or absence of increases in
total body weight during the preclinical phase of disease.
It would appear that the extent of genetically controlled
differences in scrapie agent-host interactions will expand as
we examine more agent-host combinations and analyze more
parameters.

VII.   CHANGES IN THE BLOOD-BRAIN BARRIER

In recent studies, increased permeability of brain
microvessels to intravenously injected horse radish peroxidase
(HRP) has been described in mice injected either IC or IP
with scrapie (Wisniewski *et al.*, 1983). HRP leakage was
focal and was more intense near the IC injection needle tract
than elsewhere. The areas of leakage did not correspond to
areas of vacuolation or plaques (with the exception of the
needle track where plaques and leakage are prevalent). The
increase in permeability was seen in non-plaque forming
combinations, e.g. ME7 - C57BL, 22A - VM and 139A - C57BL as
well as plaque forming combinations such as 87V in IM or VM.
The increase in HRP leakage was examined primarily in clinical
mice; however, a few mice studied during the preclinical
phase of disease showed leakage, but at a reduced level
compared to clinical mice. In the same report (Wisniewski
et al., 1983), changes in the location of plasmalemma bound
alkaline phosphatase activity were also reported. In control
mice, enzyme activity was located predominately on the luminal
surface, whereas in scrapie mice, activity was on both luminal
and abluminal surfaces. The relationship of these changes in

the brain microvasculature in scrapie to the other histopathological changes seen is not clear at this time.

It is interesting that recent studies have shown that cells of the lymphocyte series and endothelial cells interact (Burger and Vetto, 1982; Stevens, *et al.*, 1982). For example, endothelial cells can act as accessory cells by presenting antigen in an immunogeneic form to sensitized T cells (Hirschberg *et al.*, 1982). An interesting hypothesis evolves: Scrapie infection of lymphocytes affects their interaction with endothelial cells. This in turn affects the capacity of the endothelial cells to maintain the integrity of the blood-brain barrier, which leads to histopathological changes and disturbed brain function.

Increased permeability of the blood-brain barrier in scrapie provides another link with Alzheimer's Disease, since there is also evidence of similar changes in the blood-brain barrier of humans with this disease (Wisniewski and Kozlowski, 1982; Carp *et al.*, 1984a).

VIII. AN ABNORMAL FIBRILLAR STRUCTURE CONSISTENTLY OBSERVED IN SCRAPIE PREPARATIONS

Electron microscopic (EM) studies of conventional viruses have contributed to our understanding of virus-host cell interactions and have been an important tool for analyzing the effectiveness of purification protocols and inactivation procedures. In scrapie, no structure has been identified. Abnormal profiles in scrapie infected brains have been reported but these findings have not been universal with respect to agent-host combinations or consistent from laboratory to laboratory. Our own attempts began with finding an abnormal fibrillar structure in synaptosomal preparations of brains from clinical mice. These are designated scrapie associated fibrils (SAF) (Merz *et al.*, 1981). The fibrils are of 2 kinds, having either 2 or 4 distinct filaments (Figure 6). Each filament is 4-6 nm in width and the fibrils are usually 100-500 nm in length. Fibrils are usually straight, but on occasion they deflect at a single point. At their widest the fibrils are 12-16 nm in width with 2-4 nm between filaments. They narrow along their length every 40-60 nm and at these points they are only 4-6 nm wide with no visible space between filaments. The arrangement of the filaments suggests a helical structure. SAF are markedly different in appearance from normal brain fibrils such as microtubules, neurofilaments, glial filaments and F actin. However, SAF share some structural characteristics with amyloid fibers (Merz *et al.*, 1983a).

SAF have been seen in synaptosomal fractions prepared

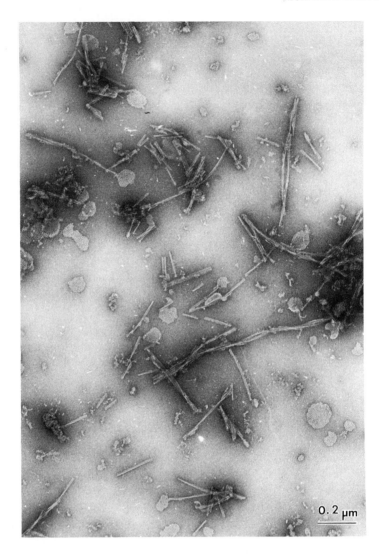

Figure 6. An electron micrograph of partially purified SAF from brains of 139A injected (IC) C57BL mice. Type 1 and 2 SAF can be seen, with membranous debris, both free and attached to SAF. The preparation was stained with 3% sodium phosphotungstate, pH7.2. The bar represents 0.2 micron.

from mice injected with various strains of agent (ME7, 139A, 87V, 22A, 22L and 79A) and in hamsters injected with 263K. They have been seen in synaptosomal fractions from C57BL, VM and IM mice injected with scrapie. In the ME7-

C57BL combination, mice injected by either IP or IC routes
have SAF. Following IC injection, SAF are first seen in
brain preparations at 63 days in a combination with an
incubation period of 150 days (Merz et al., 1983a). SAF have
been seen in spleen and the increasing concentration of SAF
in spleen parellels the rise in scrapie infectivity in this
organ. SAF have been found in every scrapie preparation in
which we would expect to find a high titer of scrapie
infectivity. In contrast, SAF have not been seen in more
than 50 control samples including brain and spleen preparations from normal brain injected hamsters and mice, uninoculated old mice, cuprizone or triethyltin treated mice (treatments which produce CNS histopathological changes similar to
some of those seen in scrapie), and brains from mice chronic-
ally infected with Semliki Forest virus. Thus, all controls
have been negative and, in fact, the only non-scrapie instances of SAF presence have been synaptosomal fractions prepared
from brains of patients with Creutzfeld-Jakob disease (CJD)
and from brains of animals injected with CJD and Kuru material (Manuelidis and Manuelidis, 1983; Merz et al., 1983b;
Merz, et al. 1984). As noted previously CJD and Kuru are
slow infection processes caused by scrapie-like agents.
     Conjecture about the relationship of SAF and scrapie
have centered on three possibilities: (1) SAF are an aberrant
fibril produced in scrapie affected animals as part of the
pathological process. The fact that SAF were found in spleen,
an organ which does not show histopathological changes, argues
against this possibility. (2) SAF are a specific aberrant
fibril, i.e. amyloid. Although SAF do not look exactly like
any of the known amyloid fibrils, (Merz et al., 1983a; Merz
et al., 1983c), there is a family of these structures so
that SAF may be another type of amyloid fibril. Pathological
deposits of amyloid in the form of plaques have been described in certain scrapie agent-mouse strain combinations
(see section VI, Genetics). However in scrapie these depos
its have never been described in any organ other than brain
(SAF are in spleen preparations) and they are not seen in
many of the agent-strain combinations that have SAF (e.g.
139A in C57BL, ME7 in C57BL, 263K in hamsters). It should be
noted that systemic amyloidosis has not been observed naturally in our mouse colony nor has it been possible to induce
systemic amyloidosis experimentally (Kozlowski et al., unpublished observations). (3) The final possibility is that SAF
are the structural manifestation of scrapie infectivity.
There are a number of findings which support this concept:
(a) the observations have been made in material prepared in 3
separate laboratories and in preparations from infected animals maintained in 5 laboratories; (b) the finding has been
limited to unconventional slow virus diseases (scrapie, CJD,

and Kuru) (c) SAF have been seen in brain and spleen, which
have high titers of agent. As indicated above, there are no
histopathological changes in spleen in these diseases; (d) in
the infected animal the increase in the number of SAF approximately correlates with increases in infectivity titer and
(e) in preliminary studies SAF and infectivity co-purify.

In order to determine which of these possibilities is
correct it would be important to purify SAF. This would lead
to analysis of the chemical nature of SAF and, perhaps, provide an opportunity to establish conclusively if SAF and
infectivity co-purify. Progress on purification of agent and
correlating infectivity with a physical entity will be difficult because of problems detailed in the next section.

IX. PROBLEMS IN CORRELATING RESULTS OBTAINED BY INFECTIVITY ASSAYS WITH EFFECTS ON SCRAPIE AGENT

The task of detecting a possible relationship between
scrapie infectivity and a specific physical entity is difficult (Cho *et al.*, 1977). The only way to assay scrapie infectivity is by animal injection. The usual method of estima-
ting titer is by diluting to an end point. Another method
described some time ago is to estimate titer from the incubation period (Hunter *et al.*, 1963, Mould *et al.*, 1967, Dickinson *et al.*, 1969). Subsequent work showed that if host
species and strain, route of injection, age and sex of the
host, scrapie agent and prior treatment of agent are kept
constant then incubation period is indeed an accurate measure
of titer (Outram, 1976). With regard to prior treatment of
agent, Prusiner *et al.* (1982) found no alteration of the dose-
incubation period relationship after inoculum had been heated
at different temperatures up to 100° and Somerville *et al.*
(1980) showed that treatment of a partially purified fraction
with Triton X-100 had no effect on the relationship. However,
boiling the inoculum (Dickinson and Fraser, 1969), treatment
of brain homogenates with sodium dodecyl sulfate or LiCl
(Kimberlin, 1977) and treatment of brain homogenate with
sodium deoxycholate (Lax *et al.*, 1983a) have led to a skewing
of the dose response curves. In a recent study we treated
synaptosomal or synaptic plasma membrane fractions with the
detergents octyl-β-D glucopyranoside or sulphobetaine 3-14.
These fractions were then subjected to differential or density gradient centrifugation (Somerville and Carp, 1983).
Determination of dose by end point analysis and comparison of
dose with incubation periods at each dilution showed that
this relationship was different for detergent treated material
compared to fractions that had not been exposed to detergent
(Table IX). For the same dose of inoculum previous treatment

Table IX

Difference in Average Incubation Period for the Same Dose of
Scrapie Injected IC with and without Detergent Treatment

Treatment of Inoculum	No. of Assays	Average Difference(in Days) from no Detergent Treatment
No Detergent	10	–
Detergent[a] still present	7	11
Detergent[a] treatment, then removed	7	19

[a] Detergents used = Octyl β-D-glucopyranoside and sulphobetaine 3-14.

and subsequent removal of detergent led to an increase in
incubation period of 19 days compared to material not exposed
to detergent. The same comparison for samples in which
detergent had not been removed showed an 11 day difference.
These findings combined with those previously referred to
(Dickinson and Fraser, 1969; Kimberlin, 1977; Somerville
et al., 1980; Prusiner et al., 1982; Lax et al, 1983a),
emphasize that incubation period can only serve as a titer
estimate after dose-response curves have been established for
each chemical and physical treatment.

There are also difficulties with the end point titration
estimate of infectivity. A number of reports have shown that
end point titer estimates of scrapie are particularly sensitive to physical and chemical treatments of the inoculum.
Extensive homogenization of scrapie brain caused an increase
in titer compared to material homogenized gently (Malone et
al., 1978). Sonication of each dilution in an end point
titration series resulted in a 17 fold increase in titer
compared to unsonicated material (Rohwer and Gajdusek, 1980).

In a recent study (Table X), we showed that incorporation of detergent (0.1% N lauroyl sarcosinate) in dilution
fluid caused increases in titer estimates of more than 100
fold for both brain homogenate and gradient fractions of
detergent treated membrane material (Somerville and Carp,
1983).

The known characteristics of scrapie and of the assay
system provide possible reasons for the findings noted in
this section. Scrapie infectivity is "sticky" and appears to
be attached to various membranous cell components (Hunter and
Millson, 1967; Millson and Manning, 1979; Prusiner et al.,
1979). The infectious units are prone to aggregation (Prusiner et al., 1978; Prusiner et al., 1979; Millson and Manning, 1979) so that chemical or physical treatments which
affect the proportion of single vs multiple units would

Table X
Effect of Inclusion of Detergent in the Diluent on
Titers of Infectivity Measured after IC Injection

Expt. No.	Inoculum	Presence of 0.1%NLS[a]	Titer in LOG$_{10}$ Units
1	Brain	No	6.4
	homogenate	Yes	>8.3
2	Detergent[b]	No	<5.4
	Treated membrane		
	fractions	Yes	>6.5

a   NLS = N Lauroyl Sarcosinate.
b   Metrizamide gradient fraction of sulphobetaine 3-14
    treated synaptosomal fraction.

change the measurable infectivity. Infectious units can attach to glass containers which decreases the amount remaining in solution (Dickinson, personal communication). We have already noted that treatment of the host's lymphoretucular system just prior to or at the time of infection can affect incubation periods of IP injected brain homogenates (Outram *et al.*, 1974; Kimberlin and Cunnington, 1978; Dickinson *et al.*, 1978; Carp and Warner, 1980). Preliminary data suggests that the number and activity levels of peritoneal exudate cells present in the peritoneal cavity at the time of IP injection can affect incubation period, and probably, have an effect on end point titer, too (Carp, unpublished). Although experimentally induced changes in pathogenesis have been produced only with peripheral injection, other treatments or the inclusion of other reagents in the inoculum for an IC injection might affect pathogenesis.

The effect of any physical or chemical treatment directed toward purifying or inactivating "agent" (defined here as the physical entity that includes the genetic information) can only be measured by analysis of infectivity in animals. As stated earlier there are no other "handles" to verify an effect, no immunological, biochemical or electron microscopic monitor of change that can be correlated with changes in the number of infectious units. It is certainly possible that scrapie "agent" will "co-purify" or "co-inactivate" with what we measure as the infectious unit. However, it is also possible that physical and chemical manipulation will not directly affect agent but will either (1) change the association of infectious units with their immediate environment (e.g. association with cell material, degree of aggregation, attachment to container) rendering them more or less capable

of causing infection or (2) affect the ability of the host to
fulfill its role in scrapie pathogenesis (Dickinson and
Outram, 1983).

X.   SCRAPIE - SUBVIRAL PATHOGEN: VIROIDS AND PRIONS

Relating scrapie to the title of this volume is fraught
with issues that are controversial and perhaps information
stressed in this chapter can contribute to the dialogue. On
a few points there would be unanimity. Certainly, all would
agree that scrapie is pathogenic (See Sections II, III, VI
and VII). Further, there is ample evidence that scrapie is
not a viroid: (1) failure to extract infectious RNA (Marsh *et*
al. 1974; Ward *et al.* 1974); (2) inactivation of infectivity
with proteases (Cho, 1980; Diener, *et al.,* 1982; Prusiner,
1982; Lax *et al.,* 1983b); (3) resistance of infectivity to
nucleases (Hunter,1972; Kimberlin 1982a; Diener *et al.,* 1982;
Prusiner, 1982). The term subviral does provoke controversy.
Certainly, most of the target size data suggest an extremely
small infectious agent and sizing by gel filtration has also
pointed toward a small structure. Another fact is the failure
to see a structure similar to conventional animal viruses in
material with high infectious titers. On the other hand,
Rohwer and Gajdusek (1980) have examined the X-ray and UV
inactivation data in the context of values obtained for
conventional animal viruses rather than from the original
target size calculations from phage inactivation studies.
Looked at in these terms, size values for the putative nucleic acid of scrapie are close to those obtained for the
smaller animal viruses. Also, these authors show that aggregation could yield data that would make target size appear to
be smaller than it actually is (Rohwer, personal communication) and we have already mentioned the propensity for aggr -
egation of scrapie infectivity (Prusiner *et al.,* 1978;
Prusiner *et al.,* 1979;Millson and Manning, 1979; Somerville
et al., 1980). The most striking data supporting a small
size for scrapie infectivity is based upon molecular sieve
chromatography using a Toya Soda TSK 4000 column (Prusiner,
1982). As pointed out, however, the size estimate is relevant
for a globular structure but would not shed light on the size
of a fibrillar infectious agent (Prusiner, 1982), such as
that proposed in Section VIII. Another explanation for the
small size estimate reported for scrapie with this technique
is that the detergent (sulphobetaine 3-14), which was part of
the sample diluent, formed micelles which eluted agent from
the TSK 4000 column (Diringer and Kimberlin, 1983). This is
consistent with the hydrophobic nature of the scrapie agent:
agent would adhere to the micelles and assume their mobility

(MW ∿ 65,000) through the column. Finally, the possibility
that components of the infectious unit could dissociate
during filtration and reassociate after filtration is remote
but cannot be excluded.

The question of the relevance of the term "prion" to
scrapie (Prusiner, 1982) evokes additional controversy (Kimberlin, 1982b; Johnson, 1982; Dickinson *et al.*, 1983).
One cannot deny that protein is important for scrapie infectivity (Cho, 1980; Prusiner, 1982; Lax *et al.*, 1983b).
However, proteins are also an important component of conventional viruses and they would be referred to implicitly, at
least, in any definition of the word virus. For example, in
the opening chapter of the virology section (page 1010) of
the book entitled *Microbiology* by Davis *et al.*, (1973) there
is the following: "A complete viral particle or virion may be
regarded as a block of genetic material surrounded by a coat
which protects it from the environment, serves as a vehicle
for its transmission from one host cell to another and
initiates its replication." Later the statement is made that
"a protein coat surrounds the nucleic acid." The small size
of scrapie and the requirement for protein would still be
consistent with a variety of possibilities for the nature of
the scrapie agent and for its mode of replication. A number
of these possibilities were presented in the paper that
introduced the term prion (Prusiner, 1982). In fact, the
possibilities presented appear to include all logical alternatives. Thus, if we permit prion to be defined in this broad
fashion, the term contributes little to the dialogue about
the nature of the agent. On the other hand, the term would
contribute significantly to the dialogue if the scrapie infectious entity is protein and nothing but protein. In fact,
this is the definition that is inherent in the derivation
of the word (prion = infectious protein) and it is this definition which has captured the attention of the scientific
community. The agent characteristics suggesting this heretical hypothesis, a protein which can perform reverse translation and/or direct its own synthesis (Johnson, 1982), are
based solely on information derived from correlating infectivity assays with scrapie agent activity – correlations which
have the potential problems noted by other investigators
(Dickinson and Outram, 1983; Kimberlin, 1982a,b) and summarized in Section IX. All of those concerned in analysis of
the situation would apear to agree that it is too early to
exclude the role of non-protein moities in scrapie (Prusiner,
1982; Kimberlin, 1982b; Johnson, 1982; Prusiner, 1984).
Certainly, if agent specific molecular species other than
protein prove to be important for scrapie replication and/or
genetic integrity, the term prion, as defined by its derivation, is inappropriate. We would therefore agree that the

proper terminology for these agents can only be arrived at following molecular characterization (Johnson, 1982).

Among the alternatives to the "protein only" depiction of the nature of scrapie agent the most appealing to us is a model suggested by Kimberlin (1982b). In this model a small scrapie specific nucleic acid supplies the genetic information to account for the data detailed in Section VI, whereas the host protein (perhaps fibrillar) that it is associated with is required to confer infectivity. The nucleic acid would not be translated, as is the case with viroids. The small size of the nucleic acid combined with its requirement for host protein would explain much of the inactivation data reported over the years for scrapie infectivity (Hunter, 1972; Gajdusek, 1977; Prusiner, 1982). Furthermore, the presence of host rather than agent coded protein would explain the lack of an immunological response by the host.

XI. FINAL COMMENTS

There are a number of points about scrapie that we know with some certainty: The agent is transmissible; it replicates in appropriate hosts; the disease is the archetypal unconventional slow virus infection; the lymphoreticular system appears to be important in the pathogenesis for agent entering the host by a non-CNS route; a number of aspects of agent-host interaction are under genetic control; there is an increase in blood-brain barrier permeability in scrapie mice; aberrant fibrils (termed SAF) are a consistent electron microscopic finding in preparations of scrapie brain and spleen, and lastly, there are problems in correlating results of infectivity assays with effects on scrapie agent, particularly after physical or chemical treatments. There are, however, important aspects of scrapie that remain to be fully analyzed: the nature of the agent, its mode of transmission in natural disease, several key steps in pathogenesis, the extent of genetic control contributed by host and by agent and the mechanisms whereby that genetic control is made manifest. The interest in scrapie derives in part from these aspects that are mysterious and unknown and in part because a number of histopathological changes seen in scrapie appear to make it an excellent model of human diseases that are characterized by dementia and premature aging (Alzheimer's disease, Creutzfeld-Jakob disease, Kuru, Gerstman-Straussler Syndrome) and perhaps make it a model for old age associated pathology of the human brain (Wisniewski *et al.*, 1975; Dickinson *et al.*, 1979; Gajdusek and Gibbs, 1982; Dickinson *et al.*, 1983; Carp *et al.*, 1984a). Advances in research on the nature of the scrapie agent, its replication and the pathogenesis of scrapie disease may provide clues needed to analyze those steps that lead to diseases affecting the aged brain in humans.

SUMMARY

Data are reviewed which establish that scrapie is caused by a transmissible, replicating agent. Those criteria that define an unconventional slow infection process are noted and reasons for regarding scrapie as the archetype of unconventional slow virus diseases are given. Evidence supporting the importance of the lymphoreticular system in scrapie pathogenesis is presented, including some initial studies aimed at using *in vitro* techniques to analyze agent-host cell interactions. The influence of genetic control on scrapie agent-host interactions is detailed with emphasis on incubation period and histopathological differences. The histopathological changes include the extent of vacuolation in various areas of the brain and the presence or absence of amyloid plaques. Data are presented which confirm the extensive literature in this area and the information is expanded to include agent-host combinations not previously examined, and a new marker, the presence or absence of weight increases during the pre-clinical phase of disease is described. Changes in the blood-brain barrier are described. Information is reviewed on an aberrant fibril which is consistently found in scrapie brain and spleen homogenates. Problems that can arise in the analysis of scrapie infectivity are reviewed and additional data on this point are presented.

Finally, in view of the characteristics reported for scrapie, we indicate how scrapie relates to the title of this volume.

ACKNOWLEDGMENTS

The authors appreciate the incisive comments and suggestions contained in reviews of the manuscript by Dr. Richard H. Kimberlin of the Neuopathogenesis Unit, Edinburgh, Scotland and by Drs. Halldor Thormar, Richard Kascsak and Michael Quinn of the Institute for Basic Research in Developmental Disabilities. We thank Mrs. Leatrice Kolodney for her assistance in preparing the manuscript, Mr. Lawrence Black for library searches and Mr. Richard G. Weed and his staff for assistance with photography and graphics.

REFERENCES

Beck, E., and Daniel, P.M. (1965). Kuru and scrapie compared; are they examples of systemic degeneration? *In* "Slow, Latent and Temperate Virus Infections"

(D.C. Gajdusek, C.J. Gibbs, Jr., and M. Alpers, eds.) pp. 85-91. NINDB Monograph No. 2, Publication No. 1378, Public Health Service, Washington, D.C.

Brotherston, J.G., Renwick, C.C., Stamp. J.T., Zlotnik, I. and Pattison, I.H. (1968). Spread of scrapie by contact to goats and sheep. *J. Comp. Path. 78,* 9-17.

Brown, P., Salazar, A.M., Gibbs, C.J. Jr., Gajdusek, D.C. (1982). Alzheimer's disease and transmissible virus dementia (Creutzfeldt-Jakob disease). *Ann. N.Y. Acad. Sci. 396,* 131-143.

Bruce, M.E., Dickinson, A.G. and Fraser, H. (1976). Cerebral amyloidosis in scrapie in the mouse: Effect of agent strain and mouse genotype. *Neuropath. App. Neurobiol. 2,* 471-478.

Bruce, M.E. and Dickinson, A. G. (1979). Biological stability of different classes of scrapie agent. *In* "Slow Transmissible Diseases of the Nervous System," Vol. 2, (S.B. Prusiner and W.J. Hadlow, eds.) pp. 71-86. Academic Press, New York.

Bruce, M.E. and Fraser, H. (1981). Effect of route of infection on the frequency and distribution of cerebral amyloid plaques in scrapie mice. *Neuropathol. Appl. Neurobiol. 7,* 289-298.

Burger, D.R. and Vetto, R.M. (1982). Vascular endothelium as a major participant in T-lymphocyte immunity. *Cellular Imm. 70,* 357-361.

Carp, R.I. (1981). Transmission of scrapie by oral route: Effect of gingival scarification. *Lancet i,* 170-171.

Carp, R.I. and Callahan, S.M. (1981). *In vitro* interaction of scrapie agent and mouse peritoneal macrophages. *Intervirology 16,* 8-13.

Carp, R.I. and Callahan, S.M. (1982). Effect of mouse peritoneal macrophages on scrapie infectivity during extended *in vitro* incubation. *Intervirology 17,* 201-207.

Carp, R.I. and Thormar, H. (1975). Pathogenesis of slow infections of the central nervous system. *In* "Biology of Brain Dysfunction," Vol. 3 (G.E. Gaull ed.) pp. 265-306. Plenum Publishing Corp., New York.

Carp, R.I. and Warner, H.B. (1980). Effect of human lymphokines on scrapie incubation. Abstract. 80th Annual Meeting Am. Soc. Microbiol., Miami Beach, p. 262.

Carp, R.I., Merz, G. and Wisniewski, H.M. (1984a). Transmission of unconventional slow virus diseases and the relevance to AD/SDAT transmission studies. *In* "Senile Dementia in the Next Twenty Years," Alan R. Liss, Inc. New York (in press).

Carp, R.I., Callahan, S.M., Sersen, E.A. and Moretz, R.C. (1984b). Preclinical changes in weight of scrapie infected mice as a function of scrapie agent-mouse strain combination. *Interivrology 21*, 61-69.

Chandler, R.L. (1963). Experimental scrapie in the mouse. *Res. Vet. Sci. 4*, 276-285.

Chandler, R.L. and Turfrey, B.A. (1972). Inoculation of voles,Chinese hamsters, gerbils and guinea-pigs with scrapie brain material. *Res. Vet. Sci. 13*, 219-224.

Cho, H.J. (1980). Requirement of a protein component for scrapie infectivity. *Interivrology 14*, 213-216.

Cho, H.J., Greig, A.S., Corp, C.R., Kimberlin, R.H., Chandler, R.L. and Millson, G.C. (1977). Virus-like particles from both control and scrapie-affected mouse brain. *Nature (London) 267*, 459-460.

Clark, M.C. and Haig, D.A. (1971a). An attempt to determine whether maternal transmission of scrapie occurs in mice. *Br. vet. J. 127*, 32-34.

Clarke, M.C. and Haig, D.A. (1971b). Multiplication of scrapie agent in mouse spleen. *Res. vet. Sci. 12*, 195-197.

Davis, B.D., Dulbecco, R., Eisen, H.N., Ginsberg, H.S., Wood, W.B., Jr. and McCarty, M. (1973). Microbiology, 2nd Edition. Harper and Row, Hagerstown, Maryland, p. 1010.

Dickinson, A.G. (1976). Scrapie in sheep and goats. *In* "Slow Virus Diseases of Animals and Man," (R.H. Kimberlin, ed.), pp. 209-241. North Holland Publishing Co., Amsterdam, Netherlands.

Dickinson, A.G. and Fraser, H. (1969). Modification of the pathogenesis of scrapie in mice by treatment of the agent. *Nature (London) 222*, 892-893.

Dickinson, A.G. and Fraser, H. (1972). Scrapie: Effect of Dh gene on the incubation period of extraneurally injected agent. *Heredity 29*, 91-93.

Dickinson, A.G. and Fraser, H. (1979). An assessment of the genetics of scrapie in sheep and mice. *In* "Slow Transmisible Diseases of the Nervous System," Vol. 1 (S.B. Prusiner and W.J. Hadlow, eds.) pp. 367-385. Academic Press, New York.

Dickinson, A.G. and Meikle, V.M.H. (1971). Host-genotype and agent effects in scrapie incubation: Change in allelic interaction with different strains of agent. *Mol. Gen. Genet. 112*, 73-79.

Dickinson, A.G. and Meikle, V.M.H. (1969). A comparison of some biological characteristics of the mouse-passaged scrapie agents, 22A and ME7. *Genet. Res. 13*, 213-225.

Dickinson, A.G. and Outram, G.W. (1983). Operational limitations in the characterization of the infective units of scrapie. Symposium Proc. "Virus non conventionnels et affections de systeme nerveux central" (L.A. Court ed.), Masson, Paris, France, pp. 3-16.

Dickinson, A.G. and Taylor,D.M. (1978). Resistance of scrapie agent to decontamination. *New Eng. J. Med. 299*, 1413-1414.

Dickinson, A.G., Mackay, J.M.K. and Zlotnik, I. (1964). Transmission by contact of scrapie in mice. *J.Comp. Path. Therapeutics 74*, 250-254.

Dickinson, A.G., Meikle, V.M.H. and Fraser, H. (1969). Genetical control of the concentration of the ME7 scrapie agent in the brain of mice. *J. Comp. Pathol. 79*, 15-22.

Dickinson, A.G., Stamp, J.T. and Renwick, C.C. (1974). Maternal and lateral transmission of scrapie in sheep. *J. Comp. Path. 84*, 19-25.

Dickinson, A.G., Fraser, H., McConnell, I., and Outram, G.W. (1978). Mitogenic stimulation of the host enhances susceptibility to scrapie. *Nature (London) 272*, 54-55.

Dickinson, A.G., Fraser, H. and Bruce, M.E. (1979). Animal models of the dementias in "Alzheimer's disease" (A.I.M. Glen and L.J. Whalley, eds.) Churchill-Livingstone, Edingburgh, pp. 42-45.

Dickinson, A.G., Bruce, M.E. and Scott, J.R. (1983). The relevance of scrapie as an experimental model for Alzheimer's disease. *Banbury Report 15*, 387-398.

Diener, T.O., McKinley, M.P. and Prusiner, S.B. (1982). Viroids and prions. *Proc. Natl. Acad. Sci. 79*, 5220-5224.

Diringer, H. and Kimberlin, R.H. (1983). Infectious scrapie agent is apparently not as small as recent claims suggest. *Bioscience Reports 3*, 563-568.

Eklund, C.M., Kennedy, R.C. and Hadlow, W.J. (1967). Pathogenesis of scrapie virus infection in the mouse. *J. Infect. Dis. 117*, 15-22.

Fraser, H. (1979). Neuropathology of scrapie: The precision of the lesions and their diversity. *In* "Slow transmissible Diseases of the Nervous System." Vol. I, (S. B. Prusiner and W.J. Hadlow, eds.) pp. 387-406, Academic Press, New York.

Fraser, H. (1981). Neuronal spread of scrapie agent and targeting of lesions within the retino-tectal pathway. *Nature (London) 294*, 149-150.

Fraser, H. (1983). A survey of primary transmission of scrapie and rida to mice, Symposium "Virus non conventionnels et affections du systeme nerveux central." Masson, Paris, France. pp. 34-46.

Fraser, H. and Bruce, M.E. (1973). Argyrophilic plaques in mice inoculated with scrapie from particular sources. *Lancet 1*, 617-618.

Fraser, H. and Dickinson, A.G. (1970). Pathogenesis of scrapie in the mouse: The role of the spleen. *Nature (London) 226*, 462-463.

Fraser, H. and Dickinson, A.G. (1973). Scrapie in mice: agent strain differences in the distribution and intensity of grey matter vacuolation. *J. Comp. Pathol. 83*, 29-40.

Gajdusek, D.C. (1977). Unconventional viruses and the origin and disappearance of Kuru. *Science 197*, 943-960.

Gajdusek, D.C. and Gibbs, C.J., Jr. (1982). Slow virus infections and aging. *In* "Neural Aging and its Implications in Human Neurological Pathology." (Aging Vol. 28) (R.D. Terry, C.L. Bolis and G. Toffano eds.). pp. 1-12, Raven Press, New York.

Gibbs, C.J., Jr., Amyx, H. L., Bacote, A., Masters, C.L. and Gajdusek, D.C. (1980). Oral transmission of kuru, Creutzfeld-Jakob disease, and scrapie to nonhuman primates. *J. Infect. Dis. 142*, 204-208.

Gibbs, C.J., Jr., and Gajdusek, D.C. (1973). Experimental subacute spongiform virus encephalopathies in primates and other laboratory animals. *Science 182*, 67-68.

Hirschberg, H., Bergh, O.J. and Thorsby, E. (1980). Antigen-presenting properties of human vascular endothelial cells. *J. Exp. Med. 152*, 249-255.

Hotchin, J. and Buckley, S. ,(1977). Latent form of scrapie virus: A new factor in slow-virus disease. *Science 196*, 668-671.

Hourrigan, J.K. Klingsporn, A., Clark, W.W. and deCamp, M. (1979). Epidemiology of scrapie in the United States. *In* "Slow Transmissible Diseases of the Nervous System" Vol. 1 (S.B. Prusiner and W.J. Hadlow, eds.) pp. 331-356. Academic Press, New York

Hunter, G. D. (1972). Scrapie: A prototype slow infection. *J. Infect. Dis. 125*, 427-440.

Hunter, G.D., Millson, G.C. and Chandler, R.L. (1963). Observations on the comparative infectivity of cellular fractions derived from homogenates of mouse - scrapie brain. *Res. vet. Sci. 4*, 543-549.

Hunter, G. D. and Millson, G.C. (1967). Attempts to release the scrapie agent from tissue debris. *J. Comp. Path.* *77*, 301-307.

Johnson, R.T. (1982). The novel nature of scrapie. *Trends in Neurosciences 5*, 413-415.

Kimberlin, R.H. (1977). Biochemical approaches to scrapie research. *Trends in Biochemical Sci.* 2, 220-223.

Kimberlin, R.H. (1982a). Reflections on the nature of the scrapie agent. *Trends in Biochemical Sci.* 7, 392-394.

Kimberlin, R.H. (1982b). Scrapie agent: Prions or virinos? *Nature 297*, 107-108.

Kimberlin, R.H. and Millson, G.C. (1967). Some biochemical aspects of mouse scrapie. *J. Comp. Path.* *77*, 359-366.

Kimberlin, R.H. and Cunnington, P.G. (1978). Reduction of scrapie incubation time in mice and hamsters by a single injection of methanol extraction residue of BCG. *FEMS Microbiol. Lett. 3*, 169-172.

Kimberlin, R.H. and Walker, C.A. (1977). Characteristics of a short incubation model of scrapie in the golden hamster. *J. gen. Virol.34*, 295-304.

Kimberlin, R.H. and Walker, C.A. (1978a). Pathogenesis of mouse scrapie: Effect of route of inoculation on infectivity titres and dose-response curves. *J. Comp. Path. 88*, 39-47.

Kimberlin, R.H. and Walker, C.A. (1978b). Evidence that the transmission of one source of scrapie agent to hamsters involves separation of agent strains from a mixture. *J. gen. Virol. 39*, 487-496.

Kimberlin, R.H. and Walker, C.A. (1980). Pathogenesis of mouse scrapie: Evidence for neural spread of infection to the CNS. *J. gen. Virol. 51*, 183-187.

Kimberlin, R.H. and Walker, C.A. (1982). Pathogenesis of mouse scrapie: Patterns of agent replication in different parts of the CNS following intraperitoneal infection. *J. Royal Soc. Med. 75*, 618-624.

Kimberlin, R.H. and Walker, C.A. (1983). Invasion of the CNS by scrapie agent and its spread to different parts of the brain. *In* "Virus non conventionnels et affections due systeme nerveux central" (L.A. Court, ed.) pp. 17-33. Masson, Paris.

Kingsbury, D.T. Kasper, K.C., Stites, D.P. Watson, J.D., Hogan, R.N. and Prusiner, S.B. (1983). Genetic control of scrapie and Creutzfeldt-Jakob disease in mice. *J. of Imm. 131*, 491-496.

Lax, A.J., Millson, G.C. and Manning, E.J. (1983a). Can scrapie titres be calculated accurately from incubation periods? *J. gen. Virol. 64*, 971-973.

Lax, A.J., Millson, G.C. and Manning, E.J. 1983b). Involv-
    ment of protein in scrapie agent infectivity. *Res.
    vet. Sci. 34*, 155-158.
Malone, T.G., Marsh, R.F., Hanson, R.P. and Semancik, J.S.
    (1978). Membrane free scrapie activity. *J. Virol.
    25*, 933-935.
Manuelidis, L. and Manuelidis, E. (1983). Fractionation and
    infectivity studies in Creutzfeldt-Jakob disease,
    Banbury Report 15, 399-424.
Marsh, R.F. and Hanson, R.P. (1979). On the origin of
    transmissible mink encephalopathy. *In* "Slow
    Transmissible Diseases of the Nervous System,"
    Vol. 1 (S.B. Prusiner and W.J. Hadlow, eds.)pp.
    451-460. Academic Press, New York.
Marsh, R.F., Semancik, J.S., Medappa, K.C., Hanson, R.P.
    and Reuckert, R.R. (1974). Scrapie and trans-
    missible mink encephalopathy: Search for infect-
    ious nucleic acid. *J. Virol. 13*, 993-996.
McFarland, D.J., Baker, F.D. and Hotchin, J. (1980). Host
    and viral genetic determinants of the behavioral
    effects of scrapie encephalopathy. *Physiol. Behav.
    24*, 911-914.
McFarlin, D.E., Raff, M.C., Simpson, E. and Nehlsen, S.H.
    (1971). Scrapie in immunologically deficient mice.
    Nature (London) 233, 233-336.
Merz, P.A., Somerville, R.A. and Wisniewski, H.M. (1983a).
    Abnormal fibrils in scrapie and senile dementia
    of Alzheimer type. Symposium Proc. "Virus non-
    conventionnels et affections du system nerveux
    central" (L.A. Court, ed.). Masson, Paris, France.
    pp. 259-281.
Merz, P.A., Rohwer, R., Somerville, R.A., Wisniewski, H.M.,
    Gibbs,C.J. Jr. and Gajdusek, D.C. (1983b). Scrapie
    associated fibrils in human Creutzfeldt-Jakob
    disease. *J. Neuropath. Exp. Neurol 42*, 327.
Merz, P.A., Somerville, R.A., Wisniewski, H.M., Manuelidis L.
    and Manuelidis, E. 1984
    Nature 306, 474-476.
Merz, P.A., Somerville, R.A., Wisniewski, H.M. and Iqbal, K.
    (1981). Abnormal fibrils from scrapie-infected
    brain. *Acta Neuropathol (Berl) 54*, 63-74.
Merz, P.A., Wisniewski, H.M., Somerville R.A., Bobin, S.A.,
    Masters, C.L. and Iqbal, K. (1983c). Ultrastruct-
    ural morphology of amyloid fibrils from neuritic
    and amyloid plaques. *Acta Neuropathol (Berl) 60*,
    113-124.
Millson, G.C., Hunter, G.D. and Kimberlin, R.H. (1976). The
    physicochemical nature of the scrapie agent. *In*
    "Slow Virus Diseases of Animals and Man" (R.H.

Kimberlin, ed.) pp. 243-266. North Holland Publishing Company, Amsterdam.

Millson, G.C. and Manning, E.J. (1979). The effect of selected detergents on scrapie infectivity. *In* "Slow Transmissible Diseases of the Nervous System," Vol. 2, (S.B. Prusiner and W.J. Hadlow, eds.) Academic Press, N.Y. pp. 409-424.

Mould, D.L., Dawson, A. McL. and Smith, W. (1967). Determination of the dosage - response curve of mice inoculated with scrapie. *J. Comp. Path. 77*, 387-391.

Outram, G.W. (1972). Changes in drinking and feeding habits of mice with experimental scrapie. *J. Comp. Path. 82*, 415-427.

Outram, G.W. (1976). The pathogenesis of scrapie in mice. *In* "Slow Virus Diseases of Animals and Man," (R. H. Kimberlin, ed.) pp. 325-357. North Holland Publishing Co., Amsterdam, Netherlands.

Outram, G.W., Dickinson, A.G. and Fraser, H. (1973). Developmental maturation of susceptibility to scrapie in mice. *Nature (London) 241*, 103-104.

Outram, G.W. Dickinson, A.G. and Fraser, H. (1974). Reduced susceptibility to scrapie in mice after steroid administration. *Nature (London) 249*, 855-856.

Outram, G.W., Dickinson, A.G. and Fraser, H. (1975). Slow encephalopathies, inflammatory responses, and arachis oil. *Lancet i*, 198-203.

Palsson, P.A. (1979). Rida (Scrapie) in Iceland and its epidemiology. *In* "Slow Transmissible Diseases of the Nervous System" Vol. I(S. B. Prusiner and W.J. Hadlow, eds.) Academic Press, N.Y. pp. 357-366.

Pattison, I.H. (1964). The spread of scrapie by contact between affected and healthy sheep, goats or mice. *Vet. Res. 76*, 333-336.

Pattison, I.H., Hoare, M.N., Jebbett, J.N. and Watson, W.A. (1974). Further observations on the production of scrapie in sheep by oral dosing with foetal membranes from scrapie affected sheep. Br. Vet. J. 130., 65-67.

Pattison, I.H. and Millson, G.C. (1961). Experimental transmission of scrapie to goats and sheep by the oral route. *J. Comp. Path. 71*, 171-176.

Prusiner, S.B. (1982). Novel proteinaceous infectious particles cause scrapie. *Science 216*, 136-144.

Prusiner, S.B. (1984). This volume.

Prusiner, S.B., Cochran, S.P., Groth, D.F., Downey, D.E., Bowman, K.A. and Martinez, H.M. (1982). Measurement of the scrapie agent using an incubation time interval assay. *Annals of Neurology 11,* 353–358.

Prusiner, S.B., Garfin, E. E., Baringer, J. R. Cochran, S.P., Hadlow, W.J., Race, R.E. and Eklund, C.M. (1979). On the partial purification and apparent hydrophobicity of the scrapie agent. *In* "Slow Transmissible Diseases of the Nervous System," Vol. 2. (S.B. Prusiner and W.J. Hadlow, eds.) pp. 425–463. Academic Press, New York.

Prusiner, S.B., Hadlow, W. J., Garfin, E.E., Cochran, S.P. Baringer, J.R., Race, R.E., and Eklund, C.M.(1978). Partial purfication and evidence for multiple molecular forms of scrapie agent. *Biochemistry 17,* 4993–4999.

Rohwer, R.G. and Gajdusek, D.C. (1980). Scrapie – virus or viroid. The case for a virus. *In* "Search for the Cause of Multiple Sclerosis and Other Chronic Diseases of the Central Nervous System. (A. Boese, ed.), Weinheim, West Germany: Verlag Chemie.

Sigurdsson, B. (1954). Rida, a chronic encephalitis of sheep with general remarks on infections which develop slowly and some of their special characteristics. *Brit. Vet. J.,110,* 341–354.

Stevens, S.K., Weissman, I.L. and Butcher, E.C. (1982). Differences in the migration of B and T lymphocytes: Organ-selective localization *in vivo* and the role of lymphocyte-endothelial cell recognition. *J. Immunol. 128,* 844–851.

Somerville, R.A. and Carp, R.I. (1983). Altered scrapie infectivity estimates by titration and incubation period in the presence of detergents. *J. gen. Virol. 64,* 2045–2050.

Somerville, R.A., Millson, G.C. and Kimberlin, R.H. (1980). Sensitivity of scrapie infectivity to detergents and 2-mercapoethanol. *Intervirology 12,* 126–129.

Ward, R.L., Porter, D.D. and Stevens, J.G. (1974). Nature of the scrapie agent: Evidence against a viroid. *J. Virol. 14,* 1099–1103.

Wisniewski, H.M., Bruce, M.E. and Fraser, H. (1975). Infectious etiology of neuritic (senile) plaques in mice. *Science 190,* 1108–1109.

Wisniewski, H.M. and Kozlowski, P.B. (1982). Evidence for blood–brain barrier changes in senile demential of the Alzheimer type (SDAT). *Ann. N.Y. Acad. Sci. 396,* 119–129.

Wisniewski, H.M., Lossinsky, A.S., Moretz, R.C., Vorbrodt, A.W. Lassmann, H. and Carp, R.I.(1983). Increased blood–brain barrier permeability in scrapie infected mice. *J. Neuropath. Exptl. Neurol. 42,* 615–626.

Wisniewski, H.M., Moretz, R.C. and Lossinsky, A.S. (1981). Evidence for induction of localized amyloid deposits and neuritic plaques by an infectious agent. *Ann. Neurol.* *10*, 517-522.

Zlotnick, I. (1968). Spread of scrapie by contact in mice. *J. Comp. Path.* *78*, 19-22.

Chapter 19

VIRAL ETIOLOGY OF MULTIPLE SCLEROSIS:
A CRITIQUE OF THE EVIDENCE

F. Gonzalez-Scarano and N. Nathanson

Departments of Neurology and Microbiology
School of Medicine, University of Pennsylvania
Philadelphia,   Pa. 19104

I.   INTRODUCTION

Multiple sclerosis (MS) must currently be ranked among the major enigmas in medicine. On the one hand, it has been the subject of a vast effort by a host of investigators, and on the other, its etiology remains elusive. During the last 20 years, when research on MS has employed modern methods, the proposal that this mysterious disease is caused by one or several viruses has been a leading hypothesis. Yet, if so, the putative agent has defied discovery. Futile efforts to identify a conventional virus suggest that, if the hypothesis is still viable, an unconventional subviral agent might be implicated. For this reason, it is of interest to review briefly the current evidence for a viral etiology of MS, in a monograph devoted to subviral pathogens.

SUBVIRAL PATHOGENS
OF PLANTS AND ANIMALS:
VIROIDS AND PRIONS

Copyright © 1985 by Academic Press, Inc.
All rights of reproduction in any form reserved.
ISBN 0-12-470230-9

II.   THE VIRAL HYPOTHESIS: BACKGROUND AND HISTORY

The idea that a virus might cause MS springs from several quite different sources, each of which provides suggestive clues. First, studies of identical twins where one has MS show that the second twin develops the disease in only about 30 percent of instances (Spielman and Nathanson, 1982). This low concordance suggests that an exogenous event must be imposed on even a proven susceptible genotype in order to cause disease. Migrant studies, described in greater detail below, also indicate that the risk of MS is influenced by environmental factors, since movement of a population from a low to high risk region alters the subsequent incidence of the disease (Nathanson and Miller, 1978).

The discovery and elucidation of persistent viral infections has provided a separate line of evidence suggesting that, even in humans, chronic neurological disease may be caused by viruses (Johnson and Herndon, 1974; Johnson, 1975). Three quite distinct diseases have been well documented in the past 15 years. Creutzfeldt-Jakob disease is a spongiform encephalopathy, one of the group of agents related to scrapie, the exact nature of which remains elusive (see Prusiner, this volume). Progressive multifocal leukoencephalopathy is a progressive disease with focal demyelination which is caused by JC virus, a human member of the polyomavirus group. Finally, subacute sclerosing panencephalitis is a fatal chronic destructive encephalitis caused by measles or, rarely, by rubella virus.

A third clue is provided by studies of the spinal fluid in patients with MS (Thompson, 1977). In most cases the level of immunoglobulins is elevated, with evidence of intrathecal antibody synthesis of oligoclonal antibodies. This suggests that a local immune response is occurring within the central nervous system (CNS) and that this response may be indirect evidence of a foreign microbial agent, conceivably a virus (Paterson and Whitacre, 1980). Furthermore, when CSF samples were tested for anti-viral antibody activity, a high proportion of patients with MS were found to have antibody against one or more of a number of human viruses (Norrby, 1978). Based on the serum to CSF ratio, these antiviral antibodies were synthesized within the CNS.

In sum, several independent lines of evidence have bolstered the hypothesis that a viral agent might trigger the development of MS. In the following sections, we will review and critique these different sets of data.

III.   EPIDEMIOLOGY OF MS:
DOES IT SUPPORT THE VIRAL HYPOTHESIS?

Prevalence of MS in Different Populations. The prevalence of MS is well-defined in only limited areas of the
world, particularly in some of the developed countries
(Acheson, 1977). Studies in North America, Europe, and
Australia indicate that risk increases with distance from the
equator. For instance, the rates are higher in northern than
southern Europe. In the northern part of the United States
and in Canada, the rate is about twice that in the southern
United States (Beebe et al. 1967).

Studies in several countries demonstrate that, following
migration between areas with different incidence, the migrating population, or its offspring, take on the risk of the
new area of residence. The evidence is particularly impressive among veterans in the United States, where movement in
either direction (North to South or the reverse), between
birth and induction into service, alters the risk(Dean and
Kurtzke, 1971; Kurtzke et al., 1979). Likewise, migration
from Great Britain to South Africa reduces incidence while
migration from North Africa to Israel increases incidence
(Alter et al., 1966; 1977).

Although the effect of migration upon the risk of developing MS is generally accepted, it is less clear what this
observation means. If the migration effect is assumed to
reflect differences in the age of exposure to an infectious
agent which causes MS (the usual interpretation), several
predictions may be made regarding age distribution, soci -
oeconomic and rural-urban differences in rates, and secular
trends in incidence and age distribution. Many of these
predictions fail to be confirmed by the epidemiological data
(Nathanson and Miller 1978). Therefore, interpretation of
the epidemiologic evidence must be viewed with scepticism.

IV.   ANIMAL MODELS

A. Persistent infection of the CNS. One of the
strongest arguments for the search for viruses in MS is that
a number of diseases of animals that are well documented to
have a viral etiology, resemble MS both pathologically and
clinically (Doherty and Simpson, 1982). Three diseases have
been studied thoroughly: Theiler's Murine Encephalomyelitis
Virus (TMEV) and Mouse Hepatitis Virus (MHV) in mice and
rats, and visna of sheep. The hallmarks of these diseases
are the presence of symptoms of white matter disease and the
pathological evidence of demyelination. Exacerbations and
remissions are seen both naturally (visna) and by manipula-

tion of the model (TMEV). Although none of the models is perfect, in combination they suggest that a disease such as MS could arise from a viral infection.

B. Theiler's Murine Encephalomyelitis. The group of viruses responsible for TMEV are picornaviruses originally isolated by Theiler in the 1930's (Theiler, 1937, 1940). Although they were a known cause of both asymptomatic enteric infection and of CNS disease, their true significance as a model for demyelinating disease was not recognized until Lipton began a systematic study of their pathogenesis in the 1970's (Lipton, 1975). TMEV is an endemic cause of asymptomatic disease in mouse colonies. In occasional animals, it spreads to the nervous system, where it results in a flaccid paralysis originally described as "mouse poliomyelitis". Experimentally, after intracerebral inoculation TMEV causes a biphasic illness, initially involving the gray matter and subsequently (in survivors) the white matter (Lipton, 1975).

The TMEV group can be subdivided according the predominance of gray or white matter disease after intracerebral inoculation. Recently, it has become clear that these biological differences reflect true genetic heterogeneity. The more virulent viruses (GDVll, FA) share large plaque size, polypeptide mobility, and T1 oligonucleotide pattern (Lipton, 1980; Lipton and Friedmann, 1980; Lorch et al., 1981). These viruses tend to cause a severe neuronal infection and a high mortality. From the standpoint of MS research, those viruses that cause a more persistent disease (DA, WW, TO4 and Yale) are more interesting, and the remainder of the discussion will be confined to them.

The demyelinative myelopathy associated with persistent TMEV infections has been studied extensively by light and electron microscopy. After an inital infection which involves both neuronal and glial cells (Penney, 1979) the virus persists in the CNS in spite of the presence of neutralizing antibody (Lipton and dal Canto, 1979). The amount of infective virus present during this late phase is small, and there is little detectable antigen seen by fluorescence studies or electron microscopy (Lipton, 1975; dal Canto, 1975). In situ hybridization has demonstrated the presence of viral RNA in glial cells during this late demyelinative stage (Brahic et al., 1981).

An autoimmune component has been postulated for the late white matter disease seen in TMEV. Immunosupression ameliorates the CNS lesions (Lipton et al., 1977) and the SJL/j mouse, known to be particularly susceptible to autoimmune phenomena, develops more intense demyelinative lesions (dal Canto, 1979).

Brahic (unpublished,1983) has suggested a credible hypothesis for the series of events that result in chronic TMEV infection and demyelination. A virulent panencephalitis kills neurons and infects glial cells, which do not support replication, at least not productively. In the animals that survive the initial disease, and where the virus belongs to the less virulent group, a low level of virus production persists. This low level replication is sufficient to either destroy a number of oliodendrocytes, resulting in demyelination, or to trigger a cellular immune response, with the same final result. In either case, the initial immune response, though adequate for clearance of the majority of virions, allows the persistence of low levels of TMEV.

C. Mouse Hepatitis Virus. The MHV group, which infects both mice and rats, was initially isolated in 1949 (Cheever *et al.*, 1949). The first isolate, JHM virus, was a neurotropic strain. Since then, these viruses have been classified as either hepatotropic (MHV-3 for example) or neurotropic (JHM and others). They are part of the family Coronaviridae, which are positive stranded RNA viruses so named because of their electron microscopic appearance. The family includes a number of human isolates, responsible for a significant proportion of upper respiratory infections in man.

The CNS pathology was initially described as demyelinative (Bailey *et al.*, 1949). It is now known that the neurotropic strains of MHV infect both neurons and oligodendrocytes. The survivors from the initial panencephalitis may go on and develop a demyelinating syndrome, with chronic persistence of the virus in oligodendrocytes (Herndon *et al.*, 1975; Weiner *et al.*, 1973).

Three recent developments have increased interest in MHV; (i) the isolation of a human coronavirus from MS brain; (ii) the isolation of mutants that are highly neurotropic yet have a low mortality associated with them; and (iii) the development of an autoimmune-type illness after adoptive immunization of rats with lymphocytes from MHV infected animals.

The isolation of a coronavirus from MS brain (Burks *et al.*, 1980) has not been duplicated, and is discussed below. Over the past several years, Oldstone and associates have isolated a number of temperature sensitive (ts) mutants of JHM, the prototypic MHV neurotropic strain. One of these, ts8, shows a low mortality when injected intracerebrally into mice, yet induces a persistent infection with recurrent demyelination (Knobler *et al.* 1982). This mutant also demonstrates high infectivity for oligodendrocytes, rather than neurons. The CNS of these animals shows demyelinated and

remyelinated axons, suggesting potential similarities with
MS. Since the disease can be induced in inbred strains of
mice, a variety of genetic parameters can now be studied with
this system.

In addition to the finding that ts mutants of MHV
can cause an exclusively demyelinating disease, recent work
has demonstrated that auto-immune mechanisms may play a role
in the demyelination caused by these viruses. Ter Meulen and
collegues (Watanabe, 1983) have now been able to infect rats
with JHM strain, restimulate the lymphocytes from these
diseased rats with myelin basic protein *in vitro*, and cause a
demyelinative disease in healthy rats adoptively immunized
with these lymphocytes. These findings are an important
confirmation of the long-standing hypothesis that viruses may
be able to trigger an immune response to self antigens. At
this point it is not clear how this sensitization takes
place, but the more likely possibilities are that: (i) injury
to oligodendrocytes exposes antigens not usually available to
the immune system; (ii) there are antigens on the JHM virus
which cross react with cellular antigens; or (iii) in the
process of infecting cells the virus acquired cellular antigens which are then presented to the immune system. Although
there is as yet no evidence for the first of these possibilities, cross reacting antigens have been established for other
viruses (Fujinami *et al.*, 1983). Whichever of these mechanisms is shown to be responsible for this unusual response to
MHV infection, this promises to be an exciting area for research related to MS.

D. Visna. Visna is a disease of sheep (Palsson, 1976)
caused by a naturally occurring retrovirus (also called
progressive pneumonia virus, or maedi virus). In the field,
the agent is spread as a respiratory infection, between ewe
and lamb or between adults, and usually causes a progressive
interstitial pneumonitis; some infected animals also develop
the CNS phase, known as visna.

Under experimental conditions,when a large inoculum of a
neurotropic strain is injected intracerebrally into genetically susceptible Icelandic sheep, a high proportion develop a
chronic subacute encephalitis (Nathanson *et al.*, 1983; 1984).
At irregular intervals of months to years, additional focal
demyelinating lesions arise in brain and spinal cord, with
consequent progressive paralysis which is eventually fatal.
All infected sheep undergo lifelong virus persistence, in
lymphoid tissues, lung, or CNS. However, the genome apparently persists as a latent provirus and most infected cells
produce little or no infectious virus and are not killed by
the infection. Virus isolation often requires co-cultivation

with permissive sheep fibroblasts. During the course of infection, sheep develop serum antibody against the envelope glycoprotein and against the major internal protein. A transient cellular response can often be demonstrated by an *in vitro* lymphocyte proliferation in the presence of viral antigens.

It appears that the slowness of the infection is due to a host cell restriction on the expression of the viral genome (Brahic *et al.*, 1981); in cultures, sheep fibroblasts are highly permissive while selected other cell lines are severely restrictive (Nathanson *et al.*, 1984). A second factor limiting infection *in vivo* is the high titer of neutralizing antibody in serum and CSF. The same mechanisms which slow the infection also account for its persistence, particularly the maintenance of the viral genome as a latent provirus. In addition, in some sheep the occurrence of antigenic variants of the virus probably contributes to persistence (Narayan *et al.*, 1978; Lutley *et al.*, 1983; Thormar *et al.*, 1983).

The mechanism of the development of the CNS lesions is less well understood. The early subacute inflammatory response is prevented by immunosuppressive intervention and probably respresents a virus-specific immune response (Nathanson *et al.*, 1976; 1981). The late focal demyelinating lesions may be due to the bystander effect of a classical delayed type hypersensitivity but this is only speculative.

E. Virus-induced demyelination. One salient observation which arises from the animal models described above is that primary demyelination, of a focal nature, can be caused by certain persistent viral infections. The pathologic hallmark of MS is the plaque, also a focal demyelinating lesion. This connection establishes the plausibility that a virus could be instrumental in the pathogenesis of MS. For this reason, the mechanisms of virus-induced demyelination are of interest.

Two different mechanisms appear to operate in different models (see above). Coronaviruses apparently demyelinate by initiating a lytic infection of oligodendrocytes (Weiner, 1973) although auto-immune mechanisms may also come into play (Watanabe *et al.*, 1983). With Theiler's virus, there is evidence that the antiviral immune response may be important, since immunosuppression will prevent demyelination under certain conditions (Lipton and dal Canto, 1977). On the other hand, virus apparently persists in oligodendroglia although no infectious virions are synthesized. Possibly direct virus lysis may also operate in this model. In visna, it is likely that demyelination is an indirect process, since there are very few infected cells in the CNS. Possibly, an immunological process could provide an amplifying mechanism to explain the very severe lesions which can occur (Nathanson *et al.*, 1976; 1981). However, this model does not lend itself to the precise testing of such a hypothesis.

A final point of importance is that, in all of the animal models, it may be very difficult to detect virus during the chronic phase of demyelination (Martin and Nathanson, 1979). This is particularly true of mouse hepatitis and visna infections. Thus, it is plausible that a putative but unidentified viral agent might go undetected in MS tissue, in the absence of agent-specific probes.

V.   AUTO-IMMUNE DISEASE INITIATED BY VIRUSES

The hypothesis that a chronic viral infection of the CNS might initiate an autoimmune demyelinating process has long been suggested as a mechanism in MS (McFarlin and Waksman, 1982). Such a hypothesis could explain two key observations: (i) the great difficulty in detecting a viral agent on CNS examination of patients with longlasting progressive MS, and (ii) the resemblance of the pathology of MS to relapsing forms of experimental allergic encephalitis (EAE). In the past, there was little evidence to support such a concept, appealing as it was. Recently, however, two sets of observations have given the concept of virus-induced auto-immunity enhanced credibility.

A.   EAE following mouse hepatitis virus (MHV) infection. ter Meulen and his colleaques (Watanabe *et al.*, 1983) have recently reported studies in Lewis rats (highly susceptible to EAE) infected with MHV. Several months after infection, these animals develop partial paralysis, and show histologic evidence of chronic demyelination; some lesions resemble those of EAE while others appear more like the demyelination produced by MHV in mice. When spleen and lymph node cells from such rats are transferred to Lewis recipients a classical EAE occurs, about one week after transfer. That the effect is due to cells not virus is indicated by the short incubation period and by the limitation of the effect to syngeneic recipients, while MHV-susceptible allogeneic recipients do not develop disease. This appears to be the first bona fide model of virus-induced EAE.

B. Virus-induced autoimmunity. The advent of hybridoma technology has permitted the isolation of clonal B cell populations from virus-infected mice. Mice infected with many viruses yield clones synthesizing anti-viral antibodies. Recently, it has been shown that, in some viral infections, the animals also raise monoclonal antibodies against a variety of self antigens (Haspel *et al.*, 1983). Appropriate controls indicate that the viral infection is required and that this response is not due to self antigens contaminating the inoculum.

C. Molecular mimicry. One possible mechanism for virus-induced auto-immunity is the sharing of epitopes between proteins and self proteins. Although long postulated, direct evidence has been lacking. However, several recent reports indicate that occasional antibody clones do indeed recognize shared epitopes on virus and self (Fujinami *et al.*, 1983; Dales *et al.*, 1983).

Taken together, these recent observations from several laboratories suggest that credence must be given to the proposal that virus infection could initiate auto-immune demyelination, and that immunologic mechanisms exist which could account for such an occurrence.

VI. SEARCH FOR VIRUSES IN MS

A. Attempts at isolation. Conventional efforts at defining a transmissible agent in MS tissue have been directed at both visualization and isolation (Johnson, 1975; Johnson and Herndon, 1974; Fraser, 1977; Sever and Madden, 1980; Melnick, 1982; Cook and Dowling, 1980). Most of the efforts, by the nature of the disease, have utilized brain tissue obtained at autopsy. Processing of such tissue prior to the onset of autolysis is difficult. Many patients with MS die in nursing homes and other chronic care institutions where initial etiology of the neurologic disorder may not be well known and where there is no interest in research. Consequently, experimental tissue is scarce, and most investigators have not limited their efforts to patients in whom the disease is known to be active, as might be judged by the continuing appearance of new symptoms and signs. Chronic "burned out" cases may have little inflammation and/or active myelin destruction and could conceivably no longer carry a putative etiologic agent.

B. Visualization. There have been several reports of visualization of extraneous virus-like particles in either MS tissue obtained at autopsy or explants from such tissues. The descriptions have ranged from "herringbone" to paramyxovirus-like particles, and they have been localized to nucleus (Prineas, 1972) and endoplasmic reticulum (Tanaka *et al.*, 1975) of astrocytes and of infiltrating mononuclear cells. Because of the persistent association of elevated measles antibody titers with MS, discussed above, paramyxovirus-like particles have been of particular interest. Unfortunately, the findings on electron microscopy have not been reproducible.

C. Isolations. Isolations of viruses or viral-like

agents from MS tissue by routine explantation and inoculation
methods, either in tissue culture or in a variety of animal
species, have been reported consistently since the late
1940's (Margulis *et al.*, 1946; Dick *et al.*, 1958). In
recent years the number of isolations has reached a frequency
of about one each year, and the reported agents range from
conventional organisms, like CMV and herpes (Wroblewska *et
al.*, 1979; Gudnadottir, 1964) to ill defined factors like
the MS- associated agent (Carp *et al.*, 1972; 1978) and
measles antigen (Pertschuk *et al.*, 1976). These isolations
have, to the present time, been disappointing, and the reported isolates have either not been confirmed in other
laboratories or, in some cases, have been shown to be mycoplasma (Mitchell *et al.* 1978) or other passenger agents such
as mouse hepatitis virus (Burks, 1979). Table 1 shows a list
of the best known reports.

Table I
Viral Isolations from Multiple Sclerosis Tissue

Year	Virus	Reference
1946	Rabies	Margulis *et al.*
1972	MSAA*	Carp *et al.*
1972	Parainfluenza/(6/94)	ter Meulen *et al.*
1978	Bone marrow "agent"	Mitchell *et al.*
1979	Cytomegalovirus	Wroblewska *et al.*
1979	Coronavirus	Burks *et al.*
1982	Unidentified	Melnick *et al.*

*MSAA: MS associated agent.

Current efforts by one group (Gilden, Wroblewska, and
colleagues) consist of explantation of tissue from diseased
areas of white matter and growth of the brain either as
primary cultures or in a variety of indicator cell lines. In
parallel, some samples are inoculated into chimpanzees and
mice. Two isolates, TMEV and CMV strains, have been properly
identified as unrelated to MS(Wroblewska *et al*, 1979 Approximately 24 other brains have been negative (D.H. Gilden,
personal communication). These extensive efforts suggest
that if an agent is present in MS tissue obtained at autopsy,
it does not grow in conventional tissue culture nor by the
more common methods of explanation.

D. Use of Nucleic Acid Probes. The rapid expan-
sion of techniques in molecular biology has added a powerful
armamentarium for those interested in the search for putative
infectious (replicating) agents in chronic systemic and neurologic diseases. A number of investigators have now begun
searching MS tissue with a variety of nucleic acid probes,
utilizing viruses which have in the past been associated with

the disease by either serological methods or isolations. A recent conference sponsored by the MS Society (Haase et al., 1983) focused on the current and potential use of these probes. Investigators are now looking at MS tissue with probes designed to detect canine distemper virus (P.C. Dowling and collaborators), coronavirus (S. Weiss), and measles virus, (A. Haase). The work with the measles probes has progressed the furthest, and it shows that both MS and control tissue contain sequences that will hybridize with measles complementary DNA (Haase et al. 1981). The sequences in brain are sensitive to ribonuclease, suggesting that the nucleic acid in brain is viral RNA and not an integrated DNA copy. As controls for this work, visna and Theiler's murine encephalomyelitis virus probes were also hybridized with brain, and these were negative in both MS and normal tissue. Work in another laboratory has shown that canine distemper virus probes do not hybridize with the brain of MS cases.

The work with other viral probes is still at a preliminary stage. Nucleic acid probes are becoming increasingly sensitive and precise, and it is unlikely that this kind of work will be completed at a level that satisfies exacting minds in the near future. In addition, the positive findings with measles will color any results obtained with other viruses; additional complementary evidence will be needed to suggest that any agent has a role in this disease.

VII.   SUMMARY AND CONCLUSIONS

The etiology and pathogenesis of multiple sclerosis is a major enigma which continues to defy solution in spite of a great deal of research employing techniques which range from epidemiology to molecular biology. Family and population studies strongly suggest that the disease is triggered by an exogenous environmental event. Viral and immunological investigations of animal models make it plausible that a viral infection can cause a chronic multifocal demyelinating process in the CNS, and recent observations suggest that this could involve an auto-immune process initiated by a viral infection. A direct viral cytolytic effect or an anti-viral immune response offer alternative mechanisms.

However, attempts directly to demonstrate a viral agent, viral genome, or viral proteins have been unsuccessful to date. This sugests that, in addition to conventional viruses, it is possible that a novel virus or virus-like agent might be involved. Clearly, the detailed investigation of viroids, virusoids, and other subviral agents will provide an essential foundation for the continuing search for the cause of MS.

REFERENCES

Acheson, E.D. (1977). Epidemiology of multiple sclerosis. *Brit. Med. Bull.* 33, 9-14.

Alter, M., Leibowitz, U., Speer, J. (1966). Risk of multiple sclerosis related to age at immigration to Israel. *Arch. Neurol. 15.*, 234-237.

Alter, M., Loewenson, R., Kahane, E. (1977). Migrants and multiple sclerosis. *Neurology 25.*, 341.

Bailey, O.T., Pappenheimer, A.M., Cheever, F.S.,and Daniels, J.B. (1949). A murine virus (JHM) causing disseminated encephalomyelitis with extensive destruction of myelin. II Pathology. *J. Exp. Med. 90,* 195-212.

Beebe, G., Kirtzke, J.F., Kurland, L.T., *et al.*, (1967). Studies on the natural history of multiple sclerosis. 3. Epidemiologic analysis of the Army experience in World War II. *Neurology 17,* 1-17.

Brahic, M., Stowring, L., Ventura, P., and Haase, A.T. (1981). Gene expression in visna virus infection. *Nature (London) 292,* 240-242.

Brahic, M., Stroop,W.G., and Baringer, J.R. (1981). Theiler's virus persists in glial cells during demyelinating disease. *Cell 26,* 123-128.

Burks, J.S., Devald-McMillan, B., Jankovsky, L., and Gerdes,J. (1979). Characterization of coronaviruses isolated using multiple sclerosis autopsy brain material. *Neurology 29,* 547.

Burks, J.S., DeVald, B.L., Jankovsky, L.D., and Gerdes, J.C. (1980). Two coronaviruses isolated from central nervous system tissue of two multiple sclerosis patients. *Science 209* 932-933.

Carp, R.I., Liarsi, P.C., Merz, P.A., and Merz, G.S. (1972). Decreased percentage of polymorphonuclear neutrotrophils in mouse blood after inoculation with material from multiple sclerosis patients. *J. Exp. Med. 136,* 618-629.

Carp, R.I., Warner, H.B., and Merz, G.S. (1978). Viral etiology of multiple sclerosis. *Prog. Med. Virol. 24,* 158-177.

Cheever, F.S., Daniels, J.B., Pappenheimer, A.M., and Bailey, O.T. (1949). A murine virus (JHM) causing disseminated encephalomyelitis with extensive destruction of myelin. I. Isolation and biological properties of the virus. *J. Exp. Med. 90,* 181-194.

Cook, S. D., and Dowling, P.C. (1980). Multiple sclerosis and viruses: an overview. *Neurology 30,* 80-91.

dal Canto, M.C., and Lipton, H.L. (1975). Primary demyelination in Theiler's virus infection: an ultrastructural study. *Lab. Invest. 33,* 626-637.

dal Canto, M.C., and Lipton, H.L. (1979). Recurrent demyelination in chronic central nervous system infection produced by Theiler's murine encephalomyelitis virus *J. Neurol. Sci. 42,* 391-405.

Dales, S.,Fujinami, R.S., and Oldstone, M.B.A. (1983). Infection with vaccine favors the selection of hybridomas synthesizing autoantibodies against intermediate filaments, one of them cross-reacting with the virus hemmagglutinin. *J. Immunol. 131,* 1546-1553.

Dean G., and Kurtzke,J. F. (1971). On the risk of multiple sclerosis according to age at immigration to South Africa. *Brit. Med. J. 3,* 725-729.

Dick, G.W.A., McKeown, F., and Wilson, D.C. (1958). Virus of acute encephalomyelitis of man and multiple sclerosis. *Brit. Med. J. 1,* 7-9.

Doherty, P., and Simpson, E. (1982). Murine models of multiple sclerosis. *Nature (London) 299,* 106-107.

Fraser,K.B. (1977). Multiple sclerosis: a virus disease. *Brit. Med. Bull. 33,* 34-39.

Fujinami, R.S., Oldstone, M.B.A., Wroblewska, Z., Frankel, M.E., and Koprowski, H. (1983). Molecular mimicry in virus infection: cross-reaction of measles virus phosphoprotein or of herpes simplex virus protein with human intermediate filaments. *Proc. Natl. Acad. Sci. 80,* 2346-2350.

Gudnadottir, M. Heldadottir, H.,Bjarnason,O., and Jonsdottir, K. (1964). Virus isolated from the brain of a patient with multiple sclerosis. *Exp.Neurol.9,* 85-95.

Haase, A.T., Ventura, P., Gibbs, C.J., Jr., and Tourtellotte, W.W. (1981) Measles virus nucleotide sequences: detection by hybridization in situ. *Science 212,* 672-675.

Haase, A.T., Pagano, J., Waksman, B., and Nathanson, N.(1984). Conference report: detection of virus genes and their products in chronic neurological diseases. *Neurology 15,* 119-121.

Haspel, M.V., Onodera, T., Prabhakar, B.S., Horita, M., Suzuki, H., and Notkins, A.L. (1983). Virus-induced autoimmunity: monoclonal antibodies that react with endocrine tissues. *Science 220,* 304-306.

Herndon, R.M., Griffin, D.E., McCormick, U., and Weiner, L.P., (1975). Mouse hepatitis virus-induced recurrent demyelination. *Arch. Neurol. 32,* 32-35.

Johnson, R.T., and Herndon, R.M. (1974). Virologic studies of multiple sclerosis and other chronic and relapsing neurological diseases. *Prog. Med. Virol.* *18*, 214–228.

Johnson, R.T. (1975). The possible viral etiology of multiple sclerosis. *Adv. Neurol.* *13*, 1–46.

Knobler, R.L., Lampert, P.W., and Oldstone, M.B.A. (1982). Virus persistence and recurring demyelination produced by a temperature-sensitive mutant of MHV-4. *Nature (London)* *298*, 279–280.

Kurtzke, J.F., Beebe, G.W., and Norman, J.E., Jr. (1979). Migration and multiple sclerosis in the United States. *Neurology 29*, 579.

Lipton, H.L. (1975). Theiler's virus infection in mice: an unusual biphasic disease process leading to demyelination. *Infect. Immun.* *11*, 147–1155.

Lipton, H.L. and dal Canto, M.C. (1977). Contrasting effects of immunosuppression on Theiler's virus infection in mice. *Infect. Immun.* *15*, 903–909.

Lipton, H.C., and dal Canto, M.C. (1979). Susceptibility of inbred mice to chronic central nervous system infection by Theiler's murine encephalomyelitis virus. *Infect. Immun.* *26*, 369–374.

Lipton, H.L. (1980). Persistent Theiler's murine encephalomyelitis virus infection in mice depends on plaque size. *J. gen. Virol.46*, 169–177.

Lipton, H.L. and Friedmann, A. (1980). Purification of Theiler's murine encephalomyelitis virus and analysis of the structural virion polypeptides: correlation of the polypeptide profile with virulence. *J. Virol.* *33*, 1165–1172.

Lorch, Y., Friedmann, A., Lipton, H.L. and Kotler, M. (1981). Theiler's murine encephalomyelitis virus group includes two distinct genetic subgroups that differ pathologically and biologically. *J. Virol.* *40*, 500–567.

Lutley, R., Klein,J., Petursson, G., Palsson, P.A., Georgsson, G. and Nathanson, N. 1983). Antigenic variation of visna virus during longterm infection of Icelandic sheep. *J. gen. Virol.* *64*, 1433–1440.

Margulis, M.S., Soloviev, JV. D., and Shubladze, A.K. (1946). Etiology and pathogenesis of acute sporadic disseminated encephalomyelitis and multiple sclerosis. *J. Neurol, Neuros., and Psychiat.* *9*, 63–74.

Martin, J.R., and Nathanson, N. (1979). Animal models of virus-induced demyelination. *Prog. Neuropath.* *4*, 27–50.

McFarlin, D., and Waksman, B. (1982). Altered immune function in demyelinative disease. *Immunol. Today. 3,* 322-325.

Melnick, J.L. (1982). Has the virus of multiple sclerosis been isolated? *Yale J. Biol. Med.55,* 251-257.

Melnick, J.L., Seidel, E.J., Inone, Y.K., and Nishibe, Y (1982). Isolation of virus from the spinal fluid of three patients with multiple sclerosis and one with amyotrophic lateral sclerosis. *Lancet 1,* 830-833.

Mitchell, D.N., Porterfield, J.S., Michelotti, R., Large, L.S., Goswami, K.K.A., Taylor, P., Jacobs, J.P., Hockley, J.J., and Salisbury, A.J. (1978). Isolation of an infectious agent from bone marrow of patients with multiple sclerosis. *Lancet 1,* 387-391.

Narayan, O., Griffin, E.E., and Clements, J.E. (1978). Visna mutation during "slow infection": temporal development and characterization of mutants of visna virus recovered from sheep. *J.Gen.Virol.41.* 343-352.

Nathanson, N., Panitch, H., Palsson, P.A., Petursson, G., and Georgsson, G. (1976). Pathogenesis of visna. 11. Effect of immunosuppression upon early central nervous system lesions. *Laboratory Investigation 35,* 444-451.

Nathanson, N., and Miller A. (1978). Epidemiology of multiple sclerosis: critique of the evidence of a viral etiology. *Amer. J. Epidemiol. 107,* 451-461.

Nathanson, N., Martin, J.R., Georgsson, G., Palsson, P.A., Lutley, R.E., and Petursson, G. (1981). Effect of post-infection immunization upon the severity of visna lesions. *J. Com. Path. 91,* 1-7.

Nathanson, N., Georgsson, G. Lutley, R., Palsson, P.A., and Petursson, G. (1983). Pathogenesis of visna in Icelandic sheep. Demyelinating lesions and antigenic drift. In *Viruses and Demyelinating Diseases.* C. Mims, ed. Academic Press, London, pp. 111-124.

Nathanson, N., Georgsson, G., Palsson, P.A., Najjar, J.A., Lutley, R., and Petursson, G. (1984). Experimental visna in Icelandic sheep, the prototype lentivirus infection. *Rev. Inf. Dis.* In press.

Norrby, E. (1978). Viral antibodies in multiple sclerosis. *Prog. Med. Virol. 24,* 1-39.

Palsson, P.A. (1976). Maedi and visna in sheep. In *Slow Virus Diseases of Animals and Man,* Kimberline, R.H. ed. North Holland, Amsterdam, pp 17-43.

Paterson, P.Y., and Whitacre, C.C. (1981). The enigma of oligoclonal immunoglobulin G in cerebrospinal fluid from multiple sclerosis patients. *Immunol. Today 2,* 111-117.

Penney, J.B., and Wolinsky, J.S. (1979). Neuronal and oligodendroglial infection by the W.W. strain of Theiler's virus. *Lab.Invest.40,* 324-330.

Pertschuk, L.P., Cook, A.W., and Gupta, J. (1976). Measles antigen in mutiple sclerosis: Identification in the jejunum by immunofluorescence. *Life Sciences 19,* 1603-1608.

Prineas, J. (1972). Paramyxovirus-like particles associated with acute demyelination in chronic relapsing multiple sclerosis. *Science 178,* 760-763.

Sever, J.L., and Madden, D.L. (1980). Viruses that do not cause multiple sclerosis. In *Search for the cause of multiple sclerosis and other chronic diseases of the central nervous system.* Boese, A., Ed. Verlag Chemie, Basel, p. 414-424.

Spielman, R.S., and Nathanson, N. (1982). The genetics of susceptibility to multiple sclerosis. *Epidemiol. Rev. 4,* 45-65.

Tanaka, R., Iwasaki, Y., and Koprowski, H. (1975). Paramyxovirus-like structures in brains of multiple sclerosis patients. *Arch. Neurol. 32,* 80-83.

ter Meulen, V., Iwasaki, Y., Koprowski, H., *et al.,* (1972). Fusion of a cultured multiple sclerosis brain cells with indicator cells: presence of nucleocapsids and virions and isolation of parainfluenza-type virus. *Lancet 11,* 1-5.

Theiler, M. (1977). Spontaneous encephalomyelitis of mice, a new virus disease. *J. Exp. Med.65,* 705-719.

Theiler, M., and Gand, S.,(1940). Encephalomyelitis of mice. 1. Characteristics and pathogenesis of the virus. *J. Exp. Med. 72,* 49-68.

Thompson, E. J. (1977). Laboratory diagnosis of multiple sclerosis: immunological and biochemical aspects. *Brit. Med. Bull.33,* 28-33.

Thormar, H., Barshatzky, M.R., Arnesen, K., and Kozlowski, P.B. (1983).The emergence of antigenic variants is a rare event in long-term visna virus infection *in vivo. J. gen. Virol. 64,* 1427-1432.

Watanabe, R., Wege, H., and ter Meulen, V. (1983). Adoptive transfer of EAE -like lesions from rats with corona virus induced demyelinating encephalomyelitis. *Nature 305,* 150-153.

Weiner, L.P. (1973). Pathogenesis of demyelination induced by a mouse hepatitis virus (JHM virus). *Arch. Neurol. 28,* 298–303.

Wroblewska, Z., Gilden, D., Devlin, M., Huang, E.-S., Rorke, L.B. Hanada, T., Furukawa, T., Cummins, L., Kalter, S., and Koprowski, H. (1979). Cytomegalovirus isolation from a chimpanzee with acute demyelinating disease after inoculation of multiple sclerosis brain cells. *Infect. Immun. 25,* 1008–1015.

Chapter 20

SUBACUTE SPONGIFORM VIRUS ENCEPHALOPATHIES CAUSED BY UNCONVENTIONAL VIRUSES

D. Carleton Gajdusek

National Institute of Neurological and Communicative Disorders and Stroke, National Institutes of Health, Bethesda, Maryland 20205

INTRODUCTION

The pursuit of the transmissibility and virus etiology of kuru (15,21,23,25,26,32,69) and the presenile dementia of the Creutzfeldt-Jakob disease (CJD) type (19,22) has led to the definition of the unconventional viruses as a new group of microbes, which because of their very atypical physical, chemical and biological properties has stimulated a world-wide quest to elucidate their structures and resolve the many paradoxes they present to the basic tenets of microbiology and to solve the enormous clinical and epidemiological problems these viruses pose. The unanticipated ramifications of the demonstration of such slow infections by unconventional viruses and the peculiar properties of the unconventional viruses have led to a series of discoveries each of which has wide implications to microbiological and neurobiological research and research on chronic diseases of man (3,4,19,41,42,54-59,62) (Tables I-III). These discov-

Copyright © 1985 by Academic Press, Inc.
All rights of reproduction in any form reserved.
ISBN 0-12-470230-9

eries and paradoxes they pose may be summarized in the
following Sections   I through XIV.

I.   MICROBES WITHOUT A NON-HOST ANTIGEN

These slow viruses first invade and replicate in the re-
ticuloendothelial cells and particularly low density lymphocytes in the spleen. Yet, they provoke no antibody response
in infected animals or in animals passively immunized with
live virus preparation of infectious titers over 10^{11} ID_{50}
/gram, when complement fixation, virus neutralization, immune precipitation, ELISA, and other tests for antibody are
used. With the inability to demonstrate any antiviral antibody response or any immune response directed against non-
host viral components or capable of neutralizing the virus
activity, these unconventional viruses become unique in their
immunological inertness in microbiology. Natural and experimental infection with them elicit no antibody response in
the host, nor does immunosuppression with whole body radiation, cortisone, anti-lymphocytic serum or cytotoxic drugs
alter the incubation period, progress or pattern of disease,
or duration of illness to death. Finally, *in vivo* and *in
vitro* study of both B-cell and T-cell function reveal no
abnormality early or late in the course of illness and cells
cultured *in vitro* from diseased animals show no sensitization
to high titer preparations of these viruses. Since high
titer infective material in both crude suspension and highly
purified fractions also fail to elicit an immunological
response against non-host components, even when used with
adjuvants, this becomes the first group of microbes in which
such immunological inertness has been demonstrated, and
evokes the speculation that the replication of these viruses
does not involve production of a virus specified non-host
antigen (19,36,46,54,68) (Table I).

II. UNUSUAL RESISTANCE TO PHYSICAL AND CHEMICAL INACTIVATION

The demonstration of the resistance of the unconventional viruses to high concentrations of formaldehyde or glutar-
aldehyde and most other anti-viral and antiseptic substances,
to ionizing and ultraviolet radiation, to ultrasonication and
to heat and the further demonstration of iatrogenic transmission through surgically implanted stereotactic electroencephalographic electrodes, contaminated surgical instruments,
and corneal transplantation and possibly through dentistry
has led to the necessity of changing autopsy room and operat-
ing theater techniques throughout the world, as well as the
precautions used in handling older and demented patients.

Many of the gentle organic disinfectants often used for disinfection, including detergents and the quarternary ammonium salts, and even hydrogen peroxide, ether, chloroform, iodine, phenol and acetone, are inadequate for sterilization of the unconventional viruses as is the use of the ethylene oxide sterilizer. This demands revision of previously acceptable procedures for decontamination and disinfection (7, 8, 9) (Table I, III).

TABLE I

Atypical properties of the unconventional viruses

Physical and Chemical Properties

Resistant to
    Formaldehyde and gluteraldehyde
    β-propiolactone
    Ethylenediamine tetraacetic acid (EDTA)
    Nucleases (ribonucleases A and III, deoxyribonuclease I)
    Cisdiamino platinum compounds (Cisplatin)
    Psoralens
    Hydroxylamine reversal of diethyl pyrocarbonate inactivation
    Heat (80°C); incompletely inactivated at 100°C
    Ultraviolet radiation: 2540 Å
    Ionizing radiation (γ rays): equivalent target 150,000
       daltons; corrected for polymeric association: 10^{11}
       daltons
    Ultrasonic energy
    Atypical ultraviolet inactivation action spectrum:
       Å = 6 x 2540 Å ; 2200 Å = 50 x 2540 Å   2370
    Not recognizable as virion by electron microscopy
       (no core and coat)
    Amyloid-like fibrils seen in infected brains (SAF-scrapie
       associated fibril) resembling aggregated scrapie associated protein ("prion")

Biological Properties

No eclipse phase
Doubling time of 5.2 days (in hamster brain), similarly
    slow in mouse brain
Long incubation period (months to years; decades)
No inflammatory response
Chronic progressive pathology (slow infection)
No remissions or recoveries: always fatal
"Degenerative" histopathology: amyloid plaques, gliosis
No inclusion bodies
No interferon production or interference with interferon
    production by other viruses
No interferon sensitivity

Table 1. continued -

No virus interference (with more than 30 different con-
    ventional viruses)
No infectious nucleic acid demonstrable by DNA hybridiza-
    tion or transfection
No antigenicity, no non-host protein demonstrated
No alteration in pathogenesis(incubation period, duration,
    course) by immunosupression or immunopotentiation by:
        (a) ACTH, cortisone
        (b) Cyclophosphamide
        (c) X-ray
        (d) Antilymphocytic serum
        (e) Thymectomy or splemectomy
        (f) "Nude" athymic mice
        (g) Adjuvants
Immune B cell and T cell function intact *in vivo* and *in
    vitro*
No cytopathic effect in infected cells *in vitro*
Varying individual susceptibility to high infection dose
    in some host species (as with scrapie in sheep)
Varying susceptibility, virulence and pathogenesis (areas
    of the brain involved) in different species

TABLE II
Classical virus properties of unconventional viruses

Filterable to 25 nm average pore diameter (APD) (scrapie,
    TME); 100 nm APD (kuru, CJD)
Titrate "cleanly" (all individuals succumb to high LD_{50} in
    most species)
Replicate to titers of 10^5/g to 10^{11}/g in brain
Pathogenesis: first replicate in spleen and elsewhere in
    the reticuloendothelial system, later in brain
"Adaptation" to new host (shortened incubation period)
Genetic control of susceptibility in some species (sheep
    and mice for scrapie)
Specificity of host range for given strain
Strains of varying virulence and pathogenicity and with
    different host ranges
Clonal (limiting dilution) selection of strains from "wild
    stock"
Interference of slow-growing strain of scrapie with replica-
    tion of fast-growing strain in mice

TABLE III

Methods of inactivating unconventional viruses
Autoclaving (121°C at 15 pounds per square inch for 60 min.)
Sodium hydroxide (0.1 to 1.0 N)
Hypochlorite (Clorox) (5.0 percent)
Phenol extraction
Chloroform of chloroform-butanol
Strong detergents
Proteinase K
Kaotropic ions (thiocyanate, guanadinium, trichloroacetate)
2-Chloroethanol
Potassium permanganate (0.002M)

III. EXPRESSION OF FAMILIAL CJD DETERMINED BY A SINGLE AUTOSOMAL DOMINANT GENE

CJD became the first human infectious disease in which a single gene was demonstrated to control susceptibility and occurrence of the disease. The autosomal dominant behavior of the disease in such families, including the appearance of the disease in 50% of siblings who survive to the age at which the disease usually appears, has evoked the possibility of slow virus infection in other familial dementias. The presence of CJD patients in the families of well-known familial Alzheimer's disease, and the familial occurrence of the spino-cerebellar ataxic form of CJD, the Gerstmann-Sträussler syndrome, which is also transmissible, have led to renewed interest in familial dementias of all types (41,42,63).

IV. AUTOIMMUNE RESPONSE TO 10 nm NEUROFILAMENT

The demonstration by Sotelo *et al.* of a very specific autoimmune antibody directed against 10 nm neurofilaments and no other component of the CNS in over 60% of the patients with kuru and CJD as a phenomenon appearing late in the disease, was the first demonstration of an immune phenomenon in the subacute spongiform virus encephalopathies and an exciting new avenue of approach for the study of the transmissible dementias (61,62). This autoimmune antibody behaves like many other autoimmune antibodies, such as the rheumatoid factor and the anti-DNA antibody in systemic lupus erythematosus and the anti-thyroglobulin antibody in Hashimoto's thyroiditis, in that it is occasionally present in normal subjects, more often present in subjects closely related to the patients. Although found in more than half of patients with transmissible virus dementia, it does not appear in 40% of patients with classical CJD. It does develop in other grey matter diseases, including Alzheimer's and Parkinson's

diseases, but at far lower incidence than in CJD. Furthermore, it is not present in patients with other immune diseases
such as disseminated lupus erythematosus and chronic rheumatoid arthritis (2). Bahmanyar *et al.* have demonstrated that
this autoimmune response is directed specifically against the
200,000-dalton component of the three proteins comprising the
10 nm neurofilament triad, and not against the 145,000-dalton
and 70,000-dalton components (1). Bahmanyar has shown that
the antineurofilament antibody of CJD, kuru and scrapie reacts also with the pooled neurofilaments produced in the
brains of rats treated with β,β'-iminodipropionitrile (IDPN)
and with Alzheimer's neurofibrillary tangles (unpublished
data).

V. SUBACUTE SPONGIFORM VIRUS ENCEPHALOPATHIES

Kuru and the transmissible virus dementias have been
classified in a group of virus-induced slow infections that
we have described as subacute spongiform virus encephalopathies because of the strikingly similar histopathological
lesions they induce; and, scrapie, mink encephalopathy, and
the chronic wasting disease with spongiform encephalopathy of
captive mule deer and of captive elk all appear, from their
histopathology, pathogenesis, and the similarities of their
infectious agents, to belong to the same group. The basic
neurocytological lesion in all these diseases is a progressive vacuolation in the dendritic and axonal processes and
cell bodies of neurons and, to a lesser extent, in astrocytes
and oligodendrocytes; an extensive astroglial hyper-
trophy and proliferation; and, finally, spongiform change or
status spongiosus of gray matter (3,4,37). These atypical
infections differ from other diseases of the human brain
which have been subsequently demonstrated to be slow virus
infections in that they do not evoke a virus-associated
inflammatory response in the brain (i.e., no perivascular
cuffing or invasion of the brain parenchyma with leucocytes);
they usually show no pleocytosis nor do they show marked rise
in protein in the cerebrospinal fluid throughout the course
of infection. Furthermore, they show no evidence of an
immune response to the causative virus and, unlike the situation in the other virus encephalitides, there are no recognizable virions in sections of the brain visualized by
electron microscopy (Table I).

There are other slow infections of the central nervous
system that are caused by more conventional viruses including
measles virus, papovaviruses (JC and SV40-PML), rubella virus,
cytomegalovirus, herpes simplex virus, adenovirus types 7 and
32, and RSSE virus (Table IV). However, unlike these "conventional" viruses, the "unconventional" viruses of the
spongiform encephalopathies have unusual resistance to

TABLE IV

Slow infections of man caused by conventional viruses

Disease	Virus
Subacute post-measles leukoencephalitis	Paramyxovirus--defective measles
Subacute schlerosing panencephalitis (SSPE)	Paramyxovirus--defective measles
Subacute encephalitis	Herpetovirus--herpes simplex
	Adenovirus--Adenotypes 7 and 32
Progressive congenital rubella	Togavirus--rubella
Progressive panencephalitis as a late sequela following congenital rubella	Togavirus--defective rubella
Verruca vulgaris (warts)	Papovavirus--warts
Progressive multifocal leukoencephalopathy (PML)	Papovavirus--JC; SV40
Cytomegalovirus brain infection	Herpetovirus--cytomegalovirus
Chronic infectious mononucleosis	Herpetovirus--Epstein Barr (EB) virus
Epilepsia partialis continua (Kozhevnikov's epilepsy) and progressive bulbar palsy in U.S.S.R.	Togavirus--RSSE and other tick-borne encephalitis viruses
Chronic meningoencephalitis in immuno-deficient patients	Picornaviruses--poliomyelitis, echovirus
Homologous serum jaundice	Hepadnavirus B, hepatitis B (Dane particle)
	Hepadnavirus D (delta antigen--defective)
Infectious hepatitis	Picornavirus--hepatitis A
Transfusion-associated non-A non-B hepatitis	Unclassified, non-A, non-B
Epidemic non-A non-B hepatitis	Unclassified, non-A, non-B
Acquired immune deficiency syndrome (AIDS)	HTLV-III Retrovirus: Lentivirus--LAV/HTLV-3
T-cell leukemia	Retrovirus: Oncornavirus--HTLV-1, HTLV-2

ultraviolet radiation and to ionizing radiation, to ultrasonication, to heat, and nucleases, and to formaldehyde,
gluteraldehyde, beta-propiolactone, ethylenediamine tetraace-
tic acid (EDTA), and sodium deoxycholate. They are moderate-
ly sensitive to most membrane-disrupting agents in high
concentration such as chloroform, ether, periodate (0.01M),
2-chloroethanol, alcoholic iodine, acetone, chloroform-butanol,
to caotropic ions such as thiocyanate and guanadinium and
trichloroacetate, and to proteinase K and trypsin when partially purified, but these only inactivated 99% to 99.9% of
the infectious particles leaving behind much highly resistant
infectivity. Sodium hydroxide (0.1 to 1.0 N) and hypochlo-
rite (5% Chlorox), however, quickly inactivate over $10^5 ID_{50}$
of the virus (7-9). Virions are not recognized on electron
microscopic study of infected cells *in vivo* or *in vitro*, nor
are they recognized in highly infectious preparations of
virus concentrated by density-gradient banding in the zonal
rotor. These unconventional properties, especially the resistance to nucleases and the atypical action spectrum of
inactivation by UV, have led to the speculation that the
infectious agents lack a nucleic acid, and that they may be a
self-replicating protein (and a derepressor of cellular DNA
bearing information for their own synthesis), even a self-
replicating membrane fragment which serves as a template for
laying down abnormal plasma membrane, including itself (19,
54).

The scrapie virus has been partially purified by density-gradient sedimentation in the presence of specific detergents. Rohwer has succeeded in a 1000-fold purification of scrapie virus relative to other quantifiable proteins in the original brain suspension (59). In such preparations the virus is susceptible to proteinase K and trypsin digestion but it is not inactivated by any nuclease. Such sedimented, washed and resuspended virus has been banded into peaks of high infectivity with the use of cesium chloride, sucrose, and metrizamide density gradients in the ultracentrifuge. Sucrose-saline density gradient banding of scrapie virus in mouse brains produced wide peaks of scrapie infectivity at densities of 1.14 to 1.23 g/cm^3 (59). Attempts to demonstrate a nonhost nucleic acid in the scrapie virus by DNA homology (6) and transfection (5) and nuclease inactivation (34) have been unsucessful. On electron microscopic examination, fractions of high infectivity (10^7 to 10^8 LD_{50}/ml) reveal only smooth vesicular membranes with mitochondrial and ribosomal debris and no structures resembling recognizable virions. Lysosomal hydrolases (N-acetyl- β -D-glucosaminidase, β -galactosidase, and acid phosphatase)and mitochondrial marker enzyme (INT-succinate reductase) show most of their activity in fractions of lower density than in the fractions having high scrapie infectivity.

The UV action spectrum for inactivation of scrapie shows a sixfold increased sensitivity at 237 nm over that at 254 or 280 nm, and 50-fold increased sensitivity at 220 nm. This atypical action spectrum for inactivation of microbes should not be taken as proof that no genetic information exists in the scrapie virus as nucleic acid molecules, since Latarjet has demonstrated similar resistance to ultraviolet and a similar UV action spectrum for microsomes (30,33,38,39). Ultraviolet resistance also depends greatly on small RNA size, as has been shown by the high resistance of the purified, very small, tobbacco ring spot satellite virus RNA (about 80,000 daltons).

Nevertheless, the unconventional viruses possess numerous properties in which they resemble classical viruses, and some of these properties suggest far more complex genetic interaction between virus and host than one might expect for genomes with a molecular weight of only 10^5 daltons. By filtration they size at 30 to 50 nm. They are, truly, slow viruses in that a fast growing scrapie in hamster brain has a doubling time of 5.2 days (58).

The high resistance to inactivation could well be the result of the high propensity of the hydrophobic scrapie virus to form aggregates. Such aggregates would require "multiple hits" for their inactivation either by chemical or physical agents rather than the "single-hit" kinetics of the inactivation of monomeric free viruses (57).

In spite of very unusual resistance of a significant subfraction of the infectious particles to heat, the majority of particles are rapidly inactivated by temperatures above 85°C (56). Autoclaving (120°C at 15 pounds per square inch for 60 minutes) completely inactivates scrapie virus in suspensions of mouse brain. We have recently proposed the use of 0.1 to 1.0 N sodium hydroxide for precautions in the medical care of and in handling materials from patients with diseases caused by these unconventional viruses (7-9).

In plant virology we have recently been forced to modify our concepts of a virus to include subviral pathogens such as the newly described viroids causing eleven natural plant diseases--potato spindle tuber disease, chrysanthemum stunt disease, citrus exocortis disease, cadang-cadang disease of coconut palms, cherry chlorotic mottle, cucumber pale fruit disease, hop stunt disease, avocado sunblotch disease, tomato bunchy top disease, tomato "planta macho" disease and burdock stunt disease to which we may turn for analogy (13,60). All of the viroids are small circular RNAs containing no structural protein or membrane and they have all been fully sequenced and their fine structures determined. They have only partial base pairing as the circle collapses on itself. They contain only 246 to 574 ribonucleotides and replicate by a "rolling circle" copying of their RNA sequences in many sequential rotations to produce an oligomeric copy which is then cut into monomers, sometimes dimers. No protein is synthesized from their genetic information and only the replication machinery of the cell is used. Australian plant pathologists have recently identified the virusoids of four natural plant diseases (velvet tobacco mottle virus, solanum nodiflorum mottle virus, lucerne transient streak virus, subterranean clover mottle virus). These contain in addition to a conventional virus RNA genome of greater than 10^6-daltons a small RNA circle which is the size of a viroid and which requires the larger genome for its replication. These subviral pathogens have caused us to give much thought to possible similarities to the unconventional viruses. However, we have shown that the unconventional viruses differ from the plant viroids on many counts (13,54,60).

Thus the intellectually stimulating analogies of the unconventional viruses to viroids and virusoids prove to be spurious, yet these subviral pathogens of plants have served to alert us to the possibility of extreme departure from conventional virus structures.

The delta antigen of infectious hepatitis, a defective replicating particle with only 1,700 bases on its genome (68,000 daltons) and requiring the infectious hepatitis B virus for its replication, offers further intriguing analogies to the unconventional viruses.

VI. SCRAPIE-ASSOCIATED FIBRILS (SAF)

In suspension of scrapie-affected brain sedimented in a density gradient, Merz and Somerville have demonstrated an amyloid-like 2- or 4-stranded fiber which increases in quantity with virus titer (49,50). We have found these structures in brains of CJD patients and in brains of primates

TABLE V

Presence of scrapie associated fibrils (SAFs), paired helical filaments and amyloid fibrils, in suspension of brain tissue from Creutzfeldt-Jakob disease, kuru, scrapie andother brain specimens

	Scrapie Associated Fibrils (SAF)	Paired Helical Filaments (PHF)	Amyloid Fibrils
Creutzfeldt-Jakob disease			
Case 1	+	−	−
2	+	−	−
3	+	−	−
4	+	−	−
5	+	+	−
6	+	+	+
7	+	−	+
8	+	−	+
Control human brain specimens			
Normal (6 cases)	−	−	−
Amyotrophic lateral sclerosis (2 cases)	−	−	−
Schizophrenia (1 case)	−	−	−
Alzheimer's disease, sporadic (5 cases)	−	++	++
Alzheimer's disease, familial (1 case)	−	+++	+++
Guamanian normal			
Case 1	−	+	−
2	−	+	−
3	−	−	−
Guamanian Parkinsonism-dementia	−	−	−
Case 1	−	−	−
2	−	+	−
3	−	−	−
4	−	−	−
Animal brain specimens			
Scrapie infected			
Sheep (natural scrapie)(1)	−	−	−
Mice	+	−	−
Hamster (2)	+	−	−
Squirrel Monkey (2)	+	−	−
CJD infected			
Squirrel Monkey (1)	+	−	−
Kuru infected			
Squirrel Monkey (3)	+ (1)	−	−
	− (2)		
Normal			
Sheep (1)	−	−	−
Mice (2)	−	−	−
Hamster (3)	−	−	−

with experimental CJD and kuru, and not in normal control brains or brains of patients with other neurodegenerative diseases (Table V) (47,48,51). It has been postulated that these structures may represent the scrapie or CJD or kuru infectious agent (14,14a,51,55) (Fig. 1). Such structures bring to mind the filamentous phage fd and filamentous plant viruses which are of about the same diameters.

These scrapie associated fibrils may be distinguished structurally from paired helical filaments of Alzheimer's disease, parkinsonism-dementias of Guam, and from classical brain amyloid fibrils of Alzheimer's disease and normal aging (47,48). However, the similarities are great. Monoclonal antibody against normal neurofilament and autoimmune oligoclonal antibodies of Creutzfeldt-Jakob disease, kuru and scrapie react with normal 10 nm neurofilaments and with pooled neurofilaments induced by IDPN in rats and with neurofibrillary tangles of Alzheimer's disease. It will be interesting to learn whether such autoantibody or some monoclonal antibody to normal neurofilaments will react scrapie with associated fibrils (SAFs) to brain amyloid and to purified paired helical filaments of Alzheimer's disease and the aging brain. This is especially true since Prusiner reports that his scrapie associated protein aggregates into fibrils which resemble amyloid structurally and in staining properties (55).

The possibility that 10 nm neurofilaments to which the autoantibodies in CJD, kuru and scrapie react show sequence homology with paired helical filaments of Alzheimer's disease and the aging brain and these, in turn with amyloid and the SAFs of Merz and with Prusiner's scrapie associated protein would suggest the hypothesis that interference with axonal transport may lead to neurofilament abnormalities (neurofibrillary tangles) and also to amyloid plaques as two aspects of the same disturbance of neurofilament metabolism. That the unconventional viruses themselves may be evolved from neurofilament and immunoglobulin genetic coding is the ultimate guess.

If such a structure does represent the scrapie virus, then it is truly "unconventional" in animal virology even if it does have its counterparts among filamentous plant viruses and bacteriophage. However, the crucial argument revolves about the assumption that the scrapie (and kuru and CJD) virus, if a structurally unusual filamentous virus, does or does not contain the information for its replication in an intrinsic nucleic acid genome. Should it prove not to have such a nucleic acid genome, then the "romantics," who have prematurely contended, on insufficient evidence, that it is a totally new form of replicating microbe, a pure protein (perhaps a neurofilament with immunoglobulin homology) devoid of DNA or RNA, will have been right. The conservatives, "non-

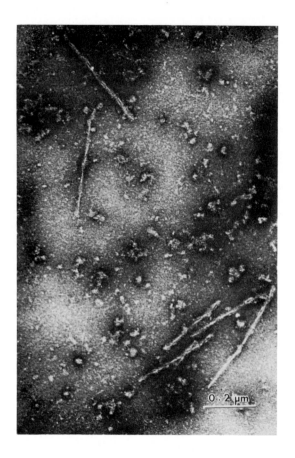

Figure 1.

a. Scrapie associated fibrils (SAF) from the brain of a
    scrapie affected hamster.
b. SAF as found in the brain of a Creutzfeldt–Jakob disease
    (CJD) patient (center, b). The SAFs can be differentiated
    structurally from paired helical filaments which are con-
    tained in the characteristic neurofibrillary tangles of
    Alzheimer's disease (right, c), and from amyloid fibrils
    from the brain of a CJD patient (left ,a), and may none-
    theless share sequence homology and represent different
    aspects of a single pathogenesis. Original magnification at
    90,000X; samples stained with 3% sodium phosphotungstate, pH
    7.2 (from Merz et al., 1984).

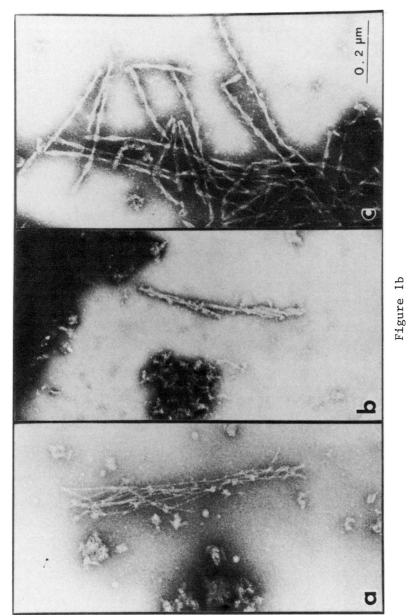

Figure 1b

heretics", who contend that it must have DNA or RNA although
they are unable to produce any demonstration thereof, do so
on the basis of their faith in the basic tenets of microbiology and their demonstration of the unjustifiability of claims
to the contrary because of the demonstrated high order of
aggregation of hydrophobic scrapie infectious units and the
large uncertainty of *in vivo* titration points in mice and
hamsters.

VII. ATTEMPTS TO DEMONSTRATE A VIRUS IN OTHER CHRONIC DEGENERATIVE DISEASES

The suspicion has been awakened that many other chronic
diseases of man may be slow virus infections. Data from both
the virus laboratory and from epidemiological studies have
accumulated which suggest that multiple sclerosis and Parkinson's disease, disseminated lupus erythematosus, and juvenile
(type 1, insulin dependent) diabetes, polymyositis, some
forms of chronic arthritis, and even the currently much-
discussed acquired immune deficiency syndrome (AIDS) may be
slow infections with a masked and possible defective virus as
their causes.

Our attempt to establish a viral etiology for Alzheimer's disease, Pick's disease, Parkinson's disease, multiple
sclerosis, progressive supranuclear palsy, amyotrophic lateral sclerosis, schizophrenia and autism in childhood, and a
wide variety of other chronic, some non-inflammatory, diseases of the central nervous system of man has led to failures
except in the group listed above. This long-standing negative data has become increasingly important as the research
on these diseases, even including hereditary Huntington's
disease, has more intensively embraced the slow virus etiological hypothesis of their causation and for research work
directed at their pathogenesis. In addition to using our
large holdings of monkeys and chimpanzees and non-primate
laboratory animals for inoculation studies for these diseases, we have used cocultivation tissue culture techniques with
many cell lines and other *in vitro* systems of tissue culture
to detect any virus which may reside in the brain. Inoculated tissue cultures are screened for the presence of viral
antigens or viral reverse transcriptase, and examined by
electron microscope for virus-like particles and by immunofluorescence using antibodies to known viruses, and by the
technique of *in situ* DNA hybridization with probes made to
the nucleic acids of known viruses.

VIII. KURU

Kuru is characterized by cerebellar ataxia and a shivering-like tremor that progresses to complete motor incapacity and death in less than 1 year from onset. It is confined to highland New Guineans living in a number of adjacent valleys in the mountainous interior of Papua New Guinea and occurs in 169 villages with a total population of just over 35,000 (Figure 2). Kuru means shivering or trembling in the Fore language. In the Fore cultural and linguistic group, among whom more than 80 percent of the cases occur, kuru had a yearly incidence rate and prevalence ratio of about 1 percent of the population. During the early years of investigation, after the first description by Gajdusek and Zigas in 1957, it was found to affect all ages beyond infants and toddlers; it was common in male and female children and in adult females, but rare in adult males. This marked excess of deaths of adult females over males had led to male-to-female population ratio of more than 3:1 in some villages, and of 2:1 for the whole South Fore group (15,17,19,21,69) (Fig. 3).

Kuru has been disappearing gradually during the past 20 years (19,37a). The incidence of the disease in children and adolescents has decreased during the past two decades, and the disease is no longer seen in persons under 25 years of age. This change in occurrence of kuru appears to result from the cessation of the practice of ritual cannibalism as a rite of mourning and respect for dead kinsmen, with its resulting conjunctival, nasal, skin, mucosal and gastrointestinal contamination with highly infectious brain tissue mostly among women and small children. In recent field work on kuru it has been possible to obtain clear documentation of incubation periods of thirty years and more in human kuru and, because of the scarcity of kuru patients, to identify small clusters of related patients and to ascertain the exact cannibal feast which caused contamination (37a). We discovered that the great majority, in fact over ninety percent of the infants and children of women present at a contaminating event of cannibalism, have already developed kuru. Continued surveillance has revealed no alteration in the unusual pattern of kuru disappearance, which indicates the artificial man-made nature of the epidemic; kuru virus clearly has no reservoir in nature and no intermediate natural biological

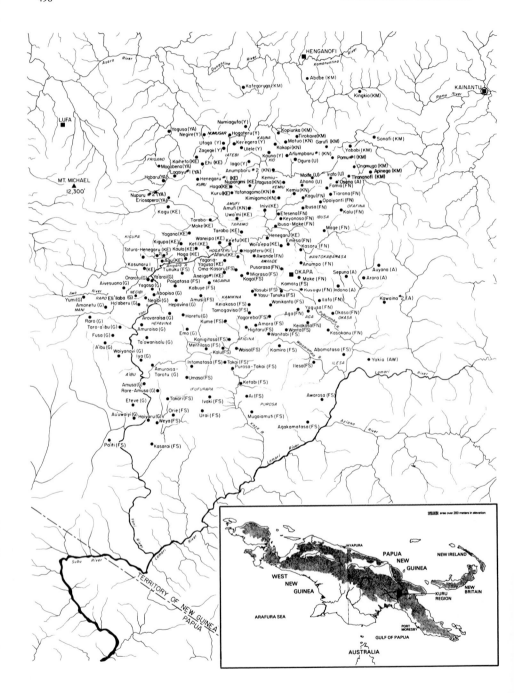

cycle for its preservation except in humans. Furthermore, there is no transplacental or neonatal transmission, even as an integrated genome or as a milk factor from a mother who is incubating kuru or already a kuru victim. There were only 12 kuru deaths in 1982 and the youngest kuru patients are now over 30 years of age (19,21) (Fig. 4).

The clinical course of kuru is remarkably uniform with cerebellar symptoms progressing to total incapacitation and death, usually within 3 to 9 months. It starts insidiously without antecedent acute illness and is conveniently divided into three stages: ambulant, sedentary, terminal (Figs. 5 - 9).

For several years all work on the kuru virus was done with chimpanzees, the first species to which the disease was transmitted (23,32) (Figs. 10-12). Eventually, other species of nonhuman primates developed the disease: first, several species of New World monkeys with longer incubation periods than in the chimpanzee; and later, several species of Old World monkeys with yet longer incubation periods. We have transmitted kuru to the mink and ferret, the first nonprimate hosts that have proved to be susceptible, although dozens of other species of laboratory, domestic, and wild nonprimate and avian hosts have been inoculated without their developing disease after many years of observation. More recently we have transmitted kuru to the goat using both human kuru brain inocula and brain from experimentally infected monkeys. In the goat, the disease resembles scrapie. Kuru does not transmit to sheep (19,29).

The virus has been regularly isolated from the brain tissue of kuru patients. It may attain high titers of more than 10^8 ID_{50}/gram of brain tissue. In peripheral tissue, namely liver and spleen, it has been found only rarely at the time of death and in much lower titers. Blood, urine, leukocytes, cerebrospinal fluid, and placenta and embryonal membranes of patients with kuru have not yielded the virus (19) (Figs. 13-14).

Figure 2.   The kuru region (shown in black area, inset map, lower right)contains more than 35,000 people living in 169 villages (census units) nestled at from 1000 to 2500 meters above sea level among rain forest-covered mountains. River drainages of the kuru region are shown in the larger map, with superimposed locations of the villages in which kuru has ever occurred. The cultural and linguistic group of each village is indicated: A, Auyana; AW, Awa; FN, North Fore; FS, South Fore; G, Gimi; KE, Keianga; KM, Kamano; KN, Kanite; U, Usurufa; Y, Yate; and YA, Yagaria.

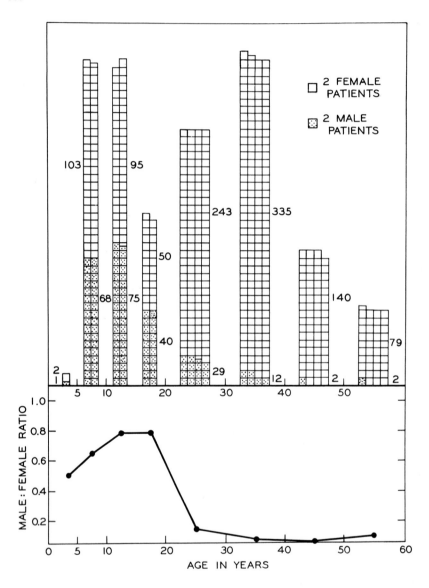

Figure 3. Age and sex distribution of the first 1276 kuru patients studied in the early years of kuru investigations. The youngest patient had onset at 4 years of age, died at 5 years of age. In recent years, with the progressive disappearance of younger patients (no one born since cannibalism ceased in a given village has died of kuru), age and sex patterns have completely changed.

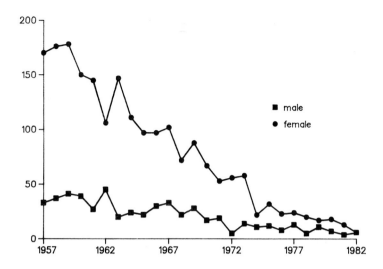

Figure 4a. The overall incidence of kuru deaths in male and female patients by year since its discovery in 1957 through 1982. More than 2,500 patients died of kuru in this 27-year period of surveillance, and there has been a slow, irregular decline in number of patients to one-tenth the number seen in the early years of the kuru investigation. The incidence in males has declined significantly only in the last few years, whereas in females it started to decline over a decade earlier. This decline in incidence has occured during the period of acculturation from a stone age culture in which endocannibalistic consumption of dead kinsmen was practiced as a rite of mourning, to a modern coffee-planting society practicing cash economy. Because the brain tissue with which the officiating women contaminated both themselves and all their infants and toddlers contained more than 1,000,000 infectious doses per gram, self-inoculation through the eyes, nose and skin, as well as by mouth, was a certainty whenever a victim was eaten. The decline in incidence of the disease has followed the cessation of cannibalism, which occurred between 1957 and 1962 in various villages.

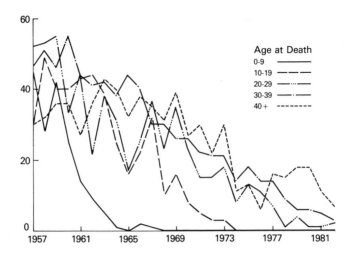

Figure 4b.   Kuru deaths by age group from 1957 through 1982.
The disease has disappeared from the youngest age group (0
to 9 years) about 10 years before it disappeared in the 10 –
to 19-year olds, and about 10 years before it disappeared in
the 20- to 29-year-old age group it has almost disappeared
and no one under 25 years of age has had kuru for the past
5 years.   The number of adult patients has declined to less
than one-tenth that seen in early years of investigation.
These changes in the pattern of kuru incidence can be explained by the cessation of cannibalism in the late 1950's.   No
child born since cannibalism ceased in his village   has
developed the disease.

Figure 5. [57-NG-VIII-34]
Five women and one girl, all victims of kuru, who were still
ambulatory, assembled in 1957 in the South Fore village of
Pa'iti. The girl shows the spastic strabismus, often transi-
tory, which most children with kuru developed early in the
course of the disease. Every patient required support from
the others in order to stand without the aid of the sticks
they had been asked to discard for the photograph.

Figure 6. [60-287]
Two women with kuru so advanced that they require the use of
one or two sticks for support, but are still able to go to
garden work on their own. Their disease progressed rapidly
to death within less than a year from onset.

Figure 7. [57-563]
The youngest patient with kuru, a boy from Mage village,
North Fore, who self-diagnosed the insidious onset of clumsi-
ness in his gait as kuru at 4 years of age, and died at 5
years of age, several years before his mother developed kuru
herself. His friend helps him stand.

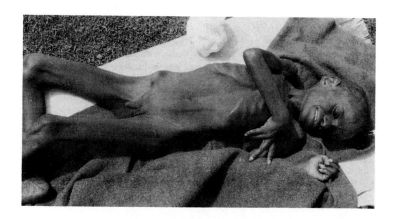

Figure 8. [57-NG-IV-9]
A Fore boy with advanced kuru. He had been sedentary for only two months before reaching the terminal stage of the disease; he was no longer able to speak, but was still alert and intelligent.

Figure 9. [57-306]
Eight preadolescent children, four boys and four girls, with kuru in 1957 at the Kuru Research Hospital in Okapa, New Guinea. All died within 1 year of photography. There have been no such preadolescent child victims of kuru in recent years; no one born since cannibalism ceased in his village in the late 1950s or early 1960s has died of kuru.

Figure 10.
Chimpanzee with a vacant facial expression and a drooping
lower lip, a very early sign of kuru preceding any "hard"
neurological signs. Most animals show this sign for weeks or
even months before further symptoms of kuru are detectable,
other than subtle changes in personality. Three successive
views of the face with early kuru drawn from cinema frames.
The face of a normal chimpanzee is drawn in three views
below, from successive cinema frames.

Figure 11.
Chimpanzee with early experimentally induced kuru eating from
floor without use of prehension. This "vacuum cleaner" form
of feeding was a frequent sign in early disease in the chimpanzee when tremor and ataxia were already apparent.

Figure 12.
Kuru transmission experiments in chimpanzees, illustrating
the early extensive use of this rare and diminishing species
and significant curtailment of chimpanzee inoculations after
the fourth chimpanzee passage. It was at this time that we
discovered that New World monkeys could be used in lieu of
the chimpanzee, although the incubation periods were considerably longer. The experiments indicate failure of the agent
to pass a 100 nm or smaller filter. They also show the failure of a conventional virus neutralization test, using only
10 infectious doses of kuru virus, to neutralize the virus
with serums from patients with kuru or from chimpanzees with
experimental kuru or antiserums made by immunizing rabbits
with kuru-infected chimpanzee brain. In these experiments,
kidney, spleen, and lymph nodes have not yielded virus, and,
although chimpanzee brain has had a titer above 10^{-6} by
intracerebral inoculation, at 10^{-5} dilutions such brain suspensions inoculated by peripheral routes have not produced
disease. In the third passage (on the left), liver, spleen,
and kidney given intracerebrally presumably caused disease
since 100 nm filtrates of infectious brain have regularly
failed to produce the disease; the affected third passage
animal had received both inocula.

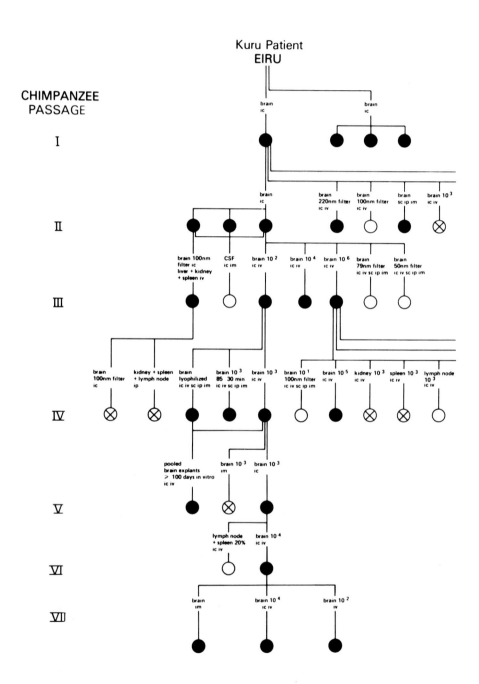

Figure 12

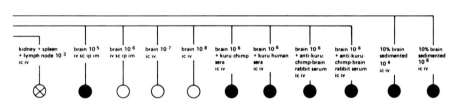

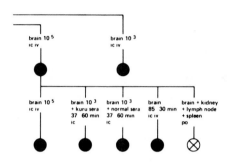

Figure 13.
All cooking, including that of human flesh from diseased
kinsmen, was done in pits with steam made by pouring water
over the hot stones, or cooked in bamboo cylinders in the hot
ashes. Children participated in both the butchery and the
handling of cooked meat, rubbing their soiled hands in their
armpits or hair, and elsewhere on their bodies. They rarely
or never washed.   Infection with the kuru virus was most
probably through cuts and abrasions of the skin, or from nose-
picking, eye rubbing, or mucosal injury.   Here, in a pig
feast, the children help themselves with officiating men; in
a cannibalism of a kuru victim, women would officiate, surrounded by participating children.

Figure 14. (a & b) Boys of prepubertal age were removed from the
women's houses to enter the *wa'e*, men's house, after elaborate first-
stage initiation ceremonies. Thereafter, and for the rest of their
lives, they would live, eat, and sleep separately from the women.
Married men did not share the houses of their wives, and sexual activity was restricted to daylight in the secluded privacy of the gardens. Three Fore boys are shown in the first stage of inititiation
during their ceremonial adornment, after having been held in seclu-
sion for several days and having their nasal septa pierced. (a)
Bark strips are braided in their hair. (b) Bands of shells of high
value to the Fore are fastened to their foreheads. (c) Youthful Awa
toxophilite, already a warrior. (d) Young Awa warriors in their
boys' house.

Figure 14 c & d.

IX . TRANSMISSIBLE VIRUS DEMENTIAS
(CREUTZFELDT-JAKOB DISEASE)

Creutzfeldt-Jakob disease (CJD) is a rare, usually sporadic, presenile dementia found worldwide; it has a familial
pattern of inheritance,usually suggestive of autosomal dominant determinations in about 10 percent of the cases (Fig.
15). The typical clinical picture includes rapidly progressive global dementia, myoclonus, and marked progressive motor
dysfunction, and paroxysmal burst of high-voltage slow waves
on electroencephalography (EEG). The disease is usually fatal
in less than one year, often within a few months of onset.
The disease is regularly transmissible to chimpanzees, New
and Old World monkeys, and some, but not all strains, are
transmissible to the domestic cat, the guinea pig, and the
laboratory mouse. Pathology in these animals is indistinguishable at the cellular level from that in the natural
disease or in experimental kuru. Human brain tissue inoculated at high dilution into goats produces a disease indistinguishable from scrapie. It does not do so in sheep.
Since the host range and incubation periods of different
isolates of the CJD virus vary greatly,many different strains
are now available in the laboratory. Strains with similar
biological properties may help in identifying common source
infections (Figs. 16-19).
    As we have attempted to define the range of illness
caused by the CJD virus, a wide range of clinical syndromes
involving dementia in middle and late life have been shown to
be such slow virus infections associated with neuronal vacuolation or status spongiosus of gray matter and a reactive
astrogliosis. Patients with CJD proven by virus isolation
have also had simultaneous and autopsy verified diagnosis of
brain tumors (glioblastoma, meningioma), brain abcess, Alzheimer's disease, progressive supranuclear palsy, senile dementia, or stroke, or Köhlmeier-Degos syndrome. Hence, the
urgent practical problem is to delineate the whole spectrum
of subacute and chronic neurological illnesses that are
caused by or associated with this established slow virus
infection. Some 14 percent of the cases show amyloid plaques
akin to those found in kuru, and many show changes similar to
those of Alzheimer's disease, in addition to the status
spongiosus and astrogliosis of CJD, and other cases also
involve another neurological disease as well as CJD. We have
started to refer to this transmissible disorder as transmissible virus dementias (TVD) (40, 63).
    Since our first transmission of CJD, we have obtained
brain biopsy or early postmortem brain tissue on over 500
cases of pathologically confirmed CJD; from 218 of these the
virus has been transmitted to laboratory primates. We have

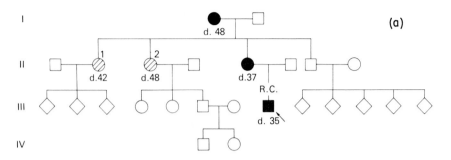

Figure 15.
Subacute spongiform virus encephalopathy has been transmitted
to chimpanzees or New World monkeys from eight patients with
transmissible virus dementias of a familial type. Ten percent of CJD patients have a history of similar disease in
kinsmen.
(a) Genealogical chart shows a family with five cases of CJD
over three generations, suggesting autosomal dominant inheritance. From patient R.C., the disease has been transmitted
to a chimpanzee. Solid, CJD confirmed pathologically; hatched, probable CJD; arrow, transmitted to chimpanzee from brain
tissue inoculated intracerebrally.
(b) This family has five cases of CJD over three generations,
again suggesting autosomal dominant inheritance. From the
brain tissue of patient H.T., obtained at autopsy, the disease has been transmitted to two monkeys.
(c) This family has eleven members suffering from CJD-like
disease in three generations. From the brain tissue of
patient J.W., obtained at autopsy, the disease has been
transmitted to a squirrel monkey.

B FAMILY

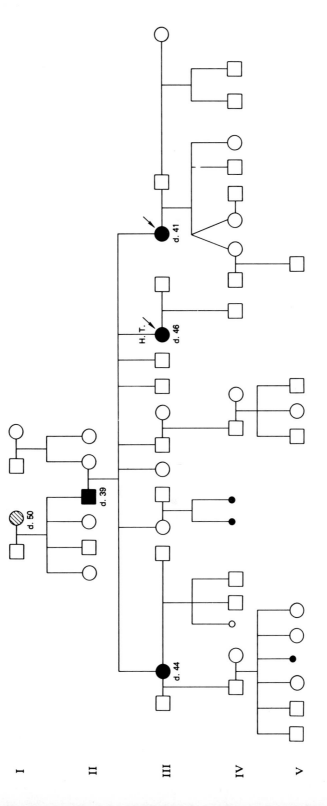

Figure 15b.

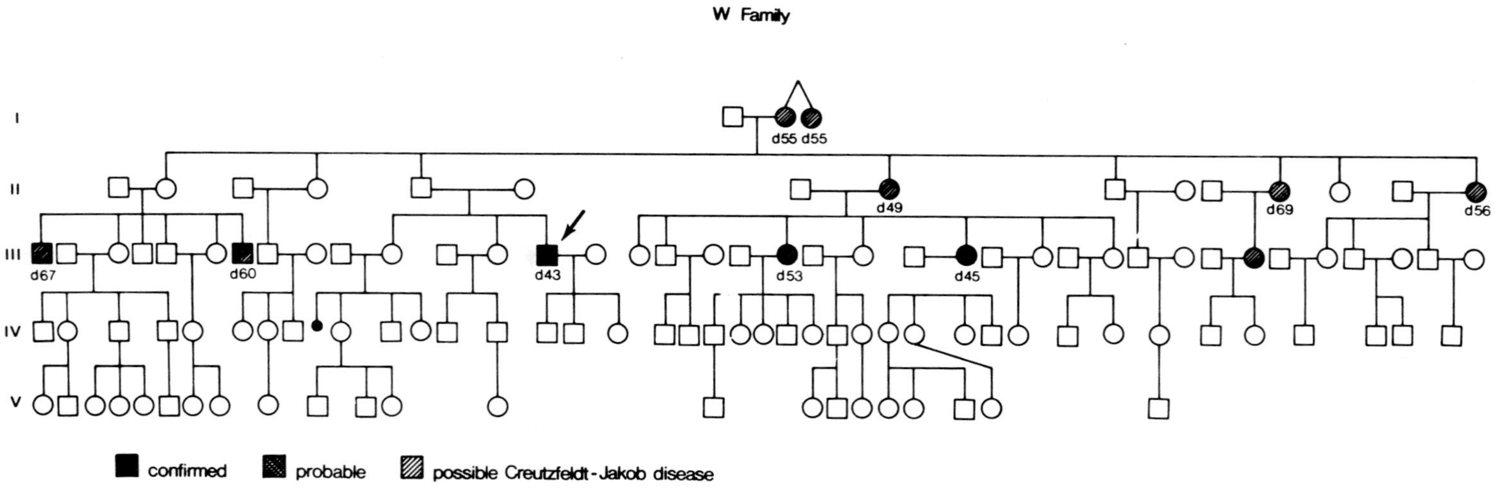
W Family
I
II
III
IV
V
d55 d55
d49
d69
d56
d67
d60
d43
d53
d45
confirmed
probable
possible Creutzfeldt-Jakob disease

Figure 15 c.

clinical records on more than 1,500 cases. We have been aware of occasional temporal and spacial clustering of non-familial cases in small population centers in Israel (35), Czechoslovakia (44,45), Hungary (44), England (43,64), Chile (27), Italy (15a) and the U.S. This geographic and temporal clustering does not apply,however, to a majority of cases, and is unexplained by the 10 percent of the cases that are familial. There are two reports of conjugal disease in which husband and wife died of CJD within a few years of each other.

The prevalence of CJD has varied markedly in time and place throughout the United States and Europe, but we have noted a trend toward making the diagnosis more frequently in many neurological clinics in recent years, since attention has been drawn to the syndrome by its transmission to primates and accidental transmission to man by surgery. For many large population centers of the United States, South America, Europe, Australia, and Asia, we have found a prevalence approaching 1 per million, with an annual incidence and a mortality of about the same magnitude, as the average duration of the disease is 8 to 12 months. An annual incidence of at least 1 per million applies to Australia, France (11), Switzerland, England (43,64), Sweden, Finland, Italy, Israel (35), Chile (27), Japan, United States and many other countries in recent years. Kahana *et al* reported the annual incidence of CJD ranging from 0.4 to 1.9 per million in various ethnic groups in Israel (35). They noted, however, a 30-fold higher incidence of CJD in Jews of Libyan origin compared to the incidence in Jews of European origin. We have further demonstrated that in familial cases a single autosomal-dominant gene pattern of occurrence is indeed true in spite of the fact the disease is caused by a virus. This is the first example in man of an autosomal-dominant single-gene inheritance controlling the appearance of an infectious disease (40-42,63) (Fig. 16).

Probable man-to-man transmission of CJD has occurred in a recipient of a corneal graft, which was taken from a donor who was diagnosed retrospectively to have had pathologically confirmed CJD. The disease occurred 18 months after the transplant, an incubation period just the average for chimpanzees inoculated with human CJD brain tissue. From suspension of brain of the corneal graft recipient we succeeded in transmitting CJD to a chimpanzee although the brain had been at room temperature in 10 percent formol-saline for 7 months. More recently we learned that two of our confirmed cases of TVD were professional blood donors until shortly before the onset of their symptoms. To date, however, there have been no transmission of CJD linked to blood transfusions. We have transfused three chimpanzees, each with more than 300 ml of human whole blood from a different CJD patient, and they have

remained well for over six years. Finally, the recognition
of TVD in a neurosurgeon, and more recently in two physicians
and in a dentist and two of his patients (64), has raised the
question of possible occupational infection, particularly in
those exposed to infected human tissue during surgery, or at
postmortem examination.

The unexpectedly high incidence of previous craniotomy
in CJD patients noted first by Nevin *et al.*, then more recently by Matthews and by ourselves (40,43, 64), raises the possibility of brain sugery either affording a mode of entry for
the agent or of precipitating the disease in patients already
carrying a latent infection. The former unwelcome possibility has become a reality with the transmission of CJD to two
young patients with epilepsy who were recipients of implanted
silver electrodes sterilized with 70 percent ethanol and
formaldehyde vapor after these electrodes had been used on a
patient who had CJD. The patients had undergone such elect-
rode implantation for stereotactic electroencephalographic
localization of the epileptic foci at the time of correction-
al neurosurgery. The same electrodes, sterilized yet another
time in formaldehyde vapor, were implanted in a chimpanzee
which has developed CJD (19).

Sporadic Alzheimer's disease is not transmissible to
subhuman primates. More than 30 specimens of brain tissue
from nonfamilial Alzheimer's disease have been inoculated
into TVD-susceptible primates without producing disease. Our
transmission of spongiform encephalopathy to chimpanzees from
two cases of the familial form of Alzheimer's disease has not
been reproducible and many further attempts to transmit
familial Alzheimer's disease have been negative (10,31).

The enormous resistance to usual decontamination procedures of the unconventional virus causing kuru and CJD of man
and scrapie in animals has resulted in altered procedures in
all autopsy rooms, surgical theaters and clinics.

The problem this resistance to inactivation may cause
has reached enormous proportions with respect to the hepatitis

---

Figure 16.
Worldwide distribution of Creutzfeldt-Jakob disease (CJD).
Countries reporting CJD are identified. For some countries
such as the Malagasy Republic (Madagascar), Algeria, Libya,
Tunisia, Indonesia, China and the eastern U.S.S.R. cases have
been reported to our laboratory, but not published. Mortality
figures usually reach one death per million population; these
have everywhere risen toward 1.0 with increased awareness and
willingness to make the diagnosis in the medical profession.
In foci of high incidence (viz. Slovakia, Chile, and Libyan
Jews in Israel), mortality rates have been considerably higher.

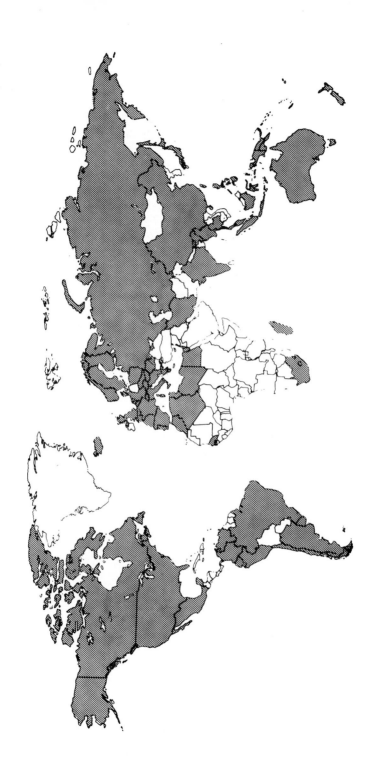

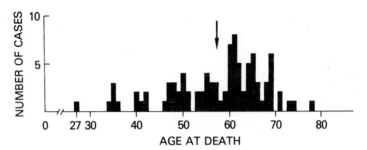

Figure 17.
Frequency distribution of age of death of 94 patients with
transmissible CJD.The mean age at death was 57 years (arrow).

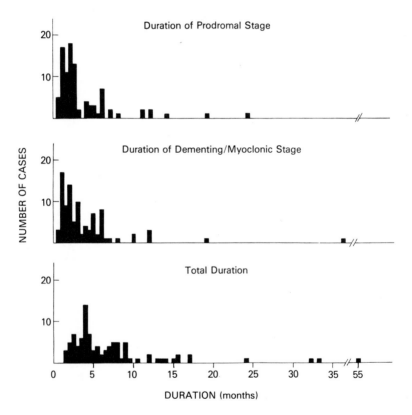

Figure 18
Duration of illness in 94 patients with transmissible CJD.
The mean durations of the prodromal stage was 3.5 months (3.9 SD;
range, 0.5 to 24.0), the mean duration of the dementing/myoclonic
stage was 3.9 months (4.6 SD; range, 0.5 to 36.0); and the mean
total duration was 7.3 months (7.5 DS; range, 1.5 to 55.0).

B vaccine prepared from the hepatitis antigen in serum of human volunteers; some of these volunteers may be incubating the Creutzfeldt-Jakob dementia syndrome. Once this has been suggested, it is apparent that there is no assay procedure sufficient to declare the vaccine safe. Even a chimpanzee assay would require decades and still be uncertain, as shown by our newer work on variation in host range of human strains of CJD. Our work with primates suggests that peripheral routes of inoculation may give irregular "takes" but would be expected to have long incubation periods of perhaps one or more decades. The infectious nature of scrapie was rediscovered in the 1930s in England by an enormous vaccine accident in which formalized louping-ill virus vaccine made using scrapie infected sheep brain caused scrapie infection in 18,000 British sheep in herds formerly unaffected by scrapie. The moral, ethical and legal aspects of continuing to use the hepatitis B vaccine once this problem has been raised and appreciated are enormous. A clonal hepatitis B vaccine should be sought.

X.   SCRAPIE

Scrapie is a natural disease of sheep, and occasionally of goats, and has widespread distribution in Europe, America, and Asia. Affected animals show progressive ataxia, wasting,

---

Figure 19.
Six serial passages of CJD in chimpanzees starting with brain tissue from a biopsy of patient R.R. with CJD in the United Kingdom. Also shown is transmission of the disease directly from man to the capuchin monkey and marmoset, and from chimpanzee brain to three species of New World monkeys (squirrel, capuchin, and spider monkeys), and to six Old World species (rhesus, stump-tailed, cynomolgus, African green, pig-tailed macaque, and sooty mangabey). Incubation periods in the New World monkeys ranged from 19 to 47 months, and in the Old World monkeys from 43 to 60 months. The pig-tailed macaque and the sooty managabey showed positive CJD pathology when killed without clinical disease. A third passage to the chimpanzee was accomplished with the use of frozen and thawed explanted tissue culture of brain cells that had been growing *in vitro* for 36 days. The fourth, fifth and sixth chimpanzee passages were done using 10^{-3}, 10^{-4}, and 10^{-4} dilutions of brain, respectively. This indicates that the chimpanzee brain contains greater than or equal to 5×10^5 infectious doses per gram, and that such infectivity is maintained in brain cells cultivated *in vitro* at 37°C for at least 1 month. The lower left shows transmission of CJD from a second human patient (J.T.) to a cat, with a 30-month incubation period, and subsequent serial passage in the cat with 19- to 24-month incubation.

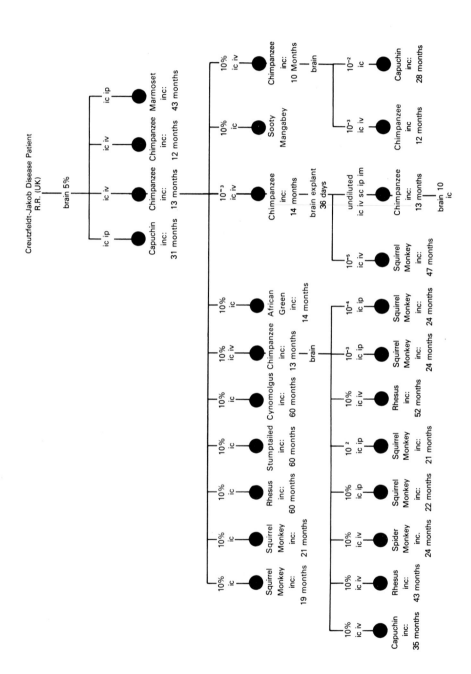

Creutzfeldt-Jakob Disease Patient
R.R. (UK)

brain 5%

ic ip	ic iv	ic iv	ic ip

Capuchin inc: 31 months

Chimpanzee inc: 13 months

Chimpanzee inc: 12 months

Marmoset inc: 43 months

10% ic — Squirrel Monkey inc: 19 months

10% ic — Squirrel Monkey inc: 21 months

10% ic — Rhesus inc: 60 months

10% ic — Stumptailed inc: 60 months

10% ic — Cynomolgus inc: 60 months

10% ic iv — Chimpanzee inc: 13 months

10% ic — African Green inc: 14 months

10^{-3} ic iv — Chimpanzee inc: 14 months

10% ic — Sooty Mangabey inc:

10% ic iv — Chimpanzee inc: 10 Months

brain explant 36 days

undiluted ic iv sc ip im

brain

brain 10 ic

10% ic iv — Capuchin inc: 35 months

10% ic iv — Rhesus inc: 43 months

10% ic iv — Spider Monkey inc: 24 months

10% ic ip — Squirrel Monkey inc: 22 months

10^2 ic ip — Squirrel Monkey inc: 21 months

10% ic iv — Rhesus inc: 52 months

10^{-3} ic ip — Squirrel Monkey inc: 24 months

10^{-4} ic ip — Squirrel Monkey inc: 24 months

10^{-5} ic iv — Squirrel Monkey inc: 47 months

Chimpanzee inc: 13 months

10^{-3} ic iv — Chimpanzee inc 12 months

10^{-2} ic — Capuchin inc: 28 months

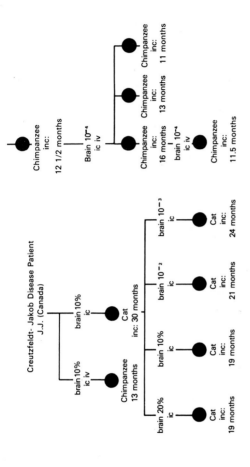

Figure 19

523

and frequently severe pruritis. The clinical picture and
histopathological findings of scrapie closely resemble those
of kuru; this permitted Hadlow to suggest that both diseases
might have similar etiologies. As early as 1936, Cuillé and
Chelle had transmitted scrapie to the sheep, and its filterable nature and other virus-like properties had been demonstrated four decades ago (12). Much more virological information
is available about the mouse- and hamster-adapted strains of
scrapie virus than about the viruses that cause the human
diseases (24).

Although scrapie has been studied longer and more in-
tensely than the other diseases, the mechanism of its spread
in nature remains uncertain. It may spread from naturally
infected sheep to uninfected sheep and goats, although such
lateral transmission has not been observed from experimentally infected sheep or goats. Both sheep and goats, as well
as mice, have been experimentally infected by the oral route.
It appears to pass from ewes to lambs, even without suckling;
the contact of the lamb with the infected ewe at birth appears to be sufficient; the placenta itself is infectious
(52). Transplacental versus oral, nasal, optic, or cutaneous
infection in the perinatal period are unresolved possibilities. Older sheep are infected only after long contact with
diseased animals; however, susceptible sheep have developed
the disease in pastures previously occupied by scrapie sheep.

Field studies and experimental work indicate genetic
control of disease occurrence in sheep. In mice, there is
genetic control of length of incubation period and of the
anatomic distribution of lesions, which is also dependent on
the strain of scrapie agent used. Scrapie has been transmitted in our laboratory to five species of monkeys, and such
transmission has occurred with the use of infected brain from
naturally infected sheep and from experimentally infected
goats and mice (Fig. 20.). The disease produced is clinically and pathologically indistinguishable from experimental
CJD in these species (Fig. 21).

Figure 20.
Scrapie has been transmitted to three species of New World monkeys
and two species of Old World monkeys. (a) Transmission of scrapie
from the brain of a scrapie-infected Suffolk ewe (C506) in Illinois
to a cynomolgus monkey, and from the fourth mouse passage of this
strain of scrapie virus to two squirrel monkeys and a spider
monkey. The incubation period in the cynomolgus was 73 months,
in the squirrel monkeys it was 31 and 33 months, and in the
spider monkey it was 74 months. A chimpanzee inoculated over
200 months ago with this sheep brain remains well. The rhesus
monkey inoculated with this sheep brain died of intercurrent
infection at 187 months after inoculation and showed no brain
pathology.

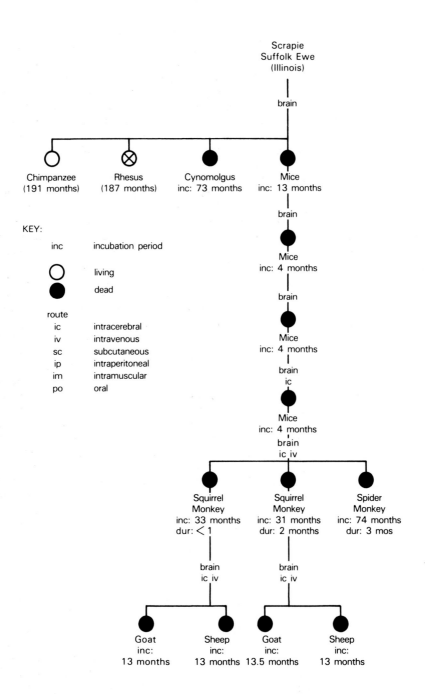

TRANSMISSION OF GOAT-ADAPTED AND MOUSE-ADAPTED SCRAPIE (COMPTON STRAIN) TO NON-HUMAN PRIMATES

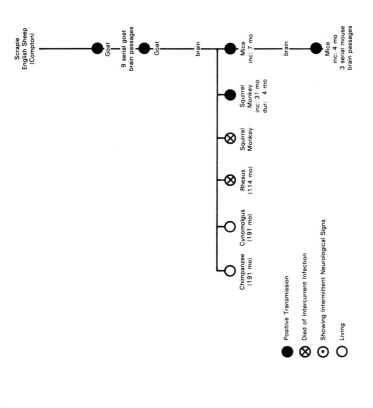

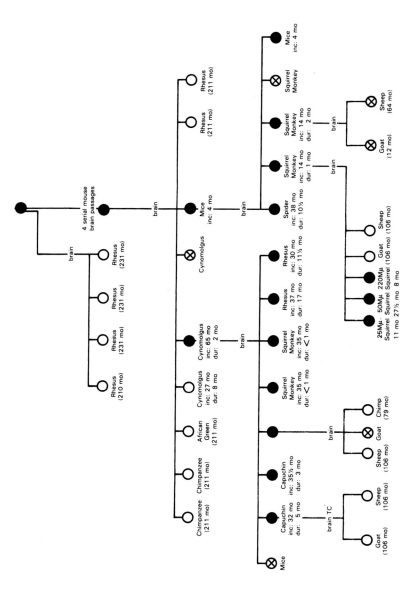

Figure 20(b). Primary transmission of goat-adapted scrapie (Compton, England strain) to the squirrel monkey and to mice and the transmission of mouse-adapted scrapie to two species of Old World and three species of New World monkeys. Numbers in parentheses are the number of months elapsed since inoculation, during which the animals remained asymptomatic.

527

TRANSMISSION OF MOUSE-ADAPTED SHEEP SCRAPIE
(U.S. STRAIN 434-3-897) TO A SQUIRREL MONKEY

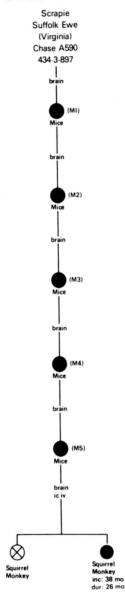

Figure 20(c).

Transmission of mouse-adapted sheep scrapie (U.S. strain 434-3-897) to a squirrel monkey 38 months following intra-cerebral inoculation with a suspension of scrapie-infected mouse brain containing $10^{7.3}$ infectious units of virus per ml. This animal showed signs of ataxia, tremors and incoordination, and the disease was confirmed histologically.

XI. TRANSMISSIBLE MINK ENCEPHALOPATHY

Transmissible mink encephalopathy (TME) is very similar to scrapie both in clinical picture and in pathological lesions. On the ranches on which the disease developed, the carcasses of scrapie-infected sheep had been fed to the mink; presumably the disease is scrapie. The disease is indistinguishable from that induced in mink by inoculation of sheep or mouse scrapie. Like scrapie, TME has been transmitted by the oral route, but transplacental or perinatal transmission from the mother does not occur. Physicochemical study of the virus has thus far revealed no differences between TME and scrapie viruses (24).

The disease has been transmitted to the squirrel, rhesus, and stump-tailed monkey, and to many nonprimate hosts, including the sheep, goat,and ferret, but it will not transmit to mice. In monkeys the illness is indistinguishable from experimental CJD in these species.

XII. TRANSMISSIBLE SPONGIFORM ENCEPHALOPATHY OF MULE DEER AND ELK

In 1978 a chronic wasting disease was noted in the captive mule deer herd at Fort Collins, Colorado, and the clinical picture and neuropathology closely resembled the subacute spongiform encephalopathy of scrapie in sheep or goats (65). This disease has been experimentally transmitted to other mule deer (67). Bahmanyar has demonstrated that amyloid plaques are developed in most of the affected mule deer. Now a similar chronic wasting disease with a subacute spongiform encephalopathy is occurring in the adjacent herd of captive elk (66).

XIII.   ORIGIN AND SPREAD OF KURU

Unanswered crucial questions posed by all of these agents are related to their biological origin and mode of survival in nature. The diseases they evoke are not artificial diseases, produced by researchers tampering with cellular macromolecular structures, as some would have it. They are naturally occurring diseases, for none of which do we know the mode of dissemination or maintenance which is adequate to explain their long-term persistence. For kuru we have a full explanation of the unique epidemiological findings and their change over the past two decades: the contamination of close kinsmen withina mourning family group by the opening of the skull of dead victims in a rite of cannibalism, during which all girls, women, babes-in-arms, and toddlers of kuru vic-

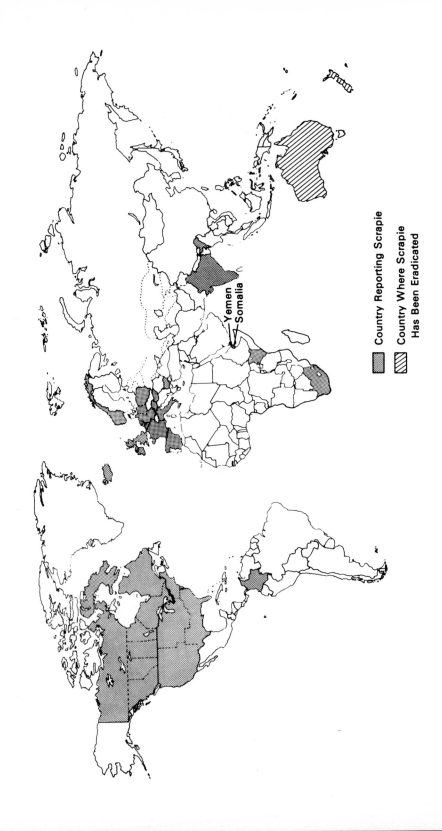

Yemen
Somalia

Country Reporting Scrapie

Country Where Scrapie
Has Been Eradicated

tim's family were thoroughly contaminated with the virus.
The disease is gradually disappearing with the cessation of
cannibalism and has already disappeared in children, adolescents, and young adults with progressively increasing age of
the youngest victims. However, this does not provide us with
a satisfactory explanation for the origin of kuru. Was it
the unlikely event of a sporadic case of worldwide CJD, which
in the usual cultural setting of New Guinea produced a unique
epidemic? A spontaneous case of CJD has been seen in a native 26-year-old Chimbu New Guinean f om the Central Highlands, whose clinical diagnosis was proved by light- and
electronmicroscopy of a brain biopsy specimen. Serial passage of brain in man in successive cannibalistic rituals
might have resulted in a change in the clinical picture of
the disease, with modification of the virulence of the original agent.

If such spontaneous CJD is not responsible for the origin of kuru, another possibility might be that the serial
brain passage of some other well-known viruses, which occurred by inoculation of brain from successive kuru victims in
multiple sequential passages into kinsmen has yielded a new
neurotropic strain. Finally, in view of what occurs in the
defective replication of measles virus in patients with
subacute sclerosing panencephalitis (SSPE), we may conjecture
that an ubiquitous or, at least, a well known virus may have
been modified into a defective, incomplete, or highly integrated or repressed agent *in vivo* in the course of its long-
masked state in the individual host. Such a new breed of
virus may no longer be easily recognizable either antigenically or structurally, because of failure of full synthesis
of viral subunits or of their assembly into a known virion.
Therefore, we may ask if kuru does not contain some of the
subunits of a known agent, modified by its unusual passage
history.

Figure 21.
Worldwide distribution of scrapie in sheep (based on data
supplied by Drs. J. Hourrigan and A. Klingsporn of the United
States Department of Agriculture). Although scrapie has not
been officially reported in the USSR, an outbreak of mink
encephalopathy occurred in Finland and the infecting material
was traced to the USSR (J. Hourrigan, personal communication,
1978). Scrapie has not been reported in the Middle East.

XIV. CONJECTURAL NATURAL HISTORY OF CJD, KURU, SCRAPIE,
TME, AND CHRONIC WASTING DISEASE
OF CAPTIVE MULE DEER AND ELK

Scrapie has now been found to cause a disease clinically and neuropathologically indistinguishable from experimental CJD in three species of New World and two species of Old World monkeys. This disease occurs after either intracerebral or peripheral routes of inoculation. Natural sheep scrapie strains, as well as experimental goat and mouse scrapie strains, have caused disease in the monkeys. The Compton strain of scrapie virus, as a result of such passage through primates, develops an altered host range, for it no longer produces disease in inoculated mice, sheep, and goats. A similar situation has been noted to prevail when scrapie is produced in ferrets or mink; the mink or ferret brain virus is no longer pathogenic for mice. This is also true for the virus of natural mink encephalopathy, which, presumably, had its origin in the feeding of scrapie sheep carcasses to mink on commercial mink farms.

CJD or kuru viruses may produce, after asymptomatic incubation for more than 2 years, an acute central nervous system disease in the squirrel monkey, with death in a few days; even sudden death without previously noted clinical disease has been seen. The same strains of kuru or CJD viruses produce chronic clinical disease in the spider monkey, closely mimicking the human disease, after incubation periods of 2 years or more. The time sequence of disease progression also mimics that in man, ranging from several months to more than a year until death. A single strain of kuru or CJD virus may cause severe status spongiosus lesions in many brain areas, particularly the cerebral cortex in chimpanzees and spider monkeys with minimal or no involvement of the brainstem or spinal cord, whereas in the squirrel monkey this same virus strain may cause extensive brainstem and cord lesions. Both kuru and CJD viruses cause scrapie-like disease in goats, but not in sheep.

From the above findings, it is clear that neither incubation periods nor host range, nor the distribution or severity of neuropathological lesions can be interpreted as having any significance toward unraveling the possible relationships of the four viruses causing the subacute spongiform virus encephalopathies.

As was mentioned earlier, we have found that the prevalence of CJD in the United States and abroad appears to be about 1 per million whenever extensive neurological survey for cases is instituted. In a study in Israel, an overall prevalence in Jews of Libyan origin is 30 times as high as in

Jews of European origin. The custom of eating the eyeballs
and brains of sheep in the Jewish households of North African
and Middle Eastern origin, as opposed to Jewish households of
European origin, has understandably given rise to the conjecture that scrapie-infected sheep tissue might be the source
of such CJD infection. Sheep heads are eaten widely by many
ethnic groups in the United States and abroad.

Figure 22 presents a conjectural schematic natural history of the subacute spongiform virus encephalopathies in
which the hypothetical origin of CJD, kuru, and TME and
chronic wasting disease of captive mule deer and elk from
natural scrapie in sheep is proposed with possible routes of
transmission indicated. However, such games of armchair
speculation provide schemata that cannot yet be tested. They
may, nevertheless, have heuristic value. In the absence, as
yet, of proven antigenicity or identified infectious nucleic
acid in the agents, neither serological specificity nor nucleic acid homology can be used to answer the compelling
question of the relation between the viruses of kuru, TVD,
scrapie, and TME, and chronic wasting disease of captive mule
deer and elk.

The possibility that the viruses of all six of the
subacute spongiform virus encephalopathies are not just
closely related agents, but different strains of a single
virus that have been modified in different hosts, is easily
entertained. The passage of sheep scrapie into other sheep
and into goats, at least by the route of feeding of material
contaminated with placenta and embryonic membrane, and into
mink from feeding carcasses of scrapied sheep, are established
paths of scrapie transmission. The transmissible spongiform
encephalopathies of captive mule deer and elk may well have
originated from scrapie contamination of pasturage. In view
of the experimental transmission of scrapie to monkeys, and
of CJD and kuru to goats to produce a scrapie-like disease,
there is serious cause for wonder whether kitchen and butchery
accidents involving the contamination of skin and eyes may
not be a possible source of CJD in man. We believe that
contamination during the cannibalistic ritual was the sole
source of transmission of kuru from man to man and have
conjectured above that a spontaneous case of CJD may have
given rise to the chain of kuru transmissions. The documented
case of CJD from corneal transplant suggests that other tissue
transplantation may also be a source of infection. It is
known that the virus is present in peripheral tissue, as well
as in the brain. The case of CJD in a neurosurgeon who had
frequently performed autopsies poses a possibility of occupational hazard to the neurosurgeon and neuropathologist;
two other physicians and several dentists are known to have

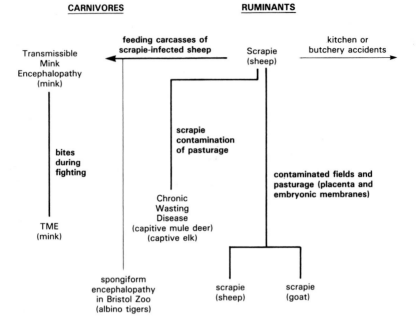

Established or probable routes are indicated in **bold face**

Figure 22.
Conjectural natural history of the subacute spongiform virus encephalopathies. Hypothetical origin of Creutzfeldt–Jakob disease (CJD), kuru, and transmissible mink encephalopathy (TME) and chronic wasting disease of captive mule deer and elk (CWD) from natural scrapie of sheep. The spongiform encephalopathy in albino tigers in the Bristol zoo has not been experimentally transmitted.

HUMANS

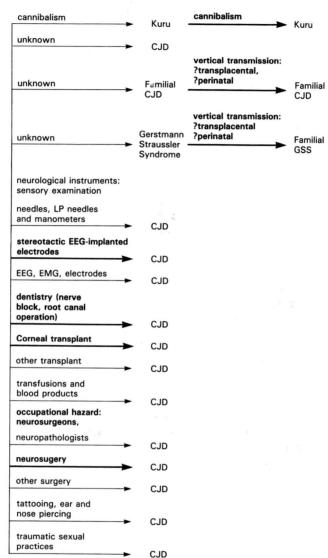

died of CJD.   Finally, the rather frequent report of neurosurgery or other surgery preceding the appearance of CJD, as
noted by us and by other workers, may indicate that such
surgery has been a source of infection, rather than a virus
activating incident.   This seems to be a real hazard in view
of the episode of transmission of CJD to two patients from
the use of CJD-contaminated electrodes in stereotactic electroencephalography (EEG) during surgery for epilepsy.   The
use of formaldehyde for their sterilization was, in view of
the resistance of the unconventional viruses to it, a very
unfortunate choice.   The appearance of CJD in a dentist and
in two of his patients suggest dentistry as a possible mode
of transmission;   scrapie virus has been isolated from the
dental nerves of experimentally infected animals.   The mode
of transmission, which at first sight would appear to be
vertical in the cases of familial CJD, remains unknown.
Whether infection is transovarian or occurs in utero or during parturation, or from a milk factor or some other neonatal
infection, also remains unknown, although from kuru epidemiological study (that is, failure to see kuru in children
born to kuru-infected mothers since the cessation of cannibalism), we have no evidence for such transmission.

PROSPECT

The elucidation of the etiology and epidemiology of
a rare, exotic disease restricted to a small population
isolate--kuru in New Guinea--has brought us to worldwide
considerations that have importance for all of medicine and
microbiology.   For neurology, specifically, we have considerable new insights into the whole range of presenile dementias
and, in particular, to the large problems of Alzheimer's
disease and the senile dementias.   The implications of vertical transmission of slow virus infections, and of host genetic control of disease expression for all genetic diseases,
and the relationship of these slow virus infectious processes
to those which may lead to neoplastic transformation, are
obvious.
However, the major problems among the degenerative dis-
eases--multiple sclerosis, Alzheimer's disease or senile dementia of the Alzheimer type, and parkinsonism, polymyositis,
schizophrenia and autism--remain etiologically unsolved although there are tantalizing laboratory and epidemiological
data pointing to the possible role of virus-like agents in
these diseases.   Perhaps the masked and defective slow infections with conventional viruses, such as are seen in PLM and
SSPE, may provide the best leads for studying these diseases.
The foci of high incidence of amyotrophic lateral scler-

osis with associated high incidence of parkinsonism–dementia complex and early appearance of neurofibrillary tangles in the normal population among the Chamorro people on Guam and the Japanese of the Kii Peninsula remain continuing challenges. Our discovery and reevaluation of the very small but very intense focus of such motor neuron disease with associated high incidence of parkinsonism, parkinsonism–dementia, and other peculiar bradykinetic and myoclonic dementia syndromes among the Auyu and Jakai people in a remote population of West New Guinea suggest strongly that some common etiological environmental factor may underlie the occurrence of all of these very different syndromes, as they occur strangely in these small isolated populations and are not found in the much larger surrounding populations of the same peoples (16,18,20). Here, techniques of slow virus investigation, including the use of *in situ* DNA hybridization using radioactive probes made from copies of the RNA of suspected known viruses have indicated that slow virus infection is unlikely. We now have evidence indicating that disordered mineral metabolism caused by secondary hyperparathyroidism in response to environmental calcium and magnesium deficiencies has resulted in hydroxyapatite depositions of calcium and aluminum and other metals in neurons early in life, which lead to neurofibrillary tangle formation and the spectrum of chronic neurodegenerative disease in high incidences in these populations (28, 53). The ultimate pathophysiological mechanism behind these diverse phenomena may be interference with axonal flow in the transport of 10 nm filament proteins down the axon. A similar mechanism may underlie neuron damage by a slow virus, a toxin such as IDPN or aluminum parenterally, or the deposition of hydroxyapatites in neurons in early life.

Furthermore, the production of paired helical filaments of which the neurofibrillary tangles of Alzheimer's disease are composed and also the formation of amyloid plaques may both be aspects of the same basic interference with 10 nm neurofilament transport down the axon. Prusiner's aggregated scrapie associated protein and the scrapie associated fibrils of Merz may be one and the same molecular complex closely related to 10 nm neurolfilament and to amyloid. Thus, interference with normal transport of 10 nm neurofilament may be the basis of pathology in scrapie and CJD and also be the underlying pathogenesis for a vast number of degenerative diseases.

The models of lysogenicity and of subviral genetically active macromolecular structures from the study of bacterial viruses and bacterial genetics and the viroid and virusoid subviral pathogens of plants and the example of filamentous plant viruses and bacteriophage supply ample imaginative

framework for an expression of our ideas of possible mechanisms of infectious pathogenesis in man. The unconventional
viruses tax even our imagination in relation to molecular
biology gained from these studies in bacteria and plant
viruses. For a now-disappearing disease in a small primitive
population to have brought us thus far is ample reason for
pursuing intensively the challenges offered by the still
inexplicable high incidence and peculiar profusion of different neurological syndromes, pathologically distinct yet apparently somehow related to each other, which have been
discovered in the several small population enclaves. We are
also pursuing avidly the causes of other chronic non-neuro-
logical diseases wherever they occur in high incidence in
isolated populations where the high incidence and restricted
environmental and cultural variables increase the likelihood
of successful inquiry.

REFERENCES

1. Bahmanyar, S., Liem, R.K.H., Griffin, J.W. and Gajdusek,
      D.C. (1984) Characterization of antineurofilament
      autoantibodies in Creutzfeldt-Jakob disease. *J.
      Neuro. Exp. Neurology* 43, 369-375.
2. Bahmanyar, S., Moreau-Dubois, M.C., Brown, P., Cathala, F.
      and Gajdusek, D.C. (1983) Serum antibodies to neuro-
      filament antigens in patients with neurological and
      other diseases and in healthy controls.
      J. Neuroimmunology 5,191-196.
3. Beck, E., Daniel, P.M., Alpers, M., Gajdusek, C.C., Gibbs,
      C.J., Jr. and Hasser, R. (1975) Experimental kuru
      in the spider monkey. Histopathological and ultra-
      structural studies of the brain during early states
      of incubation *Brain 98,* 592-620.
4. Beck, E., Daniel, P.M., Davey, A., Gajdusek, D.C. and
      Gibbs, C.J., Jr. (1982) The pathogenesis of spongi-
      form encephalopathies: an ultrastructural study.
      Brain 104, 755-786.
5. Borras, M.T., Kingbury, T.T., Gajdusek, D.C. and Gibbs,
      C.J., Jr. (1982). Inability to transmit scrapie by
      transfection of mouse embryo cells in vitro. *J.gen.
      Virology 58,* 263-271.
6. Borras, T. and Gibbs, C.J., Jr. Molecular hybridization
      studies of scrapie brain nucleic acids: I. Search
      for specific DNA sequences. *Virology, submitted.*
7. Brown, P., Gibbs, C.J., Jr., Amyx, H.L., Kingsbury, D.
      T., Rohwer, R.G., Sulima, M.P. and Gajdusek, D.C.
      (1982) Chemical disinfection of Creutzfeldt-Jakob
      disease virus. *New England J. Med. 306,* 1279-1282.

8. Brown, P., Rohwer, R.G. and Gajdusek, D.C. (1984) Sodium
    hydroxide decontamination of Creutzfeldt-Jakob
    disease virus. Letter to the Editor. *New England
    J.Med.* 310, 727.

9. Brown, P., Rohwer, R.G., Green, E.M. and Gajdusek, D.C.
    (1982) Effect of chemicals, heat and histopatholog-
    ical processing on high infectivity hamster-adapted
    scrapie virus. *J. Infectious Diseases 145,* 683-
    687.

10. Brown, P., Salazar, A.M., Gibbs, C.J., Jr. and Gajdusek,
    D.C. (1982) Alzheimer disease and transmissible
    virus dementia (CJD). In "Alzheimer's disease,
    Down's Syndrome, and Aging", F.M. Sinex and C.R.
    Meril, editors. *Annals New York Academy Sciences
    396,* 131-143.

11. Cathala, F., Brown, P., Raharison, S., Chatelain, J.,
    Lecanuet, P., Castaigne, P., Gibbs, C.J., Jr. and
    Gajdusek, D.C. (1982) Maladie de Creutzfeldt-Jakob
    en France: contribution a une recherche épidemio-
    logique. *Revue Neurologique (Paris) 138,* 39-51.

12. Cuillé, J. and Chelle, P.L. (1936) Pathologie animal la
    maladie dite tremblante du mouton est-elle inocua-
    ble? C.R.Acad. Sc.(D) *(Paris) 203,* 552-1554.

13. Diener, T.O. (1979) "Viroids and Viroid Diseases". John
    Wiley and Sons, New York. 252 pp.

14. Diringer, H. Gelderblom, H., Hilmert, H. Ozel, M.,
    Edelbluth, C. and Kimberlin, R.H. (1983) Scrapie
    infectivity, fibrils and low molecular weight pro-
    tein. *Nature (London) 306,* 476-478.

14a. Diringer, H., Hilmert, H., Simon, D., Werner, E. and
    Ehlers, B. (1983) Towards purification of the
    scrapie agent. *Eur. J. Biochem. 134,* 555-560.

15. Farquhar, J. and Gajdusek, D.C., eds. (1980) "Kuru:
    Early Letters and Field Notes from the Collection
    of D. Carleton Gajdusek". Raven Press, New York,
    338 pp.

15a. Fieshi, C., Orzi, F., Pocchiari, M., Nardini, M., Rocchi,
    F., Asher, D.M., Gibbs, C.J., Jr. and Gajdusek,
    D.C. (1983) Creutzfeldt-Jakob disease in the pro-
    vince of Siena: two cases transmitted to monkeys.
    Italian Journal of Neurological Sciences 1, 61-64.

16. Gajdusek, D.C. (1963) Motor-neuron disease in natives of
    New Guinea. *New England J. Med. 268,* 474-476.

17. Gajdusek, D.C. (1973) Kuru in the New Guinea Highlands.
    In: "Tropical Neurology", J.D. Spillane, ed. Oxford
    Press, New York, pp. 376-383.

18. Gajdusek, D.C. (1977) Urgent opportunistic observations:
    the study of changing, transient and disappearing

phenomena of medical interest in disrupted primi-
itive human communities. In: "Health and Disease in
Isolated and Tribal Societies.", J. Whelan, ed.
Ciba Foundation Monograph 49, pp. 69-102.

19. Gajdusek, D.C. (1977) Unconventional viruses and the
origin and disappearance of kuru. *Science 197*,
943-960.

20. Gajdusek, D.C. (1979) A focus of high incidence amyotrophic lateral sclerosis and parkinsonism and
dementia syndromes in a small population of Auyu
and Jakai peoples of southern West New Guinea. In:
"Amyotrophic Lateral Sclerosis", Proceedings of the
International Symposium on Amyotrophic Lateral
Sclerosis Tokyo, February 2-3, 1978, T. Tsubaki,
and Y. Toyokura, eds., University of Tokyo Press,
Tokyo, 287-305.

21. Gajdusek, D.C. (1959-1983) Journals 1954-1983, 34 volumes, published in limited edition. National
Institutes of Health, Bethesda, Maryland.

22. Gajdusek, D.C. and Gibbs, C.J., Jr. (1975) Slow virus
infections of the nervous system and the Laboratories of Slow, Latent and Temperate Virus Infections. In: "The Nervous System", D.B. Tower, ed.
Vol. 2,"The Clinical Neurosciences", T.N. Chase,
ed. Raven Press, New York, pp. 113-135.

23. Gajdusek, D.C. Gibbs, C.J., Jr. and Alpers, M. (1966)
Experimental transmission of a kuru-like syndrome
in chimpanzees. *Nature (London) 209*, 794-796.

24. Gajdusek, D.C., Gibbs, C.J., Jr. and Alpers, M., eds.
(1965) "Slow, Latent and Temperate Virus Infections"
NINDB Monograph No. 2, National Institutes of
Health. PHS Publication No. 1378, U.S. Govt. Print-
ing Office, Washington D.C., 489 pp.

25. Gajdusek, D.C. and Zigas, V. (1957) Degenerative disease
of the central nervous system in New Guinea. The
endemic occurrence of "kuru" in the native population. *New England J. Med. 257*, 974-978.

26. Gajdusek, D.C. and Zigas, V. (1959) Kuru: clinical,
pathological and epidemiological study of an acute
progressive degenerative disease of the central nervous system among natives of the Eastern Highlands
of New Guinea. *Amer. J. Med. 26*, 442-469.

27. Galvez, S. and Cartier, L. (1979) A new familial clustering of Creutzfeldt-Jakob disease in Chile. *Neuro-
cirugía 37*, 58-65.

28. Garruto, R., Fukatsu, R., Yanagihara, R., Gajdusek, D.C.,
Hook, G. and Fiori, C.E. (1984) Imaging of calcium
and aluminum in neurofibrillary tangle-bearing neu-

rons in parkinsonism—dementia of Guam. *Proc. Nat. Acad. Sci. U.S.A. 81,* 1875—1879.

29. Gibbs, C.J., Jr. and Gajdusek, D.C. (1972) Transmission of scrapie to the cynomolgus monkey (macaca fascicularis). *Nature (London) 236,* 73—74.

30. Gibbs, C.J., Jr., Gajdusek, D.C. and Latarjet, R. (1977) Unusual resistance to UV and ionizing radiation of the viruses of kuru, Creutzfeldt-Jakob disease, and scrapie (unconventional viruses). *Proc. Nat. Acad. Sci. U.S.A. 75,* 6268—6270.

31. Goudsmit, J., Morrow, C.H., Asher, D.M., Yanagihara, R.T., Masters, C.L., Gibbs, C.J., Jr. and Gajdusek, D.C. (1980) Evidence for and against the transmissibility of Alzheimer's disease. *Neurology 30,* 945—950.

32. Hadlow, W.J. (1959) Scrapie and kuru. *Lance 2,* 289—290.

33. Haig, D.C., Clarke, M.C., Blum, E. and Alper, T. (1969) Further studies on the inactivation of the scrapie agent by ultraviolet light. *Virology 5,* 455—457.

34. Hunter, G.D., Collis, S.C., Millson, G.C. and Kimberlin, R.H. (1976) Search for scrapie-specific RNA and attempts to detect an infectious DNA or RNA. *J. Gen. Virology 32,* 157—162.

35. Kahana, E., Alter, M., Barham, J. and Sofer, D. (1974) Creutzfeldt-Jakob disease: focus among Libyan Jews of Israel. *Science 183,* 90—91.

36. Kasper, D.C., Sotos, D.P. Bowman, K.A., Panitoh, H. and Prusiner, S. (1982) Immunological studies of scrapie infection. *J. Neuroimmunology 3,* 187—201.

37. Klatzo, I., Gajdusek, D.C. and Zigas, V. (1959) Pathology of kuru. *Laboratory Investigation 8,* 799—847.

37a. Klitzman, R.L., Alpers, M.P. and Gajdusek, D.C. (1984) The natural incubation period and transmission of Kuru in three clusters of patients in Papua, New Guinea *Neuroepidemiology* (in press).

38. Latarjet, R., Muel, B., Haig, D.A., Clarke, M.C. and Alper, T. (1970) Inactivation of the scrapie agent by near-monochromatic ultraviolet light. *Nature (London) 227,* 1341—1343.

39. Latarjet, R. (1979) Inactivation of the agents of scrapie, Creutzfeldt-Jakob disease and kuru by radiation. In "Slow Transmissible Diseases of the Nervous System," Vol. 2, S.B. Prusiner and W.J. Hadlow, eds. Academic Press, New York, pp. 387—407.

40. Masters, C.L., Harris, J.O., Gajdusek, D.C. Gibbs, C.J. Jr., Bernoulli, C. and Asher, D.M. (1979) Creutzfeldt-Jakob disease: patterns of worldwide occur-

rence and the significance of familial and sporadic clustering. *Annals. Neurology 5*, 177-188.

41. Masters, C.L., Gajdusek, D.C. and Gibbs, C.J., Jr. (1981) The familial occurrence of Creutzfeldt-Jakob disease and Alzheimer's disease. *Brain 104*, 535-558

42. Masters, C.L., Gajdusek, D.C. and Gibbs, C.J., Jr. (1981) Creutzfeldt-Jakob disease virus isolations from the Gerstmann-Sträussler syndrome, with an analysis of the various forms of amyloid plaque deposition in the virus-induced spongiform encephalopathies. *Brain 104*, 559-588.

43. Matthews, W.B. (1975) Epidemiology of Creutzfeldt-Jakob disease in England and Wales. *J. Neurology, Neurosurgery and Psychiatry 38*, 210-213.

44. Mayer, V., Orolin, D. and Mitrova, E. (1977) Cluster of Creutzfeldt-Jakob disease and presinile dementia. *Lancet 2*, 256.

45. Mayer, V., Orolin, D., Mitrova, E. and Lehotsky, Y. (1978) Transmissible virus dementia: an unusual space and time clustering of Creutzfeldt-Jakob disease and other organic presenile dementia cases. *Acta Virologica 22*, 146-153.

46. McFarlin, D.E., Raff, M.C., Simpson, E. and Nehisen, S. (1971) Scrapie in immunologically deficient mice. *Nature (London) 233*, 336.

47. Merz, P.A., Rohwer, R.G., Kascsak, R., Wisniewski, H.M., Somerville, R.A., Gibbs, C.J., Jr. and Gajdusek, D.C. (1984) An infection specific particle from the unconventional slow virus diseases. *Science* (in press).

48. Merz, P.A. Rohwer, R.G., Somerville, R.A., Wisniewski, H.M., Gibbs, C.J., Jr. and Gajdusek, D.C. (1983) Scrapie associated fibrils in human Creutzfeldt-Jakob disease. Abstract number 68, Abstracts of the Fifty-ninth Annual Meeting of the American Association of Neuropathologists, St. Louis, June 9-12. *J. Neuropathology and Experimental Neurology 42*, 3 (May), 327.

49. Merz, P.A., Somerville, R.A. and Wisniewski, H.M. (1983) Abnormal fibrils in scrapie and senile dementia of Alzheimer's type. In: Virus Nonconventionnels et Affections du Système Nerveux Central. L.A. Court and F. Cathala, eds. Masson Editeur, Paris, pp. 259-281.

50. Merz, P.A., Somerville, R.A., Wisniewski, H.M. & and Iqbal, K. (1981) Abnormal fibrils from scrapie-infected brain.*Acta Neuropathol. (Berlin) 54*,63-74.

51. Merz, P.A., Somerville, R.A., Wisniewski, H.M., Manuelidis, L. and Manuelidis, E.E. (1983) Scrapid associated fibrils in Creutzfeldt-Jakob disease.

Nature (London) 306, 474-476.

52. Pattison, I.H., Hoare, M.N., Jebbett, J.N. and Watson, W.A. (1972) Spread of scrapie to sheep and goats by oral dosing with fetal membranes from scrapie affected sheep. *Vet. Record 99,* 465-467.

53. Perl, D., Gajdusek, D.C. Garruto, R.M., Yanagihara, R.T. and Gibbs, C.J., Jr. (1982) Intraneuronal aluminum accumulation in amyotrophic lateral sclerosis and parkinsonism-dementia of Guam. *Science 217,* 1053-1055.

54. Prusiner, S.B. (1982) Novel proteinaceous infectious particles cause scrapie. *Science 216,* 136-144.

55. Prusiner, S.B., McKinley, M.P. Bowman, K.A., Bolton, D.C., Bendheim, P.E., Groth, D.F. and Glenner, G.G. (1983) Scrapie prions aggregate to form amyloid-like birefringent rods. *Cell 35,* 349-358.

56. Rohwer, R.G. (1984) Virus-like sensitivity of the scrapie agent to heat inactivation. *Science 223,* 600-602.

57. Rohwer, R.G. (1984) Scrapie infectious agent is virus-like in size and susceptibility to inactivation. *Nature (London) 308,* 658-662.

58. Rohwer, R.G. (1984) Growth Kinetics of hamster scrapie strain 263K: sources of slowness in a slow virus infection. *Virology* (in press).

59. Rohwer, R.G. and Gajdusek, D.C. (1980) Scrapie--virus or viroid: the case for a virus. In "Search for the cause of Multiple Sclerosis and Other Chronic Diseases of the Central Nervous System," Proceedings of the First International Symposium of the Hertie Foundation, Frankfurt am Main, September 1979, A. Boese, ed. Verlag Chemie, Weinheim, pp. 333-355.

60. Sänger, H.L. (1982) Biology, structure, functions, and possible origins of plant viroids. In: "Nucleic Acids and Proteins in Plants," II. Encyclopaedia of Plant Pathology, New Series, 14B. Springer-Verlag, Berlin, pp. 368-454.

61. Sotelo, J., Gibbs, C.J., Jr., Gajdusek, D.C., Toh, B.H. and Wurth, M. (1980) Method for preparing cultures of central neurons: cytochemical and immunochemical studies. *Proc. Nat. Acad. Sci. U.S.A. #77,* 653-657.

62. Sotelo, J., Gibbs, C.J., Jr. and Gajdusek, D.C. (1980) Autoantibodies against axonal neurofilaments in patients with kuru and Creutzfeldt-Jakob disease. *Science 210,* 190-193.

63. Traub, R., Gajdusek, D.C. and Gibbs, C.J., Jr. (1977) Transmissible virus dementias. The relation of transmissible spongiform encephalopathy to Creutzfeldt-Jakob disease. In: Aging and Dementia", M. Kinsbourne and L. Smith, eds. Spectrum Publishing Inc., New York, pp. 91-146.

64. Will, R.G. and Matthews, W.B. (1982) Evidence for case-to-case transmission of Creutzfeldt-Jakob disease. *J. Neurology Neurosurgery and Psychiatry 45*, 235-238.

65. Williams, E.S. and Young, S. (1980) Chronic wasting disease of captive mule deer: A spongiform encephalopathy. *J. Wildlife Diseases 16*, 89-98.

66. Williams, E.S. and Young,S. (1982) Spongiform encephalopathy of Rocky Mountain elk. *J.Wildlife Disease 16*, 89-98.

67. Williams, E.S., Young, S. and Marsh, R.F. (1982) Preliminary evidence of the transmissibility of chronic wasting disease of mule deer. Abstract No. 22 in Proceedings of the Wildlife Disease Association Annual Conference, August 19, 1982, Madison, Wisconsin.

68. Worthington, M. and Clark, R. (1971) Lack of effect of immunosuppression on scrapie infection in mice. *J. Gen. Virology 13*, 349-351.

69. Zigas, V. and Gajdusek, D.C. (1957) Kuru: clinical study of a new syndrome resembling paralysis agitans in natives of the Eastern Highlands of Australian New Guinea. *Medical J. Australia 2*, 745-754.

Index